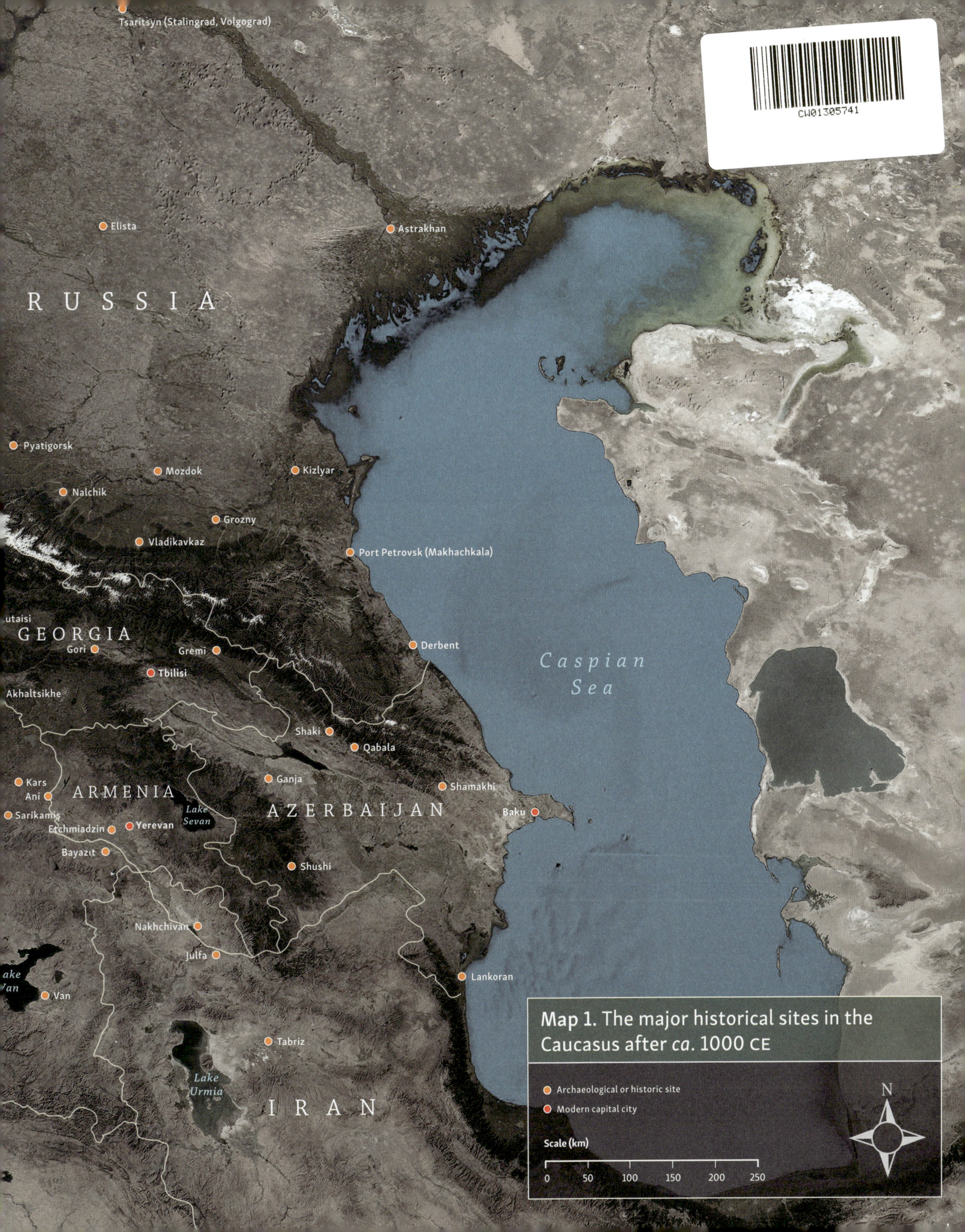

Map 1. The major historical sites in the Caucasus after *ca.* 1000 CE

- Archaeological or historic site
- Modern capital city

HISTORY OF THE CAUCASUS

Received
02 February '24.

VOLUME **TWO**

HISTORY OF THE CAUCASUS

In the Shadow of Great Powers

CHRISTOPH BAUMER

I.B. TAURIS
LONDON · NEW YORK

I.B.TAURIS
Bloomsbury Publishing Plc
50 Bedford Square, London, WC1B 3DP, UK
1385 Broadway, New York, NY 10018, USA
29 Earlsfort Terrace, Dublin 2, Ireland

BLOOMSBURY, I.B.TAURIS and the I.B.Tauris logo are trademarks of Bloomsbury Publishing Plc

First published in Great Britain 2024

Copyright © Christoph Baumer, 2024

Photographs © Christoph Baumer 2023, unless otherwise stated

Christoph Baumer has asserted his right under the Copyright, Designs and Patents Act, 1988, to be identified as Author of this work.

For legal purposes the Photo Credits on p. 351 and Acknowledgements on p. 352 constitute an extension of this copyright page.

Project managed by Carolann Young, Initial Typesetting Services
Cover design: Christopher Bromley
Cover image © Alexander Svirkin
Book design by Christopher Bromley
Copyedited by Henry Howard

Front cover image: The ruined mountain village of Gamsutl, Gunibsky Rayon, Dagestan, Russian Federation.

Back cover image: Bronze figure at the bottom of the Yerevan Cascade, Yerevan, Armenia.

All rights reserved. No part of this publication may be reproduced or transmitted in any form or by any means, electronic or mechanical, including photocopying, recording, or any information storage or retrieval system, without prior permission in writing from the publishers.

Bloomsbury Publishing Plc does not have any control over, or responsibility for, any third-party websites referred to or in this book. All internet addresses given in this book were correct at the time of going to press. The author and publisher regret any inconvenience caused if addresses have changed or sites have ceased to exist, but can accept no responsibility for any such changes.

A catalogue record for this book is available from the British Library.

A catalogue record for this book is available from the Library of Congress.

ISBNs:
HB   978-0-7556-3628-0
ePDF   978-0-7556-3630-3
eBook   978-0-7556-3629-7

Image editing and processing by Sturm AG, 4132 Muttenz, Switzerland

Printed and bound in Italy

To find out more about our authors and books visit www.bloomsbury.com and sign up for our newsletters.

Contents

I. A Fragmented Identity: An Introduction to Contemporary Ethnic and Political Conditions in the Caucasus — 1

II. In the Wake of International Great-Power Politics — 7
   1. The Golden Age of Georgia — 8
   2. The Mongol incursions and supremacy — 30

III. The Armenian Kingdom of Cilicia — 49
   1. Semi-independent Armenian warlords and Muslim Armenian viziers — 50
   2. The Rubenids of Cilicia: From principality to kingdom — 53
   3. The Kingdom of Cilician Armenia — 60

IV. The South Caucasus under Turkmen, Ottoman and Iranian Safavid Domination — 73
   1. Georgia and the devastations of Timur-e Lang — 74
   2. The partition of Georgia — 78
      Excursus: *The Armenian catholicosate's return to Etchmiadzin and a renewed schism* — 80
   3. The South Caucasus as battleground for eight Ottoman–Safavid wars — 84
   4. The South Caucasus under Safavid rule — 101
      Excursus: *The Armenian Mekhitarist congregation* — 109
   5. A brief reunification of Kartli and Kakheti and the foundation of independent khanates — 111

V. First Russian Advances into the North Caucasus — 113
1. The defence pact of 1557 between Kabarda and Russia — 114
2. The Cossacks and the first Russian military lines — 122
3. Mongol Kalmyks in the north-eastern Caucasus — 130

VI. The Caucasus under Russian Rule — 133
1. From the Treaty of Georgiyevsk (1783) to the annexation of Georgia in 1801 — 134
2. Iran's interlude with Napoleon and Russia's conquest of the South Caucasian khanates and sultanates — 139
3. The resistance of North Caucasian mountain peoples — 148
   3.1 Yermolov's first offensives north of the Greater Caucasus — 149
   3.2 The jihad of the imams — 152
   3.3 The conquest, resettlement and expulsion of the Circassians — 163
4. Russian administration and the rise of nationalism — 165
5. The Russian conquest of the former western Armenia 1877–1878 — 169
   Excursus: *Oil-drilling at Baku and the Nobel brothers* — 171
6. The emergence of nationalist and social-revolutionary parties, Armenian massacres and ethnic unrest — 174
   6.1 Armenian nationalist and socialist parties in the Russian and Ottoman empires — 175
   6.2 Georgian socialists — 179
   6.3 Pan-Turkism and socialism in the South Caucasian Muslim provinces — 181

VII. A Short-Lived Independence and Foreign Interventions — 183
1. World War I, the Armenian Genocide and the collapse of the Russian Empire — 184
2. The Transcaucasian Republic, the declaration of independence of Georgia, Azerbaijan and Armenia, and foreign interventions — 195
   2.1 The short-lived Transcaucasian Republic — 195
   2.2 Ethnic and social conflicts in Georgia — 196
   2.3 The Republic of Armenia — 199
   2.4 The race for Baku — 201
   2.5 War in Karabakh, Nakhchivan, Zangezur and Kars — 203
   2.6 Armenia and the Paris Peace Conference — 207
3. The Russian Civil Wars 1917–1920 and the short-lived North Caucasian states — 217

VIII. Under Soviet Rule — 223
1. Soviet consolidation of power, collectivization and Stalin's purges — 224
2. Operation Edelweiss: The battle for the Caucasus in World War II — 230
   Excursus: *Richard Sorge, Stalin's master spy* — 230
3. Deportations and the start of the Cold War — 240
4. Political stagnation and the rise of nationalism — 242

IX. Independence in the South Caucasus — 247
1. The disintegration of the Soviet Union — 248
2. The Armenian declaration of independence and the issue of Nagorno-Karabakh — 249
3. The Azerbaijani declaration of independence and the development of the oil and gas industry — 252
4. The First Nagorno-Karabakh War 1992–1994 — 260
5. Georgian independence and the South Ossetian and Abkhazian wars — 265

X. Autonomy and Failed Independence in the North Caucasus — 273
1. The northern region: Rostov, Krasnodar, Adygea, Stavropol and Kalmykia — 275
2. The western and central region: Karachay-Cherkessia, Kabardino-Balkaria, North Ossetia–Alania and Ingushetia — 277
3. The eastern region: Chechnya and Dagestan — 281

XI. The Caucasus in the Twenty-First Century — 289
1. Republics and regions of the North Caucasus — 290
2. The independent republics in the South Caucasus — 294
   2.1 Azerbaijan — 294
   2.2 The Second Nagorno-Karabakh War 27 September–10 November 2020 — 298
   2.3 Armenia — 302
   2.4 Georgia — 304
      2.4.1 The Georgian–Russian War 7–12 August 2008 — 306
      2.4.2 Georgia, Abkhazia and South Ossetia since the 2008 war — 309
3. Outlook — 312

Appendix: Chronology of the most important Caucasian dynasties 313

Notes 317

Bibliography 339

List of Maps 350

Photo credits 351

Acknowledgements 352

Indexes 353
    Concepts 355
    People 363
    Places 369

A Fragmented Identity: An Introduction to Contemporary Ethnic and Political Conditions in the Caucasus

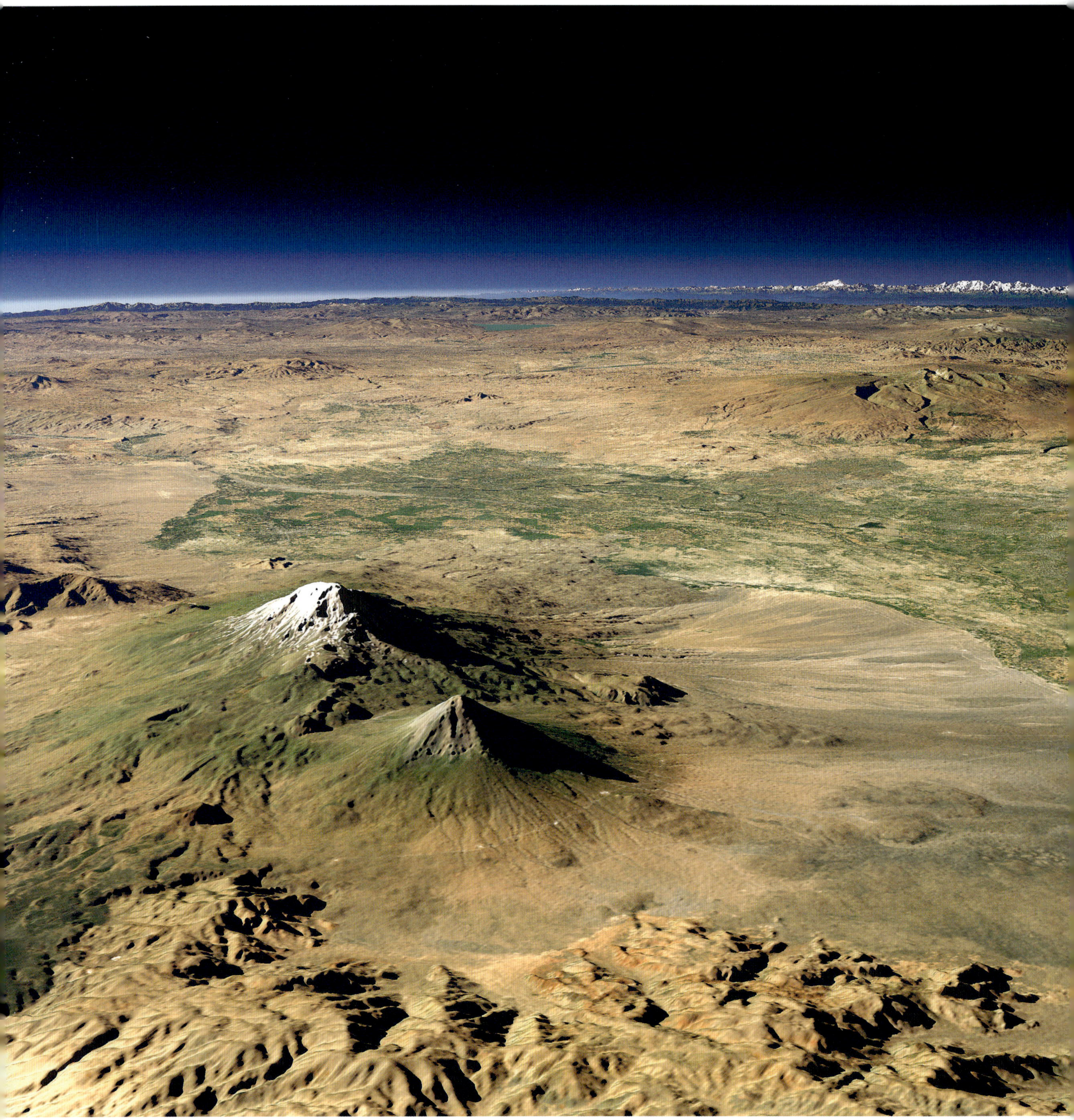

The sovereign states of the Southern Caucasus and the Russian Republics of the Northern Caucasus, as well as their adjacent neighbours, are in their present configurations rather recent polities which mostly emerged from the breakdown of the Soviet Union in the second half of 1991. In addition, several conflicts over the sovereignty of breakaway republics continue to smoulder, and occasionally burst into flames. While states define themselves by their governmental structures within a defined geographical environment, and by certain sets of ideological values, they ultimately consist, as Henry Kissinger reminds us, of a 'collection of individuals'.[1] The identity of the polities therefore stems from the collective identity of these individuals, who in the Caucasus often define themselves by their respective language and ethnicity.[2] These peoples' identities have grown historically over centuries; they are the more entrenched for having been shaped by long periods of foreign political domination: in the North Caucasus since Russia's military encroachments as of the later sixteenth century and in the South Caucasus since its absorption into the Ottoman and Persian zones of influence beginning in the early sixteenth century. In these times of foreign hegemony, ethnic identities formed the anchor points for the Caucasian communities. These identities also included distinctive religious components: in the north, the local pagan or Muslim peoples were confronted by Christian Orthodox Russians, while in the south the Christian Georgians and Armenians came under the rule of Ottoman Sunni or Persian Shiite Muslims, and then in the early nineteenth century of Imperial Russia which favoured the Russian Orthodox Church, especially in Georgia.

The peculiarities of these historic identities were preserved and reinforced by the particular geography of the Caucasus: narrow, virtually sealed-off valleys between high mountain ranges. This is why the present states and republics of the Caucasus, a mere thirty years old, are burdened with a heavy load – the burden of history of its peoples, so often embellished and dramatized in the telling, and of centuries-old mutual prejudices. While the state borders of these polities were defined on the drawing board of the Soviet administration, they didn't arise from 'greenfield sites', so to speak, but from highly historical soils. To paraphrase Kissinger, the new states attained their identity through the consciousness of ancient history: as he wrote, 'History is the memory of states.' And for this reason,

---

1. Satellite photo from a height of 19 km of the South Caucasus. In the foreground the two volcanoes Lesser Ararat (right) and Greater Ararat, in the centre the plain of the Aras and in the background the Greater Caucasus ridge.

'no significant conclusions are possible in the study of foreign affairs – the study of states acting as units – without an awareness of the historical context. For societies exist in time more than in space.'[3] If a polity is ethnically homogeneous like, for example, Armenia or, to a lesser degree Azerbaijan, the identity of this state will have a rather homogeneous character which may induce it to be more abrasive vis-à-vis its neighbours. On the other hand, if several distinct ethnicities with their own pronounced identities coexist within a single state, the polity's identity will be heterogeneous, which may lead to internal tensions in that state. Such is the case in Georgia where the South Ossetian and Abkhazian communities broke away from the Georgian majority. And in the North Caucasian republics, the ethnic Russians are often no more than tolerated, although these small republics would not be able to survive without hefty financial subsidies from Moscow. On these grounds, the present states and republics of the Caucasus have little in common beyond a shared past of Soviet domination, and political and economic cooperation within the region is often suboptimal or even nonexistent. For example, Armenia has no diplomatic contacts with neighbouring Azerbaijan and Turkey respectively, and the latter two have established a strict economic boycott of Armenia because of the Nagorno-Karabakh conflict. Georgia, on the other hand, has contacts neither with its renegade provinces of Abkhazia and South Ossetia, nor with the successor state of the Soviet Union, Russia.[4]

The state-building process in the Caucasus followed the typical nation-state model which, regardless of its type of government, aims at creating a state where a large majority of its people share the same language, ethnicity and culture. The awareness of these commonalities forms the basis for the narrative of a common history. In pronounced nation states, ethnic or distinct cultural diversity is discouraged while the adoption of the *Leitkultur*, the guiding culture, is encouraged. In fact, the high ethnic homogeneity of the sovereign states of Armenia, Georgia and, to a lesser degree, of Azerbaijan is a recent phenomenon which only took shape in the later 1910s and early 1990s due to the mass exodus of threatened communities. The trend towards nation-state building began in Europe at the turn of the fifteenth and sixteenth centuries and gained momentum in the nineteenth, during the struggles of various peoples of the Balkans and Greece to gain independence from the Ottoman and Austro-Hungarian empires. The aspiration of smaller and middle-sized peoples to statehood based on single languages and ethnicities and a consciousness of their own histories was finally sanctioned at the Congress of Berlin in summer 1878 and endorsed by the US President Woodrow Wilson's *Fourteen Points* declaration of 8 January 1918. While the Berlin Congress, which was chaired by the German Chancellor Otto von Bismarck, approved the dismemberment of the Ottoman Empire, the declaration by Wilson, who headed a federal state, was indirectly critical of empires and colonial powers in general. During the brief intermezzo between the Bolshevik Revolution of November[5] 1917 and the Soviet reconquest of the Caucasus in 1920–1921, Wilson's declaration with its rhetoric of the right of peoples to self-determination was often quoted to legitimize the claims to sovereignty of its short-lived polities.

The modern nation state is the antithesis of the older imperial state model where a single government, often personified in a single monarch, rules many nations and non-sovereign states. The empire accepts within its borders ethnic diversity and, in the ideal case, guarantees diverse ethnic, religious and even legal traditions. The Ottoman Empire was exemplary for such a state system, where ethno-religious minorities such as the Armenians were organized as autonomous communities called *millets*, headed by their religious leaders. In the case of the Armenians this was their Patriarch of Constantinople who reported directly to the Ottoman sultan. The size of the Ottoman Empire as a viable multinational state is illustrated by the fact that no fewer than 34 modern sovereign states once lay within its borders. When the Young Turk and war minister Enver Pasha began in the 1910s to transform the Ottoman Empire of nationalities into a Greater Turkish nation state, Turkish nationalism quickly replaced the previous tolerance towards ethnic diversity. In the Turkish nation state there was no more space for Armenian and Assyrian Christians.

The Russian Empire, too, represented a typical multinational state model which encompassed a plethora of ethnicities that retained their religious and cultural autonomies. However it must be noted that in the north-western Caucasus, the indomitable resistance to Russian rule by the indigenous Circassians during the nineteenth century could only be neutralized by their forced resettlement in the Ottoman Empire. As in Central Asia, proselytizing of Muslim communities by the Russian Orthodox Church in the North Caucasus was forbidden for decades. At the top of the Empire stood the tsar, and most Caucasian ethnic groups felt a commitment of loyalty towards the tsar, not to the Russian state. However, when Russia began to implement Russification programmes in the South Caucasus in the fields of education, communication and religion, it had the opposite effect to that intended: instead of a cultural harmonization, it stimulated

2. *Khachkars* and funerary chapel at the Armenian cemetery of Noratus located on the western shore of Lake Sevan. A *khachkar* is an engraved memorial stone stele featuring a cross. Gegharkunik Province, Armenia. Photo 2015.

nationalism. This emerging nationalism was not based on an awareness of a pan-Caucasian community but on ethnicity. This lack of pan-Caucasian cohesion became blatant in spring 1918 when the Transcaucasian Democratic Federative Republic, founded on 22 April to counter the danger of a hostile Turkish advance, fell apart only five weeks later on 26–28 May 1918. The interests and perspectives of the three nascent nations were too divergent. While Georgia placed itself under a German protectorate and the Turkic Muslim community of Azerbaijan welcomed the advancing Turkish troops as brothers in faith and ethnicity, the Armenians were left alone and had to accept a humiliating treaty.

The sovereignty of the South Caucasian states lasted a mere couple of years, since Soviet Russia claimed the territorial inheritance of the defunct Tsarist Empire. Soviet Russia's reorganization as the Union of Soviet Socialist Republics was imperial in character. The Union's republics and the lower entities such as Autonomous Republics, oblasts or okrugs were non-sovereign states and administrative units, while the real power was held by the Politburo of the CPSU, the Communist Party of the Soviet Union. Nevertheless, when the Soviet Union collapsed in 1990–1991, it turned out to have functioned only in the short term as a melting pot uniting different peoples under a single rule; in the long term the administrative segmentation of the Caucasus by ethnicity had worked as a catalyst of nationalism. The Soviet regime was significantly less tolerant of religious or political diversity than its predecessor, since the practice of religion was severely restricted and no ideology deviating from the official Marxist–Leninist credo was tolerated. Basically, cultural diversity was only allowed in the shape of folklore. But when the Soviet Empire imploded, the lid came off the Pandora's Box of Caucasian nationalisms, out of which by the year 2022 had emerged three sovereign states, eight Russian republics, three additional federal subjects of Russia, and three quasi-states that were internationally barely recognized. The pendulum has obviously swung from multinational empire status back to nation states.[6] Two tiny Russian republics are exceptions to the model of a nation state, as they each consist of two different ethnic groups with distinct languages. In Karachay-Cherkessia the indigenous Cherkess are politically united with the Turkic Karachay, and in Kabardino-Balkaria the indigenous Kabardians share the republic with the Turkic Balkars.

Time will tell how stable the present partition of the Caucasus is. The political future of the Caucasian states depends not only on their own dynamics but also on the strategies of the neighbouring regional powers, Russia and Turkey. While Turkey sees itself as a close ally of Azerbaijan and as a protecting power of the Azerbaijan Autonomous Republic of Nakhchivan, Russia is determined to suppress at all cost any breakaway movement of its own autonomous North Caucasian republics, as was evidenced in the two Chechen Wars. Furthermore, the Kremlin ranks the states and quasi-states of the Southern Caucasus which belonged to the former USSR as its 'Near Abroad' and pays special attention to them. While Russian diplomats claim that the Kremlin doesn't seek to establish zones of influence in its Near Abroad, any marked rapprochement of a Caucasus state to another great power, especially to US-led NATO, provokes strong and unpredictable responses. The abundance of fossil fuels in the Caspian Sea littoral states and the network of existing and planned pipelines touching the Caucasus, as well as the implacable US–Iran conflict, have added to the region's volatility. While the states of the South Caucasus are once again masters of their own destiny, their room for manoeuvre remains somewhat curtailed by the interests and conflicts of the surrounding powers.

It is one of the goals of this book to facilitate some comprehension of the specific recent developments and present situation in the Caucasus: to show how aspirations for national autonomy developed in the context of complex foreign domination, how the historical narrative – possibly perceived differently by local populations and diasporas – limits governments' scope for action, and how governments navigate between the cliffs of different interest groups, national myths, harsh economic realities and foreign agendas.

II

In the Wake of International Great-Power Politics

1. The Golden Age of Georgia

When King Bagrat III died in 1014 he left to his son and successor **Giorgi (George) I** (r. 1014–1027), then only sixteen years old, a united and relatively large kingdom, but one which was not yet consolidated and whose cohesion had only been guaranteed by Bagrat's strong personality.[1] Prince Kvirike III of Kakheti (r. 1010/14–1037), whose father Davit (David) had been forced by Bagrat to submit to Georgian authority, immediately seized the opportunity to regain sovereignty for his inheritance. He then quickly regained control over neighbouring Hereti and established his capital in Telavi. Since Giorgi's priorities lay in the west, he refrained from countermeasures and instead won Kvirike as an ally in his fight against Byzantium. Giorgi wanted to regain those territories in Tao that had been ceded to Byzantium in 1001 after Davit III Kouropalates of Tao had been forced to bequeath them to Emperor Basil II (r. 976–1025) in his will of 989/90.[2] Between 1014 and 1018 Giorgi managed to recapture several strongholds of Tao, but was then confronted by an ultimatum from Basil II who was by now in a position of strength, having crushed the Bulgarian Empire. Instead of negotiating, Giorgi entered an offensive alliance with the Fatimid caliph of Egypt, al-Hakim bin-Amr Allah (r. 996–1021) whereby the latter would launch a naval attack on Byzantium. At the same time Giorgi also won the alliance of the Armenian rulers of Ani, Hovhannes-Smbat III (r. 1017/20–1040/41), and of Vashpurakan, Senekerim-Hovhannes (r. 1003–1021). This alliance was threatening to Basil to the extent that the three kings controlled and could block vital trade routes.

When al-Hakim died in early 1021, Basil II attacked in the same year. He defeated Giorgi's retreating rearguard near Lake Çıldır in Ardahan Province and ravaged Javakheti and Trialeti. Before Basil retired to winter camp at Trebizond, he neutralized Giorgi's Armenian allies: Senekerim-Hovhannes surrendered his kingdom against territories around Sebasteia (today's Sivas) and Hovhannes-Smbat III bequeathed his realm to Byzantium.[3] As reported by Sumbat Davitis-dze, writing around 1030 and whose work on the Georgian Bagratids forms a section of *Kartlis Tskhovreba*,[4] in the first half of 1022 the conspiracy of Nikephoros Phokas Barytrachelos and Nikephoros Xiphias prevented Basil from resuming the campaign against Georgia. However, the emperor succeeded in sowing mistrust between the two rebels and Xiphias murdered Phokas, whereupon the rebellion collapsed. Basil then scored a decisive victory over Giorgi and forced him to vacate not only Tao but also Klarjeti and Javakheti and hand over his three-year-old son Bagrat as a hostage for three years. When Basil died in 1025, shortly after having restored the child hostage to his father Giorgi, the latter prepared for a renewed war to recapture the lost territories.[5]

However, Giorgi died in 1027 and the crown went to his son **Bagrat IV** (r. 1027–1072), a minor, whose mother Mariam Artsruni of Vashpurakan – Giorgi's first wife – acted as regent along with the *eristavis* (dukes) Liparit IV Baghvashi and Ivane Abazasdze. Under this constellation, the high Georgian nobility regained some of the previous power which they had lost to Bagrat III. Furthermore, Giorgi's second marriage to the Alanian

3. The cross-in-square cathedral of Samtavisi was consecrated in 1168 and restored in the fifteenth–sixteenth century. It is famous for its exterior relief on the east side. Shida Kartli, Georgia. Photo 2013.

4. The monastery of the Nativity at Katskhi, built 988–1014. It has an unusual dodecagonal ground plan with six apses. The monastery church served as burial place for the powerful noble Liparit family. Imereti, Georgia. Photo 2018.

princess Alda, who had borne a son named Demetre (d. 1042), soon developed into a serious liability for Bagrat IV and the kingdom's stability. After the Byzantine emperor Romanos III (r. 1028–1034) resumed hostilities against Georgia and several nobles opted for Byzantine sovereignty, the Queen Dowager Mariam travelled to Constantinople where in 1031 she successfully negotiated peace and a matrimonial alliance. She returned with Princess Helena Argyros, a niece of the emperor. But the young queen died after a few months and Byzantium eagerly answered the appeals for help from Alda and her son, Bagrat's half-brother Demetre, who both resided in Anakopia. A Byzantine fleet occupied Anakopia and brought the young pretender and his mother to Constantinople; the emperor thus acquired a Georgian puppet king as bargaining chip.[6]

After Duke Liparit IV defeated the Shaddadid rulers of Ganja (Gəncə) in 1034 in his capacity as commander-in-chief of the royal army, he rose to become the most powerful prince, overshadowing the young king. Around the same time, Liparit had captured the emir of Tbilisi, Jaffar III Ali (r. *ca.* 1032–1046), and handed him over to Bagrat and Mariam. Becoming aware that their strongest supporter was on the verge of turning into their most dangerous rival, they reinstated the prisoner's possessions. For the time being Liparit hid his anger. Four years later, in 1038, King Bagrat and Liparit besieged Tbilisi and Emir Jaffar prepared to flee to the Shaddadids. But Bagrat thwarted Liparit's plans for the second time; he made peace with Jaffar and confirmed him as ruler of Tbilisi. Liparit now realized that he would in turn be soon overshadowed by the young king, and sided with the exiled pretender Demetre, intending to install him as a puppet ruler answerable to Liparit. Since Bagrat had recaptured some strongholds in Tao, Byzantium retaliated by sending Demetre and an army including Varangian mercenaries; Liparit joined the invaders. Although the rebels scored some victories, Liparit was unable to decisively defeat Bagrat, and the duke's pawn Demetre died in 1042.[7]

In 1048, Bagrat seemed suddenly to be rid of his rival. When the Seljuk warlord Ibrahim Inal (d. *ca.* 1050), a brother of Sultan Tughril, threatened the Byzantine *theme* of Iberia, Emperor Constantine IX (r. 1042–1055) ordered Liparit, who held the prestigious title of *magistros*, to join the defending Byzantine army. At the nocturnal Battle of Kapetron east of Erzurum on 18 September 1048, the two Byzantine generals leading the wings were victorious but Ibrahim Inal managed to capture Liparit who was commanding the centre and deported him to Isfahan. But Bagrat's joy was premature, since Constantine ransomed Liparit from Sultan Tughril in order to keep him as a counterweight to the Georgian king. In the words of the Byzantine historian John Skylitzes (d. after 1101):

[General] *Kekaumenos had the right wing, Aaron* [son of the last Bulgarian ruler Ivan Vladislav and governor of Vashpurakan] *the left, while Liparites was stationed on the centre; it was towards evening. … Battle was joined: Kekaumenos and Aaron routed their opposing wings and pursued them till cockcrow but Liparites, desolated by the loss of his nephew, charging at full tilt, fell when his horse was wounded; then he was taken prisoner. While that was happening to him, the Romans* [Byzantines] *called off their pursuit, dismounted and offered hymns of victory to God. … When the emperor learnt of the capture of Liparites he was all for redeeming him. He sent extravagant gifts and ransom* [money] *to the Sultan.*[8]

The high esteem in which Liparit was held by the Seljuks is revealed in the account by the medieval Muslim historian 'Izz ad-Din ibn al-Athir (1160–1233) who calls him 'the Georgian king'.[9] When Liparit returned with Byzantine troops around 1051, Bagrat was unable to offer resistance and was forced to leave his capital Kutaisi. With his mother Mariam he travelled to Constantinople to negotiate an arrangement with Constantine, who, however, detained them for three years. In the meantime, Liparit manipulated Bagrat's second wife Borena, sister of the Alanian king Durgulel, into handing over the baby Prince Giorgi II. Liparit then had the infant crowned in the cathedral of Ruisi and declared himself regent, together with Bagrat's sister Gurandukht. Around 1054 or 1055 Constantine released his royal captive and Bagrat returned to Kutaisi.[10] Yet Liparit controlled extensive parts of Georgia and held Bagrat's only son Giorgi II. As stated in *Kartlis Tskhovreba*, 'Liparit exercised total authority over the Upper region [Kartli], and he had as friends Sultan Doğlubeg [Tughril] in Khorasan and the Greek king [the Byzantine emperor].'[11] Yet between 1058 and 1060 a number of dissatisfied nobles of Liparit's party arrested their ruler and handed him over to Bagrat who, in order to diffuse the tensions within Georgia, spared his life; he had him tonsured and sent in exile to Constantinople.[12]

But Bagrat and Georgia were not allowed to rest. As recounted by al-Athir, in the year 1064 Sultan Alp Arslan (r. 1063–1072) led a Seljuk army from Ray (south of Tehran) to Nakhchivan and captured some castles garrisoned by Byzantine troops. He then handed over the command to his son Malik Shah and his vizier Nizam al-Mulk. They marched westward and besieged the Armenian fortified city of Marmashen, known to the Seljuks as Miryam Nashin.[13] The Seljuks wore down the defenders with several waves of attacks, then conquered the city. 'Malik Shah and Nizam al-Mulk made their entry into the town and burnt and destroyed the churches. They killed many of the populace, although many converted to escape death.'[14] (For Christian prisoners of war, this was quite often the only way to avoid execution.) Instead of crossing the River Achuryan and attacking the stronghold of Ani which Byzantium had acquired in 1045, the Seljuks marched north and conquered the Georgian fortified city of Akhalkalaki, which they set on fire. The Seljuk army then turned southwards and captured Ani.[15] This looting campaign formed the prelude to an almost sixty-years-long war between Georgia and the Turkic Seljuks which only ended with King Davit (David) IV's overwhelming victory at Didgori in 1121.[16]

Faced with the growing threat from the east, Georgia and Byzantium overcame their decades-old enmity and entered a matrimonial alliance: Bagrat married his daughter Marta to the eldest son of Emperor Constantine X (r. 1059–1067), the future Michael II Doukas (r. 1071–1078). On the eastern front, in the mid 1060s Bagrat conquered Hereti and large parts of Kakheti, whose king Aghsartan (Akhsitan) I (r. 1058–1084) sought the protection of the Seljuk sultan Alp Arslan and, according to *Kartlis Tskhovreba*, converted to Islam and had himself circumcised.[17] This conversion shows that Christian rulers under pressure from another Christian king may have had few qualms about trading their religious affiliation in return for military support. Around the year 1068, Alp Arslan and his vassal Aghsartan attacked Bagrat, who had to vacate Kakheti and retreat to Kartli. The retreating king was saved when severe snowfalls set in and Alp Arslan left Kartli. As the sultan passed Tbilisi, he gave the small emirate to Fadhl II of Ganja (r. 1067–1073). But Bagrat quickly recovered Kartli and crushed Emir Fadhl who managed to flee with a few followers only to fall into the hands of Aghsartan, who promptly sold him to Bagrat in return for a few castles. Bagrat then forced Fadhl to relinquish his claims to Tbilisi under threat of death and installed one Sitlarabi as his own Muslim vassal emir.[18] But when Fadhl soon after betrayed his oath and occupied the fortress of Agarani south of Tbilisi, Bagrat called on his brother-in-law, the Alanian ruler Durgulel, for support. They quickly forced Fadhl to retreat and the combined forces under Crown Prince Giorgi II and Durgulel attacked and looted Fadhl's capital, Ganja. Since Alp Arslan did not retaliate, Bagrat soon stopped paying tribute and instead sent presents only.[19] Alp Arslan, however, had other priorities to pursue in Anatolia, winning an outstanding victory at Manzikert in 1071 over Emperor Romanos IV (r. 1068–1071) which precipitated a deep crisis in Byzantium from which the Empire never recovered. With Byzantium's elimination of the Armenian kingdoms in the first half of the eleventh century and disbanding of the local paramilitary border troops,[20] the accelerated retreat of imperial troops from eastern and central Anatolia now meant that the second-last Christian power in the Southern Caucasus had vanished, leaving Georgia as the only Christian bastion in the region.

5. The tiny church dedicated to Maximus the Confessor on top of the 40-m-high Katskhi limestone pillar was founded in the ninth or tenth century. The building was restored between 2005 and 2009 and a monk lived as a stylite on top of the pillar from 1995 to 2015. Imereti, Georgia.

6. Cathedral of Our Lady in the monastery complex of Gelati near Kutaisi. It was founded by King Davit IV in 1106 and was consecrated in 1130 by King Demetre I. The monastery was designed by King Davit as an academy of science in order to further develop Georgian culture and scientific learning. Several medieval Georgian rulers are buried in the monastery. Imereti, Georgia. Photo 2013.

Seen from a broad perspective, Georgia's only choice was between submitting to the dominant Seljuks and its rulers adopting Islam, or building a strong standing army. Bagrat's grandson Davit IV would choose and successfully implement the second path. He would be greatly helped in his endeavours by another development, which also took place in the fateful year 1071: the capture of Jerusalem by the Khwarazmian mercenary warlord and nominal Seljuk vassal Atsiz ibn Uvaq (d. 1079).[21] The ensuing conflicts with the Egyptian Fatimids for the control of the Holy City, internal rivalries and misgovernment, and the lack of security for Christian pilgrims crossing Anatolia would pave the road for the First Crusade and the foundation of the Crusader States within the Seljuk realm (or, more accurately, zone of influence). The war effort of the Seljuks and their Muslim vassals would henceforth focus on fighting the Crusaders, and at times distract them from the Caucasus.

Bagrat IV died in November 1072 and was succeeded by his son **Giorgi II** (r. 1072–1089). Hardly had he come to the throne before Giorgi faced a rebellion from Liparit's son Ivane, who raided parts of Kutaisi. Giorgi defeated the rebel, but instead of eliminating him, he assigned him the fortress of Samshvilde. Ivane 'thanked' the king for his leniency by betraying him twice more, finally defecting to Alp Arslan's successor Sultan Malik Shah (r. 1072–1092). When Ivane's son Liparit V showed signs of disloyalty, the Sultan seized Samshvilde and along with it Ivane, who thereafter disappears from history. In the early autumn Giorgi inflicted a decisive defeat on the invaders. He then recovered Samshvilde, captured Kars from the Seljuks and advanced to Abkhazia where the withdrawal of the Byzantines from the east allowed him to not only reoccupy Anakopia but also to take possession of some Byzantine fortresses which the retreating commander Gregory Pakourianos handed over to him.[22] This was Giorgi's last military success, for from now on in battle he would meet only defeat. He suffered a first reverse in 1077 at the hands of the Seljuks, who renewed their devastating attack three years later, looting and burning the capital Kutaisi and reaching the Black Sea. As deplored in *Kartlis Tskhovreba*, the Seljuks established a rhythm of destruction: 'In springtime the Turks would carry out [depredations]; in winter they would leave. In those times there was neither sowing nor harvest. … The holy churches were turned into stables for their horses.'[23] The Seljuks and irregular Turkmen destroyed agriculture and villages in order to turn the land into pastures for their horses, while the men fit for work were enslaved and the young males were circumcised and abducted. After three years of helplessly watching the destruction of his fertile land, King Giorgi decided to surrender and in 1083 he made the journey to Malik Shah in Isfahan. Although the Sultan forced Giorgi to pay tribute and provide soldiers, the plundering raids continued and a couple of years later, a Seljuk–Kakhetian army again ravaged Kartli. To make matters yet worse, on Easter Sunday 1088 the Tmogvi earthquake occurred, followed by aftershocks lasting a year – taken as an omen for further disasters. In view of the critical situation, the leading nobles together with Archbishop Giorgi Chqondideli (d. 1118), who was tutor to Giorgi's only son Davit, forced the unfortunate king to abdicate in favour of the crown prince whom *Kartlis Tskhovreba* introduces bombastically as 'the homonym of Davit, the father of God, and Davit's seventy-eighth descendant'.[24]

King **Davit (David) IV** (r. 1089–1125) was later given the epithet *Aghmashenebeli* which means 'the Builder', or 'Restorer' (fig. 7).[25] Indeed in due course, Davit restored the economy, introduced functioning state institutions and built Georgia into a fully sovereign and territorially compact kingdom secured by a strong standing army. But in the words of *Kartlis Tskhovreba* 'when Davit became King Kartli was ruined'.[26] Even worse, in 1089 Davit controlled only Egrisi and Abkhazia, that is western Georgia. He could not have acceded to power in worse circumstances, for the moribund kingdom was surrounded by jackals and scavengers. But Davit possessed all requisite skills: he was not only a brilliant strategist and courageous army commander, who 'did not lead his troops from behind [as others did], but he went in front at the head of all',[27] but he was also a clear-sighted administrator and reformer as well as a fine diplomat. Finally, he managed to fully exploit opportunities arising from the unforeseeable weaknesses of his key Seljuk enemy and from Byzantium's continuing decline. Right from the start, Davit realized that before he could address the disastrous security situation and restore or even expand the kingdom, he had to tackle the structural problems affecting the state and the weaknesses of regal authority. These were, first, the lack of loyalty of the leading nobles towards crown and state; second, the cronyism and

7. A sixteenth-century mural on the north wall of the north transept of the cathedral of Our Lady in the Gelati Monastery. The recognizable historical figures seen from right to left are King Davit IV (r. 1089–1125), with a model church; Catholicos Yevdemon Chkhetidze; King Bagrat III of Imereti (r. 1510–1565), his wife Elena, King Giorgi II of Imereti (r. 1565–1585), Prince Bagrat and Queen Rusudan. Photo 2013.

nepotism between gentry and church and the corruption in the latter; and third, the lack of a standing army.

Luckily for Davit, both the bellicose Sultan Malik Shah and the mastermind of the Seljuk Empire, Vizier Nizam al-Mulk died in 1092 within a few months of each other. The ensuing fragmentation plunged the Sultanate into a thirteen-year internal power struggle.[28] The resurgence of the Caliphate in Baghdad and the Crusaders' attacks, beginning in summer 1097 and culminating with the capture of Jerusalem on 15 July 1099, further rocked the Seljuk Empire. Also favourable for Davit were the ambiguous relations between Byzantium and the Crusaders, which meant that Byzantium no longer posed a threat to Georgia. When in 1093 Liparit V Baghvashi, *eristavi* of Kldekari, began to conspire against the king, he had him jailed. Davit gave him one last chance to show loyalty and pardoned him, but in 1097 after Liparit again started intriguing, Davit deported him to Constantinople. Six years later he confiscated the Baghvashi family possessions of Kldekari as well as those of the powerful *eristavi* Dzagan Abuletisdze. Whereas his father Giorgi had unsuccessfully tried to buy the loyalty of his *eristavis* and forgave rebels again and again, Davit demanded loyalty and punished the disobedient. Having broken the power of the crown's main rival, the Baghvashi family, Davit cleared Shida (Inner) Kartli of Seljuks and marauding Turkmen, captured the important stronghold of Sedaseni and prepared to reconquer Hereti and Kakheti. Because Kakheti had been since the later 1060s (with interruption) a tributary of the Seljuk Empire, Sultan Berkyaruq (r. 1092–1105) sent a strong army led by the *atabeg* of Ganja. However, at the Battle of Ertsukhi in 1104, Davit's superior battle tactics secured him a decisive victory. By this time the king had reorganized the army by raising a 5,000-strong royal guard in order to reduce the crown's dependency on soldiers provided by the nobles, and had enforced strict discipline on the troops. Over time, Davit also managed to attract elite mercenary fighters, battle-hardened former Crusaders who didn't fancy returning to Europe. Following Davit's victory at Ertsukhi, several Kakhetian nobles who despised their incompetent ruler

8. The Martyrs' monastery church of Martvili, tenth century, stands on top of a hill where in pre-Christian times an oak tree was venerated. According to legend, St Andrew preached here whereupon the sacred tree was felled. Samegrelo-Zemo Svaneti, Georgia. Photo 2018.

Aghsartan II (r. 1102–1105) seized him and handed him over to Davit, who annexed his realm. The king had now restored Georgia's unity and laid the basis for eliminating foreign enclaves such as the Emirate of Tbilisi, as well as for new conquests. Already, in the year of Jerusalem's capture by the Crusaders in 1099, Davit had discontinued the tribute payments to the Seljuk sultan and begun to resettle the depopulated and devastated regions and to rebuild agriculture.[29]

Having reined in the nobility, Davit embarked on the clean-up of the Augean Stable that was the Georgian Church. According to *Kartlis Tskhovreba*, 'the holy churches, the houses of God, had become dens of robbers; unworthy and unauthorized men had seized the principal sees by inheritance rather than by merit, like thieves.'[30] For many centuries the feudal nobles had misused church institutions in order to evade taxes and to undermine royal authority. On their feudal estates they nominated unqualified family members as bishops, and to avoid taxation transferred property to their tax-exempted bishoprics. The bishoprics and larger monasteries were practically satellite entities of the feudal estates. Davit decided to end these abuses and to make the church subordinate to the state. Together with Archbishop Giorgi Chqondideli he convened the Synod of Ruisi–Urbnisi in 1103–1104, where unworthy clergymen were deposed and rules including minimum age and qualification criteria were established for priestly ordination and appointment to bishoprics. To cut through the corrupt fabric of relations between nobility and church he subordinated the bishops and abbots in strict hierarchical order under the authority of Catholicos Ioane IV (in office 1100–1142) and Giorgi Chqondideli. Following this church reform, Davit reorganized the government, which had been hitherto a kind of itinerant court following the king's campaigns. A fixed seat of government consisting of ministers under the leadership of the grand chancellor (*mtsignobartukhutsesi*) was established at Kutaisi; as grand chancellor Davit nominated Giorgi Chqondideli, who as well as being his former tutor and chief advisor also supervised the newly created Court of Appeal. In order to prevent being caught off guard by hostile events, Davit established a domestic and foreign intelligence service. Finally, to secure a pool of well-educated clergymen and future scientists, he founded near Kutaisi in 1106 the monastery and educational centre of Gelati (fig. 6), and in Kakheti the academy of Ikalto.[31] For teachers he invited Georgian scholars from Jerusalem, Constantinople, Antioch and Cyprus to return to their homeland and contribute to its cultural revival; they not only taught ecclesiastical subjects and philosophy but also mathematics, geometry, astronomy, rhetoric and even handicrafts. At both academies, scribes were busy editing, compiling and copying manuscripts in order to make knowledge accessible. *Kartlis Tskhovreba* praised Gelati immodestly as a future 'second Jerusalem in the whole east' and 'another Athens, but much superior to it in divine doctrines'.[32] As *Kartlis Tskhovreba* reports, Davit was himself a great lover of books and an avid reader. 'In … his never-ending expeditions, in his restless labours, he loaded his books on numerous mules and camels. And wherever he dismounted from horseback, first of all he took the books into his hands.'[33] His favoured topics were theology, the Acts of the Apostles, history and astrology, and he also read the Quran in Arabic.

After Davit had laid the foundations for a stable and economically solid state, he increasingly devoted himself to foreign policy and conquests. In 1110 he conquered Samshvilde and crushed a large Seljuk army near Trialeti that had been sent by Sultan Muhammad I Tapar (r. 1105–1118) to push the Georgians back. In 1115 Giorgi Chqondideli captured Rustavi, severing Tbilisi's connections to the east. In the next year Davit cleared Tao of Turkic marauders and in the following two years did the same in Javakheti and Lori-Tashir. Although in around 1116 Davit had married his daughter Tamar to the future Shirvanshah Manuchihr III ibn Kasran, he intervened in Shirvan in 1117 because the then ruling Shirvanshah Afridun I (r. 1106–1120) was allied with the Seljuks; Davit sent his son Demetre to subdue Shirvan.[34]

In 1118, by dint of skilled diplomacy, Davit seized a golden opportunity to substantially strengthen his armed forces. At the beginning of the twelfth century Vladimir Monomakh, the ruler of Kievan Rus, had driven the Turkic Kipchaks living within his realm beyond the River Don into the Northern Caucasus. There they were battling with the Alans (Ossetians) for pasture. Since the Kipchaks were famous horsemen and mercenaries, Davit invited their prince Äträk, son of the Kipchak khan Sharukhan, to settle with 40,000 families in Georgia, on condition that each family should supply him with a mounted and fully equipped warrior. Davit mounted a military expedition to bring the Ossetians to heel and secure the Darial Pass, which the Ossetians guarded, for the Kipchaks. To seal the alliance, Davit repudiated his Armenian queen, possibly called Rusudan, and married Äträk's daughter.[35] These Kipchaks settled in Georgia and gradually adopted Christianity. To cement peace with the Ossetians, Davit gave his youngest daughter Rusudan to Jadaros, son of the Ossetian king Athon.[36] At the same time, Ossetian soldiers and about 200 Crusaders joined the Georgian army. Davit now commanded an elite guard of 5,000 men, 40,000 Kipchak

9. One of the colossal sculptures of the modern Didgori Monument celebrating King Davit's IV famous victory over a superior coalition of Seljuk armies on 12 August 1121. In the background huge swords are fixed into the ground suggesting crosses. Kvemo Kartli, Georgia. Photo 2018.

horsemen and the local border garrisons. These soldiers were professionals, not mere farmers called for temporary service. In addition, he could summon troops from his *eristavis* and vassals. In spring 1120 he continued the expansion of his kingdom by capturing the town of Qabala (Qəbələ) and winning the emir of Derbent as ally. The Emir's army soon thereafter defeated and killed Shirvanshah Afridun in battle.

The strengthening of the military proved decisive in consolidating Georgia's sovereignty. In 1121 the Seljuk sultan of Baghdad, Mahmud II bin Muhammad (r. 1118–1131), called for a Holy War against Georgia and formed a coalition composed of Seljuk troops, the *atabeg* of Ganja, various emirs of Armenia, and Tughril, the ruler of Nakhchivan. The overall command was given to Najm al-Din Ilghazi ibn Artuq, ruler of Aleppo, a notorious battle-hardened warlord who had won fame in 1119 by annihilating the Crusader army of Antioch at the Battle of Sarmeda, also called Battle of the Field of Blood, and killing its leader Roger of Salerno.[37] On 12 August 1121, at Didgori, west of Tbilisi, the Georgian–Kipchak army which allegedly numbered some 56,000 men and 200 former Crusaders, met the Muslim army, which was supposedly three to five times as large. To foil any possibility of flight by his soldiers, Davit gathered them in a gorge and had their exit barricaded by boulders and tree trunks. The narrow battle ground selected by Davit made it virtually impossible for the Seljuks to manoeuvre. A second contingent under his son Demetre, including archers and cavalry, crowned the surrounding heights in order to shoot down any fugitives and to harass the enemy's flanks. Before the battle started, a small group of heavily armoured Crusaders appeared at the Seljuk headquarters, where they pretended to be deserters. Suddenly drawing their swords they killed several of the senior Seljuk commanders, and while the Seljuks were for a moment in disarray, Davit ordered the main Crusader force to attack the Seljuk vanguard. Having crushed the vanguard and neutralized the Seljuk archers, Davit advanced with his main army while Demetre moved with his cavalry in full force downhill. The huge Seljuk army could neither react to the unexpected attacks nor regroup, and was completely destroyed (fig. 9).[38] With this overwhelming victory, King Davit and his army secured Georgia's sovereignty and dominance in the Southern Caucasus from the Black Sea to the Caspian for a full century.

This devastating victory of the Christian king Davit over the Muslim armies was one of the contributions, a few decades later, to the creation of the legend of Prester John, the mysterious and powerful Christian priest-king who was believed by some European politicians and historians to have driven back the Muslims in distant Asia. A year after the loss of the Christian County of Edessa to the emir of Mosul in 1144, the bishop and historian Otto of Freising reported that a pious Christian king called John had won a victory in Asia against a Muslim ruler. In 1157, Otto confirmed his 'report' to Emperor Frederick I Barbarossa, whereupon in the early 1160s the imperial chancellor Rainald of Dassel forged a supposed letter from this 'presbyter John' to Emperor Manuel I Komnenos of Byzantium (r. 1143–1180).[39]

As a result of this victory, in 1122 Davit IV gained full control of the Emirate of Tbilisi, which had been established around 737 and had achieved independence around 809.[40] With the conquest of the emirate, Georgia acquired a large Muslim population, as happened again in 1223 when Georgia annexed half of Shirvan. In order not to jeopardize the value of his conquest – Tbilisi was an important economic centre and trading hub – Davit guaranteed Tbilisi's Muslim population their freedom of religion and traditional way of life and even granted them preferential taxation. There was no pressure on Tbilisi's Muslims to convert to Christianity and assimilate to Georgia's majority.[41] Tbilisi regained its status as the kingdom's capital at the expense of Kutaisi. Soon after, when the Seljuk sultan Mahmud attempted to bring Shirvan back into the Seljuk zone of influence and occupied Shamakhi, Davit gathered his Kipchak cavalry and advanced to meet the Seljuks, who quickly retreated. Davit then annexed the western half of Shirvan, handing its government over to his grand chancellor Simon, bishop of Bedia and Alaverdi (in office 1118–1141), who had succeeded Giorgi Chqondideli. Davit left the eastern half of Shirvan to his son-in-law, Manuchihr III ibn Kasran (r. 1120–1160) as a Georgian protectorate.[42] Next, Davit conquered Dmanisi, which had been occupied by Turkic tribes since the early 1080s, and in 1124 he seized the former Armenian capital Ani without a fight when its population invited him to take possession of the city and to expel Emir Abu'l-Aswar Shavur (r. *ca.* 1118–1124) who intended to sell the city to the emir of Kars. Davit appointed Abuleth Orbelian as governor (in office 1124–1126).[43] In

10. Copper coin minted under King Davit IV (r. 1089–1125). On the obverse, King Davit is featured wearing Byzantine imperial clothing and a stemma. He holds a processional cross and a globus cruciger. On the reverse, a Georgian text surrounding a cross proclaims: 'Lord, aid Davit, king of Abkhazians, Kartvelians, Rans, Kakhs, Armenians.' © British Museum, London.

the same year Davit took the fortress of Oltisni west of Ani, then crossed the Southern Caucasus from west to east and conquered Derbent on the Caspian Sea. In surface area Davit's Georgia was about five times as large as today's republic.

Following Davit's conquest of Ani and parts of northern Armenia, Georgia acquired a substantial minority of Miaphysite Armenians, who were traditionally at odds with the Chalcedonian Georgians. Davit tried to defuse this potentially destabilizing issue by convening a second church council in 1123–1125.[44] While no theological compromise was achieved, Davit was wise enough not to attempt converting the Armenians to Georgian orthodoxy. His vision was the establishment of a strong state with loyalty due to its king, not the imposition of a single religion or confession. Davit died in 1125 and goes down in history as undefeated; he was buried in the monastery of Gelati. He succeeded where the Armenian kings of the tenth and eleventh centuries had failed, namely in restricting the power and autonomy of the nobility and the church and in establishing a stable, centralized state supported by a reliable standing army. As explained in *The Life of Davit, King of Kings*, one of the motivations that impelled Davit to be continuously waging war was to keep his turbulent nobles and the standing Kipchak army busy: Davit 'never left men time for plotting, idling or conspiring to take any action' of treason.[45] His great-granddaughter Queen Tamar would apply the same strategy to keep her generals and barons occupied far away from the capital. Davit's biography confirms the opinion that history is shaped by outstanding persons, and not by anonymous forces. Such leaders have a clear vision about their goals and the required strategies as well as a personality forceful enough to turn them into reality. At the same time, such rulers are sagacious enough to identify unforeseen opportunities, and are rapid in exploiting them.

According to the very brief *Life of King Demetre*, 'during Davit's lifetime ... he had set his son Demetre on the throne and crowned him with his own hands'.[46] Immediately after ascending the throne, **Demetre I** (r. 1125–1154, 1155–1156), who under his father had already proven to be a capable commander, was assailed by Georgia's Turkic enemies. Already in 1125, and again in the early 1130s, he had to expel the Seljuks from the strategically important fortress of Dmanisi which controlled one of the accesses to Tbilisi from the south. In the next couple of years Demetre's brother-in-law the Shirvanshah Manuchihr III rebelled, backed by Seljuk support. But in 1129 or 1130 Demetre forced him to accept the status quo, that is the partition of Shirvan and his authority over the eastern half restricted by obligations to pay tribute and supply troops. In the case of Ani, Demetre failed to keep the former Armenian capital firmly within the Georgian zone of influence and in 1126 Governor Abuleth Orbelian surrendered the city to Fadhl IV (r. 1126–1130), the son of the previous Muslim emir, Abu'l-Aswar Shavur.[47] Yet most of the time Ani remained within the Georgian political orbit. Five years later, Abuleth's son Ivane Orbelian plotted with Demetre's thirteen-year-old half-brother Vakhtang, whose mother was the Kipchak Gurandukht, to kill the king and set Vakhtang on the throne. Abuleth denounced his own son to the king, who reacted resolutely: Ivane was decapitated and Vakhtang blinded, as a result of which he later died.[48]

A dangerous adversary to King Demetre emerged in the person of the *atabeg* Shams al-Din Eldigüz (r. 1136–1175 or 1176), ruler of large parts of Azerbaijan, Nakhchivan and north-western Persia. Eldigüz was of Kipchak origin and initially a military slave of the Seljuk sultan Mahmud's II vizier Kamal al-Din al-Simirumi. After his master's murder, Sultan Mahmud used him as *atabeg* (tutor) for an underage emir, and Sultan Ghiyath al-Din Masud (r. 1134–1152) appointed him governor of Arran (Muslim Caucasian Albania) and gave him as a wife Momine Khatun (d. 1175), the widow of Sultan Tughril II (a son of Sultan Muhammad I Tapar). At the same time, Sultan Ghiyath appointed Eldigüz as *atabeg* of Tughril's son Arslan-Shah.[49] Feeling threatened by Eldigüz's rapid rise to power, in 1139 Demetre exploited the earthquake which wrecked Ganja, the major Muslim city of Arran, attacking the ruined city and removing the famous iron gates which he brought as spoils of war to Gelati. Four years later Eldigüz retaliated. Although Demetre remained victorious in battle, he agreed to give Sultan Ghiyath al-Din Masud his daughter Rusudan in marriage, whose dowry included the contested city of Ganja. Presumably Demetre's position was less strong than the sources suggest.

During the 1140s, the Georgian nobles who were still yearning for their lost independent power sensed an opportunity when it became apparent that Demetre had disinherited his elder son Davit in favour of the younger, Giorgi. A first attempted coup failed around 1150, but in 1155 Davit's putsch against his father succeeded; Demetre was banished to a monastery and his rebellious son ascended the throne as **Davit V** (r. 1055–1056). The reconstruction of subsequent events is obscure. According to Vardan Areveltsi (*ca.* 1198–1271), the two conspirators, the Orbelian[50] brothers Smbat and Ivane, felt they had been insufficiently rewarded by Davit V. Incited by his younger brother Giorgi or his father Demetre, or both, they poisoned him.[51] In line with the rules on regal succession, Davit's infant son

Map 2. Georgia's expansion under King Davit IV (r. 1089–1125) and Queen Tamar (r. 1184–1213)

Demna (a diminutive of Demetre) should have followed as next king. According to one tradition, the old king Demetre left his monastery to crown his son Giorgi as **Giorgi III** (r. 1156–1184) whereupon he returned to monastic life; according to another account, Demetre had been killed following his overthrow and Giorgi III took power by force at his brother's death.[52] The historian of the Orbeli dynasty, Bishop Stepanos Orbelian (*ca.* 1250–1303) suggests a third version, whereby Giorgi had sworn before ascending the throne to hand over crown and kingdom as soon as Demna reached adulthood at the age of sixteen.[53] Regardless of which account is the correct one, Ivane Orbeli was promoted to *amirspasalar*, commander-in-chief of the army, and was nominated tutor to Demna who lived in his household, further increasing his power.

As Giorgi III took control of the kingdom, Georgia's eastern and western borders were soon challenged by its Muslim neighbours. He suffered a rare defeat around 1160 or 1161 when he claimed tax arrears from Ganja and its emir responded with war, but in 1165 Georgia once more controlled Arran north-west of Ganja. Two years later, in 1167 (or in 1173 according to the historian Vladimir Minorsky) when the emir of Derbent, a vassal of Georgia, dared to attack King Akhsitan (Aghsartan) I ibn Manuchihr (r. 1160–1197) of Shirvan, which was a Georgian protectorate related by marriage to the Georgian royal family, Demetre crushed the unruly aggressor. He then confiscated territory from Derbent and gave it to Shirvan which thus gained direct access to the Caspian Sea.[54] Even more conflictual were Giorgi's relations with his western neighbours, since Georgia and several Muslim emirates fought over the spoils of the former Armenia, which had been annexed by Byzantium in the previous century and subsequently abandoned to Seljuk and Turkic conquerors after the defeat of Manzikert in 1071. In 1161 Giorgi secured Ani and appointed Ivane Orbelian (in office 1161–1164) as governor, increasing Ivane's power yet more.[55] A year later, a Muslim coalition formed by the Armen-Shahs of Akhlat,[56] the Saltukids of Erzurum and the Artuqids of Diyarbakır tried to

11. The monastery complex of Haghpat. In the foreground on the left the church of St Gregory (thirteenth century), on the right the Church of the Holy Cross (1201) and in the background the bell tower. Lori Province, Armenia. Photo 2015.

recapture Ani but suffered a bloody defeat. But in 1164 *atabeg* Shams al-Din Eldigüz attacked southern Georgia and the former northern Armenia, which he devastated. The deadlock was terminated by Georgia handing over Ani to a Shaddadid emir, Shahanshah ibn Mahmud (r. 1164–1174), who accepted nominal Georgian supremacy. In the early 1170s Giorgi turned his attention to domestic problems, among other things the then widespread banditry. He created a powerful law enforcement agency; theft and brigandage were punishable by hanging from a tree.

In 1174, Giorgi reoccupied Ani and again installed Ivane Orbelian as governor. But only two years later he returned the city to Shahanshah ibn Mahmud (second reign 1176–1198). Giorgi preferred the rule of ibn Mahmud to Ivane, who was showing obvious signs of disloyalty. Indeed, Ivane had by then decided to play his ace: Demna. Under the pretext of helping the young pretender to claim his royal rights, he and the majority of nobles planned in 1177 (or perhaps 1176) to take the king prisoner and force him to abdicate. Ivane, for his part, aspired to recover Ani and acquire for himself the small former Armenian kingdom of Lori while retaining the command of the army, thus becoming the *éminence grise* behind the inexperienced Demna. Ivane probably dreamt of reviving the former Armenian kingdom with Ani as its capital. By holding Lori, Ivane would have also controlled the narrow Debet Valley which formed the southernmost route to Tbilisi, bypassing Dmanisi. But Giorgi was alerted to the plot and escaped to Tbilisi. Qubasar, the commander of the Kipchak standing cavalry, remained loyal to his king, and the conspirators retreated to Lori. Seeing Demna's case lost, and attracted by Giorgi's promises of pardon and even promotion, several rebels switched sides. The most remarkable of them was Ivane's vassal Sargis Mkhargrdzeli (in Armenian Yerkaynabazuk, also called Zakarian) who was probably of Kurdish stock and whose forefathers had adopted Armenian Christianity.[57] He was the founder of the most illustrious and powerful non-royal dynasty of high medieval Georgia. As narrated by Stepanos Orbelian, the conspirators who had defected to Giorgi implored Ivane to surrender and hand over Demna. They corresponded with the rebel by means of letters pinned to arrows shot over the walls of the besieged fortress. Ivane refused and the royal troops stormed the fortress. Giorgi issued harsh punishments: Demna was blinded and castrated to ensure that his line would be extinguished, and he died from the after-effects. Ivane Orbelian's eyes were gouged out and his younger brother, his son and his nephew were executed. The Kipchak Qubasar was rewarded with the army command.[58]

12. Co-ruler Queen Tamar stands behind her father King Giorgi III (r. 1156–1184). Mural painted between 1184 and 1186 in the church of the Dormition, Vardzia Cave Monastery. Father and daughter are dressed in ceremonial Byzantine attire with crown and halo; they stand respectfully in front of the Virgin Mary holding the infant Jesus on her knees (not in the picture). Tamar holds the model of a church in her hands emphasizing her role of donor. Samtskhe-Javakheti, Georgia. Photo 2013.

This major revolt, putting as it did Giorgi's legitimacy into question, highlighted the necessity of addressing the matter of his succession, since he had no male heir. His younger daughter Rusudan would soon be married to Manuel Komnenos who had fought on Giorgi's side in 1167 in the punitive campaign against Derbent. His elder daughter Tamar (*ca.* 1160–1213) was now an adult, but hardly able to lead the army into battle as was expected in medieval Georgia. Nevertheless, with the extinction of the line of Davit V and Demna, the moment was propitious for Giorgi to impose his will on the unruly nobles. In 1178 he crowned Tamar as his co-ruler; her deficiency in terms of army leadership and prestige would be offset in contemporary panegyrics which exalted her to quasi-divine status. In a chronicle from the early thirteenth century, Tamar's Alanian mother Burdukhan was praised as 'equal to the Mother of God', which meant by implication that Tamar was equal to Christ. Indeed, in the same document she is elevated to the status of being the 'fourth member of the Holy Trinity'. Furthermore, according to one of the two medieval chronicles of Tamar, 'she gave birth to a son who was equal to the Son of God', which implies that she too was equal to the Mother of God.[59] Tamar's legitimacy was not derived from military virtues as with the preceding kings, but from her alleged divinity. In order to give a woman's accession to the throne the appearance of normality, her sycophants elevated Kartli's missionary saint Nino to the status of a direct envoy of the Mother of God, thereby reinforcing the impression that it was historically normal for women to play a highly significant role in Georgia.[60]

Tamar's (r. 1184–1213) accession to the throne went less smoothly than Giorgi had hoped, as the nobles believed they could take advantage of the demise of the forceful king and the relative inexperience of the young queen. She was forced to dismiss the non-Georgian commoner ministers appointed by her father, above all the Kipchak *amirspasalar* Qubasar, who had in fact suffered a stroke, and the senior minister Apridon who had started life as a serf.[61] Another ennobled commoner of Turkic (probably Kipchak) stock, who allegedly belonged to the Jaqeli family of Samtskhe, was Qutlu Arslan, Giorgi's treasurer. To avoid being dismissed, he allied himself with a faction made up of some of the nobles, rich merchants and the army. They demanded the transformation of the virtually absolute monarchy into a kind of feudal-constitutional monarchy whereby a new, representative council, the *Karavi*, would discuss and decide political issues while the competence of the existing state council, the *Darbazi*, would be extended to give it the right of approving or rejecting royal edicts. The rebellious Qutlu also demanded appointment as army commander. Tamar rejected these far-reaching reforms and ordered Qutlu's arrest, whereupon followers of both parties massed their troops. Civil war was looming, but Tamar demonstrated her diplomatic skills. Instead of attacking the insurgents, she gained time through negotiations and offered a royal pardon to every repentant rebel except Qutlu himself. The plan worked: Qutlu's companions surrendered and he was only mildly punished, though he disappeared from public life. As her new *amirspasalar* Tamar probably nominated Gamrekeli Toreli.[62] The *Keravi* was never implemented and the *Darbazi* failed to assert the right to convene itself and meet independently,

but the monarch was obliged to seek its advice and approval on the appointment of new ministers.[63] Nevertheless, Tamar had successfully mastered her reign's first major crisis. In due course, after Tamar's second marriage, to Davit Soslan, and with the appointment of the Mkhargrdzeli brothers to the kingdom's two top positions, she was to reassert her authority, although the concentration of power in the hands of the Mkhargrdzeli brothers would ultimately undermine the kingdom's unity.

On the question of her marriage, Tamar had to yield. In the words of the *Life of the Queen of Queens, Tamar,* the nobles and army commanders 'pointed out, that she was childless and the kingdom without an heir, demanding a leader for the army'.[64] Against her wishes, they selected as consort the Rus prince Yuri Bogolyubsky (king consort 1185–1188), who had been evicted from Novgorod and lived as a refugee with Kipchaks in the northern Caucasus. Prince Yuri was brought to Tbilisi and the marriage was celebrated immediately. While Yuri proved to be a capable army leader, his allegedly repulsive private behaviour rapidly alienated him from Tamar, who remained childless. He was accused of drunkenness and sodomy, and in 1188 the bishops and the *Darbazi* approved the annulment of the marriage. Yuri was richly compensated with gold and jewels and sent to Constantinople. The numerous contenders for Tamar's hand included a son of the Holy Roman Emperor Frederick I Barbarossa (r. 1155–1190), probably Duke Frederick VI of Swabia. Such an alliance would have made sense from a political point of view since Crusaders and Georgians were looking for allies against the common enemy, the Seljuk Turks.[65] Another candidate, a son of the Eldigüzid *atabeg* Qizil Arslan (r. 1186–1191) was even prepared to renounce Islam and accept Christianity in order to marry Tamar.[66] But the *Darbazi* chose, with the delighted approval of Tamar, the Alanian prince Davit Soslan (king consort *ca.* 1189–1207) who was descended from the Bagrationi on his mother's side and who later proved to be an outstanding commander. They married in late 1188 or 1189 and two children were born: the future king Giorgi IV Lasha in 1192 and the future queen Rusudan in 1193 or 1194. Yuri twice attempted to regain power in Georgia, in alliance first with rebellious nobles, later with Qizil Arslan's successor, *atabeg* Nusrat al-Din Abu Bakr (r. 1191–1210). In 1191 the insurgents advanced as far as Gori where they surrendered. Yuri obtained Tamar's pardon, but attacked again two years later from the east. After another defeat, he was probably imprisoned and is not heard of again.[67]

Strengthened by her second marriage, Tamar moved to fill the high offices of the kingdom with men she could trust. Following the brief tenure and death of *amirspasalar*

13. Palm Sunday and Christ teaching. Gospel of 1211 from Haghpat made by the scribe Hagop and the painter Markare of Ani. In the illustration on parchment, Jesus is not shown riding through a gate of Jerusalem, but through the arch of the now ruined Horomos Monastery located 15 km north of Ani. © Matenaderan, Nr. 6288, Yerevan, Armenia.

Sargis Mkhargrdzeli, the trusted follower of her father, she nominated his sons to the two most important positions: Zakare Mkhargrdzeli (d. 1212) became *amirspalasar* and was enfeoffed with Lori while his younger brother Ivane was made *msakhur-tukhutsesi*, which corresponds to Master of the Royal Household or Lord Chamberlain. Although Ivane's area of responsibility was domestic, he often joined his brother in military campaigns. Yet at the death of his brother, Ivane refused the title of *amirspasalar* and demanded to be appointed to a new Georgian office of *atabeg* which made him chief counsellor of Tamar's children.[68] These three men, Davit Soslan, Zakare and Ivane Mkhargrdzeli restored the kingdom to a position of conquest. Yet the question of confessional affiliation was an issue for the Mkhargrdzeli brothers since they were Armenian Miaphysites while the Church of Georgia was Chalcedonian Dyophysite. As recorded in a chronicle of Tamar dating from the thirteenth century, the conservative Catholicos Ioane (John) VII (in office *ca.* 1208–1210) once refused the Eucharist to Zakare as being a 'sevenfold cursed Armenian', whereupon Zakare requested a debate between Armenian and Georgian clergymen. When no debating party emerged victorious, Catholicos Ioane called for a trial by ordeal by dogs: the Armenians should hand over to the Catholicos a dog and he would give them his own. Both animals should starve three days. Then the Catholicos and the Armenians should bring a sacred host to be offered to the dogs. The devoured host would indicate which belief was wrong. While the starving Armenian dog refused the Georgian host, the equally starving Georgian dog immediately devoured the Armenian host. According to the interpretation of the Catholicos, through the dogs God had manifested his displeasure with the Armenian faith. Zakare kept his faith, but Ivane accepted, probably under political duress, a second baptism into the Georgian Orthodox Church, and thus became a 'true

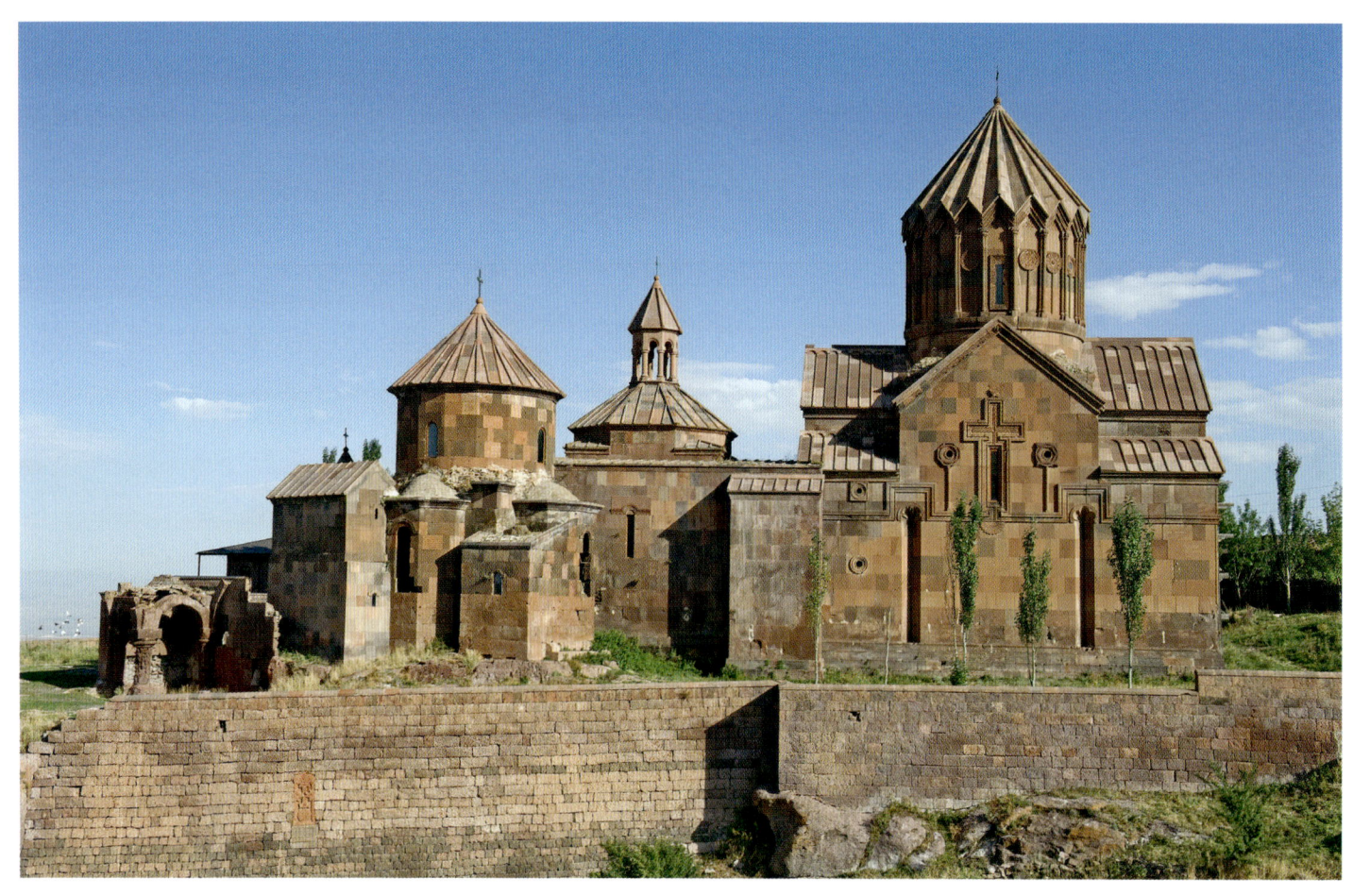

14. The fortified monastery of Harichavank. On the left the church of St Grigor the Enlightener founded in the seventh century, in the centre the *gavit* (narthex) and on the right the Astvatsatsin (Holy Mother of God) Cathedral commissioned by the brothers Zakare and Ivane Mkhargrdzeli in 1201. Shirak Province, Armenia. Photo 2018.

Christian'.[69] In reality Ivane's conversion most probably occurred much earlier than Ioane's Catholicosate, since his appointment as *msakhurtukhutsesi* brought him into close contact with the higher clergy and nobility, while the faith of the army commander fighting abroad was a less sensitive matter.

The brothers' confessional divergence turned out to be a clever move since Ivane won the acceptance of traditional Georgian circles while Zakare appealed to the Armenians who were increasing fast as a proportion of the population of Georgia as a result of conquests in former Armenia. This division of religious affiliation also greatly helped to avoid tensions between Georgian and Armenian formations within the royal army. But although both army groups had a Mkhargrdzeli as commander, problems nevertheless arose, fomented by priests who were unwilling to vary their traditional liturgical practices. As the Armenian historian Kirakos Gandzaketsi (*ca.* 1203–1271) reports, conflicts erupted during a military campaign in 1204. While the Georgians carried portable tent-churches with them, which they set up with icons and an altar in order to celebrate the liturgy while on the march, the Armenians refused to join them, and delayed their liturgy and the celebration of feast days till they reached a properly built and consecrated church. They also rejected the use of icons. Worse, divergent fasting rules meant that one part of the troops would be fasting while the other was eating. Zakare demanded that the Armenian priests harmonize their practice with what the Georgians were doing. But the Armenian priests and *vardapets* (graduate clergy) refused to comply and left the decision to the Armenian king of Cilicia, Levon I (r. 1198–1219) and the Catholicos in Hromkla (Rumkale), Ioane VI (in office 1203–1221).

The Armenian scholar and author of a code of civil and canon law, Mkhitar Gosh (1130–1213; fig. 15), recommended flexibility to the conservative priests and vardapets: 'You worry about the people that they do not mix with the Georgians through such customs, and I [will] worry about the commander [Zakare], that he does not become a Georgian like his brother [Ivane], which the Georgians are waiting for.'[70] Both king and Catholicos understood the significance of the issue and hastened to approve Zakare's request. Catholicos Ioane underscored his support by sending

Zakare a mobile tent-church and Bishop Minas as a personal legate.[71] A Church synod convened in Lori confirmed the decisions and in § 4 of the new code of laws explicitly approved the use of icons: 'Icons of the Saviour and all the saints should be accepted, and not despised as though they were pagan images.'[72] In spite of the synod's decisions, some traditional Armenian monasteries rejected the reforms, first and foremost the monastery of Haghpat (fig. 11). Its monks attacked Bishop Minas when he arrived to introduce the new rules, 'leaving him and his men half-dead'. Angered, Zakare threatened Haghpat's abbot Grigores with the death penalty and sent troops to arrest him. Grigores fled, seeking asylum with Mkhitar Gosh. While the Mkhargrdzeli brothers continued to support Haghpat, Ivane seized its subsidiary Akhtala, a strongly fortified monastery commanding the road crossing Lori to Tbilisi, whose main Holy Mother of God church he had decorated with magnificent large-scale murals (fig. 18).[73]

After Yuri Bogolyubsky's first attempt to reconquer his position failed, Davit Soslan attacked Partav (Barda) in Arran and Erzurum in Anatolia, which provoked a call to jihad against Georgia by Caliph al-Nasir (r. 1180–1225). The Muslim coalition was led by *atabeg* Abu Bakr who accepted Yuri's services in 1193 but was crushed in June 1195 at the Battle of Shamkor, 30 kilometres north-west of Ganja, by the Georgian army led by Davit Soslan and the Mkhargrdzeli brothers. While Abu Bakr managed to escape and retake Ganja, his weakened realm would remain a target for annual Georgian raids, which were as much economic as political operations since they gave the army and its commanders an occupation but also secured tax-revenues, booty and prisoners. Before the end of 1195 the Georgians had strengthened their control over Shirvan and two years later captured the important trading hub of Nakhchivan. Following the elimination of the danger in the east, the Mkhargrdzeli brothers swept through the plain of Ararat and started to systematically capture Armenian cities from their Turkic Muslim rulers, including among others Amberd (1196), Ani (1199), Dvin (1203) and later Kars (1206).[74]

15. The Goshavank Monastery. On the left a statue of the scholar Mkhitar Gosh (1130–1213). He initiated the reconstruction of the monastery which was previously called Nor Getik and was destroyed by an earthquake in 1188. Behind the statue stands the Church of St Grigor dating from *ca.* 1011, on the right the Astvatsatsin Church rebuilt by Mkhitar Gosh; at the far right the two-storeyed library. Tavush Province, Armenia. Photo 2015.

These Georgian conquests led by the Armenian Mkhargrdzeli brothers represented in political terms an Armenian reconquest since these former Armenian territories that had been held by Muslim rulers were not then firmly integrated into the Georgian kingdom, but rather, the regency over them was transferred to their conquerors. In short, the Mkhargrdzelis were enfeoffed with their own conquests within the former Armenian kingdoms. As the *Chronicles* specify, Queen Tamar 'did not take all these towns and citadels into the possession of the throne, but bestowed them, [with the exception of Kars,] on those whom she kept occupied, that is, her own troops, as Ani was witness.'[75] Benefiting from the Muslim rulers' promotion of urbanization, trade and monetarization – the best example being Ani – the Mkhargrdzelis were able to establish within the Georgian kingdom a kind of autonomous and prosperous state-within-the-state. While they remained absolutely loyal to Queen Tamar, they ruled their Armenian conquests, including Lori, like viceroys and enjoyed significantly greater autonomy than did Georgian nobles. Roughly summarized, Zakare's realm lay in the south-west stretching from Ani to Lori while Ivane's domain extended from the eastern part of the Ayrarat province, with Dvin as capital, to the regions around Lake Sevan[76] and north-eastern Syunik. Their borders were surrounded by their own or Georgian crown vassal principalities. As *amirspasalar*, Zakare held a kind of supremacy over all Armenian territories.[77] The brothers held their own quasi-princely court and awarded titles and offices within their own territory.[78] However, after the death of Tamar in 1213, cracks would start to open up in the close relationship between Bagrationis and Mkhargrdzelis. The historian Antony Eastmond has shown how the Mkhargrdzelis proclaimed their ambitions in an inscription at Haghartsin monastery (figs. 16, 17) by claiming descent from the royal Armenian Bagratunis who ruled Ani till 1045, and in another inscription at the fortress of Amberd, descent from the royal Armenian Artsrunis, rulers of Vashpurakan till 1025.[79] One may speculate that the Mkhargrdzelis would have gone on to attempt to separate from Georgia and to resurrect the

16. The complex of Haghartsin was the hereditary monastery of the Mkhargrdzeli family. On the left the Astvatsatsin Church (twelfth–thirteenth century) and its ruined *gavit*, on the right the Church of St Grigor with its large *gavit* (early eleventh century). Tavush Province, Armenia. Photo 2015.

former Armenian kingdoms of Ani and Vashpurakan, had not the Mongols shattered both powers, which by the early 1220s had become overconfident.

The conquests of the Georgian–Armenian armies alarmed the powerful sultan of the Rum Seljuks, Rukn al-Din Süleyman II (r. 1196–1204) who in 1201 occupied Erzurum, a Georgian vassal. He then sent Tamar an insulting letter, stating that he would kill all Georgians but those who would convert to Islam. His messenger added that if Tamar would adopt Islam, the Sultan would marry her; otherwise she would be relegated to his harem. Tamar rapidly mobilized the army, gathered it at the rock-hewn town of Vardzia and sent it off under the command of Davit Soslan and the Mkhargrdzelis. The two armies clashed in summer 1203 (or 1202 or 1204) at Basiani, some 60 kilometres north-east of Erzurum. After a hard and bloody fight, the Georgians won the day, forcing the sultan to flee. Thereupon the emirs of Kars, Erzurum and Erzincan were forced to submit. Tamar displayed her contempt for the disloyal Mangujakid emir of Erzincan, Nasir al-Din Vahram Shah, by fixing his ransom at one iron horseshoe.[80] About three years later, in 1206, the unruly cities of Erzurum and Kars were captured and occupied.

Georgia's next strategic move was both bold and far-sighted. At Tamar's court lived her nephews, the brothers Alexios (b. *ca*. 1182) and David Komnenos (b. *ca*. 1184) who were the grandsons of the Byzantine emperor Andronikos Komnenos (r. 1183–1185), who had been murdered in 1185, and sons of Manuel Komnenos who was blinded during the same violent unrest; their mother was Rusudan, younger daughter of Giorgi III. Both princes dreamt of restoring the Komnenos family to the imperial throne and expelling the reigning Doukas clan. An opportunity seemed to arise with the sharp tensions between the Empire and the Fourth Crusade, which had arrived at Constantinople in June 1203 in order to force it to pay its debts. Georgia's westward advance had brought it close to the former *theme* of Khaldia centred on Trebizond on the Black Sea. From Georgia's point of view, the apparent military weakness of Byzantium could tempt the Rum Seljuks to occupy Khaldia and use it as a springboard for hostile attacks. Georgia's war council therefore decided to forestall the Seljuks and to establish a friendly buffer state at its north-western border. Georgian troops occupied the southern Black Sea coast of Khaldia in April 1204 and installed Alexios Komnenos as Emperor Alexios I (r. 1204–1222) of the small Byzantine empire of Trebizond which stretched from Sinope (Sinop) to roughly the present Georgian–Turkish border as a Georgian protectorate.[81] Although

17. Relief of the brothers Ivane and Zakare Mkhargrdzeli, patrons of the Haghartsin monastery, on the eastern wall of the Astvatsatsin Church. Photo 2014.

the Sack of Constantinople occurred on 13–15 April 1204 and Alexios entered Trebizond (Trabzon) probably on 23 April, it is not possible that the Georgian attack took place as a reaction to the fall of Constantinople. News couldn't travel that fast and such a campaign required sufficient preparation time, even for a standing army. At any rate, following the Sack of Constantinople, the enemy that prevented the return of the Komnenoi of Trebizond to the throne of Byzantium was no longer the Doukas family, but the Crusader Latin Empire.

In setting up the satellite empire of Trebizond, Georgia's military capacities threatened to become overstretched, for the distance between Sinope on the Black Sea and the Caspian Sea is 1,200 kilometres as the crow flies. Although enjoying a long run of victories, Georgia remained surrounded by numerous enemies. Its armed forces had either to be dispersed over the entire territory in small units, or remain centred at a couple of key positions, leaving the kingdom's peripheral regions defenceless. Another latent risk was the dependence within the army command structure on its three most senior leaders, Davit Soslan and the Mkhargrdzeli brothers. Some of these weaknesses soon became visible. In 1207, Tamar lost her closest associate with the death of her husband Davit Soslan, and almost vanishes from historical records till her death six years later.[82] Around the same period, her trusted grand chancellor, the archbishop of Chqondidi Anton Glonistavisdze, died. To ensure a smooth transition of power, she nominated her fifteen-year-old son Giorgi IV as co-ruler. In 1208, when the Mkhargrdzelis were celebrating Easter at the royal palace of

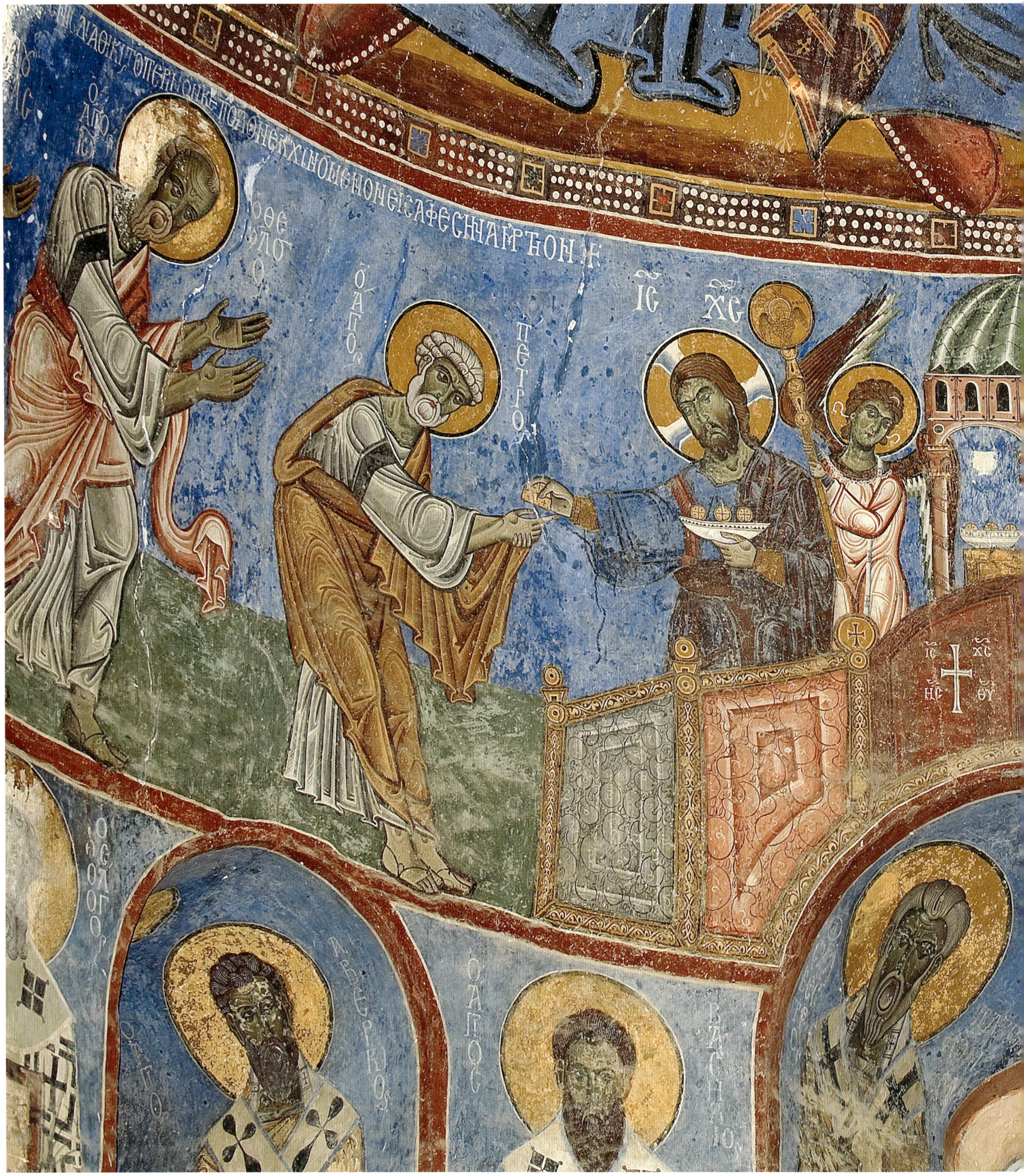
IC XC

IN THE WAKE OF INTERNATIONAL GREAT-POWER POLITICS | 29

Geguti near Kutaisi, the ruler of Ardabil, which belonged to *atabeg* Abu Bakr's realm, seized the opportunity to thoroughly plunder Ani, allegedly massacring 12,000 citizens on Easter Sunday. *Amirspasalar* Zakare took revenge during Ramadan the following year with an equally devastating raid on Ardabil.[83] One year later, Zakare embarked on a gigantic raid. He passed Nakhchivan and looted or extorted tribute in northern Persia from the cities of Marand, Tabriz, Meyaneh, Zanjan, Qazvin and even Gorgan, close to the south-eastern tip of the Caspian Sea, before returning to Tbilisi – a return journey of 3,000 kilometres.[84]

A major setback occurred in 1210. Ivane had challenged the powerful Ayyubid Sultanate which ruled over Syria and Egypt. He attacked the former *beylik* of the Ahlat-Shahs whose realm extended around Lake Van and which had been absorbed by the Ayyubids in 1207. Ahlat's ruler was al-Awhad Ayyub (d. 1210), son of Emir al-Adil I Ayyub (r. 1196–1218) and nephew of Sultan Salah al-Din Yusuf ibn Ayyub (r. 1174–1193), commonly known as Saladin. While the Georgian army besieged Ahlat, Ivane was captured, whereupon Zakare threatened to raze the city and put its population to the sword. Nevertheless, the price for Ivane's ransom was high: the return of conquered fortresses and of prisoners, a thirty-year non-aggression pact on the part of the Georgians, the payment of 100,000 dinars and the handing over of Ivane's daughter Tamta (*ca.* 1195–1254) to be al-Awhad's wife. In the words of Antony Eastmond, 'sisters, daughters and nieces were frequently regarded as commodities for their brothers, fathers and uncles to dispose of however they saw fit to further their own ends.'[85] Tamta experienced an eventful life. After her marriage she ruled Ahlat on and off as regent, until she was captured in 1230 by the Khwarazmian warlord Jalal al-Din who raped her and forced her into a brief marriage. Six years later, she was captured by the Mongols and sent on a 5,000-kilometre trek to the Mongol imperial capital Karakorum where she was detained from 1237 till about 1246. Upon her return to Ahlat she ruled the city and the surrounding region as a Mongol vassal till her death around 1254.[86] The agreement to ransom Ivane ended Georgia's expansion towards Lake Van. When Zakare died in 1212 (or late 1211), leaving behind one son called Shanshe, Tamar elevated Ivane to the rank of *atabeg*.[87]

Tamar died shortly after, in early 1213, at which time Georgia had reached virtually its greatest territorial extent.[88]

---

18. (Previous pages) Mural of the Lord's Supper in the apse of the Astvatsatsin Church of the monastery of Akhtala, dating from the first two decades of the thirteenth century. Jesus is shown twice, sharing bread and wine. Lori, Armenia. Photo 2015.

While Tamar never led the army, she was a capable ruler gifted with diplomatic skills inspiring unflinching loyalty from her close associates. Above all, she was able to choose for the highest positions in the kingdom men of extraordinary capacity and to inspire and maintain their unconditional loyalty. With the death of Queen Tamar, *amirspasalar* Zakare Mkhargrdzeli and Davit Soslan, Georgia's Golden Age was waning fast.

2. The Mongol incursions and supremacy

The years following the deaths of Queen Tamar, Davit Soslan and Zakare Mkhargrdzeli took an inauspicious turn for Georgia as several key parameters for its success turned against the kingdom. Georgia had enjoyed a united and strong leadership made up of highly competent personalities. At the same time, Georgia's enemies were numerous and far more populous, but they lacked great leaders. After this watershed, however, Georgia's two ensuing monarchs were by turns reckless and indulgent and, in the case of Queen Rusudan, anxious. With the sovereign failing to present a model of virtue, the loyalty of their closest associates, who represented the pillars of the state, weakened and the unity of the nation's leadership began to crumble. Even worse, in the Mongol commanders, Georgia was confronted with enemy generals as outstanding as they were ruthless. While the Mongols were never numerous, their superior battle tactics as well as military logistics and intelligence made them virtually invincible.

To believe the brief medieval *Life of Giorgi Lasha*, King **Giorgi IV** (r. 1213–1223), called 'Lasha', the 'Resplendent', quickly managed to alienate the senior army command and the Catholicos by his independent and headstrong behaviour. At Tamar's death, the *atabeg* of Ganja, Muzaffar al-Din Uzbek (r. 1210–1225) stopped paying tribute, whereupon Ivane Mkhargrdzeli laid siege to the city. Instead of waiting for the rebel's inevitable capitulation, Giorgi recklessly attacked with insufficient troops and, although victorious, suffered unnecessarily heavy losses. Hard pressed by the lack of supplies, *atabeg* Uzbek soon agreed to resume tribute payment.[89] A few months later, Giorgi took a married commoner as mistress, who in 1215 gave birth to the future Davit VII Ulu whom Giorgi entrusted to his sister Rusudan for education. Although Catholicos and bishops declared that they would neither accept his mistress as

19. The Mother of God Church of the fortified monastery of Pitareti from the first quarter of the thirteenth century. Kvemo Kartli, Georgia. Photo 2018.

queen nor recognize her son as legitimate heir, Giorgi refused to consider marrying any woman the *Darbazi* would recommend. In the end, Giorgi's mistress had to leave the court and the king remained childless, thus failing in his obligation to secure an appropriate succession.[90] Even worse, Giorgi distanced himself from his mother's senior ministers and surrounded himself at the palace with drinking companions. On one occasion this merry party fell in with a company of horsemen and in the ensuing brawl Giorgi lost the sight in his right eye. Zakare Mkhargrdzeli's son Vahram warned the king: 'We will not acknowledge you as king if you do not give up the company of vicious men.' Giorgi complied and thereafter scored several political and military successes while asserting his authority over the vassal states. Nevertheless, the community of interests between king and feudal nobility had been disrupted, and the powerful feudal lords begun to turn away and to search for ways to expand their own power – first and foremost among them *atabeg* Ivane.[91]

In the winter of 1217–18 an unknown enemy appeared in the east of Georgia's zone of influence when the shah of Khwarazm 'Ala al-Din Muhammad II (r. 1200–1220) crossed northern Iran and captured Tabriz. He forced *atabeg* Uzbek to submit and pay tribute, and informed King Giorgi that from now on Arran belonged to his Khwarazmian Empire.[92] The only reason an armed clash between Georgian and Khwarazmian forces never took place was that tensions were rising in eastern Khwarazm with Genghis Khan's expanding Mongol Empire. Two years later, Giorgi prepared a campaign to support the Crusaders by marching on Jerusalem. As the Burgundian crusader Gilbert de Bois wrote in a letter around 1212, Queen Tamar had already vowed to liberate Jerusalem or send her co-ruler Giorgi. Eight years later, at the beginning of 1220, the papal legate and leader of the Fifth Crusade, Pelagio Galvani, had sent an envoy to Giorgi from the Egyptian harbour city of Damietta urging him to join the Crusade and attack from the north.[93] However, the Georgian crusade never materialized, since in the autumn Giorgi received

20. Christ Pantocrator in the cupola of the Mother of God Church at the Pitareti Monastery. Photo 2018.

warnings from Ivane and Vahram Mkhargrdzeli concerning the arrival of unknown horsemen who were devastating Armenia.[94] Indeed, after Genghis Khan had crushed the Khwarazmian armies in 1219–1220, he ordered two of his best *noyans* (generals), Sübotai (d. 1248) and Jebe (d. after 1231), to pursue and kill the fleeing shah with three *tümen* (army units consisting of 10,000 horsemen each). They were then to reconnoitre northern Iran and Azerbaijan, cross the Caucasus, explore the Kipchak Steppe and return via the Volga to Central Asia.[95] Because of their superior composite bows, Armenian and Western historians called the Mongols the 'nation of the archers'.

In November or early December 1220, two Mongol *tümen* arriving from Nakhchivan appeared in north-eastern Armenia, possibly searching for suitable winter pastures. Here they were opposed by Giorgi and Ivane with an army half their size. While the Georgians were defeated, they inflicted heavy losses on the invaders. The Mongols briefly retreated to the Mughan Steppe, only to resume their attack in January 1221. On the march, the Mongol front line carried crosses, pretending to be friendly Christian troops in order to catch the populations off guard. They advanced along the River Kura, but a Georgian–Armenian army some 70,000 strong blocked the way to Tbilisi. Sübotai applied his favourite tactic of a feigned retreat, provoking the Georgians to attack his light archer cavalry, which slowly retreated while continuously firing from their strong composite bows and inflicting significant losses on the attackers. As soon as the battle line of the Georgian cavalry was drawn apart and the horses of the armoured knights exhausted, Sübotei ordered his heavy cavalry, which had been hidden in a forest, to mount a destructive counterattack, at the same time supplying fresh horses to his light cavalry. The Georgian army was crushed and King Giorgi fled for his life. But Sübotei had no interest in attacking the heavily fortified city of Tbilisi; he preferred to withdraw to the pastures of Lower Karabakh and to extort an enormous ransom from Tabriz's governor to spare the city. After having devastated the wealthy cities of Maragha and Hamadan and slaughtered their populations, the Mongols turned north, destroying several cities of Arran, till they were confronted by King Giorgi with an army, again some 70,000 strong. In spite of his two previous defeats, the valiant king was not prepared to allow the enemy to approach Georgia proper. But the two Mongol generals scored another overwhelming victory thanks to superior tactical skills. Giorgi escaped badly wounded, but the royal standing army was virtually annihilated.[96] As described in the first volume of this work, the Mongols then crossed the Caucasus and at the River Terek met a strong army consisting of Kipchak, Alanian and North Caucasian forces led by the Kipchak prince Yuri. Faced with this superior force, the Mongols once again used treachery: Sübotai bribed the Kipchaks with half of the treasures they had plundered in Iran, persuading them to abandon their Caucasian allies in the night. Then the Mongols immediately attacked the remaining Caucasians and Alans and slaughtered them. Finally they hunted down the unsuspecting Kipchaks and killed them too – thus regaining the treasures they had given them.[97] According to al-Athir, the Mongols recuperated for a while in the Kipchak Plain with its lush pastures. Later they crossed the Cimmerian Bosporus and attacked the harbour city of Sudak (Soldaia), which, according to al-Athir, 'is the Qipjaq's [Kipchaks'] city from which they trade. It is on the Black Sea and [since 1204, Venetian] ships come there, bearing textiles. The Qipjaq buy them and sell female slaves and mamelukes', that is military slaves.[98] In 1223, before returning to Mongolia, Sübotai and Jebe inflicted a crushing defeat on a strong coalition of Rus principalities at the Battle of the Kalka River in today's Ukrainian Donetsk oblast.

Before Giorgi died in January 1223, possibly as a consequence of his wounds suffered in the war against the Mongols, he arranged for the marriage of his sister Rusudan. The selected husband was Ghiyath (Ghias) ad-Din (b. 1206), a younger son of the Seljukid emir of Erzurum, Mugith al-Din Tughril Shah, who, as reported disapprovingly by al-Athir, ordered his son to convert to Christianity in order to make this alliance possible.[99] Unlike Davit Soslan, the Seljukid prince held only a weak

21. *Gavit* and burial vault of the Proshian family who were vassals of the Mkhargrdzelis in the Geghard Monastery complex. The *gavit* standing in front of the second rock church was built in 1283; the reliefs over the two arches show the coat of arms of the Proshian family. Kotayk Province, Armenia. Photo 2015.

position at the Georgian court and never assumed an army command. Rusudan's adulterous lifestyle further undermined his position and when he refused to condone her liaison with a military slave, she banished him to another city where he was kept under strict surveillance.[100] After Rusudan fled from Tbilisi to Kutaisi in 1226, he faded away; in the chronicles he is only remembered as the father of the future Davit VI Narin and of a daughter, Tamar.

Around the same time and as a consequence of the Mongol raid, bands of Kipchaks sought and were refused asylum in Georgia, whereupon they settled in the region of Ganja. In 1222 *atabeg* Ivane suffered a defeat when trying to dislodge them, but in a second battle the following year Ivane recovered their loot and chased them back over the Caucasus.[101] However, Ganja succeeded in shaking off Georgian sovereignty.[102] The handling of the Kipchak intrusion by Giorgi and Ivane stands in obvious contrast to the strategy of Davit IV, who had gladly incorporated Kipchaks eager to migrate into his army.

Although Queen **Rusudan** (r. 1223–1245) was uninterested in governmental affairs and seems to have led a voluptuous life

22. The fortress of Kveshi was built in the eleventh century and was later rebuilt several times. The only access to the castle is a ten-metre-long tunnel carved out of the rock. Kvemo Kartli, Georgia. Photo 2018.

– in the words of Donald Rayfield, she 'inherited Queen Tamar's beauty without [her] charisma and wisdom',[103] she indulged in high-flying plans. In the first year of her reign she wrote to Pope Honorius III (in office 1216–1227) explaining that her brother had been prevented from fulfilling his promise to support the Crusaders by the wicked 'Tartars' who had invaded Georgia. Believing that the Tartars were Christians, the Georgian leaders had been unprepared and suffered a defeat. But then they had conquered the invaders, supposedly killing 25,000 of them – not a figure to be trusted – and chased them away. In her judgement about the Mongols Rusudan was right: the Mongols were no potential allies of the Crusaders against their Muslim enemies, as the popes and some Western leaders believed, but atrociously cruel invaders who murdered Christians and Muslims alike.[104] Rusudan continued in her letter that she had been informed about a planned Crusade by the Emperor Frederick II (r. 1220–1250) and asked by what date the Georgian army led by Ivane Mkhargrdzeli should reach Palestine. 'The princes of our kingdom have already taken the Cross and await the campaign.'[105] Such an endeavour would have meant a more than 1,500-kilometre march through hostile territories. In view of the recent military disasters and the looming threat of renewed Mongol attacks, it seems that both Rusudan and *atabeg* Ivane had lost touch with reality. Instead of embarking on a Crusade, the Georgians were confronted with a Khwarazmian invasion. For Shah Jalal al-Din Manguberni (Manguberti, r. 1224–1231) of Khwarazm, son of 'Ala al-Din Muhammad II, had rebuilt a power base in north-western Iran after having inflicted a rare defeat on the Mongols in 1221 at Parwan in north-eastern Afghanistan.[106]

In 1225, Jalal al-Din first occupied Tabriz, whose ruler *atabeg* Uzbek had fled to the virtually impregnable fortress of Yernjak (Alinja), near Nakhchivan city. According to Jalal's secretary and biographer Muhammad al-Nasawi (d. *ca.* 1250) and the historian Ata-Malik Juvaini (d. 1283), the Georgians were well prepared for the incipient war.[107] They had assembled an army of 60,000 men; Ivane Mkhargrdzeli commanded the main force, the brothers and famous generals Shalva and Ivane Toreli-Akhaltsikheli the strong vanguard. The plan was that the vanguard should engage the enemy first and the *atabeg* keep his force in reserve. Once the battle had begun, Ivane should at a given signal encircle the enemy and destroy it. But there was disunity within the Georgian command as Ivane was jealous of his two younger rivals. After the Khwarazmians had captured Dvin, the two armies met at Garni in Armenia, in August 1225. Al-Nasawi records that the heavily outnumbered Georgian vanguard came under pressure, yet the main army did not move and left the battlefield without having engaged the Khwarazmians.[108] As explained by the anonymous author of *The Hundred Years' Chronicle*, Ivane Mkhargrdzeli begrudged the Toreli brothers the victory.[109] As a result, Ivane Toreli was killed fleeing, Shalva Toreli was captured and later executed, and the main army suffered heavy losses during the retreat when they lost their way.[110] As a consequence of his treacherous behaviour, Ivane Mkhargrdzeli had to cede the supreme command to his son Avag (d. *ca.* 1250). After his victory, Jalal offered peace in return for Rusudan's hand in marriage, which she indignantly refused, fleeing to Kutaisi.[111] Jalal resumed the war and marched to Tbilisi. The citadel there was extremely strong, but on 9 March 1226 some Muslim soldiers in Georgian service betrayed the defenders and opened the gates. Those Christians who refused to convert to Islam were massacred and all churches were destroyed. As narrated by the contemporary historian al-Athir:

The Muslims [Jalal's Khwarazmians] *took the city by force of arms without granting terms and all the Georgians there were put to death. Neither young nor old was spared, except for those who accepted Islam... They were spared* [and] *circumcised ... The Muslims plundered property there, took the women captive and enslaved the children.*[112]

When Jalal later failed to conquer Ahlat, the Georgians briefly reoccupied their capital, but on Jalal's return in 1227, the small garrison chose to put the city to the torch themselves. Although the queen remained in the safety of Kutaisi, Avag did not give up and assembled an army composed of Georgians, Kipchaks, Alans and Vainakhs (Chechens). In 1228 (or 1229) he attacked the Khwarazmians at Bolnisi, south of Tbilisi, but Jalal managed to bribe the Kipchaks who accounted for half the Georgian army's strength. The Kipchaks deserted and the Georgians again suffered defeat.[113]

However, Jalal soon left Georgia to battle against the Rum Seljuks and Ayyubids. He managed to finally conquer Ahlat in April 1230. However, his rape of the Ayyubid emir al-Ashraf Musa's wife Tamta, who had married al-Ashraf after the death of his brother al-Awhad – a provocative humiliation of al-Ashraf who had left the besieged city and Tamta in it – aroused the emir's yearning for revenge, and Jalal suffered a bloody defeat at the hands of an alliance between al-Ashraf and the Rum Seljuk sultan Kay-Qubad at the Battle of Yassıçemen in August.[114] Soon after, Jalal heard that the Mongol general Chormaghun (Chormaqan) was chasing him with a 30,000-strong army. He fled immediately, and was murdered in 1231 in Kurdistan. As reported by his secretary al-Nasawi, who accompanied the fugitive sultan, in one of his last nights Jalal, drunk, was behaving 'like a man unable to swim who had fallen into water and was clinging in to anything that he could grab'.[115] In the next two years the Mongols hunted down the remaining Khwarazmian war bands, devastated south-eastern Anatolia and around 1231 utterly destroyed the city of Ganja which was sacked again four years later. By this time, the Mongols were in permanent occupation of present-day Azerbaijan; their commander *noyan* Chormaghun (in office 1230–1241 or 1242) acted as a military viceroy, holding both military and administrative powers. After 1232 the Mongols concentrated their operations in Iran.

Meanwhile Queen Rusudan was working to ensure the future of her line of succession over that of her deceased brother. In 1230, she had her five-year-old son crowned as Davit VI, but she still had to solve the problem of King Giorgi's bastard son Davit, who would soon be an adult. The solution was to betroth her daughter Tamar in 1235 to the future Rum Seljuk sultan Kai-Khosrow II (r. 1237–1246) and hand her nephew Davit over to him to keep as a prisoner.[116] This bastard nephew, the future Davit VII Ulu, remained in Seljuk custody till 1243 when the Mongols crushed the Sultanate.

For Georgia as a state, the first Mongol and especially the Khwarazmian invasions were utterly destructive. The army was significantly weakened, its reputation had evaporated and vassals such as Shirvan, Ganja and Derbent had joined the aggressors. Even worse, Queen Rusudan and her court had abandoned central and eastern Georgia to their fates, which meant that the local nobles were left on their own; there was no longer any coordinated defence. With the disappearance of the queen and unified command, the bonds of loyalty towards the central authorities likewise dissolved. The nobles with their small armies retreated to their strong fortresses hoping to survive the hostile flood.[117] While this tactic more or less worked during the Khwarazmian raids, it would prove disastrous during the Mongol attacks that followed. For when Chormaghun resumed his attacks on Armenia and Georgia in early 1236, he came not to loot, but to conquer, stay and exploit the countries' material wealth and reservoir of young men suitable for war. Since there was no longer a Georgian royal army, Chormaghun divided the land among his *noyans*, allocating each of them a principality to subdue. In order to speed up the conquest and so as not to waste Mongol soldiers in attacking strong fortifications, Chormaghun offered relatively attractive conditions to submitting nobles: their personal security was guaranteed and they could keep their domains,

but had to take an oath of allegiance to the Great Khan, deliver hostages (usually their sons), supply provisions for the occupying troops and their messengers, submit registers of populations for taxation purposes, pay taxes and, what proved to be the heaviest obligation, provide soldiers for the Mongols' endless wars. Finally, senior local rulers were required to present themselves at the Mongol court in Karakorum in distant Mongolia or, as of the early 1240s, at the *ordu* (camp) of Batu Khan, founder of the Golden Horde, which stood near the lower Volga.[118]

The first high Georgian noble to capitulate was *amirspasalar* Avag Mkhargrdzeli in 1236. As described by Kirakos Gandzaketsi, Avag was received in honour by Chormaghun and secured his possessions, but he was forced to participate with his own troops in the Mongol attack on Ani, which belonged to his cousin Shanshe Mkhargrdzeli.[119] This meant that the son of Ivane Mkhargrdzeli had to fight the son of Zakare Mkhargrdzeli – the Mongol conquest became a Georgian civil war. Avag, in order to save his own skin and property, had to participate in the destruction of his own Armenian family empire and of the Kingdom of Georgia built by his father and uncle. As Avag dutifully continued supporting the Mongol efforts after the capture and destruction of Ani and Kars, one castle after the other surrendered. In Kirakos's words, 'there was no one to resist them [the Mongols] or offer war against them. Therefore fear was everywhere. The queen of the Georgians had fled to wherever she was able [Svaneti]. So all the princes surrendered.'[120] Avag quickly became the de facto ruler of Central Georgia and former Armenia, and around 1240 Chormaghun sent him to Karakorum where Ögödei Khan confirmed his position and gave him a Mongol wife.[121] Among the other princes who surrendered were Shanshe Mkhargrdzeli of Ani, Ivane Mkhargrdzeli's nephew Vahram Gagetsi of Shamkor, Elikum Orbelian of Syunik and Hasan Jalal Dawla (r. ca 1214–1261) of Khachen, the builder of the cathedral of Gandzasar. These nobles received the status of *enchu* which meant 'owned by the Great Khan'.[122] Hasan Jalal not only visited Karakorum twice, but also Batu Khan of the Golden Horde (r. 1227–1255) to whose son Sartaq (r. 1255–1256) he became a friend. In line with the Mongol strategy of *divide et impera*, Hasan Jalal was allowed to separate Khachen from Georgia and the Mkhargrdzelis' authority. Hasan Jalal was the founder of the dynasty of *meliks* (rulers) of Khachen which held semi-independent power with interruptions till the Russian invasions of 1804–1813 and the death of the last melik Allaverdi II Hasan Jalalyan in 1813.[123]

Smbat Orbelian, brother of Elikum Orbelian who was allegedly poisoned by Avag during a Mongol campaign against

23. Monastery of Tegher. On the right stands the Astvatsatsin Church (built in 1213) and on the left the *gavit* on whose two western roof corners two small corner chapels were built in 1221. Aragatsotn Province, Armenia. Photo 2017.

Martyropolis (probably near modern Silvan), also travelled twice to Karakorum in 1251–1252 and 1256, each journey amounting to more than 10,000 kilometres there and back, and secured the independence of Syunik from Georgia.[124] By swearing oaths of allegiance to the Mongol khan, the Georgian and Armenian nobles broke their remaining ties to the Georgian crown. The nobles also did not shrink from intriguing against each other while vying for the favour of the Mongols, for example the Mkhargrdzelis against the rising Orbelians, or the Mankaberdelis (Artsrunis) also against the Orbelians.[125] In order to maintain fighting strength, combat readiness and mobility, the Mongol *noyans* avoided the cities and stayed with their troops in the countryside. In the winter of 1238–39, the future Great Khan Möngke invaded the northern Caucasus from the north. The objective was not to occupy the inhospitable mountain regions, but to control the defile of Derbent and to secure their left flank during the first pan-Mongol campaign into Russia and Eastern Europe. While the coast regions of Derbent and Adygea were quickly subjugated, the Alans would continue to resist for three more decades.[126]

Although Queen Rusudan was well protected in her densely forested refuges in Svaneti and Imereti – the limits of Mongol cavalry deployment were the limits of their conquests – she agreed to Avag's recommendation to formally submit to the Mongols to ensure her succession; that is, the recognition of her son Davit. Previously, misjudging the nonexistent military strength of Pope Gregory IX (in office 1227–1241), she had asked him for help and had in her distress even raised the prospect that the Georgian Church might enter a union with Rome. The

24. (Overleaf) Medieval defence towers at Nij on the southern spur of the Tsorey-Loam Mountains. The upper part of the towers bear crosses indicating that the population in medieval times was Christian. Ingushetia, Russian Federation. Photo 2017.

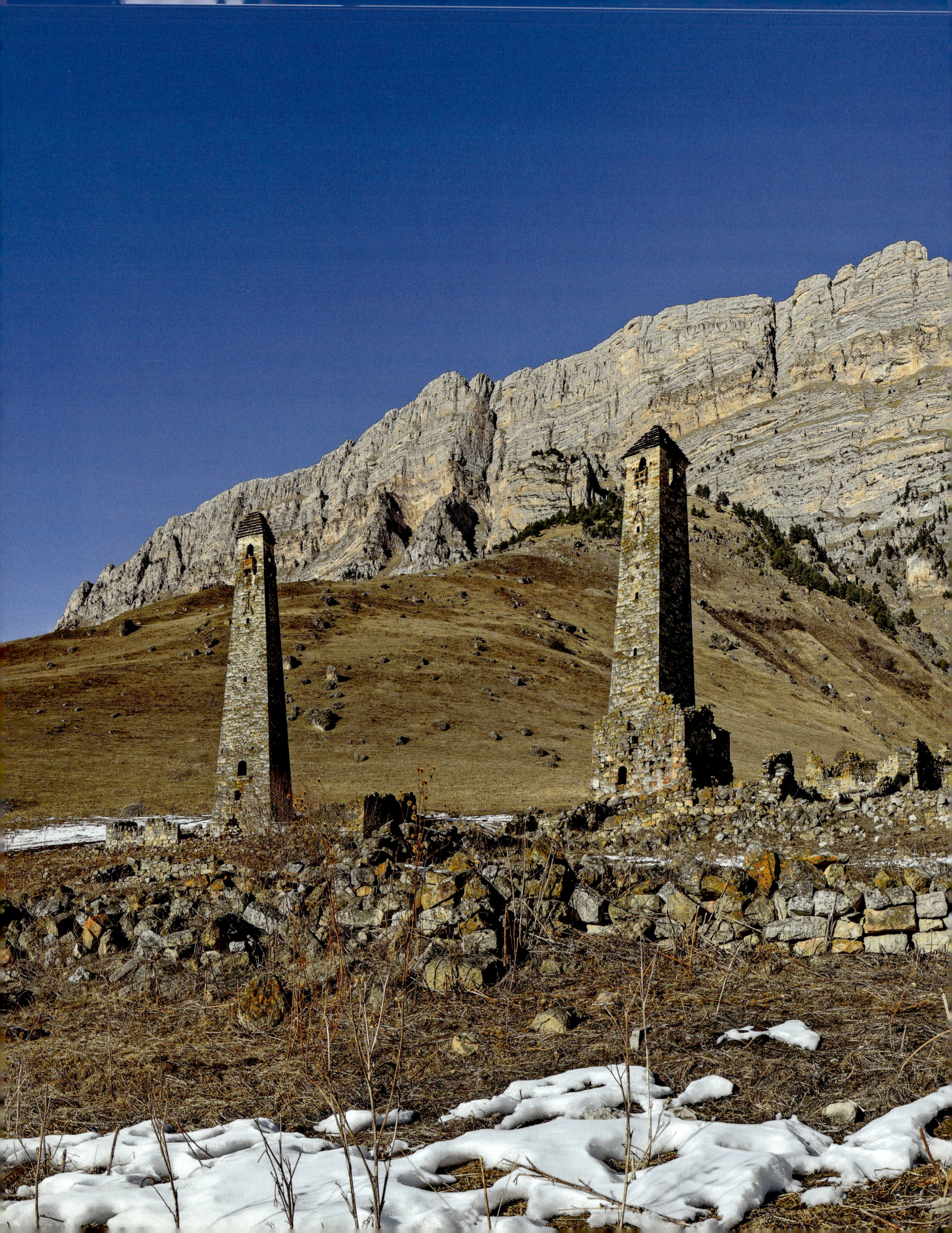

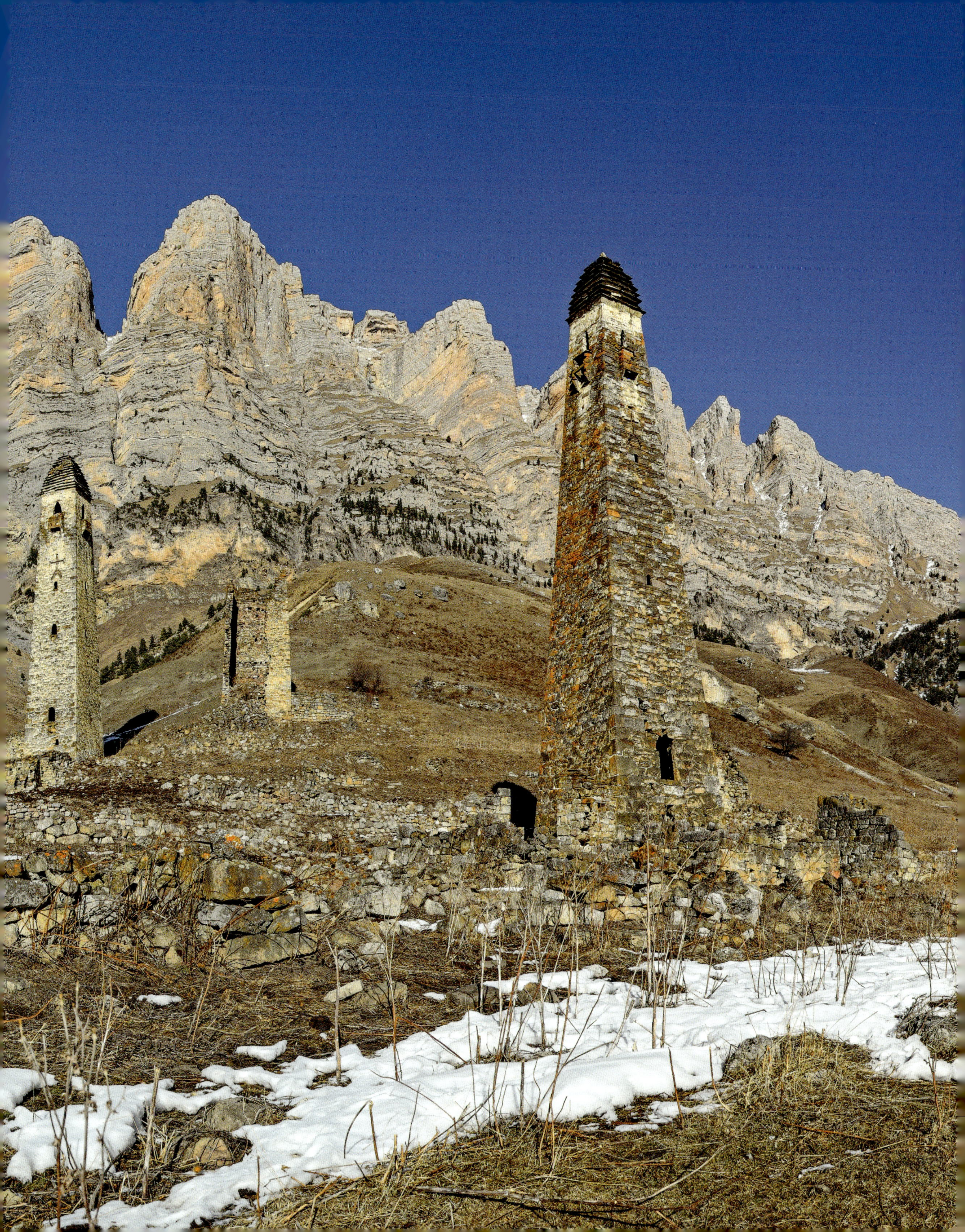

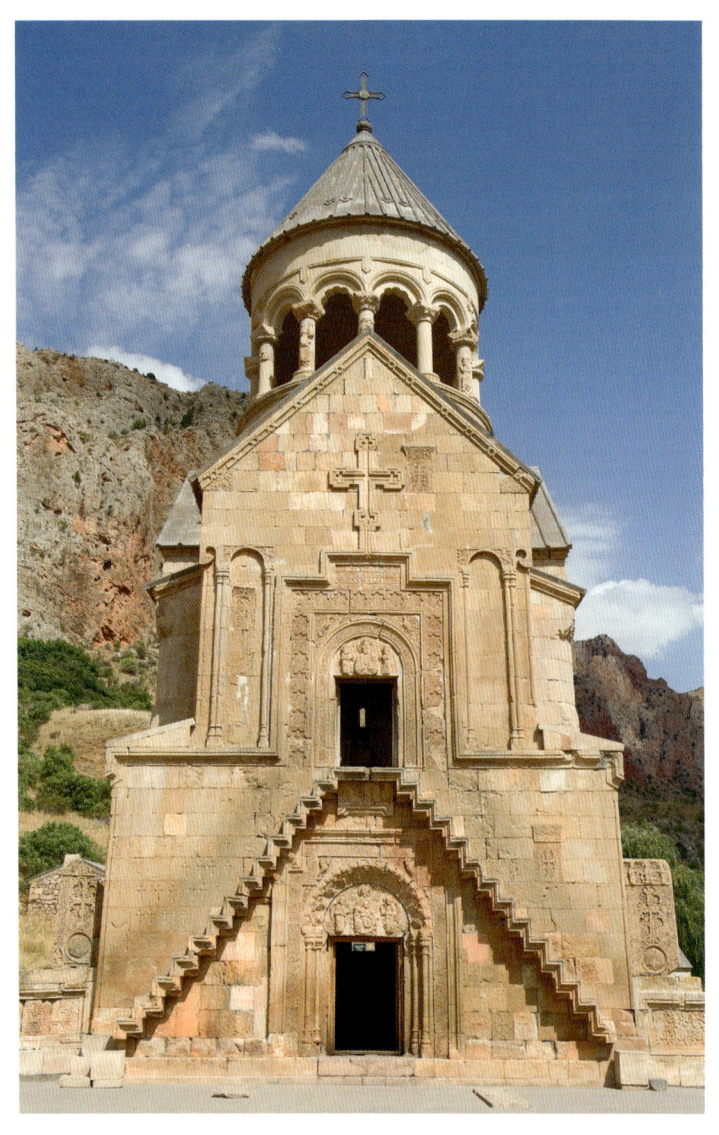

25. The three-storeyed Astvatsatsin Church of Noravank was built between 1331 and 1338. The monastery served as mausoleum for the Orbeliani family. In the lower tympanum the Virgin Mary and Jesus are flanked by the archangels Michael and Gabriel, in the upper Christ is represented between the apostles Peter and Paul. Vayots Dzor Province, Armenia. Photo 2015.

pope sent no troops, but Dominican missionaries instead, who founded, according to the Dominican friar Simon of Saint-Quentin (d. after 1248), a small convent in Tbilisi around 1240.[127] In 1243 (or 1242) Chormaghun's successor Baiju Noyan (in power 1241/42–1247, ca. 1251–1255)[128] accepted Rusudan's submission and sent her son Davit to the camp of Batu Khan and from there to Karakorum for imperial approval. By acknowledging Rusudan's submission, the Mongols introduced a dual regime insofar as they recognized the institution of royal rule and at the same time promoted regionalization by conferring on cooperative nobles the status of *enchu*. While the latter strategy hastened the kingdom's submission, the former simplified administration. When Rusudan died in 1245, her son had not yet returned and was presumed dead. The nobles therefore resigned themselves to accept Giorgi's illegitimate son Davit, who had been freed from his captivity after Kai-Khosrow II's defeat by Baiju at the Battle of Köse Dağ in 1243. He too was dispatched to Karakorum where the two Davits met at the Mongol court. The Great Khan Güyük (r. 1246–1248) recognized both and ranked them by seniority: Giorgi Lasha's son **Davit VII** (r. 1247–1270, from 1259/62 in east Georgia only) called **Ulu** (senior) and Rusudan's son **Davit VI** (r. 1247–1293, from 1258/59 in Imereti and Abkhazia only) called **Narin** (junior) were both to reign, but Davit Ulu would be the higher ranking. Kirakos summarized Güyük's decision as follows: 'And [the two Davits] went to Guyuk-Khan who received them with love. He legislated that they should rule the kingdom by turns – first Dawitʻ son of Lasha Giorg, the elder of the two; then, following his death, his father's sister's son, the other Dawitʻ, son of Rusudan, should he still be alive.'[129] As confirmed by the Il-Khanid historian 'Ala al-Din Ata-Malik Juvaini, 'Davit, the son of Qiz [maiden] Malik [that is Rusudan], he [Güyük] made subject to the other Davit.'[130] Following mediation by Avag, the condominium worked rather well for ten years, giving the appearance of a reunited Georgia. Davit Ulu resided in Tbilisi and Davit Narin often in Svaneti, although both had to participate in Mongol campaigns.[131]

The arrangements between Georgia's nobles and the *noyans* under the military rule of Chormaghun and Baiju lasted less than ten years. In this initial period, Georgia was divided into eight *tanmas*, also spelled *tamma*, military provinces administered by a local noble under the control of a Mongol *noyan*. Cordial relations between nobles and Mongol commanders were quickly established and sealed by marital ties which also led to private agreements concerning taxes. The nobles misused the opportunity to enrich themselves by demanding extra tax income for themselves, with the *noyans* withholding some of what was due to the central government in Karakorum. This relatively relaxed regime ended when the Great Khan Ögödei's widow and regent Töregene (r. 1241–1246) appointed the Muslim Arghun Aqa (in office 1243/44–1255) to be governor and supreme tax collector, endowing him also with military authority to administer an immense area from the Oxus to central Anatolia, including Georgia and former Armenia. His friend Juvaini remembered: 'Upon arriving in Tabriz, he [Emir Arghun] restored to order the affairs of that region which had been disturbed by the proximity of the great emirs such as Chormaghun, Baichu and others, who regarded that territory as their own property.'[132] In order to secure the requested volume of tax, Arghun centralized the levying of taxes by assigning their collection to special officials called *darughachi* in Mongol or *basqaq* in Turkic. These *basqaq* reported to Arghun, had no personal local ties and implacably disempowered the nobles while collecting the required taxes. In time, regional administrators known as *yeke jarghuchi* would replace the military commanders of the *tanmas*, completing the transition from military rule to civilian administration. The system was further tightened when in 1254 Möngke Khan ordered Arghun to conduct a census which again increased the tax base.[133]

The Franciscan William of Rubruck (d. after 1257), who had travelled to Karakorum by order of King Louis IX of France (r. 1226–1270) and met the Great Khan Möngke in early 1254, crossed Nakhchivan and Armenia on his return journey in winter 1254–55. In Nakhchivan, as in numerous adjoining regions, he observed the havoc wreaked by Mongols and Khwarazmians: 'Nakhchivan … was a very large and beautiful city, but it has been reduced by the Tartars [Mongols] almost to a wilderness. It contained at one time eight hundred Armenian churches, but now there are no more than two tiny ones, as they have been destroyed by the Saracens', that is the Muslim Khwarazmians.[134] Unlike the latter, who deliberately persecuted Christians and destroyed churches, the Mongols usually cared little about religious affiliation. They differentiated conquered people into obedient servants and rebels or turncoats. They were interested in exploiting human, financial and material resources, not in the beliefs of their underlings. Exceptions were the Muslim Il-Khans Ahmad (r. 1282–1284) and Ghazan (r. 1295–1304) who mainly persecuted the Nestorians, by far the largest Christian minority within Iran and today's Iraq, and ordered the destruction of their churches.[135] Rubruck then followed the River Araxes upstream and reached Ani which had by then been rebuilt. There he was a guest of Shanshe and Zakare II Mkhargrdzeli and met five

26. The medieval fortress of Ramana dating from the thirteenth to fourteenth centuries stands on the top of a small hill on the Absheron Peninsula. Baku District, Azerbaijan. Photo 2016.

Dominicans sent by the pope to Batu and Möngke Khan.[136] On the way, Rubruck stopped at the winter quarters of Baiju, who had just been informed that he would be subordinate to Hülegü. Rubruck was well received by Baiju, unlike the Dominican Ascelin of Cremona in 1247, who barely escaped with his life after his arrogant behaviour and refusal to follow Mongol customs of respect when he met Baiju in Sisian in Armenia.[137]

In 1255 Möngke Khan removed Georgia, Arran and Azerbaijan from the loose sphere of influence of the Golden Horde and assigned them to his younger brother Hülegü (r. as Il-Khan 1259/60–1265) who was preparing the second pan-Mongol westward campaign, which aimed at the final and complete conquest of Iran and the Middle East.[138] Hülegü, founder of the Perso-Mongol Il-Khan dynasty[139] quickly introduced additional taxes which were exacted with hitherto unknown brutality. Furthermore, in order to obtain the tax money quickly, Hülegü and his successors leased the tax collection to tax farmers who in turn would not hesitate to raise taxes twice or thrice a year. Those who couldn't pay the exorbitant taxes were beaten and tortured, had their cattle confiscated or their children sold into slavery.[140] Due to Hülegü's never-ending wars, first against the Assassins, then against the caliph, the Syrian Ayyubids, the Egyptian Mamelukes, and finally his cousin and rival Berke, he demanded more and more troops from the Georgian nobles, who were often placed in the most dangerous position in battle. Georgian and Armenian knights and cavalry were used as shock troops, and infantry as mere 'human arrow shields'.[141] At this point it is worthy of mention that the calamities inflicted by the Mongol wars and the reckless exploitation of Christians and Muslims alike did nothing to shake their faiths. Christian and Muslim historians usually interpreted all these disasters as God's punishments for their sins, rather than viewing these catastrophes as an indication that their God was weak or even nonexistent.

In Georgia rebellions soon broke out. According to the contemporary historian and monk Vardan Areveltsi (*ca.* 1198–1271), a first, abortive rebellion took place in 1249 when several princes gathered at Tbilisi, trying to convince Davit Ulu to join them. But 'Baiju and the other nobles [probably Avag] got wind of the presumptuousness and rebelliousness of the king and the princes … King Dawit was arrested as were other grandees who were bound and sentenced to death.'[142] Avag paid a huge ransom and the king and some of the nobles escaped execution. Ten years later in 1258 or 1259, in view of the steady and accelerating depletion of the Georgian provinces and the unfulfillable demands for troops, Davit VI Narin rebelled in Azerbaijan. After a few initial successes, he was forced to flee to Kutaisi where the western Georgian nobles crowned him as their king of Abkhazia (r. 1258/59–1293). Imereti and Abkhazia were now outside the Mongol Empire and Georgia remained divided till 1334.[143] Georgian and Armenian nobles continued to be compelled to support the Mongols in their wars in western Armenia, and also in the siege of the Ayyubid city of Martyropolis which offered tenacious resistance. As Kirakos wrote:

The city withstood the siege for more than two years while hunger grew more acute within. They ate clean and unclean animals and then started to eat people when there was no more food. The strong ate the weak. When the [supply of] poor people was exhausted they turned against one another. Fathers ate sons, and women ate their daughters; and they did not spare the fruit of their wombs.[144]

When the Mongols finally captured the city, they spared the churches out of respect for their Christian auxiliaries and allowed the Christian nobles to remove the relics which had been collected by St Marutha in the early fifth century and bring them to Georgia. In those days Davit Ulu reigned in central and eastern Georgia and held loose sovereignty over Armenia and Samtskhe in today's southern Georgia. He dutifully participated in 1258 in the attack and capture of Baghdad, but when summoned in early 1260 to join the Mongol campaign against Syria, he refused. When Arghun, now a subordinate to Hülegü, advanced on a punitive expedition, several princes chose to support him against their king. Davit fled to Sargis Jaqeli, prince of Samtskhe, where both rebels organized an obstinate resistance to Arghun. In retaliation, in 1261 Arghun executed Hasan Jalal of Khachen and Zakare II Mkhargrdzeli, son of Shanshe and grandson of Queen Tamar's *amirspasalar* Zakare I Mkhargrdzeli.[145] Soon after, Davit Ulu's wife Gvantsa, the former wife of Avag Mkhargrdzeli who had died in 1250, was also killed. This revolt ruined the fortunes of the Mkhargrdzeli clan, who were forced to sell Ani to the vizier Shams al-Din Juvaini, brother of the historian 'Ala al-Din Ata Malik Juvaini. But some years after the execution of the vizier in 1284, the Mkhargrdzeli managed to re-acquire Ani, though by this time it had been impoverished by the wars.[146]

Although Samtskhe managed to resist the Mongol attack, Davit Ulu sought refuge with Davit Narin in Kutaisi. However, quarrels soon arose between the two cousins.[147] But Hülegü's numerous difficulties were Davit Ulu's chance, for Hülegü's elder brother and supporter, the Great Khan Möngke, had died in 1259; a Mameluke army had destroyed a Mongol force at 'Ain

27. Mural of Christ Pantocrator in the ruined Chalcedonian monastery church of Khobayr. The monastery was founded in the twelfth century and acquired by Ivane Mkhargrdzeli in the early thirteenth century after he had joined the Georgian Orthodox Church. Ivane's nephew Shanshe is buried in the complex. When the author visited the ruined complex in 2015, two chapels were used as cow stables. The local Armenian authorities are rumoured to deliberately keep the buildings in a neglected and dilapidated state because the Georgian Church claims authority over the former monastery of Khobayr. Lori, Armenia. Photo 2015.

Jalut in Palestine in 1260; and an inter-Mongol war threatened.[148] Khan Berke (r. 1257–1266), half-brother of Batu Khan and ruler of the Golden Horde, did not accept the loss of the southern Caucasus and north-western Mesopotamia to Hülegü, who had expelled Berke's tribute collectors. Later, in the winter of 1259–60, the execution or poisoning by Hülegü of the three Jochid[149] princes Balagai, Tutar and Quli, who belonged to Berke's clan and had been ordered by Möngke Khan to participate in Hülegü's campaign,[150] as well as the murder of two of Berke's emissaries, triggered a massacre in which each side killed the other's traders.[151] With these events, the so-called *Pax Mongolica* that had ensured safe passage to traders throughout the Mongol Empire was definitively over. Even worse for Hülegü, in 1261 the Muslim convert Berke appealed to Hülegü's arch-enemy, the Mameluke sultan Baibars, to resume war in the name of their shared faith against his infidel cousin in Iran.[152] Of course, Berke and the Mameluke Sultan Baibars did not conclude their alliance for religious reasons, but for tangible economic and military purposes: the Mamelukes wanted to secure a constant flow of Turkic slaves from the northern steppes and a connection to the southern 'Silk Road' trade routes from which they were excluded by the axis of the two dominant branches of Toluids. The Mongol Toluids (the brothers Möngke, Hülegü and Kublai Khan, all sons of Genghis Khan's youngest son Tolui)[153] controlled the main, southern Silk Road starting in China and leading westward through (the at times insecure) Chagataid Central Asia and Il-Khanid Persia and ending at the harbour of Ayas, today's Yumurtalık, in the Il-Khanid vassal of Armenian Cilicia (fig. 38). The Golden Horde on the other hand was looking for an ally to reconquer Georgia, Arran and Azerbaijan, lost in 1255. Berke's decision to enter an alliance with the avowed enemy of another Mongol Genghisid ruler was an outrageous break with the dominant ideology established by Genghis Khan, that the world should be run by his descendants as decreed by the Heavenly Mandate. It represented the final step towards the dissolution of the Mongol Empire of which the first serious fissure had appeared in the conflicts between the Great Khan Güyük and Batu Khan.

In this dangerous situation Hülegü had no choice but to pardon Davit Ulu and restore him to his throne in Tbilisi in order to win him as ally against Berke's expected attacks. Sargis Jaqeli not only received a pardon as well, but was recognized in 1266 by Hülegü's successor Abaqa (r. 1265–1281) as a ruler independent of the Georgian king when Davit VII attempted to subjugate Samtskhe.[154] From now on, Georgia was divided into three parts: two kingdoms and one principality. Around the same time, the unity of the Georgian Orthodox Church also began to fall apart when a Catholicosate of Abkhazia re-emerged in Pitsunda.[155] In spite of all the misery that Hülegü's reign brought to Georgia, when he and his Nestorian wife Dokuz Khatun died in 1265, the Armenian historian and metropolitan bishop Stepanos Orbelian did not hesitate to compare their piety to that of the Emperor Constantine and his mother Helena.[156] As recorded by the contemporary grand vizier and historian Rashid al-Din Fadhlallah Hamdani (1247–1318), the war between the two Mongol cousins ended in a draw. In 1262 Berke's commander Nogai Noyan (d. 1299) attacked and defeated Hülegü's vanguard at Shirvan whereupon Hülegü's army inflicted a heavy defeat on Nogai near Derbent in December. Hülegü then advanced northwards as far as the River Terek where Nogai completely crushed Hülegü's army on 13 January 1263. King Davit Ulu and several nobles participated in

28. Miniature on parchment of the Prophet Jonah being spat out by the giant fish sent by God. Lectionary by the famous painter Toros Roslin from 1288. © Matenadaran, Yerevan.

this campaign and Sargis Jaqeli even saved Hülegü's life during the battle of the Terek. Nogai attacked again in 1264 but retreated without a fight when he was informed that Kublai Khan had vanquished Ariq Böke in the war for overall Mongol leadership and had sent his brother Hülegü an army of 30,000 horsemen as reinforcement. Two years later Berke led another army southwards, heading for Tbilisi, but drowned when attempting to cross the River Kura.[157] Berke's death meant no respite from the Il-Khanate since his successor Möngke-Temür Khan (r. 1266/67–1280) managed to incite Baraq Khan (r. 1266–1271) of the Mongol Chagatai Khanate to attack from the east.

The aforementioned Stepanos Orbelian, who was consecrated archbishop of Syunik in 1286, was the son of the prince and *atabeg* Tarsaich Orbelian, a member of the rising Orbelian clan. He was not only the chronicler of his ancestral dynasty, but also an eminent scholar and leader of the conservative movement prevalent in the former Greater Armenia dedicated to uphold traditional Armenian culture and, above all, the uncompromising purity of the Miaphysite Armenian Orthodox faith. Stepanos was one of the champions of Armenian orthodoxy and the independence of its church against the claimed authority of the papacy which was propagated by Catholic missionaries and supported on political grounds by some Catholicoi residing in Cilician Armenia. He is said to have declared: 'It is better to go to hell with one's forefathers than enjoy the delights of heaven with the dyophysites', that is the Catholics.[158] The archbishop was a graduate of the famous university of Gladzor, whose ruins have been tentatively identified with the monastery of Tanahativank in Syunik (fig. 29). The present buildings and ruins were built in the 1270s by the Proshian and Orbelian families; the former were also important donors at the monastery of Geghard (fig. 21). The university was founded in 1291 by *vardapet* (master) Nerses Mshetsi who taught calligraphy and theology. Other subjects taught were philosophy, geometry, mathematics and miniature painting. In 1338 the university had to close due to political unrest and was transferred two years later to the fortified monastery of Tatev from where the fight for the Armenian Church's independence continued. Stepanos Orbelian engineered and in 1297 contributed to the restoration of Tatev which was in a dilapidated condition. Finally, to remove the institution of the Catholicosate from the influence of the pro-Catholic Cilician kings, he advocated that its seat should return to Armenia proper which it had left in the eleventh century;[159] but the relocation of the main Catholicosate to Etchmiadzin in fact took place only in 1441.

When Davit VII Ulu was succeeded by his eleven-year-old son **Demetre II** (r. 1270–1289) as king of what was left of Georgia, Il-Khan Abaqa nominated Sadun Mankaberdeli as his tutor and regent. Through these offices Sadun accumulated immense wealth and when he died in 1281, Demetre tried to curtail the power of the Mankaberdeli clan by appointing Sadun's son Khutlu Bugha as *amirspasalar* but refusing him the role of *atabeg*, which he gave to Khutlu's rival Tarsaich Orbelian. Khutlu became Demetre's mortal enemy. Demetre dutifully took to the field with Georgian troops for the Il-Khans in their increasingly fruitless and costly wars against the Egyptian Mamelukes. In 1277, the Mameluke sultan Baibars (1260–1277) inflicted a heavy defeat on an Il-Khanid army at Elbistan east of Caesarea (Kayseri)[160] and in 1281 Abaqa's inexperienced brother Möngke-Temür led a strong army to Syria. On 30 October of that year, Möngke-Temür attacked the Mameluke army commanded by Sultan Qalawun (r. 1279–1290) at the Second Battle of Homs. The Mongol right wing, which consisted of Christian contingents from Georgia, Cilician Armenia and the Order of St John of Jerusalem, quickly put the enemy's left wing to flight. In the centre, however, Möngke-Timur panicked after being slightly wounded and fled, followed by most of his Mongols, turning a palpable victory into complete disaster.[161] The contemporary Armenian historian and member of the royal nobility, Hethum of Korykos (or Corycus, *ca*. 1240–after 1314) mocked: 'Temür, who had never fought a battle, retreated for fear of some Saracens … without good reason and left the victorious field.'[162] Thousands of Georgian and Armenian knights and horsemen lost their lives and King Demetre barely escaped death. The days of Mongol invincibility and superiority of leadership were long gone. Another matter affecting Georgian and Cilician Armenian vassals were the power struggles within the Il-Khanid leadership. Usually, the winner would not only execute the loser, but also wipe out his family, friends and clients. When Emir Bugha, vizier of the Il-Khan Arghun (r. 1284–1291) was convicted of conspiracy, his henchman King Demetre was ordered to court. While Arghun still hesitated to have him executed, his old enemy Khutlu Bugha recommended replacing him with Davit Narin's son Vakhtang. Demetre was beheaded In March 1289.[163]

Vakhtang II (r. 1289–1292) came to the throne with great expectations, as it was hoped that he would later succeed his aged father and thus reunite east and west Georgia. However, he died after only three years' reign and was succeeded by Demetre's son **Davit VIII** (r. 1292–1299, d. 1308). Davit pursued an active policy of intrigues when he supported the Il-Khanid Christian pretender Baydu (r. 1295) against the Il-Khan Gaykhatu (r. 1291–1295). But Baydu was toppled after a few months by the stern Muslim Ghazan (r. 1295–1304) who decided to punish Davit for his meddling in Il-Khanid policy. Instead of obeying the order to appear at court as his father Demetre had done, since this was equivalent to a death warrant, he fled to the mountains of the Greater Caucasus, from where he successfully led a guerrilla war. Since the Mongols were unable to penetrate

29. The monastery church of Tanahativank was founded in the 1270s by members of the Proshian and Orbeliani families who were related by marriage. It is believed that the famous university of Gladzor was located at Tanahativank. Of the supposed university only the foundation walls are left. Vayots Dzor Province, Armenia. Photo 2015.

his forested mountain base, they left him to rule northern Georgia as of 1304/05 till his death in 1308;[164] in 1299, however, Ghazan declared Davit VIII deposed and replaced him with his younger brother **Giorgi V** (first reign 1299–1302), whose tutor was Beka Jaqeli of Samtskhe.[165] After only three years Ghazan deposed Giorgi too and installed another brother, **Vakhtang III** (r. 1302–1311), who regularly found himself forced to command the Georgian auxiliaries in the Mongol campaigns in Syria. In the winter of 1299–1300 Vakhtang had to join the Mongol army commanded by Ghazan which succeeded in occupying Aleppo and Damascus, but wasted its victories by retreating in spring and leaving only desultory garrisons. In 1303, a Mongol army led by general Qutlugh Shah and reinforced by Georgian troops commanded by King Vakhtang, as well as Cilician Armenians under their king Hethum II, marched to Damascus, but was destroyed by a Mameluke coalition in April at the Battle of Marj al-Saffar (or Battle of Shaqhab) south of Damascus.[166] The war efforts to reconquer Syria from the Egyptian Mamelukes had become vain. The Mamelukes were former horsemen from the Kipchak Steppe familiar with the tactics of steppe warfare. By the times of sultans Baibars and Qalawun, the Mamelukes of Kipchak and Circassian origin were the best-trained military elite of the Middle Ages. They received thorough training in all aspects of horsemanship, in handling bows and lances on horseback, and in swordsmanship with the long, double-edged rider's sword. Later, in 1307, a Mongol–Georgian army also failed in an attempt to subjugate the mountain tribes living in forested Gilan, in north-western Iran.[167]

In 1311, **Giorgi V**, named 'Brtsqinvale', 'the Magnificent', returned to power, first as regent for Davit VIII's son, the minor **Giorgi VI** (r. 1311–1313), and afterwards as ruler in his own right (second reign 1314–1346). Giorgi was, like his illustrious ancestors Bagrat III and Davit IV, keen to achieve the reunification of Georgia. The conditions for realizing this goal were favourable, as infighting prevailed in Imereti and the Il-Khans were more than ever dependent on Georgian cavalry to repel the attacks of Özbek Khan of the Golden Horde (r. 1313–1341) who aimed to reconquer Georgia and, especially, Arran and Azerbaijan from the Il-Khans. By recovering autonomy in tax matters Giorgi was enabled to gradually rebuild the economy. Giorgi's greater manoeuvring space in foreign affairs is highlighted by the two embassies he could send to Egypt in order to obtain facilitated access to Jerusalem for Georgian pilgrims. Giorgi was also in contact with Pope John XXII (in office 1316–1344) who in 1328 nominated the Dominican John of Florence as first Catholic bishop of Georgia with his see in Tbilisi.[168] The establishment of this bishopric, which had a clear missionary mandate, was part of the papal strategy to exploit the Mongols' indifference towards confessional questions in their protectorates, which stretched from Cilician Armenia and Georgia all the way to Khanbaliq (today's Beijing), in order to promote a major missionary effort.[169] The eagerness of the Il-Khans between *ca.* 1260 and 1310 to form an anti-Mameluke coalition with Western European powers such as the pope further facilitated the deployment of Catholic missionaries. At the beginning of the fourteenth century the Dominicans initially

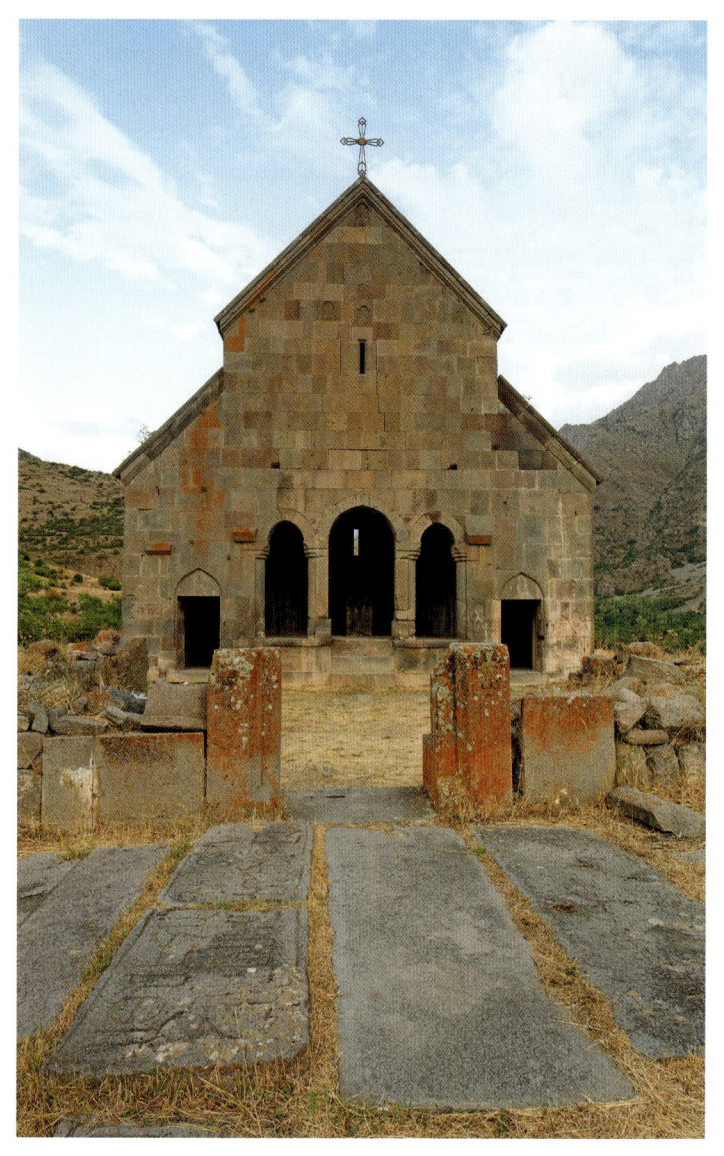

30. The so-called 'soldiers' church' of Zorats near the village of Yeghegis. The church was consecrated in 1303 by Bishop Stepanos Orbelian. At that time, warriors gathered in front of the church to receive the blessing before going to war. It is said that the wide vestibule in front of the small church remained uncovered so that knights could receive the blessing while on horseback. Zorats is the only such church remaining in Armenia. Vayots Dzor Province, Armenia. Photo 2015.

established their convents in Genoese colonies and trading towns such as Pera, Caffa and Trebizond, followed in 1318 by the archbishopric of Sultaniyeh, the Il-Khanate's capital. In 1330 the Dominican friar Bartolomeo of Bologna and the Armenian monk Hovhannes Krnetsi founded the Armeno-Catholic order of the *Fratres Unitores*, modelled on the Dominican Order, which promoted the union of the Armenian with the Catholic Church. The main base was Krna in Nakhchivan, which soon became a suffragan bishopric of the metropolitan see of Sultaniyeh, and by 1356 the *Unitores* had established a second centre in Caffa.[170]

Although Franciscans were mainly sent to the Archbishopric of Khanbaliq and to Cilicia, they were also active in the Il-Khanate, for example at the Armenian monastery of St Thaddeus south of Maku in present-day Iranian Azerbaijan where by 1321 at the latest they were directing the school of theology.[171] Hardly any of these proselytizing efforts were aimed at Muslims, but rather at the so-called heretics, that is the local Christians, with the consequence of a duplication of church structures and hierarchies. Catholic institutions competed with Greek Orthodox, Syriac Orthodox, Georgian Orthodox, Armenian Orthodox and Nestorian organizations. In terms of ordinary believers' faith, Catholicism offered little or no appeal. Its only trump card was political, inasmuch as the Cilician Armenian rulers hoped for military aid against the Mamelukes in return for a union with the Catholic Church. The see of the last Armeno-Catholic bishopric of Nakhchivan was moved in the sixteenth century to Aparan in today's Armenian Province of Aragatsotn; it became vacant around 1765.[172]

When the Il-Khan Abu Sa'id (r. 1317–1335) had Emir Choban, the Il-Khanate's strongman, strangled in 1327, the opportunity came for Giorgi to shake off the Mongol fetters. In the following year he invited his pro-Mongol nobles to a banquet where he had them all killed, thus wiping out in a single stroke the internal opponents to his strategy for independence. Then he embarked on recovering former crown lands which, since the 1250s, had been usurped by the church with the complicity of the Mongols, and on evicting the Ossetians from Kartli. In 1329 Giorgi seized the opportunity to reconquer Imereti, where for more than thirty years since Davit Narin's death in 1293 a fraternal war had been raging between Davit's son **Konstantine (Constantine) I** (r. 1293–1327) and his younger brother **Mikel (Michael) I** (r. 1327–1329) who controlled the north-east of western Georgia. After Mikel's death Giorgi occupied Kutaisi and deposed his infant child Bagrat. Five years later Giorgi coerced Qvarqvare I Jaqeli (r. 1334–1361) to acknowledge Georgian sovereignty, whereupon

the Georgian king assigned to his new vassal the hereditary title of *atabeg*, as a result of which his principality of Samtskhe long became known also as Saatabago, 'land of the atabeg'. In 1334, Giorgi had achieved his goal of reuniting Georgia. The fact that after the death of the childless Abu Sa'id the Il-Khanate fell apart into some fifteen regional dynasties and cliques, between them advancing eight puppet khans within nine years, saved Georgia from any major Il-Khanid campaigns of repression, while minor ones were repulsed.

Giorgi V was not only an astute politician but also a smart administrator and diligent legislator. Due to the guerrilla war waged by Davit VIII in mountainous northern Georgia, tribal highland law had superseded royal law. After having led a tour of inspection in the mountain areas, Giorgi issued the *dzeglis dadeba*, meaning 'the establishment of the law'. He brought all crimes, including fratricide and filicide, back under the law and laid down a clear hierarchy of punishments and blood prices according to the severity of the crime, ranging from murder down to minor injuries and theft. But while all crimes were punishable, the amount of blood money payable was a function of the offended person's rank. Giorgi's second major long-term achievement was the written codification of state government and the delineation of roles for its administrators, for during the Mongol occupation the delimitation of competences between royal and governmental authority, local princes, Mongol *noyans*, administrators and *darughachi* had been blurred and shifting. Giorgi's *khelmtsipis karis garigeba*, the 'Regulations of the Monarch's Court', defined Georgia's governance; it was based on the practice before Queen Tamar's 1184 compromises. The absolute rule of the king was assisted by a cabinet of six ministers called *Sabcho* and by the legislating *Darbazi* which did not have the authority to convene itself, but could be summoned only by royal order. In theory, neither of the two bodies could overrule the king, although in practice the ruler needed the support of his most powerful grandees to be able to act. The ranking order of the ministers was as follows: the chief minister, who directed the other five ministers, the *atabeg*, the *amirspasalar*, the palace chamberlain, the chief treasurer and the chancellor who ran the court and its properties. The *Darbazi* was convened about four times a year and was led by the six ministers and four senior monks and attended by the senior nobles and abbots, bishops and senior officials. It ratified royal appointments, but its enacted laws required royal assent.[173]

This political, social and economic upswing lasted less than two decades. Already by the late 1330s, the bloody fights between the Jalayirid ruler of Baghdad and Hamadan, Hasan-i Buzurg (d. 1356), and the Chobanid prince Hasan-i Kuchik (d. 1343) whose realm encompassed present-day Iranian Azerbaijan, had spilled over into Armeno-Georgian territory. In addition Giorgi's intervention in the civil war raging in the tiny Empire of Trebizond proved unsuccessful in restoring Georgian influence. In 1244 Trebizond had become a Mongol vassal whose value lay in the fact that it represented the terminus of the trade route leading from India via Hormuz and Tabriz to the Black Sea, from where goods were shipped to Constantinople. Since the port of Batumi (known to Westerners as Lo Vati) was then of little importance, access to Trebizond remained important for Georgia. While Venice dominated the Black Sea from 1204 to 1261, the Treaty of Nymphaion signed between Genoa and Constantinople in 1261 guaranteed Genoa an exclusive passage through the Bosporus and hence a virtual trade monopoly in the Black Sea, to the exclusion of Venice. Genoa's dominance in the eastern Black Sea was underpinned by the control of the important harbours of Pera (Galata) located on Constantinople's Golden Horn, Caffa (Feodosia) on Crimea and Trebizond.[174] Other Genoese fortified harbours or trading posts in the eastern Black Sea were Cembalo (Balaclava), Kalamita (Inkerman) and Soldaia (Sudak) in Crimea, then further east Tana (Asov), and on the eastern Black sea Coast Matrega (Phanagoria on the Taman Peninsula), Mapa (Anapa), Bata (Batario, now Novorossiysk), Kakari (Gagra), Petsonda (Pitsunda) and Sebastopolis (Sukhum). Since neither Georgia, the Golden Horde nor the Il-Khanate owned trading fleets, Genoa maintained a strong trading position till the fall of Constantinople in 1453 and would lose its last bastion only in 1475.[175] In Trebizond, Irene Palaiologina, the Byzantine wife of the Emperor Basil (r. 1332–1340), had seized power in April 1340 after having (probably) poisoned her husband. The imperial guard and a couple of nobles rebelled against her but were crushed three months later by Byzantine troops dispatched from Constantinople. Soon another pretender appeared in the person of Anna, sister of the late emperor Basil, whose mother was a daughter of Beka I Jaqeli of Samtskhe. In July 1341, Laz opposition in Trebizond and a Georgian army sent by Giorgi put the former nun Anna on the throne. Georgian influence over Trebizond seemed to have been re-established. But in September 1342 a small Byzantine–Genoese flotilla landed in Trebizond. After bloody street fights, Empress Anna was captured and strangled, and Byzantine–Genoese influence once more predominated. Later, in 1366 and 1367, King Bagrat V would marry two princesses of Trebizond in an attempt to strengthen ties with this Black Sea state.[176]

Giorgi was succeeded by his son **Davit IX** (r. 1346–1360), whose rule is not well documented. During his reign, Georgia came under foreign pressure again, losing control over Nakhchivan, central and northern Armenia, and some Laz regions. Two years into Davit's reign, calamity struck when bubonic plague, the Black Death, infested Georgia. The plague probably originated in the later 1330s in northern or northwestern China and spread along northern trade routes with Mongol troops and traders westward. It was recorded in Crimea in 1347 and expanded from there to the whole Black Sea region, the Caucasus and Europe. At the same time, it spread from Constantinople to Egypt and then the Middle East, Arabia and northern Africa. Within three to five years, Georgia, like the Middle East and Europe, lost about half of its population. But the Black Death didn't stop wars. In 1356, Jani Beg (r. 1342–1357), khan of the Golden Horde, passed the defile of Derbent and crossed today's Azerbaijan to capture Tabriz where he installed his son Berdi Beg as governor. Yet the Golden Horde's presence south of the Greater Caucasus was short-lived, since in 1357 Berdi Beg arranged for his father to be poisoned and returned to his capital Sarai on the Volga.[177] Thirty years after the plague, Georgia would again be hit by an apocalyptic cataclysm: the systematic destructions of Timur e-Lang.

III

The Armenian Kingdom of Cilicia

Medieval Armenian Cilicia was a unique political phenomenon, a kingdom in exile. Its history comprises two periods, the first of principalities (*ca.* 1080–1198), the second of a kingdom (1198–1375). It owed its existence to the power bases of its leaders: heavily fortified castles located in the thickly forested mountains of upland Cilicia; to its role as the terminus of, or gateway to a major transcontinental trade route; and to the political fragmentation of the neighbouring region. The main protagonists in this were the Rum Seljuks; the Danishmendid dynasty; the Seljuk Sultanate and their local vassals; the Ayyubids followed by the Egyptian Mamelukes; Byzantium; Cyprus; the Crusader States; and, by 1243 at the latest, the Mongols. Cilician Armenia's main weaknesses were its lack of political unity and never-ending infighting among the leading gentry, its small population, and the conflicts between rulers and church. Once the Latin Crusader states were gone and the Il-Khanate lost interest in its vassal, Cilician Armenia found itself encircled by hostile powers. In the fourteenth century it survived as long as the dominant Mamelukes preferred to exploit the land through demanding high tributes rather than waging war. Once the Mamelukes diverted trade from the Cilician harbours to Egypt, Cilicia's days were numbered.

1. Semi-independent Armenian warlords and Muslim Armenian viziers

As told in the first volume of this work, Byzantium succeeded in the tenth century in reconquering Cappadocia and Cilicia from the weakening Abbasid Caliphate; this included Antioch, which had to be repopulated in order to buttress the defensive capability of these provinces. To this end, Byzantium encouraged or even enforced the emigration of Armenians from their homelands of Vashpurakan and Greater Armenia following its occupation of those kingdoms in 1021 and 1045 respectively.[1] While most of these Armenian nobles and knights kept their Christian faith, a few voluntarily accepted Islam, while others were converted slaves who subsequently made spectacular careers rising through the ranks. To the first group, towards the end of the eleventh century, belonged the **Rubenid** and **Hethumid** princes of Cilicia (for whom see below), and **Philaretos Brachamios** (d. 1087) who controlled Western Syria. Philaretos started as a Byzantine commander who played a dubious role just before the fateful Battle of Manzikert (1071). He was described by the contemporary historian Matthew of Edessa (d. 1144) as 'the very offspring of Satan, … a perfidious man, who indeed was a precursor of the abominable Antichrist. … He was disavowed by both the Armenians and Romans.'[2] In religious matters, Philaretos was a true turncoat: born in an Armenian family of Armenian Orthodox faith, as an officer in the Byzantine army he accepted Greek Orthodoxy yet nurtured sympathies with the heretic Armenian Tondrakians and later adopted Islam to ease Seljuk pressure. Other Armenian warlords were a former officer of Philaretos, namely **Kogh Vasil**, 'Basil the Bandit' (d. *ca.* 1112/13), son of an Armenian Tondrakian, who ruled in Northern Syria thanks to his strong cavalry; **Gabriel of Melitene** (d. *ca.* 1103) ruling Melitene (Malatya); and **Thoros of Edessa** (d. 1098). The latter two had converted to Greek Orthodoxy.[3] West of Kogh Vasil's realm ruled the Armenian **Tatoul** in the region of Marash, whose western marches bordered on eastern Cilicia.

According to the historian Seta Dadoyan, the founder of the Muslim **Danishmendid** dynasty Hrahad (d. 1104), named in Turkish Gümüshtegin, was of Armenian stock and conquered areas in northern Cappadocia. The **Bene Boghusaks** in Sewawerak (Severek) north-east of Samosata and the **Nawiqis** (Awaqis) were also allegedly of Armenian descent, although the latter are also referred to as having been Turkmen.[4]

A singular case was that of the **Armenian Fatimid vizierates** in Egypt. Seven or eight Armenian viziers and army commanders dominated Fatimid Egypt with interruptions between 1074 and 1163; one of them remained Christian, the others were Muslims. The Armenian **Badr al-Jamali** (b. 1005/08, vizier 1074–94) was bought as a slave (Mameluke) by the ruler of Tripoli, Jamal al-Dawla and converted at a young age to Islam.[5] In 1063 he was nominated military governor of Damascus, and later of the harbour city of Akka (Acre) with the task of fighting the invading Seljuks. In 1073 he was called by Caliph al-Mustansir (r. 1036–1094) to Cairo, where anarchy prevailed, in order to re-establish order and prevent the collapse of the Fatimid dynasty. He brought his own Armenian guard to Cairo, increasing it to a 7,000-strong private army including numerous Armenians. Appointed vizier and *amir al-juyush* (commander-in-chief) he liquidated the unruly Turkic army leaders and turned the Caliphate into a military dictatorship. The Muslim Armenian Badr held absolute power as 'Vizier of the Sword and the Pen' and relegated the Caliph to a ceremonial and religious role.[6] Badr was succeeded by his son **al-Afdal Shahanshah** (in office 1094–1121) who installed Ahmad ibn al-Mustansir, whose mother was a daughter of Badr and hence al-Afdal's sister, as the new caliph al-Mustali (r. 1094–1100), passing over al-Mustansir's eldest son Nizar ibn al-Mustansir. After a brief civil war, Nizar was captured and died in jail. Al-Afdal's passing over of the elder Nizar came close to a putsch and triggered a schism within Ismailism into the rival sects of the Nizariyya (the Assassins) and the Mustalawiyya.[7] As narrated by al-Athir, al-Afdal retook Jerusalem from Najm al-Din Ilghazi in 1098, but lost it one year later on 15 July 1099 to the Crusaders since he arrived too late from Cairo to prevent its fall. Even worse, on 12 August a Crusader army led by Godfrey of Bouillon surprised his sleeping army at dawn near Ascalon and completely destroyed it; al-Afdal barely escaped and fled by ship. Instead of conquering Ascalon, the Crusaders withdrew in return for a substantial ransom.[8] Nevertheless, Ascalon remained disputed. After a battle in 1105 between al-Afdal's son Husayn and Baldwin I of Jerusalem (r. 1100–1118) ended indecisively, the Fatimid governor Shams al-Khilafa rebelled and entered an alliance with King Baldwin. As told by al-Athir, he then recruited an army of Armenian mercenaries that provoked the anger of Ascalon's citizens, who killed him.[9] Al-Afdal was himself murdered in 1121, probably by an Assassin taking revenge

31. The ruins of the Byzantine fortress of Anahşa, Pozantı, located near the Cilician Gates leading through the Taurus Mountains, stand on the bright promontory on the left. It may be identical with the Armenian castle of Pardzerpert, the ancestral seat of the Armenian Rubenid dynasty. Adana Province, Northern Cilicia, Turkey. Photo 2018.

32. The impregnable fortress of Lampron, from about 1073 the ancestral home of the Armenian Hethumid dynasty, stands on top of a limestone ridge. It was only captured by treachery in 1198 or 1199 by the Rubenid king Levon I (r. 1198–1219). Mersin Province, Cilicia, Turkey. Photo 2018.

for Nizar's death.[10] He may have been very briefly succeeded by his son **Sharaf al-Ma'ali ibn al-Afdal** (in office 1121?). After nine years Badr's grandson **Kutayfat ibn al-Afdal** (in office 1130–1131) came to power after the murder of Caliph al-Amir (r. 1101–1130) by an Assassin. Kutayfat withheld the nomination of a new caliph and proclaimed himself deputy of the 'hidden Imam'. According to the teachings of the Twelver Shia, the hidden Imam lives in seclusion and his return is expected at the end of the world. With such a scheme the Armenian Kutayfat hoped to establish his own dynasty, but he soon fell victim to a military coup.[11]

The next Armenian vizier, **Yanis al-Rumi al-Armani** (in office 1132), whose name translates as John the Byzantine Armenian, was, like Badr, a former military slave.[12] His tenure in office was brief, as Caliph al-Hafiz (r. 1132–1149) had him poisoned. Three years later, the Christian Armenian **Vahram** (in office 1135–1137, d. 1140) rose to power, but his title was 'executive vizier' since a Christian was not allowed to be a delegate on behalf of the Imam-Caliph. He was a prominent Christian, as he was a nephew of the Armenian Catholicos Grigor II Vkayaser, who had visited Egypt.[13] In 1154, civil strife prevailed again in Cairo and the experienced Armenian military governor **Tala'i ibn Ruzzik al-Armani** (in office 1154–1161) was called to restore order. Probably born around 1101/02 north of Urmia, Tala'i was a Twelver Shiite; he quickly put an end to the unrest and assumed, in Dadoyan's words, 'absolute military, juridical and administrative powers'.[14] His foreign policy was dedicated to fighting the Crusaders and recovering former Fatimid territories. While he scored a few tactical successes, he failed to reconquer the harbour city of Ascalon, which had been up to 1153 the last Egyptian outpost on the Palestinian coast.[15] He therefore sent embassies to Nur al-Din Zengi (r. 1146–1174), the powerful ruler of Syria who had captured Damascus in 1154, in order to achieve a military alliance directed against the Latin Kingdom of Jerusalem, with the intention of attacking the Crusader states in a pincer movement. But Nur al-Din rejected Tala'i's proposition; as a Sunni Muslim, he despised the Fatimids as dissident heretics, and furthermore, he entertained the vision of conquering Egypt himself. Eventually, Tala'i reverted to a defensive strategy; he strongly fortified the city of Bilbeis 60 kilometres north-east of Cairo to protect the capital from a Crusader attack. Nevertheless, in 1160 he could only stop the Crusaders who had reached the harbour city of al-Arish by paying them a huge tribute. In 1161 he was mortally stabbed as a consequence of his failed attempt to further strengthen his position by marrying his daughter to the infant caliph al-Adid (r. nominally 1160–1171).[16] Tala'i was briefly succeeded by his son **Ruzzik ibn Tala'i** (in office 1161–1162, d. 1163) who faced attacks from both Amaury (Amalric) of Jerusalem and Assassin forces, as well as domestic military revolts. With his fall in December 1162, the period of the Armenian vizierates in Fatimid Egypt ended.[17] Nine years later, the Sunni Kurd Salah al-Din abolished the Ismailite Fatimid Caliphate and founded the Ayyubid dynasty. As the example of the Armenian Fatimid viziers shows, in the medieval Near East ethnicity was hardly an obstacle to a rise to supreme power. Later on, ruling Mamelukes of Egypt would be of Kipchak or Circassian stock. In the case of the Armenians, the sovereign states in their homeland had disappeared, but enterprising individuals achieved success abroad.

2. The Rubenids of Cilicia: From principality to kingdom

In the mountainous uplands of Cilicia two Armenian families soon asserted themselves and went on to shape Cilician history for almost two centuries. East of the Cilician Gates, the pass leading from the plains and the Mediterranean harbours through the Taurus Mountains to Cappadocia, stood the ancestral seat of the **Rubenid** dynasty, Pardzerpert (fig. 31) which was moved after 1090 to Vahka (Feke; fig. 33) north of Sis, today's Kozan. The Rubenids were staunch supporters of the Armenian Orthodox Church and more or less antagonistic towards Byzantium. West of the Cilician Gates stood the impregnable fortress of Lampron,[18] the ancestral seat of the **Hethumid** dynasty (fig. 32), the majority of whose members adhered to Greek Orthodoxy and pursued a policy friendly to Byzantium; conversely, they enjoyed the support of Byzantium in their rivalry with the Rubenids.[19] For almost a century Byzantium would help the Hethumids to ensure that no strong Armenian state could emerge in Cilicia, which it considered as a rebellious vassal. The founder of the Hethumid dynasty was the Armenian lord **Oshin** who had left his estates around Ganja in 1073 fleeing the Seljuk threat. He entered the service of the Armenian Abul Gharib Artsruni, who since 1042 had been the Byzantine governor of Cilicia, based in Tarsus, and who assigned him the fortresses of Lampron and Barbaron. The founder of the Rubenid dynasty, **Ruben I** (r. 1080–1095) was one of the followers of King Gagik II (r. 1042–1045, d. 1079)[20] who fled from Cappadocia following Gagik's murder to the fortress of Kopitar (Gobitara) in the Taurus Mountains, from where he soon seized the fortress of Pardzerpert; in 1090 his son **Kostantin (Constantine) I** (r. 1095–1099) captured the strategically highly important castle of Vahka which blocked a direct road from Adana to Cappadocia. With possession of these two fortresses, the Rubenids controlled both main routes crossing the Taurus Mountains from the Cilician coast to Cappadocia, generating substantial income from road tolls. As has been recognized by the historian John Armenia,

the great number of fortifications built on rugged terrain was an important factor in the kingdom's ability to retain its independence until 1375 which would prove a mixed blessing for Armenian rulers. Some barons could rebel with virtual impunity, knowing that their remote strongholds would keep them safe from the reach of the king.[21]

Around 1080 Ruben declared his independence from Byzantium; yet at the same time he was till 1085 a vassal of Philaretos Brachamios who had acquired Antioch in 1078. But early in 1085, Philaretos' estranged son Barsama sold the city to the Rum Seljuk sultan Süleyman ibn Qutalmïsh.[22]

The arrival of the Latin Crusaders at the end of the eleventh century changed the dynamics in the Near East, including Cilicia. In 1090, the Byzantine emperor Alexios I Komnenos (r. 1081–1118) had appealed to Pope Urban II (in office 1088–1099) for military support against the Seljuks, purportedly to liberate the Holy Land from their grip, but in reality to divert the aggressive behaviour of Norman Sicily. Urban mobilized in 1095 and the First Crusade got underway in 1096. When the Crusaders arrived at Constantinople, Alexios seized the chance to utilize them as tool for reconquering Anatolia and Syria for Byzantium. As events would soon show, conflicts between Alexios and the Crusaders were inevitable, for the latter never considered themselves Alexios's auxiliaries. But since the Crusaders were dependent on the Byzantine fleet to cross over the Bosporus, Alexios forced their leaders to take an oath of allegiance on

Easter Sunday 1097, swearing to hand over all recovered land to Byzantium.[23] At Heraclea Cybistra, east of Iconium (Konya), the Crusader army split. The bulk followed the misleading advice of Alexios, who wanted the Crusaders to reconquer Syria for him, and chose the difficult and longer route via Caesarea; while the Norman Tancred of Hauteville and Baldwin of Boulogne (d. 1118), the future King of Jerusalem, opted for the direct and shorter road through the Cilician Gates, reaching Tarsus in September 1097. After a sharp dispute between the two leaders, Tancred left Tarsus to Baldwin to join forces with Prince Oshin of Lampron. Together they seized Adana from the Rum Seljuks; then Tancred captured Mopsuestia (Mamistra), the large fortress of Anazarbos (fig. 36) and Alexandretta (İskenderun). The winners of this side campaign to the Crusade were the Armenian princes, since the Crusaders broke the Seljuks' power in Cilicia. Baldwin, for his part, marched eastward, collecting Armenian soldiers on his march, and reached Edessa on 6 February 1098. The town's ruler, the Armenian Thoros, was disliked by his own people because of his pro-Byzantine policy and his conversion to the Greek Orthodox creed; he was also threatened by Kerbogha, *atabeg* of Mosul, while Baldwin's intentions were unclear. To save himself, Thoros adopted Baldwin as his heir. But when Baldwin briefly left for Samosata, Armenian conspirators rebelled against Thoros, who was killed while attempting to escape. The Armenians then invited Baldwin to return and take over the government. On 10 March 1098 Baldwin founded the County of Edessa, the first Crusader state in the Near East, which would last till 1144. It is debatable if Baldwin was directly involved in Thoros's fall: he was likely aware of the plot and let the conspirators accomplish their aims. According to Matthew of Edessa, Baldwin had given his approval to the conspiracy, and Kostantin I of Vahka was also involved.[24] It was obvious that Baldwin, a junior member of the family of the counts of Boulogne, had no intention of handing Edessa back to Alexios since he had conquered it without Byzantine support.

In the meantime, the main Crusader army had been besieging the strongly fortified Seljuk city of Antioch since 21 October 1097. The Crusaders took the city on 2 June, but were themselves put under siege five days later by *atabeg* Kerbogha of Mosul. While the Armenians of Cilicia supplied the Crusaders with provisions, Emperor Alexios withheld any help. He was marching with his army towards Syria to reap the fruits of the Crusaders' conquests, but when he heard of their serious difficulties he quickly retreated. Moreover, the powerful Byzantine fleet did not come to the rescue. Ultimately the Crusaders were victorious, but they judged the Byzantines to be treacherous.

The idea of returning any conquered territory to Byzantium was by now out of the question. Since Alexios had abandoned the common cause (as the Crusaders saw it) of liberating the Holy Land, they no longer felt feel bound by their previous oath. The main beneficiary of the situation was Prince Bohemond of Taranto, who founded the Principality of Antioch which lasted till 1268.[25] By 1098 at the latest it was apparent that the vision of a joint Christian effort to secure the Holy Land long term was no more than an illusion. Rivalries and fights erupted not only between the Latin states, the Byzantines and the Armenians, but also among the Armenian princes and within the Latin camp. Byzantium, the Seljuks and other Muslim warlords quickly learnt how to exploit these conflicts. As the third Rubenid ruler **Thoros I** (r. 1099–1129) found out, the cities in the Cilician plain such as Tarsus and Adana remained heavily contested. His main conquests were the city of Sis and the inland fortress of Anazarbos which he seized from the Byzantines. The Rubenid territory remained also under constant pressure from the Seljuks to the north, for example in 1108, and from Malik Shah of Iconium three years later. Both attacks were repulsed.

Thoros's rule saw schism in the Armenian Church, with the proclamation of some of the numerous anti-catholicoi of the period. Catholicos Grigor II Vkayaser, the Martyrophile (in office with interruptions 1066–1105) changed his residence often and travelled extensively. According to Matthew of Edessa, in 1074/75 he travelled to Constantinople, Rome and Egypt where the vizier Badr al-Jamali had seized power. Here he allegedly 'consecrated Gregory, his nephew, as catholicos', or rather as archbishop, which indicates that many Armenian mercenaries living in Egypt had kept their Christian faith.[26] During Grigor's difficult tenure, two monks declared themselves anti-patriarchs and his coadjutor Barsegh (Basil) I ruled the church independently, for Grigor preferred a life of reclusion to administration. At times there were three rival catholicoi besides an independent coadjutor. Since Grigor II tried to bridge the doctrinal gaps with Greek Orthodox and Roman Catholic churches, he was opposed in the Armenian homelands. He was succeeded by Barsegh I (in office 1105–1113) whose successor Grigor III (in office 1113–1166) had already been nominated by Grigor II. At the consecration of Grigor III, Davit Tornikian, the archbishop of Aghtamar, who claimed descent from the royal Artsruni family of Vashpurakan, rebelled, declaring himself catholicos; the schism lasted till 1895. In order to distance himself from political pressures, in 1147 Grigor purchased the strong fortress of Hromkla standing inside a bend of the Euphrates north-west of Edessa (fig. 37).[27] Before the arrival of the Crusaders, Hromkla belonged to Kogh Vasil who was forced to hand it over to the count of Edessa.[28] It was a bold move, for Hromkla stood outside Cilicia and was dependent on good relations with the neighbouring local Muslim rulers.

According to the thirteenth-century chronicler Vahram, Thoros's successor **Kostantin II** (r. 1129) fell victim after a few months to a palace conspiracy and was succeeded by Thoros's brother **Levon (Leon** or **Leo) I** (r. 1129–1137, d. 1140).[29] Levon was determined to put his principality on a firmer footing by expanding it into the plain adjoining the Mediterranean Sea. He exploited the rivalries between Byzantium and the Latin states of Edessa and Antioch and the threats of Imad al-Din Zengi, *atabeg* of Mosul. Before that, he had to fend off an attack by Bohemond II of Antioch (r. 1126–1130), who thought that the moment was opportune to capture Anazarbos. But Levon appealed to the Danishmendid emir Ghazi (r. 1104–1134) for help, and when Bohemond approached in February 1130, the emir crushed the invaders and the prince was killed. Levon then capitalized on the Danishmendid alliance to capture the three important cities in the plain, Adana, Tarsus and Mopsuestia, as well as the harbour of Korykos (or Corycus, fig. 34). In 1136, Raymond I of Antioch (r. 1136–1149) and Baldwin of Marash attacked Levon, who was allied with Count Joscelin II of Edessa (r. 1131–1144, d. 1159), illustrating the way that the Crusader States were also waging war among themselves. Levon and Joscelin repulsed the attack, but the losers managed to capture Levon by treachery, and he was forced to buy his freedom with a ransom.[30] However, against the next attacker Levon was powerless, for in summer 1137 the Byzantine emperor John II Komnenos (r. 1118–1143) arrived to reclaim the former territories of Cilicia and Antioch. With the support of the Hethumids of Lampron he quickly seized Seleucia (today's Silifke), Korykos, Tarsus, Mopsuestia, Adana and the fortresses of Tell Hamdun (Toprak Kale) and Anazarbos. The victorious emperor then forced Antioch to capitulate and recognize Byzantine suzerainty, whereupon he returned to Cilicia, captured Vahka and took King Levon and his two sons Ruben and Thoros prisoner. All three were deported to Constantinople where Ruben was murdered and Levon soon died. By 1138 it seemed that Armenian Cilicia had ceased to exist as a principality.[31]

Around 1143, however, having succeeded in escaping from his confinement, **Thoros II** (r. 1145–1169, d. 1170) returned to eastern Cilicia, rallied the Armenians and recaptured one by one

33. The second family seat of the Armenian Rubenids from 1090, Vahka stands north of the village of Feke. Adana Province, Turkey. Photo 2018.

34. The sea castle of Korykos, originally Byzantine, controlled access to the eponymous Mediterranean harbour. The Byzantine admiral Eustathios Kymineianos reconstructed the earlier Roman and Byzantine mainland fortification in the early twelfth century and built an additional fortress on the small island located 400 m offshore. Both fortresses were captured by the Armenian prince Thoros II (r. 1145–1169), and Korykos became a harbour of strategic importance for Armenian Cilicia. It was held by Cyprus, with interruptions, from 1360 to 1448. Mersin Province, Turkey. Photo 2018.

most of his father's territories. But Emperor Manuel I Komnenos (r. 1143–1180) refused to accept this revival of the Armenian Rubenid principality and undertook two military expeditions to bring Cilicia back under Byzantine sovereignty. The first campaign in 1152, ineptly led by Manuel's cousin Andronikos, ended in an ignominious defeat of the Byzantine–Hethumid army. Two years later, Manuel induced the Seljuk sultan of Iconium, Mas'ud I (r. 1116–1156) to attack Thoros, but Mas'ud was routed by an alliance of the Rubenids with the Knights Templar. In his next move, Manuel tried to bribe Raynald of Châtillon, prince of Antioch (1153–1160/61), to attack Thoros. Raynald, however, entered a secret alliance with the latter to attack Byzantine Cyprus which they thoroughly pillaged in spring 1156. Outraged, the Emperor Manuel invaded Cilicia in 1158 and threatened Antioch, whereupon Raynald had to humiliate himself in Mopsuestia by advancing alone, barefoot and with a rope under his neck, and throwing himself at the feet of the emperor, who pardoned him. Thoros fled into the mountains. The emperor's expedition alarmed King Baldwin III of Jerusalem (r. 1143–1163) who rushed to meet him with a strong army. As he preferred a weak Armenian buffer state in the north of the Latin realm to a threatening Byzantine neighbour, Baldwin secured a pardon for the fugitive. To keep his principality, Thoros had to swear loyalty to the emperor and accept governors from Byzantium. According to the Armenian military commander, diplomat and chronicler Smbat Sparapet (the Constable, d. 1276), however, the emperor's efforts to force *atabeg* Nur al-Din Zengi of Aleppo to submit as well were a total failure. The latter realized that Manuel was too weak to attack him, for 'he did not make his demands with sword and spear, but with paper and ink'. Manuel returned to Constantinople and Smbat's account concludes scoffingly: 'That brave emperor of the Greeks, Manuel, who had come as a mighty eagle, returned as a weak fox.'[32] Yet after a Byzantine governor reputedly boiled Thoros's unruly brother Stephen alive around 1163/64, Armenian Rubenid attacks on the Greeks resumed. King Amaury I of Jerusalem (r. 1163–1174) brokered a peace with

Byzantium.[33] In spite of several short-term setbacks, Thoros successfully expanded Rubenid Cilicia from a mountain principality to a more stable state with access to the sea.

In 1169, Thoros abdicated in favour of his underage son **Ruben II** (r. 1169–1170) and installed as regent a crusader named Thomas, but Thoros's brother Mleh, the youngest surviving son of Levon I, contested the succession. According to Smbat Sparapet, Mleh, who had taken vows as a Templar, had previously attempted to murder his brother Thoros II, who had banished him from Cilicia. Mleh had fled to Emir Nur al-Din and converted to Sunni Islam, emulating the conversion of the former Fatimid commander Badr al-Jalali. Nur al-Din provided troops to **Mleh I** (r. 1170–1175) who invaded Cilicia in 1170. The regent Thomas tried to save Prince Ruben II by sending him to Hromkla under the protection of Catholicos Nerses IV Shnorhali, but Mleh's henchmen murdered the young prince. Backed by Muslim troops, Mleh embarked on attacks against Lampron, the Templar fortress at Baghras and the Byzantine governor Kalamanos whom he made prisoner and sent to Nur al-Din. In 1173, Manuel recognized Mleh as lord of Cilicia and Cilician Armenia looked to be firmly positioned in the Muslim Ayyubid camp. But when Nur al-Din died in 1174, Mleh's power base dissolved, in spite of many Armenian mercenaries in Fatimid service having emigrated to Cilicia after 1171.[34] Weary of the uncontrollable Turkic bands, a number of leading Armenian nobles murdered Mleh and placed **Ruben III** (r. 1175–1187), the eldest son of Thoros's brother Stephen, on the throne.[35] He set about consolidating Armenian Cilicia, which had been destabilized by Mleh's military adventures and pro-Ayyubid policy. He was indirectly helped in this task by the Byzantine defeat at the hands of the Seljuk sultan Kilij Arslan II (r. 1156–1192) at the Battle of Myriokephalon in Phrygia, in 1176. From now on, Byzantium pursued a defensive strategy, renouncing its efforts to reconquer Iconium and Cilicia.[36] Ruben concluded peace with Kilij Arslan in 1180 after payment of a substantial tribute, but three years later was attacked by an alliance of Hethum of Lampron and Bohemond III of Antioch (r. 1163–1201). When Ruben's long siege of Lampron failed, he accepted Bohemond's treacherous proposal to conduct negotiations in Antioch. Upon arrival, Ruben was taken prisoner and only released after payment of a huge ransom. On his return, Ruben abdicated in favour of his brother Levon.[37]

Levon II (r. as prince 1187–1198, as king 1198–1219) took power at a turning point in the history of the Crusader States, since in July 1187 Sultan Saladin (Salah al-Din) of Egypt and Syria wiped out the strong Crusader army led by King Guy de Lusignan of Jerusalem (r. 1186–1187 and 1192, d. 1194) at the Battle of Hattin in Palestine, whereupon Saladin captured dozens of fortresses, and Jerusalem itself on 2 October 1187.[38] Saladin's overwhelming victory reduced the Crusader States to coastal territories. The deaths of so many knights were never requited and the defeat heralded the decline of the Latin presence in the Near East. In the short term, Cilician Armenia rose in significance in the view of the European Crusader powers as an entry gate and bridgehead for further military expeditions, such as the Third Crusade (1189–1192). Soon after assuming power, Levon was confronted by a Turkmen attack which advanced as far as the Cilician capital of Sis. But Levon succeeded in killing their leader Rustam in a violent counterattack and routed the invaders.

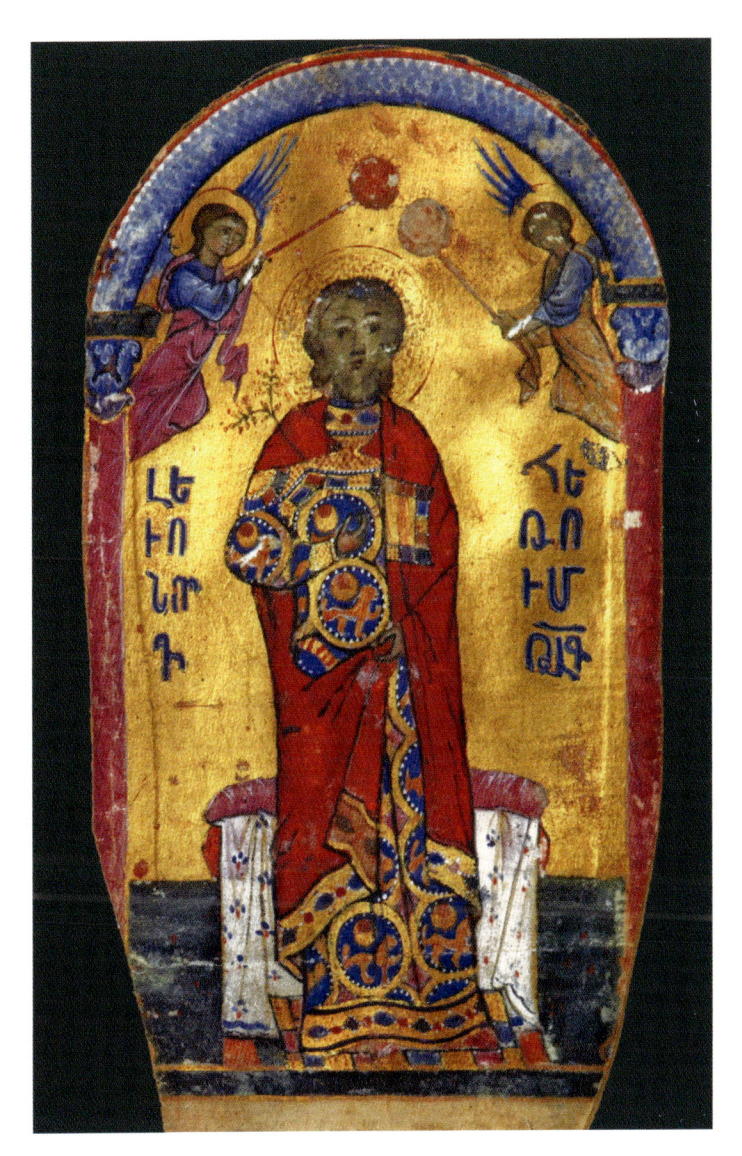

35. The future prince and king Levon II (r. 1269–1289). Miniature from a gospel commissioned around 1250 by Catholicos Kostantin I for his pupil, the Crown Prince Levon. The inscription says: 'Levon, son of King Hethum'. The painting and calligraphy were done on parchment at Hromkla, then the see of the Armenian catholicosate. MS 8321, fol. 15, Matenadaran, Yerevan.

According to legend, the Armenians were helped by the military saints George and Theodore who had taken the shape of two soldiers.[39] Soon after, Levon captured Seleucia and ordered the reconstruction and expansion of the two harbours of Ayas (Laiazzo, today's Yumurtalık) and Korykos. Following his coronation in 1198, Levon granted trading rights to Venice and Genoa as a result of which these Cilician harbours became termini and transhipment centres for transcontinental trade routes, making them a key commercial zone for the Italian trading republics and Western states, in competition with Egypt.[40] Levon was conscious of the strategic value of his small principality for the Crusaders, for when the Emperor Frederick I Barbarossa and Pope Clement III (in office 1187–1191) sought his support for the forthcoming Third Crusade, he took the opportunity to ask to be crowned king. Frederick agreed and led his army personally through Anatolia and Iconium, but his accidental drowning in the mountain river Calicadnus (Göksu) just north of Seleucia put a temporary halt to Levon's ambitions. Nevertheless, in 1191 Levon participated in the conquest of Cyprus with Richard I of England, 'the Lionheart' (r. 1189–1199), which the latter handed over to his vassal Guy de Lusignan (r. in Cyprus 1192–1194). Levon also took part in the final phase of the siege of Akka, led by the French king, Philippe II Augustus (r. 1190–1223).[41] After the Crusader victory at Jaffa in August 1192, Richard and Saladin negotiated a truce whereby Saladin kept Jerusalem, but allowed Christian pilgrims access to the Holy Sites and accepted the existing Latin presence along the coast. With his participation in two military enterprises, Levon had further strengthened his position among Western leaders.

Returning from Akka, Levon occupied the castle of Gaston, also called Baghras, which Saladin had seized from the Templars and then dismantled in 1188. Since Baghras stood at the border between Cilicia and the Principality of Antioch and

36. The huge fortress of Anazarbos, today called Anavarza Kalesi, dominates the eponymous lower city which in the Byzantine era was called first Justinopolis and soon after Justinianopolis. The upper city is built on two adjacent rock spurs more than 800 m long which were already settled in prehistoric times. In 964, the Byzantine emperor Nikephoros II Phokas had conquered the city from the Arabs; it fell to the Crusaders in 1097 or early 1098 and was later annexed by the Principality of Antioch. But as early as 1107 it fell to the Armenian Rubenid prince Thoros I (r. 1099–1129). The castle was reconquered by the Byzantines in 1137 and was subsequently disputed by both sides. In the second half of the twelfth century, Anazarbos was firmly in Armenian hands and became the principality's capal. Around 1184 CE the administrative capital of the Armenian principality was transferred to Sis. It was at Anazarbos that the Mongol emir Bilarghu had King Levon III and the regent Hethum II murdered in 1307. One year before the final destruction of the Armenian Kingdom of Cilicia, that is in 1374, the Armenians were expelled from Anazarbos by the Mamelukes. Adana Province, Turkey. Photo 2018.

Map 3. The Armenian Kingdom of Cilicia, 1198–1375

was a gateway to the city, Levon had the fortress rebuilt, for he dreamt of integrating the principality into Armenian Cilicia. When Bohemond III and the Templars demanded the restitution of Baghras, Levon flatly refused and applied to Bohemond the same treacherous ruse the latter had used on his brother Ruben in 1187. He invited Bohemond to Baghras for negotiations, took him prisoner and deported him to Sis. Levon extorted the suzerainty over Antioch from Bohemond in return for his freedom, but when the Armenian delegates arrived at Antioch to take control of the city, the Greek population rebelled. To avoid war, King Henry I of Jerusalem, who resided in Akka, mediated between both parties: Levon kept Baghras, Bohemond regained his freedom and Levon's niece, Alice of Armenia (d. after 1234) was married in 1195 to Bohemond's eldest son Raymond. It was stipulated that their oldest son should ultimately inherit Antioch, while Bohemond waived any claim to Cilicia. When Raymond died in 1197, his one-year-old son Raymond-Ruben (d. 1221/22) was sent back with his mother to Levon. However, Levon's vision never came about. The Antiochian Greek and Latin burghers rejected an Armenian regent for the infant Raymond-Ruben. Furthermore, the ongoing fights in the war of succession for Antioch not only divided the Christian states, but also the military orders. The Templars stood on Bohemond's, that is the Greek, side and the Teutonic Knights on the Armenian side, while the Hospitallers switched their support in 1204 from Bohemond to Levon.[42] Only the king of Jerusalem had enough authority to prevent wars between the Christians. In 1216, Levon installed Raymond-Ruben by military means as ruler in Antioch, but he then quarrelled with his great-uncle and even attempted to take him prisoner. Levon escaped and Raymond-Ruben was ejected from the city in 1219, fleeing to Cilicia. With Raymond-Ruben's expulsion from Antioch, Levon's strategic vision of uniting Cilicia and Antioch under Armenian rule to build a strong Christian state collapsed. Dying and utterly disappointed, Levon disinherited Raymond-Ruben of any claim to Cilicia in favour of his infant daughter Zabel (Isabella).[43]

3. The Kingdom of Cilician Armenia

In 1196 Levon, resuming his project of elevating his principality to a kingdom, had sent a delegation to Barbarossa's successor Henry VI (r. 1191–1197) and Pope Celestine III (in office 1191–1198). After some hesitation, the emperor agreed to the coronations of both Levon and of Amaury de Lusignan as king of Cyprus, which would make Cilician Armenia and Cyprus vassal kingdoms of the Holy Roman Empire under the universal rule of the Hohenstaufen dynasty. Levon recognized imperial suzerainty whereupon in 1197 Henry's chancellor, Bishop Conrad of Hildesheim (d. 1202) and the papal legate, Cardinal Conrad von Wittelsbach (d. 1200) set off with two crowns, for Cyprus and Cilicia. But the papacy set tougher conditions, namely the alignment of Armenian rites with the Catholic ones, as a further step towards rapprochement in the ongoing dialogue between both churches. In 1141, the Catholic Synod of Jerusalem had already recognized the orthodoxy of the Armenian Creed and in 1146 an Armenian Church delegation acknowledged papal supremacy, while Pope Eugene III (in office 1145–1153) reconfirmed the orthodoxy of the Armenian faith. However, this understanding was based on two misunderstandings: the Armenians understood the papal supremacy not as absolute, but as primacy within the episcopal hierarchy, while Rome was not aware that the Armenian Church rejected the Chalcedonian Creed. In 1184, Pope Lucius III (in office 1181–1185) sent Catholicos Grigor IV Tgha (in office 1173–1193) a pallium as symbol of the churches' unity.[44] While the main monasteries of the Armenian heartland remained hostile to any change to the Armenian Creed and rites, the Catholicos and the Cilician bishops were also in dialogue with the Greek Orthodox Church. A church council held in 1179 at Hromkla recognized the orthodoxy of the Greek Christology and hence the Chalcedonian Creed, but rejected Greek interferences in the Armenian rites.[45] There was no follow-up.

Anticipating papal demands, in 1194 Levon had already removed the stubborn Catholicos Grigor V (in office 1193–1194) and replaced him with the more malleable and pro-Latin Grigor VI Apirat (in office 1193–1203). This provoked the anger of the traditionalists in the heartland who supported the self-proclamation of Basil, archbishop of Ani, as anti-catholicos (in office 1194–1206).[46] King Levon was unable to react, since Ani was ruled by the Georgian vassal Sultan ibn Mahmud.[47] Levon remained powerless in 1201 too, when the Armenian archbishop of Caesarea, Ananias, declared himself catholicos under the protection of the Seljuk sultan of Iconium. When the papal legate arrived in Tarsus after having anointed Amaury of Lusignan in September 1197, he confronted Catholicos Grigor and the twelve assembled Cilician bishops with the ultimatum that they must accept three changes to the Armenian rites: as summarized by Kirakos,

to celebrate the feasts of the Lord and of all the saints on whatever days they occurred; to utter prayers in the church during the day and evening, … instead [reciting prayers] *only at the time of the administration of the sacrament during the holy Mass; and not to break the fasts on the eves of Christmas and Easter, except with fish and olives.*

When the bishops hesitated, Levon added: 'Do not worry about it. I will mollify them this time by deception.' The bishop then swore the required oath. While Levon was insistent that Cilician Armenia be recognized as a kingdom, he refrained from alienating the traditionalist bishops of Cilicia. On 6 January 1198, Prince Levon II was consecrated in Tarsus as **King Levon I** of Armenia jointly by Catholicos Grigor VI and Cardinal Conrad of Wittelsbach and received the crown from Bishop Conrad of Hildesheim. Not to be outdone, the Byzantine emperor Alexios III Angelos (r. 1195–1203) sent a second crown.[48] In spite of Levon's reassurance to the recalcitrant bishops, the dialogue with Rome continued for more than a century and a half, leading in the course of five synods to a piecemeal Latinization of the Armenian Church, which included the recognition of the Chalcedonian Creed, the adoption of the '*Filioque*' and the celebration of Christmas on

25 December instead of 6 January. (In view of obviously failing military support from the West, several such adaptations to Catholic rites were revoked by the synod of Sis in 1361.[49]) Soon after his coronation, King Levon captured the castle of Lampron by deceit. He pretended to give his niece Philippa in marriage to Oshin III, eldest son of Baron Hethum III. As soon as Hethum, Oshin and their knights arrived in Tarsus for the wedding preparations, Levon took them prisoner, and the fortress, left without a commander, was captured; Hethum was forced to become a monk.[50] The family only recovered its ancestral castle when in 1226 the crown came to the Hethumids by marriage. Seen from a distance, it seems that treachery was, in the medieval environment of Christian Cilicia and Antioch, part of day-to-day business.

While Levon had nominated his infant daughter **Zabel** (r. as queen 1219–1252) as heir and Baron Adam of Gaston as regent, there were two more claimants: Raymond-Ruben, and Zabel's elder half-sister Stephanie (also called Rita). Levon had arranged that the son of the king of Hungary should marry Zabel, but things took a different course. The Hungarian prince never came and the regent Adam was murdered by Assassins, to be replaced by the Hethumid Kostantin of Barbaron (d. *ca.* 1263). To realize his vision of the Hethumids superseding the Rubenids as the ruling family, Kostantin had only to set the right levers in motion. Baron Adam was already dead and Raymond-Ruben soon died in jail. When Stephanie, who was married to John de Brienne, king of Jerusalem (r. from Akka 1210–1225), claimed the Armenian throne in 1220, she and her infant son soon also died mysteriously. Kostantin now seems to have chosen a diversion, for he married Zabel to **Philip** (r. 1222–1224, d. 1225), son of Bohemond IV of Antioch. But Philip refused to adapt to Armenian customs and church rites and stole part of the royal treasure, bringing it to Antioch. Kostantin had Philip arrested in 1224 and, when his father

37. Ruins of the castle of Hromkla, fortified see of the Armenian catholicosate from 1147 until 1292, located in a bend of the River Euphrates, Turkey. The remaining buildings were later razed by the rebellious Egyptian Ottoman general Ibrahim Pasha in 1839. Gaziantep Province, Turkey. Photo 2018.

38. The small sea fortress of Ayas, today's Yumurtalık, Turkey, located *ca.* 400 m off the Cilician coast. The Crusaders called this strategic harbour Laiazzo and it was probably visited by Marco Polo in 1271. Ayas was looted or sacked by Mamelukes in 1266, 1275, 1283, 1322, 1335 and 1337. Adana Province, Turkey. Photo 2018.

refused to return the stolen treasures, he was killed. As narrated by al-Athir, in response Bohemond entered an alliance with the sultan of Iconium, Kay-Qubad I (r. 1220–1237) and ravaged northern Cilicia, whereupon Kostantin enticed the *atabeg* of Aleppo, Shihab al-Din Toghrul to attack Antioch, which forced Bohemond to quickly return to defend his capital.[51] Finally Kostantin could realize his dream. In June 1226, he forced Zabel to marry his son Hethum.[52] By this masterstroke, Kostantin united the two leading Armenian dynasties and ended their vicious rivalry.

King **Hethum I** (r. 1226–1269, d. 1270) was soon confronted by two bellicose and mutually hostile powers, the Mongols and the Mamelukes, whose armies and resources Cilician Armenia could in no way match. To stay neutral was no option in the Middle Ages and to fight both enemies utterly impossible. Hethum would have to choose one power as protector and ally, which would automatically attract the fury of the other. During the 1230s, Hethum had first to deal with attacks in the south-west by the Rum Seljuk sultan Kay-Qubad I, on Alanya and later the fortress of Anamur on the Mediterranean Sea (fig. 39). He lost the coastal towns and fortresses west of Seleucia, but received them back from the Il-Khan Hülegü after participating in the capture of Aleppo and Damascus in 1260.[53] Hethum had been confronted by Mongol advances by 1236 at the latest, when Chormaghun had resumed the conquest of the Southern Caucasus. He would surely have been informed by refugees, traders and ecclesiastical contacts regarding the invincible and ruthless Mongol armies and their campaigns of destruction in the east Armenian homelands and Georgia, and would know that the only escape from annihilation was to surrender without resistance, as Avag Mkhargrdzeli and other Armenian nobles had done. When the Mongols crushed the Rum Seljuks at the Battle of Köse Dağ in 1243, they stood virtually at the doorstep of Cilicia. In the same year, the Georgian queen Rusudan had surrendered and sent her son Davit to Karakorum. The options available to Hethum, who could raise at best, according to the king's nephew Hethum of Korykos, 12,000 cavalry and 45,000 infantry, were bleak.[54] To retreat to the mountain castles had been proven in Georgia to be a dead end; the arrival of a strong anti-Mongol Crusade from the West was highly unlikely, and the idea of building a defence alliance comprising Armenia, the Crusader States and military orders as well as the neighbouring Seljuk sultans and emirs was an illusion. Furthermore, the Mongols seemed to be a more dangerous threat than the surrounding Muslim states which were at loggerheads with each other. Following the advice of Hasan Jalal Dawla, prince of Khachen, Hethum and his father Kostantin, who acted as councillor, decided to pre-empt a Mongol attack by voluntarily declaring Cilician Armenia a vassal of the Great Khan. They gambled on obtaining better terms by submitting still undefeated, so as to avoid destruction and receive reliable protection from the Mongols. Kirakos Gandzaketsi summarized the situation: 'Once this [Battle of Köse Dağ] had occurred, when Het'um saw that the [Seljuk] sultan had been defeated by [the Mongols] he sent ambassadors and valuable gifts to them to make peace and to place himself in submission.'[55]

After negotiations with the Mongol commander Baiju, Hethum sent his brother Smbat Sparapet to Karakorum where he met the Great Khan Güyük. On his way, he wrote a letter from Samarkand to his brother-in-law, King Henry of Cyprus (r. 1218–1253), describing the Mongol devastation of the Central Asian cities and expressing his surprise concerning the numerous (Nestorian) Christian communities and beautiful churches he came across.[56] It seems that Smbat exaggerated the number of Christians among the Mongols and their piety in an effort to counter Giovanni da Pian del Carpine's critical report of 1247 in which he described the cruelty of the Mongols and the Great Khan's uncompromising claim to global domination. While Smbat's letter was addressed to his brother-in-law, its real intended recipient was King Louis of France (r. 1226–1270); the Armenian *sparapet* obviously wanted to give King Louis and the Crusaders the impression that the Mongols could be an ally against the Muslims. The letter was handed to the king when he arrived in Cyprus in September 1248, leading the Seventh Crusade.[57] As a result Louis possessed both del Carpine's realistic assessment of the Mongols' attitude towards Christianity and also Smbat's exuberant and biased narrative.[58] On 20 December

39. The fortress of Anamur (Mamure Kalesi) on the Mediterranean coast of Turkey. The site was fortified in Roman times in the third century, taken over by the Byzantines and changed hands several times till it became an Armenian Hethumid property in *ca.* 1188; it then marked the westernmost expansion of the Cilician Armenian principalities. The large stronghold, with 36 well-preserved towers of different shapes, fell to Kay-Qubad (r. 1220–1237) in the 1220s or early 1230s. More than a century later, the fort was briefly held from 1361 till 1373 by Cyprus, to which the Armenian king Kostantin III had ceded the coastline as far as Korykos. It then belonged to the Emirate of Karaman, which lost it to the Ottomans in 1469. Mersin Province, Turkey. Photo 2018.

1248 he met the Mongol envoys sent by Eljigidei, Baiju's successor. The Mongol viceroy pretended to offer Louis an alliance whereby he would attack Baghdad and Louis would wage war on the Mamelukes in Egypt. In reality, Eljigidei and his staff feared that Louis would attack either their Rum Seljuk vassal or Syria, and wanted to steer the Crusaders' army far away.[59] Meanwhile, Smbat was well received by Güyük who confirmed Mongol protection for his new vassal and demanded that Armenia must provide troops.[60] Smbat was back in Cilicia in 1250; but Güyük had died in 1248 and was succeeded by the Great Khan Möngke (r. 1251–1259).

As recorded by Kirakos, Batu Khan then summoned Hethum to come to him and to renew the oath of allegiance personally in front of Möngke Khan.[61] The failure of King Louis' Crusade further highlighted the fact that Cilicia could not count on any help from Western Europe. Queen Zabel's death in 1252 delayed Hethum's departure. As described by Bar Hebraeus (d. 1286), he embarked on his 7,000-kilometre journey in 1253 or early 1254 disguised as a muleteer, as he feared capture by hostile Seljuks.[62] He crossed his ancestral homeland of Greater Armenia, passed Derbent and met Batu Khan and Batu's son and future successor Sartaq, who was reputedly a Christian. Then he proceeded north of the Caspian Sea and met Möngke on 13 September 1254, staying fifty days in his camp. Möngke assured Hethum of Mongol protection and freedom of religion.[63] On his return journey via Ray, Qazvin and Sisian, the king also met Baiju and Hülegü, the designated conqueror of the Middle East. Hethum was back in Cilicia in 1255. He brought back reports not only about the Christians he had encountered, but also about Buddhists 'who worship extremely large clay idols named Shakmonia [Shakyamuni] ... and Madri [Maitreya] of whom they also made a clay image of unbelievable size in a beautiful temple.'[64] Hethum's description probably relates to Buddhist Uyghurs. Knowing Hülegü's plans from first hand, Hethum strongly advised the Latin powers of the Levant to submit as well to the Mongols. But they were suspicious of Mongol intentions, aware as they were of previous Mongol atrocities in Russia, Poland, Silesia and Hungary. They feared Mongol duplicity, and specifically that the Mongols would first, with their help, annihilate the Muslim sultans and emirs as well as the Mamelukes, and then, in a second move, turn on them, crush them and destroy their castles. Based on the detailed reports of Carpine and Rubruck as well as on the past experiences in Eastern Europe, they understood that the Mongols knew no allies, only underlings and enemies.[65] Hethum's son-in-law Bohemond VI of Antioch (r. 1251–1268) alone submitted at the last moment in January 1260, when Hülegü's attack on Syria had begun.

Less than three years after his return, Hethum was asked to prove his loyalty as a vassal and to supply troops for Hülegü's conquest of Baghdad, which was achieved in 1258; countless Muslims were slaughtered, but the Christians were spared, another reason being that Hülegü's mother Sorkaktani Beki and wife Dokuz Khatun were Nestorians.[66] Since the Mongol army counted numerous Georgian and Armenian soldiers in its ranks, many local Christians of Syria began to dream that the Mongols would deliver them from Muslim dominance. Late in 1259, Hülegü began his campaign of conquest in Palestine and Egypt by besieging Aleppo. Summoned by Hülegü, Hethum and Bohemond rushed to meet him with their troops. Aleppo fell in January 1260. As related by Bar Hebraeus, who was at that time the region's Syriac Orthodox metropolitan, Christians were not spared in the massacres. Only the intercession of Bar Hebraeus and of a relative of King Hethum saved the surviving Christians who had sought refuge inside a church.[67] Next, Damascus surrendered without a fight to the Mongol commander Ked Buqa, who happened to be a Nestorian.

On 1 March [1260] *Kitbuqa entered Damascus at the head of a Mongol army. With him were the King of Armenia* [Hethum] *and the Prince of Antioch* [Bohemond]. *The citizens of the ancient capital of the* [Omayyad] *caliphate saw for the first time for six centuries three Christian potentates ride in triumph through their streets.*[68]

The occupation of Damascus represented for King Hethum the climax of his career, for he had every reason to expect that the Mongol–Armenian army would continue its victorious march and soon conquer Jerusalem, which Hülegü might possibly even hand over to him. But within six months this vision was shattered and Hethum would be cornered in a bitter defensive war for the rest of his reign.

Soon after the capture of Damascus, Ked Buqa raided Hebron, Ascalon, Jerusalem and Nablus and placed a squadron in Gaza to impede a Mameluke advance. An Egyptian attack was expected since the Mameluke sultan Saif ad-Din Qutuz (r. 1259–1260) had crucified Hülegü's envoys, which meant war.[69] Because Palestine would be the battlefield, the Crusaders had to decide who to side with. Since Ked Buqa had destroyed the unruly town of Sidon and already ordered some Crusaders to dismantle their castles, they decided on neutrality, favouring the Mamelukes by allowing them free passage through their territories. At this moment, in summer 1260, Hülegü, whose horses could not get enough fodder in Syria and were suffering from the heat,[70] received two ominous reports: his brother and

40. Miniature of the Battle of Mari, also called Disaster of Mari, where in 1266 an Armenian army led by princes Thoros and Levon was crushed by the Mameluke commander Qalawun. In the centre, Prince Levon is taken prisoner while his brother Thoros lies dead in the grass at the right. *Livre des Merveilles*, early fifteenth century, BN Fr 2810, folio 245v. © Bibliothèque Nationale, Paris.

ally Möngke had died, and Berke Khan had begun to withdraw troops that formed part of Hülegü's army. The Il-Khan returned to Tabriz with most of the army, leaving Ked Buqa behind with only 10,000 men and the Christian auxiliaries.[71] Qutuz and his commander Baibars advanced as far as Akka and set a trap at 'Ain Jalut, north of Jerusalem. During the battle there on 3 September, part of the Mameluke army feigned retreat and lured Ked Buqa's warriors out of a secure position. The main Mameluke force then surrounded them, and destroyed them in close combat in which the professionally trained Mamelukes were superior to the Mongols. Ked Buqa fell; Hethum and Bohemond were not present at the battle.[72] The Mamelukes took advantage of the situation and advanced into Syria, where on 10 December they defeated a second Mongol army at the First Battle of Homs. The defeats were a historical turning point since this was the first time a major Mongol campaign had been successfully repelled. The Mongol advance and the destruction of the Ayyubid emirates as well as the Il-Khanid retreat behind the Euphrates that followed created a power vacuum in Syria which was quickly filled by the victorious Mamelukes. They annexed the land, including Damascus and Aleppo, but excluding Antioch and the Assassin's fortresses. Under sultans Baibars I (r. 1260–1277), who had murdered Qutuz on his return to Cairo, and Qalawun (r. 1279–1290), the Egyptian Mamelukes became the leading power in the Near East. Even though the Mongol Il-Khanate undertook five further attacks on Syria, in 1281, 1299, 1300, 1303 and 1312–1313, it was never able to drive out the Mamelukes. It was also an irony of history that the haughty Mongols who had previously demanded unconditional submissions from popes and Western European kings now came as supplicants courting these same powers for an anti-Mameluke alliance. Between 1262 and 1313, the Il-Khans sent 19 embassies to the West, none of which met a tangible response, apart from the abortive cooperation in 1272 between the future King Edward I (r. 1272–1307) of England and the Mongol general Samaghar.[73]

Sultan Baibars was as cunning and ruthless a commander as any of Genghis Khan's best generals. Having saved Egypt from the Mongol onslaught, he devoted himself to clearing Palestine of the last Crusader bastions and consolidating the Sultanate's hold on Syria. With the fall of Antioch in 1268, Armenia lost its glacis and buffer. The fortress of Crac des Chevaliers fell in 1271, Tripoli in 1289, and in 1291 Sultan Khalil (r. 1290–1293) eliminated the last Crusader bastions on the Near Eastern mainland. While the Mamelukes restored and garrisoned the captured inland castles, those on the coast were utterly razed in order to deny bridgeheads to any future Crusades. The trading Republic of Genoa reacted to the loss of the last Latin bridgeheads in 1290 by signing a treaty with Sultan Qalawun mutually granting trading rights and immunity for merchants, which reduced the attractiveness of the Cilician harbours.[74] But Cilician Armenia held out till 1375 as the only Christian state on the Near Eastern mainland. In Baibars' and his successors' assessment, Cilicia's military capabilities had to be severely curtailed and its economy exploited to the maximum. Following two raids into the regions of Antioch and Cilicia in 1261 and 1262, King Hethum managed in 1265 (or 1264) to deter the advancing Mamelukes by massing his army in the Syrian Gates (today's Belen Pass through the Nur Mountains) which guarded the direct access to Cilicia from Antioch.[75] Both passes, the Syrian and the Cilician Gates, were so strong that al-Athir nicknamed the Armenian king 'Lord of the Passes'.[76] But Hülegü's death in 1265 offered Baibars an ideal opportunity for a renewed attack on the Mongol protectorate of Armenia. In 1266 he sent his best commander, Qalawun towards Cilicia. Hethum anticipated the attack and hastened to Tabriz to ask Hülegü's successor Abaqa for military help. On 24 August 1266, in Hethum's absence, Qalawun completely destroyed the Armenian army commanded by Hethum's sons Thoros and Levon (the future King Levon II), at the Battle of Mari north of the Syrian Gates (fig. 40). According to Smbat Sparapet, the Armenian army fought badly and soon fled, abandoning its royal commanders and loyal companions.[77] Thoros was killed fighting and Levon captured.[78] The Disaster of Mari was the last attempt of the Armenians to stop an invader at their borders in a major pitched battle; from now on the nobles and knights would usually retreat to their mountain castles and abandon the cities in the plain to their fate. If we believe Marco Polo, who stayed in Ayas only five years later, the Armenians had lost their fighting qualities. 'In days of old the nobles there were valiant men, and did doughty deeds of arms; but nowadays they are poor creatures, and good at naught,

41. The fortress called by the Crusaders Tell Hamdun, today's Toprak Kale, controlled the south-eastern access to Cilicia. It was fiercely contested between Byzantines, Armenians, Crusaders and Mamelukes. While the Armenians managed to recapture Tell Hamdun which they had surrendered in the wake of the Disaster of Mari (1266), they lost it for ever in 1337. Osmaniye Province, Turkey. Photo 2018.

unless it be at boozing.'[79] Following their victory, the Mamelukes sacked Ayas, Adana, Tarsus and Sis where the citadel successfully held out. To ransom his son Levon, Hethum had to surrender several fortresses and to convince Abaqa to hand over a prominent prisoner called 'Red Falcon' who was a friend of Baibars.[80] After Levon had returned from his two years' detention, Hethum abdicated in favour of his son.

King **Levon II** (r. 1269–1289) inherited a devastated realm without significant armed forces. One of his priorities was to rebuild Ayas which rapidly profited from the fall of Antioch leaving it the last major trading harbour on the Near Eastern mainland held by Christians. In 1275, Baibars again conducted a raid on Cilicia, advancing as far as Korykos, plundering Ayas and Tarsus and deporting thousands of Armenians to Egypt as slaves. The disastrous Mongol counteroffensive supported by a large Armenian and Georgian force in 1281 further weakened Cilicia's position.[81] In retaliation, Qalawun again sacked Ayas in 1283. Levon was forced in 1285 to submit to the Mameluke sultan; to obtain a truce of ten years, he had to agree to pay a huge annual tribute, refrain from negotiating hostile alliances and grant Muslim merchants far-reaching trade privileges. By this latter clause, the Cilician harbours became free ports for the Mamelukes. Qalawun also preferred extorting high annual tribute payments to occupying the poor Cilician uplands. Cilician Armenia was now a Mameluke tributary vassal, since its previous (unreliable) protector, the Il-Khanate, proved in 1283 and 1285 unable or unwilling to rescue its Armenian client. Levon died in 1289, leaving five sons who would fight each other for succession in a singularly ferocious and brutal way.

King **Hethum II** (r. 1289–1293, co-ruler 1295–1296, r. 1299–1303, regent 1303–1307) was a complex personality, more than once exchanging the role of a king with the life of a monk and yet coming back to the throne, and never fully relinquishing power. When Hethum ascended the throne he was given little respite, since the Mameluke attacks soon resumed in spite of the truce. Following the capture of Akka in 1291, Sultan al-Ashraf Khalil (r. 1290–1293) attacked the patriarchal fortress of Hromkla. It fell in May 1292 and Catholicos Stephen IV (in office 1290–1293) – who had replaced Kostantin II (in office 1286–1290) because the latter was opposed to a church union with Rome – died in Egyptian captivity. To succeed him Hethum arranged the appointment of Grigor VII of Anazarbos (in office 1293–1307) who was in favour of the church union, in line with Hethum's strategy to obtain papal support in return for submitting the Church to the pope. At this point, popes were still perceived as potential organizers of Crusades. Grigor moved the patriarchal see to Sis, thus losing its independence from the temporal power (figs. 42, 111). Hethum was a staunch adherent of an assimilation of the Armenian to the Roman Catholic Church and in 1289 he invited the Spiritual Franciscan zealot Angelo da Clareno (d. 1337) and five other Spirituals to missionize among the Cilician Armenians. Shortly after Hethum's abdication in 1293, they were forced to leave. To avoid further Mameluke raids, Hethum surrendered the cities of Marash and Besni and the fortress of Tell Hamdun (Toprak Kale, fig. 41) whereupon he abdicated in favour of his brother **Thoros III** (r. 1293–1295, co-ruler 1295–1296). Although Hethum entered a monastery as a Franciscan friar, he continued to advise his brother and officially resumed power when the Muslim Ghazan became the new Il-Khan in 1295. Although the renewal of the oath of allegiance yielded no significant material results, Hethum and Thoros's journey to Ghazan significantly alleviated the suffering of the local Christians of the Il-Khanid Khanate. The contemporary Bar Hebraeus recorded: Emir Nauruz (d. 1297), who had put Ghazan on the throne,

issued a command that the churches, the houses of images [Buddhist temples] *and the synagogues of the Jews should be destroyed ... And no Christian was to be seen* [in the streets] *unless he had a girdle round his loins, and no Jew was to be seen unless he had a mark on his head. ... Hitâm* [Hethum] *begged from the King of Kings* [Ghazan] *that the churches should not be destroyed, because they were the dwellings of God, and also houses of prayer. ... And thus, through this believing king many churches were freed from the destroyer.*[82]

According to the eyewitness Rabban Bar Sauma (*ca.* 1225–1294), vicar general of the Nestorian Church of the East, the two Armenian kings also saved the Nestorian Catholicos Mar Yahballaha III (in office 1281–1317), who had been imprisoned and suffered tortures, from a certain death by ransoming him.[83]

When the two kings travelled one year later to Constantinople to arrange a matrimonial alliance with the Emperor Michael IX Palaiologos (r. 1294–1320), their brother **Smbat** (r. 1296–1298) whom they had entrusted with the deputy governorship of the kingdom, usurped power with the blessing of Catholicos Grigor VII and the help of yet another brother, Kostantin. Informed of Smbat's putsch, Hethum and Thoros hurried back home, but were caught by Smbat's henchmen in Caesarea and jailed in Pardzerpert. Smbat ordered Thoros to be strangled and Hethum blinded. With these infamous deeds, Smbat opened an era of fratricidal wars that lasted almost half a century. After less than two years, **Kostantin I** (r. 1298–1299) rebelled against his former ally Smbat and had him imprisoned, while Hethum was freed. As soon as Hethum had partially recovered his eyesight, he removed Kostantin and retook power. When Kostantin begun to conspire with the jailed Smbat against Hethum he had both plotters arrested and sent in exile to Constantinople, where they died in prison.[84]

Following another Mameluke raid, Ghazan undertook a renewed attempt to reconquer Syria. The coalition army, consisting of Mongols, Armenians, Georgians and Templars from Cyprus, scored a great victory at the Third Battle of Homs on 22 or 23 December 1299. While a few raids were undertaken in 1300 in Palestine, reaching as far as Gaza, Ghazan retreated in February 1300 with the bulk of the army, whereupon the Mamelukes reoccupied Syria and resumed their attacks on Cilicia.[85] As agreed between the Crusaders and Ghazan, who had promised to return towards the end of 1300, a force of Templar knights attacked the Syrian harbour of Tortosa (Tartous), and a small flotilla from Cyprus took the coastal city of Batroun in today's northern Lebanon. Since the Il-Khanid army failed to turn up, the Templars established their base on the island of Ruad three kilometres off the coast of Tortosa. In February 1301, the Il-Khanid general Qutlugh Shah led a 60,000-strong army to Syria where he was joined by Hethum II and some Crusaders. But after just a few raids, Ghazan cancelled the campaign and ordered Qutlugh Shah back. Ghazan's retreat sealed the fate of the Crusader bridgehead on Ruad which counted 120 Templar knights, 500 Templar archers and 400 Templar sergeants: the Mamelukes laid siege to Ruad and starved the garrison out. Although the Mamelukes guaranteed free passage to the surviving Templars who capitulated on 26 September 1302, in the end they were all either massacred or taken prisoner.[86] A new Mongol expedition in 1303 ended in a disastrous defeat which put an end to Cilicia's dream of sharing a stable border with its Mongol protector. Later in the year, Hethum again exchanged the crown for a monk's habit, resigning in favour of Thoros's minor son **Levon III** (r. 1303–1307) but keeping the regency.

The Catholic Church realized only in 1289, on the occasion of the visit of the famous Franciscan missionary John of Montecorvino (1247–1328), future archbishop of Khanbaliq, that the Armenian Church was Miaphysite and condemned the Chalcedonian Creed. As a result, the papacy increased its pressures on the Armenian Church, declaring the adoption of the Chalcedonian Creed and certain liturgical adaptions to be preconditions for any Western support. However, it seemed to Hethum that without such support Cilicia would eventually succumb. The regent and Grigor VII, the 'Catholic Catholicos' as he was nicknamed,[87] decided to comply and convened a synod in March 1307. Although Grigor died soon after, prior to the election of a successor Hethum and Levon imposed their will on the 32 attending bishops, against the fierce resistance of the traditionalists. Union with the Catholic Church was declared and the authority of seven ecumenical councils accepted, with the adoption of the Chalcedonian Creed. Furthermore, Christmas was to be celebrated on 25 December and water mixed with wine in the chalice during Mass.[88] These decisions caused a popular uproar, provoked the murder of the Armenian bishop of Caesarea and fuelled the notorious rebellious instincts of a number of nobles. This opposition entered into collusion with the Mongol emir Bilarghu, residing in Sis, who was already angry with Hethum for resisting the construction of a mosque in the capital; possibly he wanted to seize power himself.[89] Bilarghu summoned Hethum and Levon with a large retinue to the fortress of Anazarbos for a banquet where on 18 November 1307 he had all of them massacred. This incident highlighted the limited room for manoeuvre that future kings and catholicoi would have in matters of rapprochement with Rome. In protest four years later, Patriarch Sargis I of Jerusalem (d. 1313) declared autocephaly, but did not assume the title of catholicos, thus avoiding a schism. Quoting the historian Krzysztof Stopka, kings and 'catholicoi had to be flexible in their policy, steering clear of the Scylla of Rome and the Charybdis of the conservatives' in Cilicia and the Armenian heartland.[90] The bleak external outlook for Cilician Armenia was aptly summarized by the Venetian traveller and geographer Marino Sanuto the Elder (*ca.* 1270–1343) in an allegory included in the revised version of his treatise *Secreta Fidelium Crucis* (Secrets of the Faithful of the Cross) addressed to Pope John XXII (in office 1316–1334):

The kingdom of Armenia is under the teeth of four beasts. On one side, the lion, i.e. the Tartars [Mongols], *to whom the king of Armenia is paying a heavy tribute. On the other hand, the leopard, i.e. the Sultan* [of Egypt], *who is ravaging his country every day. The third side is held by the wolf, i.e. the* [Karamanid] *Turks* [west of Cilicia], *who undermine his power. The fourth side is the snake, i.e. the pirates, who gnaw the bones of the Christians of Armenia.*[91]

Sanuto could have well added a fifth beast, for example the hyena, i.e. the princes and churchmen who were at merciless loggerheads with each other.

Fortunately for Hethum's brother **Oshin** (r. 1307–1320), Hethum had not taken him to the murderous meeting at Anazarbos.

Oshin initially sought protection in the citadel of Sis and sent his twin brother Alinakh to the Il-Khan Oljeitu (r. 1304–1316) for confirmation. The Il-Khan condemned Bilarghu's deed and had him executed. During Oshin's reign, external political conditions became even more difficult. After the last, failed Mongol campaign against Mameluke Syria in 1312–1313, Cilicia became of little strategic value to the Il-Khanate. The peace treaty of 1321 with the Egyptian Sultanate further sealed the isolation of the small Armenian kingdom. This meant that Cilicia became all the more dependent on support from the Latin powers and Cyprus. In spite of the risks involved, Oshin pursued the pro-Catholic strategy of his murdered predecessor and had the nine articles of faith that were decided upon in 1307 reconfirmed at the synod of Adana in 1316. When riots again broke out, Oshin reacted swiftly by arresting the rebellious clergymen and nobles, and had the ringleaders executed. Four years later, King Oshin too paid with his life for his policy, and was poisoned, probably by his brother-in-law Oshin of Korykos, son of Hethum the Historian.[92] Oshin of Korykos became the regent for the underage **Levon IV** (r. 1320–1341), King Oshin's son. The regent tried to secure his position by murdering several of Oshin's relatives, marrying his widow and forcing Levon to marry his daughter Alice. Finally he made his brother Kostantin *sparapet* of Cilicia. These manoeuvres were to no avail, for when Levon reached maturity in 1329, he ordered the execution of his two uncles, the regent Oshin and *sparapet* Kostantin, as well as his wife Alice. The murderous record led a Dominican friar to warn King Philip VI of France (r. 1328–1350) who was considering a Crusade in 1332:

The leopard cannot change its spots, nor the Ethiopian his skin: they [the Armenians of Cilicia] partake in every error known in the East. Their King [Levon II] had nine children, and all, sons and daughters alike, have come to a violent end, except one daughter and no one knows what her end will be. One brother killed another with the sword, another poisoned his brother, another strangled his brother in prison, so they all murdered one another till only the last was left and he was poisoned and died miserably.[93]

Philip's plan for a renewed Crusade led nowhere, with his attention caught up by the start of the Hundred Years War (1337–1453).

As of 1322 (or 1321)[94] Mameluke strategy towards Cilicia changed, since it was now aimed at the destruction of this economic competitor of the Egyptian trading ports. That year's raid devastated Ayas to such a degree that only the castle on the mainland was rebuilt, and not the one standing on a tiny offshore islet. When the emir of Aleppo, a loyal vassal of the Mamelukes, attacked again in 1335, most of the inhabitants fled to Cyprus. The Mamelukes delivered the deathblow to Ayas two years later, when they razed all fortifications and occupied the defenceless town, which thereby lost its dominant trading position. The remaining trade shifted to Tarsus and Korykos, and when in 1360 the emir of Aleppo captured Tarsus and Adana, Korykos placed itself under the protection of the Kingdom of Cyprus to which it belonged till 1448.[95] The rump of Cilicia was now landlocked. While Cilician Armenia was struggling for political survival, the fight between the faction favouring a church union with Rome and the traditionalists continued with unabated violence, especially after 1337 and the loss of Ayas. One party wanted to gain Western military support at any price, the other advocated an appeasement strategy by breaking all political and church contacts with Western powers in order not to provoke further devastation at the hands of the Mamelukes. When the pro-union Catholicos Kostantin III (in office 1323–1326) died, he was followed by the staunchly traditionalist Jacob of Tarsus (in office 1327–1341). Jacob used a similarly drastic formulation as Bishop Stepanos Orbelian had done earlier saying 'that it would be better for his flock to go to hell as Armenians rather than to heaven as members of the Latin Church'.[96] At the same time, the *Fratres Unitores* were making headway in Cilicia and Levon pushed for a complete Latinization of the Armenian Church under papal oversight, in order to finally obtain badly needed military support. When Catholicos Jacob threatened Levon with excommunication, the king had him deposed and replaced by the more tractable Mukhitar I (in office 1341–1355). These developments angered the Armenian monk Nerses Balients (Baghon), one of the *Unitores* and reportedly a former Armenian bishop of Urmia, who had been missionizing in Cilicia since 1336 and did not shrink from rebaptizing Armenians who converted to Catholicism, nor from re-ordaining priests. He travelled to Avignon and handed to Pope Benedict XII (in office 1334–1342) a memorandum entitled *Fides Armenorum* in which he listed no fewer than 117 errors of the Armenian Church.[97] The pope reacted sternly in a letter to the king, not mincing his words: the Catholic Church would not help those who persisted in living in error in questions of faith; military support could only be considered after the eradication of the horrendous errors in the church of both Armenias.[98] In this heated domestic situation, approaching civil war over ecclesiastical issues, King Levon was murdered by angry traditionalists. Since Levon's only child had died around 1331, the Hethumid line of Armenian rulers was extinguished with his death.

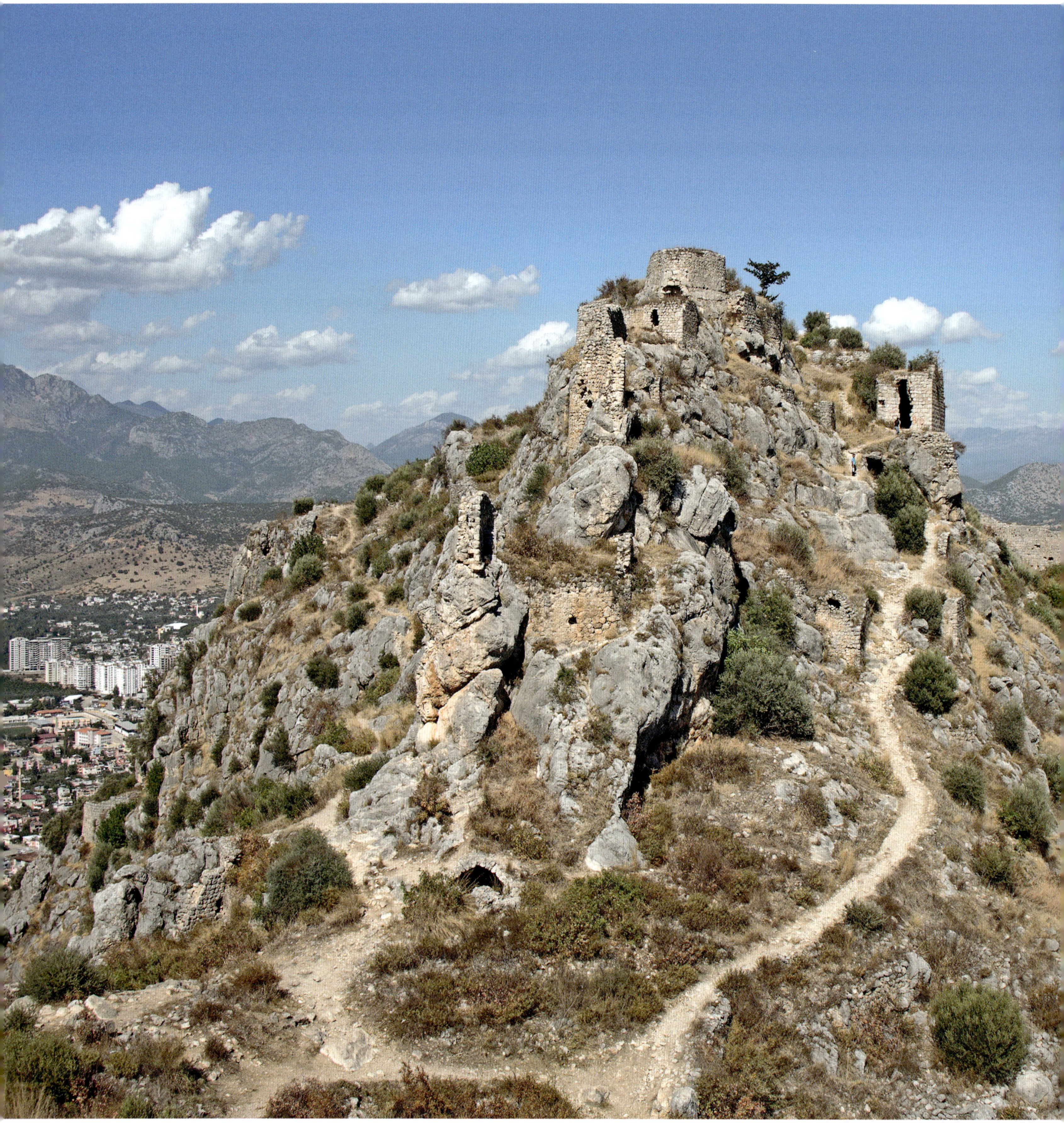

The crown passed next to Guy de Lusignan, a grandson of Levon II. Guy's mother was Levon's II daughter Isabella (murdered by Oshin of Korykos before 1323) who was married to Amaury de Lusignan (d. 1310). Initially very reluctant to accept this quasi-suicidal command, Guy finally agreed; to appease the Armenian barons, he took the regnal name of **Kostantin II** (r. 1342–1344). Caught between the two irreconcilably hostile factions and without a power base of his own, Kostantin was isolated and forced to invite French-speaking knights to fill administrative assignments. His decision to discontinue tribute payments to the Egyptian sultan provoked a renewed wave of Mameluke destruction. When Kostantin insisted on pursuing a pro-Latin policy, the traditionalist party had him, his brother Bohemond and all the Latin nobles murdered in summer 1344. Armenia had become ungovernable, torn apart by uncompromising parties. The objective of the small Crusade initiated by Pope Clement VI (in office 1342–1352) and consisting of Venetians, Cypriots and Knights Hospitaller, which captured the harbour of Smyrna in October 1344, had as its objective not the rescue of Cilicia, but a fight against Turkic piracy.[99] Cilicia's next ruler, **Kostantin III** (r. 1344–1363) was not an Armenian by royal blood, but was related by marriage to the collateral Hethumid line of Korykos. After yet another Mameluke attack in 1346, Kostantin became the last king of Armenian Cilicia to appeal to the pope for help, who sent two legates to Cilicia with almost plenipotentiary powers. Arriving in 1347, the legates not only blackmailed the Armenians into yielding to their demands, but also aimed to reduce the catholicos to the rank of a Latin patriarch subject to the pope. Mukhitar I and the king refused, however, and closed the negotiation in early 1349.[100] After Cilicia had lost its remaining harbours in 1360, it became obvious that further expectations of Western military support were futile and concessions to Rome useless. The continued existence of Armenian dioceses and monasteries under Muslim rule in Greater Armenia indicated an alternative. Under the guidance of Catholicos Mesrop I of Cilicia (in office 1359–1372) and King Kostantin, a synod held in

---

42. The northern, smaller half of the strongly fortified complex of Sis; in the background the modern city of Kozan. Sis was originally a Byzantine fortress and became in the second half of the seventh century an Abbasid border stronghold, which was reconquered by Nikephoros II Phokas in 964. The Rubenid prince Thoros I captured Sis in 1113, but it was lost to the Byzantine emperor John II Komnenos in 1137. In the 1140s or early 1150s the Armenians regained control over Sis and around 1184 the city became the administrative capital of the principality (as of 1198/99 the kingdom). Between 1266 and 1375 the region of Sis was ravaged no less than ten times by the Mamelukes and their allies. The city capitulated in 1375 to the Mamelukes which brought an end to the Armenian Kingdom of Cilicia. Adana Province, Turkey. Photo 2018.

1361 in Sis revoked the adoption of Latin practices along with many previous concessions, thus ending the 'Cilician Union' with Rome.[101] One may surmise that this victory of the traditionalist party made it possible for King Kostantin to die in 1363 of natural causes.

After Kostantin III's death, the throne remained unoccupied for two years till the accession of **Kostantin IV** (r. 1365–1373). Due to the lack of clear and accurate sources, the succession of Armenian kings is disputed. Possibly Kostantin's II nephew Levon (b. 1342, later King Levon V) inherited the crown but did not then assume power. Around 1368, King Peter I of Cyprus (r. 1358–1369) was offered the crown by a group of nobles.[102] According to the tendentious and unreliable Franciscan chronicler (and confessor of the imprisoned King Levon V), Jean Dardel, Kostantin had offered Peter his beleaguered kingdom and, when the latter was murdered in 1369, he entered into negotiations with the Mameluke Sultan al-Ashraf Sha'ban (r. 1363–1377). By now, Cilicia was reduced to Sis and its surroundings. Displeased by these negotiations, some of the barons murdered the king in 1373. In the meantime, Kostantin II's nephew Levon, who had been jailed following the murder of Peter I of Cyprus, had been set free after producing a papal letter allegedly issued by Urban V (in office 1362–1370) designating him as rightful king of Armenia. Eager to reign, Levon was allowed to leave Cyprus in spring 1374 after he had renounced any claims to Cypriot property. When he was crowned as **Levon V** (r. 1374–1375, d. 1393) in Sis in September it was already too late to determine the strategic direction of policy for, according to Jean Dardel, a number of barons, along with Catholicos Poghos (Paul) I (in office 1374–1382), had already begun negotiations with the Mamelukes and the emir of Aleppo to surrender Sis. If we believe Dardel, Poghos proclaimed 'that he preferred the temporal domination of one of Islam's rulers, rather than the spiritual supremacy of the Pope'.[103] While this position amounted, from a political and military perspective, to betrayal, it was rational from an ecclesiastical point of view: unlike the Catholic Church which demanded submission to papal authority and the adoption of Latin beliefs and rites, Muslim rulers did not normally bother about Christian creeds and rites so long as they paid the imposed taxes. Early in 1375, an Aleppian–Mameluke army besieged Sis, and the last king of Cilician Armenia was forced to capitulate on 13 April 1375.[104] Levon was jailed in Cairo until King John of Castile ransomed him in 1382. In 1385–1386 he attempted to mediate between France and England in the Hundred Years War to bring an end to this unending conflict which would have been the precondition for considering a Crusade to reconquer Cilicia. Levon died in 1393 in Paris. Even after the disappearance of the Armenian Kingdom of Cilicia and of the corresponding political pressure for a union of the Armenian with the Catholic Church, the struggle between the traditionalists and the Unionists continued unabated in the former Greater Armenia. Among the traditionalists, Malachia Krimetsi stands out for his radicalism. In the later 1370s he enrolled the support of local Muslim rulers to eject the *Fratres Unitores* from Nakhchivan, and in Koghb, in north-eastern Armenia, he arranged for a Catholic Armenian *vardapet* (archimandrite and teacher) and his students to be sentenced to death and boiled alive.[105]

After the fall of the Armenian Kingdom of Cilicia there would be no independent Armenian state for more than half a millennium, till the short-lived republic of 1918–1920.[106] But the Armenian nation survived, albeit under Turkic, Persian and, as of the early nineteenth century, Russian rule. With regard to the Armenian Cilician people, ever since the occupation of Ayas, there had been an emigration of wealthy Armenian merchants to Cyprus. In the following years, thousands more Armenians left Cilicia for Italy, France, Spain, Poland and Crimea; in the latter, an important diaspora already existed. Among the most important vectors for keeping the identity of the Armenian nation alive were the Armenian Church and its tradition of religious manuscripts and books, which enjoyed as much veneration as icons in the Greek and Russian Orthodox Churches or reliquaries in the Roman Catholic.[107] The less affluent farmers and mountain dwellers remained. In 1375, neither the Egyptian Mamelukes nor the Emirate of Aleppo established direct rule over Cilicia, but allowed the Turkmen Ramazanids to take possession of the countryside while trying to keep control over the major cities for themselves.[108] However, by 1381 the Ramazanids had captured Adana, which they turned into the capital of their emirate. Twenty years later, a new wave of destruction hit Cilicia when Timur-e Lang sacked Sis, provoking a renewed emigration to Constantinople, Crimea and Europe. The Ramazanid emirate remained a more or less independent buffer state between the Ottomans and the Mamelukes till 1516 when the Ottoman sultan Selim I (r. 1512–1520) conquered Syria from the Mamelukes. After the massacres of 1895 and 1909 and the genocide of 1915, the last surviving Armenians left Cilicia in 1921 when France renounced its mandate and handed the territory over to Turkey. In 1923, Armenian and Greek properties whose owners were no longer living in Turkey were confiscated and redistributed to Muslim immigrants. Today, only the relics of military and port architecture, as well as sparse church ruins, remain as witnesses to the once prosperous Armenian communities.

IV

The South Caucasus under Turkmen, Ottoman and Iranian Safavid Domination

1. Georgia and the devastations of Timur-e Lang

When King **Bagrat V** (co-ruler from 1355, r. 1360–1393) ascended the throne, Georgia was only slowly beginning to recover from the ravages of the Black Death.[1] In the second half of his reign, Bagrat faced an even greater challenge when he had to decide which of the two rivals who were vying for supremacy in Iran and Transoxania (western Central Asia), Toqtamish or Timur-e Lang, he should side with, if only in the spirit of benevolent neutrality. Toqtamish was a Genghisid prince of the Blue Horde who unsuccessfully attempted in 1376 to overthrow Urus, Khan of the White Horde, and then fled to Emir Timur-e Lang (Tamerlane). While Toqtamish's first two attempts to seize power in the White Horde failed, he succeeded in his third attack in winter 1377–78 thanks to the support of Timur. In 1380, he united both hordes and rebuilt the Golden Horde whose capital was New Sarai in the Lower Volga region. While Timur believed he had fostered a grateful and loyal junior ally in Toqtamish, the latter harboured greater ambitions. Having burned Moscow to the ground in 1382, he aimed at conquering the former, now fragmented, Il-Khanate as well as Transoxiana, which would have given him control over the most important transcontinental trade routes. Having already conquered Khwarazmia in 1379, Toqtamish crossed the Caucasus in winter 1385–86 with King Bagrat's support, invaded Derbent and Shirvan, and pillaged Tabriz which was the gate to Iran. Considering Iran and its valuable trade routes to belong to his domain, Timur struck back fast. He advanced to Tabriz and decided to eliminate Georgia as an ally of Toqtamish. He first destroyed the fortresses of Nakhchivan and Kars, and then laid siege to King Bagrat in the heavily fortified city of Tbilisi, where

43. The Last Supper. Mural from the late fourteenth century in the church of St Grigori, Ubisa, founded in the late ninth century. The murals reflect the influence of the late Byzantine school from the time of the Palaiologos dynasty (1259–1453). Imereti, Georgia. Photo 2018.

he had been abandoned by his nobles as they retreated to their castles. Tbilisi fell on 22 November 1386; its inhabitants were massacred and Bagrat fell into captivity. This was the first of Timur's eight attacks on Georgia between 1386 and 1403. Timur's army spent the winter in Karabakh.

To regain his freedom, Bagrat pretended to convert to Islam and Timur sent him back under the surveillance of a 12,000-strong army which was to enforce Georgia's conversion to Islam. Bagrat secretly informed his son Giorgi, the future king Giorgi VII, who raised an army and destroyed the Timurid troops in an ambush, freeing Bagrat. In the words of the medieval historian Tovma Metsobetsi (1378–1446),

[Bagarat] *came with numerous presents to submit to the detestable king, but* [Timur], *filled with Satan's evil, made him apostatize and then took him and went to Karabagh … Now the king of Georgia, filled with the wisdom of the Holy Spirit, tricked* [Timur], *saying: 'Give me numerous troops so that I may go to Georgia, take the entire land and turn it to your faith …'* [Timur] *rejoicing, dressed him in a robe of honor, gave him numerous gifts and sent him off with many troops. … Now Bagarat secretly sent to his sons … to come surreptitiously and help their father flee from Timur.* [Bagarat] *took Chaghatai* [Timur]*'s troops to the most narrow and tight places, while the king's sons held the expanse of the road. Putting their swords to work they killed many of them, more than 12,000 they say. Taking their father, they went to their dwelling* [Tbilisi].[2]

Furious, Timur immediately attacked Georgia in March 1387 but fierce resistance inflicted heavy losses on his invading troops. Concerned that Toqtamish, to whom Bagrat had appealed for help, might again invade Azerbaijan, Timur retreated without achieving any of his ends. Two years later, Bagrat managed to reduce Imereti, whose *eristavi*, Aleksandre I had taken advantage of Timur's invasion of 1387 to declare himself as an independent king, to vassal status.[3] Timur's relentless war against Toqtamish continued outside the Caucasus. The emir reconquered Khwarazmia and defeated Toqtamish in June 1391 at the Battle of the Kondurcha river in the Middle Volga region north-east of today's Samara.

Timur was burning to take revenge for Bagrat's apostasy and in 1393 sent raiding expeditions to Samtskhe. In the first half of 1394 Timur ravaged parts of southern Georgia, but everywhere met with fierce resistance. In autumn of the same year, Timur attacked Georgia again in Inner Kartli and advanced northwards through the Aragvi valley in order to occupy the strategic Darial Gorge to prevent a renewed alliance between Toqtamish and Georgia, now ruled by King **Giorgi VII** (from 1369 co-ruler, r. 1393–1405 or 1407). However, Toqtamish duped Timur again, advancing along the western Caspian coast and devastating Azerbaijan. As reported by the later historian Mir Ghiyas al-Din Muhammad Husayni, alias Khwandamir (*ca.* 1475–1535), Timur hurriedly left Georgia to confront Toqtamish, whom he narrowly defeated thanks to the improvisations of his quick-witted officers near Grozny on the River Terek.[4] In order to eliminate Toqtamish once and for all, he systematically smashed the economic foundations of the Golden Horde by razing the most important trading cities to the ground, while in Alania and Dagestan he destroyed Christian churches and villages wherever he encountered them. In Dagestan, one of the emirs of the local Kumyk people who was blind in one eye dared to challenge the invader: 'I the blind one have a question for you the lame one [Timur's Persian sobriquet *e Lang* meant "the lame"]: who are we that a king mighty like you comes to make war on us: what do we have that you want to take from us?' Timur, it is said, returned the village's property.[5] He then retreated to Shirvan whose ruler Shirvanshah Ibrahim I (r.1382–1418) had submitted in 1386 and again in 1394, thus saving his realm from destruction. According to the seventeenth-century Turkish historian Ahmad ibn Lütfullah, surnamed Müneccim-bashi, whose work was based on older Arabic documents,

Shaykh Ibrahim waited on Amir Timur when in 797 AH/1394 CE the latter was moving to Dasht (of Qipchaq) [in pursuit of Toqtamish] *via Derbent. He presented to him offerings, nine pieces of every kind, as was the wont of the Mongol kings. But as slaves he offered only eight. When asked about the reason he replied* [to Timur] *in a pleasant way: 'I am myself the ninth'. This was well received by Timur.*[6]

The emir subsequently returned to Samarkand and appointed his son Miran Shah, who was even crueller than his father, as governor of Azerbaijan. Giorgi took advantage of Timur's absence to counterattack and rescued the Jalayirid prince Tahir, son of Sultan Ahmad Jalayir, by breaking the year-long siege of the fortress of Yernjak (Alinja) by Timurid troops (fig. 187 in volume I).[7]

After having looted Delhi in 1398, Timur, who was displeased with Miran Shah's governorship, returned to Azerbaijan in 1399, subsequently devastating Kakheti and Hereti, but again meeting with stubborn Georgian resistance. This time, not only churches and monasteries were razed, but also towns and villages were wiped out and their populations eradicated, while orchards and vineyards were uprooted and arable fields devastated. Timur pursued the same strategy as Genghis Khan and some of his commanders, namely to depopulate entire landscapes and convert farmland into horse pastures. The onset of winter forced Timur to leave Georgia and spend the winter in Karabakh. In spring 1400 he sent Giorgi an ultimatum to hand back the refugee Prince Tahir, which Giorgi flatly refused to do. The emir again destroyed Tbilisi, then, *inter alia*, the Sveti Tskhoveli Cathedral in Mtskheta, the town of Gori and the cathedrals of Samtavisi and Ruisi. Several times Giorgi broke through sieges, and each time escaped to the forests to continue his guerrilla war. Unable to catch Giorgi, Timur left Georgia, deporting tens of thousands into servitude to Samarkand. Later in the year Timur captured the city of Sebasteia (today's Sivas in central Anatolia). According to the Castilian ambassador Ruy González de Clavijo, who in 1404 travelled overland to Timur-e Lang's court in Samarkand, after the surrender of Sebasteia Timur ordered 4,000 Armenians to be buried alive despite having sworn immediately prior to their capitulation that he would not spill their blood.[8] After having captured and massacred the inhabitants of Aleppo, Damascus and Baghdad, Timur's troops finally managed, after a siege of thirteen years, to conquer Yernjak, thus robbing King Giorgi of a strategic ally. When Timur required that Georgia pay tribute, taxes and the *jizia*, an additional tax levied on non-Muslims, Giorgi sent his half-brother Konstantine as negotiator, who agreed in September 1401 to the Truce of Shamkor. In exchange for Timur's sparing Georgia further attacks, Giorgi had to pay annual tribute, supply troops and allow Timurid armies unconditional transit through Georgia. However, when in 1402 Timur advanced against the Ottoman sultan Bayezid I (r. 1389–1402), he ordered a detachment to capture the fortress of Tortum, garrisoned by Georgians, who were then put to the sword.

Having annihilated Bayezid's army at Angora (Ankara) in July 1402 and captured the sultan, Timur was free to settle accounts with Giorgi, who remained undefeated. Towards the end of the year, Konstantine returned to Timur who was camping near Kars, accompanied by *atabeg* Ivane II Jaqeli of Samtskhe (r. 1391–1444) who cherished ambitions of independence. The two emissaries were *prima facie* on an official mission, but their true motivation remains open to debate.[9] At any rate, in 1403 Timur ravaged Imereti and conquered the mountain fortress of Kurtin which was considered impregnable.[10] But the way to Abkhazia was blocked by forests and swamps. Since Timur's troops had again suffered heavy losses against the Georgian guerrillas and winter was approaching, he agreed to peace with Giorgi. The Georgian king recognized Timur as suzerain, agreed to pay annual tributes and handed over gold, jewels and horses, while Timur recognized Georgia as a Christian state and the right of Georgian kings to be consecrated as Christian rulers.[11]

Although several times defeated, Georgia remained, after seventeen years of war against Timur-e Lang, unconquered; but the country was ruined and, only half a century after the Black Death, depopulated for a second time. By contrast, other regions which belonged to Timur's loose empire, such as Ganja, Karabakh and Yerevan, were forcefully settled with some 200,000 Turkic families, from Anatolia, Syria and Azerbaijan.[12]

As news of Timur's death spread in February 1405, his realm, which lacked any firm administrative structures, immediately sank into fratricidal wars between his sons and grandsons. In Azerbaijan, the mentally disturbed Miran Shah quarrelled with his own sons Abu Bakr and Omar.[13] Although King Giorgi could only raise an army of 5,000 horsemen, he swiftly exploited the opportunity to recover lost territories. He first occupied Ani and Erzurum in the west and then hurried eastwards, recapturing Nakhchivan and Ganja and crushing a Timurid army sent by Miran Shah three times the strength of his own.[14] But Giorgi and his kingdom were not allowed to rest, for they soon found themselves facing attacks from two, mutually hostile, Muslim Turkmen tribal confederations: the Qara Qoyunlu (*ca.* 1380–1468), whose name means 'black sheep', and the Aq Qoyunlu (*ca.* 1378–1503), the 'white sheep'. These two tribes of semi-nomadic pastoralists further advanced the Turkification of the South Caucasus, which had begun in the seventh century with the Western Turks and had reached its first climax with the invasions and immigrations of the Oghuz and Seljuks in the eleventh century.[15] Giorgi was killed in battle against the Qara Qoyunlu in 1405 or 1407 in the Armenian–Georgian marches known as Somkhiti, and was succeeded by his half-brother **Konstantine (Constantine) I** (r. 1405/07–1412). The new king's position was probably challenged by his eldest son and future successor Aleksandre who fled the court and sought asylum with Ivane II Jaqeli of Samtskhe. Konstantine's main adversary was Qara Yusuf, sultan of the Qara Qoyunlu, who from his base of Kars in 1406 attacked Azerbaijan and defeated Miran Shah's son Abu Bakr at the Battle of Nakhchivan. Two years later, Qara Yusuf scored another victory in the war over Azerbaijan at the Battle of Sardrud, where Miran Shah was killed. In 1412 Konstantine, who feared that Georgia would soon be Qara Yusuf's next target, forged an alliance with Shirvanshah Ibrahim I and Sayid Ahmed Orlat, lord of Shaki. However, this triple alliance was crushed in December 1412 at the Battle of Chalagan in the Lachin (Laçın) district of western Azerbaijan. Ibrahim and Konstantine were taken prisoner; the latter and 300 Georgian nobles were executed, while Ibrahim was released after having paid a huge ransom.[16]

44. Mural of Christ Pantocrator above and God the Father below. Church of St Grigori, Ubisa, late fourteenth century. Imereti, Georgia. Photo 2018.

45. The fortress of Khertvisi controlled an important road that led from Armenia to Georgia. It was built in the eleventh century and later expanded to a mighty stronghold by the Ottomans. Samtskhe-Javakheti, Georgia. Photo 2013.

2. The partition of Georgia

Konstantine was succeeded by **Aleksandre (Alexander) I** (r. 1412–1442, d. *ca.* 1446) who benefited from the ongoing war between Timur's son Shah Rukh (1409–1447)[17] and the Qara Qoyunlu, which for three decades prevented any major new attacks on Georgia by the latter. This respite allowed Aleksandre to defeat the rebellious *atabeg* Ivane Jaqeli in 1414 and coerce him into submission. At the same time, he first mediated between the ruling Dadiani of Mingrelia and the Shervashidzes of Abkhazia, and then forced both to recognize his suzerainty. Soon afterwards he married Tamar, heiress to Imereti, a Bagratid descended in the female line from Queen Rusudan (r. 1223–1245), by which he hoped to strengthen his claim to Imereti. Aleksandre devoted himself to rebuilding the Georgian economy and religious life by reconstructing churches and strategic fortresses, confiscating untilled land and redistributing it to poor villages. He also resettled people from Imereti, which had suffered less from Timur's devastations, to Kakheti and the depopulated valleys in Kartli.[18]

After reconquering Lori in 1431 which had been seized by tribes of the Qara Qoyunlu, he took the fateful step in 1433 of nominating four of his five sons as joint kings in order to keep the key regional nobles, repeatedly prone to rebellion, in check. Instead of clearly designating a crown prince and relegating his remaining sons to a lower position in the line of succession – and putting recalcitrant sons out of action as necessary by forcing them to become monks – Aleksandre turned his sons into would-be kings who each built up their own networks of followers and troops while competing mercilessly among themselves for the pole position. The three elder sons, Vakhtang, Demetre and Giorgi would indeed each seize power while the fourth, Zal, died soon after his father's abdication in 1442, and the fifth, Davit, was consecrated at the age of nine as catholicos of Georgia.[19] Aleksandre's decision brought the country's existing centrifugal tendencies into the inner circle of the monarchy, thus threatening Georgia's unity and laying the grounds for its later partition. In 1440, the Qara Qoyunlu sultan Muzaffar al-Din Jahan Shah (r. 1438–1467), a vassal of Shah Rukh, demanded tribute from Georgia. When Aleksandre refused,

enraged, [Jahan Shah] came with a countless host of troops suddenly and unexpectedly on great Easter day. Those who fell into their hands were enslaved and the grandees were killed. He besieged the city of Samshvilde. By Pentecost ... they had captured Samshvilde ... And they built a minaret of 1,664 human heads at the gate of the city, and they took captive 9,400 [people] ... Sixty blessed men, senior priests, monks and princes were sacrificed like sheep at the city gate; some had their heads quartered; some crushed, some were killed [even] after apostatizing.[20]

Disillusioned with politics, King Aleksandre abdicated in 1442 and retired to a monastery, taking the name of Atanasi; but he neglected to clarify his succession.

46. Entry to the St Gayane Church built in memory of the legendary abbess Gayane allegedly martyred by King Trdat IV (r. 298–ca. 330/31). The church was founded in 630 and belongs to the complex of Etchmiadzin; the church was reconstructed in 1652 and the entrance arch built in 1688. Armavir Province, Armenia. Photo 2015.

The Armenian catholicosate's return to Etchmiadzin and a renewed schism

The tensions and hostilities between the Armenian Church traditionalists and the pro-Catholic Armenian unionists climaxed in the year 1441 when the see of the Armenian catholicosate was moved from Sis in Cilicia to Etchmiadzin in the Ararat Plain. The trigger for this move, which would cause a schism in the Armenian Church lasting (although in a mitigated form) till the present day, were the decisions taken at the Ecumenical Council of Ferrara and Florence in 1438 and 1439. In view of two major impending threats – the Hussite anti-papal reform movement and the Ottoman expansion menacing Constantinople – Pope Eugene IV (in office 1431–1447) aimed at reuniting the Orthodox and Roman Catholic churches and invited delegates from the Eastern churches to attend the ecumenical council. From Georgia, delegates of King Aleksandre and his co-ruling sons participated in the council but they refused to sign the Act of Union with the Catholic Church, preferring to uphold the autocephaly of the Orthodox Georgian Church.[21] From the Armenian side, two different delegations attended the council, of which the first consisted of two archbishops representing Catholicos Kostantin VI of Vahka in Cilicia (in office 1430–1439). They participated in the discussions between Orthodox Greeks and Latins in April 1438, but left when the real negotiations on the question of union began. The second Armenian delegation came from the large Armenian community in Caffa on the Crimean peninsula, which was then a Genoese colony. Since, like Constantinople, the Genoese colonies and trading cities along the Black Sea Coast felt threatened by the Ottomans, they urged the Crimean Armenians to agree to a church union in order to benefit from a future Crusade against the Turks. Catholicos Kostantin, who favoured a union with Rome, endorsed the second delegation which arrived in Florence on 13 August 1439. The Armenians from Caffa accepted Rome's conditions for union and the *Decretum pro Armenis* was released on 22 October 1439; it was signed by Pope Eugene, eight cardinals, two patriarchs, five archbishops, twenty-five Latin abbots and two Armenian delegates, the *vardapets* (archimandrites) Sargis and Thomas. This declaration of union bore few consequences since Catholicos Kostantin died a few weeks later and his successor Grigor IX (in office 1439–1441, for Cilicia only 1441–1446), who had agreed to the conditions for union defined in the *Decretum pro Armenis*, was deposed in 1441 by the synod of Etchmiadzin.[22] The Armenians who were Genoese subjects remained loyal to the union in view of Genoese pressures. The Genoese authorities not only recommended that the catholicosate should move to a Genoese stronghold such as Caffa, Pera or Famagusta, but also threatened to impose punitive fiscal measures on the Armenians of Caffa should the catholicos and the Armenians under Genoese jurisdiction not follow the decisions formulated in the *Decretum pro Armenis*. The fall of Constantinople and Pera in 1453 and the Ottoman conquest of Caffa in 1475 closed the matter for good. With the Bosporus controlled and the Genoese merchants expelled, the Black Sea became an Ottoman lake.

The Union of Florence angered the traditionalists of former Greater Armenia, who took up the recommendation made by Stepanos Orbelian around 1300 to bring the catholicosate back to its roots in Etchmiadzin. Having received the approval of Emir Yaqub Beg, Jahan Shah's governor in the province of Ayrarat residing in Yerevan, who had already allowed local Armenian nobles (called *ishkhans*) to form small autonomous principalities, a local Armenian synod met at Etchmiadzin in May 1441 and decided to move the see of the catholicosate from Sis back to Etchmiadzin. Since Grigor IX, who had probably been invited, did not attend the synod, he was deposed and Kirakos I of Khor Virap elected as the new catholicos of all Armenians (in office 1441–1443). However, Grigor IX and the Cilician bishops refused to accept his deposition and the corresponding loss of prestige and revenues to themselves, and excommunicated all participants of the Etchmiadzin synod and declared its decisions invalid.[23] Although a compromise was reached in the sixteenth century between the catholicosates of Etchmiadzin and Sis, as well as Aghtamar, whereby the latter two recognized the primacy of the former while Sis retained its autocephaly and the title 'Catholicosate of the Great House of Cilicia',[24] further divisions had taken place within the orthodox Armenian Church. By the end of the fifteenth century, an ecclesiastical pentarchy had formed within the Orthodox Armenian community consisting of the three autocephalic catholicosates of Etchmiadzin, Sis and Aghtamar as well as the two patriarchates of Jerusalem and Constantinople. In addition, the Armenian Catholic Church and various Evangelical Armenian churches and groups later emerged.[25] Although the return of the Catholicosate to Etchmiadzin represented an important step towards re-anchoring the Armenian national identity in the Armenian highlands, the church and its senior clergy were not mandated by the people, but by a Muslim emir and Turkic sultan, and later by Iranian shahs or Ottoman Turk sultans. From the second quarter of the sixteenth century, the Armenian patriarch of Constantinople wielded increasing juridical and financial power over the Armenian people living outside the Iranian Khanate of Yerevan although in ecclesiastical terms his rank was below that of the Catholicos of All Armenians. However, a kind of *modus vivendi* existed for almost three centuries between the patriarch and the catholicos concerning juridical matters over the bishoprics. It was only after the Russian annexation of Iranian Armenia in 1828 that a sharp distinction between the jurisdictional authorities of catholicos and patriarch was drawn, in that the patriarch of Constantinople from now on exclusively controlled the Armenian bishoprics and parishes within the Ottoman Empire.[26]

The Georgian king Aleksandre was succeeded by his eldest son **Vakhtang IV** (r. 1442–1446) whose brother **Demetre** became his co-ruler while the third brother, Giorgi remained joint king of Kakheti. The only major event recorded during Vakhtang's brief reign was a hard-fought battle against Jahan Shah that Vakhtang could rightfully claim as a victory, since the attacking sultan left the battlefield at night and returned to Azerbaijan. While Georgia lay outside Jahan Shah's sultanate, Armenia formed a march on its northern border, which ran from Marmashen in the west to the delta of the River Kura in the east.[27] As mentioned, in Armenia Jahan Shah left the administration of their small principalities to the *ishkhans*, under the control of a governor. In mountainous Karabakh he restored five local dynasties which had been disempowered and dispossessed by Timur to their former positions and granted them the title of *melik*. In the context of Karabakh, this Arabic title meant not 'king' but 'dynast'. Of the five melikdoms of highland Karabakh, the most prominent was the house of Hasan-Jalalian which had been founded by Hasan Jalal Dawla (r. *ca*. 1214–1261) of Khachen. As described by the historian Robert Hewsen, 'the Hasan-Jalalids monopolized the katholicosate of Albania from at least the 14th century (the see passing from uncle to nephew) and treated the katholicosal seat, the great monastery of Gandzasar, as their ancestral abbey, repository of wealth, and family mausoleum.'[28]

When King Vakhtang died without an heir, his brother Demetre III (d. 1453) should have become king, but his younger brother **Giorgi VIII** (r. 1446–1465, as **Giorgi I** of Kakheti r. 1466–1476) seized power; Demetre retired helpless to Imereti. When Giorgi took charge of the monarchy, the disintegration of state unity was already well under way. Troubles began in Samtskhe in 1447, when Qvarqvare II Jaqeli (r. 1451–1498) rebelled against his brother, *atabeg* Aghbugha II (r. 1444–1451). Giorgi subdued the revolt in Aghbugha's favour, but made a mortal enemy of Prince Qvarqvare who took power in 1451 after his brother's death. As a first step towards independence, he tried to separate his principality from Georgia ecclesiastically and encouraged the bishop of Atsquri to secede from the Georgian Church. But Catholicos Davit III (in office, possibly with interruptions, 1426–1457)[29] reacted swiftly by excommunicating the bishop and all priests ordained by him, as a result of which all religious services in which they had officiated became invalid. The pressure from believers who no longer had access to valid church services and sacraments forced Qvarqvare to yield.

An epochal event occurred in 1453 with the fall of Constantinople to the Ottomans. The Byzantine Empire disappeared from the map – its last remnant, the miniature Empire of Trebizond, was conquered in 1461 – and Christian Georgia was now surrounded by potentially hostile Muslim powers: the Ottomans, the Qara and Aq Qoyunlu, followed by the Iranian Safavids. The fall of Constantinople alerted Pope Callixtus III (in office 1455–1458) to the Ottoman Muslim threat and in 1457/58 he sent Ludovico da Bologna (d. 1479) on a diplomatic mission to the East to evaluate the possibility of forging an alliance, together with European powers, against the expansive Ottomans. When Ludovico reached Georgia, both king and nobles were very receptive to the concept of an European–South Caucasian alliance as they considered themselves directly threatened by the Ottomans; they were prepared to put their quarrels aside to build a common front. When Pope Pius II (in office 1458–1464) called for an anti-Ottoman Crusade in 1459, King Giorgi and the principalities and counties of Samtskhe, Mingrelia, Guria, Anakopia, Trebizond and Armenia committed themselves to a Crusader army of 120,000 men. The alliance was joined by the powerful sultan of the Aq Qoyunlu, Uzun Hasan (r. 1452–1478), who also felt threatened by the rising Ottomans since his power base was in today's eastern Turkey. These powers sent a major joint embassy to Europe in 1460 to work out a common plan of military operations, but it was utterly disappointed by the complete lack of concrete support and commitment on the part of the Holy Roman Emperor Frederick III, Pope Pius II, the king of France, Louis XI and Duke Philippe of Burgundy. Although the project of an anti-Ottoman coalition originated in the West, the European powers refused to participate.[30]

In Georgia, the détente between king and nobles did not last. In 1462 the Christian prince Qvarqvare Jaqeli formed an offensive alliance with the Muslim sultan Uzun Hasan of the Aq Qoyunlu to defeat King Giorgi. The following year, Qvarqvare encouraged the *eristavi* of Kutaisi, Bagrat, a nephew of King Giorgi, to join the rebellion. When Giorgi marched towards Kutaisi, Bagrat entered an alliance with the *eristavis* of Svaneti, Abkhazia, Mingrelia and Guria. The rebel coalition defeated King Giorgi at the Battle of Chikhori in 1463. Meanwhile Qvarqvare Jaqeli underscored his claim to independence by minting his own coins and adopting the royal title *mepe*, meaning king. *Eristavi* Bagrat also declared himself king (r. as **Bagrat II of Imereti** 1463–1466), but he had to concede wide autonomy and tax exemption to his four allies, which accelerated the fragmentation of Georgia. Yet Giorgi still strove to restore unity and in 1465 attacked the renegade prince of Samtskhe. But he was surprised in an ambush and taken prisoner by Qvarqvare,

47. Modern statue of Uzun Hasan, ruler of the Aq Qoyunlu (r. 1452–1478). Independence Monument built in 2001 in Ashgabat, Turkmenistan. Photo 2014.

whereupon Bagrat II of Imereti seized the opportunity to capture the defenceless Kartli. Bagrat then declared himself king of all Georgia as **Bagrat VI** (r. 1466–1478) and established a separate catholicosate of Abkhazia with its see in Pitsunda which was in communion with the Syriac Orthodox Church of Antioch.[31] Qvarqvare became suspicions about his further ambitions. He freed his royal prisoner Giorgi, in the hope that if Giorgi and Bagrat would fight and weaken each other, he would be able to finally emerge as the strongest without the need of further fighting. Since most nobles of Inner Kartli had sided with Bagrat, Giorgi was not in a position to recover Kartli; he therefore resigned his claim and retired to his initial power base of Kakheti where he ruled independently as King **Giorgi I of Kakheti** (r. 1466–1476). By reforming Kakheti's administration and building new administrative structures, he laid the grounds for the new state of Kakheti. Giorgi died in 1476 and his son Aleksandre I succeeded him. Georgia had by now disintegrated into three kingdoms: Kakheti, ruled by Giorgi I, Kartli and Imereti under Bagrat VI and Samtskhe ruled by Qvarqvare. Furthermore, the western counties of Svaneti, Abkhazia, Mingrelia and Guria asserted their semi-independence, and the inner cohesion of Kartli–Imereti was at best shaky, as Konstantine II, the son of Demetre III, challenged Bagrat's authority. Bagrat had to buy a truce by conceding Kartli to Konstantine after his death and limiting the inheritance of his own son Aleksandre, the future King Aleksandre II, to Imereti.[32]

As soon as **Konstantine II** (r. 1478–1491, as king of Kartli 1491–1505) had ascended the throne, he expelled Aleksandre II from Kartli and Imereti; Aleksandre found refuge in Racha-Lechkhumi, a mountainous region in north-western Georgia. When Qvarqvare rebelled again in 1483 and defeated King Konstantine at the Battle of Aradeti, Aleksandre II used the opportunity to take control of Imereti and crown himself King **Aleksandre II of Imereti** (r. 1483–1510). Konstantine made efforts to reconquer Imereti, but plundering attacks by Yaqub Beg, also called Sultan Yaqub, of the Aq Qoyunlu (r. 1478–1490) on Samtskhe in 1486 and by the Aq Qoyunlu warlord Sufi Khalil Beg Mawsilu on Tbilisi in 1488 twice forced Konstantine to abort his campaigns against Imereti. While Sufi Khalil Beg besieged Tbilisi and captured it in February 1489, Qvarqvare II of Samtskhe and **Aleksandre I of Kakheti** (r. 1476–1511) remained passive, observing the increasing weakness of King Konstantine. Prior to Yaqub Beg's raid of 1486, his father Uzun Hasan had already devastated Georgia three times in the years 1473, 1474 and 1477, allegedly to punish Georgian princes for not supporting him militarily in his lost war against the Ottomans. Although Uzun Hasan had suffered a crushing defeat against the Ottoman sultan Mehmet II (r. 1444–1446, 1451–1481) at the Battle of Otlukbeli[33] in August 1473, he still had enough cavalry left to ravage Georgia.[34] In view of the hopelessly confused political situation, in 1490 the war-weary King Konstantine convened the *Darbazi*, the state council consisting of the senior church hierarchy and leading nobles, to evaluate possible options for overcoming the deadlock between the power-hungry and mutually hostile princes. The *Darbazi* made a rational analysis of the messy situation and concluded that a peaceful reunification of the Georgian kingdom through negotiations was, under the current conditions, totally unrealistic and that a continued war would not produce a winner, but would further ruin the country. Instead the *Darbazi* recommended partitioning Georgia between the major players and agreeing on their borders. In

THE SOUTH CAUCASUS UNDER TURKMEN, OTTOMAN AND IRANIAN SAFAVID DOMINATION | 83

Map 4. The partition of Georgia in 1491 CE

- Georgian borders in 1450 CE
- Borders between Georgian kingdoms and principalities in 1491
- Aq Qoyunlu and vassals in 1478
- Shamkhalate and vassals
- Ottoman–Safavid Treaty of Zuhab of 1639
- Major cities
- River

1491 Konstantine II was forced to recognize the kingdoms and principalities which had emerged after the Battle of Chikhori as independent from the national crown: Georgia formally split into the kingdoms of **Kartli**, **Kakheti** and **Imereti**, each of which was ruled by a separate branch of the Bagratids, and the powerful principality of **Samtskhe-Saatabago**, ruled by the Jaqelis. Imereti itself soon had to accept the virtual independence of the principalities of **Abkhazeti** (Abkhazia, ruled by the Sharvashidzes), **Samegrelo** (Mingrelia, under the Dadianis), **Guria** (under the Dadiani-Gurielis) and **Svaneti** (under the Gelovanis).[35]

3. The South Caucasus as battleground for eight Ottoman–Safavid wars

At the beginning of the sixteenth century, the South Caucasian kingdoms and principalities found themselves sandwiched between two aggressively expanding regional superpowers set on a confrontational course: the Turkic Ottomans and the Iranian Safavids. Since the former were Sunni Muslims and the latter had been compulsorily converted by the dynasty's founder Shah Isma'il from Sunni to Shia Islam, the political and military competition also carried a religious streak. Not only were the small South Caucasian states at loggerheads with each other and unable to build a common front, but the balance of power made it impossible to fight both invaders at the same time. Their only feasible option was to submit to one power in order to resist the other. For more than a century, from 1514 to 1639, the South Caucasus was a disputed battlefield between Ottomans and Iranians, who fought eight wars there.[36] The Ottomans had quickly recovered from the heavy defeat at Angora in 1402. After liquidating the remnants of the Byzantine and Trebizond empires in 1453 and 1461 and driving the Genoese from Crimea and the eastern Black Sea coast in 1475, they advanced into the south-western Caucasus. By ejecting the Genoese from the eastern Black Sea, the Ottomans and their Crimean vassals acquired the lucrative Genoese slave trade and redirected the trade in captured or bought Circassians from Egypt to Constantinople, also called Kostantiniyye and Istanbul in Ottoman times.[37] From an administrative point of view, Crimea remained divided. The former Genoese possessions along the littoral came under direct Ottoman rule and formed the *vilayet* (province) of Kefe (Caffa), while the Crimean Tatar dynasty of the Genghisid Giray (1431–1783) remained from 1478 a semi-independent vassal of the Ottomans.

On the other hand, the Iranian Safavids (1501–1736) were a new power, emerging in 1501 when Shah Isma'il (r. 1501–1524) crushed the Aq Qoyunlu and founded the Safavid dynasty of Iran with Tabriz as capital. After centuries of foreign rule and political fragmentation, Iran became once more a stable state, although its rulers had always to reckon with the powerful tribal federations. The Safavids stemmed from a militant religious order called Safaviyya which was founded around 1300 by sheikh Safi al-Din Ishaq (1252–1334) who propagated a kind of popular folk Islam venerating 'Ali, son-in-law of the prophet Mohammed. This aspect of his teaching laid the grounds for the later Shiite sympathies within the Safaviyya. One and a half centuries later, Shah Isma'il's grandfather, leader of the Safaviyya based in Ardabil (north-western Iran), the Turkmen sheikh Junaid (d. 1460), transformed the religious order into a religiously tinged military instrument of power. It is probable that Sheikh Junaid was the first Safaviyya leader to propagate Twelver Shiism.[38] Junaid fell in battle in 1460 against a Lezgian army while he was trying to convert Shirvan to Shiism. His son and successor Sheikh Haydar further militarized the order and reportedly introduced for his Turkmen fighters a white turban wrapped around a red, twelve-gored cap symbolizing the twelve imams of Shia Islam, which gave the warriors their nickname of Qizilbash (red-heads). Sheikh Haydar attacked Shirvan in 1488 to avenge his father. Feeling threatened, Shirvan's ruler Farrukh Yasar (r. 1465–1500) appealed to the Aq Qoyunlu sultan Yaqub who sent troops. The Shirvanshah defeated Haydar's Qizilbash and had their leader executed. Twelve years later, shortly after carrying out a raid on Samtskhe, Sheikh Isma'il avenged his father and grandfather when he crushed Farrukh Yasar's army near Shamakhi and the Shirvanshah fell in battle. Isma'il ordered all captured Shirvanis to be massacred and had a tower built from the severed heads.[39] After his ascension to the throne, Isma'il declared Twelver Shiism the state religion. The new state was a theocracy inasmuch as Isma'il considered himself to be the delegate of the Twelve Imams who were themselves representatives of 'Ali whom Ismail acclaimed as the manifestation of God on earth. While the Safavid army consisted mainly of Turkmen, and Iran's court language was Azerbaijani Turkic, the civil administration was run by Iranians, as Shah Isma'il needed a counterweight to the Turkmen tribes who had brought him to the throne.[40]

The first Ottoman and Safavid encroachments on the southern Caucasus started before the first Ottoman–Safavid war. In the eastern region, Shah Isma'il conquered Baku, Shamakhi and Shirvan in 1500 where he installed Farrukh Yasar's son Bairam Beg (r. 1500–1501) as his vassal. Following the murders in quick succession of the next two rulers, Sheikh Ibrahim II (r. 1502–1524) seized power. Although he expelled the Qizilbash garrison from Shirvan, he thought it prudent to submit to Isma'il, which secured relative peace for Shirvan till the death of his son Khalilullah II in 1535.[41] Confronted by fanatical Qizilbash troops in 1500, Shirvan's western neighbour, Aleksandre I of Kakheti, also chose a cautious strategy. Since the two embassies he had sent to Grand Duke Ivan III of Moscow in 1483 and 1491–1492 brought no results, Aleksandre recognized Isma'il's suzerainty, which ensured Kakheti a kind of peace with Iran for about a century. Aleksandre's wise rule ended abruptly in 1511 when his elder son **Giorgi II** (r. 1511–1513), who was eager to attack Kartli and suspicious of his younger brother Demetre, ordered the assassination of his father and the blinding of his brother. These crimes earned Giorgi the nickname 'Giorgi the Evil'. He immediately attacked Kartli, whose ruler **Davit X** (r. 1505–1525) was also hard pressed from the west by Aleksandre II of Imereti. While Davit took refuge in the fortress of Ateni, his younger brother Bagrat I, prince of Mukhrani, organized the defence of Kartli and in 1513 succeeded in capturing Giorgi the Evil in an ambush. Giorgi was put to death and Davit X annexed Khakheti, but only for five years. Davit's control over Kartli was tenuous anyway, as the kingdom was divided into several secular and ecclesiastical principalities ruled by nobles and bishops.[42] As for Aleksandre II of Imereti, he proved unable to hold the Kartlian fortress of Gori which he had snatched from Davit in 1509, since Ottoman proxies from Trabzon (Trebizond) attacked Imereti in his absence. When Aleksandre returned to his kingdom, he found Kutaisi and the monastery of Gelati looted and burned down. Three years later, the governor of Trabzon, Selim, the future Sultan Selim I (r. 1512–1520), advanced into western Georgia.[43]

Relations between the Ottomans and the Safavids had been strained since Isma'il's seizure of power, because missionaries of the Safaviyya were actively propagating Shiism among the Turkmen of eastern Anatolia. These new converts soon either rebelled against the Ottoman authorities or joined Isma'il's Qizilbash troops as mercenaries, thus strengthening the Ottoman Empire's Shiite rival and leaving the region worryingly short of men fit for war. It was the Anatolian Qizilbash revolt of 1511 which forced Sultan Bayezid II (r. 1481–1512) to abdicate in favour of his son Selim, who understood the seriousness of the Qizilbash threat to Ottoman rule in eastern Anatolia. Sultan Selim ordered a severe crackdown on Anatolian Qizilbash, some of whom had allegedly supported his rival brother Ahmad. In 1514 Selim initiated the *First Ottoman–Iranian War (1514–1517)* not least because he planned to conquer Syria and Egypt and did not wish to run the risk of being stabbed in the rear by Isma'il. Selim scored an overwhelming victory in August 1514 at the Battle of Chaldiran (in the modern Iranian province of Azerbaijan) thanks

48. The ruined three apses of the nunnery of Ninotsminda founded in the sixth century. The brick architecture and ornamentation of the bell tower from the sixteenth century on the right shows Iranian influence. Samtskhe-Javakheti, Georgia. Photo 2013.

49. The Royal Fortress and the church of the Archangels in Gremi dating from the sixteenth century. The fortress was built by King Levan I of Kakheti (r. 1518–1574) and chosen as his capital, because Gremi was easier to defend than Telavi. The blue glazed tiles on the roofs of the church and the residential tower, both built with red bricks, indicate Iranian influence. Inside the Archangels Church, built in 1565, the murals date from 1577. During the campaign of extermination by the Iranian Shah Abbas I in 1614–1616, the city was burnt to the ground and the 'useful' population, i.e. craftsmen, young women and boys were deported to Iran while the remainder were killed. The destroyed city was not rebuilt and was abandoned in 1672. Kakheti, Georgia. Photo 2013.

to his artillery, whereupon he looted Tabriz, but he then had to retreat because of the danger of mutiny among his troops. Before attacking Syria and Egypt in 1517, Selim conquered northern Mesopotamia and consolidated the Ottoman hold on eastern Anatolia, a move which marked the beginning of the Ottomans' penetration of the Armenian highlands and encroachments on Georgia. The defeat at Chaldiran not only broke Isma'il's reputation for invincibility, but also drove him to indulge in hedonistic pleasures.[44] His son Tahmasp I (r. 1524–1576), however, draw lessons from Chaldiran and equipped his army with firearms and artillery.

After the abdication of *atabeg* **Mzetchabuk Jaqeli of Samtskhe-Saatabago** (r. 1500–1515), who had paid lip service of suzerainty to Sultan Selim, a power struggle ensued between his nephew Qvarqvare and Mzetchabuk's younger brother **Manuchihr (Manuchar) I** (r. 1515–1518). At first, the pro-Ottoman Manuchihr prevailed and Qvarqvare called for help from Isma'il, who dispatched his general, Div Sultan Rumlu, to Samtskhe. The latter defeated Manuchihr in 1517 and installed **Qvarqvare III** (r. 1518–1535) on the throne. The Qizilbash army spent the winter in Nakhchivan and then occupied Gori in Kartli. While King Davit X was negotiating with the invaders over the annual tribute Kartli would have to pay to avert further Iranian depredations, Kakhetian nobles set Giorgi the Evil's son **Levan I** (r. 1518–1574) on the throne of Kakheti. Since Davit's attempts to recover control over Kakheti failed and at the same time he was attacked from the west by the Ottoman proxy **Mamia I of Guria** (r. 1512–1534), he had no choice but to recognize King Levan. Kakheti, Kartli and Samtskhe now belonged to the Iranian zone of influence while Armenia was part of the Ottoman. Two years later, in 1522, Shah Isma'il demanded that Davit X convert to Islam. When he flatly refused to betray his religion, Isma'il declared war. Although Davit's son Luarsab scored a victory, the Safavid army prevailed and conquered Tbilisi by treachery. Following Shah Isma'il's death soon after, Davit reoccupied his capital. But in 1525 his brothers challenged his rule and forced him to abdicate, giving way to his brother **Giorgi IX** (r. 1525–1527). However, **Luarsab I of Kartli** (r. 1527–1556), who had proven his military skills in the war against Isma'il, won the support of **Bagrat III of Imereti** (r. 1510–1565) and forced Giorgi IX to abdicate and enter a monastery.[45]

The *Second Ottoman–Iranian War (1533–1535)* began in 1533 when Sultan Süleyman (r. 1520–1566) occupied Kurdistan, Tabriz, Baghdad and parts of the Persian Gulf. This attack was coordinated with a group of disaffected Qizilbash leaders and Tahmasp's rebellious younger brother Sam Mirza.[46] The Safavid counterattack soon drove the Ottoman Turks out of Azerbaijan. In view of the Ottoman reversals, kings Luarsab of Kartli and Bagrat III of Imereti, together with Prince **Rostom of Guria** (r. 1534–1564), formed an alliance against Samtskhe which was in danger of falling under Ottoman control. In 1535, Rostom captured Qvarqvare III of Samtskhe and handed him over to Kartli where he died in jail, while Bagrat III and Luarsab divided Samtskhe-Saatabago among themselves. The triple alliance collapsed in 1541 when a Qizilbash army ravaged Lower Kartli and seized Tbilisi, where all males who refused to convert to Islam were massacred, and a Qizilbash garrison was installed to keep control. In the same year, King Levan of Kakheti renewed his allegiance to Shah Tahmasp and paid tribute, thus securing a continued period of relative peace. At the same time, between 1538 and 1551, Shirvan, Baku and Shaki were permanently integrated into the Safavid Empire and Tahmasp appointed his brother Alqas Mirza to be governor of Shirvan after having Shirvanshah Shah Rukh (r. 1535–1538) removed and killed.[47] As narrated by Abbas Qoli Bakikhanov (1794–1847), after some time Alqas Mirza developed a desire for independence and even struck coins in his own name. After having devastated Kartli in 1547, Shah Tahmasp attacked his rebellious brother who fled via Dagestan to Istanbul, whereupon the shah appointed his son Isma'il Mirza as governor of Shirvan.[48] Shirvan was a wealthy political entity based on its function as a trading hub and its important silk-production industry.[49] The integration of today's Azerbaijan into the Safavid Empire led to the conversion of its people to Shiism.

After a previous Ottoman invasion of Samtskhe-Saatabago had failed in 1543, Sultan Süleyman again attacked in 1545. The Turkish army ejected the Imeretian and Kartlian forces and installed Qvarqvare's son **Kaikhosro II Jaqeli** (r. 1545–1573) as puppet *atabeg* of Samtskhe. At the same time, Bagrat's vassal, **Levan I Dadiani of Mingrelia** (r. 1533–1572) declared independence in his principality. Horrified at the brutal Ottoman exploitation of Samtskhe, Kaikhosro appealed to Shah Tahmasp who invaded in 1547 and ravaged Kartli, starting the *Third Ottoman–Iranian War (1547–1549)*. Although defeated, Luarsab refused to yield and conducted a tough guerrilla war. In 1548, a Turkish army counterattacked, its artillery directed by the French Ambassador to the Ottoman Empire, Baron d'Aramon Gabriel de Luetz, whose aim was to bring about a quick Ottoman victory so that it would become free to wage war on the common enemy, the Holy Roman Emperor Charles V (r. 1519/30–1556). By 1550, the Ottomans controlled most of Georgia's Black Sea coast and south-western Samtskhe-Saatabago.[50] Meanwhile in 1548, Sultan Süleyman, accompanied by Tahmasp's rebellious brother

50. King Levan I of Kakheti offering the model of the newly built church of Gremi to the Mother of God. Mural from 1577, church of the Archangels, Gremi. Kakheti, Georgia. Photo 2013.

Alqas Mirza, attacked Iran and occupied Tabriz. Tahmasp responded by sending his son Isma'il Mirza to ravage eastern Anatolia; Süleyman retreated in 1549 and Alqas Mirza was captured trying to reach Fars. As a consequence of the repeated Ottoman conquests of Tabriz, Shah Tahmasp moved his capital inland to Qazvin.[51]

The *Fourth Ottoman–Iranian War (1551–1555)* began soon after, in 1551, when Shah Tahmasp tried to eject the Ottomans from western Samtskhe and to force the submission of Kartli. The Qizilbash began by raiding the monastery of Vardzia and murdering its monks, then conquered Erzurum, only to lose it again. The Qizilbash returned to Kartli in 1554 from where they carried off up to 30,000 people into slavery. Once again, the lack of cooperation, let alone unity, between the various Georgians made a coordinated and effective defence against the two invaders from the south impossible. In 1555, Sultan Süleyman and Shah Tahmasp decided to overcome the military stalemate and concluded the Treaty of Amasya. They divided the South Caucasus into zones of satellite states. The Likhi (Surami) mountain range was chosen for the dividing line, which represents the watershed between the Black and the Caspian seas. Ottoman Turkey took western Armenia, western Samtskhe, Imereti, Mingrelia and Guria while Safavid Iran was allocated eastern Armenia, eastern Samtskhe, Kartli, Kakheti, Karabakh, Nakhchivan and today's Azerbaijan. As long as the Ottomans and Iran agreed to divide Georgia into zones of influence, the reunification of Georgia would remain impossible. Iran retained Tabriz, but the Ottomans kept most of today's Iraq including Baghdad and Basra, which gave them access to the Persian Gulf. The peace lasted 23 years.

For the Ottomans and especially the Crimean Tatars, the main point of interest in western Georgia was its function as a supplier of slaves. The Tatar Crimean economy was essentially predatory and depended on the one hand on tribute payments from Muscovy, Poland and the Danubian principalities and on the other on the trade of non-Muslim slaves, with the latter increasing in importance as the tribute payments dwindled over time.[52] A variant of the slave racket consisted in kidnapping wealthy farmers and traders in order to extort ransoms. Some of the Circassians living in the north-western Caucasus, who had since the sixteenth century either been subject to raids by the Tatars or belonged to their sphere of influence, were not only in the habit of robbing non-Muslims from Abkhazia and Mingrelia, but were also not averse to selling their own children, especially beautiful young girls, to Crimean Turkic slave-traders who resold them in Istanbul. Later, within the increasing impoverishment of Mingrelia and Imereti, their nobles and senior clergymen too engaged in the slave trade, and Akhaltsikhe became a major slave trading centre.[53] As reported by the polymath and historian Kâtip Çelebi (1609–1657), 'these people [the Circassians] abduct persons among each other and sell them to traders. ... [The Circassians] pay every year their taxes in kind, that is slaves. They also sell their prisoners to slave traders.'[54] As a result, many people either fled from Mingrelia and Samtskhe to Kakheti or the forests of Kartli, or converted to Islam, since Islamic law forbade the enslavement of Muslims. As the scholar W.E.D. Allen pointed out, Russia too was involved in slave trading, albeit on a much smaller scale than the Ottomans and Crimeans. Russia used to sell Livonian and German prisoners of war to Iranian ambassadors in its Muslim satellite khanate of Kasimov (Qasim) (1452–1681) since it was forbidden to sell Christians in Russian cities.[55]

The Ottomans soon consolidated their hold on western Samtskhe. After they had seized the cities of Ardahan and Ardanuç in 1551, in 1578 (or 1576) they annexed Akhaltsikhe, whose name in Georgian means 'new castle'; the existing castle was expanded to a huge fortress (fig. 51). The Ottomans kept the Jaqeli *atabegs*, who had converted to Islam, in place as *beylerbeys*, that is senior governors of the now Turkish province. That the conversion of Jaqeli princes was solely motivated by political reasons is best exemplified by **Manuchihr II Jaqeli** (r. 1582–1587, d. 1614), younger brother of *atabeg* **Qvarqvare IV** (r. 1573–1581). The older brother followed a pro-Ottoman policy; the younger aspired initially to independence. In 1578 the Ottomans confirmed Qvarqvare as *atabeg* of a part of Samtskhe, which they had divided into eight *sanjaks* (an administrative unit within a *vilayet*). However, Manuchihr played the card of religion and converted to Islam, taking the name Mustafa Pasha. Endorsed by the Ottomans, he ousted his Christian brother Qvarqvare in 1581. But Manuchihr soon turned his coat again. During the retreat after a joint Ottoman–Samtskhe force had met defeat in a battle against Simon I of Kartli, Manuchihr wounded the Turkish pasha of Tbilisi (who suspected him of treachery), abjured Islam and joined the victor's camp. Not wishing to lose the important bridgehead of Samtskhe, Sultan Murad III (r. 1575–1594) looked for reconciliation and reconfirmed the renegade as *atabeg*. But when Manuchihr upheld his alliance with Kartli, Sultan Murad sent Ferhad Pasha with a strong army, who defeated both allies in 1587; Simon I had to submit and pay annual tribute to the Ottomans while Manuchihr fled to Iran.[56] In 1625, Akhaltsikhe became the capital of the Turkish *pashalik* of Çıldır.[57] The political integration of Samtskhe-Saatabago into the Ottoman Empire went hand in hand with a religious alignment. Several factors led to the Islamization of Samtskhe: first, Christians who adopted Islam were exempt from the poll tax imposed on Christians (and Jews); next, while Georgian Orthodox Christians who were unwilling to convert were emigrating to Imereti and Kartli, Anatolian Muslim settlers took their place in Samtskhe. (Some Christians converted to Catholicism since Catholics enjoyed special protection in the Ottoman Empire due to the pressure from Western European powers.) Finally, many nobles attempted to secure their privileges by adopting Islam, which then motivated their subjects to take the new religion of their masters. After Russia conquered Turkish Samtskhe in 1828 the descendants of these Georgian converts and the Turkic immigrants became known as Meskhetian Turks.[58]

King Luarsab I of Kartli refused to bow to the political order imposed by the Treaty of Amasya and persisted in waging a guerrilla war against the Iranian occupiers of Tbilisi and their garrison. In 1556, Shah Tahmasp dispatched Shahverdi Sultan, governor of Ganja and Karabakh, to bring Luarsab to heel. At the ensuing Battle of Garisi the Kartlian army was victorious, but both commanders, Luarsab and Shahverdi, were killed. Luarsab's eldest son **Simon I** (r. 1556–1569, 1578–1599, d. 1611) succeeded him as king and moved his capital to Gori. On the other hand, King Levan of Kakheti continued to accept Kakheti's Safavid vassalage and sent his son Vakhtang to the Iranian court, where he was forced to convert to Islam. Nevertheless, Levan secretly allied with his son-in-law Simon I of Kartli with the object of evicting the Qizilbash from Tbilisi. But the allied army was crushed on Easter Sunday 1561 and Levan's son Giorgi killed. At this moment of Simon's defeat, his envious younger brother Davit and a few pro-Safavid Kartlian nobles travelled to Qazvin and submitted to Shah Tahmasp. Davit converted to Islam, taking the Islamized name Daud Khan. In turn, Tahmasp appointed him king of Tbilisi and Lower Kartli and supplied him with troops to fight his brother. In the following fratricidal war from 1567 to 1569, Simon won the first two battles, at Dighomi and Samadlo, but was taken prisoner at the Battle of Partskhisi. Simon refused to bow to Islam and spent the next nine years as captive in the fortress of Alamut, north-east of Qazvin. The renegade Daud Khan, aka **Davit XI** (r. 1569–1578), became nominal ruler of Kartli. Since in Georgia there was not only disunity among the small kingdoms and principalities, but also within the individual ruling families, the protagonists became largely the plaything of the great powers, Iran and the Ottomans, thus perpetuating a history of foreign domination which had begun with the Roman–Parthian condominium over Armenia.[59] The judgement given from personal experience by the French jeweller and traveller Jean Chardin (1643–1719) applied also to Georgia's political situation in the later sixteenth century: 'The Georgians hate each other and never join forces.'[60]

Levan of Kakheti managed to save his kingdom from the victor's wrath after the Iranian victory of Partskhisi; nevertheless he strove to find an ally against Safavid dominance and turned to Russia. Under Tsar Ivan IV 'Grozny' (r. 1547–1575) whose epithet means 'the fearsome', Russia emerged as the only remaining strong Orthodox state. It had conquered the Muslim khanates of Kazan in 1552 and Hajji Tarkhan (Astrakhan) in 1556, thus gaining access to the Caspian Sea. At the same time, Russia now controlled the steppe road connecting Tatar Crimea and its satellites in the Kuban (north-western Caucasus) with Central Asia and could thus sever trade relations between the Ottomans and the Uzbek khanates. In spite of the common Ottoman and Crimean interest in keeping the steppe road open, the Crimean Tatar khan Devlet Giray (r. 1551–1577) sabotaged the Ottoman–Crimean campaign against Astrakhan in 1569 by suddenly withdrawing his troops near the Volga. The campaign failed and the majority of Turkish troops perished.[61] Meanwhile in 1557 Tsar Ivan had concluded a treaty with Temryuk, prince of Kabarda in the North Caucasus; the alliance was cemented in 1560 by Tsar Ivan's marriage to Temryuk's daughter Kuchenei.[62] The Russian expansion was mainly driven by the objective of securing trade routes with the major Eastern economies,

51. The huge fortress of Akhaltsikhe. The fortress, which was formerly called Lomsia, was founded in the ninth century and became in the thirteenth century the seat of the Jaqeli family, the *eristavis* of Samtskhe. They obtained the title *atabeg* of Saatabago as of the fourteenth century. The Ottomans conquered the city in 1578 (or 1576) and greatly rebuilt and expanded both fortress and city, which they renamed Akhaltsikhe, 'new castle'. Under the Ottomans, Akhaltsikhe became an important centre of human trafficking. During the Russian–Turkish War of 1828–1829 the Russian commander General Paskevich seized Akhaltsikhe which was incorporated into the Russian Empire at the subsequent Treaty of Adrianople on 14 September 1829. Samtskhe-Javakheti, Georgia. Photo 2013.

THE SOUTH CAUCASUS UNDER TURKMEN, OTTOMAN AND IRANIAN SAFAVID DOMINATION

India, Iran and China, as well as of finding anti-Ottoman allies on Russia's soft southern border in order to stop the attacks by the Crimean Tatars, who acted as Ottoman 'irregulars'. The Kabardians, for their part, sought protection from the Tatars' slave raiding. The Russian strategy made a confrontation with the Ottomans and their powerful Crimean vassals inevitable, since the Crimean khans sought to extend their dominance in North Caucasus east of Circassia to Kabarda, Dagestan and the western Caspian shore. The Ottomans, in turn, relied on the Crimean Tatars to control the steppes. This constellation led to a three-cornered rivalry between the Ottomans, Iran and Russia that would last till the 1860s. In 1563 Levan sent an envoy to Moscow – the first of a total of seventeen embassies exchanged between Kakheti and Russia between 1563 and 1605 – asking for a formation of musketeers, but Iran intervened and forbade the stationing of Russian troops in Kakheti.[63] Levan died in 1574 and was succeeded by his eldest son from his first marriage, **Aleksandre II** (r. 1574–1601, 1602–1605). Aleksandre's son and successor, Konstantine, who was also his murderer, later claimed in his own defence that his father Aleksandre had murdered his own father Levan, thus making clear that patricide was common practice among the Kakhetian ruling family.

[Patricide and fratricide are] *nothing new in our family, but has been happening since ancient times; my father* [Aleksandre II of Kakheti] *had put an end to the life of his father* [Levan] *who was my grandfather, and he also killed his brother. Now I have done likewise, and myself I don't know whether it will lead to good or evil. ... Though I am of the Moslem faith, I am not a Moslem of my own free will.*'[64]

The ***Fifth Ottoman–Iranian War (1578–1590)*** began with the above-mentioned Ottoman annexation of Samtskhe by the Ottoman commander Lala Mustafa Pasha.[65] His main objective was to join up with a Crimean Tatar force in Shirvan, which would arrive via the North Caucasus, and together attack Iran. In 1578 the Turks scored a difficult victory over the Qizilbash at Çıldır since heavy rain made the use of their superior firearms impossible. Daud Khan (Davit XI) fled to the mountains and Lala Mustafa occupied Tbilisi, where he left a garrison of 2,000 men. Tbilisi would remain in Ottoman hands till 1606. After Aleksandre II of Kakheti submitted to Lala Mustafa, the latter won another victory at the River Alazan and occupied Shirvan. Faced with Daud Khan's cowardly flight and Aleksandre's switch of alliance, Shah Khudabanda (r. 1578–1587) liberated the still popular former Kartlian king Simon I from his jail in Alamut and offered him military support to reconquer Kartli, so long as he embraced Islam. This time, Simon pretended to convert and returned to Kartli with a Qizilbash cavalry detachment which harassed Lala Mustafa's army when it returned to its winter quarters in Erzurum. Mustafa Pasha had left a garrison in Shirvan under the command of Osman Pasha, who in November 1578 repelled the attack of a Qizilbash army with difficulty, and only thanks to Tatar forces who had crossed the North Caucasus.[66] Tbilisi too managed to repulse Simon's attacks. In 1579, the Safavids captured the harbour of Shabran in north-eastern Azerbaijan, but the Ottomans managed to hold Derbent and Baku. Today's Azerbaijan was the helpless battleground between Turks and Iranian Qizilbash. The war flared up again in 1583 at the Battle of Torches which was fought north of Shabran during the night. The Turks won, and a few months later their commander Osman Pasha marched with part of the army to Crimea via the northern route along the River Terek. In November 1583, he was ambushed with his troops by a Russian Cossack unit at the River Sunzha; he crushed the attackers and destroyed their fort at the junction of the rivers Terek and Sunzha. This skirmish may be considered the first Ottoman–Russian clash for dominance over the Caucasus. The Turks further consolidated their hold over the South Caucasus by occupying Yerevan (1584), Tabriz (1585), Ganja (1588) and Nakhchivan (1589). Furthermore, by 1587 the Ottomans had launched a small fleet on the Caspian Sea which gave them the option of supporting the Safavids' other arch-enemy, the Uzbek Khanate of Bukhara. The Iranian Shah Abbas I (r. 1588–1629) who had inherited a weakened state from his father Khudabanda, recognized the danger of an joint Ottoman–Uzbek attack on two fronts and chose to buy time in order to restore order, rebuild the army and reconquer those territories of Khorasan which had been lost to the Uzbeks. At the Peace of Istanbul on 21 March 1590, Shah Abbas had to confirm most of the Ottoman conquests made since 1578. Iran lost to Turkey all of Iranian Azerbaijan including Tabriz, Shirvan, Ganja, Derbent, eastern Dagestan, Karabakh, Kakheti, Kartli, eastern Samtskhe, Yerevan province, Kurdistan, Luristan, Mesopotamia including Baghdad, and Khuzestan.[67] The territorial losses in today's Azerbaijan deprived the Safavids of the possibility of exporting their silk products to Europe while bypassing the Ottoman Empire. Shah Abbas was determined to regain control over this important trade route as soon as the opportunity should arise. As history was to prove a couple of decades later, the Ottomans had won a pyrrhic victory since the state treasury was empty and the army, albeit most of the time victorious, had suffered huge losses of manpower. Furthermore, the territories gained were too far from the capital of the centrally organized Ottoman Empire to be effectively controlled

52. The St George Monastery, Alaverdi, surrounded by a defensive wall. The church was founded in the sixth or seventh century and rebuilt during the reign of the Kakhetian king Kvirike III (r. 1010/14–1037). It was turned into a mosque in 1604 and reconstructed after the earthquake of 1742. Kakheti, Georgia. Photo 2013.

and the harsh winters of the Anatolian highlands prevented rapid troop deployments to unruly provinces far away in the east.

Like his father King Luarsab, Simon I of Kartli refused to accept foreign domination. From 1595 he took up guerrilla activities against the Ottomans and in 1599 liberated Gori. Sultan Mehmet III (r. 1595–1603) reacted to this challenge by sending a strong army under Jafar Pasha, who captured Simon in battle and sent him in chains to Istanbul where he died in 1611; he was succeeded by his eldest son **Giorgi X** (r. 1599–1606). Unlike King Simon, Aleksandre II of Kakheti opted for a dual-track strategy. He paid the Ottomans the requested tribute in order to secure local autonomy but in parallel engaged in close diplomatic relations with Russia. After initial diplomatic contacts had been established between Kakheti and Moscow in 1585 and 1586, a Russian ambassador, Rodion Petrovich Birkin arrived at the court of King Aleksandre, who signed an oath of loyalty to Tsar Feodor I (r. 1584–1598) on 29 August 1587. In exchange, Aleksandre requested a joint military operation against the *shamkhal* (ruler) of Tarki near today's capital of Dagestan, Makhachkala. Tarki may have been built on the ruins of the ancient Khazar capital of Samandar.[68] The Shamkhalate extended over a territory comparable to today's Dagestan and was populated by Kumyks of Turkic stock as well as by Avars. By its geography, it controlled the narrow plain on the western Caspian littoral and thus a section of the trade route connecting Muscovy with Iran. In the 1580s and 1590s the Shamkhalate was allied with the Ottoman Empire and used by the Ottomans to raid Kakheti. As well as a military operation, Aleksandre furthermore recommended building a

Russian fort in the estuary of the River Terek north of Tarki. This fort became Tersky Gorodok, 'Terek-town', which was supposed to control the Shamkhalate and to secure the trade route from Astrakhan to Iran.[69] On his return journey to Moscow, Birkin was accompanied by three Kakhetian ambassadors who were received in 1588 by Tsar Feodor and the boyar Boris Godunov, who held the real power. They confirmed Russia's protection of Kakheti. As documented in the Russian archives, in 1589 Prince Semyon Zvenigorodsky brought the letter of patent for King Aleksandre to the Kakhetian capital, Gremi (fig. 49) and confirmed Russia's protection. The agreement brought Aleksandre no positive results since the *shamkhal* attacked Kakheti in 1591 and two minor Russian expeditions around 1592 and 1594 failed to decisively defeat him. Boris Godunov, by now tsar (r. 1598–1605), attributed the second attack's lack of success to Aleksandre's failure to honour his agreement to send the Kakhetian army against the *shamkhal* at the same time.[70] Moreover, Shah Abbas resented Aleksandre's submission to Russia, viewing it as a betrayal; but he saved his punishment for later.

In 1601, Aleksandre's eldest surviving son **Davit I** (r. 1601–1602) seized power, forced his father to enter a monastery under threat of death and jailed his brother Giorgi. But since Davit died only one year later, Aleksandre regained the throne and freed Giorgi, his third son, who acted as regent during Aleksandre's stay with Shah Abbas from early 1604 to March 1605. In the meantime, Shah Abbas had modernized his army and decreased its dependence on the tribal Qizilbash. The new core of the armed forces was the cavalry formation of Ghilman, Muslim converts of Christian Georgian, Armenian and Circassian descent.[71] These Ghilman had no tribal affiliations and were loyal only to their ruler or commander. In creating the Ghilman cavalry, Shah Abbas had obviously copied the Turkish military

53. The Armenian cemetery of Noratus, located on the western shore of Lake Sevan, counts 902 *khachkars* and carved tombstones. Gegharkunik Province, Armenia. Photo 2015.

organization of the Janissaries formed from forcefully recruited, enslaved Christian boys who were compulsorily converted to Islam and underwent thorough military training. In 1602 Shah Abbas began the reconquest of the territories lost to the Ottomans in the previous war. The *Sixth Ottoman–Iranian War (1603–1612)* began with the Iranian capture of Tabriz and Nakhchivan, whereupon Shah Abbas ordered Giorgi X of Kartli and Aleksandre II to join him in the siege of Yerevan. In Aleksandre's absence, the regent, Giorgi received the Russian ambassador Mikhail Ignatyevich Tatishchev who reached Gremi with an escort of *streltsy*, the standing Russian troops armed with muskets, whose infantry units were formed by Ivan IV. When Ottoman troops from Ganja and Shamakhi attacked Kakheti soon after, Giorgi defeated them with the help of forty *streltsy* lent by Tatishchev, as a result of which Giorgi swore fealty to the tsar on 1 January 1605. It is possible that Shah Abbas was informed about Giorgi's pledge of allegiance to Russia and decided to eliminate both Aleksandre II and Giorgi. He sent the king and his fourth son Konstantine, who had grown up at the Safavid court and had become a Muslim, back to Kakheti under a Qizilbash escort. Konstantine was ordered to wage war on the Turkish ally, Shirvan and was instructed to kill his father and brother at the first sign of disloyalty towards Iran. As King Aleksandre hesitated to immediately attack Shirvan, he sealed his own fate. Although Giorgi was warned by Tatishchev of Konstantine's murderous intentions, he and his father Aleksandre attended a council of war convened by Konstantine on 12 March 1605 where they were immediately cut to pieces. As recorded by the horrified ambassador Tatishchev, 700 other Kakhetians were murdered on the same day and the patricide **Konstantine I** (r. 1605) sent the heads of his father and brother to Shah Abbas as proofs of his loyalty. As he left, Tatishchev refused to hand to Konstantine the presents which were meant for Aleksandre and he made clear that Konstantine would have to send his own embassy to the tsar petitioning for his protection should he wish to enjoy it.[72] The Russian delegation then proceeded to Kartli where King Giorgi X requested 500 *streltsy* in return for his allegiance to the tsar, but refused to give his daughter Helen in marriage to Tsar Boris's son Feodor there and then, since she was too young.[73]

Konstantine never reaped the fruits of his crimes. When the Kakhetians rejected his authority, Ketevan, widow of King Davit I, took the lead in the rebellion against Konstantine, who fell in battle in October 1605. Since the dowager queen pledged loyalty to Shah Abbas in the name of her seventeen-year-old son Teimuraz, Abbas acknowledged him as King **Teimuraz I of Kakheti** (r. 1606–1614/16 and 1634–1648 in Kakheti, 1625–1633 in Kakheti and Kartli, d. 1661). In the same period, the Russian general Ivan Buturlin fulfilled Russia's pledge to attack the Shamkhalate and captured its capital Tarki in 1604, deciding to spend the winter there. However, the Kumyks and Ottoman troops under the leadership of the *shamkhal*'s son Saltan Mahmut[74] continued to resist and besieged Tarki. Since Buturlin could expect a relief force neither from Moscow nor from Gremi, in June 1605 he accepted the Kumyks' offer of safe conduct for his army. As soon as the 7,000 Russians had left the protective walls of Tarki, they were massacred virtually to the last man.[75] This first Russian–Georgian military alliance ended in disaster, not least because Russia was too weak to wage wars almost 2,000 kilometres away from Moscow and because the leading members of the Kakhetian royal family were in a state of enmity with one another. One year later, in 1606, Shah Abbas exploited the second wave of Celali rebellions (*ca.* 1595–1610) which rocked Anatolia, to reconquer Baku, Shirvan, Shamakhi, Ganja, Karabakh, Dmanisi and Tbilisi. With this successful counterattack, Shah Abbas laid the grounds for Safavid dominance over Kartli, Kakheti and almost all of today's Azerbaijan, which lasted more than a century till Tsar Peter I's military raid along the west coast of the Caspian Sea in 1722–1723 and the fall of the Safavid dynasty (1736). Having re-established Iranian rule over Tbilisi, Shah Abbas installed Giorgi's X son **Luarsab II** (r. 1606–1615, d. 1622) as the new king of Kartli. When the Ottomans attempted to regain control over Kartli using Crimean Tatar proxies in 1609, the Georgian army led by Giorgi Saakadze (*ca.* 1570–1629) defeated the Crimean attackers at the Battle of Tashiskari. Three years later, Saakadze, who belonged to the petty nobility, became the victim of calumnies spread by jealous aristocrats and had to flee to Shah Abbas.

The Treaty of Nasuh Pasha between the Ottomans and the Safavids, signed in November 1612 and confirming the Treaty of Amasya, was only a truce which did not affect the South Caucasus. Probably provoked by a rare rapprochement between Kartli and Kakheti around 1612, Shah Abbas decided to crush this inter-Georgian alliance. As narrated by Jean Chardin, Abbas attacked Kakheti in 1614, captured Gremi and turned the cathedral of Alaverdi into a mosque (fig. 52). Worse still for Christian Georgia, Shah Abbas ordered the deportation of 30,000 Kakhetian men to Iran and resettled Muslims from Karabakh and Shirvan to fill their places in Kakheti; yet even worse was to come two years later.[76] In the meantime, Abbas installed the Muslim Bagrationi **Iese** (in Georgian) or **Isa** (in Persian) **Khan** (r. 1614–1615) as puppet king of Kakheti. King Teimuraz had fled to King Luarsab who in turn felt overwhelmed by Abbas's superior power; both kings retreated to Imereti in 1614 whose king **Giorgi III** (r. 1605–1639) refused to hand over the two refugees to the invader. When Shah Abbas threatened to ravage Kartli, Luarsab surrendered to save his country. Since Luarsab staunchly refused to convert to Islam, Abbas had him first imprisoned in Shiraz and then murdered in 1622. In Lower Kartli, Abbas installed King **Bagrat VII** known as Bagrat Khan (r. 1615 or 1616–1619), who was a Muslim. The Iranianized puppet king was despised by the Kartlians as a renegade and wielded no more authority than Isa Khan of Kakheti, who was killed in a local revolt. Angered, Shah Abbas sent an army of 15,000 Qizilbash to supress the revolt and capture Teimuraz who had returned to Kakheti, but the latter crushed the invaders with a much smaller force at the Battle of Tsitsamuri. Shah Abbas now decided to destroy the economic basis of Kakheti and to erase its population. In 1616, he personally led a huge army including a force of Lezgian Dagestanis to whom he proclaimed: 'I want to exterminate Kakheti. Kill or make prisoners all these Kakhetians who pass into the mountains on your side and I will enrich you with gifts.'[77] The Iranian army systematically destroyed towns, villages and churches. About 70,000 Kakhetians were massacred and 100,000 to 130,000 were deported to Iran and Dagestan.[78] Shah Abbas not only deported Kakhetians and Kartlians, but also Armenians. Between 1604 and 1618 hundreds of thousands of young Armenians, mainly artisans, traders and peasants, were carried off to Iran. The single largest group stemmed from Julfa (Jugha in Armenian) in Nakhchivan;

---

54. (Facing page) St John the Evangelist and his companion Prokhoros the deacon. Miniature from a gospel book illustrated by the Armenian painter Mesrop of Khizan (*ca.* 1560–1652) in New Julfa, the Armenian quarter of Isfahan, Iran. MS Ludwig II, 7, fol. 80v. © Getty Museum, Los Angeles.

THE SOUTH CAUCASUS UNDER TURKMEN, OTTOMAN AND IRANIAN SAFAVID DOMINATION | 97

55. St Luke. Miniature from a gospel book illustrated by the Armenian painter Mesrop of Khizan (*ca.* 1560–1652) in New Julfa, the Armenian quarter of Isfahan, Iran. MS Ludwig II, 7, fol. 122v. © Getty Museum, Los Angeles.

those deportees who survived the cruel forced marches were settled in the suburb of Isfahan called New Julfa, founded in 1606.[79] As observed by Jean Chardin seventy years after Shah Abbas's ravages, the once flourishing city of Julfa was nothing but a heap of lifeless ruins, since the shah had applied a scorched-earth policy to the region, destroying the city, deporting the inhabitants and even poisoning the wells in order to prevent a possible Turkish advance through the city.[80] The deportations from Nakhchivan by Shah Abbas led to the permanent depopulation of Armenians in this region. Since the Safavids granted New Julfa's Armenian merchants trading privileges with Europe, and later also with Russia, the local community thrived in the seventeenth century and expanded its trading operations to India. When the bigoted Shah Husayn (r. 1694–1722) began to discriminate against Christian Armenians, an Armenian exodus began towards India which was accelerated by New Julfa's looting by Afghan invaders in 1722 and the ensuing civil war. The estimates for today's Armenian community in Iran range from 70,000 to 200,000, of which about 10,000 to 12,000 live in New Julfa.

In the same year as Shah Abbas's campaign against Kakheti, the *Seventh Ottoman–Iranian War (1616–1618)* began, which led, among other things, to a Crimean Tatar army plundering Ganja and Nakhchivan. Although Shah Abbas severely defeated the invading Ottoman army west of Ardabil, he had to agree to the Treaty of Serav signed in autumn 1618, which confirmed the previous Treaty of Nasuh Pasha. Yet the fugitive Teimuraz of Kakheti refused to admit defeat and asked Russia for support. In revenge, in 1620 Shah Abbas had both of Teimuraz's sons castrated, from which mutilation both died, and four years later he had Teimuraz's mother Ketevan tortured to death.[81] In his cruelty, Shah Abbas surpassed even the Mongols. After the massacres and mass deportations of Kakhetians, Shah Abbas had ordered the Turkic Qizilbash chieftain Paykar Khan (d. 1625) to repopulate Kakheti with Turkic cattle breeders. But the remaining Kakhetians revolted. In 1625, Abbas had several Kakhetian leaders murdered through treachery, after which he decided to exterminate the Kartlians as he had done with the Kakhetians nine years before. He sent a large army under the command of Karachaqay Khan, to whose staff was attached Giorgi Saakadze, who had been in Safavid service since 1612. Suspicious of Abbas's intentions, Saakadze intercepted one of his messengers who was carrying the order to Karachaqay Khan to kill all Kartlian nobles and officers, including Saakadze himself. In view of Abbas's treachery, Saakadze turned his coat for the second time and forged an alliance with Zurab I (d. 1629), the Kartlian *eristavi* of Aragvi, who had himself been in Safavid service since 1619. On 25 March 1625 Saakadze and Zurab completely destroyed Karachaqay Khan's 35,000-strong army at the Battle of Martqopi, and drove Paykar Khan from Kakheti and the puppet ruler **Simon II Khan** (r. in Kartli 1619–1625, in Tbilisi 1625–1630) from Kartli, whereupon Saakadze recalled Teimuraz from exile and installed him as ruler of Kakheti and Kartli (r. 1625–1633). Kartli and Kakheti were tentatively reunited, but Simon Khan retained Tbilisi. Although the next Safavid punitive expedition achieved a costly victory in summer 1625 at the Battle of Marabda, Shah Abbas was forced to accept Teimuraz's rule. However, where Shah Abbas failed, namely in the destruction of this nascent Georgian unity, the Georgian nobles and Saakadze's ambitions succeeded. As early as 1626, a civil war broke out between Teimuraz, who was supported by most Kakhetian nobles, and Saakadze who wanted to put Prince Aleksandre of Imereti on the Kartlian throne. At the Battle of Bazaleti Teimuraz, supported by *eristavi* Zurab, was victorious and Saakadze fled to Istanbul where he was executed in 1629. In this period, Teimuraz sent an envoy to Philip IV of Spain and Pope

Urban VIII with the unrealistic plan of a joint Spanish–Papal–Georgian Crusade against the Ottomans. Nothing came of this wild initiative. When Shah Abbas died in 1629, Teimuraz wanted to eliminate two potential rivals. He first incited *eristavi* Zurab to kill Simon Khan in his sleep, after which he murdered his ally Zurab by treachery. Seemingly, in these brutal times concepts of loyalty and faithfulness were rarely applied in politics.

While the **Eighth Ottoman–Iranian War (1623–1639)** was mainly fought in Mesopotamia and Iran, Shah Safi (r. 1629–1642) decided to remove the troublesome Teimuraz. In 1632 he sent Khosro Mirza aka **Rostom Khan** (r. in Kartli 1633–1658, in Kartli and Kakheti 1648–1656) with troops to Kartli, where he seized power. Since Rostom Khan, an illegitimate son of Daud Khan (Davit XI), had been born and brought up in Isfahan, he was most probably a Shiite by birth. He enjoyed domestic autonomy, but was forced to provide troops and tributes.[82] King Rostom evicted Teimuraz from Kakheti, but the latter returned in 1634. Since Shah Safi's armies were hard pressed by the attacking Ottomans, he gave in and recognized Teimuraz as *vali* (governor) of Kakheti and promised to return deported Kakhetians. Shah Safi's concession was not enough either to stop Teimuraz swearing allegiance to Tsar Michael Romanov (r. 1613–1645) in 1639 or to prevent him waging war against Rostom and instigating his assassination. In 1639 the Treaty of Zuhab, also called the Treaty of Qasr-e Shirin, had been concluded, which allocated Mesopotamia to the Ottomans for good. Baghdad would remain in Ottoman possession till 1917. Concerning the South Caucasus, the Treaty of Amasya (1555) was essentially reconfirmed with the exception that the eastern part of Samtskhe now remained with the Turks. The regions of Shirvan, Ganja and Yerevan became Iranian provinces, the Shamkhalate and peoples of Dagestan were vassals, and Kartli and Kakheti were ruled by local *valis* who

56. The Armenian Maghardavank Monastery, also called the St Stepanos Monastery, stands 15 km south of the city of Julfa on the Iranian side of the valley of the River Araxes. The monastery was possibly founded in the seventh century; it is certainly attested in the tenth century. After several expansions and restorations it was rebuilt around 1330. After Shah Abbas I had deported the Armenians from Julfa, beginning in 1604, the monastery was abandoned. It was partially restored towards the end of the seventeenth century and again in the 1820s, but was finally abandoned in 1915. Together with the Armenian monastery of St Thaddeus, also located in Iranian Azerbaijan, it has figured since 2008 on the UNESCO World Heritage List. East Azerbaijan Province, Iran. Photo 2001.

considered themselves kings.[83] In what is now Azerbaijan and Armenia, several khanates emerged over time whose rulers held wide administrative, judicial and military powers and were even allowed to mint their own coinage.[84]

In the first half of the seventeenth century, the large migration movements into the south-eastern Caucasus came to an end, which allows an opportunity to briefly address the thorny issue of the ethnogenesis of the Azerbaijani people. Since today's Azerbaijan, and the Iranian province of Azerbaijan to its south, were from the sixth or seventh centuries CE a busy corridor of transit as well as a destination for immigration, the ethnic origin of the Azerbaijani people is complex to reconstruct. In contradiction to Turcophile claims, whereby Azerbaijanis are mainly Turks, or even that the eastern Caucasus is the cradle of all Turkish people (ignoring the fact that the Turkic peoples originate from the region between the Altai and Ural mountains), the vast majority of scholars and the few genetic studies point to a mixed ethnogenesis. It appears that Azerbaijanis have an autochthonous Caucasian background with a close relationship with the Georgians and less closely with the Medians (Iranians). Also discernible are Turkmen elements which stem from the arrival of numerous Turkic tribes such as the Oghuz, Seljuks and Turkmen, and earlier possibly the Western Turks and Khazars. In addition, Iranian Azerbaijanis show genetic closeness to the Kurds.[85]

Shah Safi could not accept an enduring conflict between his two Caucasian vassals, Teimuraz and Rostom. Thanks to the end of the Ottoman–Safavid wars, Safi now had his hands free to consolidate Iranian control in the Caucasus. He placed troops at Rostom's disposal, who chased Teimuraz once and for all out of Kakheti in 1648 and initiated a programme of rebuilding the economy and public monuments. But Teimuraz, now a refugee in Imereti, was still not giving up. He and **King Aleksandre III** of Imereti (r. 1639–1660) dispatched envoys to Moscow in 1649, offering the vassalage of Imereti and Kakheti (which Teimuraz no longer controlled) in return for Russian troops. Later, in 1653, Teimuraz also sent his grandson Erekle, the future king of Kakheti, to Moscow, yet again without any material result. Clearly, the same self-destructive pattern that had characterized Georgia and Armenia in the pre-medieval periods repeated itself in Georgia in the sixteenth and seventeenth centuries: the losing party in an internal power struggle did not hesitate to offer submission to a foreign power in exchange for military aid.[86] In 1658, Teimuraz himself travelled to the court of Tsar Alexei (Alexis, r. 1645–1676), but returned in despair to Imereti in 1659, leaving his grandson and sole heir in Russia. At this juncture, the dauntless Teimuraz ended his 55-year-long fight for independence, and took monastic vows. When Rostom's successor, the Muslim King **Vakhtang V** of Kartli, aka Shah Nawaz (r. 1658–1675) invaded Imereti in 1661, Teimuraz fell into his hands and was sent to Shah Abbas II (r. 1642–1666) who had him jailed in Astarabad (today's Gorgan) on the Caspian Sea.[87] While Teimuraz's never-ending wars and rebellions failed to restore Georgia's unity and independence, he undoubtedly contributed to keeping the Georgian fighting spirit alive. On the other hand, the pragmatic approach of the Kartlian kings Rostom and Vakhtang V in formally accepting Islam while supporting the reconstruction of churches, and submitting to the shahs while rebuilding the local economy and securing relative peace, was probably the only adequate long-term strategy for a small nation facing an overpowering neighbour.

57. Sketch by the Italian Theatine missionary Teramo Christoforo de Castelli (1597–1659) who was active in Georgia from 1632 to 1654. De Castelli's caption says, among other things: 'Il Gran Mofti fra Turchi e come il Papa fra noi.' (The Great Mufti is for the Turks what the Pope is for us.) Later de Castelli calls the Great Mufti 'Gran Pontifico del Demonio', that is 'Great Pontiff of the Devil'. In the sketch a demoness holds the pontiff by a chain wound around his neck. Source: Don Christoforo de Castelli, *Relazione e album*... (1976), ill. 393, p. 377.

4. The South Caucasus under Safavid rule

For more than seven decades from the middle of the seventeenth century, the South Caucasus remained within the Safavid zone of influence, with the exception of western Georgia and western Armenia. With the transfer of power from King Rostom to Vakhtang, the house of Mukhrani (a cadet branch of the Bagrationis), became dominant in Kartli. In 1656, the same year that Shah Abbas II deposed Rostom Khan in Kakheti, he dispatched Selim Khan, ruler of Ganja, to be *vali* in Kakheti, whose Turkification he promoted by settling about 80,000 Turkmen families from the Safavid empire in the province.[88] This ethnic displacement, to the detriment of the autochthonous Kakhetian population, triggered a revolt by the mountain peoples – Khevsurs, Pshavs and Tushetians – who in 1659 stormed the fortresses manned by Qizilbash troops and massacred the fleeing garrisons.[89] Five years later, Kakheti would once more become a political entity of its own when Archil ascended the Kakhetian throne. While King Vakhtang continued the prudent policy of his predecessor in not provoking the wrath of the Iranian shahs, in 1661 he seized the opportunity to expand his domain when unrest broke out in Imereti due to the intrigues of the widow of King Aleksandre III, Queen **Darejan** (queen consort 1639–1660, 1661–1663, 1668)[90] which would plunge Imereti into a chaos of assassinations and rapid successions of ephemeral rulers that lasted for more than a century, till King Solomon I took power in 1752. When her husband Aleksandre died in 1660, probably by poisoning, Queen Darejan had Aleksandre's son **Bagrat IV** (r. 1660–1661, 1663–1668, 1669–1678, 1679–1681) crowned king of Imereti and forced him to marry her niece Ketevan. Yet she kept all power. A few months later she ordered her stepson Bagrat to divorce Ketevan and proposed herself as his new bride. When Bagrat refused to marry his stepmother, which would have constituted a grave sin, she had him blinded and married an obscure noble called Vakhtang Tchutchunashvili, whom she crowned king as **Vakhtang I** (r. 1661–1663, 1668). These vicious events caused disgust among Imeretian nobles who asked Mingrelia and Kartli to intervene. Vakhtang V invaded in 1661 and placed his son **Archil** (r. in Imereti 1661–1663, 1678–1679, 1690–1691, 1695–1696 and 1698) on the Imeretian throne. But by this de facto union of Kartli and Imereti, King Vakhtang violated the Ottoman–Iranian Treaty of Zuhab which had allocated Imereti to the Ottomans and Kartli to the Safavids. The Ottomans swiftly protested and mobilized troops in Eastern Anatolia, whereupon Shah Abbas II, who was unwilling to restart the Ottoman–Iranian wars, forced King Vakhtang in 1663 to recall his son Archil from Kutaisi and to reinstall Bagrat IV. As compensation, Archil was nominated ruler of Kakheti under the name of **Nazar Khan** (r. in Kakheti 1664–1675) after he had converted to Islam. In the year of his ascension to the throne, he had to repulse an attack by his brother-in-law **Erekle I** (r. in Kakheti 1675–1676, 1703–1709, in Kartli 1688–1703), a grandson of Teimuraz I. However, Archil left Kakheti in 1675 and joined the Ottomans at Akhaltsikhe; between 1678 and 1698 he was four times more king of Imereti.

As for Bagrat IV of Imereti, in 1668 he obtained revenge for his blinding in an act of treachery typical of the times. Jean Chardin, who spent time in Imereti a few years after the event, described it as follows: after Vizier Khosia Lashkhishvili had won the trust of Queen Darejan and been adopted by her as her son, he pretended to be gravely ill and lured her to his house. There she was immediately stabbed to death, whereupon the vizier called for her husband Vakhtang and Bagrat IV. While Khosia's henchmen held Vakhtang, Bagrat IV pierced him with his dagger shouting 'Traitor, you ordered to tear out my eyes; now I will rip out your heart.'[91] Chardin was shocked by the social conditions in Imereti and Mingrelia. He reported that King Bagrat's third wife Tamar had a flagrant affair with the bishop of Gelati and that it was common practice for bishops to have several wives or lovers. He also commented with disgust that the upper clergy and nobility were involved in the slave trade; the catholicos of Mingrelia, Guria and Abkhazia not only sold appointment as bishops, but also western Georgian children to the Turks.[92] Basically, Christian churchmen and nobles were exploiting fellow Christians for the benefit of their Muslim overlords and their own profit. King Bagrat's son and successor **Aleksandre IV of Imereti** (r. 1683–1690, 1691–1695) also traded young people into slavery. After he tried to switch allegiance from the Ottomans to the Safavids in 1689, a Turkish expedition expelled him in 1690 but he was reinstalled one year later. In 1692, the famous Bagrati Cathedral of Kutaisi was blown up by the Ottoman occupiers.

In Kartli, **Giorgi XI** (r. 1676–1688, 1703–1709) succeeded his father Vakhtang V after he had converted to Islam, taking the name **Shah Nawaz II**. When Giorgi made contact with Pope Innocent XI (in office 1676–1689) with a view to a future alliance, Shah Suleiman (r. 1666–1694) had him removed in 1688 and installed **Erekle I** aka Nazar Ali Khan (r. in Kartli 1688–1703) on

58. Seventeenth-century mural of the main donors on the northern wall of the church of Saints Quiricus and Julitta in Zarati. The absence of inscriptions makes a secure identification of the donors impossible; they possibly belong to the local Mkhetsidze family which provided governors until the seventeenth century. Imereti, Georgia. Photo 2018.

the Kartlian throne, but his rule remained challenged by Giorgi from 1691 till 1695. In 1696, Giorgi's career took an extraordinary turn. Shah Husayn ordered him to Isfahan and nominated him governor of Kerman Province with the task of restoring the Shah's authority there. In 1703, Giorgi was rewarded by being reinstalled as king of Kartli but he was not allowed to return home. Instead he was honoured with the title of Gurgin Khan and in 1704 was nominated governor general of the Afghan province of Kandahar where the local Sunni Afghan Pashtuns were in revolt, resisting Shah Husayn's forcible Shiite proselytizing. Giorgi therefore delegated the administration of Kartli to his nephew, the regent **Vakhtang** (regent 1703–1712), the future King **Vakhtang VI** (r. 1719–1724). In Kandahar, Gurgin Khan suppressed the revolt with merciless toughness. One of the protagonists of the revolt whom he arrested was Mir Ways (d. 1715), the chief of the Hotaki tribe, who belonged to the Ghilzai tribal federation. Mir Ways was sent to Isfahan where he gained the trust of Shah Husayn who set him free. Once he had returned to Kandahar, he repaid the trust Shah Husayn had placed in him by treacherously murdering Gurgin Khan at a banquet. Then he seized power and founded the short-lived Hotaki dynasty (1709–1738). **Kaikhosro Bagrationi** (r. in absentia in Kartli 1709–1711), Giorgi's nephew, commanded a large Safavid punitive army sent to Kandahar. But Mir Ways outmanoeuvred the Iranians and annihilated the whole army. Ten years later, Mir Ways' son Mir Mahmud (r. 1717–1725) attacked Iran and conquered Isfahan on 22 October 1722. This heralded the end of the Safavid dynasty, which would have repercussions in the South Caucasus.[93]

When Vakhtang VI ruled Kartli from 1703 to 1712 as regent for Giorgi XI and Kaikhosro, he strove to restore agriculture, promote trade, and restore centralized authority by curtailing the more or less unlimited power of the leading nobles, and to regulate serfdom and the feudal system. The law code known as *dasturlamali* categorized people by the amount of blood money to be paid in the case of their murder. It confirmed the preferential position of landowners and attempted to foster the petty nobility to the disadvantage of the magnates. But it also corroborated the status of serf peasants as virtually without legal rights. Insolvency was one of the key causes due to which free peasants were degraded to serfs; in such a case the only resort for an indebted father was to sell his children into slavery to settle his debt. (Nevertheless the status of peasants was less severe than under Tsar Peter I's infamous 'passport decree' of 1719. While the vast majority of people living within Russia were already severely limited in their freedom by the Law Code of 1649 that formalized serfdom, enforced labour levies and restricted movement, the new decree ordered that 'no one is to travel anywhere from town to town, or village to village, without a travel or transit letters'. No serf or peasant was allowed to leave his village without the written approval of his owner. To shelter any traveller without such documents was a criminal offence.[94] The decrees of 1649 and 1719 had two key objectives: first, to chain peasants to an assigned piece of land in order to secure a predictable agricultural output and prevent flight from forced labour and oppressive landlords; and second, to increase the number of available soldiers by means of compulsory conscription among serfs.) Vakhtang could initiate a revival only of local and regional commerce, rather than of Georgia's (or Armenia's) previous role as hub of transcontinental trade. This trade between the Orient and Europe had for the most part long since shifted to maritime routes and alternative land trails. In Kartli, Vakhtang also tried to modernize the urban community by introducing a printing press in Tbilisi in 1709. A similar endeavour was undertaken by Archil's son Prince Aleksandre of Imereti (d. 1711) who was a friend of Tsar Peter and accompanied him in his travels to Western Europe in 1697–1698 where he studied artillery in The Hague. During this stay, he asked an acquaintance of Tsar Peter, the long-standing mayor of Amsterdam, Nicolaas Witsen (d. 1717) to develop fonts for the Georgian alphabets, which were ready by 1699.[95]

59. Mural of the Deesis, that is Christ Pantocrator flanked by the Virgin Mary and St John the Baptist. Provided the Deesis is interpreted as the Last Judgement, the book held in the left hand of Christ is the Book of Life mentioned in Revelation 20:12–15, which lists the candidates for the Kingdom of Heaven. Mary and St John humbly ask Christ for mercy for the judged people. Central apse of the cathedral of Nikortsminda. Racha-Lechkhumi and Kvemo Svaneti, Georgia. Photo 2013.

In 1712, Shah Husayn summoned his vassal Vakhtang to court and ordered him to convert to Islam. When Vakhtang refused, he was imprisoned and replaced as ruler of Kartli first by his half-brother **Simon** (r. 1712–1714) and later by his other half-brother **Iese** aka **Ali Quli Khan** (r. 1714–1716, 1724–1727) who had served in the Safavid army under Gurgin Khan (Giorgi XI) and Kaikhosro. It is again striking how the Iranian shahs appointed and removed members of the Bagrationi dynasty to be army officers or governors of the South Caucasus as they saw fit. Since during Simon's and Iese's rules Kartli was plagued by insurgencies, Shah Husayn deposed Ali Quli Khan and appealed to Vakhtang, who relented and converted to Islam in 1716. Since the shah still would not allow Vakhtang to return to his kingdom, the latter dispatched his son **Bakar** (r. 1716–1719) as regent. Finally, in 1719, Vakhtang retook power in Kartli and defeated the marauding Dagestanis four times in battle. Witnessing the increasing weakness of the Safavid government, he opted for independence and established secret contacts with the Russian ambassador to Iran and governor of Astrakhan, Artemy Volynsky (d. 1740). At that time, Tsar Peter I (r. 1682–1725) planned a military campaign into the eastern Caucasus in order to prevent the Ottomans from reconquering it, to secure the trade routes of Russia to the East via Iran and to control the business of silk-producing Shirvan.[96] Peter decided to prioritize a military advance through the eastern Caucasus after the catastrophic failure of the Russian expedition of 1717 to Khiva in western Central Asia whose aim had been to open a new, direct trade route with India.[97] He had already in 1717 begun to attract Dagestani rulers into the Russian zone of influence by offering them financial subsidies. One of the first Dagestani leaders to declare himself a vassal of Russia was the *shamkhal* Adil Giray (but this didn't stop him from taking subsidies from Iran as well).[98] Vakhtang suggested that a joint Russian–Georgian force could liberate Georgia from the Iranian yoke which would give Russia a firm ally in the South Caucasus. In November 1721, he confirmed to Tsar Peter that he and the Kartlian army would

60. The upper fortress of Ananuri was the seat of the *eristavis* of Aragvi. The lower fortress is in ruins and partially flooded by a reservoir. The smaller church of the Redeemer on the left was built in the early seventeenth century, the larger church of the Dormition on the right dates from 1689. Mtskheta-Mtianeti, Georgia. Photo 2013.

61. The southern section of the medieval city wall of Baku. The walls were built in the twelfth century and were several times restored. Baku, Azerbaijan. Photo 2016.

be at Ganja in late summer 1722 to await the arrival of Russian forces. Since the Peace of Nystad concluded on 10 September 1721 had put a final end to the Great Northern War of 1700–1721 between Russia and Sweden, Tsar Peter was now able to focus on the Caspian region. In summer 1722 he launched a combined sea and land operation and took Derbent without a fight, but he never proceeded as far as Ganja. He was anxious to avoid a confrontation with the Ottomans, who had also advanced into the eastern Caucasus and had recognized Hajji Daud as Shirvanshah. Tsar Peter retreated before winter to Astrakhan leaving garrisons along Azerbaijan's coast and abandoning Vakhtang to his fate.[99] The Russian capture of Baku in summer 1723 was of no help to King Vakhtang, and Russia lost interest in its Caspian conquests after Tsar Peter's death in 1725. The breach of promise of 1722–1723 would not be the only time that Imperial Russia betrayed Georgia by ignoring its previous commitments of military assistance: later betrayals occurred in 1787 and 1795. At best, Russia was too weak to put words into action; at worst, Russia's intention was to weaken Georgia to the extent that it would inevitably fall to the Russian Empire; this was the strategy applied by Tsarina Catherine II (r. 1762–1796).[100]

In fact, the situation between Russia and the Ottomans remained tense in Azerbaijan where their troops stood only 60 kilometres apart. Furthermore, Abraham Stanyan, British ambassador to the Porte, was constantly encouraging the Ottomans to attack the scattered Russian garrisons, since the British government feared Russia's entry into trade with India. In fact, English merchants had used the Caspian route till the late sixteenth century themselves, since the southern sea route to India around the Cape of Good Hope and the Indian Ocean were dominated by Spanish and Portuguese fleets for much of the sixteenth century. After Captain Richard Chancellor succeeded in entering the White Sea in 1553 and landing near today's port of Arkhangelsk, he travelled to Moscow where Tsar Ivan granted him and other English merchants permission to trade in Russia. Six years after the Muscovy Company was founded in 1555, a representative of the Company reached Iran, and from now on there would be annual trading journeys from England to Iran via Russia and the Caspian route. When English ships regained access to the eastern Mediterranean, and especially after the successful first expedition of the East India Company to South East Asia in 1601–1603, English traders abandoned the longer

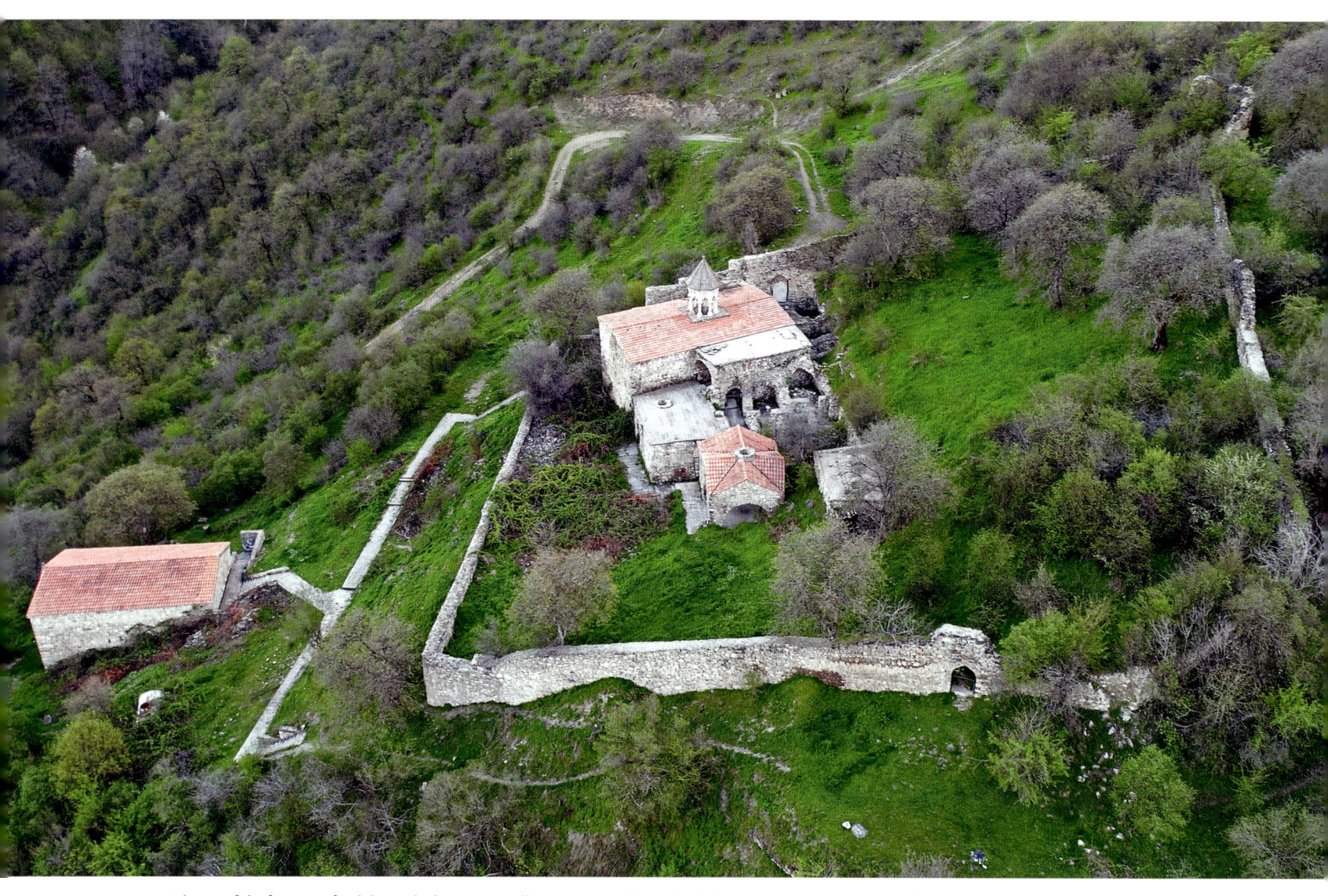

62. Aerial view of the fortress of Halidzor, which was originally a nunnery. In the 1720s Halidzor served as headquarters for the Armenian leader and Iranian vassal David Beg (d. 1728) who resisted the encroachments by the Ottoman occupation and local Muslim tribes. Syunik Province, Armenia. Photo 2019.

and more cumbersome route via the Caspian.[101] By the 1720s, Great Britain's preference was for the Caucasus to fall under the control of Ottoman Turkey rather than become part of Russia. In retrospect, British pressure on the Ottomans to eject the Russians from the eastern Caspian littoral seems like a prelude to the future Great Game.[102] It was only thanks to the mediation of the French ambassador to Turkey, Jean-Louis d'Usson, marquis de Bonnac, that war between Russia and the Ottomans was averted and an agreement achieved whereby both parties would keep their territorial gains: Russia was assigned Derbent, Baku, Astarabad and Gilan, Turkey the inland territories of Shirvan, Armenia and Georgia; Russia thus recognized Ottoman suzerainty over Kartli and Kakheti.[103] A nest of Armenian resistance against the Turkish invaders survived for a few years in Syunik (Zangezur) where from his base at the fortress of Halidzor the Armenian David Beg (d. 1728) organized the tiny, embryonic Safavid vassal state of Kapan which lasted from *ca.* 1723 to 1730 (fig. 62). Davit's successor Mkhitar Sparapet was murdered in 1730 by Armenian villagers who sent his head to the Ottoman pasha. With Mkhitar's assassination, the Armenian resistance in Kapan came to an end.[104]

Vakhtang VI's flirtation with Russia had dire consequences. Shah Tahmasp II (claimed rule 1722–1729, r. 1729–1732) encouraged the Muslim king of Kakheti **Konstantine II** aka **Muhammad Quli Khan** (r. 1722–1732) to attack Kartli in coordination with the khanates of Ganja and Yerevan as well as troops from Djaro-Belokan (today's Zaqatala). Vakhtang was ousted from Tbilisi and fled to an approaching Ottoman army. But the Ottomans installed **Iese** (second reign 1724–1727), who had defected to the Turks and become a nominal Sunni Muslim, as Turkish puppet king of Kartli under the name of **Mustapha Pasha**. Vakhtang now fled to Russia where he ended his days in exile. In 1732, the Ottomans killed King Konstantine of Kakheti (who had submitted to them in 1725), after he began playing a reinvigorated Iran against his Ottoman overlords, and replaced him with his Christian brother **Teimuraz II** (r. in Kakheti 1732–1736 with interruptions, 1738–1744, in Kartli 1744–1762), after the latter's submission. During the two campaigns of the Iranian warlord Tahmasp-Quli Khan, later to be Nader Shah (r. 1736–1747), in 1734–1735 Teimuraz II defected to the attacking Iranians who in August 1735 captured Tbilisi from the Ottomans.[105] But when Teimuraz refused to convert to Islam, Tahmasp-Quli Khan installed the Muslim Bagrationi prince Ali Mirza, aka **Aleksandre III** (r. 1735–1736) as nominal *vali* of Kakheti under the supervision of an Iranian officer. Yet Aleksandre not only failed to assert himself in Kakheti but also considered a revolt, whereupon Nader Shah replaced him in 1736 with **Abdullah Beg** (r. 1736–1738), the eldest son of Iese Khan from the house of Mukhrani-Bagrationi. But the excessive Iranian tax demands imposed on Kartli and Kakheti continued to provoke unrest. Since Nader Shah, absorbed by the conquest of Kandahar as well as the planning of a plundering raid on Delhi, was unwilling to risk a rebellion in Georgia while campaigning in India, in 1738 he nominated Teimuraz to be *vali* of Kakheti and his son Erekle, the future King Erekle II, to be commander of the Georgian troops in the expedition to India. With these nominations, Nader, who had abolished the Safavid dynasty and declared himself shah in 1736, elevated the two Bagrationi princes to positions which would be key to enabling them to reunite Kartli and Kakheti, de facto in 1744, de jure in 1762.

The murder of Konstantine II and the Iranian–Georgian reconquest of Azerbaijan and eastern Georgia were elements of the ***Ninth Ottoman–Iranian War (1730–1735)***. In 1730, Tahmasp-Quli Khan began the reconquest of Iran's western territories that had been lost in the previous decade to the Ottomans. After crushing the Afghan Shah Ashraf Hotaki Ghilzai, a nephew of Mir Ways, in 1729, he freed Hamadan, Kermanshah and Tabriz from their Turkish occupiers the following year. But he was forced to postpone the reconquest of the South Caucasus because of an attack by Abdali Afghans in the east, who besieged the important city of Mashhad. Eager to assert his authority, Shah Tahmasp II exploited Tahmasp-Quli's absence in eastern Iran by attempting to bring the latter's aborted plan to fruition, and laid siege to Yerevan. But Shah Tahmasp was an incompetent commander, his army consisted of untrained recruits and his logistical arrangements were poor. The Ottomans cut his supply line and crushed his army at the Battle of Kurijan, whereupon they occupied Tabriz and Hamadan. Tahmasp had to accept the proposal of the Ottomans whereby they would return Tabriz, Hamadan and Kermanshah, but he had to recognize Ottoman suzerainty over Armenia, Georgia and most of today's Azerbaijan.[106] After having forced the incompetent Shah Tahmasp II to abdicate in 1732, Tahmasp-Quli Khan resumed the war against the Ottomans. He aimed to recover the lost Armenian and Georgian territories by capturing Baghdad and then exchanging it for the South Caucasian regions. Although in his attack on Baghdad in 1733 Tahmasp-Quli suffered a rare defeat, his renewed attack two years later would meet with success.

Russia had already signed the Treaty of Resht in 1732 renouncing all territorial gains south of the River Kura, that is Mazandaran, Gilan and Astarabad. The Russians wanted to abandon these conquests in the south-western Caspian anyway, as a result of losing ten thousands of soldiers since 1722 to malaria and other diseases in the unhealthy climate. Three years later, the Iranian–Russian Treaty of Ganja confirmed the previous agreement and Russia agreed also to evacuate Azerbaijan's littoral, including Baku – the only good harbour on the western Caspian coast – Derbent and even the Svyatoi Krest (Holy Cross) fortress in the Shamkhalate of Tarki which had only been founded in 1722.[107] The new border followed the River Sulak, and those Russians living near Svyatoi Krest were relocated to Kizlyar on the northern side of the River Terek.[108] The treaty was advantageous to both parties: Russia 'delegated' to Iran the task of checking the Ottoman advance into the Caucasus, while Iran got rid of the Russian bridgeheads along the Caspian coast. The treaty even came close to a military alliance, for when a strong Crimean army advanced through Dagestan a few months later while Nader Shah was operating in Armenia, Russia launched a relief attack against Crimea.[109]

Tahmasp-Quli Khan first courted the large Armenian community in 1735 by visiting Catholicos Abraham III (Abraham of Crete, in office 1734–1737) in Etchmiadzin. He granted the Armenian Church tax exemption and annulled the discriminatory Safavid decree whereby Armenian converts to Islam automatically acquired the inheritances of their remaining Christian relatives. Shortly after, on 19 June 1735, he annihilated an Ottoman army far superior in number at the Battle of Baghavard (or Yeghevard) north of Yerevan with the deployment of more than 500 *zamburaks*. The *zamburak* was a piece of mobile light artillery used against infantry. It consisted of a heavy

63. Illustration of an Iranian artillerist firing a *zamburak* swivel gun from a crouching camel. Source: Pierre Amédée Jaubert, *Voyage en Arménie et en Perse* (1821), p. 281.

musket or small swivel gun which had a longer firing range than a standard infantry musket and was mounted on and fired from a camel. While the cities of Tbilisi, Ganja and Yerevan soon surrendered to Tahmasp-Quli, a strong Crimean Tatar army crossed the North Caucasus and marched through Dagestan in order to reinforce the Ottoman troops. But they arrived too late, as Turkey recognized in the Treaty of Istanbul of 1736 that the central and eastern South Caucasus belonged to Iran. Meanwhile, the Crimean campaign to Dagestan triggered the Russian–Ottoman War of 1735–1739, during which Russia captured the important harbour of Azov.[110] In spite of the peace treaty, Tahmasp-Quli Khan (now Nader Shah) and the Ottoman sultan Mahmud I (r. 1730–1754) found themselves unable to agree on religious matters. The Ottomans requested that Shiite clergy should stop cursing the caliphs Omar and Uthman while Nader

Shah wanted his modified form of Shiism to be recognized by the Ottoman sultan-caliph[111] as the fifth *madhab* (Sunni school of law), called the Ja'afariya.[112] Nader Shah's rapprochement with Sunnism was motivated by his eagerness to expand his authority beyond the limited circle of Shiites, who represented only a minority of Muslims. Sultan-Caliph Mahmud understood the implications of Nader Shah's demand and rejected it in 1736, 1742 and 1743. In summer 1743 the sultan-caliph underlined his refusal to accept moderate Shiism as the fifth Sunni *madhab* by issuing a fatwa that allowed Sunnis to enslave and kill Shiite Iranians as heretics.[113]

Since Nader Shah failed to decisively crush the marauding Lezgins in 1736, or to avenge the death of his brother Ibrahim in battle against them in late 1738, he returned in 1741 to evict them once and for all from the southern foothills of the Greater Caucasus. But Nader's Lezgian War (from summer 1741 till spring 1743) proved to be a costly failure. While the Iranian army, supported by cannons, was more than a match for Ottoman or Indian forces, it had a hard time attempting to pacify the Lezgian and Avar mountain people who avoided pitched battles and conducted a partisan war. Nader Shah won several skirmishes in the foothills, but his 6,000-strong vanguard suffered a painful defeat in a narrow valley in Avaria in August 1742 (or 1741), and the Avar fortress of Khunzakh remained unconquered. When Nader and his decimated army left Dagestan in 1743 because a new war with the Ottomans was imminent, they became the targets for repeated attacks by the victorious highlanders.[114] In view of the Ottoman threat and the previous loyalty of Teimuraz and Erekle, Nader Shah felt bound in 1744 to secure their continued goodwill through a major concession: he recognized the Christians **Teimuraz II** as king of Kartli (r. 1744–1762) and his son **Erekle II** as king of Kakheti (r. 1744–1762, in Kartli and Kakheti united 1762–1798). Thus Nadir Shah facilitated the reunification of Kartli and Kakheti, which took place in 1762 when Erekle II inherited Kartli on his father's death.[115] After Nader's failed attack on Ottoman Mosul and a Turkish defeat in 1745 the **Tenth Ottoman–Iranian War (1743–1746)** was concluded with the Treaty of Kordan (Kerden) in September 1746. It confirmed the boundary between both empires as defined in 1639 in the Treaty of Zuhab. Nader Shah also accepted that the sultan-caliph would not legitimize Shiite Ja'afariya as the fifth *madhab* of Islam. One year later, Nader Shah, who had turned paranoiac, was murdered by officers of his personal guard whom he had ordered to be killed next day by his Afghan mercenaries.

The Armenian Mekhitarist congregation

After a century without proper state institutions, when ecclesiastical structures were weak, warfare raged and economic poverty was rife, the spiritual and intellectual state of the Armenian clergy and its monasteries had declined. It was the Armenian priest Mkhitar (Mekhitar) Sebastatsi (1676–1749) who took it upon himself to tackle the task of leading the Armenian Church out of its intellectual isolation. Ordained priest in 1696, Mkhitar came into contact with learned Catholic Jesuits who since 1684 had maintained a station, and later a school, in Erzurum. Studying the Chalcedonian Creed and Catholic theology, Mkhitar concluded that there was no unbridgeable divide between the Armenian and the Roman Catholic confessions. In Aleppo in 1695 Mkhitar adopted the Catholic profession of faith; it remains unknown whether he was forced to abjure the Armenian profession, and whether he at first concealed his conversion within the Armenian religious environment. In 1699 he obtained the degree of *vardapet*, that is a religious teacher entitled to instruct students. On 8 September 1701 he and a few students founded a new order in Istanbul with Mkhitar as abbot. His aims were to lift the educational and intellectual level of Armenia's monks and clergy and to achieve a rapprochement, and ultimately a reunion, with the Roman Catholic Church, while maintaining Armenian as the language of worship, as well as the inherited traditions of the Armenian Church.[116] The small community lived for the time being according to the rules of St Anthony. However, his initiative met with fierce resistance among the Armenian community of Istanbul. Since two Armenian archbishops obtained an arrest warrant from Sultan Ahmed III (r. 1703–1730) denouncing Mkhitar as a French spy, in around 1703 he and his students had to flee to Methoni (Modon) in the Peloponnese, which belonged to Venice.

64. Aerial view of the Armenian Mekhitarist monastery of San Lazzaro in the lagoon of Venice.

In 1711, Pope Clement XI (in office 1700–1721) confirmed the new congregation, which had adopted the Rule of St Benedict.[117] Four years later, the small Armenian Catholic community had to flee again when the Seventh Venetian–Ottoman War (1714–1715) broke out and the Turks evicted the Venetians from the Peloponnese. The Mkhitarists, who also called themselves 'Armenian Benedictines' sought refuge in Venice where an Armenian printing press had existed since 1513. In 1717 they were allocated the small island of San Lazzaro where they renovated the existing church and built their monastery between 1724 and 1740. Printing work began in 1733.[118]

In theological matters Mkhitar differentiated between religion and nation as between creed and customs. In his understanding, a Catholic Armenian remained an authentic Armenian; but for his Armenian opponents a Catholic Armenian was a traitor to his nation. According to Mkhitar, under the umbrella of the Chalcedonian Creed there was room for both Latin and Armenian rites, while according to Catholic and Armenian church doctrines a communion of sacraments was strictly forbidden.[119] As emphasized by the chronicler of the San Lazzaro community Alberto Peratoner, Mkhitar's personal position 'combined a strong sense of universal Church in unity with the Holy See in Rome and a singular attachment to the traditions of the Armenian Apostolic Church'.[120] For these reasons, Mkhitar opposed the creation of a parallel ecclesiastical organization, but his views did not prevail. In 1740–42 the Armenian Catholic patriarchate of Cilicia was founded with, as patriarch, Abraham Petros I Ardzivian (in office 1740–1749), who had spent a few years in an Ottoman jail or exile after his conversion to Catholicism.[121] Today the see of the Armenian Catholic Church is located at Bzoummar north of Beirut, Lebanon; it counts about 150,000 adherents. In fact, to realize Mkhitar's vision of a universal church based on a communion of faith and creed, both the Latin and the Armenian churches would have had to drastically change their doctrines. But the Armenian Church rejected the Chalcedonian Creed as heretical while the Roman Catholic Church demanded from sister churches in communion with it an administrative submission and a uniformity of practice.

Mkhitar's successor Stephanos Melkhonian (in office 1750–1799) provoked a secession when he unilaterally extended the term of office of the abbot to life. Abbot Melkhonian forced Astvatzatur Babikian and his followers, who resisted this change in the order's constitution, to leave the monastery in 1773. The expelled monks first settled in Trieste where they founded a new monastery with Babikian as abbot, thus formalizing the schism. The community of Trieste counted nineteen monks, San Lazzaro thirteen. In 1797 French troops occupied Venice and put an end to the Republic. When in 1810 Napoleon closed all monastic institutions in Venice, he decreed that the Mekhitarist community could continue as an academy of learning. The community of Trieste fared less well. Around 1800 serious quarrels and even brawls occurred among the monks while the monastery's debts accumulated. In 1808, three years after Trieste fell to France, the new authorities ordered the monks to sell their property in order to pay their debts. In January 1811 the monastery was confiscated and closed. Abbot Babikian and some monks emigrated to Vienna where in 1811 they were allowed to settle in an empty Capuchin monastery. In the meantime, the community of San Lazzaro expanded and by reclaiming land north of the island doubled its surface area. Today, the library of the monastery treasures 4,500 Armenian manuscripts. In the year 2000, the two Mekhtarist branches finally merged under the leadership of General Abbot Yeghia Kilaghbian, based in San Lazzaro. The Mekhtarists enjoy an independent position within the Catholic Church, as they are directly subordinate to the Vatican.[122]

5. A brief reunification of Kartli and Kakheti and the foundation of independent khanates

By contrast with previous reigns where there had been violent quarrels between rulers and their sons, Teimuraz II and Erekle II worked in close cooperation with each other and crushed the revolts of pretenders such as the former *vali* Abdullah Beg and other Iranian claimants. They expanded their realm by drawing Yerevan, Nakhchivan and Ganja into their zone of influence. In 1747, both Georgian kings helped **Shahverdi Khan Ziyadoghlu Qajar** (r. 1747–1760) to gain power in Ganja, and in return he had to pay an annual tribute to his sponsors. When Shahverdi Khan was killed in a local rebellion, Teimuraz and Erekle intervened again and placed Shahverdi's son **Muhammad Hasan Khan** (r. 1760–1780) on Ganja's throne; the tribute payment to Georgia continued. When a power struggle broke out between Muhammad Hasan Khan and his younger brothers in 1778, King Erekle II and **Ibrahim Khalil Khan Javanshir** of Karabakh (r. 1763–1806) invaded and in 1780 divided the Khanate of Ganja between them.[123] In 1780–1782, Erekle prevented **Fath-'Ali Khan Quba'i** (r. 1758–1789), the powerful ruler of Quba who had subjugated Derbent and Baku around 1765, from conquering the lowlands of Karabakh.[124] But the Treaty of Georgiyevsk (see below) between Georgia and Russia led to a rupture between Erekle and Ibrahim from 1783, as Erekle had to give up the Georgian share of Ganja. However, the two Georgian kings failed to stop the devastating plundering and kidnapping raids by the Avars, since the system of defensive blockhouses they erected remained porous. The Georgian renaissance after 1744 was helped by the chaos which erupted within the Iranian political leadership following Nader Shah's death. It was not only Kartli and Kakheti that exploited the unrest within Iran but also several tribal dynasts who, within the former Safavid South Caucasus, made up eleven more or less independent khanates and a few sultanates. These khanates were: Yerevan, Nakhchivan, Ganja, the Karabakh lowlands, Derbent, Quba (Qobbeh), Shakhi, Shirvan, Baku, Javad and Talish. Added to them were the Five Melikdoms of highland Karabakh (which became vassals of the Khanate of Karabakh in the 1750s) and the sultanates of Elisu, Qazakh, Shamshedil (Shams al-Din), Shoragöl and the five self-governing communities of Djaro-Belokan which correspond approximately to the present district of Zakatala in north-western Azerbaijan.[125] In Dagestan, where most tribes had united in a common effort to repulse Nader Shah, about twenty-eight principalities emerged after his death, following linguistic boundaries.[126] Although Kartli's and Kakheti's previous experiences with Russia had been disappointing, Teimuraz II saw in St Petersburg the only potential counterbalance to the Iranians and Ottomans. Eight years after a Georgian embassy to Russia in 1752 had brought no results, King Teimuraz himself travelled to the Russian court to negotiate military support. His efforts remained inconclusive, however, and he died in Astrakhan on his way back to Kartli in January 1762. Erekle II succeeded him as king of Kartli and thus united eastern and central Georgia for the first time since the end of the fifteenth century. Yet Erekle had to remain cautious in his relations with Iran. When Iran's ruler Karim Khan Zand (r. 1751–1779) was leading a military operation in today's Azerbaijan in 1762/63 and approached Georgia's border, Erekle nominally submitted and was confirmed as *vali* of Georgia.[127]

As Erekle soon found out, not only Iran, but also the supposedly friendly Russia monitored Georgia's rise with suspicion. In 1749 (or 1752), Russia had already allowed Prince Paata Bagrationi, a bastard son of King Vakhtang VI who had been brought up in St Petersburg, to leave Russia. After he had returned to Kartli and disobeyed royal orders, he was jailed but later pardoned by King Erekle, which did not prevent him from organizing a plot to murder the king and seize power himself. The planned putsch was uncovered and the conspirators arrested. Prince Paata was beheaded, a few were burnt to death and other ringleaders were mutilated. One year later, in 1766, Tsarina Catherine II arranged for the return of another claimant to the Georgian throne living in Russian exile. This was Prince Aleksandre, grandson of Vakhtang VI. In 1779, during Erekle's absence from Tbilisi, he tried to seize power but failed miserably and fled to Dagestan. At Erekle's repeated requests, Russia applied pressure on Fath 'Ali Khan Quba'i to arrest Aleksandre, but only after the Treaty of Georgiyevsk which had turned Georgia into a Russian protectorate; Aleksandre was apprehended and incarcerated till his death in 1791. Erekle made great efforts to relaunch the Georgian economy and repopulate deserted regions. He attracted Georgians living abroad as well as Ottoman Armenian, Circassian and Russian settlers by offering them an allocation of crown land and tax exemptions. A little later, in 1774, King Erekle introduced mandatory military service in order to replace the Circassian mercenaries who constituted an important part of the Georgian army.[128]

In Imereti, King **Solomon I** Bagrationi (r. 1752–1765, 1767–1784) emulated Teimuraz II and Erekle II. He was determined to free his kingdom from Ottoman overlordship and from the higher nobility which profited greatly from the slave trade with the Ottomans. He forbade slave trading and took measures to reinvigorate trade and agriculture. However, his ban on slave trading provoked the anger of its key profiteers, the Ottoman pasha of Akhaltsikhe, *eristavi* Rostom of Racha and Ivan Abashidze. The latter led an Ottoman army into Imereti in 1757, but lost the Battle of Khresili in December along with his life. In 1758 Solomon defeated two other Ottoman armies, and in the same year he concluded a mutual defence pact with King Erekle. Not wanting to lose this important supplier of human merchandise, in 1765 the Ottomans captured Imereti's capital Kutaisi where they installed Solomon's nephew Teimuraz (d. 1768) as anti-king, he having promised to once more allow slave trading. But since Teimuraz's authority never exceeded the perimeter of the Turkish garrison, in 1768 the Ottomans struck a deal with Solomon. They recognized Imereti as an autonomous kingdom, in return for which Solomon would deliver every year sixty non-ethnic Georgians to the Turks as slaves – a promise Solomon never intended to keep. One year later, Solomon pretended to make peace with his old enemy the *eristavi* of Racha and invited him and his seven sons to a peace celebration in the course of which he had all eight men chained and blinded, after which he annexed Racha.

When the Russian–Ottoman War of 1768–1774 broke out, Solomon and Erekle agreed to enter the war on Russia's side, yet the interests of the three allies were asymmetric. Russia sought to scatter Turkey's forces by starting a fourth, diversionary front in addition to the main battlefields on the Danube, the eastern Mediterranean Sea and Crimea, while Solomon and Erekle wanted to get rid of the Turks from the whole of Western Georgia. In 1769, the German-born Russian General Gottlob Curt Heinrich von Tottleben (d. 1773) crossed the Darial Pass and entered Kartli to join King Erekle's forces. But Tottleben was incompetent, arrogant and treacherous. He quarrelled with and intrigued against his ally Erekle, and twice withdrew from a battlefield. In 1770, King Solomon, with Russian help, forced the Turks to evacuate Kutaisi whereupon Tottleben advanced towards the Ottoman harbour of Poti, against Solomon's advice not to attack in the heat of summer. But Tottleben wanted to expel the Turks from Poti without Solomon's involvement in order to acquire the port for Russia. When he failed to take Poti, he began to intrigue with Mingrelia and Guria against King Solomon. Tottleben was replaced in 1771 by Major General Sukhotin with equally little success, whereupon the Russian Caucasus army was recalled. Russia emerged in 1774 as victor in the war, obtaining by the Treaty of Küçük Kaynarca (Kainarji) free passage through the Bosporus and Dardanelles and the acquisition of Azov and, in the Caucasus, Kabarda among other places, while Erekle and Solomon lost out. Poti and coastal Guria south of the River Rioni remained firmly in Turkish hands and the alliance between the two Georgian rulers deteriorated into distrust and hostility. While Erekle found ways to mend fences with Istanbul, in 1784 Solomon suffered a serious defeat at the hands of the Ottomans and died one month later.[129] As observed by W.E.D. Allen, 'the Treaty of Kuchuk Kainarji was merely an armistice in the mighty conflict which was continued between Russia and Turkey during the six decades between 1768 and 1829, and in this conflict the fate of Georgia was no more than a minor incident.'[130]

V

First Russian Advances into
the North Caucasus

1. The defence pact of 1557 between Kabarda and Russia

Russia's spectacular expansion from the sixteenth century onwards had different objectives depending on the geographic direction.[1] The westward extension aimed at gaining access to the Baltic Sea for trading purposes; a similar commercial goal was pursued by the south-eastern advance along the River Volga to the Caspian Sea. The eastward thrust into Siberia was a commercial and strategic endeavour to obtain raw materials such as furs and metals. The southern advance into today's Ukraine and the expansion south-eastwards into the vast Pontic Steppes and the foothills of the Greater Caucasus Range followed two strategic goals. The first, earlier expansion, beginning with the rise of Muscovy in the fourteenth century, was aimed at pushing the hostile nomadic tribal federations such as the Mongol Golden Horde, the Nogais and the Crimean Tatars as far away as possible from Moscow, and later from other cities and agricultural lands. No urban or agricultural development was possible in an environment continuously ravaged by plundering and man-hunting raids, by which, moreover, immense sums were extorted from Muscovy for ransoming kidnapped Russians. According to the historian Michael Khodarkovsky, as late as the first half of the seventeenth century between 150,000 and 200,000 Russians were abducted, to be either ransomed or sold into slavery.[2] The second objective of expansion was to secure the fertile agricultural lands controlled by the semi-nomadic steppe peoples. The fertile lands within the Pontic Steppe Belt and its continuation towards the Caspian Sea acted like magnets for the Muscovite peasants, who were used to shorter growing seasons and inferior farmland. In the end, there was, at least in those days, no compromise possible between sedentary farmers governed by a centralized state and semi-nomadic steppe dwellers organized in tribal confederations. The agricultural land had to expand and the steppe had to shrink; and the semi-mobile tribes had to leave or change their way of life.

Similarly to the Roman–Byzantine Empire, Russia distinguished between two types of frontier demarcation: on the one hand firm borders between stably organized states such as Russia's with Sweden, Poland or Prussia; these 'inner' borders were controlled by the Russian government and secured by regular troops. On the other hand, there existed softer 'outer' frontiers with the realms of the steppe peoples. These frontiers lacked clear demarcations and the regions behind them were Russian protectorates without being controlled and administered by Russia. The 'outer' frontiers were secured by lines of fortifications similar to the Roman *limes*, placed at a certain distance from the frontier and manned by Cossack 'irregulars'. These defensive lines could extend over more than 1,000 kilometres, and the land between line and frontier was monitored by Cossack patrols and local spies. As long as the frontier was stable and not porous to hostile raids, this system worked well at low cost for the Russian government. But if the irregulars failed to prevent raids, or sometimes for other strategic considerations, the inner border was advanced to the outer frontier and the new outer frontier was accordingly pushed forward, thus reducing the habitat of the nomadic peoples. The vacated land would then be settled by Cossacks, and later by non-Cossack Russian peasants as well.

As history would prove, Russia's advance into the North Caucasus turned out to be the most costly and difficult of all its territorial expansions. The main reason was a clash of incompatible social structures and sets of values which in turn were conditioned by the region's geography. As outlined by Robert Ware and Enver Kisriev, the lowlands and foothills of the North Caucasus were 'vertically', hierarchically organized with a pyramidal social fabric which included several ranks and was dominated by a leader, most usually a prince, who wielded supreme, though not absolute, authority. Decision-making was top-down. The mountain regions with their narrow valleys, on the other hand, had 'horizontal', egalitarian social structures which were regulated by the principles of self-determination, kinship and decision-making in local councils of free men. These alpine societies rejected class distinctions and privileges of nobility. Since Russia's state and society organization was highly centralized and hierarchical it shared similarities with the former while being incompatible with the latter.[3] For example, Russia could conclude a treaty with a lowland prince who in turn secured its implementation among his subjects. In alpine societies however, there was no regional authority to negotiate with and the self-determined communities excluded from the outset the idea of any subjugation under a distant tsar or his representative. At best, there existed intercommunal fraternities. They may be compared to the medieval Swiss mountain confederations which had no superordinate executive body. Decisions of more than local scope were taken by the assembly of community leaders who would in times of war elect a military commander whose authority would expire when the conflict was concluded. The conflict between egalitarian mountaineers and hierarchical lowlanders was especially exacerbated in Kabarda by a clash of incompatible seasonal economic interests: whereas the lowlanders were farmers and their feudal lords were bound to protect their fields from outer aggression, in winter the highlanders would occupy the lowlands with their flocks. Since farmland cannot be used at the same time as pasture, contention over land use was inevitable. Later, in the nineteenth century, a third social model entered the North Caucasus: universalistic and absolutist 'political Islam', whose social model was hierarchical and whose leader, the imam, claimed absolute, God-given authority which he partially delegated to his chosen *na'ib*, or representatives. The Islamic model as typified by Imam Shamil (d. 1871) was in opposition to both the egalitarian and the aristocratic (including the Russian) systems.[4]

The first official contacts between tsarist Russia and the North Caucasian peoples occurred under Tsar Ivan IV 'Grozny'.[5] At that time the south-western part of the North Caucasus belonged to the zone of influence of the Crimean Tatars, who also controlled the Lesser Nogai horsemen roaming in the Kuban. The Nogai Horde was of Mongol stock. In the middle of the sixteenth century, under Muscovite pressure part of the Nogai left their pastures in the lower reaches of the Volga and migrated to the steppes of Azov and the Kuban.[6] The Tatars extorted tribute and slaves and used the region as a transit route for their armies fighting the Iranians in today's Azerbaijan. On the orders of the Ottoman Turks, the Crimean Tatars had conducted four devastating campaigns against Circassia (Cherkessia) and Kabarda in the years 1545, 1546, 1547 and 1551. When Tsar Ivan advanced Russia's border to Kazan (1552) and Astrakhan (1556), several princes and tribal leaders of Circassia, Beshtepe (near today's Pyatigorsk) and neighbouring Kabarda seized the opportunity to seek Russian protection from the predatory Crimeans.[7] Among the Circassians[8] both types of society existed: the egalitarian, such as the Abzakh (Abadzekh), Natukhai and Shapsugs who

65. Medieval defence and residential towers in Egikal. Jeyrakh Valley, Ingushetia, Russian Federation. Photo 2016.

came together in rather loose associations called *jamaats*, and the aristocratic, of which the Kabardians, who spoke an east Circassian language, were the most prominent.[9] At the top of aristocratic Circassian societies stood the princes, called *pshi*, of whom the most prominent was the ruler or *pshi-tkhamade*. Below the princes ranked the hereditary nobility, *tlakotle*, and below them the impoverished petty nobles, *dezhenugo*, who ruled individual villages called *auls*. The executive arm of the *pshi-tkhamade* consisted of the *biekol* who enforced law and order and collected taxes. The majority of Circassians were peasants who were divided into free farmers (*tfokotl*), who had to fulfil duties imposed by the nobility, and the former slaves (*azat*) who had either bought their freedom or had been set free by their masters. The free peasants, the *biekol*-officers and the nobility formed the armed retinue of the rulers. Then followed the tiny category of slaves (*og*) who nevertheless possessed some property rights and those slaves called *pshitl* whose property their masters could confiscate at any time. At the bottom ranked the domestic slaves, *unaut*, who were without any rights and remained the unrestricted property of their owners.[10]

Kabardian society too was highly structured and counted up to eleven different classes ranging from slaves without rights up to the princes. Kabardians and Circassians cultivated an interesting custom, the *ataliq* educational system, which was designed to ensure a tight social cohesion between princely and gentry classes, and which was described in the early nineteenth century by European travellers such as the Frenchman Taitbout de Marigny who travelled to Circassia three times between 1818 and 1824, and the German Karl Friedrich Neumann.[11] Princely young boys were given to their vassal nobles for education, above all in the military arts. The teaching vassal became the foster-father (*ataliq*) and his sons the foster-brothers of the young prince. The latter would in adulthood become brothers-in-arms.[12] Since there existed no national authority enforcing law and order, travelling through Circassia was dangerous. Several travellers of the nineteenth century described that it was impossible to travel without having a *konak* (or *kinak*), a 'friend of the guest' from the tribe whose area one was crossing. The *konak* acted as a

66. The medieval graveyard of Dargavs. Archaeological investigations showed that some of the dead were buried in a kind of small wooden boat which was then placed inside a burial house. It was probably believed that souls had to cross a river on the way to the underworld. The dead were buried clothed and usually with grave goods. When the plague broke out in the seventeenth century, the burial houses were also used as quarantine stations. In the burial houses which had deep crypts, members of the same family were laid to rest over generations. North Ossetia–Alania, Russian Federation. Photo 2011.

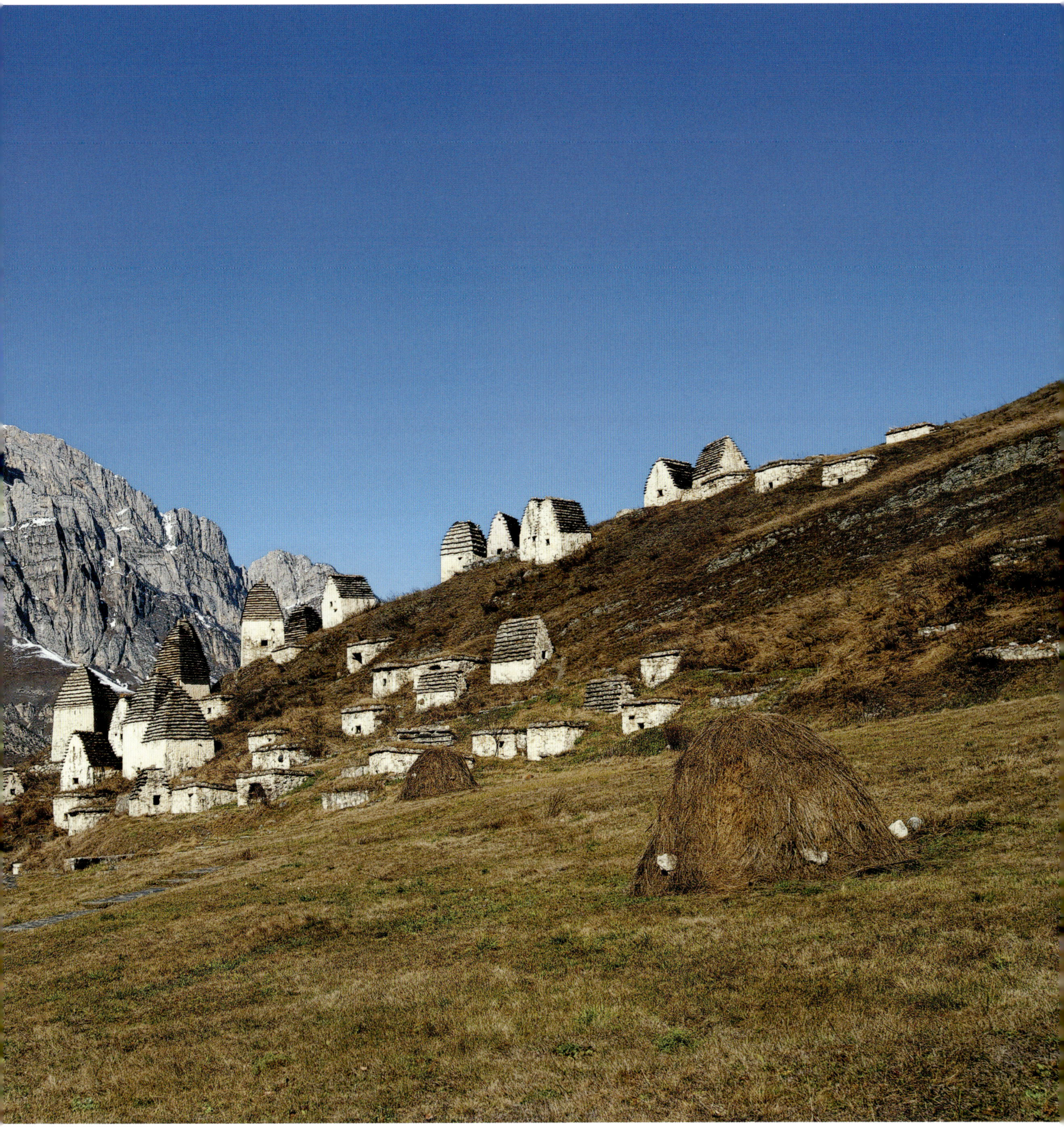

67. Defence tower in the ruined village of Galiata. Digor Valley, North Ossetia-Alania, Russian Federation. Photo 2017.

protector, guaranteed the safety of the foreign traveller and was his potential avenger should he suffer harm.[13]

East of the Kabardians lived the Ossetians, a part of whom were their vassals. The Ossetians, too, had a hierarchy of social classes. As described by the British traveller and explorer John F. Baddeley, the lowest two classes were the serfs and slaves. The serfs whom he called 'Kasaks' were attached to the land and could only be sold with it, but the slaves, 'the *Karavesh*, were bought and sold like cattle'.[14] Further east were the self-determined and egalitarian societies of the Ingush and Chechens and, south of them, the Khevsurs who lived on both sides of the Greater Caucasus Range, the Tushetians north of the range and the Pshavs south of the range. Like the Svans in Georgia, these peoples built mountain villages with numerous stone towers which served as secure dwellings in case of attacks from other, hostile villages and as protection from blood-vengeance – these towers were symbols of egalitarian micro-societies without any law enforcement by external authorities. The Chechens, Ingush and numerous mountain Dagestanis represented no nations, only communities of people speaking the same or a similar language; their identity derived from their tribal affiliation and tribal alliances.[15] In the East Caucasus, in Dagestan, the Laks and Dargans were structured in classes; the alpine Avars and Lezgians lived in self-determined *jamaats*, while the lower-dwelling Avars and Lezgians were often ruled by khans.[16] Finally the Turkic Kumyks, who shared linguistic and cultural affinities with the Ottoman Turks, lived in a highly hierarchical social structure led by the *shamkhal*.

As mentioned above, in 1557 Prince Temryuk (Kemirgoko) of Kabarda (d. 1571) concluded an alliance with Tsar Ivan which was sealed in 1561 by Tsar Ivan's marriage with Temryuk's daughter Kuchenei (Gueshchenei), who in Russia was called Maria Cherkasskaya. A year before, Temryuk had sent one of his sons, called Saltanuk (Sultanuko), to Moscow where he converted to Christianity.[17] He adopted the name Mikhail Temryukovich and became a powerful member of Ivan's *oprichnina*, his military administrative body. But in 1571 the Kabardian prince was executed when Tsar Ivan suspected him of treacherous contacts with the Crimean Tatar khan Devlet Giray (r. 1551–1577).[18] While several Kabardian rulers cultivated Russian alliances up to the mid-eighteenth century, others opted for arrangements with Crimea. However, it soon became obvious that Russians and North Caucasian rulers had different interpretations of such treaties. For Russia, a treaty sealed by an oath of loyalty to the tsar represented an 'eternal' submission under the tsar's sovereignty and to cancel it was perceived as rebellion. But for the North Caucasian rulers, such treaties were pacts between equals and they felt free to conclude parallel alliances with other powers. For them, to end the validity or to request a renegotiation of such a treaty was no rebellion, but merely an assessment that the arrangement was, within the frame of a new political constellation, no longer favourable. In brief, the North Caucasian rulers had multiple loyalties, just as they easily exchanged religious confessions according to who was their main overlord. That the Kabardian ruling classes had a relaxed approach to religious matters is also clear from the fact that Russian Orthodox Christians and Sunni Muslims could coexist in the same family, an arrangement that would have been inconceivable in Chechnya or Dagestan. It must be stressed that the first Kabardian–Russian defensive pact in no way meant that Kabarda had opted for a 'voluntary unification' with Russia, as claimed by some Soviet and post-Soviet Russian historians.[19] The Kabardians valued Russian help against the Tatars, but did not feel bound by any 'eternal oath' to the tsar. When in 1720 Tsar Peter failed to give military support to the Kabardians as they faced a major Crimean Tatar invasion, many Kabardian leaders turned away from Moscow and submitted to the Tatars.[20] Nor can the Ottoman-Russian Treaty of Küçük Kaynarca (1774) be claimed as the date of Kabarda's becoming part of Russia, for its allocation to Russia was decided without the involvement of the Kabardian leaders, who refused to submit. As explained by Michael Khodarkovsky,

when in 1779 the nobles of Greater (western) Kabarda refused to swear allegiance to Russia and declared that they had traditionally been under Russian protectorship as guests or allies (kinaks) but not subjects, Russian troops marched into Kabarda, forcing the Kabardians to sue for peace and to pledge unconditional allegiance.[21]

In 1552, a Circassian delegation secured a rapid agreement from Moscow to form a mutual defence alliance, which was quickly followed by joint military operations. As soon as 1553, a joint Circassian–Russian army repulsed a Crimean Tatar attack on Kaluga and Serpukhov, south of Moscow. While in 1554 a new and bloody Tatar slave raid on Circassia found the Circassians unprepared, in the next year a strong detachment of Russian musketeers warded off another Tatar attack. Following up on their success, in 1556 a combined Circassian–Russian force attacked Crimean possessions in western Circassia. However, in 1559/60, the joint attack of Circassian troops and Zaporizhzhian Cossacks from central Ukraine under the *ataman* (military commander) Dmytro Vyshnevetsky failed to capture the Ottoman fortress of Azov (Azaq). This failure prompted several rulers of western Circassian aristocratic tribes who had previously been pagan or nominally Christian to convert to Islam.[22] In the absence of Russian protection, such conversion was the only easy way for western Circassians dwelling within the reach of the Crimean Tatars to escape enslavement. The Ottoman–Crimean Tatar slave-hunting raids into Circassia were a plague. They began in 1475, even before the Ottomans had subjugated the Crimeans, when Sultan Mehmet II ordered a raid into Circassia in which thousands of Circassians were kidnapped.[23] As with the future Russian involvement in Kabarda, the Circassian–Crimean and Kabardian–Crimean conflicts also bore characteristics of a proxy war between the Ottomans and Russia. These intricate conflicts forced many other Circassian tribes to decide which side to take. The large western Circassian Zhane tribe and the Turkic Karachais opted for the Crimean Tatars while the equally Turkic Balkars chose Moscow. As for the Shapsug, Abzakh and Natukhai tribes who dwelled in remote mountains, they could afford to ignore both opponents. In the words of the historian of the region, Walter Richmond, 'it would be these three tribes who presented Russia with the fiercest and most uncompromising opposition in the nineteenth century.'[24]

For Russia, Kabarda's value rested not only in its opposition to Crimean sovereignty, but in its strategic geographic location, for it controlled both the through-route from Crimea to Dagestan, and also the northern approach to the Darial Pass leading into Georgia, the future Georgian Military Highway. The Kabardian nobles, for their part, sought from Russia protection from the rapacious Crimean Tatars and military

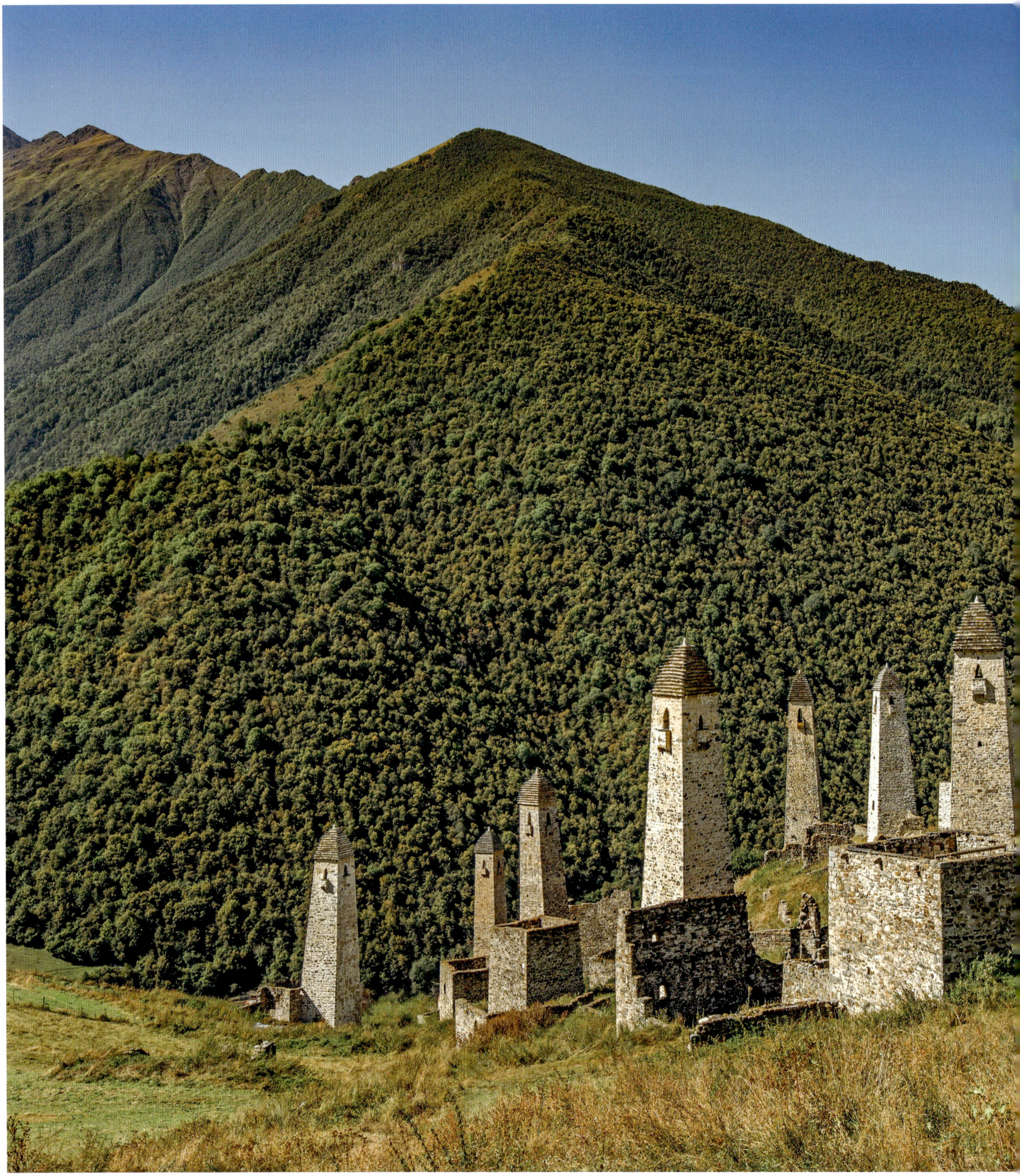

support in containing the highlanders. Not surprising for a tribal confederation such as the Kabardian, internal conflicts arose when Temryuk concluded his alliance with Russia, since his opponent in Kabarda, Sheapshoko Kaitukin (Qeitiqwe) allied himself with the Tatars. In the ensuing war of 1562–1563, Russian forces assisted Temryuk in crushing Kaitukin's revolt. In order to establish a permanent military presence in the central North Caucasus, in 1567 (or 1563) Russian musketeers built a fort called Terskaya Krepost at the junction of the Rivers Sunzha and Terek, north-east of Grozny in today's Chechnya, which was in those days part of Lesser Kabarda.[25] Feeling provoked by the Kabardian–Russian pact, in the same year Ottoman Crimean forces invaded Kabarda and abducted countless young women and children. When the Ottoman army returned two years later from its failed attack on Astrakhan, the Kabardians took revenge by annihilating the retreating Turkish troops. In the ensuing peace negotiations, Russia agreed in 1570 to dismantle Terskaya Krepost. It was rebuilt in 1578, but, as mentioned in the previous chapter, again destroyed in 1583 by Osman Pasha. As a replacement, the fortified town of Tersky Gorodok was built in 1588 in the estuary of the Terek north of the Shamkhalate. However, setbacks occurred when the Crimean Tatars first defeated Temryuk in 1570 and then in 1571 burned Moscow, at the time a wooden city, with the exception of the Kremlin which was built from stone and brick. According to some historians, when the Tatars returned via the Kuban, Temryuk launched a counterattack during which he lost his life. According to other, more plausible sources, Devlet Giray defeated Temryuk in 1570 and forced him to join his subsequent attack on Moscow.[26] This latter version would explain why Tsar Ivan had Temryuk's son Saltanuk executed in 1571. At Temryuk's death, power passed to his younger brother Kanbulat (d. 1589). However, under his and his successor Mamstruk's rule their hold on the Kabardians slipped. In the 1590s, Kaitukin's son Prince Ghazi seized power from Temryuk's clan, which dealt a blow to Russian prestige.[27]

It was not only in Kabarda, but also in the Shamkhalate that Russia's early expansion bore no fruit. While the local title of *shamkhal* appears as early as the end of the fourteenth century, the historically verifiable dynasty of the *shamkhals* of Kumyk (Kumuk) and Tarki emerged for the first time in 1553. The Shamkhalate had two poles, which reflected its hybrid nature: the stronghold of Kumyk in the Lak Mountains and the Caspian harbour of Tarki.

---

68. The former village of Erzi counts eight medieval defence towers up to 30 m high and the ruins of 49 residential towers. Ingushetia, Russian Federation. Photo 2016.

The first served the *shamkhals* as summer residence, the latter as a winter dwelling since the winter pastures were located in Tarki's hinterland. In 1641 the Shamkhalate finally split into the principalities of Kumyk and Tarki.[28] As mentioned above, in the last two decades of the sixteenth century the Shamkhalate was in league with the Ottomans, which brought it into conflict with Russia. Unlike the majority of Kabardian nobles who welcomed the Russian intervention, the *shamkhals* remained opposed to Moscow's interference and the campaign of General Buturlin of 1604–1605 ended in total disaster for the Russians (see above). At the death of Tsar Boris Godunov in 1605, the 'Time of Troubles' known as *Smuta* engulfed Russia, lasting till Michael Romanov's ascension to the throne in February 1613.[29] During these trouble-filled years, the Caucasus moved far out of the political focus of the mutually antagonistic, short-lived rulers in Moscow. Nevertheless the Cossacks upheld a Russian presence in the North Caucasus; but between 1606 and 1636, the Tatars conducted seven major slave raids into Circassia and Kabarda which were left defenceless.[30]

2. The Cossacks and the first Russian military lines

While the Cossacks were far from being autochthonous inhabitants of the North Caucasus, they nevertheless shaped its history and culture. To begin with, in the sixteenth century, the Cossacks were formed of freebooting communities, called hosts, of self-governing horsemen who also took non-combatant women into their groups. Their designation 'Cossack' has the same Turkic Cuman root as Kazakh, meaning 'free man', 'freebooter'. Their medieval predecessors from the thirteenth century on were mainly of Turkic stock, but from the sixteenth century the Cossacks were increasingly joined by Slavs such as Russians and Poles, Balto-Slavic Lithuanians and people from today's Ukraine, thus becoming a Slav–Tatar ethnic hybrid. While Muscovy as a state had fought the mobile steppe horsemen since the fourteenth century, from the sixteenth century numerous impoverished Russian peasants and other individuals restricted by servitude found a self-determined, mobile way of life more attractive than remaining chained to a piece of land owned by some boyar. Moscow quickly realized the value of these unruly communities and with presents and subsidies incited them to harass its Ottoman enemy and their Crimean Tatar vassal. They acted as commissioned pirates of the steppes, similar to the English 'Sea Dogs' enlisted by Queen Elizabeth I as raiders against Spain. While the Ukrainian hosts were the most numerous, the largest host existing at the fringes of the North Caucasus was the **Don Host** which dwelled along the middle and lower Don. The Don Cossacks were valued allies of Tsar Ivan IV and in 1569 played a decisive role in the destruction of the Ottoman expeditionary force sent against Astrakhan. The tsars deployed the Don Cossacks as an unofficial tool to harass the Ottomans in the same way that the Ottomans themselves used the Crimean Tatars to raid and weaken Russia. Both governments disavowed any responsibility for the actions of their clients whom they officially discredited as runaway serfs and bandits.[31] Sometimes the Don Cossacks were too audacious, as in 1637 when in a *coup de main* they captured the Ottoman fortress of Azov and offered it to Tsar Michael. But the tsar feared war with Turkey and ordered the Cossacks to withdraw.

South of the Don Host was the **Black Sea Host** whose members lived along the northern shore of River Kuban. The nucleus of the Black Sea Host grew in the seventeenth century after the destruction of the Lesser Nogai Horde, and again when survivors of the failed uprising of the rebellious Don Cossack leader Stenka Razin (d. 1671) sought a sanctuary from tsarist repression in the Kuban. Their ranks were strengthened after 1783 by resettled Zaporizhzhian Cossacks. In 1860, the Black Sea Host became the **Kuban Host** within the Kuban Province. Considerably older than the Kuban Host was the **Terek Host** whose settlement area lay along the middle and lower River Terek. The earliest free Cossacks to construct their *stanitsas* (military settlements) in the Terek and Sunzha region probably arrived in the early sixteenth century. Before the nucleus of the Terek Host emerged with the reconstruction of Terskaya Krepost in 1578, the smaller Cossack **Greben** (Ridge) **Host** had been involved in the construction of the first fort in 1567 (or 1563). Although the second fort was razed in 1583, several Cossack *stanitsas* were by then established along the Terek, and the Cossack ranks were reinforced by unaligned Cossacks emigrating from the Volga. The Terek Cossacks served the tsar's orders several times, for example when they suppressed a revolt in Astrakhan in 1614 or when they fought the Nogais. In 1646, after the **Belgorod Line** some 600 km south of Moscow had come under renewed Tatar attacks, Terek and Don Cossacks jointly repelled the Tatar invaders. Although Terek Cossacks helped suppress Stenka Razin's revolt, many defeated Cossack rebels fled from the tsarist army to the Terek Host where they were welcomed as refugees.

The schism (or *Raskol*) which occurred within the Russian Orthodox Church between the majority of believers who accepted the ritual and liturgical reforms introduced by Patriarch Nikon (in office 1652–1666) and a minority of so-called Old Believers, provoked tensions and fights among the Cossacks. Following the anathematization of the Raskolniki at the 1666–1667 synod and their ensuing persecution, a few Raskolnik Cossacks fled to the Greben Host which was traditionally more religious and conservative than the Terek Host.[32] The majority of Old Believer Don Cossacks were less fortunate. They had found traditional Cossack refuge in the Host, but when they began to propagandize around 1683 for their Old Belief, troubles began. A Cossack delegation was sent to Moscow to hear the position of the tsar who in his response condemned the rebellious Old Believers and the Don Cossacks sheltering them. The Raskolnik Don Cossacks fled to Kabarda in 1688. In 1689 they retaliated by launching a counterattack on the Don Host. But feeling insecure, about a thousand Raskolnik Cossacks migrated in the winter of 1690–91 to northern Dagestan where they placed themselves under the protection of the Muslim *shamkhal* of Tarki. When Russian officials approached the *shamkhal* to hand over the 'renegades', he refused, since it would go against local custom to betray his guests. The Raskolniki replied to the official offer of pardon, that the Muslim *shamkhal* was 'a just tsar who would

69. Ruins of the village of Alagir located high above the modern town of the same name. North Ossetia–Alania, Russian Federation. Photo 2019.

124 | HISTORY OF THE CAUCASUS: VOLUME 2

Sea of Azov

DON COSSACKS

AZOV-MOZDOK LINE (1778)

BLACK SEA COSSACKS

Pavlovska

Temryuk (1778)

BLACK SEA–KUBAN–TEREK LINE (1793)

River Kuban

Anapa (1828)

CIRCASSIANS
1864

Yekaterinograd (Krasnodar) 1793

Sucuk-Kale (Novorossiysk, 1829)

BLACK SEA COAST
1829

Veliyaminovskoye (Tuapse, 1838)

KARACHAIS
1828

Gagra (1830)

ABKHAZETI
1810

Sukhumi (1810)

Black Sea

OTTOMA

Map 5. The Russian conquest of the Caucasus by late 1829 and the foundation of Russian forts to 1838

- ••• Russian military lines and year of completion
- -- Border of the Russian Empire in late 1829
- -- Regions under firm Russian control in 1801
- ▪ Conquered states and peoples
- ◨ Regions under no or weak Russian control in 1829
- ♜ Major Russian fort (and year of construction)
- ♛ Major fort of the Imamate
- — Georgian Military Highway, 1783 (Mozdok branch completed 1817, Yekaterinograd branch 1825)
- ○ Major cities
- — River

FIRST RUSSIAN ADVANCES INTO THE NORTH CAUCASUS | 125

RUSSIAN EMPIRE

ASTRAKHAN GOVERNORATE

Astrakhan

River Volga

Alexandrovsk
Stavropol, 1777

CAUCASUS GOVERNORATE 1803

River Kuma

AZOV–MOZDOK LINE (1777/78)

Georgiyevsk (1777)

TEREK COSSACKS

GREBEN COSSACKS
(merged 1712 with Terek Cossacks)

Mozdok (1762)

Kizlyar (1735)

KIZLYAR–MOZDOK LINE (1763)

Nalchik (1818)

River Terek

SUNZHA LINE (1817/18)

Terskaya Krepost (1567)

Svyatoi Krest (1722)

KABARDIANS
1774/1827

Grozny (1818)

Caspian Sea

UPPER SVANETI 1858

GREAT CAUCASUS

Vladikavkaz (1784/90)

Dargo

CHECHENS 1859

SHAMKHALATE 1786/93

Khunzakh

Akhulgo

Gunib

Kakhib

Gamsutl

MINGRELIA 1803

IMERETI 1804

OSSETIA

EAST DAGESTAN 1859

KAITAG 1813–1825

DERBENT 1806

GURIA 1810

GEORGIAN MILITARY HIGHWAY

Tbilisi

SAMTSKHE/ AKHALTSIKHE 1829

KARTLI–KAKHETI 1801

DJARO–BELOKAN 1803

KURA
VASSAL, 1812

QUBA 1806

ELISU 1804

River Kura

SHAKI 1805

SHURAGEL 1805

GANJA 1804

SHIRVAN 1805

BAKU 1806

YEREVAN 1828

Lake Sevan

KARABAKH 1805

EMPIRE

NAKHCHIVAN 1828

River Aras

TALYSH 1813

Lake Van

IRAN

N

not impose upon their religion or liberties'.[33] Trusting in their protector, the Raskolnik Cossacks grew bolder and harassed Cossack forts and *stanitsas* loyal to the tsar, threatening to isolate the Terek Cossacks. In 1692, tsarist musketeers and local Chechens ambushed the Raskolnik Cossacks near the River Sunzha and wiped them out.[34] Soon afterwards, in the early 1700s, the Terek Cossacks reconstructed the Russian forts which had been destroyed or abandoned after Buturlin's debacle of 1605. When Tsar Peter undertook his Caspian Campaign in 1722, the Terek Host was moved southwards again to man the newly built Svyatoi Krest (Holy Cross) fortress which stood near the northern shore of the River Sulak. As was most often the case, the role of the Cossacks consisted in first advancing a frontier and subsequently defending it.

The cooperation with tsarist Russia profoundly changed the spirit and structure of the Cossack hosts over time. In the beginning they were egalitarian communities open to newcomers and refugees, provided they were combative. Their military and political leader, the *ataman*, was elected in an assembly called a *krug*, yet the *krug* retained the authority to decide on policy towards external powers and on war. Cossack hosts were military democracies of free men. As of 1635, with the construction of the 800-kilometre-long defensive Russian **Belgorod Line**, the Cossacks' role and *modus operandi* began to change. The period of *Smuta* had revealed only too clearly that the southern frontier of Russia remained exposed to Tatar and Zaporizhzhian attacks that could depopulate entire regions, which is why the Russian government decided to replace the previous porous frontiers with fortified and patrolled demarcation lines. The new Belgorod Line, whose command was located at Belgorod, was around 400 kilometres south of the previous **Abatis Line** which had followed the middle course of the River Oka. As an intermediary step, a chain of fortified and garrisoned towns were built further south, including Voronezh and Liven (1586), Kursk (1587), Yelets (1592), Belgorod (1598), Valuyki (1599) and Tsarev Borisov (1600). Thanks to the Belgorod line, the settled agricultural zone moved about 100 to 200 kilometres to the south; it stretched over 500 kilometres from Okhtyrka in the west to Kozlov (Michurinsk) in the north-east. Its continuations, the **Simbirsk Line** (1636–1648) and the **Trans-Kama Line** (1652–1686) extended it to a shield 1,800 kilometres long protecting Moscow from attack from the south and east. These lines were boundaries which could not be

---

70. The ruined mountain village of Gamsutl. The village once counted almost 3,000 inhabitants; the last villager died in 2015. Gunibsky Rayon, Dagestan, Russian Federation. Photo 2021.

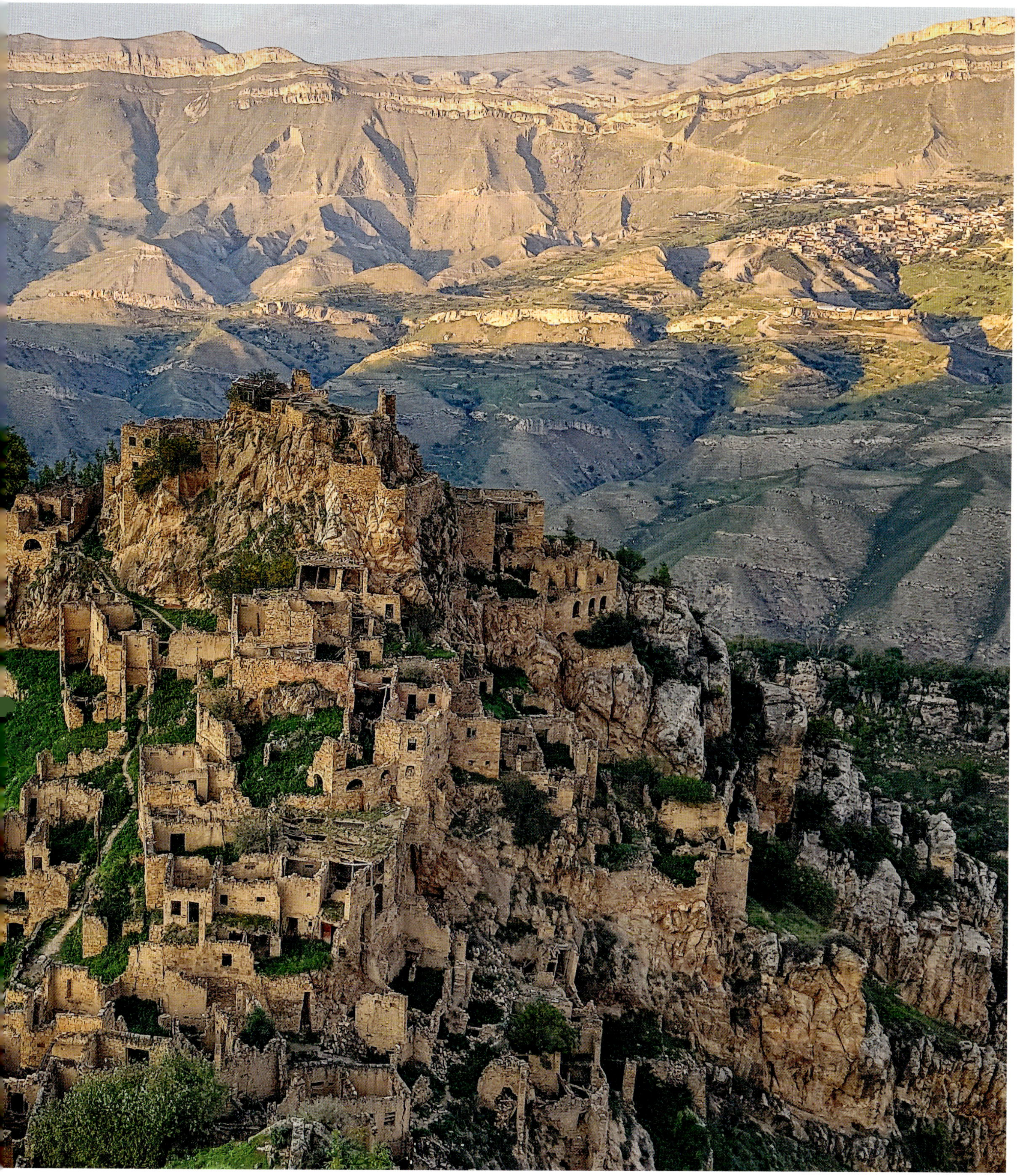

71. Abandoned castle of Mansau from the fourteenth century at the village of Khanaz. Digor region, North Ossetia–Alania, Russian Federation. Photo 2019.

crossed without official authorization. Since the Belgorod Line marked the separation of Russian agricultural land under the rule of government in the north from the realm of Cossacks and nomads in the south, it also signalled the transition from serfdom and legal prosecution to self-determination and freedom. Exactly like the Great Walls of China, the Russian lines were also built to prevent Russians from emigrating into the steppes.

In spite of these obstacles, the increasingly heavy taxes and burdens of compulsory work inflicted on the peasants, as well as compulsory military service, led to a growing flow of serfs and oppressed people illegally crossing the border to join the Cossack hosts. This created problems for both Cossacks and tsar. The Don and Terek Hosts had only limited economic resources and there was a dearth of young women, while the Russian government and the boyars could not afford to lose thousands of soldiers, forced labourers and taxpayers every year. In 1685, the government banned the Cossacks from accepting fleeing serfs, whereupon the Don Host strictly forbade any agricultural activity. Already, seven years earlier, the Don Host had begun to impose on newcomers a tough trial period before they were admitted as Cossacks. More drastic restrictions were to follow at the Treaty of Constantinople in 1700 when the Ottomans and Russia decided to stop all raiding in the steppe, and in Tsar Peter's *ukaz* (decree) of 1701 which forbade all raids against the Ottoman Empire unless they were sanctioned in advance by Moscow.[35] In a sense, the Cossacks found themselves on the same side of the fence as their traditional opponents, the Tatar steppe raiders. They were forced by the Russian government, which paid them with ammunition, arms and grain, to change their economic model and way of life. After a renewed Don Cossack civil war, between the traditionalists and those prepared to adapt, came to an end in 1708 in the complete victory of the latter, Tsar Peter took drastic measures. From 1709, the *ataman* was no longer elected by the *krug* in the Don Host's capital of Cherkassk, but was instead nominated by the tsar to whom alone he answered. Twelve years later, the Don Host lost its special status of a stand-alone political entity, since responsibility for managing Cossack affairs was transferred from the Foreign Ministry to the Ministry of War. The Cossacks were downgraded from a free force which cooperated with the tsar on an ad hoc basis to an irregular army which was expected to fight when and wherever ordered. The Don Host and other Cossacks traded their freedom for lifelong military service in order to secure their traditional law, customs, and tax exemption. The various hosts kept their juridical and territorial enclaves to which access was barred to state bureaucrats and ordinary, non-Cossack Russians.[36] By the latter measure, the government ensured that the Cossacks maintained their combativeness and *esprit de corps*. The Cossacks were no longer an open fighting community which made up losses by welcoming newcomers, but a closed society where membership was hereditary. The Russian government now exercised full control over its population: the peasants and serfs had to serve in the regular army and the Cossacks were lifelong irregulars. It was this system that allowed Russia to embark in its countless wars during the nineteenth century; the sheer amount of available manpower usually compensated for deficiencies in armament, often poor General Staff planning and, in the case of the Caucasus, ignorance of the battle terrain. The various Cossack hosts used different combat methods: the Black Sea and Kuban Cossacks fought mainly with long lances, but the Cossacks serving on the central and eastern Caucasian front lines preferred to use sabres. This variation in armament meant that the lancers were superior as cohesive formations fighting on flat ground while the sabre fighters were superior in close combat and in hilly terrain.[37]

Russia applied the expansionary strategy of constructing military lines also on its eastern flanks.[38] After the Belgorod Line had proven its value, the **Tsaritsyn Line**, stretching from the Volga to the Don, was completed in 1718, which was succeeded in the 1750s by the more easterly **Orenburg Line**. In the south-west, the **Dnieper Line** connected the rivers Dnieper and Donets and hindered the Crimean Tatars in their attacks northwards. In the North Caucasus, General Admiral Fyodor Matveyevich Apraksin (d. 1728) launched a murderous attack on the Kuban Nogai Horde in 1711 with the help of a strong Kalmyk cavalry army, which showed that combined attacks by Russian musketeers and Kalmyk riders could defeat the feared Nogai horsemen.[39] In the following years, civil war-like conditions prevailed in Kabarda where pro-Russian and pro-Crimean factions struggled for supremacy. The Terek Cossacks too came under heavy pressure in around 1718 from the Chechens, who harassed them as soon as they left the protective walls of their *stanitsas*. In 1720 the Chechens were defeated by a combined force of Terek and Don Cossacks as well as Russophile Kabardians. But this success was short-lived and the Chechens' fight against Russian dominance would last till 1859.[40] Although Tsar Peter's death cut short Russia's Caucasian ambitions, in 1736 the German-born Field Marshal von Münnich (d. 1767) formulated what would become Russia's grand strategy in the south for almost two centuries: to annex Crimea and conquer the North Caucasian plains in order, ultimately, to capture Istanbul (Constantinople) and win free access to the Mediterranean Sea.[41] The stage was set for a foreign policy that lasted till the tsardom collapsed in 1917. Slightly more than a century after von Münnich's vision, Tsar Nicholas I (r. 1825–1855) wrote in a memorandum to his son and successor, Alexander II (r. 1855–1881):

Our aim is, and remains, Constantinople ... For a long time England has had the supremacy on the ocean; but the same position which we have attained on land will be occupied by our maritime power. The possession of Constantinople, the Dardanelles, the whole littoral of the Black Sea is indispensable for us. The Emperor Alexander [I, r. 1801–1825] *claimed Constantinople and the Dardanelles, when Napoleon proposed the partition of Turkey to him;* [...] *We have to continue our struggle with the tribes of the Caucasus.*[42]

In the North Caucasus, the **Kizlyar–Mozdok Line**, completed in 1763, ran from Kizlyar in the Terek Delta to Mozdok in Kabarda. The continuation westward from Mozdok to Pavlovskaya and in 1778 to the Black Sea coast north of the Taman Peninsula formed the **Asov-Mozdok Line.** Following the kidnapping and death in Dagestan of the German botanist and explorer Samuel Gottlieb Gmelin (d. 1774), who was in Russian service, by Ahmad Khan Usmi of the Kaitag, a brief punitive expedition was conducted to Derbent without further consequences.[43] Five years after the completion of the Asov-Mozdok Line, in 1783, the western Nogai were ejected from the plains on the right, that is the northern and eastern banks of the River Kuban and the vacant land was given to the Cossack Kuban Host. Many Nogai moved south into Crimean Circassia and the **Kuban Line** was established south of the previous central section of the Asov-Mozdok Line. The practice of ethnic engineering was of course nothing new in the Caucasus. By now Byzantium, the Abbasid Caliphate, the various Turkic conquerors and Iran had all practised ethnic displacement on a large scale; in the nineteenth century Russia would 'only' magnify its scope. The new combined **Black Sea–Kuban–Terek** Line was completed in 1793; it extended the whole way from the Black Sea to the Caspian and cut the North Caucasus into a Russian-dominated northern half and a tribal-dominated south whose western part was under nominal Ottoman suzerainty. However, Greater and Lesser Kabarda and also North Ossetia remained outside the Terek Line; Russia claimed these territories, but was unable to control them consistently. Both Kabardas were ceded by Ottoman Turkey at the Treaty of Küçük Kaynarca in 1774 and pacified five years later.[44] South of Azov, which was conquered for good by Cossacks and Russian troops in 1736, the Cossacks built a *stanitsa* near the site of ancient Tmutarakan which had been settled by the Kiev Rus at the end of the tenth century.[45] Out of the *stanitsa* the town of Temryuk emerged in 1860. The Ottomans reacted to the continued advance of Cossacks and Russian troops which threatened Crimea and Tatar Kuban by erecting the fort of Sucuk-Kale (in Russian Sudzhuk-kale), whose bay and port had been occupied in the Middle Ages by the Genoese, and by employing French engineers around 1781 to fortify the harbour of Anapa located 50 kilometres to the north-west.[46] Nevertheless, in 1828 Anapa fell to Russia and in 1829, the Ottomans were forced to cede Sucuk-Kale to Russia which greatly expanded the harbour now called Novorossiysk. The foundation of new Cossack and Russian cities went hand in hand with the advance of the military lines: after Mozdok (1762), Alexandrovsk (today's Stavropol) and Georgiyevsk on the Mozdok–Azov Line (1777), Vladikavkaz (1784/90) and Yekaterinodar (today's Krasnodar, 1793) were founded by Kuban Cossacks, followed by Nalchik (1818), today's capital of Kabardino-Balkaria, and the Chechen capital Grozny in the same year.[47] Simultaneously with the construction of forts and new cities, Cossacks established their *stanitsas*, which often meant that local peasants had to move to the mountains. When freed Russian serfs began to pour into the North Caucasus from the 1860s on, the competition for fertile land expanded into a triangular conflict between local Caucasians, Cossacks and Russian settlers.

3. Mongol Kalmyks in the north-eastern Caucasus

In the seventeenth and eighteenth centuries a Mongol people interfered in the Caucasus for the last time in history, albeit only at its northern and north-eastern fringe and sporadically. The westward migration of the western Mongol Oirat Kalmyks,[48] which occurred in several waves between 1606 and the 1680s, was triggered by the heavy pressure exerted by the expanding eastern Mongols and Kazakhs.[49] The first to emigrate was the Torghut tribe led by **Khoo-Örlög Tayishi**[50] (r. before 1604–1644) to be followed in the next year by Dalay Bagatur Tayishi's Dörbet nomads. They soon clashed with the Russian garrisons posted in the former khanate of Sibir. Since both Oirat groups refused to acknowledge Russian sovereignty, they continued their peregrination in a south-western direction and displaced the Nogai as they advanced. By the year 1632 they had reached the River Volga and then poured into the Caspian lowlands and the north-eastern Caucasian steppe while the Nogai sought refuge first in the region of Azov, later in the Kuban and finally in Tatar Crimea where they reinforced the Crimean troops. By evicting the Nogai from the Volga region, the Kalmyks did Russia a great service, since the Volga Nogai used to kidnap numerous Russians to sell as slaves.

The Buddhist Kalmyks now formed a veritable Mongolian Buddhist island between the Muslim Turkic peoples, the Bashkirs, Kazakhs, Nogai and Crimean Tatars, and the Orthodox Russians. Around the year 1641/42, however, other Oirat groups of the Dzungar and Khoshut migrated westward as well, putting pressure on Khoo-Örlög's Torghuts and causing him to move to the south-west. There, he met his death in 1644 attacking Kabarda. Under Khoo-Örlög's son and successor **Daichin Tayishi** (r. 1647–1661) a rapprochement took place between the Kalmyks and Russia. In January 1654, Zaporizhzhian Cossacks had taken an oath of allegiance to the Russian tsar Alexei I which led Poland–Lithuania to forge an offensive alliance with Crimea against Russia. Russia now needed an ally. The Kalmyks, who had a strong cavalry and an inexhaustible reservoir of horses, formed a perfect complement to the Russian foot-soldiers, armed with musket and cannon, and the slow Russian cavalry. The first three Russian–Kalmyk treaties of 1655, 1656 and 1657 were ineffective. Like the Kabardians, the Kalmyks interpreted such treaties as military alliances between equals, whereas the Russians understood them as a commitment between vassal and monarch.[51] Only the fourth Russian–Kalmyk treaty between

Moscow and Daichin Tayishi and his son and successor **Puntsuk Tayishi** (r. 1661–1669) had beneficial results for both sides: the Kalmyks and the Zaporizhzhian Cossacks dealt the Crimean Tatars several devastating defeats. In return, the Russians allowed the Kalmyks to nomadize along the Don, erecting for their defence against further Dzungar attacks a fortification line along the Ural River manned with 2,000 musketeers.[52] Russia had understood that it was much more advantageous to enlist the Kalmyks as raiders and enemies of the Crimean Tatars than to try driving them back east again.

This strategy, which the Russians pursued from 1661 until about 1722/23, aimed at establishing a single powerful ruler among the Kalmyks, who, in return, would defend the south-eastern edge of the Russian Empire. In several respects, the Russian tsars used the Kalmyks in a similar way to how they did the Cossacks: they brought them into their dependency by payments and gifts and by restricting their access to firearms and ammunition. At first, the tsars forbade any sale of muskets, bullets and gunpowder to the Kalmyks; as of 1697 they occasionally granted a few light cannon, but these were operated by Russian gunners. As with the Cossacks, the Russians chose to let the Kalmyks fight with bows and arrows and assist them with units of Russian musketeers and dragoons. During the seventeenth century, this combination was ideal against the Tatars and Nogai, since the handling of a musket was cumbersome and in the course of a short battle it would fire no more than twelve to fifteen bullets, while a skilled Kalmyk horseman could accurately fire an arrow every ten seconds.[53]

Puntsuk's successor **Ayuka Khan** (r. 1669–1724) attempted to implement an independent policy, but internal Kalmyk conflicts and threats from Khoshut tribes forced him to seek Moscow's help. On four occasions (1672/73, 1697, 1699 and 1701), he owed his throne to Russia's continued military support.

72. The Burkhan Bakshin Altan Sume, the Golden Abode of Buddha Shakyamuni, built in 2005, is the largest Buddhist temple in Europe and has 27 monks (as of 2017). Elista, Kalmykia, Russian Federation. Photo 2017.

Nevertheless, from 1680 to 1697 he followed an anti-Russian policy. Obviously the mobile Kalmyks were more difficult to control than the comparatively settled Cossacks. Following the Russian–Kalmyk treaty of 1697, the Kalmyk cavalry decisively contributed to Tsar Peter's suppression of the Don Cossacks' revolt in 1708 and in 1711 to Admiral General Apraksin's victories over the Nogai in the Kuban region. Eleven years later, Tsar Peter requested Ayuka's support in his Caspian campaign. As witnessed by the Scottish doctor and traveller John Bell of Antermony who was a member of Tsar Peter's Russian military expedition, the tsar and the Kalmyk khan met on 22 June 1722 near the present city of Saratov on the Volga.

The Ayuka-Chan came on horseback, attended by two of the princes his sons, and escorted by a troop of about fifty of his officers and great men, all exceedingly well mounted. [...] When the Emperor saw him advancing, he went on shore, saluted him, and, taking him by the hand, conducted him on board the galley. [...] The Emperor intimated to the Ayuka-Chan, that he would be desirous of ten thousand of his troops to accompany him to Persia. The King of the kalmucks replied, that ten thousand were at the Emperor's service, but that he thought that one half of that number would be more than sufficient to answer all these purposes.[54]

Ayuka, however, was double-dealing: he provided only 3,727 unusable cavalrymen of poor fighting spirit, among whom was a Nogai spy. Presumably, this convinced Tsar Peter to change his strategy in 1723. Instead of supporting a single strong Kalmyk ruler, a 'divide-and-conquer' philosophy prevailed.

Ayuka was succeeded by his son **Kheren Donduk Khan** (r. 1724–1735). His power, however, was restricted by the intrigues of his mother Darma Bala and her lover Donduk Ombo, himself a grandson of Ayuka. Following the new strategy, after Tsar Peter's death Russia divided a reduced financial support between the quarrelling Kalmyk factions. When the rivalry between Kheren Donduk and Donduk Ombo degenerated into a bloody civil war, Russia dropped the khan, and recognized **Donduk Ombo Khan** (r. 1735–1741) as the new ruler. Under him and his successors **Donduk Dashi Khan** (r. 1741–1761) and **Ubashi Khan** (r. 1761–1771, d. 1774/75) the economic situation of the Kalmyks worsened dramatically. As a result of the resettlement of the Don Cossacks and German immigrants on the Volga, the number of pastures converted into arable land increased. The expansion of military lines severely hindered the Kalmyks in their traditional nomadic way of life and hurt their livestock economy. In the south-west, the Dnieper line sealed off Crimea, while in the south the Mozdok line shielded the Northern Caucasus from the steppe between the Don and Astrakhan. In the north-east, the new Orenburg line threatened to limit the freedom of movement to the east, and in the north-west the Tsaritsyn line forced the Kalmyks to ask for permission to use their pastures west of the Volga.[55] The Kalmyks were effectively trapped between the defence lines, and from the second quarter of the eighteenth century the Kalmyk cavalry armed with bow and arrows was fast losing its military value. In contrast to the Cossacks, the Kalmyks were too homogeneous as a nation and too little adaptable to the changing economic and military situations to cope with the new state of affairs. In military terms, for Russia they always remained a subordinate, foreign auxiliary force and were never considered as irregulars of the Russian army. Faced with this impasse, under Ubashi Khan's leadership most of the Kalmyks decided to return to Dzungaria, which had been depopulated since the Dzungars were wiped out by China in 1757. On 5 January 1771, 150,000 to 170,000 Kalmyks began their exodus eastwards, while about 60,000 stayed behind. The Russian border troops were too slow to stop them. On the way, they were repeatedly attacked by Kazakhs and lost about 85,000 people;[56] the survivors were initially allowed to settle in Dzungaria. The Kalmyks who remained in Russia were placed under the rule of the governor of Astrakhan in 1771 and the title of Kalmyk khan was abolished. But for Russia, the unimpeded escape of the Kalmyks had unpleasant consequences, as it revealed the weakness of its frontier garrisons and encouraged other peoples to rebel. Those Kabardians who were opposed to Russian suzerainty stiffened their resistance and began to harass remote *stanitsas*, and the dissatisfied Yaik (Ural) Cossacks who had lost several of their former privileges rebelled in 1773–1774 under the leadership of Yemelyan Pugachev (d. 1775).

VI

The Caucasus under Russian Rule

73. Equestrian statue of King Erekle II of Kakheti (r. 1744–1762) and of the united Kakheti and Kartli (1762–1798) in the city of Telavi. King Erekle managed to reunite Kakheti with Kartli but in 1783 signed the fateful Treaty of Georgiyevsk. Kakheti, Georgia. Photo 2013.

1. From the Treaty of Georgiyevsk (1783) to the annexation of Georgia in 1801

The foundation and piecemeal fortification of Vladikavkaz between 1784 and 1790 was a milestone on the way to fulfilling von Münnich's vision: the conquest of Constantinople (Istanbul). The name of the fortress – 'Master of the Caucasus' – proclaimed Russia's strategic determination to command the Caucasus. To control the Black Sea was a precondition for acquiring Constantinople, and so the South Caucasus had to come under Russian rule. Furthermore, Russia had, since the First Partition of Poland (1772), followed an expansionist strategy; in the south-west this lasted until the Third Partition of Poland in 1795 and in the north-west till the annexation of Finland from Sweden in 1809. Thereafter, Russian territorial gains would only be achieved in the south and the east, until Stalin and Hitler divided Poland for the fourth time on 23 August 1939 and the Soviet Union annexed most of Karelia from Finland following the two Soviet–Finnish Wars (1939–1940, 1941–1944). The mastery of the South Caucasus offered the additional promise of access to the Persian Gulf and the Indian Ocean, should Iran become weak. In the short term, a Russian initiative in Iran would secure a new trade route with India and South East Asia.[1] In this latter respect, the first two Russian attempts to establish trading branches in the Iranian city of Astarabad (Gorgan) in 1781–1782 and in Gilan, where Russia asked for the usage of the port of Anzali in 1785–1786, failed miserably.[2] In the 1770s and 1780s only one door was open for Russia to the south: via the Darial Pass to Georgia. In the west, the majority of the eastern Black Sea coast was still under Ottoman control and the littoral lacked roads. In the east, the route along the western coast of the Caspian Sea was topographically easy but it was open to attacks from the bellicose coastal tribes of Dagestan, and any Russian advance would mean war with Iran. But in the central sector, Georgia was struggling to secure its independence against its stronger opponents, Iran and Turkey, and its king Erekle II still hoped to get Russian support. For Russia, Georgia was the gateway to the south; the only prerequisite for lasting hegemony was the enlargement of the Darial Pass into the future Georgian Military Highway, which was provisionally achieved by October 1783 and concluded by 1817. In the year 1783, Russia took two important steps on its road to Constantinople: it annexed Crimea and concluded the Treaty of Georgiyevsk with King Erekle II of Georgia. That the goal of a conquest of Constantinople represented official Russian foreign policy was symbolically highlighted in 1787 when Tsarina Catherine II (r. 1762–1793) visited Crimea. When she arrived in Cherson, she was greeted by a triumphal arch on which was painted 'This is the way to Constantinople', which had been erected by Prince Grigory Potemkin.[3] A couple of years later, her last favourite, Prince Platon Zubov (d. 1822), confirmed the plan to seize Constantinople.[4]

During the Ottoman–Russian War of 1768–1774, the Turkish fleet was destroyed at the naval Battle of Çeşme in 1770. The loss of the fleet was devastating for Crimea since its only connection to Turkey had been by sea. The resulting military and geographical isolation left Crimea vulnerable to Russian attacks and in four campaigns between 1771 and 1783 Catherine occupied and finally, in April 1783, annexed the peninsula. However, in the early 1780s, a push towards Georgia was more promising still. Timing was favourable as King Erekle's luck seemed to have run out. Neighbouring Imereti was under increasing Ottoman pressure and, much worse, his favoured and very promising son Levan had died in 1781 in suspicious circumstances, probably a victim of political intrigue. At the time of his death Levan commanded the small Georgian standing army, which thereupon disintegrated. Furthermore, Kakheti was increasingly becoming a target for the Avar ruler Omar Khan (r. 1774–1801).[5] Erekle was now prepared to trade Georgia's independence for Russian protection. On 24 July 1783, the Georgian delegates, princes Ivane Mukhrani and Garsevan Chavchavadze and the Russian lieutenant general Pavel Potemkin, a cousin of Catherine's favourite Grigory Potemkin, signed the **Treaty of Georgiyevsk**. It consisted of a preamble, thirteen articles along with four separate secret articles, and an instruction concerning coronations and the oath of allegiance. Article 1 obliged the king of Kartli and Kakheti to reject all allegiances to external powers but Russia. Article 2 guaranteed Georgia's territorial integrity and article 3 obliged any new Georgian king to seek Russia's approval and to swear the oath of allegiance at his coronation. Article 4 prohibited Georgian kings from establishing diplomatic relations with foreign powers without Russian consent. Article 5 stipulated a Russian minister at the Georgian court. Article 6 defined an enemy of one state as the enemy of the other and guaranteed that Erekle and his descendants would remain Georgia's kings. Article 7 forced Georgian kings to supply Russia with troops and article 8 downgraded the catholicos, the patriarch of the autocephalous Orthodox Georgian Church, to a mere member of the Russian synod ranking only eighth among the Russian archbishops. Secret article 1 installed Russia as arbiter between Georgia and Imereti in case of disputes. In secret article 2 Russia promised to garrison two infantry battalions in Georgia and in secret article 4 to 'offer all possible military aid' in case of war.[6] Within eighteen years, Russia had broken all its obligations. It seems that the Georgian side negotiated the treaty rashly and concluded it in haste, for it reduced the independent and unconquered state of Georgia to a Russian protectorate which forbade its vassal rulers to conduct an autonomous foreign policy, and it annihilated the autocephaly of its state church.

Only four years after signing the treaty of Georgiyevsk Russia ignored its commitments towards Georgia when Tsarina Catherine recalled the Russian troops stationed there at the outbreak of the Ottoman–Russian War of 1787–1792. Erekle had no other choice but to seek an arrangement with the Sublime Porte. In the meantime, for Agha Muhammad Khan Qajar (r. 1789–1797), who had gradually risen to power in Iran since 1779, Georgia was, like the various khanates of Azerbaijan, nothing but a rebellious Iranian province which had to be brought to heel. In September 1795 Agha Muhammad issued an ultimatum to King Erekle demanding that he cancel his treaty with Russia and submit once more to Iranian sovereignty. Although Erekle appealed for Russian military help, based on articles 2, 6 and secret article 4 of the 1783 treaty, General Gudovich, who was based in Georgiyevsk, refused, remaining passive; just as he had in 1791, when Erekle, concerned about Agha Mohammad's military build-up, had asked Gudovich for the return of Russian troops to Tbilisi. Following their victory at the Battle of Krtsanisi, the Iranians stormed Tbilisi on 11 September 1795, massacring the population and putting the city to the torch. About 15,000 Georgians were deported to Iran. Agha Mohammad then turned east and ravaged Shirvan.[7] However, he omitted to install a new ruler or to leave an Iranian garrison in Tbilisi in order to prevent Russia's return to Georgia. Judging from a distance, one has to concur with Donald Rayfield and other historians that Tsarina Catherine intentionally refused to honour her own treaty with

Georgia in order to further weaken Erekle and annex his debilitated kingdom.[8] Almost 150 years later, a similar fate befell Poland: when the Warsaw Uprising broke out in August 1944, Stalin ordered the Red Army, which had reached the city's eastern suburbs, to cease combat so as to allow the Wehrmacht to wipe out the Polish pro-Western resistance. Once Agha Muhammad had left the region, in early 1796 Tsarina Catherine dispatched an army under the command of Valeriyan Zubov (d. 1804) who was briefed to invade Iran and topple Agha Muhammad. Tbilisi was again occupied by a Russian detachment while Zubov took Derbent, Shamakhi, Baku and Ganja. But when the tsarina died in November 1796, her son and successor Paul I (r. 1796–1801) put an end to the campaign and recalled the army to the Caspian Terek Line. It was only Agha Muhammad Khan's assassination in June 1797 in Shusha (Shushi), Karabakh, which spared Georgia a second devastation.[9] Half a year later, Erekle too died.

Erekle's son and successor **Giorgi XII** (r. 1798–1800) was ill and weak. He created unrest within Georgia when he ignored Erekle's will and testament and nominated his own son Davit as crown prince instead of Iulon, Erekle's son by his second marriage. At the same time, Agha Muhammad's successor Fath-'Ali Shah Qajar (r. 1797–1834) issued an ultimatum to Giorgi threatening him with even worse devastation than that of 1795. Overwhelmed, Giorgi asked Tsar Paul to turn Georgia into a Russian protectorate while maintaining the rule of the Bagrationi dynasty. Worried that Georgia would either slip into chaos or return to the Iranian zone of influence, in November 1799 Tsar Paul sent Pyotr Ivanovich Kovalensky with substantial troops to Tbilisi, instructing him one year later that upon Giorgi's expected imminent death no successor should be enthroned. On 18 December 1800 Tsar Paul issued unilaterally a decree annexing Georgia to the Russian Empire. Then events came to a head. Giorgi died on 28 December and the next day the Russian general Ivan Lazarev declared the tsar's decision to the nobles. On 18 January 1801 Tsar Paul's decree was published and Georgia became part of Russia. Less than two months later, on 11 March, General Carl Heinrich von Knorring became governor general and gave orders to deport male and female members of the Bagrationi family to Russia. On 12 April the Georgian nobles were forced under military duress to swear an oath of allegiance to the tsar. Finally, on 12 September 1801 Tsar Alexander I (r. 1801–1825), who had succeeded his assassinated father Paul, confirmed Georgia's annexation to the Russian Empire.[10] Like his father, Alexander was convinced that in order to firmly control Georgia, Russia had to acquire all the khanates and emirates of today's Azerbaijan up to the Rivers Kura and Aras (Araxes), which set the stage for the next Russian conquests. If we take *kouropalates* Ashot I Bagrationi (r. 813–ca. 830) as the forefather of the Kingdom of Georgia,[11] in 1801 a thousand-year-old kingdom that had been ruled by the same Bagrationi dynasty came to an end. This survival in such a contested environment was an outstanding achievement.

At the end of 1802, Tsar Alexander replaced Kovalensky and Knorring, who had turned out to be incapable, with General Pavel Tsitsianov, a Russified Georgian. The new military governor silenced the disaffected nobles by granting nominal army ranks and pensions, efficiently quelled the remaining pockets of resistance, captured Ganja in early 1804 and successfully

74. Mural from the seventeenth century of eristavi Giorgi I Dadiani (d. 1323) on the northern inner wall of the monastery of the Dormition at Nojikhevi near Khobi. Giorgi I Dadiani was the founder of the monastery and holds a model of the church in his left hand. The inscription states: 'Eristavi Giorgi ordered this house of prayer to be built and frescoed. May God have mercy on him.' Samegrelo-Zemo Svaneti, Georgia. Photo 2013.

75. Entry to the ruined palace of the Shervashidze family in Likhny. The palace was destroyed by Russian troops in 1866 during the suppression of an anti-Russian rebellion. Autonomous Republic of Abkhazia. Photo 2018.

repelled raids from Lak highlanders. Three years before, General Lazarev had decisively beaten the invading Avar khan Omar.[12] The last member of the Bagrationi dynasty remaining in power was Catholicos Anton II (in office 1788–1811, d. 1827), who decisively defended the privileges, legal corpus and traditions of the Orthodox Georgian Church. Anton, a son of King Erekle, resisted the Russification of his church for ten years before he was deported to Russia in November 1810. In July 1811 Tsar Alexander abolished the Georgian patriarchate and replaced it with a mere exarchate of the Russian Orthodox Church; at the same time the patriarchate of Abkhazia and Imereti was abolished and its bishoprics integrated into the Georgian exarchate.[13] While the first exarch Varlaam was a Georgian, he was dismissed in 1817 for resisting Russification, and all his successors till 1917 were ethnic Russians nominated by the tsar. The upper clergy was now swiftly Russified; Russian liturgy replaced the Georgian and many beautiful ancient murals were whitewashed.[14] More than a century later in 1943, when Stalin appealed to the patriotism of all citizens and institutions, the autocephaly of the Georgian Church was again recognized by the Soviet Union. Concerning the Armenian Apostolic Church, Russia confirmed the position of the Catholicos of Etchmiadzin as its supreme authority in 1828 and regulated the latter's election whereby the Armenian higher clergy could submit two candidates to the tsar, who chose one of them. In 1836 Tsar Nicholas confirmed the autocephaly of the Armenian Apostolic Church. Six years earlier, the nominal Albanian catholicosate, which had been vacant since 1816, was downgraded to the metropolitanate of Karabakh.[15] Soon after the Russian regulation of the Armenian catholicosate, the Ottoman government empowered the Armenian patriarch of Constantinople to fully and exclusively control all Armenian bishoprics and parishes within the Empire.[16] Within the Ottoman Empire the Armenians lived primarily in the cities of Constantinople and Smyrna (İzmir) and in the eastern and south-eastern Anatolian *vilayets* (provinces) of Erzurum, Van, Hakkari, Bitlis, Hozat/Dersim, Kars-Çıldır, Trabzon, Sivas, Adana and Diyarbakır.[17] According to the official Ottoman census from 1844, about 2,400,000 Armenians lived in the Empire of which 225,000 resided in the capital.[18] Worldwide, *Encyclopaedia Britannica* of 1875 estimated a population for 1850 of about 4 million Armenians, of which 1,200,000 lived in the Russian Empire and 150,000 in Iran.[19]

In the western parts of Georgia, the Russian occupation was slower; it dragged on from 1803 till 1810 by which time Mingelia, Guria, Imereti and the Abkhazian littorals near Sukhumi and Gagra were incorporated into the Russian Empire. As in the eastern south Caucasus, these military operations were an element of two distinct wars, the Ottoman–Russian War of 1806–1812 and the Russian–Iranian War of 1804–1813, which in turn were for Tsar Alexander merely sideshows compared to the struggle against Napoleon. As a result Russian commanders in the Caucasus had only small numbers of troops at their disposal. **Mingrelia** became a Russian protectorate in 1803 while its ruling family, the Dadiani, kept some internal autonomy till 1867. A similar arrangement was chosen in **Guria** which became a protectorate in 1810; but when regent-dowager Sophia Gurieli began in 1826 to resist Russian domination and three years later asked the Ottomans for military support, Russia intervened and annexed the principality. In **Imereti**, at King Solomon's I death in 1784, **Davit II** (r. 1784–1789, 1790–1791) became regent for the underage Prince Davit, nephew of Solomon and grandson of King Erekle of Georgia. Five years later, King Erekle intervened and forced Davit II to vacate the throne in favour of the seventeen-year-old Prince Davit who took the regal name of **Solomon II** (r. 1789–1790, 1791–1810, d. 1815). In 1790 the deposed king Davit II briefly evicted Solomon II with the aid of Ottoman troops but soon had to flee again. Solomon II returned and quickly found himself embroiled in conflicts with his pro-Russian vassals, which led him to consider asking for Ottoman or Iranian support. General Tsitsianov ended this unstable situation in 1804 by forcing Solomon to acknowledge Russian suzerainty. Since Solomon displayed little loyalty towards his new masters, the Russian viceroy Alexander Tormasov (in office 1809–1811) occupied Imereti early in 1810 and deposed Solomon, who fled to Turkey.[20] Imereti became part of the Empire and Georgia was 'reunited' under Russian command and very soon broken up again into various administrative units.

In **Abkhazia**, the ruling Shervashidze family was divided into pro-Ottoman and pro-Russia factions which were locked in a murderous dispute. The Muslim Abkhazian ruler **Kelesh Ahmed Bey** (r. 1780–1808) held power with Ottoman support till around 1806 when he sought a rapprochement with Russia. He was murdered in May 1808, possibly by his elder, pro-Ottoman son **Aslan Bey Shervashidze** (r. 1808–1810) who had the protection of Turkish troops.[21] Two years later, Russian marines captured the port of Sukhumi, forcing Aslan Bey and the Ottoman garrison to flee to Turkey. Tsar Alexander then placed Kelesh Bey's younger son **Sefer Ali-Bey Shervashidze** (r. 1810–1821), who had converted to Christianity, on the throne of Abkhazia, which became a Russian protectorate. However, Russia's control over Abkhazia was limited to the littoral near Sukhumi and the coastal region of Gagra; the remaining mountainous areas were under the authority of free communities or local nobles. In the south, the Russian attack on Akhaltsikhe (1810) failed due to the spread of plague among the troops.[22] According to the Treaty of Bucharest (1812) which ended the Ottoman–Russian War with favourable terms for Turkey, Russia kept Sukhumi, but was forced under British and Prussian pressure to return the other captured ports of Anapa, Poti and Batumi, as well as Akhalkalaki, to Turkey.[23] Neither Great Britain nor Prussia judged a Russian territorial expansion at the cost of Ottoman Turkey as desirable. The port of Poti was recaptured by Russia in 1828, Batumi only in 1878. In 1864 the last Shervashidze prince, Mikhail (r. 1823–1864), who had been obliged to cooperate with the Ottomans during the Crimean War (1853–1856), was exiled to Russia and Abkhazia was annexed.

2. Iran's interlude with Napoleon and Russia's conquest of the South Caucasian khanates and sultanates

The Napoleonic Wars engulfed all major European powers, including Russia. For Napoleon's main adversaries Great Britain, Austria and Prussia, the war sought to maintain a balance of power on the European continent and to prevent dominance by the (initially revolutionary) French. Great Britain, moreover, wanted to secure its colonies and its naval supremacy. For Russia, the starting position was less clear. On one hand, Tsar Alexander abhorred the revolutionary French Directory (1795–1799) and its successors the Consulate (1799–1804) and the First Empire (1804–1815) with the parvenu Napoleon Bonaparte as emperor. On the other hand, Russia and France shared enough common interests to consider a tactical alliance. While Great Britain represented Napoleon's arch-enemy, Russia was well aware that London viewed its southward advance towards the Mediterranean and, potentially, also to the Persian Gulf with suspicion. For this reason Britain tended to support Ottoman Turkey, historically Russia's main adversary along with Sweden. As already mentioned, in the early 1720s Britain had encouraged Turkey to attack the Russian troops stationed in today's Azerbaijan.

76. The Emperor Napoleon I receives the Iranian plenipotentiary ambassador Mirza Muhammad Reza Qazvini on 27 April 1807 at the Palace of Finckenstein in West Prussia, today Poland. Painting by François Henri Mulard (1769–1850) from 1810. The treaty was signed one week later on 4 May. © Musée national du château de Versailles, France.

Additionally, Russia and France felt their expansionist ambitions curtailed by the superior British navy; then, since Russia and France shared no borders, there were no demarcation disputes. Finally, both powers knew that a possible route for invading India went through Iran. Britain had become alerted to that risk by Napoleon's Egyptian campaign of 1798. With these considerations in mind Russia and France, which had been at war since the days when Napoleon was general of the Directory, formed an opportunistic, tactical partnership that lasted from 1807 to 1812, before resuming a brutal war that ultimately led to France's collapse. These two foreign policy reversals had noteworthy repercussions for Iran. A major difference in Russian, French and British policies towards Iran and implicitly the South Caucasus was that Russia followed a consistent, long-term strategy while for Britain and especially France Iran had only a short-term, tactical relevance depending on developments in Europe.

The Russian–Iranian War began with General Tsitsianov's invasion of Armenia early in 1804 when an Iranian army blocked his progress, preventing him from conquering Etchmiadzin and Yerevan. After having suffered two defeats, Tsitsianov was forced to retreat. He commanded too few troops and they were of secondary quality, often raw recruits, drafted serfs or deported criminals who were not properly trained in handling their arms. On the Iranian side, the bulk of the army consisted of a wild congeries of different tribal cavalry units that were more interested in looting than in disciplined warfare. In spite of the insufficient troops available, the Russians managed to occupy several khanates and sultanates that were nominally Iranian vassals: Djaro-Belokan (Jar-Balakan) in 1803, Elisu (Ilisu), Ganja in 1804, Shirvan, Shaki and Karabakh in 1805, Quba, Derbent and Baku in 1806. Baku was only taken at the second attempt in autumn 1806, as during the ceremony of handing over the keys after the city

77. The Ishak Palace built in 1784 near Doğubayazıt. It was here that Napoleon's envoy Pierre Amédée Jaubert was kept prisoner by the Ottoman pasha for eight months in 1805/6. Ağrı Province, Turkey. Photo 2016.

surrendered in February of that year, Tsitsianov was treacherously murdered. One year before, in 1805, a Russian attack through Gilan aiming at the important city of Qazvin met with disaster, and in 1808 General Gudovich's attack on Yerevan again failed.[24] On the Russian side, there was a clear lull in fighting intensity from 1806 or perhaps 1808 to 1812 due to the need to concentrate on the European theatre of war. But Iran failed to exploit this favourable window of opportunity by forging a military alliance with the Ottomans, who were also at war with Russia.

Iran was, however, active on other diplomatic fronts in order to find support against the Russian menace. In 1801 Shah Fath-'Ali concluded commercial and political treaties with the East India Company, represented by Captain John Malcolm (1769–1833). The main political clause stipulated that Iran would prevent any transit of French troops through its territory or the occupation of any of its islands by France. In case of war with France, Britain was bound to give military help. As of 1804, when the Russian invasion of the South Caucasus resumed, Fath-'Ali appealed to Britain for support. London, that is the Company, ignored his pleas since France had been ejected from Egypt and Russia was now an ally in the Third Coalition (1803–1806) against Napoleon. Furthermore, Britain felt bound to assist Iran in case of a French attack, but not a Russian one.[25] Disappointed, Fath-'Ali turned to the French, Russia's enemy, and renewed previous Iranian–French contacts. He was prepared to enter an alliance with France provided the latter helped him reconquer Georgia. Already in 1795 the Directory had sent two envoys to Tehran to investigate the option of a Franco-Iranian alliance against Russia; they also recommended that Iran should invade Mingrelia before Russia did.[26] When Fath-'Ali's letter to Napoleon reached the French foreign minister Talleyrand (1754–1838), it piqued his interest, for he understood the chance to forge a triple alliance between France, the Ottomans and Iran which could tie up substantial numbers of Russian troops far away from Europe.[27] Napoleon and Talleyrand decided to send two envoys to Tehran: Antoine-Alexandre Romieu (1764–1805) and Pierre Amédée Jaubert (1779–1847). Romieu arrived first in Tehran, in September 1805, after surviving an assassination attempt on his way. The Iranians played a game of double-cross, for while one minister negotiated with Romieu, another proposed to the British diplomat Harford Jones a treaty of friendship with Great Britain provided it would secure the return of Georgia and the lost Azerbaijani khanates to Iran. Shortly after, Romieu died suddenly in Tehran, probably by poison.[28] Jaubert finally reached Tehran in June 1806 after having escaped several plots to murder him and spending eight months in a dungeon of the fortress of Doğubayazıt near Anatolia's border with Iran (fig. 77). When Jaubert arrived in Tehran, Fath-'Ali's first son Muhammad 'Ali Mirza (1789–1821) was preparing a military campaign against Ottoman Baghdad after efforts to secure an Iranian–Ottoman alliance had failed.[29] Having received no commitment from Great Britain, Fath-'Ali went ahead with the French proposal and dispatched Mirza Muhammad Reza as plenipotentiary ambassador to France. The project of a triple alliance started to take shape when Ottoman Turkey declared war on Russia in December 1806.

In April 1807, Napoleon nominated General Claude Matthieu de Gardane as French minister plenipotentiary for Iran and received Ambassador Mirza Muhammad on 27 April 1807 at the castle of Finckenstein in West Prussia (today Poland) where a Franco-Iranian treaty was signed on 4 May (fig. 76). In article 2, France guaranteed Iran the integrity of its present territory. Article 3 recognized 'Georgia as legitimately belonging to ... Persia' and in article 4 Napoleon promised 'to make every effort to force Russia to evacuate Georgia and Persian territory'. In article 8, Iran committed itself to end all contact with Britain, 'to declare war [against Britain] and to start hostilities without delay'.[30] In theory, Iran had acquired the strongest military land power of Europe as ally against the menace of Russia and could dream of recapturing Georgia. In practice, French involvement in Iran was for Napoleon only an option should he consider attacking India. Furthermore, should Iran declare war on Russia, it would probably have to wage war on two fronts, in the north against Russia and in the south against Britain whose navy would quickly secure Iran's islands and coast. Bold as it was, Fath-'Ali's project was a mirage, but it showed how desperate he was to recover Georgia and the lost Azerbaijani khanates. In fact, the Franco-Iranian treaty became obsolete after only two months. For after Russia's bloody defeat at Friedland on 14 June 1807, Tsar Alexander changed sides, joined the French continental blockade against Great Britain and on 7 July signed the Treaty of Tilsit. This nullified the Treaty of Finckenstein, for the Treaty of Tilsit made no reference to France's promise to force Russia to return Georgia to Iran. Napoleon had obtained from Alexander a free hand in Europe and gave Russia in return free rein in the Caucasus and Asia.

Although the Finckenstein treaty had become obsolete, Minister Gardane nevertheless left for Tehran where he arrived in December 1807. But several months before, the Russian general Gudovich had passed on the news of the Treaty of Tilsit to Shah Fath-'Ali, who immediately understood that he had been betrayed by Napoleon since he, as the victor, had not put pressure on the loser, Alexander, to compromise on Georgia. Having no better

78. The seven türbe (Turkish, 'tombs') from the early nineteenth century at Yeddi Gumbaz near Shamakhi (Şamaxı). Shamakhi District, Azerbaijan. Photo 2016.

option, however, the Shah ratified the Treaty of Finckenstein; he approved the execution of the commercial agreements but withheld the enforcement of Iran's political obligations pending the realization of article 4, that is the return of Georgia and the lost khanates to Iran. After Gudovich had rejected Iranian proposals for French mediation, Tsar Alexander confirmed in August 1808: 'The Treaty of Tilsit came after the Finkenstein Treaty. [...] My frontier is the line my troops are occupying; the peace will be at that price; and if this does not suit them [the Iranians] he [General Gudovich] will start war again.'[31] In fact, Gudovich resumed hostilities by besieging Yerevan, which resisted his attack. At the same time, the British ambassador Sir Harford Jones (since 1807 a baronet) put before the Shah the following alternative: either Iran should accept an alliance with Britain directed against France and receive military support were France to invade, or Iran would suffer a British attack if it refused. Although in January 1809 Fath-'Ali had already correctly predicted that Napoleon would renew his war against Russia once he had mastered the crisis in Spain, in March he signed the Preliminary Treaty between Britain and Iran according to which Iran agreed to hinder any European force from crossing Iran's territory in the direction of India; in return, Great Britain promised military help with Indian troops should an European army attack Iran and mediation efforts failed.[32] While the latter stipulation was attractive for Iran since it implied that Great Britain would support Iran in case of a Russian attack, the British government never intended to fulfil this obligation, as became obvious during the next Russian–Iranian War of 1826–1828 when Britain remained passive. Not only the South Caucasus, but also Iran had become a plaything of expansionist powers.

The year 1812 marked a turning point for Russia and the South Caucasus when Russian forces, with the help of a fierce winter, completely annihilated Napoleon's invading Grande Armée. Then, in May 1812 the end of the Ottoman–Russian War freed Russian troops for the Caucasian front, making Russia's domination of the South Caucasus unavoidable. In the night Battle of

Aslanduz on 31 October–1 November 1812 on the north bank of the River Aras the Russian major general Pyotr Kotlyarevsky destroyed a large army under Crown Prince Abbas Mirza (1789–1833) which had been trained by British officer-instructors commanded by Joseph d'Arcy, a major in the Royal Artillery.[33] While most British officers had been recalled in October 1812 when a renewed Russian–British alliance was emerging, the two leading instructors Captain Charles Christie (infantry) and Lieutenant Henry Lindsay (cavalry) remained in active Iranian service; Christie was killed at the battle of Aslanduz.[34] Soon thereafter, General Kotlyarevsky's troops managed to storm the strong fortress of Lankaran, capital of the khanate of Talish, which was defended by superior Iranian forces. At the same time, Russia also scored successes in Georgia. A peasant revolt over low grain prices was suppressed and the final attack by Erekle's rebellious son Alexander (d. 1844), who had fled Tbilisi in summer 1800, was crushed in November 1812. When Russian troops stormed Shatili, the stronghold of the Khevsur mountain tribe, in May 1813, Prince Alexander fled to Dagestan.[35] As narrated by the German explorer Gustav Radde (1831–1903) the Khevsurs, who were nominally Christians though also preserving pagan beliefs, were notorious for their relentless application of a code of blood vengeance which put all relatives of the killed person under obligation, and which allowed any relative of the killer to be struck down. For this reason, Khevsur men, and even boys, would not leave their villages without arms and chain mail. 'Even the peasant tilling his field wears chain mail and arms. Possibly he has killed nobody, but has inherited blood debt from an ancestor.'[36] A similar tyranny of blood feud also existed among the Svans.[37]

Britain's Iran policy had also changed in Russia's favour. While from 1809 till 1811 Britain had encouraged the shah to continue his war against Russia, it pressed him to make peace as soon as Napoleon's Russian campaign had begun.[38] Ambassador Gore Ouseley even threatened to cut British subsidies unless Fath-'Ali agreed to peace with Russia. Since Iran stood no chance against Russia without an ally, Shah Fath-'Ali had to agree to the harsh terms of the Treaty of Gulistan signed on 14 October 1813. Russia obtained the exclusive rights for warships on the Caspian Sea and kept, as previously proclaimed by Tsar Alexander, all its conquests. Iran had to cede and waive all claims to its former territories north of the Aras–Kura Line except Yerevan and Nakhchivan, but including Talish. The Russian Empire now definitively acquired Kartli–Kakheti, Djaro-Belokan, Elisu, Ganja, Shirvan, Shaki, Karabakh, Quba, Derbent, Baku and Talish.[39] Iran also dropped any claim to the south-eastern parts of Daghestan, Mingrelia, Abkhazia and Imereti.[40] Although the treaty produced clear results, it was probably viewed by both signatories as a mere truce, for Iran still aimed to recover its losses and Russia had failed to capture Yerevan and Nakhchivan north of the Aras–Kura Line. The new commander-in-chief Alexei Petrovich Yermolov (in office 1816–1827, d. 1861) was convinced that a defensible border with Iran had to follow the Aras and Kura rivers, which meant that Yerevan and Nakhchivan needed to be incorporated. After negotiations with Iran had failed to generate results, Yermolov occupied in 1825 the northern shore of Lake Sevan which controlled a northern approach to Yerevan. Crown Prince Abbas Mirza interpreted this Russian advance correctly as a preparation for a forthcoming offensive and decided to attack first. The crown prince coordinated his campaign with some of the dissatisfied former khanates, for when the Iranian army attacked suddenly on 31 July 1826 without declaring war, several Muslim cities rose in revolt and either destroyed or expelled their Russian garrisons. Yermolov had just returned from a campaign in Chechnya and, taken by surprise, was unprepared. Yelisavetpol (Ganja) and Lankaran capitulated, Karabakh was devastated, but Baku, Gimry and Shushi (Şuşa) resisted. Yermolov remained strangely passive and resisted the order of Tsar Nicholas I (r. 1825–1855) to counterattack and seize Yerevan. Tsar Nicholas then nominated Ivan Fyodorovich Paskevich (in office 1827–1831, d. 1856) as field commander of the Russian forces in the Caucasus, reporting directly to him. Since Yermolov refused to cooperate with Paskevich he was sacked in April 1827 and Paskevich became commander-in-chief.[41]

79. Khevsurs armed with sword and shield prepare for a duel in the region of Gudani, northern Georgia. Photo from the later nineteenth century. Source: *Материалы по археологии Кавказа* (1904), image 6.

Once winter had ended, Paskevich moved against the Iranian enclaves north of the Aras–Kura Line. In spite of tough Iranian resistance, the Russians captured the Khanate of Yerevan in October 1827 after having occupied the Khanate of Nakhchivan in July. Only ten days after the fall of Yerevan, Tabriz capitulated to a Russian vanguard. Shah Fath-'Ali had to sue for peace and Russia dictated the conditions. It requested Yerevan and Nakhchivan as well as the right to establish Russian consulates anywhere in Iran. Since Russia insisted on extraterritorial rights for its consulates and subjects, this was in reality a first step towards establishing a protectorate over Iran. Furthermore, Iran had to accept commercial agreements as requested by Russia. Finally, Russia demanded a large reparation payment which would make Iran indebted to Russia. Fath-'Ali resisted this latter provision and in January 1828 allowed the crown prince to resume hostilities, leading to Russia's capture of Urmia and Ardabil. Faced with the rapid disintegration of the Iranian army, Fath-'Ali had to accept the Russian terms for peace which was sealed on 21–22 February by the Treaty of Turkmenchay[42] (fig. 82). Paskevich had argued that Russia should also keep Iranian Azerbaijan, but the tsar refused fearing protests from European powers, above all Great Britain. This new Russian–Iranian border along the River Aras still divides the Azerbaijani people today; one third live in Azerbaijan, the rest in Iran.

More importantly, having gained the complete Aras–Kura Line as its border, Russia changed its strategy towards Iran. Although Russia held powerful levers, based on its consulates, extraterritorial rights and commercial treaties, it now strove for friendship rather than antagonism towards Iran. The latter, for its part, conscious of having been within the last two decades twice betrayed by Britain and once by France, came to the conclusion that treaties with European powers with only short-term, tactical interest in Iran, were of no use, and that it was more advantageous to find common ground with the overwhelming northern neighbour, Russia. This shared interest lay in Iran's east, in today's Afghanistan, where Iran could dream of expanding its territory

80. The Armenian Sevanavank Monastery stands on the northern shore of Lake Sevan. The older, small church of the Apostles on the right is dated by an inscription to the year 874, the larger Astvatsatsin Church is probably from the tenth century and was restored in the seventeenth and eighteenth centuries. Gegharkunik Province, Armenia. Photo 2015.

81. The Blue Mosque in Yerevan was completed in 1766 during the period of the Yerevan Khanate. The mosque is leased to the Iranian embassy in Yerevan for 99 years until 2114. Yerevan, Armenia. Photo 2014.

and thus compensating for the losses incurred in the Caucasus, while Russia would obtain a foothold in the direction of British India. Britain acknowledged its loss of influence and credibility in Iran in 1828 by paying recompense for the abrogation of its treaty of 1814.[43] Nevertheless, the Iranian war of 1833 against the emirate of Herat (1793–1863) which was the key to entering India, and especially the ten-month joint Iranian–Russian siege of Herat in 1837–8, were direct results of the new Russian strategy towards Iran.[44] By 1829 at the latest, when the British navy stopped Russia from seizing Constantinople, the tsars understood that Russia's ambitions on Constantinople would be thwarted by Britain unless her forces were tied up somewhere else – in India. To quote George Nathaniel Curzon, later Viceroy of India (1899–1905),

[The Russian's] *object is not Calcutta, but Constantinople; not the Ganges, but the Golden Horn. He believes that the keys of the Bosphorus are more likely to be won on the banks of the Helmund* [river near Herat] *than on the heights of the* [Bulgarian] *Plevna* [where Russia crushed the Ottomans in 1877]. *To keep England quiet in Europe by keeping her employed in Asia, that, briefly put, is the sum and substance of Russian policy.*[45]

This strategy would determine Russia's policy in the Caucasus, as well as London's counter-strategy, till the Anglo-Russian Convention of 1907.

Iran was not the only loser in the Gulistan and Turkmenchay treaties, since many Caucasian peasants who had previously not been bound to the land now found themselves under Russian rule, and when their land was granted to a noble, they were transferred with it. As the German explorer and biologist Moritz Wagner (1813–1887) noted, in Kabarda 'the Cossacks watched over them [the serf-peasants] like shepherd dogs the sheep'.[46] Among the winners were the Armenian merchants who gained access to the Russian market and those South Caucasians

82. Following the Russian–Iranian Treaty of Turkmenchay signed on 21–22 February 1828, the Iranian delegation pays Russia the agreed indemnity. Painting by Marcin Zaleski (1796–1877) from 1835. © Hermitage Museum, St Petersburg, Russian Federation.

who joined the Russian administration. And, of course, the *Pax Russica* put an end to the never-ending rivalries and conflicts between the small South Caucasian statelets; daily life became more peaceful. While the South Caucasian economy benefited in the short term from integration into the Russian Empire, it would suffer in the long term due to the economic strategy implemented by Ivan Paskevich who wanted to limit the role of the region to being a mere supplier of raw materials. He and his successors aimed to restrict South Caucasian manufacturing enterprises to the local markets and ensuring that Caucasian raw materials were processed in Russia proper.[47] The same colonialist strategy was later adopted in Central Asia where no large-scale cotton processing industry was built up, with most of the cotton being transported to Russia.

Two months after the signing of the Turkmenchay Treaty, the Ottoman–Russian war of 1828–1829 began. Although the main operations took place in what is now Bulgaria, the war was also fought in the Caucasus. Paskevich's objectives were to clean the eastern Black Sea coast of Turkish garrisons, to advance into Anatolia and to tie up Ottoman troops in the east. The Russians took Kars quickly in June 1828, but had to fight hard to conquer the huge fortress of Akhaltsikhe (fig. 51). Since winter was approaching, they retreated the bulk of their army to winter quarters which gave the Ottomans and Laz the opportunity to slaughter the town's Armenian population. In June, Paskevich resumed his advance and seized Erzurum, but in Europe the British Royal Navy hindered the Russians, who had captured Adrianople (Edirne), from progressing to Istanbul.

Russia had to accept Turkey's peace proposal. Concerning the Caucasus, the Treaty of Adrianople of September 1829 awarded the ports of Anapa and Poti, the towns of Akhaltsikhe and Akhalkhalaki and most of the eastern Black Sea littoral to Russia while Kars, Bayazıt (as of 1934 Doğubayazıt) and Ardahan were returned to the Ottomans; Kars was reconquered by Russia in 1855 and 1877. When Paskevich returned to Georgia in late 1829, between 60,000 and 90,000 Armenians attached themselves to his retreating army for fear of Turkish reprisals.[48] At the same time, 55,000 Muslims left the former khanates of Yerevan and Nakhchivan for Iran while some 30,000 Iranian Armenians migrated to the recently acquired Russian territories.[49] For the British, the preservation of the Ottoman Empire from Russian encroachments had now become a key priority. The Treaty of Adrianople had severe consequences for the local populations of the west Caucasian littoral since it transferred suzerainty over the Abkhazians and Circassians from the Ottomans to Russia. The Abkhazians and Circassians protested that they were no taxpaying subjects of the Ottomans, although many of them living close to the shore had till 1783 de facto recognized Crimean Tatar suzerainty, that is Ottoman supremacy. But throughout history, people impacted by territorial cessions have not been asked about their preferences and have had to choose between adaption, armed resistance or emigration.

83. The four medieval defence towers and twenty ruined towers for dwellings at Targim. On the left is a small necropolis with around twenty dilapidated burial houses. Ingushetia, Russian Federation Photo 2017.

84. Three medieval defence towers in the ruined and abandoned ancient village of Goor some 40 km north-west of Gamsutl. Shamilsky Rayon, Dagestan, Russian Federation. Photo 2021.

3. The resistance of North Caucasian mountain peoples

In 1829 Russia found itself in the strange situation of having two southern borders, the Black Sea–Kuban–Terek Line and, 350 to 450 kilometres further south, the Aras–Kura border. Between the two borders there were the recently conquered South Caucasus and the fiercely independent mountain-dwellers' enclaves of Dagestan and Chechnya (including today's Ingushetia), as well as the territories of some highland Kabardians and Circassians. The Greater Caucasus Range separated these two different universes. No land empire, however forbearing, could accept such hostile enclaves within its borders, whose inhabitants did not hesitate to conduct raids against its settled subjects in the plains. In general, Imperial Russia followed a tolerant strategy towards its non-Christian ethnic minorities.[50] It requested only minimal allegiance to the tsar – not to the Russian state – and usually allowed Muslims and Buddhists to continue worshipping according to their religious prescriptions. In the North Caucasus, it accepted local traditional laws (*adat*) and even Islamic *sharia* law alongside Imperial state law. This policy contrasted sharply with the ruthless missionary efforts of the Catholic colonial empires. The successor state of Imperial Russia, the Soviet Union, applied a radically different social policy since it not only demanded an unconditional allegiance and obedience to the state and its dominant Communist Party, but also claimed control of the speech and thoughts of its entire people. The Russian advance into the North Caucasus was also a clash of political systems, between a highly centralized state and traditional tribal societies. Furthermore, there remained the risk that the Ottomans could exploit their former closeness with the Circassian elites to re-establish bridgeheads in the north-western Caucasus.

The conquest of the North Caucasus proceeded in three steps:

- First, in the period 1785–1826, Sheikh Mansur's 'holy war' against Russia was defeated, after which Yermolov consolidated Russia's control of the Georgian Military Highway and made a first attempt to subjugate Dagestan and Chechnya.

- The second stage, lasting thirty years (1829–1859) was marked by the resistance of three Dagestani imams, ending with Shamil's capitulation in 1859.

- In the third period, 1859–1864/67 the Circassians were defeated, resettled or expelled to Ottoman Turkey.

3.1 Yermolov's first offensives north of the Greater Caucasus

The resistance against Russian presence stiffened in the North Caucasus around the period of the Treaty of Georgiyevsk. In the early 1780s Ottoman Turkey fortified the port city of Anapa and undertook great efforts to Islamize the pagano-Christian Circassians. The Ottomans sensed that the common Islamic religion would be a powerful banner to rally people unwilling to submit to Russia. And around 1785 a Chechen preacher named Ushurma (d. 1794), who called himself Sheikh Mansur (the victorious), organized anti-Russian resistance. He did not appeal in a traditional way to the desire of tribes for secular freedom, but applied a religious dimension by claiming that the Prophet had ordered him to declare *ghazawat*[51] or holy war against the Russian unbelievers. In order to overcome the particularism of local tribes, he propagated Islamic *sharia* law and encouraged the abandonment of the traditional *adat* laws as well as the rule of blood revenge. In line with *sharia*, he also prohibited the consumption of alcohol and tobacco. After he had defeated a Russian detachment, his two attacks on Kizlyar failed with heavy losses and he retreated first to Kabarda where he met some acceptance among dissatisfied peasants but was rejected among the aristocracy. In 1787 he tried to win the Circassians (Cherkess) for his *ghazawat*, but his eschatological sermons and likely Sufi tendencies met with disapproval among the tribal leaders and the Sunni scholars, the *ulama*; his followers dwindled fast. While staying in Anapa in 1791, he was captured by General Gudovich in his conquest of the port. Sheikh Mansur was jailed in the fortress of Shlisselburg (Schlüsselburg) near St Petersburg, where he died in 1794.[52] To the extent that Sheikh Mansur proclaimed an Islamic basis for his call for an anti-colonial war in order to achieve a supra-tribal alliance, he was a predecessor of the three Dagestani Avar imams, Ghazi Muhammad, Hamza Bek and, above all, Shamil (for whom see below).

At the beginning of his assignment General Yermolov took two strategic decisions: his first priority was to secure the Georgian Military Highway by establishing a firm territorial corridor between the Imperial province of the Caucasus and Vladikavkaz situated at the northern end of the Military Highway. He achieved this objective by moving the border from the Kizlyar–Mozdok Line to the River Sunzha and by founding in 1817 the fortress of Nazran and in 1818 those of Grozny and Nalchik. This corridor gave Russia a secure link from Mozdok via Vladikavkaz to Tbilisi. At the same time it functioned as a robust wedge dividing the still independent southern North Caucasus into two halves, Circassia in the west and Chechnya and Dagestan in the east.[53] By founding the fortresses of Vnezapnaya south-east of Grozny (1819) and the fort of Burnaya (1821) near the city of Tarki close to the Caspian shore, Yermolov cut the Kumyk region into two and pushed the eastern end of the Kizlyar–Mozdok Line further south. This latter move reflected Yermolov's second strategy. He was well aware that the independent mountain and forest dwellers were militarily superior to Russian troops in several respects. The specific geography with its deep valleys and inaccessible forests divided the population into countless self-determined tribes and villages, which impeded the usual strategy of destroying an enemy with superior forces in one blow. The fragmented nature of mountain and forest society also made it impossible for the Russians to make arrangements with regional leaders. The North Caucasian resistance was hydra-headed, and each valley and *aul* (fortified village) had to be conquered one after the other. Furthermore, the valleys could not feed large numbers of invading troops. Finally, the Russian army consisted of compulsorily drafted peasants with little motivation, who were often poorly led by officers ignorant of mountain and forest warfare; they moved slowly and relied on artillery. Since mountains and forests were ideal ground for guerrilla wars, Yermolov's chief of staff Aleksei Velyaminov designed a step-by-step strategy. Comparing the North Caucasus to a giant fortress, Velyaminov recognized the futility of frontal attacks and recommended a siege strategy.

The Caucasus may be likened to a mighty fortress, strong by nature, artificially protected by military works, and defended by a numerous garrison. Only thoughtless men would attempt to escalade such a stronghold. A wise commander would see the necessity of having recourse to military art, and would lay his parallels [i.e. forward lines], *advance by sap and mine, and so master the place.*[54]

A tight economic blockade should be enforced against the resisting regions strengthened by military defensive lines. From these lines, rapid strikes into hostile territories should be launched to burn down villages and destroy crops in order to force the natives to further retreat. In the forests, broad roads should be cut and troops should only advance with their flanks protected by sharpshooters on both sides. In this way, the siege ring would be tightened stepwise and fertile conquered land should be given to Cossacks for colonization, which would force the mountaineers to starve, submit or emigrate.[55] In brief, the axe had to precede the bayonet.

As time would prove, some Russian commanders discarded Velyaminov's recommendations and Yermolov himself torpedoed the strategy by his harsh treatment of locals who resisted. He was convinced that the toughness of the resistance fighters should be answered by at least comparable toughness and that leniency would be understood as weakness. 'I desire that the terror of my name should guard our frontiers more potently than chains of fortresses, that my word should be for the natives a law more inevitable than death.'[56] One may surmise that Yermolov's ruthlessness added fuel to the fire of the fanatical independence which drove the local Chechens and Dagestanis. And to burn down villages built from wood was no lasting measure since they were quickly rebuilt once the Russian troops had left, but the hatred of the foreign invaders remained. In military terms, Yermolov first concentrated on pacifying Kabarda, a process which lasted till the mid 1820s. One of his major successes was to stop the kidnapping and slave trade via Anapa. Turning to Dagestan, in 1819 he crushed the revolt by the Avar khan Ahmad then marched into Chechnya where he devastated the *aul* of Dadi-Yourt, some of whose inhabitants had stolen troop horses. Most of the Chechen fighters fell after having killed their own wives to prevent them from being captured by the infidels; those women and children who were taken were sold in Russia as serfs.[57] Returning to Dagestan, on 31 December 1819 he crushed the powerful Dargin Confederation and captured its capital Akusha. In the next year, Major General Madatov, a native of Karabakh who had previously conquered the Dagestani principality of the Tabasarans, subdued the large khanate of Kazi-Kumyk (Kumuk).[58] In Dagestan, the Russian administration tried to break the power of the self-determined communities by confiscating their land and redistributing it to more cooperative local elites who were socially promoted to become a new, malleable aristocracy.[59]

Having tamed the Kumyks, Yermolov was confronted in the next few years by other 'hydra heads'. In late 1821, the Chechen bandit leader known to the Turks as Beybulat Taymazoğlu and in Chechnya as Taymi Bibolt gathered angry peasants who had lost their pastures and agricultural lands as a result of the new Sunzha Line. He was supported by the *qadi* (Islamic judge) 'Abd al-Kadr who declared the fight a *ghazwa* against the Russian infidel and condemned those Chechens collaborating with Russia as enemies of Islam. The commander of the Russian left wing in the Caucasus, General Nikolai Vasilyevich Grekov destroyed the Chechen army on 11 February 1822, but Beybulat managed to escape. One year later, on 19 July 1823, the Kumyk leader Amak Bek murdered his benefactor and fellow officer Colonel Verkovsky and joined the rebellion in the Shamkhalate, to which Yermolov immediately hastened. He ordered his troops to winter in Dagestan and, concerned that the latest rebellions had clear religious overtones, secretly met the famous *alim* (theological scholar) Said al-Harakani (1764–1834). He convinced al-Harakani that prolonged resistance would only destroy Dagestan's economy and society, whereupon the *alim* issued a renunciation of the *ghazwa*.[60] Worse was to come, however, in 1825 when Chechen fighters annihilated a Russian unit and began besieging the fortress of Gherzel. Generals Grekov and Lissanevich rushed to its relief. The besiegers fled but Lissanevich, the senior commander, insisted on punishing the inhabitants of the neighbouring *aul* of Aksai who had joined in the siege. On 16 July 300 leading men from Aksai, armed with *kinjals* (double-edged, long daggers), were gathered in the fort, where General Lissanevich abused them in Tatar. When they refused to hand over their *kinjals*, Grekov slapped one man in the face; he immediately drew his dagger and killed both generals. The garrison retaliated by massacring them all, even though several of them were pro-Russian.[61] Yermolov had to make speed to Chechnya to quell the insurrection, returning to Tbilisi in summer 1826, just in time for Abbas Mirza's attack. The Chechen revolt had collapsed not so much as a consequence of Yermolov's intervention but because of its own weak leadership. During his ten years of service, Yermolov had secured the Mozdok–Tbilisi land corridor and in the short term partly pacified Dagestan, but Chechnya and Circassia, which was still under Ottoman influence, remained unconquered.

With the Treaty of Adrianople, Russia gained the eastern Black Sea littoral from Poti in the south to Anapa in the north, and rapidly secured it with a chain of shore fortifications. Within ten years, at least twelve Russian sea forts were built between Anapa and Gagra in today's Abkhazia. Russia also established a maritime blockade to force the western Circassians to submit by obstructing their supply of salt, weapons and ammunition from Turkey. The Circassians, for their part, found themselves virtually encircled by the Kuban Line in the north, the new Russian coastal forts in the west and the Greater Caucasus in the south, and, as Moritz Wagner noted in 1843, with the loss of Anapa to the Russians they lost the traditional outlet for the slave trade, which was still their major source of income.[62] Yet even now Russia was unable to proceed with impunity, since in 1834 those Circassian tribes – the Abadzekh, Natukhai, Shapsug, and Ubykh – which had been resisting Russian encroachments since 1829, formed a defensive alliance and the following year declared their independence.[63] Furthermore, the events in Circassia came into the purview of Great Britain because of the Ottoman–Russian Mutual Defence Treaty of Hünkâr İskelesi of July 1833. This treaty could be interpreted as a first step towards a Russian protectorate over Turkey. To hinder further Russian expansion, Britain began with anti-Russian covert operations which were most probably approved by the Foreign Secretary Lord Palmerston. The most prominent agent was David Urquhart (1805–1877) who reached the north-western Caucasus in 1834 and urged the Circassians to unite and to form an anti-Russian alliance with the Avar Imam Shamil. He formulated their Declaration of Independence and incited them to attack the poorly built and quite vulnerable Russian forts, as well as those Circassian tribes which were collaborating with the Russians.[64] Travellers like Moritz Wagner and the Swiss historian and archaeologist Frédéric Dubois de Montpéreux (1796–1850) noted the weakness of the Russian forts which could only be provisioned or reinforced by sea since Circassian sharpshooters controlled the near hinterland. They also recorded that

85. Cossack irregulars from the Kuban. Source: Friedrich Heinrich Albrecht, Prinz von Preussen, *Im Kaukasus 1862* (1865), p. 54.

the garrisons consisted in part of conscripted Poles, who tended to rapidly desert to the mountains, where they would either be enslaved or fight for the Circassians.[65] In several respects, the British covert operations shared similarities with the not-so-covert US operations in Afghanistan in the 1980s, albeit on a much smaller scale. That the rebellious Circassians fought Russia also as Britain's proxy was confirmed by the British agent James Stanislaus Bell (1796–1858) who wrote that 'the heroic Circassians […] are fighting *our battles*'.[66]

The British agents supplied the Circassian with arms and ammunitions and Polish, Hungarian and French volunteers reinforced the ranks of the rebels. Urquhart was rewarded for his efforts by his appointment as Secretary to the British embassy in Constantinople in 1836. He then embarked on a project – whether endorsed by the British authorities remains unknown – that was nothing less than a provocation to war. Together with the agent and arms smuggler Bell, and a number of Polish immigrants, Urquhart chartered the schooner *Vixen*, loaded it with 100 tons of gunpowder and weapons and instructed the captain to sail to Sucuk-Kale (Novorossiysk) where it would inevitably be stopped by Russian warships. Exactly this happened in November 1836 when the *Vixen* was seized and confiscated, creating uproar in St Petersburg and London. The British government, however, did not rise to the bait when Tsar Nicholas put Russian sea and land forces into battle readiness. Urquhart was expelled from the embassy, but the Circassians continued to be supplied through other agents such as Bell, John Longworth and Edmund Spencer, even though in 1837 Britain officially recognized the validity of the Treaty of Adrianople, including Turkey's transfer of Circassia to Russia. Bell remained in Circassia till 1839, training the Circassians how to use captured Russian guns.[67] The effectiveness of British covert arms and ammunition supplies was shown in early 1840 when the Circassians succeeded in capturing four of the vulnerable Russian forts. As a consequence the Russian General Nikolai Rayevsky, who commanded the littoral fortifications line and had followed a policy of accommodation regarding the Circassians, was forced to resign. The historian Walter Richmond has concluded that British (and Ottoman) covert operations were in the end counterproductive, since they strengthened Russia's resolve 'to blockade and quarantine Circassia [which] caused mass starvation'.[68] General Rayevsky's resignation confirmed the belief of the hardliners, such as the cavalry General Grigory Khristoforovich von Zass, General Pavel Khristoforovich Grabbe and Admiral Lazar Markosovich Serebryakov (of Armenian descent), that only tough measures could achieve results. Zass adapted Velyaminov's strategy to the mountainous landscape of Circassia by adopting the highlanders' own style of warfare. He first gathered intelligence and spread misinformation about his intentions, then surprised enemy villages with long-distance lightning attacks, and retreated with the same speed, giving the locals no chance to ambush his troops. In one instance, he hid in a house and spread the rumour that he had died from illness only to launch a lightning assault on a rebellious *aul*.[69]

3.2 The jihad of the imams

In the 1780s and '90s Sheikh Mansur had waged war against Russia in the name of Islam, preaching unity in place of blood feuds and tribal antagonisms. As a consequence, his rebellions were no longer based on pragmatic demands but instead became holy wars. The same strategy was adopted, refined and extended by the three Avar Dagestani imams, Ghazi Muhammad (as war commander 1829–1832), Hamza Bek (commander 1832–1834) and Shamil (commander 1834–1859). The three imams waged a thirty years' war whose epic history inspired the Chechen struggle for independence after the collapse of the Soviet Union; hence it will be traced here in greater detail.

Since in an Imamate the imam is at the same time the political leader of his community, military commander and supreme authority in judicial and religious matters, he stands far above secular tribal chiefs and legal scholars. His will, when formulated in Islamic concepts, becomes law. In an imamate, neither language nor ethnicity nor a *jamaat* but only religion can serve as vector for creating identity. The three imams were also inspired by the order of Naqshbandi Sufism in which the blind obedience of the *murid*, the student, to the commands of the *murshid*, the religious teacher, is a key element in their respective relations. This system of personal and strictly hierarchized relations eclipsed all local clan and tribal relations; it may be compared to the organization of the present Afghan Taliban. In Dagestan, the Khalidiyah branch of the Naqshbandiyah dominated, named after its founder Sheikh Khalid al-Baghdadi (1779–1827) who not only abhorred Christians, but also any Muslim rulers who did not lead an Islamic life, as well as Shiites and Saudi Wahhabis.[70] The movement inspired by these three imams in Dagestan and Chechnya is also called Muridism, and stood in opposition not only to Russian rule, but also to the local aristocrats and khans who did not rule by the principles of Islam. Muridism was in conflict equally with the free communities of self-determined highlanders who would not bow to the authority of an imam, who stood against the customary laws or *adat*, which were the basis of the *jamaat*, and for the comprehensive and exclusive introduction of *sharia*. *Adat* consisted of historical juridical decisions taken by the community, transmitted orally or compiled in *adat*-books, a kind of village constitution evolved over generations. Since *adat* was not necessarily in accordance with *sharia* law and did not derive its authority from the Quran, Ghazi Muhammad castigated the adherents of *adat* as idolaters, since they valued their ancestors higher than the commands of God.[71] Because the three imams not only fought the Russian occupiers but aimed at the establishment of a *sharia*-based, military Islamic state, the struggle against the Russians turned also into a struggle against the traditional egalitarian way of life of self-determined *jamaats*. As history would prove, those Dagestanis and Chechens who had hoped to regain and secure their traditional freedom with the imams' help found themselves confronted by an implacably strict Islamic rule regulating every aspect of life. The alleged champions of liberty turned out to behave like despotic tyrants – a development again anticipating the rise of the Afghan Taliban.

Ghazi Muhammad[72] (*ca*. 1794–1832) was born in the same Dagestani village of Gimry (Gimrah) as his schoolfriend, fellow fighter and later third imam Shamil. He began to gather followers around 1826 and preached the introduction of *sharia*, the abandonment of *adat*, the need for *ghazwa* against the Russians and Muslim collaborators as well as a ban on alcohol, tobacco and dancing. In the following year, he convinced the villagers of Gimry and its surroundings to adopt *sharia*; those who resisted were beaten. In 1829 he first attacked several villages in Dagestan who refused to obey his command; later in the year his followers proclaimed him imam. In January 1830 he started the war (1830–1859) by sending an ultimatum to Pakhu-Bike, regent of the Avar khanate for her underage sons, to break all contact with the Russians. When she failed to comply, Ghazi Muhammad and his commander Shamil attacked the Avar capital of Khunzakh where on 14 February they suffered a total defeat. Ghazi Muhammad subsequently went to Chechnya to gain new followers. The initial Russian responses to this uprising were weak and when General Paskevich was recalled in spring 1831 to suppress the Polish rebellion, Ghazi Muhammad exploited the lack of Russian leadership by briefly capturing Tarki, then defeating General Georgy Arsenyevich Emmanuel in forest country, and finally plundering Kizlyar. In a next step, Ghazi Muhammad sent preachers to the Ingush, who were related to the Chechens, and to the Khevsurs. However, the Khevsurs were nominally Christians, with crosses worked into the masonry of their tall defensive towers (fig. 24), and chased his emissaries away.[73] When the imam threatened Vladikavkaz in April 1832, lieutenant generals Grigory Vladimirovich Rosen (1782–1841), the new commander-in-chief, and Velyaminov made haste to Chechnya, arriving in June, having destroyed all hostile *auls* on their march. On 6 August 1832 the *ghazwa* army of Chechen and Avar fighters was badly mauled by Velyaminov's troops at the Battle of Germenchuk (Kermenchik). Ghazi Muhammad and Shamil retreated to their fortified home village of Gimry, to which the Russians laid siege on 27 October. Gimry was protected by a deep canyon, but Velyaminov, who had arrived on the other side of the canyon, brought his soldiers and mountain artillery down under the cover of morning fog with the help of ropes and ladders. That the cohesion among Ghazi Muhammad's fighters was questionable became apparent two days later when Hamza Bek, the future second imam, who was leading a strong relief army, turned around in front of Gimry instead of engaging the besieging Russians. In the evening of the same day Gimry fell. Almost every defender, including Ghazi Muhammad, was killed, but two managed to escape; one of them was Shamil who would turn out to be a much more dangerous adversary to the Russians.[74]

After the death of Ghazi Muhammad a successor needed to be nominated quickly in order to avoid the movement falling apart. Since Ghazi Muhammad's trusted lieutenant Shamil was recuperating from serious wounds received at Gimry and unable to lead the *ghazawat*, **Hamza Bek** (1789–1834) was elected as the second imam in spite of his dubious behaviour during the siege of Gimry. His main action as imam was the massacre of what was left of the Avar royal family. As an adolescent, Hamza Bek had been brought up in the house of the regent Pakhu-Bike who had all but adopted him as her son. Now, having subjugated most of Avaria, he advanced in August 1834 against Khunzakh. In view of his military superiority, Pakhu-Bike agreed to submit and sent her eight-year-old son Bulakh Khan as hostage to Hamza. The imam then demanded that her two remaining elder sons, Abu Nutzal and Omar, come for negotiations. When the two young princes arrived, the trap snapped shut. Hamza had them both murdered, and after his fighters had seized Khunzakh he ordered Pakhu-Bike to be beheaded. A few months later, Shamil had the young Bulakh Khan murdered too, thus wiping out the dynasty of Avar khans. The imam then declared himself khan, but just one month later, he paid the price when the Avar Hajji Murad and his

---

86. (Overleaf) Like Gunib, the fortified village of Kakhib stood in an almost impregnable location about 3 km east of Goor. Shamilsky Rayon, Dagestan, Russian Federation. Photo 2021.

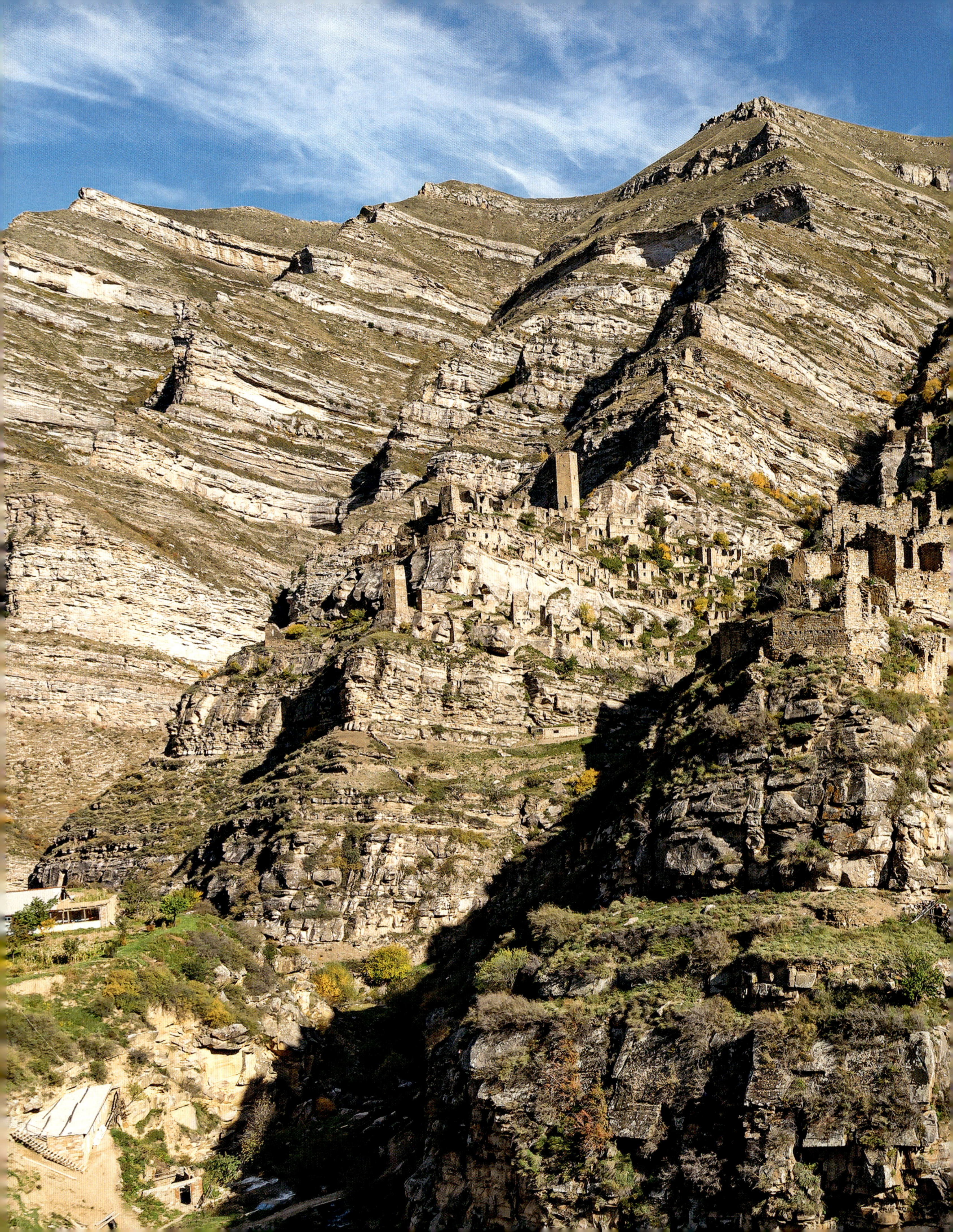

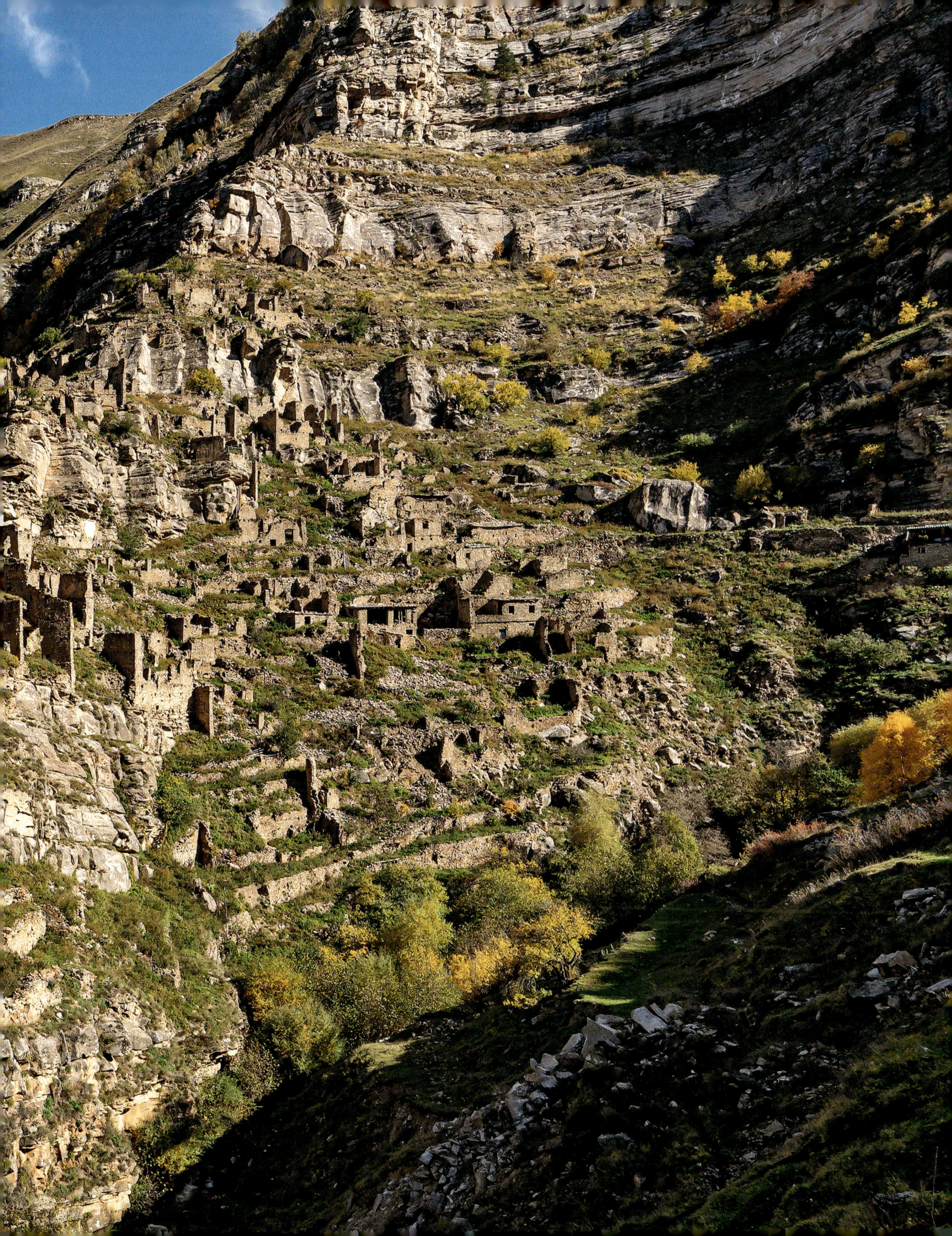

brother Othman, who were foster-brothers of the murdered prince Omar, shot him dead during mosque prayers, in accordance with the law of blood vengeance. The Avar conspirators went on to cut down Hamza's followers who had fled into Khunzakh's palace, and Hajji Murad seized power as deputy ruler.[75] When Shamil heard of Hamza's death, he hurried to the Avar village of Gotsatl to seize the treasury stored there and had himself proclaimed as the third imam. During his brief tenure, Hamza Bek laid the ground for a state administration by appointing trusted regional deputies called na'ib (plural nawwab) who reported only to him, and by hiring paid mercenaries, murtaziq, to form the nucleus of a standing professional army. To finance the mercenaries the nawwab levied taxes and very soon mutated from being mere deputies of the imam to becoming powerful regional governors who commanded their own armed guards and passed judgements according to sharia. Furthermore, since the nawwab received no salary from Shamil, they had to finance themselves, their family and bodyguards through extortion, confiscation and corruption.[76] This development rapidly downgraded the importance of the local jamaat councils. The sphere of influence of the imam changed from a loose association of independent jamaats to a hierarchically organized state, a process which Shamil would refine and complete.

The first two years of the imamate of **Shamil** (1797–1871) were rather quiet. Soon after his proclamation as imam, he concluded an informal truce with Franz Klüge von Klugenau (1791–1851), the Russian major general of Austrian descent who was based in the eastern wing of the Caucasus. Von Klugenau had only very few troops at his disposal since the bulk of the Russian forces were engaged in Circassia, while Shamil needed time to consolidate his rule. Shamil nominally accepted Russian suzerainty and promised not to bring war to the lowlands while von Klugenau committed himself to 'benevolent neutrality'.[77] In his domestic politics Shamil was implacable. As Moritz Wagner reported, he ordered his followers who had accepted Russian bribes to be buried alive.[78] Hostilities resumed in 1837 when the Russians become aware of the extent to which Shamil was strengthening his military position. In February, the new commander of the Russian eastern line in Dagestan and Chechnya, Major General Johann Kaspar Fäsi (1797–1848), a Zurich-born Swiss, ordered von Klugenau to execute a diversionary manoeuvre against the Ashitla Bridge north of Gimry, while he occupied Khunzakh. Due to the disobedience of Major General Ivelich who was commanding the vanguard, this tactical operation turned into a fiasco and the advance party was wiped out in a canyon by Shamil's fighters. Nevertheless, the main Russian army led by Fäsi won several minor engagements and captured the villages of Ashitla and Akhulgo, but was unable to force Shamil, who had entrenched himself in the fortified mountain village of Tilitl (Tiliq) south of Khunzakh, into a major field battle. Fäsi then besieged Tilitl and on 17 July, after a bloody fight, captured half of the stronghold. Shamil, who was unaware that Fäsi had run out of ammunition and that his cavalry had lost all its horses, offered negotiations to which Fäsi agreed. Shamil again nominally recognized the suzerainty of the tsar and Fäsi withdrew, a hair's breadth from victory, due to a complete logistical breakdown. Fäsi was later blamed for having missed the opportunity to put an end to the war by capturing Shamil, but he understood better than others the nature of the ghazwa: 'The fight against the Russians doesn't result from the efforts of single leaders such as Ghazi Muhammad, Hamza Bek or now Shamil, but from the religious and social prejudices [rather concepts] of these peoples.'[79]

The agreement was no more than a truce. Shamil had escaped capture or death for the second time. At the time, Tsar Nicholas was making plans to inspect the Caucasus and, based on Fäsi's report that Shamil had submitted, General Rosen ordered him to convince the imam to come to Tbilisi to present his allegiance to the tsar personally. Fäsi passed the order to von Klugenau who met Shamil on 30 September. Not trusting the Russians, Shamil refused. As a consequence, General Rosen was replaced as commander-in-chief of the Caucasus by the infantry general Yevgeny Alexandrovich Golovin (1782–1858) and the war in the north-eastern Caucasus received higher priority. In spite of the desire, expressed with increased urgency by the tsar, to finally pacify Chechnya and Dagestan, little in the way of operations took place in 1838, which allowed Shamil to build a new fortress at Akhulgo. In 1839, Lieutenant General Grabbe was given orders to capture Shamil and destroy Akhulgo. Seizing the strong fortress of Arguani en route, Grabbe laid siege to Akhulgo on 24 June with a total of 10,100 soldiers; Shamil commanded something over 1,000 fighters. The siege and capture of Akhulgo was described in detail by Dmitry Alekseyevich Milyutin who was chief of staff in the Caucasus from 1856 to 1860 and later minister of war (1861–1881).[80] Although the second major Russian assault had failed, Shamil, who had lost numerous fighters, asked for negotiations and sent his son Jamal al-Din as hostage. However, Shamil refused to surrender, whereupon on 2 September Grabbe ordered the third and final assault. After two days of house-to-house fighting, the Russians controlled Akhulgo and took about 900 prisoners, mostly women and children. All defenders were

87. The Russian army of Prince Argutinsky-Dolgorukov crosses a Caucasus mountain pass in winter 1853. The prince was supposedly a descendant of the famous medieval Mkhargrdzeli family which dominated Georgia's politics in the late twelfth–early thirteenth century. Painting by Franz Roubaud (1856–1928) from 1892. © State Art Museum of Dagestan, Makhachkala.

killed, and the victory cost Grabbe 2,200 dead and wounded. But the trophy eluded the Russians again, for Shamil and his young son Ghazi Muhammad managed to escape by climbing down the near-vertical cliffs. The imam had broken out of a hopeless situation for the third time.[81]

Having lost his Dagestani stronghold, Shamil moved to Chechnya where he gained many followers, for anger was spreading among the Chechens as a result of Russia's efforts to disarm them. By late spring of 1840, all of Chechnya rose up in rebellion. Shamil received further reinforcement when Hajji Murad, who since 1834 had stood in the Russian camp, switched sides and joined him. The imam made Hajji Murad *na'ib* of Avaria, quickly regaining power over the khanate's rural territory and tripling the size of Shamil's imamate.[82] Hajji Murad turned out to be a fighter and strategist of at least the same calibre as Shamil, which later aroused the latter's jealousy. In Chechnya, Shamil and his *nawwab* changed their strategy: instead of entrenching themselves in mountain fortresses, they now adopted guerrilla tactics, fighting in smaller, highly mobile cavalry units and avoiding pitched battles. At the same time, Shamil applied a scorched-earth policy to the border regions of his imamate, transferring its populations to the heartland. This strategy was a double-edged sword, for on one hand it established a defensive ring of barren land without provisioning and fodder, and on the other hand the heartland of the imamate became grossly overpopulated compared to its meagre resources. Even worse for the freedom-loving Chechens, Shamil strictly forbade anyone to leave the imamate, under penalty of death; even the hajj, the pilgrimage to Mecca, was prohibited.[83] These measures brought poverty and frustration to Shamil's Chechen followers and became one of the main reasons for the collapse of the imamate in 1859, when most Chechens abandoned his cause and welcomed the Russians as liberators.

In the years 1840–1841 Shamil lured the Russian commanders von Klugenau and Galafiyev into undertaking erratic marches through Chechnya. While they chased an uncatchable enemy and burnt deserted villages, they suffered continuous losses. In the meantime, General Grabbe had lobbied with the tsar for Fäsi's command not to be renewed and for himself to become commander of the eastern line directly reporting to the minister of war, thus bypassing Golovin. When in April 1842 Shamil attacked the town of Kazi-Kumyk in southern Avaria, Grabbe seized the opportunity given by Shamil's absence to make an assault on his new capital of Dargo in eastern Chechnya, which was defended by two of Shamil's *nawwab*. Since the approach to Dargo from the north led through the forest of Ichkeria, the highlands of eastern Chechnya, Grabbe's force – with more than 10,000 men, 3,000 horses and a huge baggage train – was much too cumbersome. In the dense forest, the army was unable to march in battle formation, being obliged to move forward in a narrow line. Chechen sharpshooters easily picked out their targets from behind trees while other fighters blocked the path with wooden barricades and ambushed the kilometre-long column. Having covered no more than 25 *versts* (27 kilometres) in three days and suffered heavy losses, Grabbe was forced to order the retreat, which turned into a rout. Between 11 and 16 June Grabbe lost 66 officers and over 1,700 soldiers, with precisely nothing to show for it. Grabbe resigned and Golovin was replaced by General Alexander Ivanovich Neidhardt (1784–1845).[84] Two years later, Russian forces would suffer another defeat of even greater magnitude in a Chechen forest. Following Grabbe's defeat, Shamil expanded his standing army and built a

88. The abandoned village of Gamsutl in winter fog. As proved by Imam Shamil (commander 1834–1859), such fortified mountain villages were easy to defend and succumbed only to long sieges. Gunibsky Rayon, Dagestan, Russian Federation. (See also above, fig. 70).

mountain-artillery unit out of captured Russian guns, manned by Russian deserters. In 1843 Shamil used his newly reinforced army to take all the Russian forts in Avaria except Khunzakh. In the next year, Daniyal, sultan of Elisu, who stood on Russia's side and wore the honorary rank of a Russian major general, defected to Shamil when the Russians planned to abolish his small sultanate.[85] Unable or unwilling to understand why Neidhardt's counter-offensives, launched in 1844, and employing the traditional method of powerful incursions into mountain and forest territory, failed to achieve significant results, and ignoring that only a patient war of attrition could annihilate the imamate, in January 1845 Tsar Nicholas and his bureaucratic advisors replaced Neidhardt with General Mikhail Semyonovich Vorontsov (1782–1856). As viceroy from 1845 to 1853 Vorontsov had wide-ranging powers. However, Vorontsov had been, since the Napoleonic Wars, an administrator without military command, and when Tsar Nicholas ordered him to quickly seize Dargo, he obeyed against his better judgement and the advice of his generals.[86]

Vorontsov attacked Dargo from Andi in the south and soon faced the same problems as had Grabbe two years before. His army of 21,000 men and 42 guns was too large for forest warfare and his baggage train was further obstructed by numerous 'military tourists', young aristocrats from St Petersburg or noble staff officers without combat experience who wanted to quickly gain a decoration. All these useless men – known as *fazany*, pheasants – travelled with numerous servants and extensive luggage. Moreover, as so often, Russian logistical preparations were bad. Shamil, for his part, emphasized his intransigence by having all the Chechen leaders in Andi who had conducted negotiations with Vorontsov beheaded. On 18 July 1845 Vorontsov marched with 9,500 men from Andi through the forest to Dargo, suffering severe losses on the way. But it was an advance into the void, for Shamil had evacuated all inhabitants of Dargo and burnt the village down. Vorontsov's army sat in ruined Dargo trapped with short supplies, since the Chechens blocked all outward routes. The situation became desperate after Shamil managed to destroy a supply convoy before it reached Dargo and ammunition began to run out. Desperate, Vorontsov decided to break out north to the *aul* of Gerzel and sent messengers to General Robert Karlovich Freytag (1802–1851), based in Grozny, asking for rescue. On the death march north, it seems that Vorontsov travelled safely in an armoured palanquin. By 31 July, when Freytag's relief force finally arrived to save Vorontsov's moribund army, it had lost three generals, 195 officers and four in ten of its men. In 1848, as a 'reward', Vorontsov had Freytag, whose continuing success overshadowed him and showed up his own mediocrity in non-conventional warfare, promoted away to Army Headquarters.[87] Vorontsov's ill-conceived and badly planned campaign was the worst Russian defeat in the Caucasus so far, which greatly enhanced Shamil's prestige.

The viceroy learnt his lesson and returned to the siege strategy outlined by Velyaminov, of systematically clearing forests and cutting broad roads, concentrating on Lesser Chechnya southwest of Grozny. This not only allowed for safe army movements but forced the Chechen peasants to choose between remaining loyal to Shamil and starving in the heartland of the imamate, or accepting Russian rule. As a result, Shamil's Chechen imamate gradually reduced in size. The only two Russian offensives against Gergebil, east of Khunzakh, in 1847 and 1848, failed. On the other side, Shamil retook the initiative in 1846 and marched into Greater Kabarda, the majority of whose nobles had previously refused to join the *ghazwa* and pay war taxes. In reply to this rejection, Shamil publicly proclaimed that God's wrath would send those Kabardian Muslims who refused to fight the Russians to hell.[88] But his campaign was foiled by some brilliant manoeuvring by General Freytag who, against Vorontsov's express orders, had kept troops under arms after the previous year's disaster at Dargo. Thanks to his excellent intelligence network, Freytag knew of Shamil's plans and was able to block his advances each time. Furthermore, in the plains of Kabarda Shamil's fighters lost the advantages of terrain that they had enjoyed in the mountains and forests. Above all, Freytag's tactical dispositions saved the crucial Darial Pass, controlling the Georgian Military Highway, from being captured by Shamil who was forced to flee back to Chechnya.[89] In spring 1848 Shamil took a fateful decision. He imposed his own son Ghazi Muhammad as his designated successor without consulting his key *nawwab* beforehand. By handing over the imamate to his son as if it was his private property Shamil caused much discontent. Then, as he resented Hajji Murad's fame and popularity and feared that he might dispute his son's future imamate, he condemned him to death in absentia three years later. Hajji Murad almost fell into the treacherous trap, but he escaped to the Russians. Kept under respectful surveillance in Tbilisi, he escaped again, but was caught on 5 May 1852 by a unit of Russian militia and killed.[90]

Since 1842 Shamil had been attempting to forge a pan-North-Caucasian alliance with the various Circassian tribes in the west, the majority of which refused to accept subordination under Russia. The key weakness of the Circassians was their fragmentation into tribes and clans. James Bell and other British agents had urged the Circassians to unite in their war effort, without success. Shamil now decided to try uniting them in the name of Islam and to establish a Circassian satellite imamate. His first *na'ib* Hajji Muhammad met with a positive response among the Shapsug and Ubykh but hostility from the Abadzekh and Natukhai, since he insisted in replacing the *adat* system with *sharia* law. Hajji Muhammad died in 1844, and Shamil's next envoys were Suleiman Efendi and Hajji Bakr who produced as their credentials a faked *firman* (decree) from the Ottoman sultan. The Circassians, Karachay and Kabardians refused to introduce *sharia,* to pay a *ghazwa* tax or to allow volunteers to join Shamil in Chechnya. They furthermore resented Hajji Muhammad's prohibition on trade with the Russians. Shamil's next *na'ib* Muhammad Asiyalav (known as Amin), who arrived in late 1848, was more successful. He succeeded in gaining sufficient followers to oblige the Shapsug and Natukhai to abandon their pagan rituals for Islam. He established a rudimentary administration in Circassia and mountainous Abkhazia, mainly winning the sympathies of poorer, egalitarian communities, whereas the hierarchically organized tribes tended to support the local noble Sefer Bey Zaneqo (*ca*. 1798–1860) who had worked with Urquhart. The two leaders fought for supremacy, which led to a civil war lasting from 1856 to 1858, including skirmishes between the Abadzekh and Bzhedug supporting Muhammad Amin and the Natukhai fighting on Sefer Bey's side.[91] The rivalry between the Circassian *pshi* (prince) and Shamil's *na'ib* had intensified in 1854 when the Ottoman sultan Abdulmejid (r. 1839–1861) nominated Sefer Bey pasha and supreme commander of the Circassian forces.[92]

During the Crimean War of 1853–1856, which engaged Russia against a French–British–Sardinian alliance, the Caucasus was a secondary theatre of war, as it had been in the Ottoman–Russian conflict of 1828–1829. Although Shamil made several bids for joint military operations with the Circassians and Ottomans, it never came to anything. Before the start of the Crimean War on 16 October 1853 Shamil had already crossed the Greater Caucasus in August and briefly occupied Zakatala in today's northern Azerbaijan, but he was soon pushed back. Then, in autumn, three Turkish armies attacked Georgia and forced the Russians to abandon the ports of Poti and Redut Kale, but the central Turkish army was stopped before Akhaltsikhe. Later, on 1 December 1853, General Vasily Ossipovich Bebutov (1791–1858) defeated the retreating northern Turkish army at the Battle of Başgedikler east of Kars. At the beginning of 1854, an Anglo-French fleet cleared the eastern Black Sea of Russian ships and forced Russia to abandon its littoral fortifications south of Anapa.

Anapa itself and Novorossiysk were later evacuated. Although in this early stage of the war the Ottomans pushed for a massive allied landing on the west Caucasian coast, France and Britain prioritized a landing in Crimea in order to destroy Russia's naval power and capacities. The Crimean landing began in September. At the same time, Muhammad Amin failed to rally the Circassians behind Shamil in order to launch a coordinated pan-Caucasian attack on the weakened Russians who had redeployed troops from the Caucasus to the Danube and Crimea. In Tbilisi General Nikolai Andreyevich Read had temporarily replaced Vorontsov as commander-in-chief in March 1854. Without any experience in the Caucasus, he first hesitated about the course of action to take, and then panicked. He recommended to Tsar Nicholas to evacuate the whole southern Caucasus and to retreat behind the Greater Caucasus Ridge. Outraged, the tsar replaced him with General Nikolai Nikolayevich Muravyov and secured Iran's neutrality in the war by waiving due reparation payments.[93] In July 1854, Shamil crossed the Greater Caucasus once more and ravaged Kakheti, securing a huge quantity of plunder, including four Georgian princesses whom he exchanged for his son Jamal al-Din who since 1839 had been living in Russian custody.[94] When no Ottoman troops appeared to form a pincer attack on Kartli, Shamil ordered a withdrawal in August. He was confirmed in this decision when he learnt that the Ottomans had suffered three defeats between 15 June and 5 August along the Turkish–Russian border. The imam experienced another setback when a renewed effort to join forces with Muhammad Amin again failed.

In May 1855 Muravyov, who had delegated administrative tasks to General Bebutov, laid siege to the mighty fortress of Kars. In order to reduce pressure on Kars, the Ottoman commander Omar Pasha (1806–1871) landed in Batumi in September and proceeded to Redut Kale and Sukhumi. He planned to join forces with Abkhazian and Circassian forces, but they and Shamil preferred to wait and observe developments. In the meantime, the Crimean capital Sevastopol had capitulated on 11 September and Muravyov's assault on Kars had failed at the horrendous cost of 8,000 Russian casualties either dead or wounded. Omar Pasha then marched south-westwards towards Kutaisi and scored a victory at Zugdidi, only 80 kilometres away from his goal, but was then held up by severe winter rains. Although Omar Pasha's army was marooned in the mud, the Russian commander in Mingrelia, the Georgian prince Ivane Bagration-Mukhransky, panicked and destroyed his supplies.[95] But on 28 November the Nova Scotian-born British commander of Kars, General William Fenwick Williams (1800–1883) surrendered the fortress to Muravyov, whereupon the Ottoman troops were withdrawn from Zugdidi. The Treaty of Paris ended the war on 30 March 1856. Russia returned Kars to the Ottomans but its possession of Circassia and the eastern Black Sea littoral were not challenged; Crimea was returned to Russia which was forced to renounce a Black Sea war fleet, and the Russian Black Sea coasts were demilitarized. Although Russia had been defeated, the imposed peace conditions were rather lenient since Britain was war-weary, France had no interest in the Black Sea and the Ottomans were too weak to make demands. Furthermore, Russia's capture of Kars had demonstrated Turkey's vulnerability. But the lack of unity among the various north Caucasian peoples and tribes robbed them of the chance to assert their independence, or at least autonomy.[96] For Russia's part, the Crimean War had shown how dangerous it was to host hostile powers inside its own borders that could in case of war become enemy bridgeheads. As soon as the war ended, Russia's military priority was to pacify the North Caucasus once and for all.

Four months after the Treaty of Paris, on 3 August 1856, Tsar Alexander II (r. 1855–1881) nominated three senior commanders of highest quality to lead the Caucasus army to victory: General Prince Alexander Ivanovich Baryatinsky (1815–1879) became viceroy and commander-in-chief of the Caucasus, General Dmitry Alekseyevich Milyutin (1816–1912) his chief of staff, and General Nikolai Yevdokimov (1804–1873) field commander of the left flank, that is of operations in Chechnya and Dagestan. Yevdokimov's experience in the North Caucasus was equalled by none; as early as 1824 he had distinguished himself by extraordinary intelligence and *sang-froid* and in 1837 he had accompanied von Klugenau to his meeting with Shamil. One of the first measures taken by Baryatinsky was to end the unrest reigning in the tribal region of Upper Svaneti where members of the ruling Dadishkeliani, who had shown pro-Ottoman sympathies, were quarrelling among themselves. The ruler of western Upper Svaneti, Konstantine Dadishkeliani was brought to Kutaisi and ordered to live in exile in Yerevan. Prince Albrecht of Prussia, who visited the Caucasus in 1862, narrated how during a meeting with Prince Alexander Gagarin, the governor of western Georgia, Dadishkeliani killed the prince and three staff members with his *kinjal*. The murderer was executed and all of Upper Svaneti annexed to the Empire in 1858.[97]

As recommended by Milyutin in a memorandum to Tsar Nicholas in 1854, all forces were first concentrated against Shamil; the Circassians would be dealt with in a second step. The strategy designed by Velyaminov, of cutting down forests and building broad roads at least double the range of a rifle[98] was systematically continued, and in spring 1857 Yevdokimov undertook two major deforestation campaigns in Lesser and Greater Chechnya. In the words of chief of staff Milyutin, 'he used not the bayonet as weapon of conquest but the axe'. The experienced commander was also famous for his tactic of feints to confuse the enemy and to lure them into an unfavourable position.[99] Viceroy Baryatinsky praised Yevdokimov's masterly tactics to the tsar: 'Yevdokeemoff never once gave the enemy a chance of fighting where they meant to and where the advantage might have been on their side. The strongest positions held by Shamil and his hordes fell almost without resistance as a result of well-planned movements only.'[100] By autumn 1857, Yevdokimov had brought Lesser Chechnya under Russian control. Indefatigable, he began his next campaign in December 1857 and in a winter operation conquered the Argun Valley which separated western Chechnya from what was left of

89. Imam Shamil (seated) with two of his sons, Ghazi Muhammad Pasha (left) and Muhammad Şefi (Shafi, right). Ghazi Muhammad later served in the Ottoman army, Muhammad Şefi in the Russian army. Photo by Alexander Roinashvili, before 1871.

Shamil's realm in the east. Since Shamil's fighters would burn down *auls* while retreating and carry the inhabitants off eastward, the local Chechens invited the Russians to move in before their villages were put to the torch by the retreating Islamist fighters. After Shamil's failed counterattack against Vladikavkaz in August 1858, the Chechens began to rebel in great numbers against the imamate, chasing Shamil's *nawwab* away or killing them; other *nawwab* choose to submit, bringing their subjects with them. The Chechens, who had been under siege for almost two decades and had suffered starvation, harsh rule and restricted movement, realized that Shamil's cause was lost and that submission to Russia might be a better alternative.

After Yevdokimov's storming of Vedeno near Dargo, the last capital of the imamate, on 19 April 1859, the remaining Chechen communities loyal to Shamil submitted to the Russians and the imam fled to Gunib in Dagestan. Soon the fortresses of Ullu Kala, Tilitl, Chokh (fig. 90), Ichichali and Irib, which protected the roads to Gunib, capitulated. Baryatinsky showed great leniency towards the capitulating Chechens and Dagestanis. Virtually all *nawwab*, *qadis* and other functionaries who willingly surrendered were pardoned and many of them kept their positions within the new Imperial administration. Only those officials who fought for the imamate till the end were either exiled or jailed. Gunib was an extremely well-defended mountain fortress built on a slope whose highest point stood at 2,354 metres above sea level (vol. I, fig. 20); to properly man it a garrison of about 4,000 men would have been required but only 400 fighters and armed women remained with Shamil. The assault began in the night of 5–6 September 1859 and the imam surrendered with two sons the following afternoon. He was brought to St Petersburg and lived in comfortable exile in Russia; he died in Medina in 1871 after undertaking the hajj.[101] Shamil's lasting impact on

90. The fortified village of Chokh, one of Imam Shamil's last strongholds, capitulated on 7 August 1859, one month before Shamil surrendered in nearby Gunib. Gunibsky Rayon, Dagestan, Russian Federation. Photo 2021.

Dagestan and Chechnya was on the one hand the deepening of the Islamization of their populations, and on the other his success in overcoming tribal particularisms and the creation of supra-tribal state institutions. In the latter respect, Shamil paved the way for the Russian Imperial state administration. The next task for the Russians was the conquest of Circassia.

3.3 The conquest, resettlement and expulsion of the Circassians

In Circassia and mountainous Abkhazia the starting position for Russia around 1859 was different from that in Chechnya and Dagestan. Imam Shamil had imposed on the clans and tribes of his imamate a state-like administration whose merciless harshness made the Russian Empire seem the lesser evil. The Circassians however were even more warlike than most of the Chechens and Dagestanis; they had never experienced the yoke of the imamate; and they were bitterly divided into mutually hostile clans and tribes. Furthermore, wealthier Circassians maintained close relations with the Ottomans based on the slave trade, and many coastal Circassians had a pro-Ottoman orientation that could be instrumentalized by the Turks. General Milyutin outlined in November the alternatives which applied to the whole northern Caucasus.

The conquest of a region is carried out by two methods: either (1.) by subjugating the local inhabitants and allowing them to remain on the land they inhabit, or (2.) by taking the land away from its inhabitants and placing the victors on it.[102]

The second method, of population displacement and exchange, was of course nothing new and had been practised since antiquity; it would later be applied on a vast scale at the end of both world wars. Although much fertile land was confiscated in the eastern part of the northern Caucasus and handed over to Cossacks, it was the first method that was mainly implemented there, while the second one prevailed in the west. The objective of the Russian Army High Command was to prevent insurgencies in the hard-to-control mountain areas once and for all, without having to permanently station large troop units in the region. Based on a recommendation by generals Baryatinsky, Milyutin and Yevdokimov, on 10 May 1862 Tsar Alexander II approved the plan to displace the Circassian highlanders, offering them the choice of either settling in the lowlands of the Kuban or emigrating to the Ottoman Empire. Their vacated land would be allocated to Cossacks, or left unoccupied. Contrary to allegations that Imperial Russia had intended genocide,[103] 'there is no evidence that the intention of the Russian Empire was to destroy them [the Abadzekh, Circassians and Ubykh] as ethnic groups, but simply to rid the Empire of their presence.'[104] The Circassians were exposed not only to the Russian pressure to push them out, but also to an Ottoman 'pull'. The Ottoman military was interested in acquiring bellicose young men for the Turkish army, and especially the famous cavalry units. Ottoman emissaries promised houses, fertile land and tax exemptions for North Caucasian settlers in Turkey, and furthermore spread the rumour that Russia planned a forced Christianization of the North Caucasian peoples.[105]

The large-scale emigration to Turkey began in 1858/59 when 30,000 semi-nomadic Nogai left their pastures on both sides of the River Kuban, followed in 1861 by 10,000 Kabardians. On 18 March 1864 the final Russian ultimatum expired and in May the remaining Circassian fighters were crushed in a last series of battles near Sochi. In total 500,000 to 750,000 Circassians and mountain Abkhazians migrated to Turkey in 1864–6, while about 100,000 settled in the plains of the Kuban.[106] Further, smaller waves of emigrations occurred in 1867, 1877/78 and in the 1890s.[107] These Circassians preferred to migrate to Muslim Turkey than to settle under non-Muslim rule in lowlands far away from their homeland. In Circassia, lands were granted initially to Cossacks, and later also to liberated Russian serfs. In Abkhazia, the autonomous princedom was abolished in 1864 and, alongside Russians, Greeks and Armenians, it was mainly Mingrelians who settled in the region that was now named the Sukhum Military Sector.[108] When the Circassian migrants entered Turkey, the Ottoman authorities were hardly prepared for them and their arrival had a destabilizing effect. The refugees were packed into insanitary lodgings and camps and contagious diseases soon began to spread, even in Constantinople. Although the refugees received state supplies and allowances, migrants formed armed gangs which clashed with the similarly armed bands of Kurds. The gangs also harassed the Armenians of eastern Anatolia, usually with impunity. These attacks and the lack of security precipitated an exodus of numerous Anatolian Armenians and Greeks to the Russian Empire, whereupon their abandoned houses and fields were occupied by the Circassians.[109] Another issue was slavery, since Islamic law did not permit the enslavement of Muslims. But among the refugees there were tens of thousands of slaves who were more or less Muslims. The Ottoman government proceeded with caution, recommending in March 1867 that slave-owners willing to liberate their slaves should be compensated by receiving land. On the other hand it acted to prevent Circassian slaves from escaping.[110]

Since most young Circassians underwent a thorough training in horsemanship and the handling of arms in adolescence, many of them entered the Ottoman army, mostly as irregular cavalry units. A few made spectacular careers as officers. One of them was the Ubykh, Osman Ferid Pasha (1844–1912) who became chief of the Ubykh Shapli sub-tribe when he was seventeen years old. He survived the Ubykhs' last stand in the Hodz Valley near Sochi in May 1864 and migrated to Constantinople. Due to an outstanding performance in an equestrian tournament, he entered the sultan's guard regiment, the Circassian Musketeer Guards. In 1867 he accompanied Sultan Abdulaziz (r. 1861–1876) on his European tour to London, Paris and Vienna. In 1877 he fought in Bulgaria against the Russian invaders and significantly contributed to the recapture of the strategic Shipka Pass. In 1887 Osman Ferid was promoted to major general and sent to Medina as commander of its garrison. Here he befriended Shamil's son Ghazi Muhammad who had been banished in 1882 to the Prophet's town. One year later he married Ghazi Muhammad's daughter, Shamil's granddaughter Nefiset. In 1902, Osman Ferid became Sheikh al-Haram (Keeper of the Prophet's tomb in Medina) and commander of the Hejaz. In this function he supervised the construction of the Hejaz railway with responsibility for military protection from the Bedouin. The railway reached Medina on 1 September 1908, and one year later Osman Ferid retired with the honorific title of a field marshal, but had to spend a year in exile at Mytilene on the island of Lesbos for refusing to swear an oath of allegiance to the Young Turk Union and Progress Party.[111] Not all Circassian refugees remained in Anatolia: about 250,000 of them were settled along the borders of the Balkans. Allegedly, Circassians who were enrolled in the Turkish *bashi-bazouk* irregulars distinguished themselves by special cruelty during the suppression of the Bulgarian April Revolt of 1876.[112] Forty years later, Turks of Circassian descent formed, together with Albanians, a sizeable part of the Special Organization (Teşkilat-ı Mahsusa) which played a key role in the Armenian genocide of 1915–1917.[113] While the bulk of the Circassian refugees settled in the Ottoman Empire, others emigrated to the Middle East, mainly to Syria and Jordan.

4. Russian administration and the rise of nationalism

After the conquest of the imamate most people in Dagestan were allowed to stay in their villages and keep their barren lands, not least because the Cossacks were unwilling to settle in the arid mountains. The situation was different in Chechnya where the Russian authorities confiscated much fertile farmland and gave it to Cossacks and later to former Russian serfs. Most Chechens had to be content with what land was left, but a significant number migrated to Turkey. Most famous was the exodus of 5,000 Chechen families organized in 1865 by the Ossetian general, Musa Kunduchov (b. 1820). The rift within many North Caucasian communities during Shamil's struggle also tore Kunduchov's Muslim family apart. While he made a brilliant career in the Imperial Army, two of his brothers sided with Shamil. During the Crimean War, Kunduchov commanded the important Vladikavkaz Military District where he forbade blood feud. In 1860 he was nominated head of the Chechen administration. He resolutely suppressed some rebellions, but it became increasingly difficult for him to bridge the tension between his two loyalties, as a soldier to the tsar and as a man to his people. When the discussion arose whether to resettle the Chechens north of the River Terek or in Lesser Kabarda, or even to expel them to Turkey, Kunduchov took the initiative to organize the migration of strongly dissatisfied Chechens. The Ottoman government agreed to accept 5,000 families, about 23,000 persons in all, and the tsar approved the plan in May 1864. While Kunduchov continued his military career in the Ottoman Empire, the ordinary Chechens and Ossetians who migrated with him fared badly. They soon fell into abject poverty and many of them would have returned to their homeland, but this Russia refused to allow.[114]

Following the end of the war, the administrative divisions of the Caucasus were redrawn. From north to south and west to east the following provinces were created: Don Host, Astrakhan, Kuban, Stavropol, Terek, Black Sea District, Kutaisi, Tbilisi, Dagestan, Kars (as of 1878), Yerevan, Yelisavetpol (Ganja) and Baku; Tbilisi remained the seat of the viceroy and his administration.[115] One of the first measures was the general prohibition of slavery. When the viceroy Baryatinsky resigned in 1862, the Georgian Grigol Orbeliani briefly became acting viceroy, followed by Grand Duke Mikhail Nikolayevich (in office 1862–1882, d. 1909), the fourth son of Tsar Nicholas I, who delegated most of the executive and administrative tasks to his predecessor Orbeliani. One year before, in 1861, the grand duke's elder brother Tsar Alexander II set in motion a major reform, namely the abolition of serfdom, which took place in 1864/65 in Georgia, 1868 in the Kuban and 1870 in the provinces of Yerevan, Yelisavetpol and Baku. Tsar Alexander had already declared in 1856 that 'it is better to abolish serfdom from above than to wait until the serfs begin to liberate themselves from below.'[116] It is noteworthy that the autocrat Alexander not only declared the abolition of serfdom but also succeeded in enforcing it in the same year as a terrible civil war started in the United States of America over basically the same issue. The two major problems linked with the abolishing of serfdom were the questions of land ownership and of compensation of serf-owners who lost their human 'property'. The serf-owners received a fixed *per capita* indemnification from the government, and freed serfs had the right to buy about half of the land they previously cultivated, for which purpose they could obtain a government loan. The government compensated the landowners and the peasants had to repay the corresponding loan in annual instalments, normally over seven to nine years; peasants who were too poor to pay for their land received a small lot for free depending on where they lived. Over time, with demographic growth, the reform created huge pressure on available land which led freed serfs and their descendants to migrate to the Empire's peripheries, including the North Caucasus, where the newcomers were made less than welcome by natives and Cossacks alike. It was a triangular conflict between native highlanders, Cossacks and the ordinary Russian settlers, known as *inogorodnye*. The Russian government was aware of the sensitivity of the issue: in the South Caucasus, Russian peasants were only allowed to freely settle in 1899. The huge reservoir of suddenly mobile people later fed the need for cheap labour demanded by Russia's industrialization, which would create urban proletariats prone to social-revolutionary propaganda. As in Russia, there was much resistance by the large land- and serf-owners in the provinces of Tbilisi and Kutaisi, and especially in Svaneti. The peasants, too, were angry at being obliged to pay for 'their' land, especially since repayments often extended over decades. While they were personally free, they remained in economic serfdom. Redemption payments of impoverished peasants to former landowners were only abolished in 1912.[117]

In the North Caucasus, the abolition of slavery and serfdom went less smoothly. In those regions where feudal structures were widespread, such as Kabarda and Balkaria, the aristocratic slave-owners threatened to revolt. In order to avoid unrest, the grand duke agreed to the serf-owners' demand that the serfs and slaves should buy their freedom in money or goods, which left the farmers in a state of financial dependence for many years. For many freed serfs or slaves, the only viable option was to seek seasonal work at the Cossacks' *stanitsas*.[118] On the other hand, in the North Caucasus, especially in Dagestan and Chechnya, the Russian authorities took religious and traditional sensitivities into account and chose a type of indirect rule called 'military–civil administration'.[119] Power was concentrated among higher army officers while the locals were allowed to run their internal affairs according to their *adats*. Large concentrations of Cossacks such as the Terek or the Kuban Host remained autonomous under military supervision, while scattered *stanitsas* were structured into Cossack military organizations reporting to the military administration. In the North Caucasus, as in Russian Central Asia, the natives were not subject to military conscription; they had to pay a substitute tax or, if they were suitable, they could serve as volunteers. In addition, for the higher administration at district or provincial level, Russia made a deliberate effort to hire local officials. In contrast to the Ottoman Empire where the governments' enduring weakness had forced them to allow Catholic and Protestant missionaries to evangelize among its Christian populations including Greek Orthodox, Armenians and Assyrians (Nestorians), in the Russian Empire foreign proselytizing and missionization were prohibited. In this sense, the Armenian Orthodox Church was protected within the boundaries of the Russian Empire from competition from Western Catholics or evangelicals. However, one may speculate that such missionaries would have met far less success in the Russian Empire than they did in the Ottoman. The Ottoman Christians who converted were not generally motivated by adherence to a different creed but, rather, hoped to enjoy as Catholics or Protestants the protection of European powers.

In Turkish western Armenia timid reforms took place around the middle of the nineteenth century. The Armenians within the Ottoman Empire, around three-quarters of whom were farmers, suffered from numerous fiscal discriminations. They not only had to pay the various state taxes which were collected by notoriously corrupt tax-farmers,[120] but they were additionally obliged to pay a poll tax imposed on Christians and further taxes to Turkish or Kurdish feudal landlords, and to perform various forced labour. If an indebted farmer was unable to pay his taxes, his land would be confiscated. Finally, Armenian peasants were also exploited by their church which required payments and donations at regular feast days and at events such as births, baptisms, marriages and funerals. Due to strong political pressure from Great Britain and France which had de facto saved the Ottoman Empire from Russia's grip in the Crimean War, Sultan Abdulmejid I issued a decree in 1856 which abolished the poll tax.[121] However, the Armenians' subordination to the Armenian patriarch of Constantinople remained unchanged. In the Ottoman Empire, non-Muslim religious communities were organized as *millets*. The *millet* was headed by the religious leader of the community, who was responsible for the good behaviour of its members. Provided no Muslim was involved in litigation, court cases were judged according to the community's law. In the earlier nineteenth century the major *millets* were the Greek Orthodox, Armenian and Jewish. In 1831 a Catholic Armenian *millet* emerged, and in 1847 a Protestant Armenian *millet*.[122] In distant Anatolia however other, more or less independent, rules existed. For example, large Kurdish landowners were accustomed to buying and selling whole villages, including their Armenian peasants.[123]

In January 1881, the assassination of the reform-minded tsar Alexander II by social-revolutionary terrorists put an abrupt end to the reforming spirit both in Russia proper and in the Caucasus. His successor Tsar Alexander III (r. 1881–1894) recalled Grand Duke Mikhail, replaced the viceroyalty with generals reporting to the interior minister and nominated as chief of the Caucasus administration Alexander Dondukov-Korsakov (in office 1882–1890), who was of Kalmyk descent on his mother's side. The new tsar reversed his predecessor's relatively liberal policies and initiated a programme of increased centralization and, in the Caucasus, of Russification. This latter measure was a first step towards Russian nationalism, since the term 'Russian' began to change from meaning a subject of the Russian Empire irrespective of ethnicity to denoting an ethnic Russian of Slav descent. Of course, Russia being a contiguous land empire, the question of national homogeneity stood more in the foreground than in a maritime empire like Great Britain where it was a non-issue or even considered undesirable. By, at the latest, the Berlin Congress of 1878, states began to define themselves by national and ethnic criteria, most famously to start with in the Balkans. The basis for this new political paradigm was the axiom that a well-defined ethnicity of a certain size had the right to form a national self-government, that is to live in a state of its own (smaller ethnicities were defined as minorities). This meant that national borders had to follow ethnic borders and, as a consequence, minorities had either to accept their status or to migrate to another state where their ethnicity was in the majority. As history would prove, the ultimate results of this new paradigm were population exchanges and ethnic cleansings. At the same time the Congress marked the opening point of the dismantling of land empires, since the new nation-biased paradigm even allowed for foreign intervention in empires in favour of single ethnicities.[124] By 1918, the three main European land empires, the Ottoman, Russian and Austro-Hungarian, had disappeared.

Until the 1880s Russia was careful not to erect artificial walls dividing ethnic Russians and the other peoples of its empire. Non-Russian Muslim peoples and vassal states had to give their oaths of allegiance to the tsar, and not to the Russian state which was perceived as a bulwark of Christianity *par excellence*. But from now on in the South Caucasus, Russification meant that schools were discouraged from teaching in native languages, the Russian language become dominant in the administration, and native civil servants were replaced by ethnic Russians. The Georgian Orthodox Church additionally lost privileges in favour of the Russian Orthodox Church and in 1904 the Georgian language was even forbidden to be taught in parish schools.[125] Armenian schools too were temporarily closed or the senior classes suppressed so as to force eager Armenian pupils to attend Russian higher schools. This discriminatory policy against the local people brought counterproductive results. Rather than achieving a national and cultural homogeneity, instead it brought about a sharpening of ethnicities' self-consciousness and their political radicalization, leading in turn to demands for ethnic autonomy. This development stiffened the divisions not only between ethnic Russians and non-Russians, but also among the various ethnicities themselves. Rivalries and even hostilities emerged between Georgians and Armenians and Armenians and Muslim 'Tatars', that is Muslim Azerbaijanis who are today popularly called Azeris.[126] In all three regions, Armenia, Georgia and, to a different degree in Azerbaijan, the policy of Russification instead provoked nationalism, which took an especially virulent turn in the shape of the Armenian Socialist Democrat Hunchakian Revolutionary Party (SDHP) and the Armenian Revolutionary Federation (ARF, also called Dashnaktsutyun or Dashnaks), which were inspired by the Greek and Bulgarian liberation movements.[127] In Azerbaijan, opposition to Russian rule manifested itself less in the shape of nationalism than as pan-Islamism or pan-Turkism.

Among Russian Armenians the nationalist and anti-Russian movement gained momentum under Tsar Nicholas II (r. 1894–1917, d. 1918) who nominated as head of the Caucasus administration Grigory Sergeyevich Golitsyn (in office 1897–1904), whose leitmotif was 'coldness and fear' – the best possible strategy to antagonize the local people. He soon closed Armenian and Georgian schools and banned local newspapers and cultural societies. In the first years of his administration the local middle and upper classes put up with this increased Russian repression since they distanced themselves from the anticlerical social-revolutionaries who advocated violence. Among the traditionally rather pro-Russian Armenian bourgeoisie the turning point came in 1903 when on 12 June Tsar Nicholas II signed the decree recommended by Golitsyn concerning the confiscation of the Armenian Church's revenues stemming from its properties.[128] In the words of the Italian traveller, historian and diplomat Luigi Villari in 1905, 'the Church was placed under [Russian] tutelage'.[129] In 1882, the governor Dondukov-Korsakov had already accused the Armenian Church of supporting Armenian nationalism. In the later 1890s the suspicion arose that the Armenian Church was promoting revolutionary nationalism among Armenians living in the Ottoman Empire.[130] The Golitsyn administration feared that an Armenian revolutionary struggle against the Ottoman administration would radicalize the Armenians in the Russian Empire who in turn would rise against Imperial rule. Golitsyn and the minister of the interior Vyacheslav von Plehve (in office 1902–1904) recommended that the Russian government should stop positioning itself as protector of the Ottoman Armenians since their aspirations to an independent Armenia would sooner or later include the reunification of Ottoman and Russian Armenia to create a new national entity. In this respect, the two traditional foes, the Ottoman and Russian empires, shared a common interest in suppressing Armenian nationalism.

The consequences arising from the decree on church revenues were disastrous for Russia, since it united previously bitter opponents into an anti-Russian front. The upper Armenian bourgeoisie, especially, had previously disliked the revolutionary Dashnaks who applied mafia-like methods by extorting 'protection'-money from affluent Armenians under threat of assassination.[131] The church, which had previously condemned the anticlerical

91. The citadel of the huge Ottoman fortification of Kars, built from basalt masonry. In 1386 or 1389 Kars surrendered to Timur-e Lang and was then contested by the Kara Qoyunlu and Aq Qoyunlu, and later by the Safavids and Ottomans. In 1731, Ottoman Kars withstood an attack by the Iranian Nadir Shah, but in 1745 a large Ottoman army suffered a crushing defeat by Nadir. In 1807 Kars defied a Russian attack, but was captured by General Count Paskevich in 1828. Under British pressure, however, Russia had to return Kars to the Ottoman Empire. During the Crimean War, the British general in Ottoman service Sir William Fenwick Williams defended the modernized fortress, but was forced to surrender to General Muravyov after an epidemic of cholera on 28 November 1855. At the end of the Crimean War, Russia had to cede Kars back to the Ottomans. In the Ottoman–Russian War of 1877–1878, the Russians again stormed Kars on 17–18 November 1877 and made the city the capital of an oblast of the same name. Kars Province, Turkey. Photo 2016.

Dashnaks as impious, now viewed them as possible allies; and Dashnaks as well as Hunchaks, recognizing the huge potential among the angered Armenian middle and upper classes, suddenly embraced the church's cause. While remaining critical of religion in general, they toned down their anticlerical rhetoric. In 1903 the Dashnaks founded a Central Committee for Armenian Self-Defence and in February 1904 they published their *Plan of Action for the Caucasus* which added to their previous objective – the liberation of Ottoman Armenians from the Ottoman yoke – the liberation of the Russian Armenians from tsarist rule as a step towards building a South Caucasus-wide Armenian entity.[132] Dashnaks and Hunchaks organized demonstrations throughout the South Caucasus[133] and widespread strikes, as well as a wave of assassinations of tsarist officials. The Hunchaks badly wounded Golitsyn in October 1903, who is said to have proclaimed in fury, 'in a short time there will be no Armenians left in the Caucasus, save a few specimens for the museum.'[134] Plehve was murdered in St Petersburg in July 1904 by the terrorist branch of the Russian social-revolutionaries and in Tbilisi Golitsyn narrowly escaped another assassination attempt in the same year, this time by the Dashnaks, at which he resigned his position. Dozens of state officials were murdered.[135] As Villari observed with surprise, the Russian authorities in the Caucasus at times did not hinder, or even encouraged, internationalist, socialist propaganda since they viewed it as a means to fight nationalism and constitutionalism, given that communism called for the mobilization of working classes beyond borders and ethnicities.[136] In fact, among the middle and upper Armenian classes a new understanding of national and secular identity emerged which no longer located its self-consciousness in the traditional equation of Armenian subject with Armenian Christian believer. The new self-consciousness was ethnic, secular and anticlerical.

Tsar Nicholas was forced to backtrack. He reintroduced the role of viceroy reporting directly to the tsar, and nominated Ilarion Vorontsov-Dashkov (in office 1905–1915). In August 1905 the tsar followed the new viceroy's recommendation to cancel the 1903 Armenian Church decree and to return to the church the administration of the revenues from its real estates.[137] This retraction pacified the Armenian bourgeoisie, which, as Vorontsov-Dashkov correctly perceived, was in favour of capitalism and private property and loathed socialism; moreover the church feared expropriation of its vast holdings of real estate, which was a demand of the Dashnaks. But the latter did not soften their anti-tsarist stance and moved closer to the socialists; in 1907 they called for the confiscation and nationalization of all means of production.[138]

5. The Russian conquest of the former western Armenia 1877–1878

Russia's victory in the Ottoman–Russian War of 1877–1878, while failing to secure its objectives on the main Danube front, achieved a few territorial gains in the south-western Caucasus, which was once again a secondary theatre of war. Having swiftly recovered from the defeats of the Crimean War, in 1876 Russia formally renounced clause 3 of the 1856 Paris Treaty which stipulated a neutralization of the Black Sea. Following Serbia's defeat (brought upon itself) by the Ottoman Empire in 1876, the brutal suppression of the Bulgarian revolt in April–May of the same year and the subsequent inconclusive Constantinople Conference to evaluate the creation of an autonomous Greater Bulgaria, Russia declared war on Turkey on 24 April 1877.[139] In Russia, Milyutin was now war minister. The two senior Russian commanders, brothers of the tsar, were both incompetent figureheads. In the western theatre, in today's Bulgaria, where Grand Duke Nikolai (1831–1891) was commander-in-chief, the actual leader was chief of staff General Arthur Nepokoychitsky (1813–1881), while in the Caucasus Grand Duke Mikhail's deputy Prince Dmitry Svyatopolk-Mirsky (1825-1899) was no less inept; the latter's subordinate, the Armenian Lieutenant General Mikhail Loris-Melikov (1824–1888) at least had some military competence, but was over-cautious. Ardahan and Bayazıt were soon captured, but the siege of the important port city of Batumi, which could be resupplied from the sea, dragged on and ended in failure. When in May 1877 the Ottoman fleet launched a diversionary attack by landing Circassian soldiers in Abkhazia,[140] the Russian general Kravchenko panicked and gave orders to evacuate Abkhazia, but in fact Russian troops, with the protection of the mountains, stopped the Ottoman attack.[141] General Loris-Melikov also suffered reverses. He first launched, without artillery preparation, a futile frontal infantry attack against the heavily fortified Turkish position of Zevin. Then he had to call off the offensive against Kars and evacuate Bayazıt.

In the North Caucasus, Ottoman emissaries, who were recruited among Caucasian migrants, had not been idle, and prior to the war had circulated propaganda material and letters allegedly from Shamil's son Ghazi Muhammad calling on the Muslims to rebel. In the same month as the Ottoman–Russian War began, in April 1877, an uprising broke out in Dagestan and Chechnya. Although the highland Chechen insurgents proclaimed the creation of a new imamate and elected Alibek

Haji (Khadzhi, 1850–1878) as their imam, the lowland Chechens refused to join the *ghazwa*, and coordination with the Avar rebels remained weak. Even worse, many former Dagestani *nawwab* and commanders of Shamil's imamate remained loyal to the Russian Empire and even fought on the side of the Imperial troops. Clearly the insurgents lacked a charismatic leader able to inspire combat readiness and optimism about the prospects of success. After six months the rebellion collapsed. Several thousand North Caucasian mountain people emigrated to the Ottoman Empire, while others were exiled to distant provinces of the Russian Empire and thirteen ringleaders, including Alibek Haji, were hanged.[142]

After another Russian defeat in eastern Anatolia at Kızıltepe, Milyutin sent his staff officer General Nikolay Obruchev (1830–1904) to the Caucasus, and it was he who created the meticulous plan of battle at Aladja Dagh (Alacadağ) on 15 October which resulted in a complete Russian victory, and for Turkey in the loss of almost 300 officers and 18,000 men killed or captured. After having scored another victory on their march to Erzurum, the Russians' night assault on Erzurum failed and the approaching winter forced them to settle down to a siege of the strongly fortified city. But under the Armenian general Ivan Davidovich Lazarev they achieved a decisive success on 17–18 November with the capture of Kars, where they took 17,000 prisoners and 303 guns. The fortress had been fully rebuilt since the Crimean War and possessed no fewer than twelve outlying forts which were partly connected by trenches.[143] In the west, the war was decided when Russian forces conquered the fortified city of Plevna on 10 December and then captured Adrianople (today's Edirne) on 21 January 1878. One day before the armistice was signed on 31 January, a final assault on Batumi had again failed. When the peace negotiations collapsed and Russian troops advanced to San Stefano (Yeşilköy), a western outskirt of Constantinople, on 15 February the British prime minister Benjamin Disraeli ordered a Royal Navy squadron to cross the Dardanelles and anchor near Constantinople to prevent Russia from seizing the city. The Russian–Ottoman Treaty of San Stefano, signed on 3 March 1878, which de facto ended Ottoman supremacy in the Balkans, temporarily defused the highly tense situation between Russia and Great Britain. But the terms of the Treaty of San Stefano were vetoed by Great Britain which concluded the so-called Cyprus Convention with the Ottomans on 4 June. The latter ceded administrative and military control of Cyprus to Britain while retaining nominal rights of sovereignty. In return, Britain forcefully supported Turkey at the ensuing Congress of Berlin. When Turkey entered World War I on the side of the Central Powers, Britain annexed Cyprus.

At the Congress of Berlin, which was attended by Russia, Turkey, Germany, Great Britain, Austria–Hungary, France and Italy and lasted from 13 June till 13 July 1878, the Treaty of San Stefano was nullified. As a result, Russia lost most of its gains in the Balkans but in the Caucasus obtained Batumi, Ardahan and Kars, while Bayazıt was returned to the Ottomans.[144] As a corollary of the transfer of the Batumi Province (Adjara) to Russia, some 30,000 ethnic Georgians of Muslim faith migrated to the Ottoman Empire between 1879 and 1882.[145] By far the most fateful consequence of the Berlin Treaty was the administrative transfer of Bosnia and Herzegovina to Austria–Hungary. Austria's annexation of the two provinces in 1908 enraged the Serbian nationalists, one of whom six years later assassinated the Austrian crown prince Archduke Franz Ferdinand in Sarajevo, the final trigger for World War I. What was unusual in this multilateral peace treaty is the fact that the real winners from this war were all non-belligerents: Austria–Hungary and Britain gained substantial territories and Germany, in the person of its chancellor, Otto von Bismarck, scored a diplomatic success. The losers were the two warring states. The Ottomans had to yield territories and administrative control over some of their western provinces, as ordered by the Great Powers, albeit the terms were less severe than those of the San Stefano Treaty. In the east, Turkey would recover part of its lost Caucasian territory in the Treaty of Kars signed on 13 October 1921. Russia, for its part, was robbed of its conquests in the west and the envisaged new Russian quasi-protectorate of Greater Bulgaria was shelved; it made only modest territorial gains in the Caucasus. Along with the Congress of Vienna of 1814–1815, this was the second time that the European powers drew state borders with rulers – a practice that would continue at the end of World Wars I and II. In terms of military tactics, both theatres of war exemplified the growing importance of temporary, rapidly built field fortifications, redoubts and trenches as countermeasures to the increased range and firing speed of new breechloaders. On European battlefields the war of motion began to give way to the war of position which would be the dominant mode of warfare until the introduction of tanks towards the end of World War I. Four years after the Berlin Congress, Tsar Alexander III chose to contravene clause 3 of the Treaty of Paris and create a new Russian Black Sea fleet which entered into service in 1888, and Batumi, whose status as a free port ended in 1886, was remilitarized.[146]

Oil-drilling at Baku and the Nobel brothers

The triumph of the combustion engine from the 1860s became the catalyst for a worldwide oil boom, depending as it did on an ever-increasing oil supply. Two of the key pioneers in the oil drilling business were the Swedish Nobel brothers, Ludwig (1831–1888) and Robert (1829–1896), brothers of Alfred Nobel (1833–1896), the inventor of dynamite and founder of the Nobel Prize. Their father Immanuel (1802–1872) researched explosives and invented an underwater explosive mine whose devastating power he demonstrated to the tsar's brother Grand Duke Mikhail in 1842. Nobel's underwater mines proved their defensive power during the Baltic War (1854–1855) which was fought in parallel with the Crimean War.[147] In the Gulf of Finland Russia had mined the approaches to the huge fortifications at Kronstadt and Sveaborg (today's Suomenlinna) which protected St Petersburg. Twice, in 1854 and 1855, Nobel's minefields prevented enemy fleets from approaching close enough to bombard Kronstadt.[148] Strangely enough, the Russian admiralty did not mine the ports of Crimea in order to prevent or at least hamper an enemy naval landing, something which might have changed the course of the war. In spite of this contribution to Russia's security in the Baltic War, Immanuel Nobel went bankrupt in 1859, since Russia itself stood at the brink of insolvency and its government had moreover been forced by the Treaty of Paris to purchase heavy equipment exclusively from the victorious allies. As a consequence, Russia cancelled its orders from Nobel and refused to pay financial compensation.

In 1862 Immanuel's son Ludwig founded a machine and weapons factory producing shrapnel shells and converting muzzle-loaders to breechloaders. Two years later, Immanuel's youngest son, Emil (1843–1864) was killed in an explosion while experimenting with glycerine. In March 1873 Ludwig Nobel sent his brother Robert to Baku to purchase local walnut wood for the production of rifle stocks. In Baku, Robert learnt that the government had relinquished its oil drilling monopoly as of 1 January and that licences for oil drilling were being auctioned to private investors since the state lacked the capital for investment. Robert quickly recognized the immense opportunity and with

92. Oil derricks of the Branobel Company owned by the Nobel brothers. Absheron Peninsula, Azerbaijan. Photo from the later nineteenth century. © Baku Nobel Heritage Fund.

93. The residence of the local oil baron Isabey Hajinsky (1862–1918) in Baku, built in 1912 next to the so-called Maiden Tower (Qız Qalası) dating from the twelfth century. Baku, Azerbaijan. Photo 2016.

the money he had been given for buying walnut trees purchased, without consulting with Ludwig or Alfred, several oil drilling licences and a small refinery. Like his brothers, Robert was an ingenious inventor and soon his refinery was producing the highest-grade kerosene in Russia and within a few years pushing the previous, American suppliers out of the Russian market. In 1876 Ludwig Nobel personally analysed the oil business in Baku and decided to expand the business from drilling and refining to include pipelines, pumping, rail transport and storage. As so often, revolutionary inventions provoked the wrath of the beneficiaries of the established system, and armed Cossacks had to protect the first pipeline built in 1877 connecting an oil well to the refinery from the attacks of furious horse- and mule-cart owners. Ludwig Nobel also revolutionized the method of storing oil. Instead of using artificial lake basins where much of the oil either evaporated or soaked away into the ground he built above-ground oil reservoirs made of iron which greatly reduced waste and removed the danger of oil lakes burning. The next innovation followed in 1878. This was the world's first oil tanker, *Zoroaster*, which had 21 watertight compartments. Two years later, Ludwig invented a new kind of tanker, in which the ship's hull became part of the oil storage, and introduced flat-hulled barges on the Volga to bring refined oil products to Nobel's storage centre at Tsaritsyn (today's Volgograd, formerly Stalingrad). After having created a fleet of ships, Ludwig built in addition his own fleet of railway oil-tank wagons. The first oil-carrying train reached St Petersburg in 1881 and two years later Nobel had 1,500 tank wagons in operation, including (as of 1883) on the Baku–Batumi Railway, which had been financed by the Rothschild banking group which was aiming to establish a new oil business independent from Rockefeller's leading Standard Oil. With the Rothschilds the Nobel brothers were dealing with the largest financial power in Europe, which had financed the British participation in the Crimean War and would in 1904 contribute to financing Japan's attack on Russia.[149] The recently acquired coastal city of Batumi became an important oil terminal and port, with access to the Mediterranean Sea from where textiles, cotton and manganese were also exported. Batumi experienced a rapid economic boom which laid the ground for the existence of a troublemaking proletariat prone to strike action.

Within Russia, oil products were brought by rail and water from the local Nobel storage tanks to the major retail centres. Thus the company was vertically integrated, controlling the whole chain of supply from the oil well to retail. As the historian of the industry Robert Tolf noted, 'from well to wick it was all Nobel'.[150] Further Nobel milestones were Russia's first gasoline refinery and by the late 1870s the world's first fleet of ships equipped with oil burners. To procure the necessary investment capital, in 1879 the three Nobel brothers founded the shareholder company Branobel which ran dominant businesses in oil production, processing, transport and sales. Branobel also produced oil in Derbent, Grozny and Maikop.[151] Ludwig Nobel died in 1888 and was succeeded by his son Emanuel (1859–1932). In late 1885 Standard Oil initiated a price war in Europe including sabotage actions against Branobel and Bnito, the Rothschild oil company. After a first oil syndicate founded by Emanuel Nobel failed, in 1894 a new European-wide syndicate was created consisting of Branobel, Bnito and the Russian-Armenian oil tycoon Alexander Mantashev, in order to put an end to the counter-productive and costly price wars and rivalries. One year later, on 14 March 1895, Standard Oil joined the syndicate which became a worldwide cartel. Around 1897, the oilfields of Baku and the adjacent Absheron Peninsula produced 45 per cent of the worldwide output, and of this Branobel owned 20 per cent, that is 9 per cent of world production. Branobel's extremely strong position was amplified by its bulk purchasing of crude from competitors in Baku and its tight vertical business organization, especially its dominance in transport and storage within Russia.[152] A financial crisis occurred in 1897 after Alfred Nobel's death the previous December, as he had bequeathed his fortune to his future Alfred Nobel Foundation which meant that his shares in Branobel had to be sold. Since Alfred was the largest single shareholder, selling his shares at the stock exchange would have severely weakened the Nobel family's hold on the company. Against the fervent wishes of his family, especially Robert's heirs who had already filed law suits, and even of the king of Sweden Oscar II, Emanuel refused out of respect for his dead brother to legally contest Alfred's will. He took out a loan from a German bank and bought up Alfred's holdings. In 1897 Branobel initiated the construction of the 835-kilometre Transcaucasian Baku–Batumi pipeline, which ran in parallel to the railway line which was completed in 1906.

Baku's oilfields were the source not only of great fortunes – the region generated around 90 per cent of the wealth produced within the South Caucasus[153] – but also of poverty among its workers and therefore a hotbed for all kinds of revolutionaries. Lenin quickly identified the revolutionary potential among the Baku oil workers and sent some of his best agitators there, such as Leonid Krasin (1870–1926), who was also a bomb maker and co-planner of the infamous 1907 Tbilisi bank robbery (see below); Lev Kamenev (1883–1936); and Ioseb Jughashvili, later Joseph Stalin (1878–1953). The main tools of these Bolsheviks[154] for promoting their goal of a proletarian revolution were propaganda, strikes, violent demonstrations which would provoke bloody reprisals by the security forces,[155] and the murder of class enemies. Major strikes in the oil industry began in Batumi in 1901–2, directed against the Rothschild and Mantashev facilities and instigated by Stalin.[156] In 1903 an oil workers' strike at Baku, also involving Armenian socialists[157] rapidly spread – thanks not least to the speed of communications by railway and telegraph – to Tbilisi and Batumi and then to other Russian industrial centres. This country-wide general strike incited a violent reaction in the ultra-nationalist movement of the Black Hundreds. In December 1904 the Mensheviks crippled the Baku oil business with a general strike which flared violently up again after the Bloody Sunday massacre in St Petersburg on 22 January 1905 when Imperial guards fired at unarmed demonstrators. The strikes culminated in early September in anti-Armenian pogroms and in the devastation of more than a thousand oil wells mainly belonging to the Rothschilds.[158] These outbursts of blind destruction and hate were provoked by the Black Hundreds and by Stalin's proclamation 'Workers of the Caucasus, the hour of revenge has struck', and they were carried out by Muslim Tatar workers.[159] About 2,000 people were killed, the majority of them Armenians. In 1906 strikes and bloody unrest extended also to Grozny.

The xenophobic excesses of the 1905 Baku unrest had three main causes: first a general tendency to discriminate against Jews in the Russian Empire; second the intensified anti-Semitism that welled up when it became publicly known that the Rothschilds had financed Japan's victorious attack on Russia.[160] Third, the class struggle in Baku, Batumi and Tbilisi was at the same time a clash of ethnicities, since in the oil industry the vast majority of managerial and clerical jobs were held by Armenians and Russians while the dangerous and unhealthy job of drilling, and other menial and underpaid jobs in docks and factories, were performed by Muslim Tatars, that is people from today's Azerbaijan and Dagestan, and by Iranians. For the exploited Muslim Tatars the class enemies were thus first the Christian Armenian employees, managers and capitalists, and second the Russian capitalists and state officials. For poor Tatar workers, Stalin's proclamation meant revenge on the economically more successful and wealthy Armenians. Next to territorial issues this social conflict was one of the main causes for the persistent Azerbaijani–Armenian antagonism.

Branobel also attracted excellent engineers and inventors, above all Karl Wilhelm Hagelin (1860–1955) who in the late 1880s built Russia's first propeller-driven oil tanker to replace the paddle wheelers which as well as being slower also had a lower load capacity and consumed more fuel. In 1900 he became CEO of Branobel and three years later introduced Russia's first diesel-powered oil barge. In 1907 Hagelin designed and began construction of the world's first diesel-powered oil tanker. In 1908, two Nobel diesel engines each of 120 horsepower propelled the first diesel submarine, *Minoga*; in 1909 the submarine *Akula*, driven by three 300-horsepower Nobel engines was so successful that it became the base for a whole class of early submarines. In 1911 Branobel suffered a setback when the newly formed Royal Dutch Shell bought the Rothschilds' oil companies Bnito and Mazut.[161] Emanuel Nobel not only refused the proposed takeover of the Rothschilds' Russian business but had also rejected a Rothschild proposal to jointly expand into the Far East together with Royal Dutch Shell. Instead, in 1916 Emanuel bought his main Russian competitor Russian General Oil Corporation (RGO) to which Mantashev & Co. also belonged. In 1914 RGO had launched a hostile takeover bid for Branobel but, having bought Branobel shares at highly inflated prices, RGO ran into financial problems and two of its anchor shareholders were forced to sell their RGO shares to Emanuel. In 1916, Branobel controlled almost half of Russia's oil business. But calamity was near. Russia had entered World War I fully unprepared, with mediocre senior command. In 1917 the army and government collapsed, public security broke down and anarchy spread and in 1918 the Bolsheviks nationalized – that is confiscated – all production facilities and transport operators, and seized bank deposits. The Nobel empire was gone. While Hagelin fled to Sweden in spring 1918 Emanuel took refuge in Mineralnye Vody in the North Caucasus which was controlled by the Whites.[162] When units of the Red Army approached, Emanuel, who was a virtual prisoner of the Whites, fled with forged passport and permission to travel to Stavropol where he boarded a train a few hours before Red Army troops entered the city. Since in early 1923 Royal Dutch Shell broke the embargo on Soviet oil and purchased huge quantities of Baku oil directly from the Soviet Union, in which it was soon followed by France, Great Britain and Italy, the Nobels had no chance to regain any of their property. Furthermore, being a Russian national, Emanuel Nobel had no support from any of the Great Powers for compensation from the Soviet Union for the loss of his assets. In retrospect, Baku was, during the four decades of the Nobel oil empire, one of the world's two leading crude producers, a major European business centre and a key player in Russia's industrialization and modernization. It never regained this position and, in spite of the later discovery of off-shore oil and gas fields, Azerbaijan ranks today as a secondary producer of fossil fuels.

6. The emergence of nationalist and social-revolutionary parties, Armenian massacres and ethnic unrest

In the 1880s, two closely interrelated megatrends emerged and gained increasing momentum in Europe and Russia, namely industrialization and socialism. The rapid rate of industrialization gave rise in urban centres to a new class of industrial workers, poorly paid and living in precarious conditions. They were a fertile ground for socialist ideologies and their programmes of action. While industrialization, trade and socialism shared international dimensions, a third megatrend had the opposite orientation: nationalism, and especially ethnically based nationalism. In the Caucasus, socialism and nationalism emerged – mainly in the more industrialized south – in the later 1880s and 1890s; but their objectives were often at odds. The social situations of the three major ethnic groups of the South Caucasus were different. In general, the Georgians were rather rural: landlords, farmers or low-skilled workers in the major conurbations of Tbilisi, Batumi and Kutaisi. In Azerbaijan, apart from the merchants, the majority of the natives were peasants or low-skilled workers in the Baku region. The social fabric of the Armenians was more complex for they lived in two mutually hostile empires. Within the Ottoman Empire the vast majority were peasants who suffered discrimination and the remainder were urban traders. Within the Russian Empire Armenians had quickly adapted to the different conditions and seized the new opportunities available, for example access to the huge Russian market. Besides the peasants living in the rural and underdeveloped Yerevan Province, many Armenians in Russia were urban traders or, to a lesser degree, industrialists belonging economically to the middle or upper classes; others were skilled or white-collar workers. In Tbilisi and Baku the Armenian bourgeoisie and Russians dominated the economy. The largest Armenian community lived in Tbilisi where they formed the majority of the city's population. Georgians were a minority in Tbilisi; their largest community lived in Kutaisi.

6.1 Armenian nationalist and socialist parties in the Russian and Ottoman empires

The formation of radical opposition parties in the South Caucasus was facilitated by young men studying in Russia or Europe – the Russian administration refused to open any universities in the South Caucasus – where they picked up radical ideas which they then brought home. In 1887 in Geneva young eastern Armenian revolutionaries formed the Social Democrat Hunchakian Party (or Hunchaks) whose goal was to free the western Armenians from the Ottoman yoke and to establish an independent socialist Armenia. Three years later, other revolutionaries in Tbilisi founded the Armenian Revolutionary Federation (or Dashnaks), whose objective was to achieve autonomy including political and economic freedom for Turkish Armenians, in the form of some kind of Armenian state within the Ottoman Empire; the fight against Russian rule was a secondary objective to be pursued at a later stage. The Dashnaks were less concerned with socialism and much more nationalistic than the Hunchaks. The strategy of the Dashnaks consisted of guerrilla war in the countryside fought by their *fedayi* (Armenian militia), and in the cities, terrorism.[163] The Hunchaks for their part used mass demonstrations and strikes. The Dashnak *fedayi* in eastern Anatolia also strove to protect Armenian villagers from the robberies and extortions committed by Kurdish bands. This strained situation came to a head in 1894. By the Berlin Treaty of 1878 at the latest the plight of the Armenians had been internationalized and the treaty's article 61 had requested that the Ottoman Empire end the Armenians' persecution.[164] Repeated European pressure to implement reforms led Sultan Abdul Hamid II (r. 1876–1909) to integrate the unruly Kurds, Circassians, Turkmen and Arabs into an irregular cavalry formation called Hamidiye Alayları, 'Hamid's Regiments'. The Hamidiye were supposedly created on the model of the Russian Cossacks, but in fact their objective was to fight rebellious tribes and Armenian social revolutionaries. In the end, they took an active part in the forthcoming Armenian massacres.

Even before the ARF/Dashnaks began their armed resistance within the Ottoman Empire, there had been clashes between Armenian communities and Turkish troops. Such an event occurred in 1862 when Turkish troops and Circassian and Kurdish irregulars attacked the previously autonomous Zeitun region (today's Süleymanlı) east of Cilicia in southern Turkey. When the Armenians repulsed the Ottoman troops, the latter established a tight blockade around Zeitun to starve the Armenians out. Thanks to French diplomatic intervention the blockade was lifted but Zeitun had to tolerate a Turkish garrison nearby.[165] The great massacres of Armenians of 1894–1897 began in summer 1894 when Armenians of Sasun in the province of Bitlis resisted excessive tax demands using arms supplied by the Dashnaks, whereupon army troops and Hamidiye irregulars struck, leaving some 3,000 Armenians dead. Soon after, mass Armenian demonstrations were answered by massacres throughout eastern Anatolia and in Istanbul which grew in violence after France, Russia and England again protested in May 1895 against the mistreatment of the Armenians. The situation was further aggravated by a failed Dashnak terrorist attack against the sultan. In order to draw further attention to the ongoing persecution, in August 1896 armed Dashnaks attacked the Ottoman Bank in Istanbul which was run by European creditor states, and took its personnel hostage. They demanded the swift implementation of the promised reforms in the six Armenian *vilayets* of Van, Diyarbakır, Bitlis, Erzurum, Sivas and Kharput. This desperate act brought no positive results, and thousands more Armenians were murdered in the capital. That armed resistance could be successful, however, was again exemplified by the autonomous Armenian community of Zeitun where the Hunchak party had opened a branch office. In October 1895 regular Turkish troops armed with cannons and reinforced by thousands of Circassian and Kurdish irregulars again attacked Zeitun but the defence held out, and this time the attackers suffered heavy casualties. After international mediation Zeitun received a Christian governor and the excessive tax demands were reduced.[166] When the pogroms ended, some 2,500 towns and villages had been plundered and 88,000 Armenians, as well as 15,000 Assyrians (Nestorians) had been murdered. In the words of the historian Richard G. Hovannisian, 'the twenty-five-year process of eliminating Armenians of the Ottoman Empire had begun'.[167] It must be specified that Sultan Hamid was no racist; he wanted to restore his authority, and to do so used cruel and brutal measures. By contrast, the Young Turks who would organize the genocide of 1915–17 built their actions on ethnic criteria, since they wanted to wipe out Armenians from Turkish soil.[168] Unlike the previous killings, the massacre at Adana in 1909, which cost more than 20,000 Armenian lives, was for the most part a local pogrom linked to a counter-putsch in the capital and Abdul Hamid's fall.[169]

As mentioned above, the year 1903 was a turning point in the strategic orientation of the ARF/Dashnaks. When Russia seized the revenues of the Armenian Church, the ideologically anticlerical Dashnaks not only began to defend the church for nationalistic reasons but also declared war on tsarist rule and began a campaign of assassinations of Russian high officers and officials. From 1904 to 1908 about 250 people were murdered or mutilated by bomb explosions.[170] The party's long-term goal now became the creation of an independent socialist confederation consisting of the six Ottoman Armenian *vilayets* and the South Caucasus. By moving to the left and incorporating socialist goals into their programme, the Dashnaks changed in the years 1906–1907 from a nationalist avant-garde to a revolutionary nationalist-socialist popular party, which also sought cooperation with Russian revolutionaries. The Dashnaks' pro-church swing had only been a tactical, temporary one. However, their robust intervention on behalf of the persecuted Baku Armenians had the side-effect of stimulating the Muslim Tatars to form their own organizations. When it became obvious that the Dashnaks threatened the stability not only of the South Caucasus region but also of neighbouring Iran where a large Armenian community lived, the Russian government and the viceroy Vorontsov-Dashkov came to the decision in 1908 that the party had to be stamped out across the Empire. To this end, several strategies were applied. First they courted the Armenian bourgeoisie, which loathed the Dashnaks for their mafia-like methods of extorting subsidies, and the Armenian Church. Second the Tbilisi authorities recruited the famous Dashnak guerrilla fighter Gabriel Keshishian aka 'Mihran', who had fallen out with the party over its reorientation towards socialism and had become the target of its gunmen. Keshishian's information on the Dashnak network enabled the police to arrest more than a thousand party members or suspects. However, when 159 Dashnaks were brought to trial in 1911–1912, the verdicts handed down were, for political reasons, surprisingly mild: two-thirds were acquitted and the remaining 52 were sentenced either to an easy exile or to no more than a few years in prison.[171] Finally the Armenian Church had to be cleared of its Dashnak sympathizers and supporters, but the main stumbling block towards achieving this was Patriarch-Catholicos Mkrtich Khrimian (in office 1893–1907) who was a fervent nationalist and maintained contact with Dashnak activists. His death in late 1907 gave Russia the chance to impose a friendly incumbent. After several tribulations and the brief term of Matteos II Izmirlian (in office 1908–1910) Tsar Nicholas followed the viceroy's recommendation and chose Gevorg V Surenian (in office 1911–1930).[172] By now, the Dashnaks had virtually lost their support base among Russian Armenians and, given the fact that only St Petersburg offered any chance of theoretically helping the Ottoman Armenians,

the party recommended a moratorium on terrorist acts against Russia. As Vorontsov-Dashkov guessed, in view of the rise of pan-Turkish nationalism and growing unrest among the South Caucasian Muslims, the Armenians and Georgians had no choice but to submit to Russian rule, since the likely alternative was Turkish Muslim supremacy.

In the Ottoman Empire at the beginning of the twentieth century a heterogeneous movement called Young Turks emerged, which counted much of its support among the younger army officers and aimed to replace the existing absolute monarchy with a constitutional form of government. One of their groups was the revolutionary party known as the Committee of Union and Progress (CUP) which in the revolution of July 1908 forced the sultan to accept a constitutional democracy. Five years later, in 1913, the CUP seized power and established the dictatorship of a triumvirate consisting of interior and prime minister Mehmet Talaat Pasha (1874–1921), war minister İsmail Enver Pasha (1881–1922) and navy minister Ahmed Jemal (or Cemal) Pasha (1872–1922). Since the CUP initially fought for a democratic system, the Dashnaks concluded a tactical alliance with this Young Turk party in 1907. In the 1908 parliamentary elections the Armenians even gained seats and the official status of the Armenians was raised from 'non-Muslim subject' to 'normal citizen'.[173] This equalization of status for Christian Armenians and Assyrians aroused the wrath of the Kurds and their leaders, including the Hamidiye commander Ibrahim Pasha Milli, which erupted first in the Adana massacres and later in the genocide of 1915–1917. The alliance of the Dashnaks with the CUP was however double-edged, for there existed within the CUP a powerful and ever-growing trend in favour of Turkish nationalism. For the nationalists, it was shocking that in the new Ottoman parliament elected in 1908, of the 288 deputies 141 were non-Turks. Of the latter, the 60 Arab and 27 Albanian deputies were Muslims, but the 26 Greeks, 14 Armenians and 10 Slavs were Christians, and in addition there were four Jews.[174] The Dashnaks hoped that their cooperation with the ruling Young Turks would secure security of life and property for the Ottoman Armenians as well as their civil rights and would lead to autonomy for the six Armenian *vilayets*. But, as observed by the German World War I general Friedrich Freiherr Kress von Kressenstein, who knew Enver Pasha personally, the latter advocated transforming the multi-nation Ottoman state into a Turkish national state, and ideally a Greater Turkish state that would reach from reconquered territories in the Balkans in the west to Russian Kazan in the north, encompassing the Caucasus and Iranian Azerbaijan and

94. Armenian gilt silver episcopal crozier (staff) from Van, eighteenth century. The hook is ornamented with six dragon or snake heads opening their mouths. Although in the Bible the serpent often carries a negative connotation, this crozier was associated with the miraculous staves of Moses and Aaron. © Inv. metal N 163, Cathedral Museum, Holy Etchmiadzin, Etchmiadzin, Armenia.

stretching as far as Central Asia.[175] In fact, the nationalist Young Turks had learned the lessons of the lost 1877–1878 war against Russia which had led to the expulsion of half a million Muslim Turks from the Balkans, and of the Congress of Berlin which questioned the legitimacy of multi-ethnic land empires.[176] From all this the Young Turks concluded that the Ottoman Empire had to become Turkified in order to survive; and whereas there was space for non-Muslim and non-Turkish people in the Ottoman Empire, in an ethnically defined Turkish national state there was none. Talaat Pasha's slogan 'Turkey for the Turks' perfectly encapsulated this new ideology. In a nutshell, empires are inclusive of various nationalities, pure nation states are exclusive. For Talaat, the Armenians formed an obstacle to the successful establishment of a Turkish nation state; and it was an obstacle that had to be eliminated.

In spite of this dangerous political stance, the Dashnaks confirmed their alliance with the CUP in 1909 and maintained it till January 1913 when the ultranationalist CUP triumvirate seized power in a *coup d'état*.[177] When the Ottomans suffered a catastrophic defeat in the First Balkan War of 1912–1913, Russia worried that in the case of the Empire's collapse a subsequent armed insurgency of the Ottoman Armenians might spread to the Russian Armenians and destabilize the whole South Caucasus. Of course, Russia's policy towards the Ottoman Empire was highly contradictory since at the same time as criticizing the Ottomans for failing to keep order in eastern Anatolia and protect the Armenians from Kurdish attacks, it also supported the Kurdish rebels.[178] The Imperial Russian government exerted the greatest pressure on the CUP regime to implement immediate reforms in the six Armenian *vilayets*, insisting that they should be unified into a single Armenian province placed under European control, a severe infringement of Ottoman sovereignty. The Ottoman government had no choice, but the plan raised apprehensions among European powers that Russia intended to annex eastern Anatolia. The Russian and German ambassadors to the Ottoman Empire, Mikhail Nikolayevich de Giers and Baron Hans von Wangenheim, worked out a compromise whereby two Armenian provinces would be created. The first should consist of the *vilayets* of Erzurum, Sivas and Trebizond (Trabzon), the second of Van, Bitlis, Kharput and Diyarbakır. Two inspectors general with far-reaching powers should control the provinces' executive and legislative bodies as well as the regional armed forces. For the Erzurum province, the Norwegian major Nicolai Hoff was nominated, and for the Van province the Dutch colonial administrator Louis Westenenk.

Both inspectors arrived in Constantinople in June 1914 ready to take up their positions. The Ottoman Armenians placed great hopes into this solution of the so-called 'Armenian Question' and one may wonder if an independent Armenian state would have emerged in due course. But when World War I erupted and the Ottoman Empire declared general mobilization on 3 August, the reforms were stalled and the two inspectors recalled. The experiment was scrapped before it started and less than a year later the Armenian Genocide would begin.[179]

After the Baku unrest, the ARF/Dashnaks became active in Iran too, where Iranian oil workers from Baku radicalized opposition to the regime of Shah Muzaffar al-Din Qajar (r. 1896–1907), who was forced to accept a constitution and to convene the national parliament (*majlis*) in summer 1906. Unlike the Ottoman Empire, which remained politically independent albeit financially dependent on credit-granting European powers,[180] Iran was both financially and politically subordinate to European directives. This was exemplified by the Anglo-Russian Convention of 31 August 1907 which, among other things, divided Iran into three zones: the northern provinces fell into the Russian zone, the south-eastern into the British one and the remaining central and south-western provinces formed the neutral zone which the Iranian government was allowed to administrate.[181] In June of the following year, Shah Muhammad 'Ali Shah Qajar (r. 1907–1909) organized a counter-putsch with the help of the Iranian Cossack Brigade[182] which triggered a second revolution, beginning in Tabriz. Constitutional leaders and troops rejected Shah Muhammad's authority and for ten months withstood the siege by monarchist governmental forces thanks to the vigorous assistance of Armenian guerrilla fighters. The stalemate ended on 30 April 1909 when Russian troops scattered the monarchists and arrested several Armenian *fedayi*, while the remainder fled to the Ottoman Empire.[183] One of those *fedayi* who stayed in Iran was the Armenian Yeprem Khan (1868 or 1873–1912) who joined the Iranian revolutionary Sattar Khan and the Bakhtiari tribe, which supported the constitution. Yeprem Khan's armed units then seized Rasht, Qazvin and Tehran in July 1909 where the *majlis* deposed the shah in favour of his underage son Ahmad Shah Qajar (r. 1909–1925). Abandoning the revolution, the former Armenian Dashnak Yeprem Khan became police chief of Tehran. In this function he disarmed the constitutionalist Sattar Khan and his followers and closed the *majlis* in December 1911 which earned him the hostility of the Dashnaks. He fell in combat against supporters of the ousted Muhammad 'Ali Shah in 1912.[184]

6.2 Georgian socialists

After the Russian Social Democratic Workers' Party split between Bolsheviks and Mensheviks in 1903, the latter formed the leading opposition group in Georgia, although Bolsheviks including the two Georgians, Joseph Stalin and Sergo Konstantinovich Ordzhonikidze (1886–1937) continued their murderous activities, including the attack in Tbilisi on 26 June 1907 on a bank stagecoach transporting money. Raiding banks and money transports was a method of procurement often used by the Bolsheviks. This hold-up was ordered by Lenin, Krasin, Stalin and Litvinov. It was planned by Stalin (nicknamed 'Koba') who was based in Tbilisi and had been organizing workers' walk-outs since 1898, and the attack was carried out by the Armenian Bolshevik Ter-Petrosian (aka 'Kamo') who ran a gang of bandits. The attackers acted with great brutality and ruthlessness; their bombs killed forty people and wounded another fifty. The robbers escaped with 241,000 roubles.[185] The murderous attack was counterproductive for the Bolsheviks, since even in Western Europe they were unable to exchange the numbered large-denomination banknotes into smaller units, while most Georgians found the blatant ruthlessness of the hold-up repulsive and daunting. Leon Trotsky, then a Menshevik, accused Lenin of degrading the socialist revolution to the level of banditry and robbery.[186] What the Bolsheviks lost in sympathy, the Mensheviks gained.[187] Their moderate nationalist stance also increased their attractiveness. This stance was sharply criticized by Stalin's future henchman, the Georgian Lavrenti Beria (1899–1953). He accused their leader Noe Zhordania (1868–1953), later prime minister of Georgia, of being a 'bourgeois-nationalist' aiming to unite all classes within the nation state instead of fighting for the dictatorship of a supra-national proletariat.[188]

The social revolutionaries enjoyed an increasingly broad range of sympathizers in Georgia due to the fact that native Georgians were virtually excluded from the administration, the military and the wealthy bourgeoisie whose ranks were dominated by Russians and Armenians. There existed a deep resentment among the powerless and marginalized gentry and the poor peasants towards the wealthy and influential Armenians. While not comparable to the hostility between Tatars (Azerbaijanis) and Armenians, antagonism between Georgians and Armenians certainly existed.[189] For Georgia's lower and disadvantaged classes the main enemy was Armenian capitalism. As enumerated by Luigi Villari, the Georgian opposition consisted of the following groups:

1. The Federalists, who aimed at a federation of the various ethnicities within the Russian Empire which would 'form a federal republic on the basis of the United States of America'.[190] Like the socialists, they wanted to expropriate the nobles and nationalize the Church's properties, but to keep private and industrial property.

2. The revolutionary Social Democrats, demanding in the short term political reforms, universal suffrage, the abolition of standing armies and rural reforms through land expropriations. The Social Democrats were also inspired by the Russian Populist movement of the 1870s which called for the abolition of the monarchy and the equality of persons and possessions.[191] In the medium and long term the anticlerical Social Democrats likewise aimed at the removal of the Imperial system, to be replaced with a centralized Russian republic as well as a classless society. As Villari observed, their appeal was limited by their anti-national orientation, specifically by their refusal to give consideration to 'the existing and very real racial [i.e. ethnic] and religious antagonisms'.[192]

3. The Anarchists, who seemed to lack a concrete vision of a new social order. A prominent protagonist of the Anarchists was Varlam Cherkezov (Cherkezishvili, 1846–1925) who openly advocated terrorism against representatives of the state. The Anarchists were strongly opposed to the Social Democrats and their ideal of a state monopoly of the means of production.[193]

4. The Progressive Democrats, who wanted the full independence of the Caucasus from the Russian Empire and its organization into autonomous states within a Caucasian federation.

5. The Party of Independence, which also aimed at an independent Caucasian federation. Like the Progressive Democrats their programme included social reforms, but not the abolition of private property.[194] As already mentioned, the Russian governor general Golitsyn feared the nationalists demanding full independence more than the socialists and their socioeconomic theories.

Social unrest spread in Georgia not only among urban industrial workers but even more among the peasants in the countryside. Typical was the peasant revolt in the west Georgian regions of Guria, Imereti and Mingrelia. Here about two-thirds of peasants owned too little land for their families to live on and they had to rent land from noble landowners at exorbitant prices. The ownership structure of agriculturally usable land was in the early 1900s very unbalanced. The Russian government owned 58 per cent, landowners 31 per cent, merchants 2.4 per cent, the Imperial family 1.9 per cent and tens of thousands of farmers only 6.3 per cent between them, although they accounted for 85 per cent of the total population.[195] In May 1902 the Gurian farmers began refusing to pay land rents, taxes and tithes to the clergy. With the help of workers from Batumi they organized themselves into village committees which acted as the supreme authority on all aspects of community life as well as serving as law courts. Governmental orders and court judgements from Kutaisi, Tbilisi or St Petersburg were ignored. Luigi Villari, who visited the so-called 'Gurian Republic', described one such popular court:

There are no judges, no jury, no public prosecutor, no counsel; but every person present, whether man, woman or child ... has the right to act in any of these capacities, and verdict and sentence are decided by the vote of the majority.[196]

These village committees differed from the traditional highland communities by the fact that all community members, including women, could participate in the decision-making meetings and that elders enjoyed no privileged position. When the rebellious peasants sought support from the social-democratic revolutionaries, they met with a rebuff from orthodox Marxists who claimed that the proletariat was the spearhead of revolution, not the peasantry. The Batumi socialist and later parliamentary president of Georgia Nikolai (Karlo) Chkheidze (1864–1926) declared: '[We] cannot have a peasant movement under our banners.'[197] But the Gurian Menshevik Noe Zhordania was less haughty and answered his compatriots' call for help, although he suspected that the rebellious peasants remained petty bourgeois at heart, with their insistence on maintaining private property.[198] In the next three years the revolutionary movement of peasants' communes spread to Mingrelia and Imereti, and gained further momentum after Bloody Sunday, when unrest erupted in Tbilisi.[199] One of the first measures that the viceroy Vorontsov-Dashkov took in this explosive situation was to repeal the confiscation of the Armenian Church revenues, which partially neutralized the Dashnaks. Vorontsov's conciliatory act towards the Armenians motivated the Georgian clergy to ask for the restoration of their church's autocephaly, but to no avail.

The situation worsened during summer 1905 when a general strike deprived Tbilisi of running water, electricity and food supplies while the Gurians blocked the Baku–Tbilisi–Batumi railway line, isolating western Georgia from Tbilisi. The unrest was not only fuelled by the activities of the social revolutionaries in stirring up workers and mobilizing criminal gangs, but also by demands for Russia to end the disastrous war against Japan. When the ethnic strife between Muslim Tatars (Azerbaijanis) and Armenians spilled over into Tbilisi, Vorontsov lost his nerve and armed the socialist People's Militia with 500 army rifles to act as a 'neutral' peacekeeper. While the socialist militia did indeed curb the Tatars' anti-Armenian fury, this brief cooperation between government and revolutionaries was not enough to control the prevailing state of anarchy. Officers continued to be murdered, railways and telegraphs ceased to function. Furthermore, in November 1905, frustrated Cossack units attacked demonstrators and local people in western Georgia. In the meantime, Russia had made peace with Japan under very disadvantageous terms, which at least freed troops to quell the various insurgencies in the Empire. On 26 December Vorontsov-Dashkov finally reacted forcefully by nominating General Maksud Alikhanov-Avarsky as military governor of Tbilisi, who quickly restored order in the capital, although even now Cossacks would occasionally exact revenge for previous casualties inflicted on them. Meanwhile, leading Bolsheviks such as Stalin and the Armenian Stepan Shahumyan (Shaumian, 1878–1918) left for Baku. In January 1906 General Alikhanov-Avarsky was nominated military governor of western Georgia, where he forcefully restored governmental control and put an end to the Gurian Commune. Nevertheless, the assassinations continued: chief of staff General Gryznov was killed in January 1906 and General Alikhanov-Avarsky himself in July 1907.[200] One month later, the respected poet and moderate nationalist Ilia Chavchavadze, who had condemned socialist terrorism, was murdered. His assassination was probably ordered by Stalin and Ordzhonikidze as punishment for his critique.[201] While Vorontsov-Dashkov survived an assassination attempt, the Russian exarch of Georgia, Archbishop Nikon Sofiysky was shot in May 1908 and died. It remains unclear if the killers belonged to a Black Hundreds gang or came from the Georgian clergy acting in revenge for Nikon's appeal to the police in May 1905 to dissolve a meeting of clerics demanding Georgian autocephaly.[202]

After the Bloody Sunday incident in January 1905 the Russian tsarist system was in imminent danger of being swept away by a revolution, which was averted in October by Nicholas' concession allowing the election of a State Duma, the lower house of the parliamentary legislative assembly. Whereas the Russian Social Democrats boycotted the 1906 election to the First Duma, the Georgian Social Democrats ignored the boycott and Georgia's Menshevik group won six of the Duma's 497 seats. The Armenian Dashnaks and Hunchaks did boycott the election, however, which is why the five Armenian deputies in the Duma were politically close to the Russian Constitutional Democrats, known as the Kadets. Under the leadership of Noe Zhordania the small Georgian delegation quickly developed a leading role within the leftist opposition. The politicians elected from the Muslim Azeri community were co-founders of the Union of the Muslims of Russia, Ittifaq, which was dominated by Volga Tatars. They had a liberal and constitutional programme and entered a tactical alliance with the Kadets. In the First Duma, there were 25 Muslim deputies of whom six were Azeris. When a stalemate occurred between Duma and government, the tsar dissolved parliament in July. The Social Democrats participated in the election to the Second Duma of 1907, as a result of which the parliament moved to the left; the South Caucasian socialist democratic faction led by the Georgian Irakli Tsereteli counted eight Georgians and five Armenians, while the Azeris again held six of a total of 36 Muslim seats. In the Second Duma, which numbered 518 deputies, the Social Democrats (SDs, Mensheviks and Bolsheviks) had 65 seats and the Socialist-Revolutionaries (SRs) who advocated terrorism, 37 seats.[203] After only three months, the Second Duma was dissolved by Prime Minister Pyotr Stolypin who manipulated the law for the election of the Third Duma in such a way that peasants and ethnic minorities were widely disenfranchised; the number of deputies allocated to Georgians was reduced to three, while Armenians and Azeris had a mere one each.[204]

6.3 Pan-Turkism and socialism in the South Caucasian Muslim provinces

In the eastern provinces of Baku and Yelisavetpol the social position was different from that among Georgians and Armenians. Till the late nineteenth century in the territory of today's Azerbaijan there was hardly any sense of national identity, since until its annexation by Russia it had consisted of various autonomous khanates under more or less nominal Iranian suzerainty.[205] The majority of the population were Turkic-speaking Azerbaijanis, or Iranian immigrants. Until the Russian invasion, they belonged as Muslims to a socially superior class compared to the Christians or Jews. But once within the Russian Empire, the social order dramatically changed: the formerly despised Christian infidels became their new masters and the hated Armenians now shared the same religion as their rulers. Even worse for the Azeris,[206] the Armenians swiftly seized the new opportunities offered in education, trade, banking, industry and public administration whereas the Azeris remained mainly farmers and landlords engaged only in small businesses. In mountainous Karabakh the antagonism between the Turkic and Kurdish semi-nomadic pastoralists and the settled Armenian peasants was amplified by disputes over land and pastures.

Another dimension to Azerbaijan's socio-political life was pan-Islamism, or rather pan-Islamism under Turkish leadership, which soon developed into pan-Turkism. The idea was fostered by the sultan-caliph Abdul Hamid II, who presented himself as the spiritual head of all Muslims, including those living in European colonies.[207] It spread to intellectual circles and was also propagated by the Crimean politician and publicist Ismail Gaspıralı (Gasprinsky, 1851–1914) who stressed the need for modern education and modernization in Muslim societies. He co-inspired the jadidist movement[208] and propagated the idea of a cultural convergence of Muslim Turkic peoples. A third element contributing to the social conflicts that erupted in the early twentieth century was the widespread poverty among the peasants. Like their Georgian and Armenian counterparts, the Azerbaijani peasants had been assigned too little land, which again they were expected to pay for; the result was a rural exodus to Baku's oil industry, as well as a growth in criminal gangs. Other impoverished peasants had to work for very low income on the fields of large landowners. The Russian government's opening up of the South Caucasus to migrating Slavic farmers in the late 1890s caused further resentment and unrest among the locals, since the new Russian settlers were often allocated more land than the local Azeri peasants possessed.[209] But the most explosive source of unrest was the fact, outlined above, that for the underpaid Azerbaijani oil and industrial workers the capitalist class enemy was at the same time the Armenian ethnic foe. In brief, the two eastern provinces of Baku and Yelisavetpol were torn by several conflicts: oil and industrial workers against capitalists, Turkic Azeris against Armenians, Azeri peasants against landowners, Azeri peasants and small landowners against Slav immigrants, impoverished Azeri landowners against Armenian bankers and, in Karabakh, agriculturalists against semi-nomadic pastoralists. Due to these numerous social antagonisms a great number of violent conflicts broke out and the very heterogeneity of the antagonisms made it impossible for one single opposition movement to offer an alternative to all the discontented groups – in other words no political party could prevail. Even among the Baku proletariat, class consciousness remained low, whereas ethnic nationalism grew stronger.

In the wake of the large strikes of 1905 at the Absheron oilfields and in the refineries, a series of massacres broke out, which at the time was sometimes called the Armeno-Tatar War of 1905–1906. At this time, Baku was the most populous city in the South Caucasus due to a large influx of immigrants, impoverished Azeri peasants, poor Iranian workers, urbanized Armenians and Russians. The Azeri–Armenian fighting, which in Azerbaijan also had an anti-colonial dimension, quickly spread from Baku to Nakhchivan, Yerevan, Şuşa (Shushi) and Ganja, and led to episodes of ethnic cleansing within the cities, which became divided on ethnic lines.[210] In Baku the government at first remained passive and reacted belatedly. Before the strikes turned into ethnic strife they had been mainly fuelled by the Social-Democratic revolutionaries, who had established themselves with the support of Georgian socialists in 1900.[211] But the Baku Social Democrats faced a strong local competitor in the followers of the brothers Lev and Ilia Shendrikov, who had been expelled from the Social Democratic Party by the dominant Bolshevik faction. Unlike the Bolsheviks who used strikes and violence as a political tool to attack capitalism with the ultimate aim of establishing a socialist government, the Shendrikovtsy 'gained a real base of support among the workers by articulating their purely economic demands'.[212] When a mainly Azeri mob set the oil derricks on fire in August–September 1905, they alienated many workers who lost their jobs. Later in the year, the Shendrikovtsy formed Workers' Soviets (councils) which focused single-mindedly on economic objectives. The Bolsheviks despised the successful Shendrikovtsy as mere trade unionists and as late as 1914, when the Shendrikovtsy movement was long dead, Stepan Shahumyan wrote to Lenin disdainfully: 'In general the workers here [Baku] are a terribly mercantilistic group. The rapaciousness of the oil industrialists has affected them. [They think only] to snatch another greasy piece and to increase "bonuses" … There is not the slightest interest in politics.'[213] As Lavrenti Beria explained, strikes organized by the Bolsheviks were not aimed at improving workers' living conditions but at destabilizing the tsarist regime by provoking armed clashes with the police and the army.[214] The oil strikes had declined rapidly as of 1907–1908 along with the influence of the Shendrikovtsy, due to stringent punishments and a depression in oil prices.

The ethnic conflict between Armenians and Azeris gave a significant boost to the Muslim Social Democratic Party Hummet (Hümmət, meaning 'Effort' in Azerbaijani) which had been founded in 1904 by Mahammad Amin Rasulzade (Məhəmməd Əmin Rəsulzadə, 1884–1955). Hummet was more focused on action and economy than the Bolsheviks with their political propaganda.[215] Razulzade had to flee Baku in 1909; when he returned in 1913 he joined the secret Muslim Democratic Müsavat (Equality) Party, founded in 1911, which followed a Turkophile pan-Islamist strategy. During World War I it morphed into Azerbaijan's leading nationalist party. As the ARF/Dashnaks had been virtually expelled from Russian Armenia, Muslim nationalism became Russia's major concern in the South Caucasus. St Petersburg feared that a strong pan-Islamist movement might spread like wildfire to the large Muslim communities along the River Volga and to Muslim Central Asia. Russia's apprehensions were additionally fuelled by the activities of Ottoman covert agents in the Caucasus and the increasingly aggressive stance of the German Emperor Wilhelm II (r. 1888–1918, d. 1941) who actively pursued a policy of gaining influence over the Ottoman Empire and positioned himself as a protector of all Muslims. For Russia in the early 1910s, the spectre of Turkic pan-Islamism sponsored by Germany was a source of serious concern. When in 1913 the new Turkish CUP government adopted a forceful pan-Turkic strategy, Russian apprehensions were confirmed.

ID # VII

A Short-Lived Independence and Foreign Interventions

1. World War I, the Armenian Genocide and the collapse of the Russian Empire

In the second decade of the twentieth century the fates of the South Caucasus and the Ottoman Empire were closely linked to each other. Following the Berlin Congress, the Ottomans no longer viewed Great Britain as a protector but rather as a robber state which had seized Egypt[1] and Cyprus and had failed to prevent the substantial losses of territory after the 1877–1878 war. This conviction was reinforced after the First Balkan War of 1912–1913 when the dismemberment of the Empire continued, and the opinion now prevailed that Great Britain was prepared to accept the Russian seizure of Istanbul and the Dardanelles. The secret Anglo-Russian agreement of April 1915 soon proved Ottoman apprehensions to be justified. In this dangerous situation, Germany's courting of close political and economic cooperation was more than welcome. This pro-German reorientation resulted first in the Berlin–Baghdad Railway project, which was to bypass the British-controlled sea lanes and give Germany access to the raw materials and markets of the Middle and Far East. Railways were also superior to fleets for rapid troop deployments. From a military point of view, the early twentieth century was a competition between the continental powers who relied on railways, and maritime powers. Naval powers operating from an island were only able to conduct restricted land wars, but their reach was global.[2]

Further results of the Ottoman–German cooperation were the dispatch of senior German army instructors such as General Liman von Sanders, who became Ottoman inspector general, and General Friedrich Bronssart von Schellendorf, Ottoman chief of staff, and the delivery of state-of-the-art Krupp heavy guns. Turkish nationalism was further intensified at the end of the First Balkan War when the government was confronted with about 700,000 ethnic Turk refugees who had been expelled from the Balkans. As the Armenian catholicos Gevorg V feared in 1913,

95. Re-enactment by Turkish troops of the failed Ottoman attack on the Russian fortifications at Sarıkamış in winter 1914–15. Kars Province, Turkey. Photo December 2006.

these refugees would be settled in eastern Anatolia at the expense of the Armenians.[3] Of the Ottoman triumvirate, Enver Pasha was the most eager to capitalize on Germany's superior military power. His chance seemed to come with the assassination of Archduke Franz Ferdinand of Austria on 28 June 1914, setting in motion the fateful machinery of great-power alliances that no one had the courage to stop. When Germany declared war on Russia on 1 August, Enver manoeuvred the German ambassador, Wangenheim into signing a secret mutual defence treaty the next day. Germany guaranteed the territorial integrity of Turkey, while the Ottomans committed themselves to declare war on Russia, 'should Russia actively engage in military measures against Germany.'[4] Also on 1 August, the British First Lord of the Admiralty Winston Churchill confiscated for the British navy two dreadnoughts which the Ottomans had ordered at a British shipyard and fully paid for.[5] Needless to say, this requisition destroyed any remaining chance that the Ottoman Empire would join the Entente.[6] A few days later, Enver staged another coup: two German warships, the battle-cruiser *Goeben* and the light cruiser *Breslau* sought refuge from the British fleet in the still neutral Dardanelles (Turkey not having yet declared war) where they were trapped. Enver now organized a mock purchase of the two German warships including their German crews and integrated them into the Ottoman navy which became at a single stroke superior to the Russian Black Sea fleet.[7]

Although the Ottomans were not yet officially in the war, they closed the Dardanelles on 27 September and mined its entry, which not only cut Russia off from its allies but also crippled its imports and exports, 90 per cent of which went by that route. The closure of the straits had a very negative impact on the Russian economy and was a key contributor to the February (March) 1917 Revolution. Four days later the Ottomans abrogated all capitulations[8] and on 29 October the Ottoman navy launched a surprise attack on the harbours of Odessa, Sevastopol and Novorossiysk. Russia answered by declaring war on Turkey on 31 October, with France and Britain following on 4 November.[9] From the start, Russian high command subscribed to the French doctrine that the war would be decided in the West, and as a result neglected the eastern front.[10] For three years the Russian Caucasus Army remained understaffed, and was not allowed to capitalize on any significant success that it achieved. The situations of the Armenians in the two empires were highly conflicting. On the one hand, Russian Armenians volunteered to serve in the Imperial army under famous commanders such as Andranik Ozanian (popularly known simply as Andranik), who went on in 1918–1919 to establish a semi-independent stronghold in Zangezur (Syunik),

or Garegin Nzhdeh who in 1920–1921 defied the Soviet occupants of Armenia by founding the Republic of Mountainous Armenia in the same area. Another renowned Armenian commander was Drastamat Kanayan (known as Dro) who fought with Nzhdeh in Zangezur, briefly became Armenian defence minister and in World War II formed the German Armenian Legion in the hope that the Wehrmacht would liberate Armenia from Soviet occupation.[11] On the other hand, the Dashnaks urged the Ottoman Armenians to obey the Turkish general mobilization order. However, the minister of defence, Enver Pasha had other plans; since he was not in favour of armed Armenian units within the Turkish army, he offered Armenian men the option of avoiding conscription by paying for a substitute. Late February 1915 saw a sinister portent of the future, when 10,000 Armenian volunteer soldiers were disarmed and downgraded to auxiliaries, and made to dig trenches and carry loads.[12] By then the Armenians' expulsion and extermination had obviously been decided upon; and they needed to be unarmed and defenceless. It also quickly became clear that the caliph's call to a jihad against the Entente powers had fallen flat, including among the Arabs living in the Ottoman Empire. The Arab tribes were not interested in pan-Turkism but did want independence, while the Muslims living in the Russian Empire or the British and French colonies could make no sense of this appeal that stemmed from the puppet ruler Sultan Mehmed V (r. 1909–1918).

The Ottomans had three war objectives in the east: first, the reconquest of the territories lost in 1878, namely Ardahan, Kars and Batumi; second, an advance to Baku in order to seize access to the oil resources from Russia; and third, a bridgehead on the Caspian Sea which would allow pan-Turkism to be carried into Central Asia. Russia, on the other hand, was ill prepared. There were no plans for combined land and sea operations, nor for cooperation with British forces. Furthermore, the nominal commander of the Russian Caucasus Army, the viceroy Vorontsov-Dashkov, had no military experience and his deputy, General Aleksandr Myshlayevsky was a military historian without war experience, and field commander General Georgy Bergmann (1854–1929) lacked field experience as well. Only the chief of staff, General Nikolai Yudenich (1862–1933) had gained experience, in the Pamir, in the Russo-Japanese War and in the Caucasus. Since half of the Caucasus Army's 100,000-strong force were made to redeploy to Prussia following the Tannenberg disaster in late August 1914, its task was limited to 'active defence'.[13] In November the first Russian attack commanded by General Bergmann failed due to an inadequate deployment of troops, and the Ottoman counteroffensive not only succeeded in pushing the Russians back but on 15 December captured the city of Ardahan. These early successes motivated Enver Pasha to launch the 95,000-strong Ottoman Third Army on a risky winter expedition against the Russian garrison of Sarıkamış (Sarikamish) south-west of Kars. The campaign, which lasted from 22 December to 17 January 1915, turned out a complete disaster. Although Enver had no war experience, he personally took command of the army. From Erzurum to Sarıkamış the mountain roads were abominable in winter; the Third Army had no reliable maps and its soldiers no winter clothing. In the blizzards and snowstorms during the approach to Sarıkamış the army had already lost 25,000 men, who had frozen to death or deserted. In the chaos two Turkish columns had even shelled each other, resulting in more than 1,000 casualties. As the Turks approached, Voronzov-Dashkov, Myshlayevsky and Bergmann were in favour of retreating to Kars without a fight but General Yudenich ignored their order, electing to stay in Sarıkamış and defend it at all costs. The Russian defence, supported by numerous Armenian volunteers, fended off the attackers with well-targeted machine-gun fire, leaving the Turks to begin their retreat to Erzurum on 7 January 1915 once again in appalling weather conditions. Total Ottoman losses amounted to 75,000 men, and all their artillery.[14] At the southern edge of the Caucasus, General Myshlayevsky's loss of nerve had disastrous repercussions for the local Armenian and Assyrian populations,[15] as he ordered the evacuation of Urmia and Tabriz. Ottoman troops and Kurdish irregulars led by the tribal leader Agha Simko Shikak (who in 1918 would murder the Nestorian patriarch Mar Shimun XIX) filled the vacuum in January 1915 and looted Armenian and Assyrian villages while cruelly massacring their inhabitants.[16] As soon as victory had been secured at Sarıkamış, General Yudenich ordered Tabriz to be reoccupied. An ugly massacre of civilians occurred in January 1915 on the Russian side too, when General Vladimir Lyakhov, the former commander of the Iranian Cossack brigade, ordered his troops to kill Muslim civilians in the Chorokhi Valley indiscriminately, after he had reconquered Adjara from the Ottomans.[17] In February Yudenich was promoted to field commander of the Caucasus Army, replacing Bergmann, whereas Enver Pasha had abandoned his retreating troops and hastened back to Istanbul. To detract from his own military incompetence, Enver blamed the Armenian brigades for the defeat; the Armenians became the scapegoats for the Turkish disaster, which set the course for the Armenian genocide.

February 1915 saw the start of the British-led Gallipoli campaign, instigated by Winston Churchill (1874–1965) with the objectives of knocking Turkey out of the war, seizing the straits and removing the Ottoman threat to the Suez Canal. Although Russia had a vital interest in reopening the straits and regaining access to the Mediterranean Sea, and albeit the conquest of Istanbul had been a dearly held Russian objective since the 1780s, the Russian army took no part in the allied attack. To attack Istanbul (Constantinople) in a pincer movement from the south through the Dardanelles and from the north on the Bosporus looked an obvious strategy, but it never happened, and in May the Russian Fifth Caucasian Corps which was waiting to attack was moved to Galicia to fight against the Austrians.[18] Nevertheless, Britain and France secretly acceded on 10 April 1915 to Russia's demand that in case of victory it should gain control over Istanbul and the straits. In return, Russia agreed that Britain could occupy Iran's neutral zone to better control the southern oilfields, and France Cilicia.[19] In the Gallipoli operation the British grossly underestimated the Ottoman defences and artillery capabilities, which included mobile howitzers and dummy fortifications with mock batteries. The British and French fleets failed to force the Dardanelles while sustaining heavy losses, and the landing troops were beaten back. The Allied evacuation was completed by 9 January 1916. Nevertheless, at the end of the war the victorious Allies did occupy Istanbul from November 1918 to October 1923; but the secret agreement with Russia had been nullified when the latter opted out of the war in March 1918. Had Russia gained control of the Dardanelles it might well have changed the course of Europe's – and the Caucasus' – history.

The first indication of the impending genocide of the Armenians took place in late December 1914 when Enver's brother-in-law, Cevdet (Jevdet) Bey, the governor of Van, ordered a massacre of recalcitrant Armenians in his *vilayet*. Jevdet was notorious for his cruelty and was nicknamed *Nalband*, 'Blacksmith' for having ordered horseshoes to be nailed to the feet of Armenian prisoners in order to force confessions.[20] In February 1915, after Enver had declared the Armenians collectively guilty of high treason, the deportation of Armenians from Cilicia to Konya was decided on. One month later, the deportation of Armenians was extended to the front lines, mainly in eastern Anatolia. The pogroms really started on 23–24 April 1915 when Armenian political leaders and intellectuals were arrested in Istanbul, depriving the Armenian community of its leadership. Finally, between April and July 1915, the interior minister Talaat extended the deportation of Armenians of both sexes to the major cities and to all of central and eastern Anatolia including Cilicia. During one of the numerous diplomatic interventions of the US ambassador Henry

96. Irregular Caucasian cavalry serving during World War I in the Imperial Russian army.

Morgenthau to try to stop the deportations, the war minister Enver Pasha proudly retorted: 'The Cabinet itself has ordered the deportations.' Talaat Pasha was even more explicit in expressing to a German journalist his will to exterminate the Armenians:

We have been reproached for making no distinction between the innocent Armenians and the guilty; but that is utterly impossible, in view of the fact that those who were innocent today might be guilty tomorrow. [...] We will have no Armenians anywhere in Anatolia. They can live in the [Syrian] *Desert but nowhere else.*[21]

As emphasized by Enver Pasha, the mass deportation and killing of Armenians was not the result of subordinates exceeding their competence but a planned ethnic cleansing of Turkey of its Armenian and Assyrian citizens, ordered by the ruling Ottoman triumvirate.[22] The triumvirate had an additional motivation for deporting the Armenians from their villages, since it needed to relocate some 700,000 Muslim refugees who had been ejected from their homes by the Balkan League (the kingdoms of Bulgaria, Serbia, Greece and Montenegro) during the First Balkan War. As soon as the Armenians had been deported from their Anatolian villages, these Balkan refugees would take possession of their houses and lands.[23]

The deportation of Armenians and Assyrians to the hostile Syrian Desert was purposely executed as a planned extermination. The procedure was always the same: army troops would encircle an Armenian or Assyrian village, then gather all young, fit men and lead them outside the village where they would be shot, bayoneted or sometimes drowned. Next, the young and beautiful women were picked to be distributed among the local Turkish and Kurdish men. Occasionally the remainder, that is other women, older people and children were locked into a large building which was set on fire and all those trapped inside burnt alive. More commonly these remaining people were forced on death marches to the Syrian Desert. They were supplied with neither food nor water and were escorted by members of the paramilitary irregulars from the Teşkilât-ı Mahsusa, the 'Special Organization' formed by Enver. These were recruited among the former Hamidiye Alaylar which consisted mainly of Circassians and Kurds, and, as reported by German consuls and military officers, of criminals released from prison, the infamous *çeteler* or 'chettes'.[24] As recorded not only by German, American and Italian consuls and German army officers and businessmen based in Anatolia and Syria, but also by low-ranking Muslim Ottoman officers, these irregulars would rape, rob and savagely murder refugees at will; sick or exhausted people were bayoneted on the spot. Those who survived the death marches and reached the Syrian Desert were either locked into concentration camps, allocated to Muslim families, or sold into slavery.[25] The escape of the 4,000 Armenians from Musa Dagh in summer 1915 was a lucky exception. When the Turkish henchmen from the Teşkilât-ı Mahsusa approached five villages near Antioch (today's Antakya), the villagers who had armed themselves retreated to Mount Musa Dagh where they resisted the attacks for almost two months. They were saved *in extremis* on 12 September by French warships which had seen their distress signals and brought them to Port Said.[26]

In total, of the *ca.* 2 million Armenians living in the Ottoman Empire, about 1,500,000 were deported in 1915–1916, of whom (depending on estimates) between 664,000 and 1,000,000 were killed. Possibly up to 250,000 Armenians were forced to convert to Islam in order to survive,[27] and *ca.* 200,000 survivors found asylum in Lebanon. In time most of them acquired Lebanese nationality. A few months after the Armistice of Mudros (30 October 1918) the Turkish interior minister Cemal (Jemal) Bey[28] officially gave the number of 800,000 Armenians killed during the war; this number was accepted and cited several times by the grand vizier, Damat Ferid Pasha (1853–1923).[29] Before this, Cemal Bey's predecessor as interior minister Mustafa Arif Değmer had already declared:

They [the CUP triumvirate] *decided to exterminate the Armenians, and they were exterminated.*[30]

Taking the UN General Assembly Resolution 96 from 11 December 1946 as a yardstick there is no doubt that the massacre of Armenians in 1915–1916 was a state-organized genocide. The resolution states:

97. The Armenian Genocide Memorial built in 1967 on the hill of Tsitsernakaberd near Yerevan. The 44-m-high stele symbolizes the national strength of the Armenian people and the twelve slabs standing in a circle represent the 'twelve lost provinces' in today's Turkey. Yerevan, Armenia. Photo 2015.

Genocide is a denial of the right of existence of entire human groups, as homicide is the denial of the right to live of individual human beings; such denial of the right of existence shocks the conscience of mankind, ... and is contrary to moral law and to the spirit and aims of the United Nations. ... The General Assembly, therefore, affirms that genocide is a crime under international law ... whether the crime is committed on religious, racial, political or any other grounds.[31]

As of 2021, parliaments and governments of 33 states had formally recognized the Armenian genocide, among them the United States, Canada, France, Germany, Italy, Switzerland and Russia.[32] In some of these states such as Switzerland, the public denial of the Armenian Genocide is considered a criminal offence, but not at the juridical body of the Council of Europe, the European Court of Human Rights, as was revealed in the court's verdict in the case of *Doğu Perinçek* v. *Switzerland*. Following a public denial in 2005 in Switzerland of the Armenian Genocide as 'an international lie', a Swiss court condemned the accused in 2007 to a fine based on the Swiss law against racism. This judgement was subsequently confirmed by the cantonal court of appeal and in the same year by the Federal Supreme Court of Switzerland. Perinçek then appealed to the European Court of Human Rights which ruled in 2013 against Switzerland, accusing it of having violated the right of free speech. Two years later the Grand Chamber of the European Court of Human Rights confirmed the ruling in favour of Perinçek, de facto proclaiming that the public denial of the Armenian Genocide is not punishable.[33] As for the Turkish governments, they have always denied that the massacres had been genocide and belittled them, referring to them merely as part of war operations.

Under Allied pressure and in the face of strong nationalist resentment, the Ottoman post-war governments chaired by Damat Ferid Pasha prosecuted the worst culprits of the genocide. The massacres were mainly attributed to the CUP leaders and out of the eighteen pronounced death sentences only three were executed, as several culprits had fled abroad. The three main culprits who were condemned to death *in absentia*, namely Talaat Pasha, Enver Pasha and Jemal Pasha, were evacuated on a German torpedo boat on 1 November 1918; they settled in Berlin. Outraged, a small group of Dashnaks decided to take justice into their hands and to kill the key offenders themselves. In Operation Nemesis – Nemesis being the Greek goddess of just retribution – they killed not only the two principal co-founders of the Teşkilât-ı Mahsusa, Bahaeddin Şakir and Cemal Azmi, but Talaat Pasha in 1921 and Jemal Pasha in 1922.[34] Enver Pasha escaped Armenian vengeance by fleeing Berlin for Moscow and espousing Bolshevism. However,

98. Armenian defenders during the siege of Van, Turkey, in spring 1915.

when he was sent by Lenin against the anti-Bolshevik Basmachi guerrillas in today's Tajikistan, he defected (still hoping to revive his pan-Turkic dream) and was killed in battle by Bolshevik forces.

Armenians resisted their extermination not only at Mount Musa Dagh but also in Van in eastern Anatolia.[35] There, the governor, Jevdet made a start to the planned murders and deportations on 14 April 1915 with the order that young Armenian men must submit their arms and gather at notified places. The Armenians understood that mass killing was imminent and, having no other option, prepared their defence: if they surrendered their arms, they would be slaughtered. Two days later, Jevdet lured the Dashnak leader Ishkhan into a trap and had him murdered. When the Ottoman attacks began on 19 April, the day before Easter, the Armenians repulsed the attackers, took control of the city and placed it a defensible state. The siege of Van lasted 27 days, with all attacks by Ottoman troops and irregulars failing to overcome the defenders. In revenge, Jevdet ordered the massacre of Armenians across the province, where approximately half the Armenian population was murdered.[36] When General Yudenich heard from Armenian informants about the resistance of Van, he dispatched a relief column strengthened by the First Armenian Volunteer Regiment commanded by Andranik, which reached Van on 16 May. The Armenians quickly formed a provisional government which worked well till the end of July. However, while Cossacks and Armenian volunteers led by the commanders Andranik, Hamazasp (Srvandztian) and Dro cleared the southern shores of Lake Van and were on the march to relieve some 100,000 Armenians encircled in Bitlis, Muş and Sasun, Russian troops to the north of the lake came

99. The Armenian city of Van stood till late summer 1915 in the plain below the ancient fortress of Van. Only the dilapidated ruins of four Armenian churches, two Seljuk minarets and a caravanserai remain. Van Province, Turkey. Photo 2016.

under pressure from an Ottoman counteroffensive and suffered a serious defeat. Russia announced its withdrawal from Van, which began on 4 August 1915; a chaotic flight of some 150,000–200,000 Armenian refugees followed the retreating troops to the Russian frontier. As reported by witnesses, the Armenians shot those of their own people too sick or too old to walk in order to spare them being murdered by the advancing Ottoman troops.[37] Many of the refugees who marched under the volunteers' protection survived, but most of those without it were killed. The unlucky Armenians of Bitlis, Muş and Sasun were put to death without mercy. A few weeks later General Yudenich's counteroffensive defeated part of the Turkish Third Army and in September again occupied Van, which was now without an Armenian population.

The situation of the Armenian refugees worsened further after Grand Duke Nikolai replaced the viceroy Vorontsov-Dashkov and ordered the disbanding of the Armenian volunteer regiments and the incorporation of the volunteers into the regular Russian army. Needless to say, the Armenian volunteers who had fought in stand-alone units for the liberation of their former homeland became utterly demotivated and their commanders left the service. Furthermore, in the course of 1916 the grand duke forbade the Armenian refugees who had fled to the province of Yerevan to return to their villages within the Russian zone. The reasons for this refusal were to be found in the secret pacts among the Allies concerning the post-war partition of the Ottoman Empire, such as the Anglo-Franco-Russian agreement about the straits mentioned above, and the Anglo-French Sykes–Picot Agreement of 16 May 1916 which allocated the provinces of Van, Bitlis, Erzurum and Trabzon to Russia. The southern Ottoman Armenian provinces such as Sivas, Kharput and Diyarbakır, as well as Cilicia, would be attributed to the French zone.[38] Obviously an autonomous West Armenia under Russian suzerainty was not on the Allies' drawing board. The Russian government, for its part, preferred, as recommended by General Yudenich, to settle Cossacks and other Slav colonists in the now depopulated, eastern Anatolian provinces rather than allow the return of the Armenians, who were judged to be unruly and unreliable.[39] In early January 1916 General Yudenich began a winter campaign to seize those provinces secretly allocated to Russia, which took the Ottomans by surprise. At the Battle of Köprüköy between 10 and 19 January he inflicted a heavy defeat on the Turkish Third Army. In the following months, Yudenich captured the cities of Erzurum, Bitlis, Muş, Erzincan, Bayburt (fig. 101) and the important port of Trabzon (Trebizond). In spite of these successes, achieved with relatively few troops, the Russian high command persisted in considering the South Caucasian–Anatolian front as secondary. In the Brusilov offensive from June to September 1916 Russia had achieved a pyrrhic victory over the Central Powers. While the territorial gains were modest, it forced Germany to relocate forces from France to Galicia which reduced pressure on Verdun. But the human losses were horrendous, with one million men killed, wounded or taken prisoner on each side.[40] The Austro-Hungarian army was decisively weakened, but the Russian army's offensive power was utterly destroyed and the hecatomb of human life led to demoralization among the troops and at home. The blurred war aims were incomprehensible for both soldiers and the broad mass of peasants alike. All this meant that Yudenich had to prepare himself to withstand an attack by Turkish troops released from Gallipoli (some 20 divisions) without any reinforcements. In early August 1916 the Ottoman Second Army started a counterattack masterminded by Mustafa Kemal Pasha (1881–1938, later called Atatürk) who had distinguished himself during the defence of Gallipoli. It managed to recapture Bitlis and Muş but by later September its offensive had ended in a stalemate. During the very severe winter of 1916–17 no major operations took place.[41] In retrospect, it is clear that the huge Ottoman losses suffered and the tens of thousands of prisoners and deserters lost during 1916 decisively weakened the Ottoman army and paved the way for the relatively easy British reconquest of Kut and the seizure of Baghdad in February–March 1917.

The history of the Caucasus took a new, unexpected turn when the 'February Revolution' broke out in Russia on 8 March 1917 (according to the 'new style' or Gregorian calendar) which saved the Ottoman forces from collapse at the eastern front

100. Russian commander-in-chief and viceroy of the Caucasus, Grand Duke Nikolai (1856–1929) reviews Imperial troops at Erzurum after General Yudenich had captured the city on 16 February 1916.

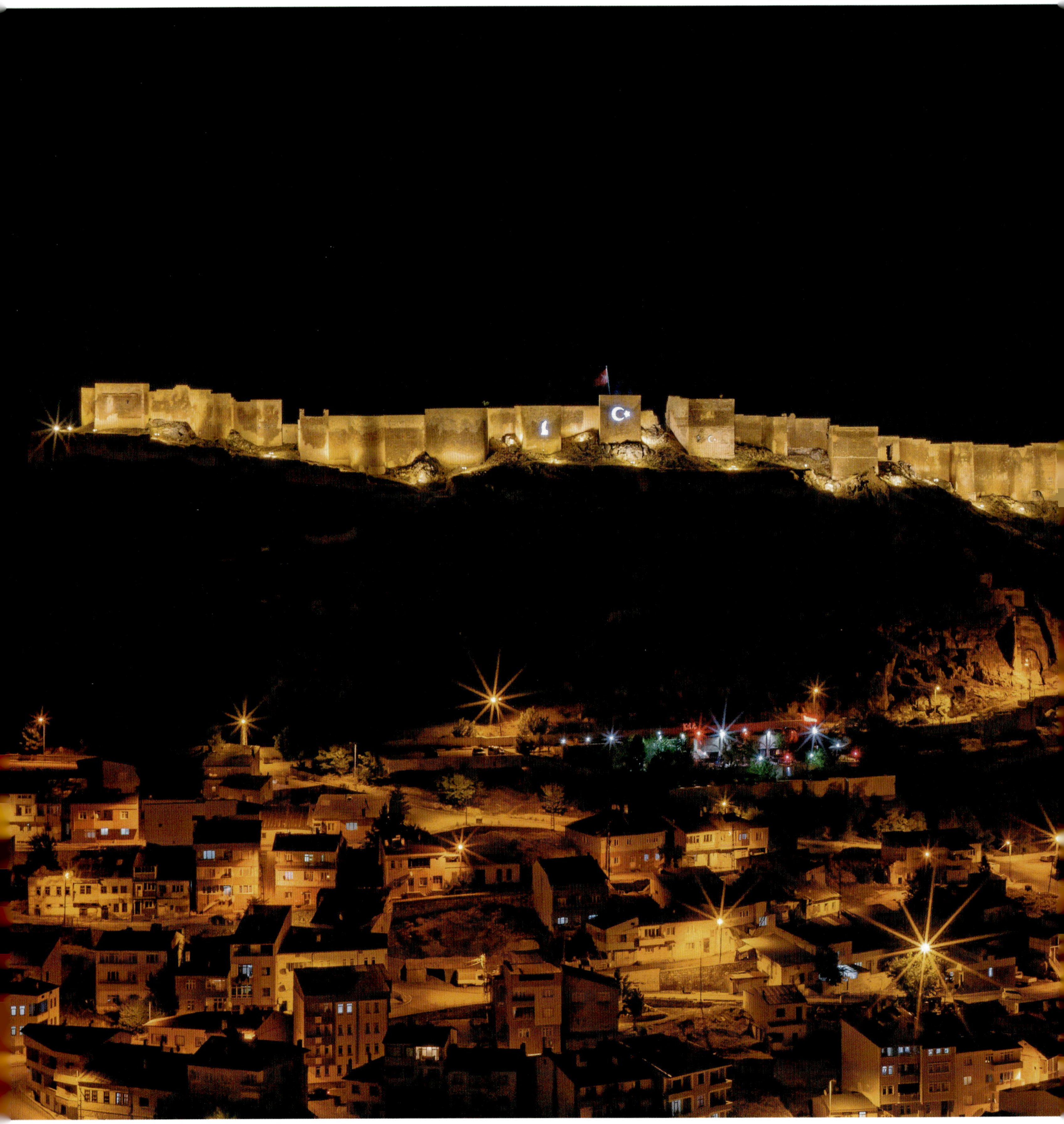

and allowed Enver Pasha to start a second campaign aimed at conquering the South Caucasus and reaching the Baku oilfields. The outbreak of the revolution was triggered in the short term by the misery, threat of famine and gigantic human losses endured during two and a half years of war, and in the longer term by a deep social malaise and discontent with the autocratic tsarist regime.[42] People wanted an immediate end to the war; the urban classes wanted the abolition of the tsardom. In the face of increasing chaos in Russia's capital Petrograd,[43] Tsar Nicholas abdicated on 15 March whereupon the Duma elected a liberal Provisional Government. At the same time the Petrograd Soviet, that is a 'Council of Workers and Soldiers' Deputies', was formed by revolutionary socialists. Russia had now two power centres. Since the social revolutionary Aleksandr Kerensky (1881–1970) was both vice chairman of the Petrograd Soviet and a member of the Provisional Government, he became – till the October Revolution on 7 November (new style) – Russia's strong man.[44] The February revolution and the tsar's abdication had an immediately disastrous effect on the Russian army: soldiers formed their own soviets which refused orders and elected their own commanders; mutinies were almost daily occurrences. As discipline rapidly slackened, the troops became unreliable and action plans could no longer be executed. In case of conflicts, soldiers turned fire on their own officers, in line with the Bolshevik propaganda that the imperialist war should be turned into an armed class struggle, in other words a worldwide civil war. The planned combined Anglo-Russian attack on Baghdad and northern Iraq was aborted in May 1917. When the Bolsheviks spread the rumour that comprehensive land redistribution to peasants would soon take place, hundreds of thousands of soldiers deserted *en masse* and marched home.[45] In spring and summer 1917 little fighting took place and the Russian generals made no more than minor adjustments to the front line in order to be able to hold it with dwindling forces. General Yudenich, whose freedom of action was becoming increasingly restricted by the soldiers' soviets, various committees and the Provincial Government, resigned in June and handed over command to General Mikhail Przhevalsky. In the autumn the latter ordered the formation of Armenian and Georgian corps to fill the gaps in the Caucasus Army.[46] Meanwhile the war minister Kerensky made the mistake of not pulling quickly out of the war, before the defeatist Bolshevik propaganda could spread further among the soldiers, and the Russian army disintegrated.

---

101. The huge fortress of Bayburt dating from the 1220s was dismantled by the Russian general Ivan Paskevich in 1829.

In the Caucasus, in March 1917 the **Special Transcaucasian Committee (Ozakom)** based in Tbilisi replaced the viceroy, Grand Duke Nikolai as the highest civil authority in the South Caucasus, while commissars were appointed to head the administration in the Terek and Kuban oblasts. All three bodies reported to the Provisional Government. At the same time, local soviets emerged and the ARF (Dashnaks) once again became active. It was the Dashnak Hakob Zavriev (1866–1920) who advised the Provisional Government to build a separate administrative unit out of the occupied Ottoman territories, called the 'land of Turkish Armenia'. Zavriev served as its civil administrator from May to November 1917 and allowed some 150,000 Armenian refugees to return to their destroyed villages in spite of dwindling Russian forces to guarantee their security.[47] This short-lived administrative unit raised hopes among Armenians for an autonomous Western Armenia under Russian protection. But the October Revolution accelerated the decay of the Russian army and the **Transcaucasian Commissariat** chaired by the Georgian Menshevik Nikolai Chkheidze which had replaced the Transcaucasian Committee on 11 November 1917, was forced to agree to the Armistice of Erzincan signed on 18 December. The armistice temporarily ended hostilities between Russia (as represented by the Transcaucasian Commissariat) and the Ottomans, and Armenian volunteers under the command of General Tovmas Nazarbekian advanced to the front to replace the Russian troops that had deserted; only a few hundred Russian officers had remained.

However, the international status of the Commissariat was ambiguous: whereas it viewed itself as still subordinate to the Provisional Government, the Ottomans considered it as an independent and sovereign entity – a confusion which would soon create major problems. The status of the Commissariat was further complicated by the fact that it rejected Bolshevism and refused to recognize the Bolshevik government – only the Baku Soviet, chaired by the Bolshevik extraordinary commissar for the Caucasus, Stepan Shahumyan who had seized power on 31 October 1917,[48] welcomed Bolshevik rule. As the Menshevik leader Noe Zhordania deplored on 7 November 1917: 'A misfortune has now befallen us. The connection with Russia has been broken and Transcaucasia has been left alone.'[49] The Commissariat found itself reluctantly on the road to independence. About six weeks earlier, the Russian bishops were expelled from Georgia and the autocephaly of the Georgian Church was restored.[50] The rift between the Commissariat and the Russian Bolshevik government (Sovnarkom) deepened when on 18–19 January 1918 Lenin ordered the Red Guards to shut down the All Russian Constituent Assembly, where the Bolsheviks were in the minority with 23 per cent of seats compared to the Russian Social Revolutionaries' 38 per cent, with the latter and their non-Russian sister parties totalling 58 per cent.[51] In a nutshell, the Commissariat had acted like an independent state by signing the Erzincan Armistice, yet it considered itself a part of the Russian Empire whose government it refused to recognize.

In the meantime, the Russian–German peace talks at Brest-Litovsk, which began on 22 December 1917, had made no progress, since Lenin, who hoped for an imminent socialist revolution in Germany, applied a delaying tactic. Germany resumed its attacks on 18 February against the virtually defenceless Russian positions in the direction of Petrograd, forcing the Sovnarkom to sign the Treaty of Brest-Litovsk on 3 March. Russia lost more than 2.5 million square kilometres of territory mainly in its west, southwest and south, along with some 60 million people and, with the loss of Ukraine, the most fertile agricultural land. As Germany's ally, Turkey also demanded war gains, which were recorded in article 4 of the treaty:

Russia will do all in her power to have the provinces of eastern Anatolia promptly evacuated and returned to Turkey. The territories of Ardahan, Kars and Batumi will also be cleared without delay of Russian troops. Russia will not interfere in the new organization of internal juridical and international juridical relations of such territories, but will allow the populations of these territories to establish new governments in agreement with neighbouring states, especially with the Ottoman Empire.[52]

Basically, the treaty was a return to pre-1878 borders. A secret addendum stipulated: 'The Russian Republic assumes the responsibility to demobilize and dissolve the Armenian militias.'[53] The treaty gave Germany and the Ottoman Empire a second wind and allowed the latter to launch a major campaign against the South Caucasus. When the Commissariat heard about the treaty it protested that the Bolsheviks had no authority to give the western parts of its territory away. But since the Commissariat had refused the invitation of General Mehmed Wehib Pasha (1877–1940), commander of the Ottoman Third (Caucasus) Army, to attend the Brest-Litovsk conference, all protests were in vain.[54]

2. The Transcaucasian Republic, the declaration of independence of Georgia, Azerbaijan and Armenia, and foreign interventions

2.1 The short-lived Transcaucasian Republic

The situation of the South Caucasian Commissariat had further worsened since mid February after the Ottomans broke the Erzincan Armistice and began a new attack. Russia's withdrawal from the war gave Enver Pasha, who was de facto Ottoman commander-in-chief, the opportunity to compensate in the Caucasus for what Turkey was likely to lose to the British in the Middle East, and to realize his dream of a pan-Turkic federation under Turkish leadership. The Ottomans seized Erzincan at the end of February, and on 12 March, two days before the Ottoman–South Caucasian peace conference began at Trabzon, the Turkish First Army under Kâzım Karabekir Pasha (1882–1948) seized Erzurum without a fight, where General Andranik had abandoned 400 heavy guns, a huge quantity of ammunition and an enormous amount of food which was most welcome to the starved Turkish soldiers. A few days later Bayburt too fell. Thousands of Armenians who had previously returned to eastern Anatolia were forced to flee again from the Turkish troops. If one considers that the Armenian and Georgian forces together numbered 31,000 well-armed men with ample ammunition, the historian Michael Reynolds is probably correct in his assessment that 'What the formations of Russian Armenians lacked ... was the will to fight for the lands of their Anatolian co-ethnics. Instead of attempting to mount any form of defence, they preferred to withdraw.'[55] Six weeks later, after having abandoned Sarıkamış on 5–6 April and Van on 7 April, General Nazarbekian obeyed without demur the order of the prime minister-designate of the Transcaucasian Republic, the Georgian Akaki Chkhenkeli, to surrender the mighty fortress of Kars on 25 April without a fight and without even bothering to spike the many guns or destroy the immense stockpile of ammunition.[56] With the loss of Kars, the defence of Anatolian Armenia crumbled. A properly planned and organized defence had been sabotaged by the deep animosities between the three main peoples involved: the Georgian Mensheviks wanted to sacrifice Turkish Armenia to save Batumi and Akhaltsikhe, the Turkic Muslims of the Müsavat Party welcomed the Turkish Ottomans as related allies and invited them to size Baku, and the Russian Armenian Dashnaks concentrated on their own territory.

Eleven days before the fall of Kars, General Wehib had captured the highly important harbour and oil pipeline terminal of Batumi, again without a fight. Now the Transcaucasian parliament (Sejm), which had been formed on 23 February, had no choice but to bow to the unconditional Ottoman demands without which continued negotiations would not be possible, namely a declaration of independence from Russia and the recognition of Turkey's territorial claims. On 22 April 1918, the Sejm proclaimed the independent **Transcaucasian Democratic Federative Republic** and nominated Akaki Chkhenkeli (1874–1959) as prime minister. The Transcaucasian Republic was to last only five weeks, until 26 May, as the conflicts of goals among the various peoples were insurmountable. The idea of South Caucasian unity was an illusion that shattered when the Russian clamp was removed and the Ottomans resumed their attacks. The German general Friedrich Freiherr Kress von Kressenstein (1870–1948), who was commander of German troops stationed in Georgia from 23 June 1918 to 7 January 1919, wrote in his war diary a lucid analysis of the mutual hostilities within the Transcaucasian Republic:

It is a great tragedy of the Caucasian peoples that they cannot get along with each other, although they inhabit an area that is a single economic entity. ... Georgia is dependent on oil from Baku [which boycotts Georgia and Armenia], Azerbaijan needs for economic reasons access to the Black Sea which is [now] blocked by Georgia, and Armenia has no free access to either the Black Sea or the Caspian Sea. ... The Transcaucasian Federative Republic was not viable because of the strong ethnic distinctions and the different foreign orientations of the peoples united in it. While Georgia relied on Germany, the Muslim Azerbaijanis were completely devoted to the Turks, and the Armenians still hoped for their salvation from the Entente.[57]

The situation is fundamentally the same today, with the exception that Georgia is oriented towards the European Union and the US, and Armenia towards Russia. In Baku, ethnic tensions had already escalated in late March 1918 when the **Baku Commune** had been formed under the Armenian Bolshevik Shahumyan, excluding Muslims. The power fight of the Dashnaks and Bolsheviks against the Müsavat Party quickly degenerated into a general pogrom of Muslims; up to 12,000 Azeri Muslims were murdered and a significant proportion of Baku's Muslims fled the city.[58]

The Ottomans recognized the Transcaucasian Republic on 28 April, but when the belligerents resumed peace negotiations on

11 May in Batumi the Ottomans made it clear that article 4 of the Brest-Litovsk Treaty had become obsolete, since the Republic had neither signed nor ratified it. Hence they ultimately demanded additional concessions: the Georgian districts of Akhaltsikhe and Akhalkalaki, the Armenian city and district of Alexandropol (Gyumri) and part of the district of Etchmiadzin. Above all, the Ottomans wanted to take hold of the Kars–Alexandropol–Julfa railway, which led to Baku and would give them full control of rail transport from Turkey to Baku. A few days later, they demanded control of all South Caucasian railways. To further increase pressure, Wehib Pasha occupied Alexandropol on 15 May and General Khalil Bey threatened to seize Tbilisi unless Georgia surrendered its railways. Threatened by the impending Turkish attack on Tbilisi, the Georgian Mensheviks turned to the German military attaché for the Caucasus, General Otto von Lossow. Haydar Bamatov, foreign minister of the United Mountain Peoples of the North Caucasus (for which see below), also appealed to von Lossow, who was interested in securing for Germany the region's oil and mineral resources, for protection. But following the failed Spring Offensive in France, German troops were exhausted and overstretched, so that no troops were available for a German North Caucasian adventure.[59] Although the Ottomans and Germany were war allies, they were economic competitors for Baku's oilfields and the regional manganese and copper deposits, as well as for Caspian cotton, since cotton was widely used to make nitrocellulose for the manufacture of ammunition and explosives. Hydraulically compressed cotton was also used in train armour. For this reason, Germany and Bolshevik Russia had concluded a secret agreement in April which was formalized on 27 August 1918, whereby Russia committed to sell to Germany a third of the production of Baku oil and Caspian cotton, providing the Germans prevented the Ottomans from occupying Baku and Azerbaijan.[60] However, as far as Caspian cotton was concerned neither the Ottomans nor Germany won, but Great Britain. In summer 1918, the British master spy Reginald Teague-Jones discovered a whole trainload of cotton bales in Krasnovodsk on the eastern Caspian littoral which had been bought by Germany and was awaiting shipment to Astrakhan. Thanks to a fictitious telegram from Astrakhan to Krasnovodsk, Teague-Jones succeeded in unloading the already full freight ships and turning away further ships arriving from Astrakhan.[61] After a short-lived pro-British government took power in Ashgabat soon afterwards in a coup, no more cotton left Turkestan. The British had thus temporarily won the 'war for cotton'.[62]

When asked for help, von Lossow outlined that Georgia must leave the Federation, declare independence and ask for German protection. **Georgia** declared its independence on 26 May 1918, and placed itself under German protection at the Treaty of Poti two days later.[63] Germany had previously concluded an agreement with the Central Council of Revolutionary Ukraine and thus obtained control over the Black Sea. German troops under General Kress von Kressenstein and the envoy Friedrich-Werner von der Schulenburg landed at Poti and reached Tbilisi on 10 June 1918, saving Georgia from a full-scale Turkish invasion. Nevertheless, on 4 June Turkey forced Georgia to sign a disadvantageous peace treaty which Kress von Kressenstein managed to mitigate by bringing the Georgian railways under German control and stipulating that the ownership of Akhaltsikhe and Akhalkalaki was to be decided by a referendum. Five months later at the **Armistice of Mudros** (30 October 1918), Britain and France forced Turkey to return its annexed territories to Georgia.[64] **Azerbaijan** followed with its declaration of independence on 28 May and **Armenia** three days later, though dating its independence retroactively to 28 May. It was revealing that the Ottomans entered a treaty of friendship with the Azerbaijani government based in Ganja but refused to either recognize its independence or to consider a federation with Azerbaijan, as Enver wanted to turn Azerbaijan into a Turkish protectorate.[65] Between 28 May and 15 September 1918 Azerbaijan was divided in two since the nationalist and pro-Turkish Müsavat party ruled over the western part of Azerbaijan from Ganja, while the Bolshevik People's Commissariat in Baku controlled eastern Azerbaijan and most of the littoral.

2.2 Ethnic and social conflicts in Georgia

The German vanguard had arrived none too soon, for on 12 June 1918 a mixed German–Georgian unit was obliged to stop an Ottoman column advancing from the south towards Tbilisi. The attackers were thrown back but several German and Georgian soldiers were taken prisoner. In reaction, German supreme command in Berlin threatened to withdraw all German soldiers, officers and officials from the Ottoman Empire unless all prisoners were released.[66] Enver yielded and abstained from further attacking Georgia. The internal fragility and regional conflicts that plague the Georgian state today were already becoming apparent in 1918. The Muslims of Adjara resisted the 'Georgification' efforts of the Menshevik government in a similar way to how the Georgians had previously resisted the tsarist regime's Russification measures. The Menshevik government repeated the Russians' earlier mistake by imposing Georgian as the mandatory school language. In the years 1918–1920, the ruthless methods used by the Mensheviks to integrate the South Ossetians living north of Gori into the Georgian state also triggered three Ossetian revolts which were supported by Bolshevik Russia, since the Bolsheviks were eager to recover as much of the territory of the defunct Tsarist Empire as they could. The armed Ossetian–Georgian clashes also had the character of class struggles, as the poor Ossetian peasants had responded to Lenin's tactical slogan 'the land to the peasants' by demanding and occupying farmland belonging to Georgian landlords. South Ossetian–Georgian tensions culminated in May 1920 with the South Ossetians rejecting Georgian statehood and opting for Russian suzerainty. After the South Ossetian nationalists captured the provincial capital Tskhinvali, the Georgians launched a ferocious punitive campaign, killing thousands of civilians.[67] Unlike in August 2008, Russia was not in a position to intervene since the Roki Tunnel linking Russian Vladikavkaz with Tskhinvali by road was only built in 1985. After Bolshevik Russia regained possession of Georgia in 1921, it granted to the South Ossetians the status of an Autonomous Oblast (province) within the Georgian Soviet Socialist Republic on 20 April 1922.[68] While this solution defused South Ossetian–Georgian tensions, it contributed to maintaining the South Ossetian identity and therefore the potential for future conflicts.

It was not only the Adjarians and South Ossetians that refused Menshevik Georgian suzerainty, but also the Abkhaz, who in November 1917 established the Abkhaz People's Council. Abkhazia had been annexed by the Tsarist Empire in 1864 and was quickly colonized by Georgians, Armenians and Russians. For example, in the district of Sukhumi 42 per cent of the population was Georgian, 12 per cent Russian and Ukrainian, 12 per cent Greek, 10 per cent Armenian and only 21 per cent Abkhaz.[69] Georgia claimed Abkhazia on historical grounds since the region had been part of the medieval Kingdom of Georgia, and later of its successor state Imereti. As in South Ossetia and

102. The New Athos (Georgian: Akhali Atoni, Russian: Novy Afon) Monastery was built in the 1880s north of Sukhumi on the eastern littoral of the Black Sea. Autonomous Republic of Abkhazia. Photo 2018.

103. The Sardarapat war memorial celebrating the Armenian victory over superior Turkish forces on 21–29 May 1918 which saved Armenia from annihilation. Armavir Province, Armenia. Photo 2022.

Georgia, the conflicts were not only along ethnic lines but also to a very great degree along social class divisions: the poorest peasants and deserted soldiers sympathized with the Bolsheviks and the prosperous farmers and business community with the Georgian Mensheviks, while the long-established Abkhaz landlords and nobles did not hesitate to appeal to the Ottomans for a military intervention since they feared the Mensheviks' land-reform programme.[70] One of the main trump cards of the Mensheviks was that since early summer 1918 they had upheld the independence of Georgia while the Bolsheviks were pushing for reintegration into Soviet Russia.

Within a year, Abkhazia experienced Georgian, German, Ottoman, Bolshevik Russian, White Russian and, indirectly, British military interventions. The first to invade Abkhazia was Soviet Russia in March 1918, for Lenin's proclamation in April 1917 of the peoples' right to self-determination was mere propaganda and applied only to the peoples of the British and French Empires. By spring 1918 it became obvious that proclamations of independence of non-Russian peoples and political entities within the borders of the former Tsarist Empire would be answered by military intervention. In terms of territorial claims Soviet Russia (as of 30 December 1922 the Soviet Union) was the true successor of the tsarist regime. The Soviets occupied Sukhumi on 8 April 1918 but were pushed back in May by pro-Georgian forces as far as Gagra. When the Soviets invaded again in June, the Abkhaz People's Council requested help from Tbilisi. The Georgian general and military governor Giorgi Mazniashvili (1870–1937), who had successfully repulsed an Ottoman attack in Guria, cleared Abkhazia of Soviet troops in June and July with German support, seizing Novy Afon (New Athos) north of Sukhumi, Gagra, Adler, Sochi and Tuapse as a result of which the latter four cities became part of the Black Sea Province.[71] With this renewed Georgian support, on 24 July the Abkhaz People's Council declared its association with the Georgian Republic provided it retained autonomous self-government.[72] In the meantime, Kress von Kressenstein had formed a small army out of Georgian German settlers and liberated German POWs. When Ottoman forces landed at Sukhumi in summer, he dispatched troops to establish small German garrisons at Ochamchira, Sukhumi and Adler.[73]

The situation got even more complicated when General Mazniashvili was confronted by troops of the White general Anton Ivanovich Denikin's Volunteer Army,[74] whom the Georgians viewed as a potential ally. The Bolshevik seizure of power had triggered rebellions throughout the Empire of former tsarist officers collectively known as 'Whites'; Denikin was the leader of one of these White armies. Although his Volunteer Army was the Bolshevik regime in Moscow's principal adversary, Denikin (1872–1947), with his credo of 'Russia, one and indivisible', was as eager as Lenin to rebuild Russia to its former Imperial size, which included the South Caucasian republics. Specifically he declared: 'All of Transcaucasia within the borders before 1914 war must be regarded as an integral part of the Russian State.'[75] Already, in early September 1918, the Georgians, badly defeated by retreating Soviet troops, had lost Tuapse to Denikin's vanguard. It was only the German garrisons which prevented the Volunteer Army from overrunning the district of Sukhumi. At the same time, in October 1918, a faction of the Abkhaz People's Council opted for an anti-Georgian alliance with the Volunteer Army, which provoked Tbilisi to send in troops to establish a more docile Council.[76] When Germany capitulated on 11 November 1918, Denikin resumed hostilities against Georgia but was told not to proceed in December 1918 by Major General George Milne, chief of the British Command in Istanbul that controlled the South Caucasus from Batumi to Baku. Denikin advanced again in December 1918 and seized Sochi, Adler and Gagra but in February was ordered by Milne to retreat from the district of Sukhumi. The Whites' December advance had been greatly facilitated by the redeployment of Georgian forces south of Tbilisi to protect the capital from the attacking Armenians.

The British were also annoyed at Denikin for battling the Georgians in Abkhazia instead of attacking the Bolsheviks. Since Denikin depended on supplies of British arms and ammunition, he had to obey the instruction not to attack Georgia or Azerbaijan.[77] When in April 1919 General Mazniashvili recaptured Gagra with the help of the anti-Bolshevist and anti-Denikin 'Green Russian' guerrillas, the British intervened again and defined the River Psou, whose delta lies between Gagra and Pitsunda, as the new border between Russia and Abkhazia (and so Georgia), which was confirmed by the Soviet Russian–Georgian treaty of 7 May 1920. Almost one year earlier, the Abkhaz People's Council had confirmed its position as an autonomous polity within the Georgian Republic.[78] However when the Red Army occupied Sukhumi on 4 March 1921 without Georgian resistance, the Abkhaz Revolutionary Committee (Revkom) declared Abkhazia an independent Soviet Socialist Republic (SSR)[79] which was confirmed on 28 March by Sergo Ordzhonikidze, chairman of the all-powerful Kavbyuro.[80] However, the independence of the Abkhaz SSR from Georgia came to an end on 16 December 1921 when it was obliged to enter a political, military and financial-economic union with its larger neighbour. The same kind of union had also been imposed on Adjara and South Ossetia. Article 1 of the Georgian Constitution of 1922 specified: 'The ASSR Ajaria, … the AO Oblast of South Ossetia and the SSR Abkhazia, which is joined to the SSR Georgia by the special union treaty, between them, all compose the Socialist Soviet Republic of Georgia.'[81] At the dissolution of the Soviet Union, these three hotspots of conflict re-emerged violently and in 2022 the Abkhazian and South Ossetian situations are further than ever from resolution.

2.3 The Republic of Armenia

At the moment of its independence Armenia was riddled with problems. The Armenian population was not concentrated in the province of Yerevan but spread throughout the South Caucasus; the largest Armenian urban communities lived outside Armenia in Tbilisi and Baku. The new capital, Yerevan was underdeveloped in comparison with Tbilisi and the young republic was flooded with around 300,000 refugees. In the last week of the Transcaucasian Federation's existence, General Wehib launched his final attack on Yerevan from Alexandropol (Gyumri). Kress von Kressenstein, who several times alerted German high command and Chancellor Georg von Hertling to the situation, judged that 'There is little doubt that the Turks are systematically intent on exterminating through systematic starvation the few hundred thousand Armenians they have so far left alive.'[82] From Enver's point of view, Armenia stood in the way of a union of Turkic Muslims stretching from the Bosporus to Central Asia; it was an obstacle obstructing free passage from Turkey to Azerbaijan and Central Asia, which had to be removed. In its distress, Armenia appealed twice to von Lossow for German protection, but in vain.[83] Germany clearly enjoyed high prestige in the Caucasus, since Georgia, Armenia and the Union of Mountain Peoples all asked for German protection from their foes – be it the Ottomans, Bolshevik Russia or the Volunteer Army. In the face of acute danger of final annihilation, the

Armenians mobilized their last resources and in three long and hard-fought battles defeated a three-pronged attack by Ottoman forces some 40 to 50 kilometres west of Yerevan, at Bash Abaran (21–29 May 1918), Karakilisa (25–28 May) and especially at Sardarapat (21–29 May) (fig. 103). On the same day as the victory of Sardarapat was secured, General Nazarbekian cautiously ordered his troops to halt in line with a ceasefire suggested by General Wehib. Feeling betrayed, General Andranik refused to recognize the new Republic of Armenia and marched to Nakhchivan with his followers and between 20 and 30 thousand refugees, later moving to Zangezur which he controlled independently from Yerevan until March 1919. On 4 June 1918, the Armenian prime minister-designate Hovhannes Kajaznuni (in office 6 June 1918–7 August 1919) together with the two strongmen, generals Aram Manukian and Dro,[84] agreed to the Peace of Batumi which left Armenia with a hardly viable, rather mountainous territory of some 10,000 square kilometres, about one third of today's Armenia.[85] Furthermore, it had to concede unhindered transit of Ottoman troops and supplies, which reduced the new republic to the status of a de facto Ottoman vassal. But after the Armistice of Mudros, Armenia recovered Alexandropol and 16,500 square kilometres of territory. Once Turkish troops evacuated Kars in February 1919, Armenian forces with British support seized the province of Kars in April and Nakhchivan in May, which increased Armenia's territory to 47,000 square kilometres. But in autumn 1920 much of these gains would be lost again.[86]

In spite of Armenia's very difficult military and economic situation, it had no hesitation in starting a brief war against Georgia over the regions of Lori and Akhalkalaki, both of which had substantial Armenian populations;[87] more extreme Armenian nationalists also claimed the harbour of Batumi. After the Ottomans left Lori and southern Borchalo, which separated Armenia from Georgia,[88] in early October 1918, the Armenians occupied this zone on 18 October and advanced further north; only the warnings of Kress von Kressenstein forced them to evacuate northern Lori which was secured by small German–Georgian platoons. The Georgians then attempted to defuse the conflict by calling a South Caucasian peace conference, but the Armenians refused to attend.[89] By 5 December 1918, Georgia controlled Akhaltsikhe and Akhalkalaki.[90] When the German retreat became apparent, the Armenian prime minister Kajaznuni issued his Georgian counterpart Zhordania with an ultimatum on 12 December 1918 to withdraw his troops from Borchalo north of Lori, where a pro-Armenian rebellion had broken out with Armenian support.[91] The next day General Dro attacked and expelled the Georgians from Sanahin, Haghpat, Alaverdi and Akhtala. Since the Armenian offensive coincided with Denikin's attack on Abkhazia, Zhordania accused Armenia of having secretly coordinated its attack with Denikin.[92] As the last German troops left Tbilisi on 23 December, Dro launched a full offensive and by the next day had advanced within 45 kilometres of Tbilisi; at the same time, he sent Zhordania an ultimatum to immediately vacate Akhalkalaki; otherwise he would attack Tbilisi.[93]

At this point General Mazniashvili took charge of the defence and threw the Armenian invaders back, whereupon the British major general William Rycroft imposed a ceasefire and ordered the Armenians to evacuate Georgia and northern Lori where the British established a neutral zone. A preliminary peace was concluded on 17 January 1919.[94] The war ended inconclusively, but Georgia retaliated by expelling Armenians in Tbilisi from administrative and police functions. Armenia won the copper mines of Alaverdi but paid a high price for them, since the concentration of most of its armed forces against Georgia led to a neglect of the strategically more important regions of Sharur (Şərur) and Nakhchivan. Even more serious was the negative impression left by the war on the Allies who in a few weeks' time were to decide on the future of the region, and especially Armenia, at the Paris Peace Conference.[95] This perception of the South Caucasians was epitomized by Major General Milne:

They [the South Caucasians] *are certainly not worth the life of one British soldier. The Georgians are merely disguised Bolsheviks ...The Armenians are ... a despicable race. The best are the inhabitants of Azerbaijan, though they are in reality uncivilized.*[96]

The reputation of Armenia and Georgia was further tarnished by the Armenian–Georgian conflict over the port of Batumi and the left bank of the River Chorokh in spring 1920.[97] Another consequence of the 1918–1919 war was that Georgia and Azerbaijan moved politically closer, and on 16 June 1919 concluded a pact of mutual defence directed against a potential coordinated attack on Georgia and Azerbaijan by Armenia and Denikin's forces.[98] In 1921, the Soviets allocated the neutral zone to Armenia and Akhalkalaki to Georgia.[99] During the winter of 1918–19 more than 100,000 Armenians succumbed to famine, cold and contagious diseases; while industrial production dropped by 92 per cent compared to 1913, agriculture by 80 per cent and livestock by 65 per cent.[100]

104. German troops on the march in Georgia in 1918.

2.4 The race for Baku

In summer 1918, a dramatic race began for the Baku oilfields during which World War allies became adversaries and World War enemies turned into allies. In the competition for the world's second-largest oil supplies and the huge cotton plantations in the Mughan Steppe, seven powers were involved: the Müsavat government in Ganja, the Baku Commune, the Ottomans, Germany, Bolshevik Russia, Denikin's Volunteer Army and Great Britain. The two Azerbaijani governments fought for supremacy in the country, the two hostile Russian regimes claimed Baku as an integral part of the Russian Empire, and Turkey aspired to unite the Turkic-speaking nations under its leadership. Germany for its part was not aiming for long-term territorial gains but for satellite states rich in raw materials such as fossil fuels, minerals, cotton and grain. By the end of April 1918 Germany had installed Hetman Pavel Petrovich Skoropadskyi as puppet ruler in Kyiv, and German and Austrian troops occupied Ukraine as far as Kharkiv, Crimea, the Donets and Don Basins as far as Taganrog, Azov, Rostov-on-Don and even the harbour of Novorossiysk on the Kuban littoral.[101] Naturally the Don Basin and Crimea served Germany as bridgeheads to the Caucasus and its rich deposits of raw materials. In theory, the Caucasus could serve as a military access point to Central Asia and Afghanistan, from where British India might be attacked. The German economic strategy not only threatened British interests but also clashed with Turkey's pan-Turkic aims. Once the British became aware of the German–Soviet oil and cotton deals they decided to intervene in Baku.

When Kress von Kressenstein put an end to the Ottoman advance to Baku via Georgia, Enver Pasha changed tactics. He replaced Wehib Pasha with Khalil Pasha as commander of the Ottoman Eastern Army Corps and created the pseudo-volunteer Caucasus Army of Islam which consisted of Turkish troops and officers, ex-tsarist cavalry units, ex-tsarist Christian officers, Daghestanis and irregulars. Although the initially 14,000-strong Army of Islam[102] was officially a local Ganja Azerbaijani force and not under the control of Istanbul, its commander was none other than Enver's half-brother Nuri Pasha (Nuri Killigil, 1889–1949).[103] The contribution of local Muslim Azeris to this nominally Azerbaijani army was minimal, as Nuri Pasha admitted: 'The Muslims of the South Caucasus talk a lot but do little.'[104] Baku was defended by the Cossack brigade of the Ossetian former tsarist colonel Lazar Bicherakov (1882–1952) and an Armenian militia. A first Turkish attack on Baku failed on 5 June 1918.[105] When the next attack of the Army of Islam again failed on 31 July, Kress von Kressenstein sought permission from Berlin to conquer Baku in a joint operation with Nuri's force, which would secure partial control of the oilfields for Germany. But Kress received no response.[106] In Baku, the commissar Shahumyan, whose power was based on a fragile Bolshevik–Dashnak coalition, was in a dilemma: since no military help could be expected from Moscow and parallel negotiations with Kress von Kressenstein remained inconclusive, the Dashnaks wanted to appeal to British forces with whom contacts had been established via the consul, Major Ranald MacDonell (1875–1941). But the Bolsheviks categorically rejected this and on 21 July Stalin, an old rival of Shahumyan since 1905, forbade him from any cooperation with the British.[107] Just before the Army of Islam attacked on 31 July, Baku's opposition overthrew the Bolshevik Commissariat. Shahumyan and his commissar colleagues fled by boat towards Astrakhan but were soon intercepted by an anti-Bolshevik warship and arrested. In the meantime, Baku's Dashnaks, Mensheviks and Social Revolutionaries seized power under the name of the **Central Caspian Dictatorship** and launched an urgent appeal for British military aid, which was all the more desperate since Bicherakov's brigade had left Baku for lack of governmental support and occupied Derbent.[108] As General Dunsterville would also experience, Baku's Armenian troops were unreliable and shirked battle; instead of obeying orders, they would hold meetings to debate whether to fight or not.[109]

To thwart Ottoman or German advances towards Baku, Britain had already in January 1918 appointed Major General Lionel Dunsterville (1865–1946) as head of a Caucasus Mission and British representative in Tbilisi. The German protectorate over Georgia brought this plan to nothing, and Dunsterville was instructed to stabilize northern and central Persia and to prevent Ottomans or Germans from seizing Baku.[110] However, Dunsterville was not allowed to land in Baku without Soviet consent; but when the Central Caspian Dictatorship asked for military aid, he sent a vanguard under Colonel Claude Stokes which reached Baku on 4 August; Dunsterville himself arrived on 17 August. The 'Dunsterforce' mission was a tough assignment: 900 British Indian soldiers, some hundred Cossacks and 6,000 battle-averse Armenians faced 14,000 combat-hardened Turks possessing strong artillery. A second, larger Turkish force counting more than 16,000 men was also approaching. As Dunsterville reported, the Armenians either deliberated whether to fight or simply refused to engage in battle, so that the burden of defending Baku rested on the shoulders of the British and the Cossacks. As Colonel Alfred Rawlinson (1867–1934) of the British Intelligence Corps discovered, the local director general of Baku's artillery was, even on the eve of a major Turkish attack on 31 August, selling advanced ammunition stocks to the enemy.[111] When the Turks broke through the defence on 14 September, Dunsterville re-embarked for Anzali with his decimated troops under cover of night.[112] On the following day, Azerbaijani volunteers marched into Baku, where they slaughtered approximately 9,000 Armenians in retaliation for their own heavy losses the previous March. The day after that, the regular Turkish troops occupied Baku and established a short-lived Ottoman protectorate over Azerbaijan. However, the victorious Army of Islam was prevented by a small flotilla under the British commodore David Norris (1875–1937) from crossing the Caspian Sea in order to land in Krasnovodsk, today's Türkmenbaşy in Turkmenistan. In spite of the previous German–Ottoman clashes, Kress von Kressenstein and Nuri Pasha managed to align their interests concerning the Baku oilfields, agreeing that Germany and the Ottomans would jointly exploit the oil reserves. Whereas the Ottomans controlled Azerbaijan, Germany would run the refineries, the Baku–Batumi railway and the parallel pipeline.[113] The end of the war, however, prevented the implementation of the agreement.

As for the Bolshevik commissars, they were freed just before Baku fell, and boarded a ship to Astrakhan. But the ship's captain sailed instead to Krasnovodsk, where they were again arrested. The anti-Bolshevik Transcaspian Provisional Government (aka Ashgabat Executive Committee) sentenced them to death, and on the night of 19–20 September, 26 commissars including Shahumyan were shot.[114] Only the later Soviet Politburo member Anastas Mikoyan was spared, on account of his youth. But in March 1919 Stalin and Trotsky launched a political campaign against the British political representative in Transcaspia, Reginald Teague-Jones and blamed him for the shooting of the Bolshevik commissars.[115] In danger of being assassinated, after leaving Transcaspia Teague-Jones later assumed a new identity and for the rest of his life was known as Ronald Sinclair.[116] Having captured Baku, the Army of Islam expanded its conquests, taking Derbent in the north on 6 October and Karabakh's capital Shushi (Şuşa) in the south-west three days later.[117] Since Enver also wanted to control the oilfields of Grozny, on 5 November an Ottoman battalion under Major General Yusuf Izzet Pasha, who was unaware that the Armistice of Mudros had ended the war on 30 October, attacked Port-Petrovsk (Makhachkala) on the Caspian, which capitulated three days later.[118] It remains noteworthy how much territorial gain could be achieved by audacious commanders such as Yudenich or Izzet Pasha with small numbers of rapidly moving troops, while in France hundreds of thousands of soldiers would die in futile trench warfare.

2.5 War in Karabakh, Nakhchivan, Zangezur and Kars

No sooner had the Ottoman occupation of parts of the South Caucasus ended than several territorial disputes arose, mainly triggered by the existence of ethnic enclaves within a state with a different majority ethnicity: for example the Armenians of Karabakh within Azerbaijan, the Armenians of Akhalkalaki within Georgia or the Muslims of the short-lived Republic of Aras within Armenian-majority Nakhchivan. Invoking President Wilson's proclaimed right of national self-determination, these minorities claimed the right to choose either independence or incorporation into their ethnic motherland. While the British tried to mediate these conflicts, their priority was to support General Denikin who denied the right to independence of any South Caucasian entities.

In the Armistice of Mudros on 30 October 1918, article 1 required the opening of the Dardanelles and Bosporus and granted Allied access to the Black Sea. Article 5 insisted on the immediate demobilization of the Turkish army except for the purposes of securing internal order. Article 11 demanded the immediate withdrawal of Turkish troops from north-west Iran and Transcaucasia (the southern Caucasus). However, it did allow Turkey to maintain troops in parts of western Transcaucasia such as the province of Kars and parts of the district of Batumi which was 'to be evacuated [by the Turks] if required by the Allies after they have studied the situation there'. This meant that the Allies, that is the British, were not insisting that Turkish troops

105. The capital of Armenia, Yerevan. In the background on the left is Lesser Ararat (3,896 m), on the right Greater Ararat (5,137 m). Yerevan, Armenia. Photo 2012.

106. The palace of the khans of Nakhchivan built in the 1780s. Nakhchivan city, Azerbaijan. Photo 2016.

retreat behind the 1914 boundaries, which greatly dampened Armenian hopes of regaining Kars, let alone of a unification of all the Ottoman Armenian provinces with the Republic of Armenia. For obvious reasons the British were more interested in occupying the straits than in eastern Anatolia. Article 15 required that all Turkish railways, including the Transcaucasian, come under Allied control and that Baku and Batumi be occupied by Allied troops. Article 24 stipulated that 'in case of disorder in the six Armenian vilayets, the Allies reserve to themselves the right to occupy any part of them'.[119] Six weeks later, on 17 November, General William Montgomerie Thomson (1877–1963) arrived in Baku with the 5,000-strong North Persia Force (known in short as 'Norperforce') to secure the oilfields; senior officers were soon stationed in key cities such as Tbilisi and Batumi. Seen from the point of view of international law it remains highly questionable whether the British occupation of Georgia was justified, since the republic had never declared war on Britain and had only sought German protection to avoid Ottoman conquest. Nor did Britain have a mandate to rule Georgia *ad interim* until Denikin had gained power in Moscow. Nevertheless, General Thomson proclaimed in early November 1918: 'Britain considers the Caucasus as part of her ally, Russia [i.e. Denikin's Whites], and therefore the recognition of any new governments is not considered.'[120] When a British colonel told Zhordania in December 1918 that the objective of the Allies was 'to restore the Caucasian viceroyalty in the name of Russian authority' and that the Georgian government had to carry out his orders,[121] Zhordania politely replied: 'Colonel, I must brief you about our country. This is an independent land. We are not at war with your country and you are here not as a conqueror, but as a guest.'[122] Towards the South Caucasian governments the British behaved like henchmen of Denikin.

Upon their arrival the British were rather welcomed by Azerbaijani politicians since they hoped that Great Britain would prevent a feared Russian reconquest, whether by the Bolsheviks or the Whites. General Thomson noted that the Transcaucasians 'hate Russia and would vastly prefer to be a protectorate of Britain or France as a guarantee against oppression … They ask "do the Allies mean to live up to their word about self-determination of small nations so far as the subject races of Russia are concerned?'"[123] The outcome of the Paris Peace Conference revealed that the Allies cared for the principle of self-determination in Europe, but not in the Caucasus. In fact, Britain was war-weary and its economy shaken. It had no plans either to annex Caucasian territory or to establish a protectorate, and its main objective was to prevent the Bolsheviks from seizing Baku. Norperforce left Baku in August 1919. One month later, the British also withdraw from Tbilisi without having recognized de jure Georgia's independence. Not only were the British suspicious of the Georgian government on account of its cooperation with Germany, but they still gambled on Denikin's victory over the Bolsheviks, and Denikin was adamant that South Caucasia belonged to Russia: the British commitment to Denikin took priority over the desire for independence of Russia's former South Caucasian provinces. The British cabinet was divided on the issue of Georgia's independence: Lord Curzon, a member of the War Policy Committee, favoured the independence of the three South Caucasian republics as a future bulwark against rising pan-Turkism and to shield Iran from Russian aggression; whereas the foreign secretary, Arthur Balfour despised the Caucasians stating: 'If they [Georgians, Armenians and Azerbaijanis] want to cut their own throats why not let them do it … We are not going to spend all our money and men in civilizing a few people who do not want to be civilized.'[124] Balfour's words, though arrogant, were also a reflection of the recent Armenian–Georgian war. As a result, neither Armenia nor Georgia was invited to actively participate at the Paris Peace Conference. The Allies recognized the governments of Georgia and Azerbaijan as de facto governments on 10 January 1920 and the Armenian on 19 January when Denikin's defeat was sealed.[125] However, a de facto recognition did not mean a recognition as a right of law, and did not imply diplomatic relations. The last British troops left Batumi in early July 1920.

Once Azerbaijan's partition had ended with the Ottoman conquest of Baku, the Ganja government relocated to the capital and the defence minister, Fatali khan Khoyski (Fətəli xan Xoyski) of the Müsavat Party became the first prime minister of the Azerbaijan Democratic Republic (in office 1918–1919); he was assassinated on 19 June 1920 by a Dashnak in revenge for the September 1918 massacres. On 28 December General Thomson recognized Khoyski's government as the de facto authority, and it seems that the prime minister won the trust of the general to such a degree that the latter and his staff officer Colonel Digby Shuttleworth favoured the Azerbaijani position in the conflict with Armenia over Zangezur and Nagorno-Karabakh. The latter's name means Mountainous (Russian *nagorny*, 'highland') Black Garden (Turkish *kara*, 'black' and Persian *bagh*, 'garden') and thus represents a three-way linguistic inheritance from the three great regional powers. When General Andranik advanced from his power base of Zangezur towards Shushi (Şuşa) to bring **Nagorno-Karabakh**, which was overwhelmingly populated by Armenians, into the political orbit of Armenia, General Thomson ordered him to stop. Thomson outlined that the World War had ended and that the Peace Conference would settle all border issues. Andranik obeyed and withdrew on 4 December 1918.[126] As a next step, on 15 January 1919 Thomson approved Prime Minister Khoyski's appointment of Nuri Pasha's former collaborator and fellow pan-Turkist, Khosrov bey Sultanov (Xosrov bəy Sultanov), as governor general of Karabakh and Zangezur.[127] By this approval General Thomson accepted these provinces as part of Azerbaijan although the vast majority of their population were Armenians. To secure Karabakh's allocation to Azerbaijan, Thomson posted 400 soldiers under the command of Major Monck-Mason in Shushi. Addressing the Armenians Monck-Mason proclaimed in the name of General Thomson: 'Any belligerent action against the government of Azerbaijan will be regarded as if it were directed against the government of Great Britain.'[128] Disillusioned with both the British and the Armenian government, General Andranik demobilized his troops in March 1919 and went into exile.[129] Yet **Zangezur** remained under Armenian control, even when faced with Colonel Shuttleworth's threat of aerial bombardment. The Zangezur Regional Council proclaimed in May 1919 that 'all acts of aggression against Zangezur, an integral part of the Republic of Armenia, would be met by ironfisted contravention'. The British didn't insist.[130] However, in late October 1919 the Karabakh governor Sultanov and other pan-Turkic Azerbaijani leaders decided on subjugating Armenian Zangezur. Azerbaijani troops, whose officers were mostly former Ottoman Turkish officers, attacked on 4 November but by the 9th they had suffered a bitter defeat at the hands of lieutenant colonels Arsen Shahmazian and Garegin Nzhdeh (Ter-Harutyunyan). However the latter was forbidden to advance and secure the district of Goghtn (today's Ordubad in Nakhchivan); as a consequence, a force made up of vengeful Muslim refugees from Zangezur and Azerbaijanis murdered about 1,400 Armenian civilians in Agulis (Yuxarı əylis). Nzhdeh retaliated by ravaging Muslim villages located south-east of Goris.[131] This brief but cruel war further damaged the reputation of Armenia and Azerbaijan among the Allies.

When in spring the Armenian National Council of Karabakh refused to submit to the governor, Sultanov, and sought a union with the Armenian Republic, Sultanov implemented with British approval a tight economic blockade of Karabakh to starve the recalcitrant Armenians into submission.[132] To break the Armenian resistance, Sultanov attacked a village near Shushi on 5 June with 2,000 Kurdish-Azeri irregulars, massacred hundreds of Armenians and occupied Shushi. By the end of June, British troops had withdrawn from Karabakh and Sultanov remained master of the region. Since the British were leaving the South Caucasus, the Armenian National Council of Karabakh capitulated on 22 August 1919 and affirmed that 'the Armenian-populated mountainous sector of Karabakh … regards itself to be provisionally within the boundaries of the Azerbaijan Republic'.[133]

In summer 1919, Armenia also lost **Nakhchivan** where some 40 per cent of the population was Armenian. After the Ottoman defeat the autonomous Muslim **Republic of Aras** (Arasdayan) had been formed with the support of the Müsavat Party, consisting of Nakhchivan including Sharur (Şərur) along the River Aras (Araxes). On the order of General Milne it was dissolved in mid May 1919 and on 20 May Armenian troops occupied the region.[134] As a result of this Armenian expansion Azerbaijan's prime minister Nasib bey Yusifbeyli (Nəsib bəy Yusifbəyli, in office 1919–1920) was afraid of a joint Armenian–Denikin attack on Baku. When the British Indian Rajput battalion stationed in Nakhchivan withdrew in early June 1919, he appealed to the Turkish general Kâzim Karabekir, who had never demobilized all his troops, and had kept several thousand Turkish soldiers under arms as a nucleus of the future Turkish Nationalist Army commanded by Mustafa Kemal. The latter had been nominated inspector general of the Ninth Army on 30 April 1919 and his authority extended over the military and the civil administration of major parts of central and eastern Turkey. Both Karabekir and Kemal had secretly sworn to resist any foreign domination, be it British or Armenian.[135] Karabekir foresaw that the eviction of Armenian forces from Nakhchivan would reopen the corridor connecting Turkey with Azerbaijan. He sent agents to Nakhchivan under Khalil Bey to organize the local Muslim irregulars and in July 1919 instigated an uprising in Sharur in north-western Nakhchivan. When confronted by the French military representative, Captain Antoine Poidebard,[136] Khalil Bey explained that the events were not a rebellion, but the rightful self-determination of the Muslim majority, in line with President Wilson's concept of national self-determination.[137]

In spring 1920, the fate of **Karabakh** too was decided. Yerevan had sent an undercover covert agent, Arsen Mikaelian to Karabakh in December 1919 to secretly prepare an uprising in coordination with General Dro and Nzhdeh's troops. However, the governor Sultanov's intelligence network swiftly detected the Dashnak agent. Sultanov called the Assembly of Armenians of Karabakh to discuss a full and definite integration of Karabakh into Azerbaijan. The Assembly split on this issue along regional lines with around two-thirds of delegates rejecting such a union, and one-third approving it on economic grounds. The badly coordinated uprising began on 23 March 1920 but failed to overcome the Azerbaijani garrisons of Khankendi (Xankəndi, Armenian Stepanakert) and Şuşa (Shushi) where hundreds of Armenians were killed in retaliation. Dro and Nzhdeh prepared a counteroffensive yet when the news came that Soviet troops had crossed the Azerbaijani border on 26–27 April Dro halted the attack, to the anger of Nzhdeh who wanted to continue the military operation. With most of the Azerbaijani army stationed in Karabakh, Baku fell to the Bolsheviks without a fight on 28 April 1920 and the **Azerbaijan Soviet Socialist Republic** was proclaimed on the same day. The Soviet Eleventh Army reached Shushi on 12 May, liquidated Sultanov's regime and forced Dro to retreat to Zangezur. Nagorno-Karabakh now became part of the Azerbaijani Socialist Soviet Republic,[138] but the Armenian resistance was so tenacious that in July Mustafa Kemal had to send Turkish troops to help the battered Red Army units.[139]

Concerning the south-western Caucasus front, on 11 November 1918 the Allied Supreme War Council demanded that Turkish troops should retreat to the pre-war Russian–Turkish frontier and thus evacuate, among other regions, **Kars Province**. The British planned to hand the civil administration to Armenians. But the Turkish general Yakub Şevki delayed the withdrawal of his troops and encouraged the Muslim population of Kars to found, based on the principle of self-determination of peoples, the **Provisional National Government of the South-Western Caucasus** or **Kars Republic** on 18 January 1919, stretching from Adjara on the Black Sea to Nakhchivan.[140] The Kars Shura (Council) forced the appointed Armenian administrators to leave the province and made it clear that it would take no orders from the British. General Milne at first hesitated to dispatch troops since a War Office directive had outlined that British soldiers should not get involved in putting down local disturbances. However, at the end of March, with the British withdrawal planned for 30 April, Milne brushed the War Office directive aside and ordered the South-West Caucasus

Republic to be dissolved. The republic was abolished on 12 April 1919 and the transfer of authority from the British to the Armenian governor designate Stepan Korganian took place on 28 April 1919, as a result of which the province of Kars was united with the Republic of Armenia.[141] As a next step, on 26 May the Armenian government proclaimed the unification of Russian and Ottoman Armenia and invited western Armenians to send twelve deputies to the expanded national parliament.[142] However, Kurdish and Turkish chiefs remained in control of much of the countryside and soon a dangerous rivalry developed between the conciliatory governor and the two repressive generals Hovsepian and Pirumian. Also the general outlook was bleak. With the withdrawal of British troops, the South Caucasian republics were exposed to attacks from three sides, namely from the Turkish nationalists, the Russian Bolsheviks and Denikin's Whites.

2.6 Armenia and the Paris Peace Conference

Having claimed victory in World War I, the Allies – France, Great Britain, Italy and the USA – faced the daunting task of securing a lasting peace for Europe and the Middle East. To this end the Paris Peace Conference opened on 19 January 1919. The Allies not only had to decide on the conditions to be imposed on the defeated Central Powers, but also to redraw the political maps of the three vanished empires, Germany, Austria–Hungary and the Ottoman. But it was the disintegrated multinational Tsarist Empire that posed the biggest challenge, not only because it was torn by several civil wars but also because a plethora of large and small nations were looking for independence from Russia. Since the two main Russian contenders for supremacy, the Bolsheviks and the Whites, claimed the entire territory of Imperial Russia as theirs, any recognition by the Allies of a former Russian province as new, independent state required a robust military guarantee to prevent it from falling prey to the future victor of the civil war. As the US Senate soon adopted an isolationist policy, against the will of President Woodrow Wilson (in office 1913–1921),[143] the three European powers set the tone and they understandably prioritized European and Middle Eastern issues; questions concerning the Caucasus were at best secondary. Basically, the victorious European powers had no strong objection to the return to the pre-war status quo of Russian sovereignty over the South Caucasus. It was only due to the chaotic situation in Russia itself that the question of the independence of the South Caucasian republics was considered at all.

The Caucasian states and self-proclaimed entities were not officially invited to the congress as powers in their own right, but their delegations were allowed to present their cases and they lobbied intensively with allied politicians and delegates. All three South Caucasian delegations started their lobbying by demanding the maximum. Georgia's remained relatively modest by claiming roughly the territory of the Georgian kingdom in the early twelfth century, that is the extent of the republic along with Zakatala in the east and Ardahan, Olti, Artvin, Batumi and Abkhazia including Sukhumi in the west (map 6). The conference granted Georgia northern Borchalo, Javakheti, Abkhazia (but without Sochi and Batumi) and Adjara.[144] Azerbaijan's demands were much greedier, claiming in addition to the republic Derbent, Karabakh, Zangezur, Nakhchivan, the Aras Valley in the Yerevan District, Kars, Olti, Ardahan, Akhaltsikhe, Artvin and Batumi, thus encompassing a vast territory stretching from the Caspian to the Black Sea; in other words virtually every territory in the South Caucasus where Muslims lived. In this plan, Armenia would be a tiny enclave within Greater Azerbaijan. Azerbaijan's claims were rejected as excessive.[145] At the same time, political groups from Nakhchivan lobbied to join Iran as a means to avoid Soviet or Armenian occupation.[146] The affiliation of Karabakh, Zangezur and Nakhchivan was to be decided later by Stalin. The Armenian demands (map 7) were even more megalomaniac than the Azerbaijani, as they encompassed the whole, short-lived empire of King Tigranes II (95–55 BCE).[147] The territory claimed extended from Shushi in the east to Mersin on the Mediterranean Sea in the south-west and from Ardahan and Trabzon on the Black Sea in the north to İskenderun (Alexandretta) on the Mediterranean in the south. As summarized by the joint memorandum dated 12 February 1919, the Armenian claim encompassed the republic, the seven Ottoman *vilayets* of Van, Bitlis, Diyarbakır, Kharput, Sivas, Erzurum and Trabzon, Cilicia plus İskenderun, Lori and Akhalkalaki, Karabakh, Zangezur and Kars.[148] This was a total of *ca.* 300,000 square kilometres for slightly more than 3 million Armenians (as estimated by the US State Department in 1922).[149] To further complicate the issue, Kemal's Turkish nationalists not only rejected any territorial cession in Anatolia but claimed the pre-1878 borders and a land corridor to Azerbaijan. The landing of Greek forces at Smyrna (today's İzmir) on 14–15 May 1919 created an immense wave of Turkish patriotism and gave Kemal's nationalism the momentum which would ultimately destroy the Armenians and Greeks alike. The Armenian claims also clashed with the interests of France in Cilicia, Sivas, Kharput and Diyarbakır which had been confirmed in the Sykes–Picot Agreement of 1916. Finally, Iran claimed the return of the former Russian and British zones, major parts of Central Asia and, in

Map 6. Territorial claims of Azerbaijan and Georgia at the Paris Peace Conference, June 1919

- ---- Territorial claim of Azerbaijan
- —— Present borders of Azerbaijan
- ---- Territorial claim of Georgia
- —— Present borders of Georgia
- ···· Armenia according to the proposal of Azerbaijan
- ● Capital city
- ○ Main city
- — River

the north-west, Azerbaijan, southern Dagestan, Armenia and the Ottoman provinces of Van, Bitlis, Diyarbakır and Kharput.'[150] These demands were so exorbitant and out of touch with reality that the Iranian delegation was refused an official hearing.

Although the Armenians enjoyed an advantage of sympathy due to their recent horrific tribulations, their excessive demands were judged by allied politicians and military as utopian. The French delegate to the Conference, Philippe Berthelot accurately diagnosed that 'the great difficulty in establishing Armenia is that the Armenians practically nowhere constitute a majority. ... Reality and logic are equally opposed to the dream of a Great Armenia stretching from Trebizond to Alexandretta.'[151] Colonel Rawlinson, who served in the British Intelligence Corps from 1918 to 1922, had a realistic assessment of the military and administrative potential of the Armenians. 'The Armenians have [with Kars] already bitten off more than they can chew and show no aptitude for Government.'[152] The American King–Crane Commission appointed by President Wilson reached a similar conclusion: 'The Armenians are in genuine danger of grasping at too much and losing all.'[153] During the deliberations in 1919

Map 7. Territorial claims of Armenia at the Paris Peace Conference, June 1919 and US President Wilson's arbitration, November 1920

- - - Territorial claim of Armenia
- - - Territorial arbitration according to President Wilson
— Present borders of Armenia
● Capital city
○ Main city
— River

it became apparent that none of the Allies had any interest in a mandate for Armenia, which was a poor country without raw materials but rich in troubles; and before the Armenian question could be tackled, the Turkish one had to be resolved. On 29 August 1919 France seized the opportunity to secure Cilicia by offering an expeditionary force of 12,000 men to support the Armenians there. The motivation for the French was not really to help the Armenians but to place a small army in striking distance of Syria, which the Sykes–Picot Agreement had allocated to France. At this point Syria was still occupied by British forces with a target date for withdrawal set for 1 November 1919. Britain agreed in September that France could occupy Cilicia and quickly began (in the word of the historian Richard Hovannisian) 'dumping' large numbers of Armenian refugees from Aleppo into Cilicia, that is into French guardianship.[154] In fact, more than 120,000 Armenian refugees returned or migrated to Cilicia believing they would be protected by France and Britain.[155]

In March 1920 Britain tried to rid itself of the Armenian question by suggesting that the League of Nations, founded on 28 June 1919, handle the issue, although it had no military forces of its own. Another major complication arose on 23 April 1920 when Mustafa Kemal founded a Turkish counter-government in Angora (Ankara) which had control of central and eastern Anatolia.[156] Three days later, Kemal offered Bolshevik Russia an offensive military alliance against Georgia and Armenia:

We accept to join forces and operations with Bolshevik Russia against the Imperialist Governments and for the liberation of oppressed people … If the Bolshevik forces conduct military operations in the direction of Georgia …, the government of Turkey will undertake to conduct military operations against the imperialist Armenian government.[157]

At that moment, the Red Army forces in the Caucasus were busy invading Azerbaijan and not yet ready to attack Georgia; moreover Russia wanted to seize Armenia for itself to create a barrier between Turkey and Muslim Azerbaijan. Anyway, in May 1920 Armenian Bolshevist agitators incited alarming revolts against the government and mutinies in the army in Alexandropol, Kars and Sarıkamış.[158] Besides, the territorial ambitions of Russia and Turkey and their common hostility to the Allies led to a Turkish–Russian alliance which would crush Armenia within a few months.

At the end the San Remo Conference (19–26 April 1920) run by Great Britain, France and Italy, the French field marshal Ferdinand Foch estimated that 60,000 Allied soldiers would be needed to seize the Turkish *vilayets* for the Armenians and that 120,000 soldiers would have to be deployed over a longer time to disarm the Turkish nationalists and to protect the Armenian minorities.[159] In view of the Bolshevik victory over Denikin's Whites and the strengthening of Kemal's Turkish nationalists, the British prime minister David Lloyd George (in office 1916–1922) recognized that it was politically totally out of the question to commit so many troops long-term to the Armenian cause; the same would be true for France.[160] He therefore declared that the Allies would supply arms to the Armenians but that they would have to fight for their aspired territories themselves. He added that 'if they are not in a position to defend their own frontiers, then there was no use for a nation of that kind in the world, and not one of the Allied Governments … would be prepared to assist them to the extent of even a single battalion.'[161] The British chief of the Imperial staff Sir Henry Wilson (1864–1922) summarized the Allies' position: 'They had decided to arm the Armenians and to let them fight it out with the Turks; if their cause was just, and if they were strong enough, they would win, and if not then they were not worth saving.'[162]

This point of view may sound cynical, but the Allies had neither a treaty with Armenia nor a broadly based mandate to act as a kind of 'world police'. Instead, the San Remo Conference appealed to US President Wilson 'to accept the mandate for Armenia' or, if the US refused the mandate, 'to arbitrate the boundaries' of western Armenia with Turkey.[163] But whereas the Democrat Wilson accepted the task of arbitration, the majority Republican Senate refused any international commitment. It twice rejected the **Treaty of Versailles** on 19 November 1919 and 19 March 1920 and thus vetoed America's membership of the League of Nations.[164] The Senate would not even consider sending peacekeeping forces or providing arms and funds.[165] Finally, on 1 June 1920, the Senate turned down Wilson's request to accept the Armenia mandate by 52 votes to 23.[166] In the course of 1920 the British government also refused to send troops or instructors to Armenia, to sell it any of its 700 surplus aircraft parked in Egypt or machines for manufacturing small-arms ammunition. It sold only some surplus arms at three-quarters list price, among them thousands of inferior Canadian Ross rifles which had proved unsuitable in general warfare and had been decommissioned by July 1916.[167] All Armenian hopes for external help had vanished.

On 10 August 1920 the Allied Powers (excluding the USA) signed the **Treaty of Sèvres** with the Ottoman Empire, which amputated virtually all the latter's territories outside Anatolia. Within Anatolia, Turkey lost the region around İzmir to Greece and in north-eastern Anatolia it lost the future 'Wilsonian Armenia'. Article 89 stated:

Turkey and Armenia … agree to submit to the arbitration of the President of the United States of America the question of the frontier to be fixed between Turkey and Armenia in the vilayets of Erzerum, Trebizond, Van and Bitlis, and to accept his decision thereupon, as well as any stipulations he may prescribe as to access for Armenia to the sea, and as to the demilitarisation of any portion of Turkish territory adjacent to the said frontier.

Article 90 specified:

In the event of the determination of the frontier under Article 89 involving the transfer of the whole or any part of the territory of the said vilayets to Armenia, Turkey hereby renounces as from the date of such decision all rights and title over the territory so transferred.

Concerning the borders between the Caucasian states, Article 91 ruled:

107. The city of Erzurum, Turkey, which was reconquered from the Armenians by the Ottoman general Kâzim Karabekir Pasha on 14 March 1918.

The frontiers between Armenia and Azerbaijan and Georgia respectively will be determined by direct agreement between the States concerned. If in either case the States concerned have failed to determine the frontier by agreement ... the frontier line in question will be determined by the Principal Allied Powers.[168]

In Turkey, the treaty fuelled the nationalist cause, and since the Allies assigned no military means of enforcing articles 89 and 90, it remained irrelevant. The Grand National Assembly led by Mustafa Kemal immediately denounced the treaty as void and in the subsequent War of Independence expelled all foreign occupants from Anatolia. The treaty was from the day of its signature a dead letter. It was superseded in 1923 by the Treaty of Lausanne.

Now events came to a head. On the same day as the signing of the Treaty of Sèvres Armenia was forced to yield Zangezur, Nakhchivan and Karabakh to the Soviet Eleventh Army, but kept the right to operate the Yerevan–Nakhchivan–Julfa Railway.[169] One day later, General Karabekir emphasized to Chairman Kemal that he had an ideal opportunity to reconquer the region of Kars and attack Armenia, since Russia had been forced to postpone its planned Sovietization of Armenia and Georgia due to its wars against Poland and Denikin's successor General Pyotr Nikolayevich Wrangel (1878–1928) in Crimea. Now was the moment to outpace Russia. Secret contacts between the Bolsheviks and Kemal had already in June 1919 evaluated their possible cooperation in the Caucasus.[170] Then, on 14 August Lenin hinted to a Turkish delegation that Soviet Russia would not intervene in case of a Turkish attack on Armenia, and ten days later, on 24 August 1920, the draft of a **Soviet–Turkish Friendship Treaty** was signed which abolished all previous Russian–Ottoman treaties. Two days later, Chairman of the Executive Cabinet Kemal

108. The upper part of the citadel of Kars. The Turkish Nationalist troops reconquered Kars on 30 October 1920 from the Armenians virtually without a fight. Kars Province, Turkey. Photo 2016.

ordered General Karabekir to begin the offensive against Armenia while he personally prepared the Turkish counteroffensive against the invading Greeks.[171]

Turkey's attack against the Armenian forces stationed in eastern Anatolia was a direct challenge to the Principal Allies, emphasizing that nationalist Turkey did not care about their diktats in the Sèvres treaty. Colonel Rawlinson, who was part of an Allied delegation to supervise Turkey's disarmament, had already observed in 1919 that in eastern Anatolia neither had Turkish troops been disarmed nor was there any intention to do so.[172] As Kemal had anticipated, the Allies did not react. Karabekir's attack on 13 September 1920 was immediately successful and captured Olti and the Peniak coal deposits. Sarıkamış was seized on 30 September, along with stockpiles of arms abandoned by the fleeing Armenians. When the Armenians sent one of their numerous appeals for help to the British Foreign Office, D.G. Osborne of the Eastern section commented: 'If the Armenians with their trained & equipped forces cannot hold Kars with its strong modern fortifications ... they had better make what terms they can as soon as possible.' The War Office concurred that Britain should write off Armenia as a hopeless issue and seek an understanding with Kemal's nationalists in order 'to revert to the traditional strategy of using Turkey as a bulwark against Russia'[173] – a strategy later also adopted by NATO. After the conquest of Sarıkamış, Kemal ordered Karabekir to briefly interrupt the offensive in order to assess the reactions of the British and Russia. Britain did not react, while on 14 October Lenin took the decision to reconquer Armenia.

In fact, Kars was doomed due to serious deficiencies in the Armenian army where morale was low and the troops were permeated with Bolshevik propaganda. Furthermore, the Armenian high command remained aloof from the actual war situation as the commander in chief Nazarbekian remained in Yerevan and the field commander Silikian in faraway Alexandropol. The Turkish troops on the other hand were highly motivated and General Karabekir stayed with his men at the front in full control of developments. When the Turks attacked the Kars defensive complex on 27 October, the Armenians abandoned their forward fortifications and trenches and fled. Three days later, on 30 October, the Turks captured the huge fortification of Kars within three hours while the Armenian gunners and infantrymen deserted and fled in panic. Just as in 1918, the Armenians did not even bother to destroy the immense stockpiles of arms and ammunitions, light and heavy artillery, railway engines and freight wagons and the huge stocks of uniforms and food which were once again highly welcome to the poorly dressed and underfed Turks. To all intents and purposes, the Armenian army had ceased to exist and on 7 November the Turks seized Alexandropol without a fight and agreed to a temporary ceasefire. Two days later General Karabekir sent Yerevan an ultimatum with new demands. When the Armenian government refused to yield, Karabekir resumed his march on Yerevan, which led to the government's capitulation on 18 November 1920.[174] As a footnote in the history of Armenia, President Wilson's report was published on 22 November, assigning to Armenia a territory of 160,000 square kilometres.[175] It was worth less than the paper it was printed on, for on 26 November Karabekir forced Armenia to repudiate the Treaty of Sèvres and on the 30th he confronted Armenia with the draft for a peace treaty. It demanded restoration to Turkey of its pre-1878 territories of Olti, Kars, Ardahan and Kağızman (Kaghisman) along with the new concession of Surmalu south of Yerevan; in addition, Armenia was ordered to cut off all relations with the Allied Powers and to reduce its army to 1,200 men.

In the meantime, on 18 October 1920 Soviet Russia had concluded an armistice with Poland, and Wrangel had fled Crimea in November, which allowed Lenin to concentrate on the South Caucasus. The Soviet Eleventh Army entered Armenia on 29 November and numerous Armenian soldiers quickly joined the invaders. Armenia had no other choice than to either become a Turkish protectorate or take refuge under the Russian umbrella and become a Soviet satellite. The proclamation on 2 December 1920 of the **Armenian Soviet Socialist Republic**, along with the simultaneous transfer of power, ended Armenia's independence. As a result, Turkey had now to negotiate peace with Soviet Russia. Nevertheless, it was an Armenian delegation headed by Foreign Minister Alexander Khatisyan who that night signed the **Treaty of Alexandropol** with Turkey which established the border along the Rivers Achuryan (Arpaçay) and Aras, thus giving the province of Kars and the district of Surmalu (including Mount Ararat) to Turkey but leaving Alexandropol (Gyumri) to Armenia. However, since the Armenian government had resigned on 2 December and the treaty was signed around 2 am on 3 December, it was invalid.[176] In the ensuing negotiations with Turkey the Soviets preferred the friendship of Kemal's nationalists to insisting on the return of the troublesome Kars Province. Article 1 of the Turkish–Soviet **Treaty of Moscow** (16 March 1921) confirmed the borders outlined in the Treaty of Alexandropol, which were advantageous terms from Turkey's point of view, since they gave back most of the territories lost in 1878. According to article 2, however, Turkey had to renounce the port of Batumi. Lenin also accommodated the Turks regarding Nakhchivan (including Sharur), since article 3 established its status as an autonomous region of Soviet Azerbaijan, and forbade Azerbaijan ever to cede this protectorate to a third country (that is Armenia) without

109. Monument in honour of General Garegin Ter-Harutyunyan aka Garegin Nzhdeh (1886–1955) in Yerevan. Nzhdeh defended Zangezur in 1920/21 against the attacking Soviet Red Army. Yerevan, Armenia. Photo 2017.

the express consent of Turkey.[177] From this clause Turkey derives the right to militarily intervene should Armenia threaten Nakhchivan. This clause was activated in September 1993 when the Turkish prime minister Tansu Çiller warned Armenia not to attack Nakhchivan and sent troops to the Armenian border. The **Treaty of Kars** (13 October 1921) signed between Turkey, Russia and the Soviet Republics of Armenia, Azerbaijan and Georgia confirmed the Treaty of Moscow.[178] At the end of World War II Stalin unsuccessfully claimed back the territories conceded to Turkey in 1921, which resulted in Turkey's joining NATO.

Although the Armenian Dashnak Government had vanished, a strong pocket of resistance remained in **Zangezur** where the indomitable General Nzhdeh refused to yield to the treaty of 10 August 1920 which allowed the Red Army to occupy that province. Defying orders from Dro to remove his troops, he waged a successful guerrilla war and in September–October defeated an attack by Red Army troops as well as Azerbaijani and Turkish regulars. Then, in November, Nzhdeh liberated the town of Goris and chased the invaders out of Zangezur. Since he refused to bow to Bolshevism, he declined to submit to the Soviet Armenian Government and on 25 December proclaimed his realm as **Autonomous Syunik**, whose name implied that it considered itself as part of Armenia. With the failure of the Armenian anti-Soviet uprising, which lasted from 18 February till 2 April 1921,[179] thousands of civilians fled from Yerevan to Zangezur where a new popular assembly declared the independent **Republic of Mountainous Armenia** in defiance of Soviet Armenia's authority. In summer, after four weeks of intense fighting, the Red Army conquered Zangezur, and Nzhdeh was forced to flee to Iran on 15 July 1921.[180] Since Tbilisi had capitulated to the Red Army on 25 February and Batumi on 17 March, the Soviets now controlled the entire South Caucasus. The Kavbyuro, headed by chairman Ordzhonikidze and Sergei Kirov, now had to tackle the thorny issue of the affiliation of **Nagorno-Karabakh** and **Zangezur**.[181]

110. The Armenian cathedral of the Holy Saviour in Shushi. The cathedral was consecrated in 1888 and damaged by wars in 1920, 1991–1992 and 2020. Shushi, Artsakh/Nagorno-Karabakh. Photo 2015.

111. The strongly fortified former see of the Armenian catholicosate in Sis, Cilicia. In Hadjin, north of Sis, about 8,000 Armenian civilians were massacred in 1920 by Turkish Nationalist troops and irregulars. Adana Province, Turkey. Photo 2016.

Whereas Nakhchivan had been contractually assigned to Azerbaijan, the other two regions, both with overwhelmingly Armenian populations, remained disputed. On 30 November 1920 Nariman Narimanov (Nəriman Nərimanov, 1870–1925), foreign minister of Azerbaijan and later its executive chairman, had hastily conceded Zangezur and Nagorno-Karabakh to Armenia, a course of action which he soon regretted.[182] The Kavbyuro met in Tbilisi on 4 July 1921 and in the presence of Stalin, who abstained from voting, decided to allocate Nagorno-Karabakh to Armenia. Enraged, Narimov threatened civil unrest and an oil boycott, and appealed to Stalin. The next day, the Kavbyuro revoked its decision and without voting allocated Nagorno-Karabakh to Azerbaijan. No doubt Stalin, to whom the populous and oil-rich Azerbaijan was of greater interest than Armenia, and who had no desire to provoke Turkey, had imposed his will. Furthermore, Nagorno-Karabakh had much stronger economic ties with Azerbaijan than with Armenia,[183] a fact which carried weight with Stalin, who drew Soviet national borders not only according to ethnic criteria but also economic ones. Nagorno-Karabakh became in November 1923 an Autonomous Oblast, but lost its northern districts of Shamkhor, Khanlar (since 2008 called Göygöl), Dashkesan and Shahumyan (Gulistan) which were mainly inhabited by Armenians but became part of Azerbaijan.[184] However, by allocating Zangezur to Armenia, Stalin denied Azerbaijan one contiguous territory, leaving Nakhchivan isolated from the rest of Azerbaijan. He obviously feared pan-Turkish irredentism and did not want a direct land corridor from Ankara to Baku. The Nakhchivan ASSR was formally established on 9 February 1924.[185]

Finally, the Armenian stronghold in **Cilicia** which sheltered some tens of thousands of Armenian refugees also came to a painful end. Willing to defend their sanctuary, Armenians formed a volunteers' unit which in November 1916 became an auxiliary force of the French Army under the name Légion d'Orient (as of October 1918 renamed Légion arménienne), totalling 4,100 officers and men. During the war, the legion was deployed not in Cilicia but in Palestine, to fight alongside Allenby's British soldiers. At the end of the war, British troops occupied Cilicia till November 1919 when they were replaced by French forces, albeit in insufficient numbers and consisting mainly of Algerian and Senegalese soldiers. After a clash between Armenian and Algerian legionnaires in March

1919, the demobilization of the Armenian Legion began and the Armenian stations were replaced by Algerian legionnaires.[186] Only six weeks after French troops had replaced the British in Cilicia, Kemal's nationalists and bands of çeteler (released criminals) attacked the French troops based in the neighbouring cities of Maraş and Aintab (Gaziantep). The French troops, as previously in Ukraine, showed poor combat spirit and bad leadership, and they lacked heavy artillery, armoured cars, aeroplanes and even wireless radio communication. During the siege of Maraş, the French entrenched themselves in their garrisons and left the çeteler to murder the terrified Armenian civilians who had sought shelter in the churches which were set on fire, while those who fled the burning churches were struck by hails of bullets. The French finally left Maraş secretly in the night of 12–13 February 1920 and abandoned the Armenians to their fate.[187] The final exodus of Armenians out of Cilicia to British or other French zones began. At the end of May 1920, the weakened French withdrew from Sis and northern Cilicia abandoning the Armenian town of Hadjin (Saimbeyli) which had been resisting Turkish attacks since March. When the isolated town finally fell in October, about 8,000 Armenians were massacred. In desperation, the Armenian Dashnaks, Minas Veradzin and Mihran Damadian proclaimed on 2 and 5 August respectively an independent **Republic of Cilicia** under French protection; both attempts were swiftly stifled by French troops. When France withdrew completely from Turkey in October 1921, all Armenians left in Cilicia departed for the French Mandate in Syria and Lebanon.[188]

Having reintegrated Azerbaijan and Armenia into the Russian Empire, the Soviets turned to Georgia. Several skirmishes had already taken place in early May 1920 at the Azerbaijani–Georgian border where the Georgians had removed the railroad tracks from the bridge of Poili (Poylu) to hinder Soviet armoured trains from attacking. At the same time, Lenin and Stalin forbade Ordzhonikidze from continuing military operations against Georgia for fear that the British, who still held Batumi, would rapidly reinforce its garrison. Another reason for ending hostilities against Georgia was the unfavourable course of the war against Poland, which had seized Kyiv on 6 May. As a result the following day, a Soviet–Georgian Treaty was signed: the Soviets recognized the Republic of Georgia and its possession of Batumi (once the British had left) in return for which Georgia was forced in a secret amendment to legalize the Communist Party and its agitation – which represented a lethal Trojan horse.[189] The Georgian government was well aware of the danger of its position and lobbied in vain for robust foreign support. But by December 1920, Georgia was encircled by hostile powers: Russia and its Azerbaijani and Armenian satellites, and nationalist Turkey. Since Britain had left Batumi and an armistice had been concluded on 18 October with Poland, Lenin ordered the Eleventh Army to prepare for the invasion of Georgia. Ordzhonikidze and Kirov arranged for an anti-Menshevik, pro-Bolshevik uprising in the Georgian part of Lori, which started on 11 February 1921. Then came a favourite trick: the rebellious Bolsheviks established a Georgian 'Revolutionary Committee' in Lori, which appealed to Moscow for support in liberating Georgia from Menshevik rule. On 14 February the Red Army attacked with 36,000 men, but met with fierce resistance even though the Georgian forces were numerically inferior and divided into the mutually hostile regular army and paramilitary National Guard. Tbilisi fell on 25 February and Zhordania fled first to Kutaisi then Batumi and finally embarked in mid-March on French cruiser. On 25 February 1921 the **Georgian Soviet Socialist Republic** was declared.[190]

With the occupation of Georgia, Soviet Russia re-established in the South Caucasus the former territorial extent of Imperial Tsarist Russia with the exception of the province of Kars. But at the south-eastern end of the Caucasus, two attempts to expand the Soviet Empire into Iran failed. The anti-Müsavat **Soviet Republic of Mughan** (May–July 1919) in the district of Lankaran collapsed after three months to be succeeded by the British-backed military **Provisional Dictatorship of Mughan** (August 1919–April 1920), while the **Soviet Republic of Gilan** (June 1920–September 1921) came to an end when Soviet Russia abandoned its goal of instigating a worldwide Socialist revolution, having concluded the Treaty of Friendship with Iran on 26 February 1921 and the Anglo-Soviet Trade Agreement of 16 March 1921. In retrospect, the experiments of the three South Caucasian republics were a success insofar as they established political systems which were much more democratic and humane than the brutal Soviet dictatorship that followed, with its systematic repression of opposition and its waves of Red Terror. But the three republics ultimately broke down not only due to the territorial conflicts and hostilities between them, but also because they utterly failed to form strong and reliable armies and relied far too much on real or hoped-for allies. While Georgia, as an ex-German protectorate, experienced difficulties in winning trust among the Allies, Armenia's wished-for protectors Britain and the USA had no interest in this poor, landlocked country. Only Azerbaijan possessed in nationalist Turkey a supporter based on kinship, which however had to prioritize relations with Soviet Russia over distant Azerbaijan.

3. The Russian Civil Wars 1917–1920 and the short-lived North Caucasian states

In the North Caucasus the political situation after the March 1917 Revolution became complicated as numerous mutually hostile political entities emerged, including Cossack hosts, liberal federations, Islamic emirates and Soviet republics. Furthermore, the wider Civil War between the Bolsheviks and Denikin's Whites was waged in the North Caucasus too. In May 1917 at the First Congress of the **United Mountain Peoples (UMP) of the North Caucasus** in Vladikavkaz, about 340 delegates from most ethnicities, including Cossacks, elected the Chechen colonel and oil magnate Abdul Mejid (Tapa) Chermoyev (1882–1937) as Chairman of its Central Committee.[191] The UMP remained loyal to Petrograd's Provisional Government. At the Second Congress of the UMP in August, serious disagreements emerged between the liberal and the Islamist wing. The latter aspired to transform the UMP into an independent imamate and requested that the Avar Najmuddin Gotsinsky, the son of one of Shamil's *nawwab*, be declared imam. At the Third Congress Gotsinsky was forced to settle for the apolitical title of mufti. In October, the UMP extended its claim of full sovereignty to cover the **South-Eastern Union of Cossack Hosts** and the **Free Peoples of the Steppe**, which included the Kalmyks. However, the UMP's Central Committee remained a 'paper government' as it did not control a clearly defined territory and lacked a standing army and police. Additionally, Gotsinsky and his deputy Uzun Hajji (Saltinsky) replaced Russian officials in the administration with conservative Muslims, bypassing the Central Committee. The combined **Terek–Dagestan Government** formed in December 1917 also

112. The fortified village of Chokh, Dagestan, was part of the United Mountain Peoples Republic. Photo 2021.

foundered when ethnic clashes and violent conflicts arose between Cossacks and highlanders who were looking for land in the plains.[192] The social, ethnic and political fragmentation of the North Caucasus doomed any attempt at voluntary supra-tribal unification to failure.

At the beginning of 1918, Bolshevik troops led by Kirov and Ordzhonikidze revitalized the Bolshevik presence in the North Caucasus and founded the **Stavropol Soviet Republic** on 1 January 1918, the **Terek Soviet Republic** and the **Black Sea Soviet Republic** on 17 March, and the **Kuban Soviet Republic** in April. These ephemeral Soviet republics were mainly supported by non-Cossack Russian or Ukrainian peasants. They were opposed by the **Terek Cossack Host** and **the Kuban Cossack Host** (or **Kuban People's Republic**). The Terek Soviet Republic decreed a land reform in May that met the approval of poor or landless highlanders and Slav *inogorodnye* but strong opposition from Ingush and Kabardian landlords and the Cossacks. In early July the four Soviet republics were merged into the **North Caucasus Soviet Republic**.[193] As in other fertile regions of Russia, the Bolsheviks put in train their infamous requisitioning policies of 'War Communism' by sending Red Army units into the villages where they confiscated grain and other foodstuffs to be sent to Russian cities.[194] Famine spread in the looted villages. As a result, at the end of July angry peasants and small landowners who had been despoiled of their goods joined Georgy Bicherakhov's bloody Cossack uprising. While the Soviets succeeded in forcing Bicherakhov to retreat to coastal Dagestan to join his brother General Lazar, these conflicts weakened the Soviets and cost them much sympathy among the local people.[195] In view of the Cossack resistance to the land reforms, the Bolshevik leadership decided to deport the reluctant Cossack communities, which were vilified as counter-revolutionaries and class enemies – a precedent for the future Soviet deportations of entire ethnic groups. The brutal deportation and systematic killing of Cossacks lasted till the mid 1920s when the *kulaks* (property-owning peasants) became the new public enemies. The Soviet 'de-Cossackization' policy aimed at the annihilation of the Cossacks as a socio-ethnic group and led to the massacre or deportation of about 300,000 to 500,000 Don Cossacks out of a total population of 1.5 million.[196] Since the indigenous people welcomed the dispossession of Cossacks and Slavs, this only increased the ethnic animosities. The establishment of the Terek Soviet Republic forced the Terek–Dagestan Government to flee to Temir-Khan-Shura (today's Buynaksk) in Dagestan where the Bolsheviks held Port-Petrovsk, while the UMP's Central Committee fled to Georgia. Its chairman Tapa Chermoyev declared the **Republic of the Union of Mountain Peoples of the North Caucasus** (UMPR) as fully independent from Russia on 11 May 1918. Nine days later, the UMP's Muslim traditionalists proclaimed Najmuddin Gotsinsky as imam and revived Shamil's **North Caucasian Imamate**.[197] Finally, one month after Chermoyev's declaration of independence, the UMPR in exile signed a Friendship Treaty with the Ottomans, who dispatched a Turkish battalion to Gunib.[198]

During 1918, several rebellious 'White' armies challenged the authority of the Bolsheviks. Some of them attempted to establish power bases and aimed to topple the hated Soviets in order to restore the Russian Empire, be it as monarchy or military dictatorship. Others led roving armies which lived from looting and selling their services to the highest bidder. Other combatants were the numerous ethnicities and Cossack hosts who claimed independence and rejected both Bolsheviks and Whites, since both wanted to restore Russia to its previous Imperial size. As aptly expressed by the historian Jonathan Smele, there existed 'wars within the main Civil War' and since dozens of self-proclaimed governments competed with each other, the period from summer 1917 to November 1920 may be compared with the *Smuta*, the 'Time of Troubles' at the turn of the seventeenth century.[199] The account that follows concentrates on the events of the war involving the Caucasus and Caucasian armies, which was only one aspect of the civil wars throughout the former Russian Empire. The formation of the White **Volunteer Army** began in November 1917 when, following his failed putsch against Kerensky, General Lavr Kornilov (1870–1918) arrived in Novocherkassk near Rostov-on-Don and joined General Mikhail Vasilyevich Alekseyev (1857–1918), former Imperial chief of staff. The Volunteer Army initially counted some 3,000 men, mainly ex-tsarist officers, cadets (officer trainees) and Cossacks; Kornilov became commander-in-chief, General Anton Denikin his deputy and Alekseyev political leader. Also in November, the Don Cossack *krug*, headed by Ataman Aleksei Kaledin declared independence; but the Cossacks were deeply divided between royalists and Bolshevik sympathizers. When the advancing Red Army threatened the Don Cossack capital Novocherkassk, the pro-Bolshevists refused to fight while the monarchists joined the Volunteer Army escaping to the Kuban. Left without troops, Ataman Kaledin shot himself on 11 February 1918 as the Volunteer Army began, in freezing weather conditions, its 'Ice March' through the Kuban.[200] Although the Kuban Cossacks, led by Ataman Alexander Petrovich Filimonov (in office 1917–1919),

Map 8. Greatest extent of advance of the Armed Forces of South Russia, early October 1919

were mainly anti-Bolshevik, they distrusted the Volunteer Army because of its imperialist tendencies, and only a minority joined the Volunteers. The fights against the numerically far superior Red troops were merciless; the Bolsheviks shot all prisoners while the Whites incorporated some Red soldiers into their units and shot the rest. Disaster struck the Whites on 9–13 April 1918 when they attacked the capital of the Kuban, Yekaterinodar (today's Krasnodar), as the attack failed with high losses and Kornilov himself was killed. Denikin took over as commander-in-chief.[201]

The decimated Volunteer Army was saved by the anti-Soviet uprising of the **Don Cossack Host** (**Don Republic**) in March–April 1918 which had retaken Novocherkassk. Their new ataman, General Pyotr Krasnov (1869–1947), joined forces with Denikin and the Kuban Cossacks and in the Second Kuban Campaign of July–August 1918 conquered Yekaterinodar and the port of Novorossiysk. It was at Novorossiysk that the British Military Mission to the Caucasus disembarked in January 1919 with huge stockpiles of arms including rifles, artillery, tanks and warplanes as well as crews to operate the heavy machinery.

113. An armoured train used by the counter-revolutionary Whites during the Russian Civil War. General Denikin's slogan '*Единая Россия*' (*Yedinaya Rossiya*, United Russia), is painted on the first carriage on the right. Photo probably from 1918/19.

On 8 January 1919 the Armed Forces of South Russia (AFSR) were formed out of the Volunteer Army, the Don Army,[202] the Crimean–Azov Army and the North Caucasus Army. Denikin remained supreme commander. However, his conviction that Russia must be 'one and undivided' deterred the new states which had formed at Russia's periphery and made his Cossack allies suspicious of his intentions. Before attacking the Soviets head on, Denikin decided to secure his rear and in January–May 1919 conquered the whole North Caucasus from the Black to the Caspian Sea, eliminating the Soviet Terek Republic and what was left of the UMPR. Denikin's intransigence towards the Chechens and Dagestanis, who partly welcomed him as anti-Bolshevik ally but not as subjects to be subjugated, was counterproductive. He not only refused them local autonomy but forcefully drafted their young men into the AFSR. This led to an opportunistic alliance between three previously mortal enemies: Soviet guerrilla units, Terek Cossacks and the reshaped **North Caucasian Emirate** headed by Uzun Hajji. Instead of consolidating his Caucasian rear, Denikin lost control of it due to his uncompromising stance. By October 1919 the emirate and the Soviets had expelled the Whites from Dagestan and Chechnya. As was to be expected, the Soviets then turned against their Muslim allies and by March 1920 had liquidated the emirate.[203]

Denikin's North Caucasus Campaign not only ended in a self-inflicted failure, it turned out to be a decisive strategic mistake. For while the Volunteer Army was active in the Caucasus, the powerful White warlord Admiral Aleksandr Kolchak (1874–1920) began his massive offensive, starting from Omsk on 4 March 1919, against the Soviet industrial centres on the Volga and ultimately Moscow.[204] Coordination between the two strongest White warlords was nonexistent. Denikin insisted on first conquering the North Caucasus, while Kolchak refused to wait till the ASFR was ready.[205] The distance between the two armies was 600 kilometres; as a result, the Red Army could first meet Kolchak's attack at the Volga and then redeploy to the south to fight Denikin, instead of having to repel two simultaneous attacks in the region between Samara and Tsaritsyn (today's Volgograd, formerly Stalingrad). Kolchak's offensive almost reached Samara on the Volga at the end of April, but when Denikin finally started his attack in May, Kolchak was already retreating.²⁰⁶ The AFSR consisted of three armies: The Volunteer Army commanded by the cavalry general Vladimir Mai-Mayevsky (1867–1920) formed the strong left wing aiming at Kharkiv, Kursk and Moscow, while the Don Cossack Army under General Vladimir Sidorin (1882–1943) made up the centre, and on the right wing was the Caucasus Army under General Pyotr Wrangel whose initial target was Tsaritsyn (map 8). The offensive at first achieved lightning successes. Tsaritsyn fell thanks to British tanks and planes on 30 June 1919, whereupon Denikin issued the 'Moscow Directive' to attack on all fronts towards the capital. While the Fourth Cossack Cavalry Corps under General Konstantin Mamontov made swift advances as far as Voronezh, it lacked discipline, as the victorious Cossacks preferred to loot and then return home with their booty than to continue the attack. This turned a potentially decisive victory into defeat.²⁰⁷ The Whites' spearhead was the western wing which rapidly seized Poltava, Kherson, Odessa, Kyiv, Kursk and on 14 October 1919 Orel, less than 400 kilometres from Moscow.²⁰⁸ The military advance was impressive, but the situation within the territory controlled by the ASFR was chaotic since Denikin's administration was dysfunctional and the populace rejected any return to monarchism.

So far, the ASRF forces had enjoyed the advantage of its large cavalry formations which allowed for a highly mobile form of warfare. Mai-Mayevsky attacked cities along the thickly populated railway lines with armoured trains carrying long-range cannons supported by aerial monitoring and reinforced by vast outflanking cavalry manoeuvres – a creative combination of modern technologies and pre-mechanized warfare. But the other White commanders, including Denikin, never mastered the coordination of cavalry and infantry with tanks and planes.²⁰⁹ Denikin's front, more than 1000 kilometres long,

114. The Russian warship *Admiral Kutuzov* in the Black Sea harbour of Novorossiysk, Russia. The bronze statue honours the wives of Soviet sailors who fought in World War II. It was from Novorossiysk that the survivors of the defeated Whites embarked on French and British battleships to be evacuated to Crimea in March 1920.

was overextended and it was now that Trotsky's reform of the Red Army produced results. Under the slogan 'Proletarians, to horse!' the First Cavalry Corps was formed under General Semyon Budyonny (1883–1973), which was supported by eight armoured trains and an aircraft squadron. On 20 October 1919 Budyonny made his attack at the weak point between the Volunteer Army and the Don Cossacks near Voronezh and rapidly drove a wedge between the two White Armies. At the same time, the Red Army reconquered Tsaritsyn, Astrakhan and the Kalmyk Steppe, and newly formed units of Latvian and Estonian riflemen successfully harassed the Volunteer Army near Orel and recaptured Kursk on 17 November.[210] Denikin had neglected to keep a strong reserve and the White retreat rapidly turned into a rout. The White draftees deserted en masse, the Cossacks abandoned the lost war and the remnants of the AFSR retreated to the Kuban. When the Kuban *Rada* (the Kuban Cossack parliament) dared to sign an agreement with the North Caucasian UMPR and affirmed its independence from both sides, on 6 November Denikin ordered ten deputies to be arrested and one member of the Paris Peace delegation executed. Then he forced Ataman Filimonov to resign. Denikin's rough treatment of the Kuban *Rada* confirmed the Cossacks' suspicions of him.[211] Desperate, Denikin recognized the independence of Georgia and Azerbaijan on 14 January 1920, showed willingness to grant minorities such as the Cossacks or the North Caucasians regional autonomy and promised land ownership to peasants.[212] But Denikin's volte-face came much too late to impress anyone, since he and his remaining soldiers were now mere fugitives. Some 125,000 Whites and civilians flocked to the Black Sea Coast, refusing to fight. Up to 26 March 1920 British and French warships evacuated about 35,000 Whites from Novorossiysk to Crimea and later 5,000 Cossacks from Tuapse. About 85,000 Whites left behind in Novorossiysk and Sochi were taken prisoner by the Red Army.[213] The North Caucasian peoples had escaped Denikin's military dictatorship but would soon fall prey to the Soviets. The anti-Bolshevik Whites had failed in the Caucasus because of their internal dissensions, their lack of military unity, their lack of solutions for the pressing social problems and, above all, because their political objectives were incompatible with the aspirations of non-Russian minorities.

VIII

Under Soviet Rule

1. Soviet consolidation of power, collectivization and Stalin's purges

As soon as the Bolsheviks had consolidated their hold over the Caucasus they first tried to implement Lenin's vision of overcoming the differences of nations and ethnicities by building a single socialist nation. The three southern Soviet Republics of Armenia, Azerbaijan and Georgia were united, against the will of the Georgian and Azerbaijani Soviets, on 12 March 1922 into the **Federative Union of Socialist Soviet Republics of Transcaucasia**. This administrative unit was further centralized on 13 December 1922 and renamed the **Transcaucasian Socialist Federative Soviet Republic (TSFSR)** which was integrated into the USSR on 30 December. Due to increased discontent among Georgian and Azerbaijani Communist Party leaders, the TSFSR was in turn dissolved into the **Armenian, Azerbaijani** and **Georgian Union Republics** on 5 December 1936. In the north, the Soviets revived the UMP on 20 January 1921 as the **Autonomous Gorskaya (Mountainous) SSR** which stretched from Kislovodsk in today's Stavropol Kray to the Caspian Sea. To its east was the **Dagestan SR**, in the north the **Terek**, **Kalmyk** and **Stavropol Autonomous Regions**, and in the north-west the **Kuban-Black Sea Oblast**; all Cossack Hosts were abolished.[1] However, due to the persistent ethnic antagonisms within the central North Caucasus, the Gorskaya Republic failed to function and broke apart bit by bit, just as had the UMP. Armed conflicts between ethnicities erupted and it became obvious that the urge for ethnic autonomy represented less a dissociation from Moscow than a desire to be distanced from one's own neighbours. Lenin's hope of erasing ethnic differences was swiftly dropped and Stalin's concept of autonomy adopted. He had already defined a nation in 1913 as 'a historically developed stable community of people, characterized by a community of language, territory, economic life and psychic nature revealed in common culture'.[2] As People's Commissar for Nationalities Stalin did not draw borders of nations according to ethnic criteria only, but also took into consideration linguistic, economic and cultural parameters. Autonomy was granted within the provisions of the Soviet Constitution.[3] Stalin argued that in the absence of developed capitalism and a class-conscious proletariat, national identities should be deliberately promoted in order to overcome the existing feudal clan-order and to lay the ground for a future socialist economy and society. Nevertheless, Stalin's form of ethno-federal system failed to breed the desired *Homo sovieticus* but rather laid the seeds of future nationalism. By 1924 the Gorskaya SSR had fragmented into the following AOs: Kabardino-Balkaria, Karachay-Cherkessia, Chechnya, Ingushetia, North Ossetia, the Sunzha Okrug and, in the west, Adygea.[4] Stalin's assertion of the interests of non-Russian peoples provided him with a weighty power base.

Although many North Caucasian men had fought alongside the Bolsheviks against Denikin's Volunteer Army, the implementation of Soviet rule did not run smoothly, as the Red Army behaved like an occupying force, requisitioning food and leaving the locals starving. Discontent spread rapidly and in August 1920 in mountainous Dagestan and Chechnya Imam Najmuddin Gotsinsky organized the Sharia Army of Highlanders. The rebels scored several victories over Soviet troops who were ignorant of mountain warfare but succumbed in 1921 when the Soviets deployed warplanes and artillery. At the same time the Soviet secret police, the Cheka (as of 1922 the GPU), hunted down rebels and their sympathizers; nevertheless Gotsinsky escaped and went underground along with a few hundred fighters. To calm the situation the Soviets allowed the reintroduction of traditional *sharia* courts and *jamaat* village councils. However, their competences were soon restricted and by 1927 they had been abolished. The uprising flared up in 1923 when the Sufi sheikh Ali Mitayev, who in 1919 had formed an alliance with the Soviets to combat the Volunteer Army, declared jihad. But Mitayev was arrested in 1924 during disarmament operations in Chechnya, and Gotsinsky in 1925; both Muslim leaders were shot. The suppression of Islam started in 1927 with the closing of mosque

115. Portrait of Stalin on Stalin Avenue near the Stalin Museum in Gori. Shida Kartli, Georgia. Photo 2013.

116. The meeting room in Stalin's dacha (country house) in Novy Afon, Abkhazia. The former residence of Tsar Alexander III was rebuilt in 1947 for Joseph Stalin. The dacha was hidden in subtropical vegetation and not visible from the street. Autonomous Republic of Abkhazia. Photo 2018.

schools and madrasas and the deportation of imams; mosques too were closed. In many instances the so-called class struggle was nothing other than power contests between hostile clans, since in villages or collective farms quite often one single clan controlled the whole Soviet administration. The dominant clan then abused its power by denouncing rival clans as counter-revolutionaries or kulaks.[5] Even so, although the Soviet repression in Chechnya and Dagestan was tough, it was not comparable to the forthcoming comprehensive and brutal collectivization campaign or the arbitrary Stalinist purges.[6] In the first years of Soviet rule, the Mongol Kalmyks fared relatively well. Although numerous Kalmyks had fought in General Wrangel's cavalry, the Soviets refrained from excessively harsh measures and from attacking their religion, Tibetan Buddhism, head on. They most probably wanted to create the impression of a tolerant government for the benefit of the people of Buryatia and Mongolia, whose territories they wanted to bring into the Soviet orbit.

Before the Georgian communists established their dominance within the TSFSR, whose capital was Tbilisi, they had to suppress several uprisings. Discontent began as early as April 1921 when all land was nationalized and the persecution of the Orthodox Georgian Church began. A first rebellion occurred in summer 1921 in Svaneti, followed by an uprising in spring 1922 in Khevsureti and in August 1924 a failed insurrection in western Georgia, especially in Guria. All these rebellions were mercilessly crushed by the Cheka/GPU with many thousands of insurgents executed or sent to Siberian concentration camps. Later, in the 1930s, not only former commanders of the Volunteer Army were assassinated in exile, but also the first prime minister of independent Georgia, Noe Ramishvili, who was murdered on 7 December 1930 in Paris.[7] In all three South Caucasian republics the formerly dominant parties of Mensheviks, Dashnaks and Müsavat were forcibly dissolved.[8] Within the Transcaucasian GPU the Georgian Lavrenti Beria (1899–1953) distinguished himself by his efficiency in liquidating counter-revolutionaries. Beria was promoted in 1922 to deputy head and in 1926 to head of the Georgian GPU. In 1931 he became the all-powerful First Secretary of the Georgian Communist Party and in 1932 of the Transcaucasian, and implemented Stalin's purges of 1934–1938 with utter ruthlessness, eliminating virtually all veteran communists. In November 1938 Beria was nominated head of the People's Commissariat for Internal Affairs (NKVD) which had absorbed the GPU and which ran all internal state security and police forces within the Soviet Union. During the war, he additionally became member of the State Defence Committee together with Stalin, Molotov, Malenkov and Voroshilov.[9] Beria was one of the most powerful men behind Stalin. To strengthen his position, Beria enthusiastically developed Stalin's personality cult which elevated him above the competing factions within the highest echelons of leadership.[10] Although now based in Moscow, Beria still dominated South Caucasian politics through his network of local cronies. After the atomic explosions at Hiroshima and Nagasaki, Beria became head of the Soviet atomic bomb programme in August 1945. Following Stalin's death on 5 March 1953, Beria lost a power struggle against Khrushchev, Molotov and Marshal Zhukov and was shot on 23 December 1953.

In Georgia, the Church had come rapidly under intense pressure, with Catholicos-Patriarch Ambrosi (in office 1921–1930) and some bishops being arrested in 1923. They were subjected to a public trial in 1924 and escaped execution only because the regime had no desire to create martyrs. In Armenia, Catholicos Kevork (Gevorg) V (in office 1911–1930) put up no resistance to Soviet rule and his successor Khoren I (in office 1932–1938) cultivated good working relations with the Soviet regime and the diaspora alike. Nevertheless, Catholicos Khoren was probably murdered by Beria's NKVD in 1938; two years earlier they had assassinated Aghasi Khanjian, the First Secretary of the Armenian Communist Party as well as Nestor Lakoba, Abkhazia's executive chairman.[11] Another henchman of Stalin was Mir Jafar Baghirov (Mircəfər Bağırov), head of the Azerbaijani GPU (in office 1921–1930) and First Secretary of the Azerbaijani Communist Party 1933–1953, who diligently implemented the Stalinist purges. Among his earlier victims figured former members of the Müsavat party, prosperous farmers and Mirsaid Sultan-Galiev, a Tatar who had propagated Islamic communism. The Great Purge arose not only from Stalin's paranoia: the dictator also wanted to avoid Party and administration becoming immobile or developing their own momentum contrary to his will. In that respect Stalin's Great Purge anticipated Mao's Cultural Revolution.

In one respect Georgia and Armenia remained privileged as they were allowed to keep their own scripts, whereas the other non-Russian nationalities such as the Azerbaijanis were forced to switch first in 1926 to the Latin alphabet and ten years later to the Cyrillic, which rendered most of their populations abruptly illiterate.[12] These changes in alphabets were particularly hard on the Kalmyks since they were obliged in 1924 to change from their old Mongol-Kalmyk *Todo Bichig* vertical script (written from top to bottom) to a modified Cyrillic script, in 1928 to Latin script and in 1938 to standard Russian Cyrillic script.[13] In Armenia, the assigning of Zangezur to Armenia had separated Turkey from Azerbaijan, but Armenian Zangezur bordered the Azerbaijani Oblast of Nagorno-Karabakh whose population was 90 per cent Armenian. In order to cut this ethnic cross-border link, a separate administrative unit was built out of eastern Zangezur which was mainly populated by Kurds and from which Armenians were expelled. This **Kurdistan Uyezd** (district) belonged to Azerbaijan, meaning that Nagorno-Karabakh was now an enclave without a border with Armenia. The Kurdistan Uyezd was liquidated in 1930 and became known as **Lachin Corridor**.[14] Two years later, after a small territorial exchange between Iran and Turkey, the latter acquired a 10 kilometre-long frontier with Nakhchivan.[15]

Russia's and the Caucasus' catastrophic supply situation had been redressed in 1922 by the temporary New Economic Policy (NEP) which allowed private property, free enterprise and a free market within the narrow frame of state control. But Stalin decided in 1928 in favour of a rapid, state-directed industrialization programme which would be implemented by strict central planning formulated in ruthless five year plans and by the nationwide collectivization of all means of production, including agriculture. His goal was to transform the rather agricultural Soviet Union into a major industrial and military power. Since the industrialization could not be implemented without purchasing foreign technology and machinery, the USSR needed hard currency which it planned to acquire through the export of grain. The collectivization of agriculture by means of the establishment of *kolkhozes* (collective farms) and *sovkhozes* (state farms) was intended to increase and better control agricultural yields. Collectivization began in the Caucasus in 1929 and took the form of a frontal attack on family farming, since the peasants were coerced into collectives and were made to surrender their harvests and livestock to state agencies. Farmers were treated as resources to be exploited at will. Since they were not allowed to leave their assigned *kolkhoz*, Soviet agrarian collectivization represented nothing other than a new twentieth-century serfdom. Stalin's proclamation that 'the kulaks had to be liquidated as a class' led to the programmatic deprivation of hundreds of thousands of peasants and their banishment to distant labour camps, since they were barred from entering collective farms.[16] The depleting system of War Communism which left peasants without sufficient grain reserves had already provoked a terrible famine in Crimea,

Ukraine and southern Russia in 1921–1923 which cost millions of human lives. Nevertheless, the Soviet government had been so cynical as to accept American relief in the form of huge free grain imports while at the same time selling requisitioned grain abroad for hard currency.[17] Collectivization, industrial urbanization and the associated indoctrination of workers also aimed at diluting the peasants' ethnic identities and dissolving their attachment to their homelands in favour of an identification of proletarian workers with Soviet socialism. The collectivization and mechanization of Soviet agriculture was also a militarization of worker-peasants – tractor drivers were easily trained as tank drivers. At the same time, industrialization and collectivization gave women the chance for work and activities outside home, yet without conceding them political power.

The very rapid collectivization of farmers was especially brutal in the mainly agrarian North Caucasus where by March 1930 80 per cent of peasant households were compulsorily collectivized, but also in Armenia with a 65 per cent collectivization rate. Since Georgia produced little grain, a 'mere' 25 per cent of farmers were collectivized.[18] But many peasants resisted, by slaughtering their livestock rather than surrendering them to the state; in addition a massive rural exodus began, as young men left the countryside for the industrial centres. The result of these lightning expropriations, loss of agricultural know-how and gross mismanagement was not long in coming: a terrible man-made famine began in the North Caucasus and the Ukraine[19] – the Soviet Union's two granaries – bringing about millions of deaths. In the North Caucasus alone about one million perished from hunger.[20] That such large-scale food confiscation is not only a story of the past was revealed by the theft of hundreds of thousands of tons of grain by the Russian army in occupied Ukraine in the spring of 2022, when Russia pretended to sell the stolen wheat to Syria, which acted as a middleman, generating revenue for Moscow and provoking famine in Ukraine.[21] In the early 1930s, the reintroduction of a strict passport regime prevented starving peasants from fleeing to the better-supplied cities. At the same time, as highlighted by the historian Alex Marshall, in the early 1930s the Soviet Union produced 'tens of thousands of tanks and aircraft that by 1941 would be on the brink of obsolescence'.[22] Between 1928 and 1932 the expropriations and deportations triggered spontaneous rebellions in freedom-loving Chechnya and Dagestan, as well as in Karachay, Balkaria and Cherkessia, which were brutally suppressed by the GPU. Mountainous Svaneti also rebelled. The GPU and army units crushed the uprisings with tanks and aeroplanes. Often it was not only the people directly involved who were punished, but also their families, and quotas were set of people to be shot, deported or imprisoned.[23] Faced with sharply declining harvests and spreading unrest, the Soviet leadership was forced to roll back many malfunctioning *kolkhozes* and to apply more nuanced strategies. To save its position, the leadership found culprits for the disaster among the lower and regional party ranks, who were then shot or deported. In the South Caucasus, the collectivized peasants were now allowed to cultivate small personal plots in addition, and to sell the proceeds at fixed prices.[24]

In July 1936 Stalin unleashed the Great Terror which lasted till November 1938 and purged most of the party, army and administrative elite, religious communities, the intelligentsia and the remaining kulaks. Victims were arrested by the secret police on faked charges and shot or deported.[25] The Georgian Sergo Ordzhonikidze, one of the very few of Stalin's old companions who still had influence in the Party, also fell victim of the Great Terror. Rumours were circulating that Ordzhonikidze was planning to accuse Stalin at the Central Committee meeting of 19 February 1937 of destroying the Party and the upper management of the Soviet Union's heavy industry. The day before, on 18 February, Ordzhonikidze was found shot dead in his bedroom. It is probable that Stalin had offered him the alternatives of killing himself or being arrested by the NKVD. Ordzhonikidze chose suicide, but the official cause of death was given out as heart failure.[26] As in the late 1920s and early 1930s, quotas were set at regional and district level as to how many people should be immediately shot and how many condemned to long-term imprisonment. Especially obedient or ambitious underlings would even ask permission to exceed their quotas. In total, officially 700,000, in truth probably more like one million people were shot without trial, including about 6,000 in Armenia, 15,000 in Azerbaijan, 17,000 in Georgia and possibly 40,000 in the North Caucasus. A similar number of people were deported to Siberia or sentenced to long-term imprisonment. Wives of convicts were mostly exiled to northern Central Asia and children were sent to orphanages.[27] In view of these multiple hecatombs and the deprivations caused by Soviet Communism it is not surprising that some Caucasians welcomed the German Wehrmacht in 1942 as liberators. Today, a certain distrust and aversion against Russia still persists across the region, except among Armenians and Abkhaz.

117. (Overleaf) The Kremlin of Rostov-on-Don built in the sixteenth–seventeenth centuries. Rostov is the north-western entry gate to the Caucasus. The first German attack on Rostov on 21 November 1941 failed to hold the city which the Red Army reconquered one week later. In late July 1942 the Wehrmacht captured Rostov for the second time, but lost it again in February 1943.

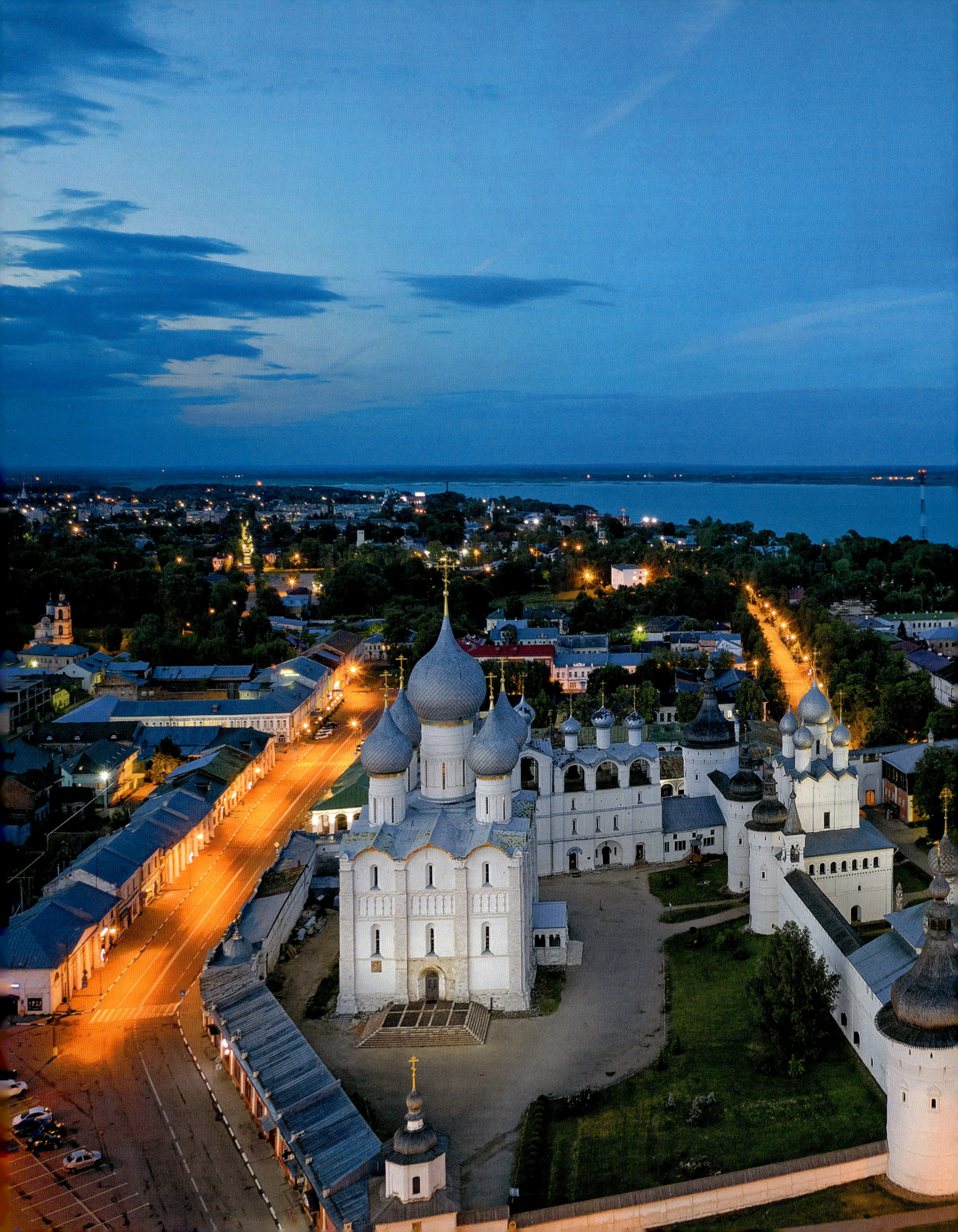

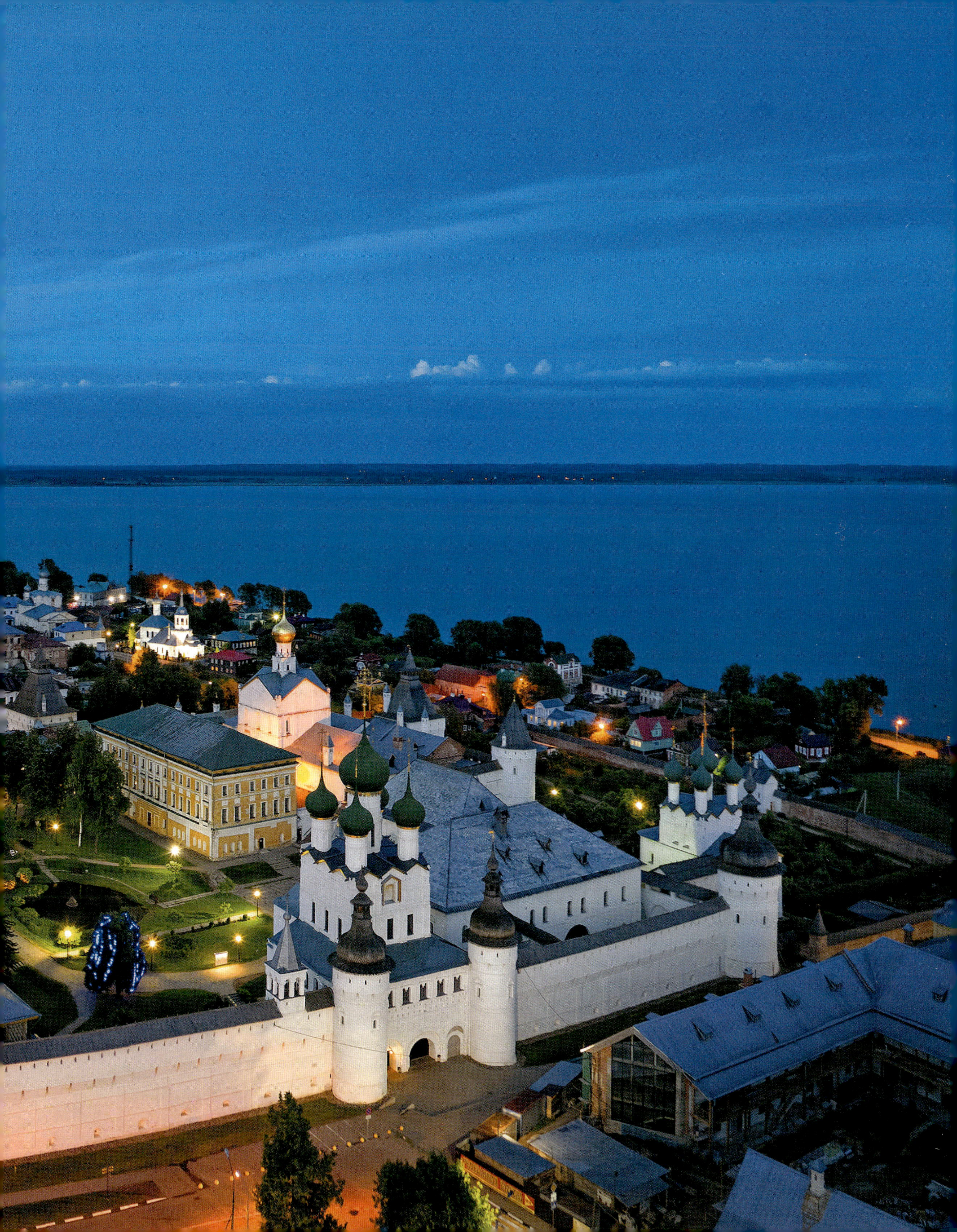

2. Operation Edelweiss: The battle for the Caucasus in World War II

In 1939, on the eve of World War II, the Caucasus was of paramount strategic importance for the USSR since its oilfields of Baku, Grozny and Maikop accounted for 96.5 per cent of known Soviet oil and fuel reserves, of which 58.5 per cent flowed through the Baku–Batumi pipeline and 27.5 per cent via Grozny. During the war, the Baku oilfields alone supplied 76 per cent of the Soviet army's, and 96 per cent of the air force's total fuel requirements.[28] (The fourth important oil-supplying area was the Urals.) This huge concentration of oil reserves made the Caucasus a key target for the Soviet Union's main enemy, Nazi Germany, whose Achilles heel was its lack of oil. At the outbreak of the war, the British navy cut off German access to the USA and the Middle East which made the Wehrmacht dependent on its own reserves, which were exhausted by late 1941, on synthetic production and on the Romanian oilfields.[29] At first, Hitler secured additional resources by the pact with Stalin signed on 23 August 1939 and subsequent trade agreements. From the USSR Germany obtained oil, chrome ore, asbestos, manganese, phosphates, cotton and grain, and it paid in war materiel, industrial goods and credit. But after Germany's failed blitzkrieg of 1941 against the USSR, Hitler and Hermann Göring became convinced in December 1941 that to win the war Germany had to acquire the Caucasus oilfields and deny them to the Soviets. The occupation of the Caucasus would also interrupt US arms supplies to Russia via Iran. Obviously the German High Command (OKW)[30] underestimated the Soviets' ability to wreck their oilfields if needed.[31]

Richard Sorge, Stalin's master spy

When Germany attacked the Soviet Union on 22 June 1941, Stalin faced the key question of whether he could move troops from the Soviet Far East to defend Moscow without risking the loss of Siberia to a Japanese attack, since it was obvious that the Red Army would be unable to fight a war on two fronts against Germany and Japan simultaneously. The Kremlin had to know what the Japanese war plans were. The man to answer this cardinal question was Richard Sorge. Born in 1895 in Baku to a Russian mother and a German father who worked as mechanical engineer for Branobel, in World War I young Sorge served in the German army as a private soldier and described his deployment and those of tens of thousands of other ill-trained young recruits as the transfer 'from the schoolhouse to the slaughter block'. Having met Russian communists he became convinced that only international socialism could prevent such senseless wars.[32] He joined the Communist Party in 1919 and worked as an underground agitator in Europe. As cover, Sorge was publicly expelled from the Comintern[33] in 1929, but he was secretly hired by Soviet Army Intelligence (GRU) and sent, purportedly as a journalist, to Shanghai. In autumn 1931 the Japanese invasion and occupation of Manchuria alarmed the Kremlin, and Sorge was instructed to find out whether Japan intended to invade the poorly defended eastern Siberia as a next step. Sorge recruited the Japanese journalist Hotsumi Ozaki and could soon reassure Moscow that Japan had no plans for an invasion of the USSR. In 1933, Sorge was posted as a Soviet agent in Tokyo with the mission of keeping the Kremlin continuously informed about Japan's intentions towards the USSR. Given the high professionalism of Japanese counter-intelligence, Tokyo represented a tough assignment for a Soviet spy. As a disguise, the journalist Sorge became a member of the Nazi Party (NSDAP).[34] Sorge was one of the very few people to be a member of the Soviet Communist Party and the NSDAP simultaneously. In Tokyo, the charming and outgoing Sorge quickly managed to penetrate the German embassy and befriended not only its German military attaché Colonel Eugen Ott, but also pro-German Japanese military officers and Colonel Kenji Doihara, chief of Japanese military intelligence.[35] In November 1936 Sorge refused to report in Moscow as ordered and remained in Tokyo. His insubordination saved his life, since almost the whole Army Intelligence section was erased by Stalin's Great Purge. In the same month, Germany and Japan announced their **Anti-Comintern Pact**, which was virtually a mutual defence treaty. For Moscow the danger of a war on two fronts became more acute, especially after the Russo-Japanese skirmish over the Changkufeng Heights in July 1938. In the meantime, Sorge had become the best placed Soviet spy worldwide. He not only had multiple contacts in the Japanese Army and its intelligence, but Ott had become German Ambassador to Japan – Sorge was his trusted confidant and had an office within the embassy – and Ozaki had become assistant to Japan's prime minister.

Sorge's importance for the Kremlin grew further as a debate raged within the Japanese armed forces about the next war target. The Japanese army had conquered Manchuria and the important parts of industrial China and now wanted to seize the eastern provinces of the USSR. But the Japanese navy wanted to capture the Philippines and the oilfields of the Dutch East Indies (Indonesia). The army's standing within Japan was weakened when it lost the Battle of Khalkhin Gol to Russia in summer 1939.[36] During 1941, Sorge proved his outstanding value several times with accurate warnings and judgements. From May 1941 Sorge warned at least four times of an impending German attack. Twice the GRU's chief, General Filipp Golikov, rejected the warnings and failed to inform Stalin. Sorge's third warning on 1 June specified that Germany had prepared 170 to 180 divisions to attack the USSR around 15 June. Stalin rejected Sorge's message as a provocation, and also Sorge's fourth warning on 20 June. Forty-eight hours later the Wehrmacht invaded a wholly unprepared USSR.[37] In early July Sorge answered Stalin's question about Japan's war plans: Japan would attack the Philippines and Indonesia in the south but 'if the Red Army suffers defeat, then there is no doubt that the Japanese will join the war, and if there is no defeat, then they will maintain neutrality.'[38] This time Stalin trusted Sorge and moved a great number of troops from the East to fight the Wehrmacht. In August and September Sorge twice confirmed that Japan would not attack the USSR in 1941 and that the next German target was the oilfields of the Caucasus.[39] But Japanese counterintelligence was on Sorge's trail and began to unravel his network. Ozaki was arrested on 12 October and Sorge on the 19th. Both were sentenced to death and hanged on 7 November 1944. Moscow had refused to exchange Sorge for a captured Japanese spy. A huge memorial monument was built in the 1960s in Sorge's hometown of Baku.

118. Monument in honour of the Soviet master spy Richard Sorge (1895–1944). Baku, Azerbaijan. Photo 2016.

Hitler's initial war directive, No. 41 dated 5 April 1942 for Case Blue (*Fall Blau*), the German strategic offensive of 1942, stated:

The aim is to destroy once and for all the living [Soviet] military power that remains and to deprive them as far as possible of their most important sources of war-economy strength. General goals: holding attacks of the Army Group Centre [before Moscow], capture of Leningrad in the north and establishing land connection with the Finns; in the south, breaking through into the Caucasus. … The first step is to unite all available forces for the main operation in the southern sector with the aim of destroying the enemy before the River Don and then to seize the oilfields of the Caucasus and to cross the Caucasus itself.[40]

In this first directive, the occupation of the Caucasus was Hitler's first priority, the capture of Leningrad second and Stalingrad was not mentioned. In Directive No. 43 (11 July 1942) the seizure of the Black Sea ports of Anapa and Novorossiysk were added and a commando ordered to secure the oilfields of Maikop.[41] The failure of this operation was to rob the successful German capture of Maikop in August of its fruits.[42] Although the Wehrmacht had scored an overwhelming victory at the Second Battle of Kharkiv (12–28 May 1942)[43] and the subsequent offensive had an excellent start on 28 June, the bulk of the Soviet forces managed to escape encirclement and annihilation by retreating eastwards. As a result it became obvious that the Army Group South could not move against the Caucasus with its left flank unprotected from Soviet attacks from the north (Voronezh) and north-east (Stalingrad). For this reason the OKW divided the Army Group South into two smaller groups as per Directive No. 45, dated 23 July 1942:

- Group B, code name Fischreiher (heron), was ordered to destroy the Soviet forces at Stalingrad, to occupy the city and then to seize Astrakhan and block the Volga delta.

- Group A, code name Edelweiss and commanded by Field Marshal Wilhelm List (1880–1971), had as targets the Black Sea and Caucasus regions.

The instructions for Group A clarified that after the destruction of the Soviet enemy south of the Don, the most important task of Army Group A was, with the 17th Army under General Richard Ruoff, to seize the entire east coast of the Black Sea. The Kuban was to be crossed and Maikop and Armavir taken. All feasible passes over the main Caucasus ridge were to be used by the 49th Mountain Corps to capture the Black Sea coast in cooperation with the 11th Army advancing southward from Kerch in Crimea, via the Taman Peninsula. At the same time, the region of Grozny was to be taken by the First Panzer Army commanded by General Ewald von Kleist (1881–1954) while the Military Highway from Ossetia to Georgia was to be blocked, if possible on the heights of the pass. Subsequently, in the advance along the Caspian Sea, the area around Baku was to be captured.[44] (Leningrad was no longer mentioned in the directive, since the OKW realized that it lacked the troops to renew the attack on the city; but the blockade was maintained.)

The German plan for Operation Edelweiss had several flaws:

1. It was no longer prioritized, but had to achieve its objectives simultaneously with Operation Fischreiher. As the course of operations would show, the neutralization of Stalingrad developed from a flank protection measure into a major battle whose outcome was decisive for the war as a whole.

2. Edelweiss had three separate targets, namely the occupation of the West Caucasian coast, the capture of the mountain passes and finally the seizure of the Baku oilfields; the capture of the oilfields had decreased in priority.

3. The plan was imprecise and the staffs were supplied with outdated maps and the exact locations of the 150 oil wells of Maikop, which were spread over a wide area, were unknown.

4. The specialized Italian Alpine Corps was sent against Stalingrad instead of to the Caucasus.

5. The OKW's organization of supplies for Group A was poor, especially in terms of fuel.

6. Group A lacked sufficient air support since the Luftwaffe was focused on supplying Group B.

7. According to Field Marshal von Kleist, the Fourth Panzer Army which initially supported Group A was unnecessary, and should have instead immediately attacked Stalingrad which in early August was still poorly defended.[45]

8. Operation Edelweiss was further handicapped by its own commander, Field Marshal List who remained stuck in a World War I mentality and had no experience in mechanized warfare. For example, in August he committed two mechanized divisions to support an operation in mountainous terrain while in September he deployed two infantry divisions in the flat Kalmyk Steppe instead of armoured tank forces.[46]

On the Soviet side, General Ivan Tyulenev (1892–1978) commanded the Transcaucasian Army and General Yakov Cherevichenko (1894–1976) the Black Sea Group. The Soviet Caucasus armies lacked specialized mountain units and also top combat troops since these were deployed around Moscow.

At first the German Caucasus offensive advanced well, capturing Rostov and crossing the River Don in late July. As it seemed that the Red Army would be unable to hold its ground, STAVKA, the Soviet High Command, dispatched six airborne brigades of battle-hardened veterans from Moscow to reinforce the Terek front, and Stalin issued his famous Order No. 227 (28 July 1942):

Cling to every scrap of Russian soil! ... Scaremongers and cowards are to be destroyed on the spot, not a step back without orders from higher command. ... Well-equipped detachments of 200 men are to be posted in the rear of unreliable divisions with the task of ruthlessly shooting all panic-mongers and cowards in the event of a panic and a disorderly retreat.[47]

At the same time Stalin sent Beria to the Caucasus where he swiftly enforced several successful reshuffles in the Soviet Caucasus army's organization. Nevertheless, von Kleist's Panzer Army seized the last remaining railway line linking the Caucasus with Russia (29 July), then Salsk (31 July) and Stavropol (5 August), reaching Maikop on 9 August only to find in the course of the following weeks that the Soviets had sabotaged the oil rigs

119. German tanks in a North Caucasian village in winter 1942–43.

120. German mountain troops crossing the Greater Caucasus in autumn–winter 1942.

121. Wehrmacht mountain trooper with machine gun in the Greater Caucasus, autumn–winter 1942.

Map 9. *Operation Edelweiss 25 July 1942 – 9 October 1943 with the key army commanders*

beyond repair – it was an empty German victory, for the oil wells were useless.[48] Furthermore, massive fuel shortages increasingly slowed down German tank divisions which had to wait for days and even weeks till camel caravans brought fuel.[49] Nevertheless, the First Panzer Army captured Krasnodar (12 August) and Mozdok (25 August), crossed the River Terek (2 September) and occupied Malgobek (6 October). In the east, German troops seized Khulkhuta (1 September) on the eastern border of Kalmykia, but failed to capture Astrakhan (fig. 124).[50] Dissatisfied with Field Marshall List's performance and mistaken deployment of troops, Hitler replaced him with von Kleist on 10 September.[51] Lacking air support and reserves, von Kleist captured Nalchik on 28 October and launched a desperate attack on Ordzhonikidze (Vladikavkaz) which failed in the face of stiff Soviet resistance in which Georgian mountain troops proved themselves outstanding. Von Kleist put an end to the offensive on 12 November and the oilfields of Grozny and Baku remained unconquered.[52] As told in late 1945 by Field Marshal von Kleist to the military historian Liddell Hart, the Caucasus campaign failed for lack of fuel and because essential sections of his forces were diverted to Stalingrad.

The primary cause of our failure was shortage of petrol. The total [petrol] that came through was insufficient to maintain the momentum of the advance, which came to a halt just when our chances looked best. But that was not the ultimate cause of the failure. We could still have reached our goal [that is Grozny and Baku] if my forces had not been drawn away bit by bit to … Stalingrad. Besides part of my motorized troops, I had to give up the whole of my flak corps [anti-aircraft defence] and all my air force.[53]

Although small minorities of North Caucasian peoples such as the Karachay, Chechens[54] or Cossacks volunteered in 1942 to fight with the Wehrmacht in order to liberate their homelands from Soviet tyranny and to reverse the hated land expropriations, the Nazis' racial policy which categorized Russian and Asiatic people as *Untermenschen* (sub-humans) torpedoed the potential for widespread collaboration among North Caucasians. The 3,000-strong *Sonderverband* (special unit) Bergmann was such a unit of Caucasian collaborators fighting on Germany's side in the North Caucasus. It distinguished itself during the battle for Nalchik, in sabotage activities behind Soviet lines and in a daring commando operation at Kizlyar near the Caspian Sea where it destroyed an armoured train.[55] Although the Caucasus was not subordinate to Alfred Rosenberg's infamous Ministry for Occupied Eastern Territories but to the Wehrmacht's administration, which was relatively tolerable by comparison, the SS death squads or *Einsatzgruppen* ('task forces') operated unhindered in the German-occupied Caucasus, since they reported to Heinrich Himmler, thus bypassing the army. In the Caucasus, *Einsatzgruppe* D under SS-Brigadeführer Walther Bierkamp (1901–1945) murdered between 10,000 and 35,000 individuals, mostly Jews and people with disabilities.[56] More lucky were the Caucasian Mountain Jews, who were descended from Jews in the Iranian empire. Bierkamp classified them as Tats – an indigenous Iranian people unrelated to ethnic Jews – and they escaped death, with the exception of 850 Mountain Jews killed in Nalchik.[57] German officers such as Colonel Claus Schenk von Stauffenberg, known for his later assassination attempt on Hitler (20 July 1944) and Friedrich-Werner von der Schulenburg, Germany's ambassador to the USSR from 1934 to 1941, exhorted the Nazi leaders to win the hearts of the occupied peoples, but in vain. The Germans further disappointed the North Caucasians by only hesitantly dismantling the hated *kolkhozes* and restoring land property to the farmers.[58] In the

122. At 2,816 m the Klukhor Pass crosses the Great Caucasus and connects Cherkessk with the Kodori Valley and Sukhumi. Wehrmacht mountain troopers from the 49th Alpine Corps stormed the pass on 17 August 1942 and advanced into the Kodori Valley from where they were pushed back after a few weeks to the top of the pass by the Red Army. They held the pass till January 1943.

end, Germany failed to turn the war of aggression against the USSR into a war of liberation against the Bolsheviks.

The mopping up of the Kuban and the Taman Peninsula by Ruoff's 17th Army was slow, not least due to General Nikolai Kirichenko's highly mobile 17th Kuban Cossack Cavalry which was well adapted to mountainous warfare. As a consequence, the 49th Mountain Corps of General Rudolf Konrad (1891–1964) was ordered to cross the Caucasus Ridge and capture the port of Tuapse. Von Kleist criticized the deployment of 49th Mountain Corps as a mistake, since Tuapse was of lower priority than the oilfields of Grozny.[59] The crossing of the Caucasus was a suicide mission: the attackers would receive only minimal supplies, there was no support from the Luftwaffe, heavy snowfalls were threatening and it was impossible to carry heavy artillery over the mule tracks to fight the entrenched defenders of Tuapse. The assault was launched on 13 August and the four columns of highly skilled mountain troops seized a number of passes which were insufficiently defended, namely the three Elbrus Passes (up to 3,550 m) and the three Klukhor Passes (up to 2,995 m) on 28 August, the five Sancharo Passes (up to 2,723 m) on 24 August and the Marukh Pass (2,748 m) on 5 September. Since the troops had several accomplished mountaineers in their ranks, Field Marshal List permitted them to climb the 5,642-metre-high Mount Elbrus on 21 August, an achievement which infuriated Hitler as being militarily purposeless (fig. 123). General Andrei Grechko (1903–1976), who commanded various armies in the Caucasus and later became Soviet defence minister, wrote critically in his memoirs:

Since the majority of the [Soviet] front's commanders were unexperienced in mountain warfare, their defences and fire systems were organised directly in the passes and no guns were positioned at their near or distant approaches. The Soviet troops did not set up perimeter defences nor did they thoroughly reconnoitre the adjoin territory.[60]

Hence the Germans could attack from the flanks with mountain howitzers and occupy the heights. The conquest of the passes was a masterpiece of military alpinism, but strategically useless. Whereas from the western passes the Germans could see the Black Sea less than 30 kilometres away, the targets of Sukhumi and Tuapse were, for the vastly out-gunned Germans stuck in the mined forests of the foothills, simply unreachable. In order to save the remaining troops, they were ordered back to secure the main ridge and its passes. The conquest of the virtually impregnable passes was in vain, but the Soviet counteroffensive of September–October to recapture them failed at a high cost in casualties.[61]

123. Propaganda photo of Wehrmacht mountain troopers placing the flag of the Third Reich on top of Mount Elbrus (5,642 m) standing on the border of Kabardino-Balkaria and Karachay-Cherkessia, Russian Federation. The selected troopers climbed Mt Elbrus on 21 August 1942.

The 17th German Army captured Anapa only on 31 August and Novorossiysk on 7 September. STAVKA reacted by replacing the head of the 47th Army, General Kotov with General Grechko. Grechko successfully reorganized resistance and, together with Major General Fyodor Kamkov's 18th Army, brought a halt to Ruoff's offensive before Tuapse by late October 1942.[62] All three German attacks, on Astrakhan, Grozny and Tuapse, had come to a standstill without achieving their goals. There was an impasse with the advantage on the Soviet side as the counter-attacks against the First Panzer Army steadily increased[63] and the Sixth German Army became encircled at Stalingrad. Even worse, when on 19 and 20 November the Red Army broke through the Third and Fourth Romanian armies deployed as flank protection west of Stalingrad, Army Group A was in acute danger of losing both its supply lines and its only means of retreat. When it became clear that the Sixth Army and Stalingrad were lost, on 28 December commander of the new Army Group Don, to immediately recall Army Group A from the Caucasus and to use it in conjunction with the Army Group Don in the relief of the Sixth Army. As a result, Unternehmen Wintergewitter ('Operation Winter Storm'), which was tasked with the relief of the Sixth Army but had too few forces, failed and became stuck 50 kilometres from Stalingrad.

In total, about 1 million Soviets served as combatants or non-combatants in the Wehrmacht, of which 170,000 to 250,000 came from the Caucasus, Crimea, the Volga region and Central Asia. The vast majority were POWs who preferred the life of well-fed and well-clad auxiliary soldiers to the miserable existence in German prison and labour camps. Within the Wehrmacht, there were five different types of units where Caucasians served:

1. 53 battalions of the *Ostlegionen* under Colonel Ralph von Heygendorff (1897–1953) consisting mainly of Slavs.

2. 26 battalions of the 162nd Infantry Division commanded by Major General Oskar von Niedermayer (1885–1948) consisting of Caucasians, Volga Tatars and Central Asians.

3. Three battalions of the *Sonderverband* Bergmann.

4. Eight battalions of Crimean Tatars.

5. Five battalions of Kalmyk Cavalry.[68]

In total this amounted to 95,000 men. The Don Cossacks were also grouped in separate units. Towards the end of the war, several units were transferred to the Waffen-SS: among them the 21,000-strong First Cossack Division commanded by General Helmuth von Pannwitz (1898–1947) became the 15th Waffen-SS Cossack Corps.[69] The bulk of these 95 battalions, namely the 79 battalions of the *Ostlegionen* and of Niedermayer's division, were mainly deployed on the western and south-western fronts, that is in France, Italy and the Balkans, but also during the Warsaw Uprising. Having to fight far from their homelands, these auxiliary troops were of varying combat value. Most of these battalions were dispersed among the Wehrmacht to prevent any security risk. In terms of nationalities, they included *ca.* 9,000 North Caucasians,[70] 25,000 to 35,000 Azerbaijanis, 25,000 Georgians, 18,000 Armenians, 5,000 Kalmyks and about 65,000 Cossacks serving in different units. Depending on the nationality, 50–90 per cent of the auxiliaries were combatants. Of them, the Germans valued the North Caucasian, Cossack and Kalmyk soldiers highest.[71]

124. The Khulkhuta memorial stands at the place where the Red Army stopped the Wehrmacht advance towards Astrakhan in late 1942. Kalmykia, Russian Federation. Photo 2017

1942 Hitler reluctantly agreed to follow the urgent appeal of his Chief of the General Staff of the German Army High Command, Kurt Zeitzler (1895–1963). He ordered the retreat of Army Group A which was in danger of being trapped in the Caucasus should Soviet armies seize Rostov.[64] Von Kleist managed to escape the encirclement.[65] He saved his army and the mountain troops, and crossed the Don on 6 February 1943, while the German 17th Army held Novorossiysk till 16 September and the Kuban bridgehead till 9 October.[66] The Battle for the Caucasus cost the Germans 72,000 casualties, including 22,000 dead or missing, their Romanian allies 45,000 casualties (12,000 dead or missing) and the Red Army an enormous 511,000 casualties (247,000 dead, missing or captured) plus countless civilian victims.[67]

In retrospect, it should be noted that Hitler made a capital mistake when, towards the end of November 1942, he refused to grant the request of Field Marshal Erich von Manstein,

Among the Caucasian expatriates siding with Germany, the Armenian General Drastamat Kanayan (Dro) was especially prominent. It seems that Dro and the Dashnaksutyun Party worried that Turkey might attack Soviet Armenia should the Wehrmacht cross the Caucasus ridge, which is why they wanted to gain German protection. Ideally, Armenian volunteers would enter Yerevan together with the Wehrmacht before Turkish troops reached the border, and Armenia's independence would be re-established. On the other hand, in order not to alienate the Allies, the party also declared its allegiance to them after the Japanese attack on Pearl Harbour on 7 December 1941. Ultimately this dual strategy saved thousands of Armenian Legionnaires from extradition to the USSR at the war's end. Dro's cooperation with Germany was twofold. He recruited volunteers to perform reconnaissance, guerrilla and sabotage missions behind Soviet lines. They were part of the *Abwehrgruppe 101*, a section of German Military Intelligence which rated the Armenian agents highly; in 1943 they were regrouped into the *Sonderkommando Dromedar* and operated, together with the Georgian *Sonderverband Tamara*, in the Taman Peninsula, Armenia, Georgia, North Caucasus and Crimea.[72] Dro also participated in the creation of the Armenian Legion attached to the 162nd Infantry Division; of its twelve battalions only two, Nos 808 and 809, fought in the North Caucasus.[73]

According to the Yalta Agreements of February 1945, all Soviet subjects who had fought for the Wehrmacht and surrendered to the Western Allies had to be extradited to the Soviet Union, as did expatriates hostile to the Soviet regime.[74] At the end of the war, 35,000 Cossacks alone, who had retreated to Austria, were compulsorily handed over to the Soviets; the officers were shot and most of the soldiers deported to Siberia or Central Asia.[75] But the vast majority of South Caucasian men eligible for service fought with great sacrifice on the Soviet side, often in

125. The Georgian Red Army sergeant Meliton Varlamis dze Kantaria hoists the Soviet flag over the German Reichstag in Berlin on 30 April 1945, together with his companions, the Dagestani Abdulkhakim Ismailov and the Russian Mikhail Yegorov. The scene was re-enacted on 2 May 1945 for the benefit of photographers.

national units. Of the 500,000 Azerbaijanis drafted, 210,000 fell (6.4 per cent of the total population) and of the 550,000 Georgians 190,000 died (5.3 per cent of the population). Of ca. 450,000 Armenians engaged in the Red Army, 150,000 were killed in battle or died in German POW camps, which represents 11 per cent of the Soviet-Armenian population.[76] In addition, ca. 18,000 Armenians fought in the US and British armies.[77] Several Armenians reached senior army positions during the war, including Marshal Ivan Bagramyan (1897–1982), Admiral Ivan Isakov (1894–1967), Chief Marshal of Armour Hamazasp Babadzhanian (1906–1977) and Aviation Marshal Sergei Khudyakov (1902–1950) who was shot for alleged espionage and posthumously rehabilitated in 1965. In total, 550,000 South Caucasians died for a state which somehow wasn't theirs. As for the North Caucasians, their loyalty towards the USSR is hard to guess since recruitment among them was halted in September 1941 and soldiers were transferred to the reserve due to high rates of desertions. In July 1942 Chechens, Ingush, Kabardians, Balkars and Dagestanis were excluded from recruitment; only volunteers, mainly Dagestanis and Ossetians, were accepted.[78]

3. Deportations and the start of the Cold War

The German retreat did not bring peace to the Caucasus, since NKVD units followed on the heels of the victorious Soviet troops and cleared the North Caucasus and Kalmykia of real or alleged collaborators.[79] Under the pretext of a necessary collective punishment of disloyal peoples, Stalin decided to get rid of, among others, the 'troublesome' North Caucasian nationalities by deporting them *en masse* to Central Asia and Siberia and so breaking their national identities. The frightful and forceful deportations organized by Beria and Mikhail Suslov began in November 1943 with the banishment of 69,000 Karachays followed by more than 93,000 (or by some accounts 127,000) Kalmyks, although ca. 23,000 Kalmyks had bravely fought in the Red Army. Next, 387,000 Chechens and 91,000 Ingush were deported in February–March 1944, 38,000 Balkars on 8 March, and 95,000 Meskhetian Turks plus 20,000 Kurds and Khemshins (Armenian Muslim converts) in November from southern Georgia. In total, about 800,000 Caucasians were deported under awful conditions and many died on the transport. Arriving at their destinations, the deportees were made less than welcome by the local inhabitants since they were labelled as Nazi collaborators. Having provided so many volunteers to the Red Army, the Ossetians and Dagestanis were mostly spared, although 62,000 Avars, Laks and Dargans were forced to relocate to the now depopulated Chechnya.[80] As a consequence of the massive deportations, the administrative borders in North Caucasus were redrawn. The Karachay AO, the Kalmyk and Chechen-Ingush ASSRs were abolished and the Kabardino-Balkar ASSR became the territorially reduced Kabardin ASSR.[81] While in the South Caucasus purges of collaborators also took place, the Soviet Union appealed to Armenian expatriates to return to Armenia. About 100,000 seized the opportunity but they quickly realized that they were unwelcome. With the onset of the Cold War, many of these returnees were thrown into prison camps; they were only freed after Stalin's death in 1953.[82]

By the Conference of Yalta at the latest, Stalin had imposed a massive expansion of the Soviet Empire upon Eastern Europe which would last for 45 years. By contrast, Stalin's attempt to expand towards and even beyond the southern edges of the Caucasus failed due to the firm line taken by the USA. Already on 7 June 1945 the Soviet foreign minister Molotov had unequivocally requested from Turkey the return of Kars and Ardahan districts, which had been ceded by Lenin in 1921, to the USSR. He also requested a revision of the 1936 Montreux Convention which gave Turkey control over the Bosporus and the straits and regulated the passage of warships. Hard pressed by the Soviet Union to cede Kars and Ardahan and feeling threatened by the two neighbouring Soviet puppet states, the Azerbaijan People's Republic and the Kurdish Republic of Mahabad (see below), Turkey abandoned its neutrality, moved close to the USA and Britain and joined NATO in 1952.[83] In 1945, the USSR also tried to expand towards the Persian Gulf by keeping control of parts of its Russian zone within northwestern Iran. Back in 1941, Reza Shah (r. 1925–1941) had refused to expel the Germans from Iran whereupon on 25–28 August the Soviets and British occupied their former zones of influence and forced the Shah to abdicate in favour of his son Mohammad Reza (r. 1941–1979).[84] Although in the Tripartite Agreement of 29 January 1942 the USSR and Britain had guaranteed to 'respect the sovereignty and territorial integrity of Iran' and to withdraw their forces 'not later than six months' after the final end of the war, the Soviets only withdrew from the eastern and central parts of their zone and maintained troops in the west in Iranian Azerbaijan.[85] Stalin wanted access to the oil deposits in five provinces of northern Iran[86] and ordered Soviet Azerbaijan's first secretary Baghirov to encourage Azeri and Kurdish separatism and to establish a Soviet puppet state, similar to the Soviet-occupied Eastern European states.

126. Don Cossack veterans of World War II celebrating at Novocherkassk, 30 km north-east of Rostov-on-Don. Rostov Oblast, Russian Federation. Photo 1994.

Whereas the British dutifully left Iran, Baghirov sponsored and organized armed Communist rebellions under Beria's supervision. On 21 November 1945, the **Azerbaijan People's Republic**, headed by the Communist Sayyed Ja'far Pishevari, was proclaimed in Tabriz and on 22 January 1946 the **Kurdish Republic of Mahabad** headed by Mullah Mustafa Barzani and Qazi Mohammad; the latter 'republic' was a narrow strip located between Lake Urmia and the Turkish and Iraqi borders. Soviet separatist propaganda also undermined Iran's unity in Gilan, Mazandaran, Astarabad and Khorasan. For the USA and Britain, a threatened Soviet annexation of northern Iran and a Soviet presence close to the Iraqi and Iranian oilfields was unacceptable. In this complicated situation, the Iranian prime minister Ahmad Qavam cleverly chose a dual strategy. Whereas he feigned conciliation in negotiations with Moscow, he asked for and obtained robust support from the USA. Events came to a head in early March 1946: on the 2nd the Soviets failed to withdraw their troops as stipulated by the Tripartite Agreement and on the 4th fifteen Soviet armoured brigades entered the two puppet republics and approached the Turkish and Iraqi borders. On the same day, Soviet tanks began to advance towards Tehran, and both the Mahabad Republic and Soviet Georgia claimed territories in north-eastern Turkey. It was clear that the Cold War had begun at the southern border of the Caucasus. The US president Harry Truman reacted by ordering his forces into combat readiness and issued Stalin an ultimatum to leave Iran by 23 March, failing which US forces would move in.[87] Stalin shied away from a military confrontation and on the 24th ordered that all Soviet troops should retreat to Baku by May 10th at the latest. Stalin had underestimated Iran's and Turkey's will to resist, and also Truman's determination. Deprived of Soviet military and financial support, the Azerbaijan People's Republic entered a provisional agreement with Tehran on 13 June. Nevertheless, the Iranian army reoccupied Tabriz on 14 December 1946 and put an end to both renegade republics.[88] An additional outcome was that the USA supplanted Britain as the dominant power in Iran.

4. Political stagnation and the rise of nationalism

The end of the war brought to the Caucasus, as to the rest of the USSR, no easing of conditions on the domestic front – rather the contrary. Relaxations in religious and nationalist matters which had been introduced during the war to gain the sympathy of non-Russian peoples were rescinded. The three South Caucasian republics had also suffered population decline due to war casualties. The Cold War triggered a militarization of these three border states which shared boundaries with US-friendly Turkey and Iran. Workers were refused passports and obliged to stay in their allocated jobs. Furthermore, state finances had to focus strongly on the reconstruction of the war-ravaged parts of the USSR. At Stalin's death on 5 March 1953, Beria attempted to seize power and initiated a package of reforms as well as the liberation of hundreds of thousands of Gulag prisoners, but he was arrested on 26 June and shot six months later. For the Caucasus, a key socio-political event was the return of deportees following Nikita Khrushchev's trenchant condemnation of Stalin's deportations in his so-called 'Secret Speech' of 25 February 1956:

All the more monstrous are the acts whose initiator was Stalin ... We refer to the mass deportations from their native places of whole nations ... This deportation action was not dictated by any military considerations. Thus, already at the end of 1943, when there occurred a permanent breakthrough at the fronts ... a decision was taken and executed concerning the deportation of all the Karachay, the Kalmyks, the Chechens, Ingush and Balkars.[89]

While Khrushchev (in office 1953–1964) did not mention the Meskhetian Turks, Crimean Tatars or Volga Germans, the five named peoples were allowed to return to their re-established homelands (that is, ASSRs) over the next two years. This resettlement created new problems, especially in Chechnya where many of those Avars, Laks and Dargans who had been settled here in 1944 had to be moved back to Dagestan; other returning Chechens and Ingush met armed resistance from Ossetian and Russian settlers.[90]

Khrushchev's dismantling of Stalin and Stalinism triggered an ideological crisis which was progressively exploited by revived nationalist movements as the tyrannical autocracy of the Stalin years was significantly relaxed. Marxism had long since lost its revolutionary verve and become an unconvincing legitimation of an inflexible socio-political order. Highly visible expressions of this renewed national consciousness and pride were the erection of the huge statue of *Kartlis Deda*, 'Mother of Kartli' on the Sololaki hilltop above Tbilisi (fig. 137) in 1958 and the replacement of Stalin's gigantic statue on top of the Victory Memorial in Yerevan in 1962 with a 24-metre-high statue of Mother Armenia in 1967 (figs. 127, 128). The South Caucasian republics also succeeded in designating their native languages as official state languages in their constitution. In all three republics Khrushchev replaced the Stalinist leadership with new personnel: in Georgia, General Vasil Mzhavanadze (in office 1953–1972) replaced Beria's crony Aleksandre Mirtskhulava as first secretary of the Georgian Communist Party and General Aleksi Inauri became chief of the Georgian KGB.[91] In Armenia Grigor Harutyunyan (Grigory Arutinov, in office 1937–1953) was succeeded by two rather insignificant secretaries before the instalment of Anton Kochinyan

127. The giant statue of Joseph Stalin inaugurated on 29 November 1950 overlooked the city of Yerevan till 1962 when it was dismantled.

128. In 1967 the 24-m-high copper statue of Mother Armenia replaced the former statue of Stalin. The pedestal is 27 m high and hosts a military museum. Yerevan, Armenia. Photo 2017.

(in office 1966–1974) who had previously been Armenian prime minister, while in Azerbaijan Stalin's henchman Baghirov was deposed in 1953 and shot three years later. After five years as first secretary, Imam Mustafayev (in office 1954–1959) was accused of nationalism[92] and replaced by Vali Akhundov (Vəli Axundov, in office 1959–1969) who in turn was succeeded by the KGB general Heydar Aliyev (Heydər Əliyev, in office 1969–1982), the future third president of independent Azerbaijan. These new first secretaries seized the opportunity given by the relaxation of repression and Khrushchev's modest economic decentralization to build their own power bases and act increasingly independently from Moscow, coming to resemble communist 'feudal princes'.[93] Common to all three republics was a thriving shadow economy. The Soviet command economy was not only highly inefficient; it also prioritized heavy and military industries to the blatant detriment of consumer goods and foodstuffs. Department store racks were often empty. This huge unmet consumer demand created a parallel shadow market which was lubricated by an all-pervading corruption which also permeated the Communist Party. Thanks to the distance from Moscow, this shadow economy blossomed especially well in the South Caucasian republics and accounted for *ca.* 25–30 per cent of the republics' respective GNP.[94]

In Stalin's homeland of **Georgia**, Khrushchev's denunciation of his predecessor's crimes was not well received and led within a week to mass demonstrations and riots in Tbilisi which had to be suppressed by security forces.[95] On the other hand, the political thaw allowed Catholicos Eprem II (in office 1960–1972) to revive the Georgian Orthodox Church and in 1962 to join the World Council of Churches (WCC).[96] Whereas Eprem cautiously appealed to Georgian patriotism and national pride, his successor Davit V (in office 1972–1977) instead propagated loyalty to the Soviet Union. Catholicos Ilia II (in office 1977–present), was from 1979 to 1983 co-president of the WCC, although after the end of the Soviet Union he was forced to cancel the affiliation of the Georgian Church with the WCC in 1997 by an anti-ecumenical group of monks and prelates who threatened it with schism.[97] The reduced control from Moscow also allowed the development of a parallel nationalism in several Caucasian republics and ASSRs. In Georgia, the officially sanctioned nationalism allowed the local party leadership to strengthen

129. The Eternal Flame stands inside the circle formed by the twelve slabs representing the 'twelve lost provinces'. The Armenian Genocide Memorial, Tsitsernakaberd near Yerevan, Armenia. Photo 2015. (See also fig. 97).

its autonomy vis-à-vis Moscow, but a dissident, underground nationalism opposed the corrupt communist regime. One of its protagonists was Zviad Gamsakhurdia (1939–1993), son of the famous writer Konstantine Gamsakhurdia and future first president of Georgia. He sympathized with independence, wrote about the degradation of Georgian architectural monuments and was a human rights activist who was arrested in 1977 and condemned in 1978 to three years' imprisonment.[98] Common to both types of Georgian nationalism was a certain sense of superiority over the non-Georgian minorities such as the Abkhaz, Adjarians and South Ossetians who were viewed at the same time as a potential threat to national unity. In the case of Gamsakhurdia and other radical nationalists, this intransigence towards minorities would lead them in the early 1990s straight into civil war. In 1972, Leonid Brezhnev (in office 1964–1982) made an attempt at cleaning out the Augean Stable of Georgian corruption and nominated Eduard Shevardnadze (1928–2014), who had served since 1965 as Georgian minister for internal affairs, as first secretary of the Georgian Communist Party, replacing Mzhavanadze whose wife was implicated in the theft of church treasures from the patriarchate, a crime which had been revealed by Zviad Gamsakhurdia.[99] Shevardnadze continued the nationalist policies of his predecessor but actively fought corruption, favouritism and nepotism. Although Shevardnadze was unable to eradicate corruption, his economic reforms based on rewarding initiative and performance yielded spectacular results with substantial growth rates in industrial and agricultural production. Impressed by Shevardnadze's solid performance, Gorbachev nominated him as full Politburo member and foreign minister of the USSR in July 1985.

In **Armenia**, which lacked energy resources, an ambitious programme was put into action in 1949 to exploit the high-altitude Lake Sevan. A tunnel to tap its water for the Yerevan region was opened and six hydroelectric plants went into operation. As a consequence, the level of the lake began to drop by a metre per year and the water turned turbid. To compensate for the loss, two tunnels were built conducting water from other rivers to the lake. Thanks to the increase in available electricity Armenia launched and successfully developed its own mechanical and chemical industries. To meet the steadily increasing energy demands the nuclear power plant at Medzamor near Yerevan was commissioned in 1976. Following the Chernobyl catastrophe in 1986 and a powerful earthquake in December 1988, the plant remained closed till November 1995, causing a severe electricity deficit. As in Georgia, so in Armenia, two kinds of nationalism arose. On the one hand there was an official version, which was directed less against Moscow than against the Turks. A major monument was built celebrating the Armenian victory of Sardarapat (1968, fig. 103), and a Genocide Memorial at Tsitsernakaberd (1967, figs. 97, 129). The construction of the latter had been decided after angry mass demonstrations had broken out in April 1965 on the fiftieth anniversary of the 1915 genocide; as a further consequence of the demonstrations, First Secretary Yakov Zarobyan (in office 1960–1966) was replaced by Anton Kochinyan. Dissident nationalism, meanwhile, was represented by the National United Party (NUP), founded in 1966, which demanded full independence and the reunification with Nagorno-Karabakh, Nakhchivan and Turkish Western Armenia. When a bomb killed seven people in a Moscow subway on 8 January 1977, a co-founder and two members of NUP were accused of terrorism and executed two years later.[100] After Kochinyan made no attempt to combat corruption, he was replaced by Karen Demirchyan (in office 1974–1988) who made no significant progress in curbing bribery but did succeed in improving the economy. Like the Georgian Church, the Armenian experienced a revival under Catholicos Vazken I (in office 1955–1994); his predecessor Kevork VI (in office 1945–1954) had been installed after a seven-year vacancy during which the patriarchal see of Etchmiadzin was closed by the Stalinist government.

After the war **Azerbaijan** suffered from its huge contribution to the war in terms of oil supply, since its known oilfields were to a great degree exhausted. Furthermore, the discovery of gigantic oilfields in western Siberia channelled all Soviet investment in that direction, and Baku's obsolete drilling and refinery installations were not renewed and upgraded, in spite of the excellent quality of Caspian oil. By the mid 1980s,

130. The building of the former Ministry for Road and Highway Construction erected in 1975 in Tbilisi. It is now the headquarters of the Bank of Georgia. The structure consists of five horizontal, two-storey building blocks. They appear as if they had been stacked on top of each other. The buildings rest on three cores; the tallest base has 18 floors. The supporting structure is made of steel and reinforced concrete and stands on solid rock. Tbilisi, Georgia. Photo 2013.

Azerbaijan's share of Soviet oil production had dwindled to 2 per cent.[101] Under First Secretary Vali Akhundov, the official nationalism took a revisionist, anti-Armenian turn. It was not only claimed that Nagorno-Karabakh and Nakhchivan had belonged since time immemorial to Azerbaijan,[102] but also that the Azerbaijanis were the descendants of the Caucasian Albanians – a statement that downplayed the Azerbaijanis' Turkic ethnic heritage.[103] An even more fanciful interpretation identified the Albanians with Oghuz Turks.[104] As for the existing Armenian churches, monasteries and cemeteries, they were either destroyed, as happened in Nakhchivan, or – in the case of the churches and monasteries of Nagorno-Karabakh and even eastern Armenia, such as Tatev – were declared, for example by Gulchohra Mammadova (Gülçöhrə Məmmədova), president of the Azerbaijan University of Architecture, to have been originally Albanian but later usurped by Armenians who had replaced their Albanian inscriptions with Armenian ones.[105] Mammadova went so far as to claim that Albanian churches located in northern Azerbaijan, such as Kiş, had been founded in the first century CE.[106] This quite untenable dating was meant to demonstrate the alleged primacy of the Albanian Church over the Armenian. As regards the Azerbaijani economy, its development under Veli Akhundov was one of the poorest performances in the whole of the USSR. Brezhnev therefore replaced Akhundov with Heydar Aliyev who quickly purged the Communist Party of its most corrupt members and adopted a policy of rotating cadres. Although Aliyev ensured that no Slavs were appointed to key state functions but only Azeris, he remained cautious in his approach to nationalism and especially pan-Turkism. He had the pan-Turkist dissident Abulfaz Aliyev (Əbülfəz Əliyev), who argued for Azerbaijan's independence and unification with Iranian Azerbaijan, arrested and jailed from 1975–1976. Later Aliyev took the name of Elchibey (Elçibəy, 'the messenger') and became the second president of Azerbaijan. Whereas corruption remained widespread, industrial production and agricultural output recovered and achieved significant growth. In 1982, Yuri Andropov (in office 1982–1984) promoted Aliyev to deputy prime minister and Politburo member but he was sacked by Mikhail Gorbachev five years later. As in Armenia and Georgia, religious tolerance increased in the 1960s, which led to a re-opening of mosques and to the emergence of an underground form of Islam which manifested itself in pilgrimages to the *mazars* (memorial shrines) of Shiite saints.

In the **North Caucasus**, the socio-political situation was even more complicated than in the South due to the multitude of nations and languages and the mass deportations. As mentioned above, Dagestanis who had settled in Chechnya in 1944 had to vacate their new homes thirteen years later to make space for returning Chechens. The Ossetians faced a similar problem, since after the deportation of the Ingush the Ossetian ASSR had been allotted parts of former Ingush territory including Malgobek, Mozdok and the eastern Prigorodny District. Since the Ossetians were mainly Russophile Christians and the Ingush were Russophobe Muslims, a shared ASSR was not an option. With the return of the Ingush and Chechens, Ossetia had to cede parts of its recently allocated eastern territories such as Malgobek back to the Chechen-Ingush ASSR. Contrary to an opinion occasionally advanced, North Caucasian identities were not solely tribal but also included an awareness of belonging to certain nationalities. So far from breaking these peoples' national consciousness, the mass deportations actually sharpened it. The concept of a titular nation with preferential rights within a defined territory also bore the seed of endless territorial conflicts with neighbouring republics over ethnic exclaves. Dual republics such as Kabardino-Balkaria or Karachay-Cherkessia for their part provoked virulent internal rivalries about the distribution of power and privileges. Even more complex was the situation within Dagestan since its inhabitants perceived themselves not so much as Dagestani or as affiliated to the ten official non-Russian ethnicities, but as members of their tribe within one of the over thirty actual ethnicities.[107] An additional platform for identification also re-emerged in the form of Islam. As in Azerbaijan, its revival took place less in the few reopened mosques than in underground prayer rooms and madrasas as well as at shrines of venerated sheikhs. Fundamentalist trends began to spread in the later 1980s. Parallel to the tolerated resurgence of Islam, traditional mediation courts run by 'Soviets of Elders' reappeared, which dealt with local civil issues.[108]

Contrary to the creation of a single atheistic Soviet nation as promoted by Khrushchev in the early 1960s, in reality there came about an increase of ethnic and, mainly in Dagestan and Chechnya, religious self-awareness. Since history is not only steered by politics, economics and social struggles, but also decisively by the mind-sets of individual people, the Soviet Union failed to become a melting pot of nations. As the appeal of Soviet ideology vanished, the platform for identification provided by a common Soviet nationhood crumbled, at the latest by the time of the ill-fated war in Afghanistan of 1979–1989. As will be shown in the next chapter, the resilient and often incorrigible ancestral mind-sets and prejudices re-emerged with full force as soon as the Soviet Union collapsed.

IX

Independence in the South Caucasus

1. The disintegration of the Soviet Union

The disintegration of the Soviet Union began in 1988 in the South Caucasus and the Baltic States. With the unravelling of the Soviet Empire, what had previously been domestic administrative boundaries became, overnight, international state borders. Nations which looked back on a long past but had been absorbed into the USSR resurfaced and re-entered history. The Caucasian nations and ethnicities had kept their identities, their myths and aspirations, but also their prejudices – which would set the future political course. As the Soviet Union vanished on 26 December 1991, so did the *Pax Sovietica*, and old simmering conflicts erupted again. Whereas the North Caucasian nations would remain *nolens volens* within the new Russian Federation, the three small South Caucasian states achieved independence but found themselves once again surrounded by three great regional powers, Russia, Turkey and Iran. Instead of opting for a close mutual cooperation, each Caucasian state defined its own national interests and attempted to win a regional power to its side, often to the detriment of its neighbour, in a typical zero-sum perspective. Obviously there was no such thing as a South Caucasian identity and the communist state ideology managed to suspend the simmering ethnic conflicts only by applying repressive measures. In a sense, the history of the relations between all the Caucasian states in the 1990s, and in the South to the present day, is a loud echo of the conflicts of 1917–1922. As Karl Marx had observed,

Men make their own history, but they do not make it just as they please; they do not make it under circumstances chosen by themselves, but under circumstances directly encountered, given and transmitted from the past. The tradition of all the dead generations weighs like a nightmare on the brain of the living.[1]

When Mikhail Gorbachev (in office 1985–1991, d. 2022) came to power in 1985, he was painfully aware that its economic stagnation would lead to the USSR falling further behind the USA and that radical political and economic reforms were needed to avoid the USSR slipping into the status of an economically 'underdeveloped country'. Gorbachev, born in 1931 in the North Caucasian Krai of Stavropol, had begun his political career in 1946 in the *Komsomol*, the All-Union Leninist Young Communist League. He served in the agitation and propaganda department and supported Khrushchev's de-Stalinization programme. In his subsequent function as First Secretary of the Stavropol Kraikom (regional committee) Gorbachev directed the extension of the Great Stavropol Canal built for irrigation purposes after which he left the Caucasus and moved to Moscow as Secretary of the Central Committee. Unlike the Georgian Eduard Shevardnadze, Gorbachev played no role after his resignation as President of the Soviet Union in the post-Soviet Caucasus.

As General Secretary of the Communist Party, Gorbachev quickly launched an ambitious reform programme under the slogans of *glasnost* (openness and transparency), *perestroika* (restructuring) and *demokratizatsiya* (democratization). He hoped that the removal of misleading propaganda and censorship as well as the freedom to address problems and suggest solutions would initiate a modernization of the Soviet society and economy and dramatically increase the latter's efficiency. Gorbachev wanted to achieve the prosperity and strength of the Western powers by adopting their way of running state and economy. It meant replacing the command economy with a free-market and entrepreneurial model. But three factors, one external and two domestic, caused his strategy to end in disaster. At the beginning of 1986, Saudi Arabia broke a deadlock within OPEC by flooding the world market with cut-price oil provoking a 70 per cent crash in the price of oil, from $32 to $10 per barrel.[2] This rash price war not only seriously hit the Saudi and other OPEC members' finances, but robbed Gorbachev of the financial means to revamp the USSR's ailing industry, causing hyperinflation and a steep rise in external debt. The modernization of Soviet industry became unfinanceable. Second, Gorbachev failed to understand that the successful Chinese economic reform programme did not allow for any critique of the Communist Party and its state structures, which secured stability. Finally Gorbachev grossly underestimated the strength of resentment against the centralized Moscow regime, the deep aspirations to self-determination and also traditional ethnic hostilities. *Glasnost* opened a Pandora's Box of grievances and nationalism. What began as a reform from above ended as a revolution from below and by 16 December 1991 the Union had fragmented into fifteen independent states, among them Georgia (9 April 1991) Armenia (21 September) and Azerbaijan (18 October).[3] As Russia's president Boris Yeltsin (in office 1991–1999) and other presidents of newly independent states quickly found out, the centrifugal forces were not going to stop at the borders of the former SSRs: tendencies to fragmentation also affected former ASSRs and AOs – in the South Caucasus Abkhazia, Adjara, South Ossetia and Nagorno-Karabakh. Gorbachev's attempt at restructuring and reconstruction of the Soviet Union led to its dismantling. Everywhere, ruthless politicians exploited the rapid raise of nationalism to advance their own interests. In the South Caucasus conflicts were driven by issues of ethnicity and territorial control, and hardly at all by religion.[4] In addition, although the downfall of the USSR had changed the world order in the South Caucasus, Central Asia and Eastern Europe, Russia remained a potentially bellicose superpower.

2. The Armenian declaration of independence and the issue of Nagorno-Karabakh

The recent histories of Armenia and Azerbaijan are closely linked with the Nagorno-Karabakh conflict which will be dealt with later in this chapter. Armenia's starting position at independence was difficult. Whereas it was ethnically homogeneous, with 90 per cent of its population ethnically Armenian and with no internal separatist movements, it was in geographical terms a landlocked country trapped between two hostile neighbours, Azerbaijan and Turkey. Furthermore, it lost in the course of 1993 its only railway link with its protector Russia due to the Georgian–Abkhaz war. The ongoing conflict with Azerbaijan over Nagorno-Karabakh decisively impeded its economic development. In spite of decades-long Azerbaijani harassments, the Armenian share of the population in Nagorno-Karabakh had 'only' declined from 94 per cent in 1923 to 79 per cent in 1979. By comparison, the Armenian population in Nakhchivan dwindled from 40 per cent of the total in 1920 to 1.4 per cent in 1979.[5] Exploiting their freedoms under *glasnost*, in February 1988 Armenian demonstrations began in Nagorno-Karabakh's capital Stepanakert and in Yerevan in favour of Nagorno-Karabakh's unification with Armenia, which the Nagorno-Karabakh Soviet then, on 20 February, demanded with an overwhelming majority. This declaration immediately provoked anger in Azerbaijan and on 27–28 February a violent

131. The National Museum and National Gallery of Armenia building stands on the Republic Square in the heart of Yerevan, Armenia. Photo 2017.

132. The Eternal Flame Monument at Martyrs' Lane in Baku. In the background are the three Flame Towers, built between 2007 and 2013. The monument was inaugurated in October 1998; it is dedicated to the victims of the violent Soviet intervention of 'Black January' 1990 and of the First Nagorno-Karabakh War 1992–1994. Baku, Azerbaijan. Photo 2016.

mob attacked Armenians at random in the industrial city of Sumqayıt (Sumgait), with dozens killed. Soviet troops intervened and 14,000 Armenians were evacuated. This pogrom, along with another incident in Ganja in November and the concomitant reprisals in Armenia, triggered a massive population exchange which highlighted Moscow's impotence to control its own member republics. There is no doubt that the ethnic Armenian–Azerbaijani conflict contributed to the fall of the Soviet Union. By the end of November 1988, about 180,000 Armenians had been forced to leave Azerbaijan for Armenia and 160,000 Azeris had to flee Armenia for Azerbaijan. By late 1990, these numbers had increased to 260,000 Armenian and 200,000 Azerbaijani refugees.[6]

Although the Nagorno-Karabakh conflict had slipped out of Moscow's control, the Presidium of the Supreme Soviet of the USSR refused to consider a political solution and on 23 March 1988 rejected Nagorno-Karabakh's appeal for an administrative transfer to Armenia.[7] This refusal spurred Armenian nationalism and led to the rise of the Karabakh Committee which advocated Nagorno-Karabakh's unification with Armenia. The Soviet Autonomous Region of Nagorno-Karabakh represents, with an area of 4,388 square kilometres, only a part of the historical Nagorno-Karabakh, called by Armenians Artsakh. In 1988 Gorbachev replaced Karen Demirchyan with Suren Harutyunyan as First Secretary of the Armenian Communist Party (in office 1988–1990). Under pressure from the street and the Karabakh Committee, the Armenian Supreme Soviet voted on 15 June unanimously to unite Artsakh with Armenia, which was again vetoed by Gorbachev on 28 June. Nevertheless, the Nagorno-Karabakh Soviet defied Moscow and voted on 12 July to unilaterally secede from Azerbaijan, which move was for a third time rejected by Moscow. In the same month Gorbachev attempted to regain control of the tense situation and appointed Arkady Volsky representative of the Politburo in Nagorno-Karabakh, in other words governor. Whereas Nagorno-Karabakh remained formally part of Azerbaijan, the Autonomous Oblast was now directly ruled by Moscow via Volsky. Although Volsky imposed martial law in Stepanakert, fighting increased and ethnic cleansing spread which forced Volsky to extend martial law over the whole oblast.[8] Armenia's economy was additionally hit in December 1988 by a devastating earthquake which killed *ca.* 25,000 people and left hundreds of thousands homeless for the winter. Harutyunyan took advantage of the emergency situation to arrest the leaders of the Karabakh Committee, but was forced by popular pressure to release them on 31 May 1989; they then formed the Pan-Armenian National Movement (ANM) with Levon Ter-Petrosyan (b. 1945) as de facto leader. In 1989, an undeclared guerrilla war raged in Nagorno-Karabakh between Armenian and Azerbaijani paramilitary forces. On 22 August the National Council of Nagorno-Karabakh declared its secession from Azerbaijan and appealed to the United Nations for assistance whereupon the Azerbaijan Supreme Soviet abolished Nagorno-Karabakh's autonomous status. Azerbaijan increased pressure on 20 August by imposing an oil and gas boycott as well as a rail and road blockade on Armenia and Nagorno-Karabakh, against which Armenia later retaliated by cutting the Baku–Nakhchivan railway. To avoid famine in Nagorno-Karabakh, Moscow organized an airlift to Stepanakert which had to be escorted by Soviet fighter jets. This new airlift from Yerevan to Stepanakert further detached Nagorno-Karabakh from Azerbaijan.[9] Since direct administration of Nagorno-Karabakh from Moscow had failed to control events, it was replaced on 26 November by military rule headed by General Safonov with the objective of re-establishing Azerbaijani rule over Nagorno-Karabakh. The Armenian Supreme Soviet countered on 1 December by declaring Nagorno-Karabakh part of Armenia, as a result of which the Armenian Soviet was now in open rebellion against Moscow. Gorbachev responded by annulling Armenia's declaration on 10 January 1990.[10]

Several days later, on 13–14 January 1990, an anti-Armenian pogrom broke out in Baku followed by a Soviet military intervention (known as 'Black January', see also below). Most Armenians living in Baku were evacuated and their apartments and houses given to Azeri refugees. Meanwhile in Armenia the Communist Party was losing authority further. In May the non-Communist ANM won a majority in the Armenian Supreme Soviet and on 4 August Ter-Petrosyan was elected its chairman.[11] Strengthened by popular support, on 23 August Armenia officially declared its will to achieve independence and unification with Nagorno-Karabakh. In spring 1991 Gorbachev ordered Operation Ring, purportedly to disarm Armenian-Karabakh guerrillas, but in fact Soviet troops and Azerbaijani special police forces concentrated on deporting thousands of Armenians from their villages along the Armenian–Azerbaijani border and in Nagorno-Karabakh, an act which was branded by Ter-Petrosyan as a Soviet war operation against Armenia.[12] In early summer, Operation Ring did put the Nagorno-Karabakh Armenians under pressure to revisit their proclaimed plan for secession, but with the failed anti-Gorbachev putsch in August this Soviet–Azerbaijani pressure vanished. In the previous year, Ter-Petrosyan had countered Gorbachev's order to disarm all paramilitary forces by integrating them as the nucleus of the new Armenian national army. Thanks to Ter-Petrosyan's foresight and his anticipation that a full-scale war with Azerbaijan was looming over Nagorno-Karabakh, Armenia was better prepared when war broke out in 1992 than Azerbaijan which neglected to build up an army of its own and relied on the Soviet Union for military support almost till the USSR disappeared. When the Soviet armed forces disintegrated in 1991–1992, discipline vanished and troops stationed in Armenia and Azerbaijan either sold their arms (including artillery, GRAD multiple rocket launchers,[13] armoured personnel carriers and tanks) to the highest bidder or offered their combat services for hire as single fully armed units; indigenous Soviet soldiers simply deserted with their arms to join local militias.[14] This development transformed what had previously been a lightly armed conflict into a fully fledged war.

In spite of Ter-Petrosyan's dislike of Gorbachev, he forcefully condemned the reactionary putsch against the latter of 19–23 August 1991, the failed move which spelt the final doom of the USSR. On 21 September, 95 per cent of Armenian voters approved Armenia's independence from the USSR, and on 16 October they elected Ter-Petrosyan as the first president of the Republic of Armenia (in office 1991–1998). Nevertheless, Armenia was well aware that it needed close political, economic and military ties with Russia. For this reason on 21 December 1991 it signed the Alma-Ata Protocol which established the Commonwealth of Independent States (CIS), as did Azerbaijan; Georgia joined in 1993, but left again in 2008. As for Nagorno-Karabakh, its government declared independence on 2 September and on 10 December a popular referendum approved with a 99.9 per cent majority the independence of the Republic of Artsakh (in Armenian, Artsakhi Hanrapetutyun).[15] However, the sovereignty of Artsakh is not recognized by any UN member state, including Armenia, which means that it remains internationally viewed as part of Azerbaijan. Artsakh and Armenia refrained from proclaiming unification in order not to give Azerbaijan a pretext for attacking Armenia directly. In fact, the situation in Artsakh and Armenia anticipated the political construct of the second Albanian state of Kosovo imposed by NATO on Serbia in 1999,[16] but, to put it bluntly, Artsakh lacked a powerful sponsor to allow it to become a second Armenian state. Soviet troops and police forces withdrew from Artsakh in December–January 1991/92. In Armenia proper, the unfavourable economic situation in the 1990s led to a surge of emigration to Lebanon where the community of people of Armenian descent numbers some 200,000 to 250,000 individuals.[17]

3. The Azerbaijani declaration of independence and the development of the oil and gas industry

In Azerbaijan, Gorbachev replaced First Secretary Kamran Baghirov (Bağirov, in office 1982–1988) with Abdurrahman Vazirov (Əbdürrəhman Vəzirov, in office 1988–1990) at the same time as dismissing Demirchyan in Armenia. A native of Nagorno-Karabakh, Vazirov failed to control events there. Besides the Nagorno-Karabakh conflict, another crisis erupted in December 1989 in Nakhchivan and Lankaran along the Azerbaijani–Iranian border when activists supported by the radical pan-Turkic Azerbaijani Popular Front Party (APF), founded by Abulfaz Aliyev aka Elchibey, attacked Soviet border posts and demanded the unification of Soviet and Iranian Azerbaijan. Soviet MVD (Ministry of Interior) troops restored order in January 1990.[18] A turning point in Azerbaijan's relations with the USSR occurred with the attacks on Armenian residents in Baku by a violent mob strengthened by Azeri refugees on 13–14 January 1990. While the Azerbaijani police remained passive, the Presidium of the Supreme Soviet of the USSR imposed a state of emergency on Baku on 15 January and organized the evacuation of 200,000 Armenians to Yerevan or across the Caspian Sea to Krasnovodsk. Exploiting the inactivity of the police and the Azerbaijani government's inertia, guerrilla groups of the APF blocked major roads with barricades and took control of Baku, as a result of which Gorbachev and the Presidium became convinced that Azerbaijan's Communist Party was losing control and that the APF would seize power. About 17,000 troops were mobilized and in the night of 20 January tanks and armoured vehicles entered Baku smashing the barricades. According to official figures some 133 civilians and 20 Soviet soldiers were killed, and hundreds of protesting civilians were wounded during 'Black January'.[19] From now on, most Azerbaijanis viewed the USSR as a hostile power. The demarcation from the former Soviet rule was visualized in the construction of the huge memorial besides the Martyr's Cemetery in 2010 (fig. 132). Indignation concerning the Soviet intervention was so great that the Nakchivan ASSR not only proclaimed on 20 January its intention to secede from the USSR but also appealed for Turkish support. For the next three years, Nakhchivan remained virtually independent from Baku. In November 1990, Heydar Aliyev began his comeback when he was elected to the Supreme Soviet of Nakhchivan, becoming its chairman in December 1991 after having resigned from the Communist Party. In this capacity he conducted independent diplomatic relations with Turkey and Iran;[20] the latter appreciated his open political stance as a counterweight to President Elchibey's rabid anti-Iranianism. Also on 20 January 1990, the inefficient First Secretary Vazirov was replaced by Ayaz Mutallibov (Mütəllibov) who in May became the first president of Azerbaijan (in office 1990–1992).

Resentment over the Azeri death toll from Black January manifested itself in the widespread de-Russification of personal names by dropping the suffix '-ov' (whereby Gambarov became Gambar, etc.) and in the return to previous traditional place names, so for example Kirovabad reverted to Ganja.[21] In view of the increasing popularity of the APF, President Mutallibov quickly adopted a nationalistic stance and requested a substantial increase on the very low price the Soviet Union paid for Azerbaijani oil (which was then resold abroad after refinement at a huge profit). Nevertheless, Mutallibov continued to rely on Moscow to solve Azerbaijan's problems in Nagorno-Karabakh and only agreed to create a national army after the anti-Gorbachev putsch. Driven by events, Mutallibov and Azerbaijan's Supreme Soviet announced on 30 August their will to restore independence, which was accomplished on 18 October. A referendum held on 29 December 1991 approved Azerbaijan's independence with a 95 per cent majority.[22] Meanwhile Elchibey's APF not only declared the unification of independent Soviet Azerbaijan with Iranian Azerbaijan as a long-term goal but also the establishment of a Turkish–Azerbaijani Confederation.[23] A few weeks after the referendum a major crisis emerged when Armenian irregulars, reinforced by units of the 366th ex-Soviet Motor Rifle Regiment, began an offensive to expand Armenian-controlled territory in Nagorno-Karabakh. Its first target was the Azerbaijani-populated town of Khojaly (Xocalı), which controlled Stepanakert's airport and from where missiles were fired on Artsakh's capital. Although the Armenian fighters warned the people of Khojaly of an impending attack and advised them to leave the city, its Security Council decided against an evacuation of the remaining 3,000 inhabitants. On 25–26 February 1992, almost the anniversary

133. Offshore oil rig platform standing in the Azerbaijani sector of the Caspian Sea. Photo 2013.

of the Sumgait massacre, the Armenians attacked Khojaly and destroyed its defences. The town was cleared of its population whereupon Armenian irregulars opened fire on the fugitives, killing about 500 civilians. The massacre created a shock among the Azeri population both in and outside Nagorno-Karabakh, which was probably the intention: wherever Armenian-Karabakh troops later advanced, Azerbaijani civilians would flee before their arrival for fear of being massacred.[24] The APF subsequently denounced President Mutallibov as the culprit for the Khojaly disaster since he had deliberately torpedoed the creation of a national army. Mutallibov resigned on 6 March and a presidential election was scheduled for 7 June. When a group in parliament reinstated Mutallibov on 14 May, Elchibey and Iskender Hamidov (İsgəndər Həmidov), leader of the APF's well-armed militia and of the far-right Bozkurt (Grey Wolf) organization, occupied parliament on the next day. Mutallibov fled to Moscow and Elchibey was elected president with 59 per cent of the vote, nominating Hamidov as interior minister.[25] Elchibey's political strategy, pan-Turkic and anti-Russian as well as anti-Iranian, became self-defeating when he applied pan-Turkic rhetoric to foreign policy. He withdrew Azerbaijan from the CIS, which drew Moscow and Yerevan closer to each other. The result of this rapprochement was highlighted by Russia's deployment of an aircraft defence system around Stepanakert and additional arms shipments. Furthermore, Elchibey's anti-Iranian polemic angered Tehran which retaliated by saying that both Azerbaijans should indeed be reunited – but within Iran, since Iranian Azerbaijan was double the size of the former Soviet Azerbaijan and the latter had belonged to Iran till the Russian aggression of the 1820s–1830s.[26] Elchibey's antagonistic rhetoric motivated Tehran to assist Armenia by supplying food and energy to Azerbaijan's main adversary. Finally, his missionary-like pan-Turkism embarrassed even Turkey which for geopolitical reasons was keen to maintain stable relations with Moscow and Iran. Turkey was well aware that Russia could counter any excessive Turkish assistance of Azerbaijan in the war over Nagorno-Karabakh by supporting the militant Kurdistan Workers' Party (PKK). In addition Turkey's NATO membership did not allow for pan-Turkic adventures. To summarize, Elchibey utterly failed to develop sustainable foreign relations for Azerbaijan. Although Azerbaijan's counteroffensive in Nagorno-Karabakh in summer 1992 initially scored some successes, Elchibey's war strategy failed as well. The counteroffensive was not really conducted by the national army, but by three semi-private armed formations, namely those of the interior minister Hamidov, of Yagub Mammadov (Yaqub Məmmədov) and of Surat Huseynov (Surət Hüseynov) who commanded several thousand soldiers and Russian mercenaries and recaptured the town of Martakert. But when in March–April 1993 Huseynov's passive attitude allowed the Armenian spring offensive to occupy the Azerbaijani district of Kalbajar (Kəlbəcər), President Elchibey accused him of collusion with Moscow and stripped him of his command in northern Nagorno-Karabakh. Furious, Huseynov removed his private army including its heavy artillery to his home base of Ganja where he acquired additional Russian armoury from the 104th airborne regiment.

The fact that Huseynov could so easily obtain this armoury strongly supports the suspicion that Moscow intended to provide him with the means to topple Elchibey, which he did in early June 1993. After governmental troops had failed to retake the rebellious Ganja, Huseynov ordered his force to seize Baku. In desperation, Elchibey asked Heydar Aliyev, the president of Nakhchivan, to help with mastering the crisis and prevent Huseynov from seizing power. On 10 June Aliyev arrived in Baku and was nominated speaker of parliament. Elchibey fled to Nakhchivan on 18 June and Huseynov's forces seized Baku on the 23rd. On the next day, parliament nominated Aliyev as acting president, who appointed, as a compromise, the warlord Huseynov as prime minister and defence minister. As the journalist Thomas Goltz succinctly remarked, 'Surat Huseynov had just been given a long, oily rope with which to hang himself', since Aliyev anticipated that Huseynov would not be up to the task.[27] Heydar Aliyev was elected president on 3 October. Dissatisfied with his position as subservient to Aliyev, one year later on 4 October 1994 Huseynov attempted to stage a *coup d'état* in Aliyev's absence, which was suppressed the next day. Huseynov fled to Moscow but was extradited to Baku in 1997 where he was sentenced to life imprisonment (he was pardoned in 2004).[28] Six months later, in mid-March 1995, Aliyev faced another putsch attempt, by Colonel Rovshan Javadov (Rövşən Cavadov), leader of the OPON Military Police, along with a number of military officers. Its objective was to remove or kill Aliyev and to reinstall Elchibey in the presidency. An incendiary aspect of this planned coup was the involvement of members of Turkish National Intelligence (MİT) and the Turkish embassy in Baku. Close associates of Turkey's prime minister Tansu Çiller (in office 1993–1996) and the prime minister herself were apparently also involved. Aliyev escaped the conspiracy only because Turkish Intelligence had detected the plot and informed the Turkish president Süleyman Demirel who immediately warned Aliyev. The regular army crushed the rebels on 17 March.[29] Demirel's warning salvaged Azerbaijani–Turkish relations, but the plot confirmed Aliyev's conviction that he needed to move closer to the West, and above all the USA. After the failed Javadov putsch and the disbanding of the private militias, Aliyev's authority was rarely challenged and Azerbaijan became stable. In November 1995, Aliyev secured his power through a constitutional referendum which defined Azerbaijan as a presidential republic with far-reaching powers for the incumbent.[30] Elchibey's Turkification efforts had also alienated non-Turkic Azerbaijani peoples such as the Lezgins who had been separated by the new national border with Russia from their kin in Dagestan, to which they would prefer to belong. And when turmoil broke out in June 1993 in Baku, the Talish nationalist, Colonel Alikram Gumbatov (Hummatov) proclaimed the short-lived Talysh-Mughan Autonomous Republic in Lankaran.[31] Heydar Aliyev's resolute intervention and termination of the Turkification policy defused tensions in both potential trouble spots.

Aliyev's two main objectives were to reduce Azerbaijan's economic dependence on Russia by securing new markets for Azerbaijani oil and gas, and to end the disastrous Nagorno-Karabakh War. In 1994, he set the course to ensure the long-term economic independence of Azerbaijan. He understood that neither the US nor any major European state would jeopardize its relations with Russia on account of a new small state located within Russia's 'Near Abroad';[32] Western powers would only get involved in the South Caucasus if they obtained long-term benefits. Oil, and later gas, was the only foreign-policy leverage Azerbaijan possessed.[33] Aliyev skilfully used fossil fuels to tie various states and economic groups to Azerbaijan, giving them a vested interest in the stability of his country. This oil strategy ensured significant foreign investments and the diversification of transportation routes of crude oil, in other words pipelines. Azerbaijan signed the so-called 'Contract of the Century' concerning the exploitation of the Azeri, Chirag, and the Azerbaijani part of the Gunashli off-shore oilfields (ACG) on 20 September 1994.[34] The contract, worth $7.4 billion and sharing production for thirty years, involved eleven international oil companies, namely the Azerbaijani State Oil Company SOCAR (20%), the project operator BP (17.1%), Amoco (17%), Lukoil (10%), Penzoil (9.8%), Unocal (9.5%), Statoil (8.6%), McDermott (2.5%), Ramko (2.1%) Turkish Petroleum TPAO (1.8%), and Delta (1.6%) from seven countries (Azerbaijan, USA, Great Britain, Russia, Turkey, Norway and Saudi Arabia). The oil reserves of the three fields are evaluated at 1.07 billion tons of crude oil.[35] The contract was followed by 26 additional agreements with 41 oil companies from 19 countries.[36]

Aliyev made a point of including the Russian Lukoil in the deal in order to mollify Russian apprehensions; by this move, he gained the Russian energy-interest groups as allies against Russia's Foreign Ministry which opposed the contract.[37] Furthermore, insofar as Russian Lukoil had access to the Caspian ACG fields and would transport Caspian oil through the Baku–Grozny–Novorossiysk (BGN) pipeline, Russia had to indirectly recognize Azerbaijan's claim to ACG in spite of the fact that no agreements among the Caspian littoral states had yet been achieved regarding oil and gas exploitation. Aliyev's move paved the way for the three agreements between Azerbaijan, Russia and Kazakhstan on the exploitation of the northern and central sectors of the Caspian Sea, signed in 2001, 2002 and 2003. They delimited 64 per cent of the Caspian seabed (with its fossil fuel reserves), assigning 18 per cent to Azerbaijan, 19 per cent to Russia and to Kazakhstan 27 per cent. On the other hand, the water and its surface were declared common property and it remained prohibited for ships to sail under the flag of non-Caspian states.[38] Originally Aliyev wanted to grant Iran a 5 per cent share in the ACG project, but the US forced him to recant his promise to Iran. To alleviate the consequences of the rigid US trade embargo, Washington granted Azerbaijan (as well as Kazakhstan and Turkmenistan) an exemption allowing for oil swaps with Iran.[39] Nevertheless in retaliation, in the controversial question of how to divide the fossil fuel resources under the Caspian Sea among the five riparian states, Iran adopted the Russian position which is disadvantageous to Azerbaijan.[40] As a side effect, the contract motivated Russia to launch the First Chechen War in December 1994 in order to regain control of the Chechen section of the Baku–Novorossiysk oil pipeline.[41] Following Russia's defeat in the war, a bypass circumventing Chechnya in the north had to be built, due to Azerbaijani pressure. The offer by the Russian pipeline company Transneft of an oil-swap arrangement was unacceptable to Azerbaijan, since Russian Ural crude oil was of lower quality than ACG crude.[42]

In the formulation of the Caucasus specialist Svante Cornell, 'the Western investments in oil cut the proverbial umbilical cord that had tied Azerbaijan's economy and politics to Moscow.'[43] By acquiring major foreign investors Aliyev increased Azerbaijan's security, and six days after signing the contract Heydar Aliyev met President Bill Clinton. By involving major American oil companies in Azerbaijan's oil business, Aliyev gained direct access to Washington.[44] Otherwise, Aliyev took care in 1994/95 to follow a balanced strategy in foreign policy, applying for membership neither to NATO nor to OPEC and refusing to allow

Map 10. Main gas and oil pipelines in the Caucasus

INDEPENDENCE IN THE SOUTH CAUCASUS | 257

134. The mosque in Nardaran on the Absheron Peninsula is said to stand over the tomb of Rahima Khanim, a sister of the eighth Shiite Imam 'Ali ibn Musa al-Rida (d. 818). The mosque and the small city are a stronghold of devout Shiites and since the riots of 2002, 2006 and 2015 have been under police observation. Baku District, Azerbaijan. Photo 2016.

foreign troops on Azerbaijani territory. Aliyev wanted to avoid dependence not only on oil customers but also on oil carriers. Like the Central Asian energy suppliers Kazakhstan and Turkmenistan, Azerbaijan suffers from the major competitive disadvantage of being virtually landlocked and thus being reliant on pipelines.[45] Aliyev's strategy accorded with the American and European wish for 'pipeline diversity' in order to bypass and thus contain Russia which in the earlier 1990s still commanded a virtual pipeline monopoly for Caucasian and Central Asian fuels. Azerbaijan wanted an alternative to the BGN pipeline not only to reduce its dependence on Russia, but also because Russia mixed lower-grade Ural oil into the high-quality ACG crude.[46] However, the matter was further complicated by the Azerbaijan–Armenian War and the American embargo on Iran which forbade a pipeline through Iran to the Persian Gulf. Azerbaijan remained potentially blocked by Russia, the US–Iran conflict and the war with Armenia.

In the end, Azerbaijan decided on seven transport solutions:

1. The Russian Baku–Grozny–Novorossiysk (BGN) oil pipeline.

2. Temporary oil swaps with Iran.

3. The Baku–Tbilisi–Supsa (BTS) oil pipeline (start 1999) which links Baku with the Black Sea. It replaced the ancient Baku–Batumi oil pipeline which had been dismantled in 1942 when the German Wehrmacht threatened the South Caucasus. Its capacity is limited by the Bosporus bottleneck since Turkey has for ecological and safety reasons severely restricted the amount of oil allowed to pass through the straits.[47]

4. The 1,768 km-long Baku–Tbilisi–Ceyhan (BTC) oil pipeline (start 2006) leading to the north-eastern tip of the Mediterranean Sea. A preliminary agreement with Turkey had already been concluded in March 1993, but Heydar Aliyev cancelled all contracts made by the Elchibey government. In return, Turkey severely limited oil tanker transit through the straits and lobbied among US oil multinationals and the US government for a pipeline passing through Turkey rather than Russia or Iran. The BTC contract was finally signed in November 1999. President Aliyev was so concerned about Russian punitive measures in retaliation for his concluding the BTC contract that in January 1999 he offered NATO a base on the Absheron Peninsula. Not wanting to involve NATO in the Caspian region, which would be perceived by Russia as a provocation, the US turned the offer down.[48] The capacity of the Ceyhan terminal is three times larger than that of the Novorossiysk terminal.[49] The BTC pipeline as well as the BTE gas pipeline (see below) resulted from a close cooperation between Azerbaijan, Georgia and Turkey, where each country possesses a leverage over the other two: Azerbaijan has the resources but no access to world markets except via Russia; Georgia has a transit corridor and Black Sea ports but no resources; and Turkey has access to world markets, especially Europe, but no resources. Thus the cooperation is highly beneficial to all three partners.

5. The Baku–Tbilisi–Erzurum (BTE) gas pipeline (start 2006) transporting gas from the Shah Deniz Caspian Sea field by way of the Azerbaijani Sangachal natural gas processing and oil production plant.[50] BTE is linked to the Trans-Anatolian Pipeline (TANAP, start 2018) which connects to the Trans-Adriatic Pipeline (TAP, start 2020) ending in Southern Italy. BTE, TANAP and TAP form the 3500-km Southern Gas Corridor.[51] The BTC and BTE pipelines elevated Georgia to the status of a key energy corridor for Turkey and Europe and made the country independent from Russian energy dependence. In this respect Georgia benefits from the Armenian–Azerbaijani conflict and the US sanctions against Iran which made a pipeline from Azerbaijan via Iran to the Persian Gulf impossible. The discovery of the huge Shah Deniz gas field and its increasing output led Azerbaijan to lose interest in a planned Trans-Caspian Gas (TCG) pipeline carrying gas from Turkmenistan to Baku since Turkmen gas would be in competition with Azerbaijani gas. Whereas Turkmenistan was only prepared to concede Azerbaijan some 17 per cent of the planned TCG pipeline, Azerbaijan demanded half, whereupon the TCG project was cancelled.[52] By the early 2020s, gas production from Shah Deniz was eventually able to fill the BTE pipeline to its full capacity.[53]

6. As of 2010, Azerbaijan exports gas to Russia via the Baku–Novo Filya (BNF) pipeline. The export of gas to Russia via Novo Filya in Dagestan not only followed a geopolitical requirement, it also served as a lever against Turkey which insisted on purchasing Azerbaijani gas at a heavy discount

in order to resell it to Europe at world market prices. In the end, Azerbaijan succeeded in reducing the discount granted to Turkey.[54] The Azeri–Chirag–Gunashvili (ACG) Agreement was renewed on 14 September 2017 with the following stakeholders: the operator BP (30.37%), SOCAR (25%), Chevron (9.57%), Inpex (9.31%), Statoil (7.27%), ExxonMobil (6.79%), TPAO (5.73%), Itochu Japan (3.65%), ONGC India (2.31%).[55] The contract runs till 2049. In 2020 Chevron sold its share in the ACG consortium to MOL Hungarian Oil and Gas PLC.

7. The Baku–Tbilisi–Kars (BTK) railway line (operational start 2017) bypassing Armenia, which gave Azerbaijan a direct rail connection with Turkey and further isolated Armenia. The railway can carry both crude oil and liquefied gas (LNG).

Other important Caucasian pipelines are TurkStream (start 2020), carrying gas from Anapa via the bottom of the Black Sea to Kıyıköy north-west of Istanbul, and the Mozdok–Tbilisi–Yerevan (MTY) gas pipeline.[56] In conclusion, Azerbaijan succeeded in breaking free from Russia's grip by independently developing and exploiting its off-shore oil and gas fields and by transporting the major part of its exported hydrocarbons bypassing Russia.

The BTC pipeline also allowed Azerbaijan to strengthen and expand its diplomatic and economic relations with Israel which had recognized Baku's independence as early as 25 December 1991. Israeli–Azerbaijani cooperation is based on mutual essential needs in the fields of energy and defence. According to the *Jerusalem Post* of 16 November 2018,[57] Baku supplies about 40 per cent of Israel's oil and is the third-largest importer of Israeli arms behind India and Vietnam.[58] The more recent Azerbaijani arms purchases include sophisticated anti-aircraft missile systems and anti-tank combat drones.[59] Moreover, in 2011 the government-controlled Azerbaijani defence corporation Azad Systems began the production of military Unmanned Aerial Systems – that is, drones – as a joint venture with the Israeli company Aeronautics Defence Systems.[60] Furthermore, in 2021 Azerbaijan also acquired the Israeli Iron Dome missile defence system.[61]

According to *Haaretz*, dated 30 September 2012, Azerbaijan and Israel evaluated allowing Israeli warplanes to use Azerbaijani airbases.[62] Certainly Heydar Aliyev and his son and successor Ilham Aliyev (İlham Əliyev, in office 2003–) were masters at turning Azerbaijan's assets to strategic advantage. In terms of religious policy, Azerbaijan is a determined secular state with secular education whereas 85 per cent of its population are Shia Muslims, as in Iran.[63] In Azerbaijan, Shiites and Sunnis live peacefully together and often pray together in the mosque, which is a positive contrast to Christian Georgia where the Georgian Church called on its believers to boycott joint services and prayers with the Catholic pope on the occasion of Pope John Paul II's visit to Tbilisi in 1999. The Georgian Church repeated its boycott call in 2016 when Pope Francis visited Tbilisi.[64] When the Islamic Party, founded in 1991 in Nardaran and financed by Iran, adopted a pro-Iran, pro-Hezbollah and anti-US policy, Heydar Aliyev banned it in 1995. Rioting in Nardaran in the years 2002, 2006 and 2015, possibly caused by social discontent over local living conditions, was swiftly supressed.[65] By establishing his son as successor, Heydar Aliyev turned Azerbaijan into a quasi-monarchy where parliament is dominated by the ruling Yeni Azərbaycan Partiyası (New Azerbaijan Party).

4. The First Nagorno-Karabakh War 1992–1994

Following the independence referendum of the Republic of Artsakh and the painful Operation Ring, the Nagorno-Karabakh Armenians regained the initiative early in 1992 by capturing Khojaly, which gave Nagorno-Karabakh control of its only airport and ended the shelling of Stepanakert. The Nagorno-Karabakh army numbered *ca.* 35,000–40,000 fighters, about a quarter of them irregular volunteers with some Russian mercenaries, while the bulk of the Armenian army guarded the Armenian–Turkish border to prevent a Turkish attack. From the Armenian point of view, the worst-case scenario was a joint Azerbaijani–Turkish attack as Turkey could muster an army of half a million men. However, as a member of CIS, Armenia could count on Russian support should Turkey attack. In fact, Marshal Yevgeny Shaposhnikov, commander-in-chief of the joint armed forces of the CIS, warned in May 1992 that a Turkish attack would provoke a Russian response and could ignite a third world war (since Turkey was a NATO member).[66] The Azerbaijani army numbered around 45,000–50,000 men; it was a patchwork of national forces, private armies like those of Huseynov and Hamidov, Turkish officers, some Russian mercenaries, Chechen volunteers and, especially in 1993/94, Afghan and Arab Afghanistan veterans. In terms of tanks and artillery the Armenians were outgunned two

135. The Armenian Dadivank Monastery built between the ninth and the thirteenth century. During the First Nagorno-Karabakh War the monastery came under the control of the self-declared Republic of Artsakh; it returned to Azerbaijani control after the Second Nagorno-Karabakh War which ended on 10 November 2020. At present, a member of the Christian Caucasian Albanian Udi community has been named preacher at Dadivank. Kalbajar District, Azerbaijan.

to one, in helicopters three to one and in warplanes twenty to one. What the Nagorno-Karabakh Armenians lacked in weaponry they compensated for in fighting motivation. For the Armenians, the struggle for Nagorno-Karabakh represented a fight for their national identity and pride, whereas the average Azerbaijani attached less significance to Nagorno-Karabakh.[67] Unlike the Armenian troops who had mostly served in regular Soviet combat units, Azerbaijanis had often been relegated to auxiliary functions and lacked proper combat training.

After Khojaly the Nagorno-Karabakh Armenians next captured the strategically important city of Shushi (Şuşa) which had been defended by the notorious Chechen commander Shamil Basayev and a few hundred Chechen fighters, among them possibly the Saudi Wahhabi and future terrorist Ibn al-Khattab. Chechen fighters were also posted behind Azeri troops to shoot retreating soldiers and deserters.[68] Shushi fell on 9 May 1992; ten days later, on 18–19 May, the Armenians sized the town of Lachin (Laçın) which was of the utmost strategic importance since it commanded the Lachin Corridor linking Armenia with Shushi and Stepanakert; this road link had been closed for more than two years. The Kurdish population of Lachin was deported to Azerbaijan. In June, regular Azeri units and troops led by the warlord Huseynov, who had recruited Afghan mujahidin and Russian mercenaries driving Russian tanks, launched a successful counteroffensive which recaptured two-fifths of Nagorno-Karabakh. Armenia asked for Russian help and the Azerbaijani advance was stopped by attack helicopters piloted by Russian crews. As a response, Azerbaijani war planes and bombers piloted by Russian and Ukrainian mercenaries bombed Stepanakert. Russia then put a stop to these attacks by installing an aircraft defence system in the city.[69] To strengthen Nagorno-Karabakh's defence, a State Defence Committee was put into place in August headed by Robert Kocharyan and later Serzh Sargsyan, the future second and third presidents of Armenia, which declared a partial mobilization. The peace initiative spearheaded by the Minsk Group of the OSCE (Organization for Security and Co-operation in Europe) was unsuccessful, since Russia vetoed the stationing of a multinational NATO peacekeeping force.[70] The Minsk Group was ineffective since its delegates were often second-rank diplomats lacking knowledge of the conflict and because the Nagorno-Karabakh War became embedded in the rivalry between Washington and Moscow. In Ter-Petrosyan's words 'the mediating countries and international organisations are not interested so much in settling the conflict, as in settling their own accounts ..., which are unconnected with it.'[71] In winter 1992–93 no major operation took place, especially since Armenia and Nagorno-Karabakh had to save fuel for domestic heating. Having no fossil fuel source, Armenia is highly dependent on the north–south Mozdok–Tbilisi–Yerevan (MTY) gas pipeline, which is however vulnerable to North- and South Ossetian sabotage. Its operation is furthermore unpredictable due to Georgia's poor relations with Russia and Azerbaijan's attempts to become a shareholder of the pipeline by purchasing the segment of the pipeline owned by Georgia.[72] Should Azerbaijan become a co-owner of the MTY pipeline, it could interrupt Armenia's supply. When the MTY pipeline is closed, Russia delivers energy via the low-capacity Tabriz–Meghri–Kajaran gas pipeline which is operated by the Russian energy corporation Gazprom.[73]

In early 1993 Armenia launched a major counterattack to recapture its losses from the previous summer. This culminated on 3 April with the seizure of Kalbajar near the Armenian border which gave Nagorno-Karabakh a second road link with Armenia. The local Azeri and Kurdish population was expelled and the district repopulated with Armenians. Exploiting the leadership crisis in Azerbaijan, Armenian-Karabakh forces continued their advance almost unhindered and captured the towns of Martakert (Aghdara/Ağdərə, 27 June) in the north, Aghdam (Ağdam, 23 July) in the east and in the south Füzuli and Jebrayil (Cəbrayıl, 23 August). Within five months, Azerbaijan lost not only northern Nagorno-Karabakh but also five Azeri districts outside Nagorno-Karabakh, in total almost 5,000 square kilometres.[74] In view of the Armenian conquests Turkey's prime minister Çiller warned Armenia not to attack Nakhchivan and requested Armenia's withdrawal from Azerbaijani territory. Iran also threatened to intervene should Armenia continue its advance.[75] Since Russian troops were guarding the Armenian–Turkish border, however, Turkey did not dare to attack. In this desperate military situation, in summer 1993 Heydar Aliyev and Rovshan Javadov asked Gulbuddin Hekmatyar, the Afghan prime minister and leader of the Afghan militia Hezb-e Islami, for permission to hire Afghan fighters, who were paid for by Saudi Arabia.[76] About 1,500 to 2,000 Afghan mercenaries fought for Azerbaijan in 1993–1994, but while their fighting spirit was praised, violent clashes soon arose between the Sunni mujahidin and the Shia Azeris concerning the latter's alleged failure to observe Quranic precepts. Further deadly clashes occurred between the mujahidin and Azeri soldiers who had fought in Afghanistan on the Soviet side, between Afghan Muslim and Slavic mercenaries employed in Azeri service and even between Afghans from different tribes. However, the lease of mujahidin mercenaries paid off for Hekmatyar since they not only brought in cash, but also opened up the Azerbaijani market to Afghan heroin exports. After the end of the war, some Afghans settled in Azerbaijan where they founded *soi-disant* 'Islamic charity organizations' that coordinated military and financial supplies from Turkey to Chechnya during the Chechen wars.[77] In January 1994, the Afghan–Azeri forces succeeded in recovering some territory, but failed to reconquer the cities of Kalbajar and Füzuli. In view of the heavy losses suffered in the previous unsuccessful offensive, Azerbaijan sought a truce to which Armenia, which had successfully defended its territorial gains, agreed. Russia mediated a ceasefire which took effect at midnight on 11–12 May 1994. Although Heydar Aliyev vetoed the stationing of Russian or CIS peacekeeping forces on Azerbaijani soil, the ceasefire was indefinitely confirmed on 26 July.[78] In spite of several violations of the truce, the ceasefire held for 26 years till the start of the Second Nagorno-Karabakh War on 27 September 2020. Beginning in 1992, all Azerbaijani citizens were forced to leave Artsakh and the other seven districts fully or partly occupied by Armenian forces, creating some 450,000 to 500,000 additional Azerbaijani refugees.[79] At the same time, the population of Artsakh declined from 189,000 in 1989 to 138,000 in 2005.[80] Including Nagorno-Karabakh, Azerbaijan had lost almost 14 per cent of its territory and 10 per cent of its population were internal refugees.[81]

In the following years, various solutions were explored to end the conflict. A major stumbling block was the tactical approach to the negotiations: whereas Azerbaijan insisted on a step-by-step approach whereby Armenia should surrender the seven occupied districts and allow Azeri refugees to return to their homes prior to the real negotiation over the status of Nagorno-Karabakh, Armenia remained adamant that it would keep control of all occupied territories until a comprehensive solution had been reached. Armenia's insistence on a comprehensive and final settlement also stems from its past experiences that international guarantees, such as the Sèvres Peace Treaty, have often been absolutely worthless. Armenia also categorically rejected any plan which would re-establish Azerbaijani sovereignty over Artsakh. As an alternative, territorial exchanges were evaluated whereby Armenia would keep Artsakh and the Lachin Corridor but would return the occupied districts and cede a land corridor in Zangezur linking Azerbaijan to Nakhchivan; but this latter swap would have deprived Armenia of its border with friendly Iran and made it dependent on hostile Turkey and Azerbaijan. The exchange proposals were soon dropped. After the failure of the OSCE's efforts in 1996 and 1997, a kind of palace revolt took place in Armenia, led by the Armenian defence minister Vazgen Sargsyan, who also commanded the powerful veterans' organization Yerkrapah, the former president of Artsakh and now prime minister of Armenia Robert Kocharyan (in office

136. The cathedral of St Grigor the Illuminator in Yerevan was consecrated on 23 September 2001. On the left is an equestrian statue dedicated to General Andranik (1865–1927). Yerevan, Armenia. Photo 2017.

1997–1998) and the interior and security minister Serzh Sargsyan, forcing President Ter-Petrosyan to resign in February 1998.[82] Unlike the three 'rebel' ministers, he was prepared to accept a step-by-step approach to peace negotiations and valued the long-term national interests of Armenia more highly than those of Nagorno-Karabakh. Armenia's economic situation was disastrous and dependent on remittances from expatriates and the worldwide Armenian diaspora. Furthermore, since 1991 hundreds of thousands of well-educated, mainly male Armenians had left the country, leading to a technological brain drain. He also believed that Armenia's bargaining position would weaken over time as Azerbaijan would invest its oil revenues in defence. After Ter-Petrosyan's resignation, Kocharyan became president (in office 1998–2008) and Armen Darbinyan prime minister (in office 1998–1999). Since Kocharyan and both Sargsyans were hardliners, the political interests of Nagorno-Karabakh outweighed those of Armenia proper.

Nevertheless, in April 1999, presidents Kocharyan and Aliyev opened direct and secret negotiations under US auspices. They resumed discussions about territorial exchanges whereby Armenia would gain Artsakh and Lachin, and Azerbaijan the occupied districts and the Meghri region in the southernmost part of Zangezur. When Aliyev's foreign minister was informed about the plan, he resigned on 24 October. But Aliyev rated the restoration of Azerbaijan's unity and a land bridge with Turkey more highly than renewed control over the troublesome and poor province of Nagorno-Karabakh. Three days later, on the 27th, immediately after a visit by US deputy secretary of state Strobe Talbot to Baku and Yerevan, five killers stormed Armenia's parliament and murdered Prime Minister Vazgen Sargsyan (in office 11 June–27 October 1999), the speaker Karen Demirchyan and six other MPs. The planned land deal was dead; it had many adversaries. Azerbaijani and Armenian hardliners rejected any territorial compromise. Iran also disapproved of a land bridge between Azerbaijan and Turkey and the loss of the Tehran–Yerevan–Moscow axis. Finally, Moscow could not tolerate a US-sponsored peace deal within its Near Abroad and feared that the reform-minded prime minister Sargsyan and speaker Demirchyan would reorient Armenia towards the United States. According to the former FSB (Russian Federal Security Service) agent Aleksandr Litvinenko, probably murdered in 2006 by the FSB, the assassination of Sargsyan and Demirchyan was masterminded by Russia's GRU (Foreign Military Intelligence) 'to prevent the signing of the agreement on Karabakh settlement'.[83] While Litvinenko produced no

137. The 25-m-high Mother of Georgia statue stands on the top of the Sololaki Hill overlooking Tbilisi. Built in 1958, the statue holds in her left hand a cup filled with wine to welcome friendly guests and in her right a massive sword to frighten off enemies. Tbilisi, Georgia. Photo 2013.

evidence for his claim, Russia would probably have been the loser in a reconciliation between Armenia, Azerbaijan and the NATO member, Turkey. As a consequence of the 1999 killings, the leaders of Armenia and Azerbaijan would from now on refrain from considering territorial exchanges. One year before his death, Heydar Aliyev made a last attempt to unblock the deadlocked conflict by offering to normalize economic relations in return for Armenia's handing back four of the occupied districts.[84] President Kocharyan refused to even discuss the proposal, at which Ilham Aliyev concluded that Armenia was not interested in a negotiated peace and would continue to play for time forever. He became convinced that the territorial integrity of Azerbaijan could only be restored by military means. Azerbaijan therefore systematically invested in its army, purchasing state-of-the-art weaponry. In the event, Ilham Aliyev had to wait seventeen years before realizing part of his objective. As for Armenia, its geographical, political and economic constraints are so limiting that the republic has no other option than to pursue the patronage of Russia as its protector.

There is another group which benefited from Armenia's landlocked geography and economic blockade by Turkey and Azerbaijan, namely those Armenian oligarchs who, via cartels, control the import and export of commodities. These groups are a continuation of the black market of Soviet times. They have privileged access to governmental ministries, are in collusion with tax and customs authorities and control the limited options for importing and, to a lesser degree, exporting consumer goods. These commodity-based cartels exploit the lack of open borders to establish monopolies that can dictate prices.[85] The same groups also assured the supply of commodities and logistics to Artsakh, which prior to 1988 had been supplied solely by Azerbaijan. As of 2003, some oligarchs entered parliament in order to secure immunity for themselves.[86] Since the preconditions for the oligarchic cartels were rooted in the Nagorno-Karabakh War and the resulting Turkish–Azerbaijani economic blockade, these groups had no interest in ending the war and much preferred the 'neither war nor peace' status quo, in other words playing indefinitely for time. As far as the Republic of Artsakh is concerned, it had virtually become an Armenian province as its inhabitants were given Armenian passports, its currency was the Armenian dram and its budget was met by Yerevan. On the other hand, Artsakh had no access to the United Nations and its numerous organizations and was internationally viewed like a pariah, similarly to Chechnya.

5. Georgian independence and the South Ossetian and Abkhazian wars

Georgia, on the eve of its renewed independence, found itself in a similar situation to Russia, albeit on a much smaller scale. It was a multi-ethnic state with a high potential for internal antagonisms, not least because many Georgians were ardent nationalists. Not only were there living in the Georgian SSSR native Georgians (70%), Armenians (8%), Russians (6%), Azeris (6%), Ossetians (3%), Abkhaz (3%) and Greek (2%), but there existed also three specific ethnic territories, namely the Abkhaz ASSR, the Adjarian ASSR[87] and the South Ossetian AO, all of which in the 1910s and 1920s had a fraught history with Tbilisi.[88] In Abkhazia the situation was especially tense, for the Abkhaz accounted for only 18 per cent of its population compared to 46 per cent Georgians (Kartvelians and Mingrelians).[89] The Abkhaz resented the pressure from Georgian immigration while the Georgians begrudged the Abkhazian minority their political and economic privileges. When First Secretary Shevardnadze left Georgia for Moscow in 1985, he was succeeded by Jumber Patiashvili (in office 1985–1989). Under his government, Shevardnadze's reforms were stalled and nationalism gained momentum. Nationalism and Russophobia were further strengthened by Gorbachev's clumsy order to destroy the famous Georgian vineyards in his fight against the widespread Russian problem of alcoholism. The spark that made the powder keg explode was the demand made on 18 March 1989 by tens of thousands of Abkhaz nationalists that Abkhazia become a full Soviet Republic independent from Georgia.[90] Feeling provoked, Georgian nationalists under Gamsakhurdia's leadership mobilized mass demonstrations in Tbilisi demanding independence. When Soviet MVD troops attacked the demonstrators on 9 April with spades and gas pistols, twenty people were killed and thousands suffered injuries from gas. Patiashvili was replaced by Givi Gumbaridze (in office 1989–1990), a former director of the Georgian KGB, who, however, remained powerless against Gamsakhurdia's outspoken nationalist coalition Round Table–Free Georgia. As in other Soviet republics, *glasnost* had opened the door to a populist nationalism that appealed to the broad masses. Gamsakhurdia not only propagated 'Georgia for Georgians', denigrating the South Ossetians and Abkhaz as separatists and criminals, but also raised a 12,000-strong 'National Guard' commanded by Tengiz Kitovani. One of Gamsakhurdia's main rivals, the former bank robber Jaba Ioseliani, created a private militia called Sakartvelo Mkhedrioni,

138. Church dedicated to the Blessed Virgin Mary from the fourteenth century in South Ossetia. The Georgian inscription on the funeral stele says: 'This morning I, the above-mentioned woman, twenty years old, will go to the otherworldly city.' Based on the phallic shape of the stele one may guess that the deceased woman mentioned was unmarried. South Ossetia. Photo 2018.

'Georgia's Knights'. When Gumbaridze saw no way out of the chaotic situation, he agreed to hold multi-party parliamentary elections in October–November 1990. Gamsakhurdia's coalition won 62 per cent of seats, while the Communist Party gained only 26 per cent. Gamsakhurdia became chairman of the Supreme Soviet on 14 November. He quickly established an autocratic regime and ordered his National Guard to disperse Ioseliani's Knights. After a popular referendum on 31 March 1991 with a 90.6 per cent turnout had approved Georgia's independence by an overwhelming majority – the South Ossetians and Abkhaz boycotted the referendum – independence was declared on 9 April 1991. Riding on a wave of popularity, Gamsakhurdia also won the presidential elections on 26 May.[91]

Gamsakhurdia's rhetoric of hate provoked anxieties among non-Georgian minorities that led to an increasing separatism combined with rapprochement with Moscow. In August 1990, the Abkhaz Supreme Council put into force the previous year's popular demand and proclaimed state sovereignty as a full republic of the Union, meaning secession from Georgia. One month later, on 20 September, the South Ossetian Supreme Soviet declared its territory an 'Independent Soviet Democratic Republic', which also meant secession. Three months later, the Georgian Supreme Soviet abolished the autonomous status of what it termed the 'Tskhinvali and Java regions', Tskhinvali being the capital of South Ossetia. Gorbachev's cancellation of both decisions had no effect. When Georgia changed its status to a non-federative unitary state in January 1991, it automatically abolished the autonomous status of Abkhazia, Adjara and South Ossetia.[92] Gamsakhuria decided to forcefully reintegrate South Ossetia at once and aimed at nothing less than the expulsion of the Ossetians from

Georgia.[93] Meanwhile the South Ossetians armed themselves and installed roadblocks. Fighting broke out in January 1991 although Soviet MVD troops attempted to separate the two adversaries; Georgia later accused the Soviet forces of assisting the Ossetian rebels. Georgian forces were expelled from Tskhinvali in March whereupon the city was shelled by Georgian artillery. Villages along the Ossetian borders were torched while Georgians living in Ossetia were forced to flee, as were Ossetians living in Georgia proper. Both sides applied brutal methods of ethnic cleansing. Undeterred by civil war, in late autumn 1991 Gamsakhurdia ordered a full-scale attack on Tskhinvali, which however never took place due to a *coup d'état* in Georgia. This small South Ossetian war, just like the massive population displacements in Armenia and Nagorno-Karabakh, showed the extent to which Moscow had lost control of the South Caucasus.

In Adjara, Aslan Abashidze, a descendant of a noble Muslim family and chairman of Adjara's Supreme Council, followed a more cautious course although he also commanded his own army. When Gamsakhurdia dispatched an official to oversee Adjara's reintegration into Georgia, Abashidze had him shot. Abashidze's avoidance of anti-Russian rhetoric now paid off, for the Soviet commander of the military base near Batumi made clear that he would defend Adjara should Gamsakhurdia's forces attack. Otherwise Abashidze abstained from involving himself in the power struggles in Tbilisi and made no attempt to seek independence, but maintained an armed political and economic autonomy which included the important harbour of Batumi. Abashidze did however incite, probably on instructions from Moscow, the Armenian-majority populations of Akhalkalaki and Akhaltsikhe in southern Georgia, who demanded to be allowed to join the Adjar Autonomous Republic. But since Armenia was highly dependent on Georgia as a transit route for Russian supplies to the country, Yerevan refrained from encouraging the separatists of Akhalkalaki and Akhaltsikhe and endeavoured to quieten things down.[94] The Russian military base near Batumi guaranteed Adjara's quasi-independence till May 2004 when

139. The Batumi Alphabetic Tower, on the right, is 130 m high and combines the double-helix pattern of DNA; in the centre is the Porta Tower. Batumi, Georgia. Photo 2018.

Abashidze failed to enlist Russian support and Adjara came once more under the control of Tbilisi.[95] The Russian base at Batumi was closed in November 2007.[96]

Gamsakhurdia's erratic rule provoked mass demonstrations which he quelled using troops. When he demanded the subordination of the National Guard to the MVD, Kitovani rebelled, removing part of his militia from Tbilisi and joining those of Ioseliani's Knights who had survived Gamsakhurdia's previous ban. Skirmishes broke out in and around Tbilisi between troops loyal to Gamsakhurdia and the Mkhedrioni reinforced by National Guard units: Georgia stood on the brink of civil war. On 22 December 1991 the joint militias of Ioseliani and Kitovani seized official buildings in Tbilisi and besieged the president in the parliament building where he was hiding. Street fighting spread, causing hundreds of casualties and much damage through Tbilisi, until on 6 January 1992 Gamsakhurdia escaped first to Armenia and then to Chechnya where the rebel general Dzhokhar Dudayev granted him asylum. Ioseliani and Kitovani then formed a Military Council with the former prime minister Tengiz Sigua. Since Georgia was internationally isolated, the troika urgently needed a figurehead which they found in Shevardnadze, who returned from Moscow in March 1992.[97] He was elected first chairman of parliament on 5 November 1992; later he became the second president of Georgia (in office 1995–2003). Based on his high prestige in the West, Shevardnadze rapidly obtained international recognition for Georgia, which allowed for foreign investment, and achieved UN membership. Nevertheless, Ioseliani and Kitovani, who retained control of the National Guard, continued to pursue their own policies and often clashed with each other. In May 1993 Kitovani was forced to resign as minister of defence, but Shevardnadze remained relatively powerless till the end of 1994 since the rump of the Georgian army was hardly a match for the Mkhedrioni. Whereas Shevardnadze managed to avoid a military escalation in South Ossetia, his lack of authority over the armed forces contributed to the unfortunate war in Abkhazia.

140. Monument to the Russian 'peace-keeping force' stationed in Abkhazia during and after the Abkhaz–Georgian War of 1992–1993. Autonomous Republic of Abkhazia. Photo 2020.

141. Above, the presidential palace; below, the concert and exhibition venue in Tbilisi designed by the Italian architects Studio Fuksas, nicknamed the 'double exhaust pipe'. Tbilisi, Georgia. Photo 2018.

Concerning South Ossetia, its government announced after Georgia's declaration of independence that it would remain an autonomous republic within the USSR. After Gamsakhurdia's fall, the Military Council refused to restore South Ossetia's previous autonomy, and fighting and shelling resumed in April 1992. On 29 May, Tskhinvali declared independence from Georgia as the Republic of South Ossetia. Although the former Soviet troops had officially left, the Ossetian rebels enjoyed the support of ex-Soviet units. Anti-Georgian rhetoric from Russian and North Ossetian hardliners fuelled the conflict. With a Russian–Georgian war seeming imminent, Shevardnadze met President Yeltsin in Sochi and the two statesmen agreed on 24 June to a peace settlement whereby a Joint Control Commission consisting of 600 Russians, 400 North and South Ossetians and 300 Georgians would monitor the demilitarized zone along the Georgian–South Ossetian border.[98] The status of South Ossetia itself remained undefined, in other words the conflict was 'frozen' and the South Ossetians continued to seek unification with Russian North Ossetia, although the North Ossetian government remained opposed to it. South Ossetia had become de facto a political entity although the border with Georgia proper remained open. Thanks to the Roki Tunnel linking Tskhinvali with Vladikavkaz, South Ossetia developed into a smuggling hub for consumer goods, cars, drugs and arms. The Republic was dependent on Russian finances and became integrated stepwise into the Russian Federation since most Ossetians opted for a Russian passport rather than a Georgian. The internationally unrecognized South Ossetia became a Russian protectorate within Georgia's internationally recognized borders.[99] The issuing of Russian passports to citizens of another country is a proven means by which Moscow can declare itself to be the protecting power of these new 'Russian citizens', whose alleged need for protection ultimately becomes the pretext for a military intervention.

Developments in Abkhazia were more dramatic. The chairman of Abkhazia's Supreme Soviet, Vladislav Ardzinba (in office 1990–1994) had created an Abkhaz National Guard and ejected ethnic Georgians from the higher echelons of administration in favour of ethnic Abkhaz. Although Abkhazia had proclaimed its sovereignty in August 1990, Ardzinba proposed in June 1992 a federative solution to the Abkhaz–Georgian conflict which would grant Abkhazia wide autonomy yet maintain Georgia's territorial integrity. When Shevardnadze and the Military Council rejected this conciliatory proposal, Ardzinba responded on 23 July 1992 that Abkhazia would now apply for CIS membership regardless of Georgia's decision in this matter. Defence Minister Kitovani reacted to Ardzinba's challenge by mobilizing his private 'National Guard' and attacked Abkhazia on 14 August. However it remains unclear whether Shevardnadze had approved Kitovani's military operation or not. After Abkhazia's capital Sukhumi fell on 18 August, Arzinba fled northwards to the Russian military base at Gudauta, but shortly afterwards Ioseliani's Mkhedrioni disembarked further north at Gagra; both Georgian forces looted freely. The Abkhaz government was threatened from north and south. If the two Georgian warlords thought that they could easily crush the rebellious Abkhaz government, they were quickly disabused of this idea. Ardzinba had maintained contacts with former Soviet, now Russian, hardliners and managed to form a strange yet superior coalition consisting of unidentified Russian units including artillery and T-72 and T-80 tanks manned by Russian crews as well as unmarked Sukhoi-25 and -27 fighter planes,[100] Slav mercenaries, Circassian volunteers from the North Caucasus and Turkey as well as Chechen fighters led by Shamil Basayev. The North Caucasian fighters were recruited by the self-declared Confederation of Mountain Peoples of the Caucasus which had been founded by a group of little-known academics and writers in 1990. The Confederation had no constituency and their delegates were self-appointed representatives of ethnicities. It called for volunteers to wage war on Georgia in Abkhazia and to carry out terrorist attacks in Tbilisi.[101] The Chechen fighters were trained by the Russian intelligence services. When they recaptured Gagra on 3 October, they killed hundreds of Georgian civilians.[102] In February 1993, unmarked aircraft began bombing Sukhumi which was held by Georgian forces. After a brief ceasefire, the Abkhaz–Russian–Chechen coalition resumed shelling Sukhumi and twice almost killed Shevardnadze, who was coordinating the defence from inside the city. Towards the end of July, Russia 'mediated' a ceasefire and a bilateral demilitarization around Sukhumi. Not for the first time, Russia had first contributed to fomenting and fuelling an armed conflict only to come in later as an alleged 'peacemaker' to mediate the conflict it had itself stirred up. For many Georgians, Russia remained the imperialist power which had crushed its independence in 1921 and was now amputating its territory, whereas for most Abkhazians Russia was, on the contrary, Abkhazia's protector against Georgian imperialism.

Russia's partiality as 'peacekeeper' was blatant; whereas Georgia withdrew its heavy weaponry to Poti, the Russians returned to the Abkhaz army the arms that they had taken into custody a couple of weeks before. When in August armed gangs of 'Zviadists', supporters of Gamsakhurdia, launched attacks on governmental, police and public buildings from their stronghold of Zugdidi (located in north-western Georgia between Abkhazia and Kutaisi), part of the demoralized Georgian forces which had retreated from Sukhumi joined the rebellious Zviadists. The Abkhaz exploited this second front in the civil war and on 16 September broke the ceasefire by attacking Sukhumi whose defenders were now without heavy weaponry. On the 27th, Sukhumi fell and Shevardnadze had to be evacuated by helicopter. The victorious coalition forces, above all the Chechens and Circassians, excelled themselves in plundering the battered city and massacring Georgian civilians. The remaining Georgian troops withdrew from Abkhazia, with the exception of the isolated Kodori Gorge in north-eastern Abkhazia. The war cost about 10,000 lives, and between 200,000 and 240,000 ethnic Georgian civilians were expelled from Abkhazia into a miserable life as refugees in Georgia. When the advancing Zviadists threatened to seize not only Kutaisi but also the port of Batumi, Russia revised its anti-Georgian policy, insofar as it offered Shevardnadze military help on condition that Georgia joined the CIS and accepted Russian troops on its territory. Having no alternative, Shevardnadze agreed to Yeltsin's offer, or rather ultimatum. Russian troops cleared north-western Georgia of Zviadists in October–November and recaptured Zugdidi on 6 November. Gamsakhurdia fled and either committed suicide or was shot on 31 December 1993, which brought the civil war to an end.

At the end of both wars, Georgia had lost 18 per cent of its territory, had to relocate almost a quarter of a million refugees and was forced to come back into the Russian orbit by joining the CIS and granting Russia three military bases at Batumi, Akhalkalaki and Vaziani near Tbilisi. Abkhazia in turn declared full independence on 26 November 1994 and became a Russian protectorate under the autocratic leadership of President Ardzinba (in office 1994–2005). Although Abkhazia had concluded peace with Georgia in April 1994 agreeing to the return of the Georgian refugees, it soon reneged on its agreement; in the event no refugees were allowed to return home. Thanks to its favourable climate, fertile soil and hydroelectric plants, Abkhazia is almost self-sufficient, but its borders with Georgia are virtually closed. Today the internationally isolated republic is only recognized

142. Holy Trinity Cathedral or Tsminda Sameba in Tbilisi was mainly financed by the Georgian oligarch and later Prime Minister Bidzina Ivanishvili and consecrated in 2004. Tbilisi, Georgia. Photo 2013.

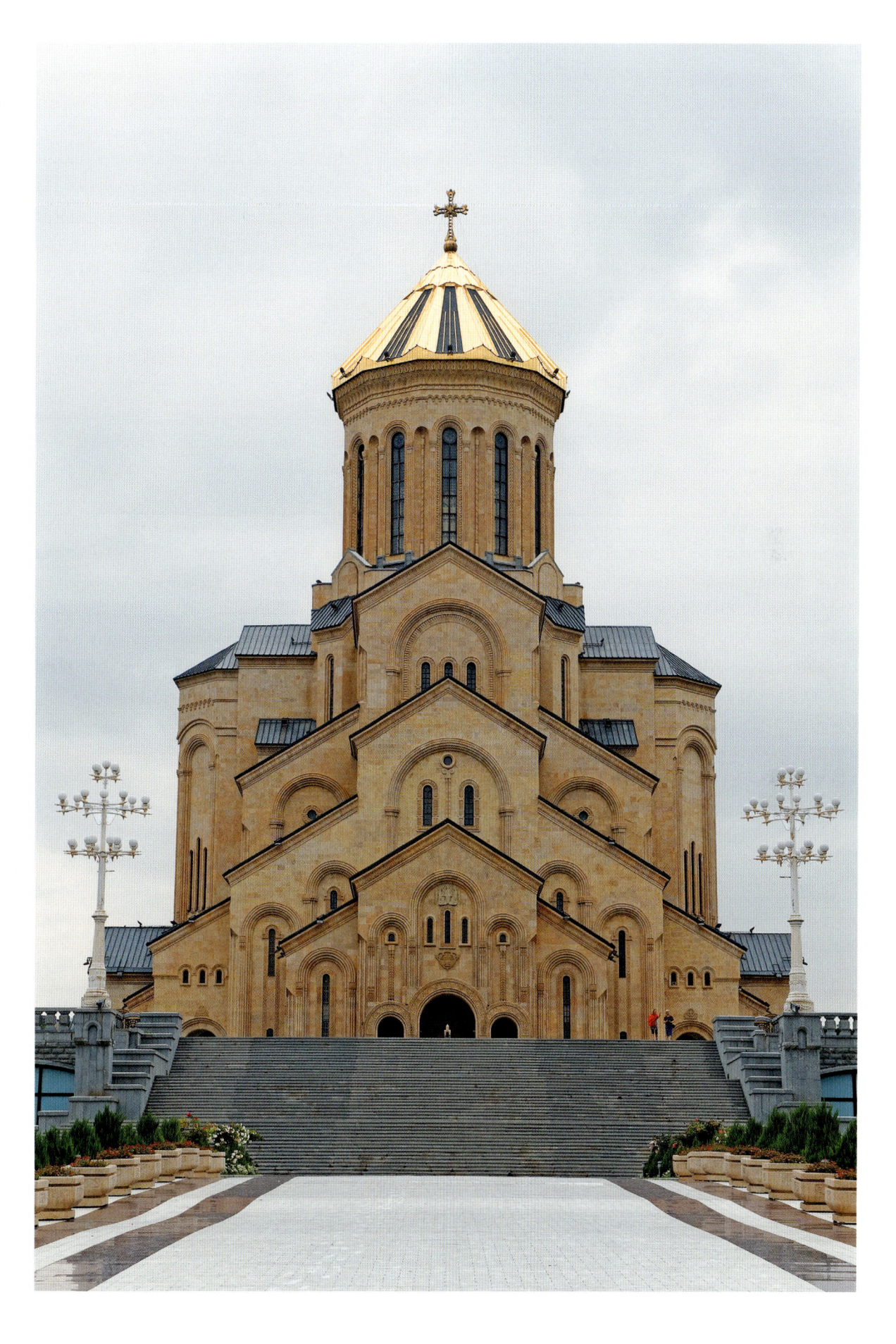

by Russia, Nicaragua, Venezuela and Nauru. Russia had at last successfully demonstrated its will to keep control at one remove over its Near Abroad, and had prevented the return of the virulently anti-Russian Gamsakhurdia regime.[103] In Georgia, Shevardnadze had first to supress angry mass demonstrations against his capitulation to the Russian ultimatum, then he had Ioseliani and Kitovani arrested and their militias disbanded. Several murders of military commanders have never been solved. As the writer Donald Rayfield has noted, by 1995 'all his opponents were dead, in gaol or in Russia' in exile.[104] But the economy remained dangerously weak and was dependent on the remittances of around one million expatriates. Although corruption was rampant, Georgia received for strategic reasons huge aid and a high level of credit from the USA, the IMF and the European Bank for Reconstruction and Development (EBRD) towards vital infrastructure projects such as the BTC and BTS oil pipelines. After a brief resurgence of the civil war in 1998 instigated by militias and Zviadists, Shevardnadze cleverly exploited Russia's short-term insolvency to negotiate the closure of the Russian base at Vaziani.

In 2002 Shevardnadze succeeded in turning a threatened Russian military intervention into a major political success. When the Second Chechen War began in 1999, thousands of Chechens crossed the Greater Caucasus and fled into the 30-kilometre-long Pankisi Gorge in northern Georgia. Among the *ca.* 12,000 Chechen refugees there were hundreds of fighters and even Arab jihadists who were able to recuperate and train here sheltered from Russian attacks. The valley also became a centre of drug smuggling and kidnapping which was carried out in cooperation with corrupt Georgian police officers. As Georgia did nothing to expel the fighters, President Putin (in office de facto 1999–) not only exerted pressure by introducing visa requirements for Georgian citizens and providing Abkhazians with Russian passports, but also authorized the gorge to be bombed several times. After al-Qaeda's terrorist attacks on the USA of 11 September 2001, Putin publicly accused Georgia of sheltering international terrorists, which alerted the USA to the matter. At this moment the Georgian interior and security ministers Kakha Targamadze and Vakhtang Kutateladze transported hundreds of Chechen fighters to the Kodori valley from where they launched attacks on the Russian protectorate of Abkhazia. Outraged, Putin ordered further bombing of the Kodori and the Pankisi valleys. Anticipating a Russian intervention in the Pankisi Gorge with ground troops, Washington pre-empted such an attack by concluding a military cooperation programme with Georgia in April 2002 and sending some 200 US instructors to train Georgian forces. For the first time, NATO soldiers were stationed in the South Caucasus. Within a few months, the Pankisi Gorge was cleared of Chechen fighters who retreated to Ingushetia where they were crushed by Russian troops. Although Shevardnadze had, with American help, averted a Russian violation of Georgian sovereignty, Georgia's neverending corruption and the blatantly rigged parliamentary elections of November 2002 provoked his fall. The US was no longer willing to tolerate his obstinacy in refusing reforms and Moscow wanted to get rid of the turncoat president. Since Putin had agreed to remove Shevardnadze, the young minister of justice Mikheil Saakashvili, opposition leader Zurab Zhvania and speaker of parliament Nino Burjanadze organized the bloodless *coup d'état* nicknamed the 'Rose Revolution' with the support of US ambassador Richard Miles and financial help from foreign NGOs such as George Soros' Open Society Institute (OSI).[105] On 22 November 2003 Saakashvili and a group of protesters stormed parliament and forced Shevardnadze to flee and hide; he resigned the next day. Six weeks later, Saakashvili won the presidential elections with a hardly credible 96.2 per cent of the vote.[106]

Autonomy and Failed Independence in the North Caucasus

143. The 'Exile and Return' monument in Elista, Kalmykia, commemorates the forced exile of the Kalmyks from 1943 to 1957. Kalmykia, Russian Federation. Photo 2017.

As in the southern Caucasus, so in the North, with the disappearance of Soviet ideology, institutions and repressive apparatus, the resulting void was immediately filled by ethno-nationalist aspirations and territorial claims as well as prejudices concerning neighbouring ethnicities. In diametrical contrast to Francis Fukuyama's thesis of an 'end of history', which in neo-Hegelian, almost eschatological thinking postulated the inevitable global triumph of democracy over autocratic regimes and thus proclaimed the end of armed conflicts provoked by autocracies, history never stopped in the Caucasus.[1] For no sooner had the Soviet clamp been loosened than not only did old conflicts and wars long thought dead re-ignite, but new ones emerged, often fuelled by resurgent nationalism. President Putin's wars in Chechnya (1999–2000), Georgia (2008), Crimea (2014) and Ukraine (2022–) exemplify the way in which history, of which armed conflicts are one of the few constant parameters, returned with all its force not only in the Caucasus but also in Europe.[2] Fukuyama's thinking also neglected the significant potential for conflict stemming from ethnic and tribal rivalries as well as from extreme religious ideologies such as jihadism. In general, the triumph of democracy announced by Fukuyama has been reversed – if anything, democracy is retreating.

However, substantial differences existed between the North and South Caucasus. Based on its mountainous geography, especially pronounced in Dagestan, the north is not only ethnically more fragmented than the south but also economically more vulnerable. Several North Caucasian republics were, under Soviet rule, economically unviable and have remained so to the present day. Their dependence on central subsidies became dramatically apparent in the early 1990s when Russia initially oriented itself unilaterally towards the West and applied a shock therapy to its economy according to IMF concepts, provoking a sharp economic decline.[3] The temporary drying up of subsidies from Moscow and the disruption of the former Soviet, now Russian market for Caucasian products caused havoc in the economies and budgets of the North Caucasian republics. But in the face of economic hardship and the perceived intent of the West to build a unipolar world to the detriment of Russia, opinions changed in Russia's leadership and the so called 'Atlanticist' strategy was replaced by an 'Eurasianist' one, simultaneously with the replacement of the ultra-reformist Russian Prime Minister Yegor Gaidar by the more moderate Viktor Chernomyrdin (in office 1992–1998) in December 1992. Eurasianism also implied Russia's reorienting itself towards the Caucasus, which was perceived as its 'vulnerable underbelly' and towards its former Central Asian republics in order to restore Russia's role in world politics. On the other hand, North Caucasian leaders were well aware that – with the exception of the Chechens – the functioning and welfare of their republics directly depended on subsidies from Moscow and on free access to the Russian market for both products and expatriate workers.[4] In the following pages the post-Soviet development in the various North Caucasian republics, oblasts and krais[5] will be briefly addressed in order, going from north to south and from west to east. It will be noted that the closer a region was to Chechnya, the more problematic was the transition period. In contrast to the titular republics where either one or two ethnicities are dominant and enjoy certain privileges, Dagestan is a multi-ethnic entity, while the two *krais* are mainly Russian and were established without reference to ethnic criteria. Overall, after 1990 the Russian Federation tried to avoid having to redraw the Soviet administrative borders.

1. The northern region: Rostov, Krasnodar, Adygea, Stavropol and Kalmykia

On the north-western edge of the Caucasus is **Rostov Oblast**, whose population of 4.2 million in 2010 was 90 per cent Russian. Whereas its western part is quite industrialized, the east remains agricultural and is sparsely populated. South-west of Rostov Oblast lies **Krasnodar Krai** with an estimated (2018)

144. The Seven Days Pagoda and the office building on the right in the centre of Kalmykia's capital, Elista, were designed by the local architect Akhmet Boschayev in 2005. Kalmykia, Russian Federation. Photo 2017.

population of 5.6 million of which 85 per cent is Russian.[6] It roughly corresponds to the Kuban region. At the time of writing the krai is administered by Governor Veniamin Kondratyev who was nominated by President Putin in 2015. The krai is the largest and wealthiest region in North Caucasus. It benefits from its connection to the Black Sea and its two major ports, Novorossiysk and Tuapse. Its relative distance from the potentially destabilizing Chechnya also significantly facilitated investments in its economy. Moreover when ethnic clashes between Chechens and Russians erupted in the krai in 2007, Moscow gave Krasnodar Krai high priority in terms of attention and support. In the centre of the krai, however, the Adyghe people succeeded in having their oblast of Soviet days elevated to the status of the **Republic of Adygea** with Maikop as capital.[7] It is a landlocked enclave of 7,800 square kilometres entirely surrounded by Krasnodar Krai. Although the Adyghe account for only 25 per cent of the population of *ca.* 450,000 people (estimate, 2018) they enjoy certain privileges.[8] The economy of Adygea is mainly agrarian, as the oil and gas reserves have dwindled to almost nothing. All three attempts between 2005 and 2007 to incorporate the enclave into the surrounding Krasnodar Krai failed due to opposition from the Adyghe of Maikop.[9] Other minorities failed to obtain their own designated territory; for example the Kuban Cossacks and the tiny minority of Circassian Shapsugs who had asked for the restoration of the former **Shapsug** National District (1924–1945) around Tuapse.

East of Krasnodar is **Stavropol Krai** where *ca.* 85 per cent of its 2.8 million inhabitants are Russian; the main minorities are Armenians, Ukrainians and Greeks. The krai's vulnerability to Chechen terrorism was highlighted in June 1995 when a Chechen terrorist commando of up to 150 or 200 fighters led by Shamil Basayev attacked the city of Budyonnovsk and captured the city hall, seizing up to 1,800 civilians as hostages. They then entrenched themselves in a hospital after having murdered 100 civilians. Basayev demanded the immediate termination of the First Chechen War and the withdrawal of Russian troops from Chechnya. When a delay occurred in the negotiations, Basayev began to shoot hostages, whereupon the security forces launched three attacks; about 290 hostages were freed or released. The drama ended only on the sixth day when Chernomyrdin agreed to a ceasefire in Chechnya. The kidnappers then returned with hostages to Chechnya. Between 130 and 166 hostages and 25 to 36 security force members were killed and more than 400 hostages were wounded. Of the terrorists, twelve were killed during the operation and more than forty were later tracked down and killed, among them Basayev in 2006.[10]

North-east of Stavropol Krai, on the north-eastern edge of the Caucasus, lies the **Republic of Kalmykia**, the only European republic where adherents of Tibetan Buddhism form a (slight) majority. Kalmykia's Buddhists belong to the Tibetan Gelug School whose head is the Dalai Lama. The spiritual head of the Kalmyk Gelug is the Shadjin Lama who has been confirmed by the Dalai Lama as a reincarnation of the Buddhist master Tilopa (d. *ca.* 1069).[11] At the dissolution of the USSR, Kalmykia kept its status as a republic of the Russian Federation. Kalmykia is thinly populated, for the 76,000-sq.-km republic counts only 275,000 inhabitants (estimate 2018), of which 57 per cent are Kalmyks of Mongol descent and 30 per cent Russians. Following Khrushchev's 'Secret Speech', the Kalmyks were allowed to return home from their Siberian and Kazakh exile and the Kalmykian AO was re-established on 9 January 1957, and upgraded to an

145. In front of the Buddhist Golden Temple of Elista stands a statue of the originally pre-Buddhist deity called the 'old wise man'. Its devout veneration by Buddhists shows that Kalmyk Buddhism successfully integrated pre-Buddhist deities. Kalmykia, Russian Federation. Photo 2017.

146. The central mosque in Nalchik, capital of Kabardino-Balkaria, Russian Federation. Photo 2010.

ASSR on 29 July 1958. In the early 1960s, Kalmykia was also affected by Khrushchev's agricultural and meat production offensive. But over-irrigation of dry soils and overgrazing by huge numbers of sheep provoked a man-made desertification of vast stretches of land.[12] Today, the economy remains oriented towards agriculture and food processing. The small industrial sector is concentrated in the capital Elista, which from 1943 to 1957 was called Stepnoy. In the east of the republic, along the Caspian littoral, Lukoil and Gazprom exploit the oil and natural gas deposits. The Tengiz–Atyrau–Novorossiysk oil pipeline, running from Kazakhstan to the Black Sea and built by the international Caspian Pipeline Consortium, crosses Kalmykia south of Elista, while a gas pipeline runs from Makat (Kazakhstan) through Kalmykia to several terminals in the north-eastern Caucasus. A special feature of Kalmykia is the widespread popularity of chess which was promoted by past president Kirsan Ilyumzhinov (in office 1993–2010); the 33rd Chess Olympiad took place in 1998 in Chess City, a suburb of Elista.[13]

2. The western and central region: Karachay-Cherkessia, Kabardino-Balkaria, North Ossetia–Alania and Ingushetia

South-east of Krasnodar lies the **Republic of Karachay-Cherkessia** which combines two different ethnicities, the autochthonous Cherkess (or Circassians, who are related to the neighbouring Kabardins) and the Turkic Karachay. Of its 466,000 inhabitants (estimate, 2018) 41 per cent are Karachay, 31 per cent Russian and 12 per cent Cherkess. Although plans were mooted in 1991/92 to divide the ASSR into a Karachay, a Cherkess, an Abazin and a Batalpashinsk Cossack Republic, a referendum held on 28 March 1992 resulted in 76 per cent of voters rejecting the split. Cherkessk remained the capital. When in 1999 the Karachay Vladimir Semyonov won the regional 'presidential' election against the

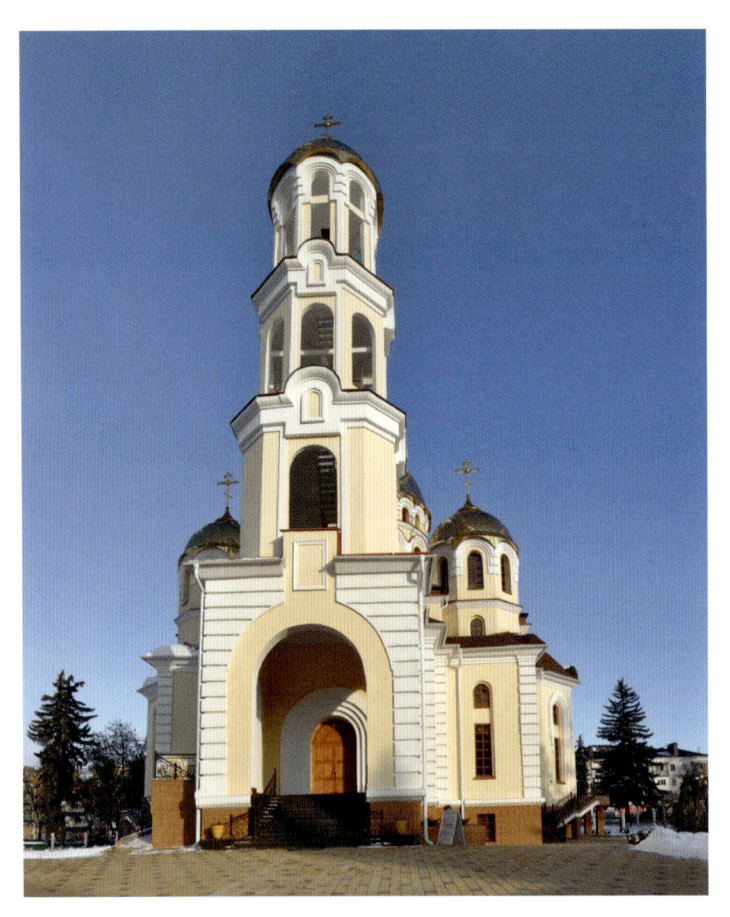

147. The Orthodox church of St Mary Magdalene in Nalchik. Kabardino-Balkaria, Russian Federation. Photo 2017.

Cherkess Stanislav Derev, unrest broke out and Cherkess groups demanded their own Cherkess republic. Nevertheless, Karachay-Cherkessia is labelled 'a stable republic within the unruly North Caucasus'.[14] The republic has the potential to flourish since it is rich in mineral deposits such as gold, silver, copper and tungsten, and has fertile soils. The Elbrus region in the south of the republic additionally has potential for tourism; however the economic situation in the 2010s remained under pressure.[15]

To the east of Karachay-Cherkessia is the **Republic of Kabardino-Balkaria**, which is also bi-ethnic: of its population of 866,000 (estimate, 2018) about 55 per cent are autochthonous Kabardian, 23 per cent Russian and 13 per cent Balkar-speaking Turkic. As in Karachay-Cherkessia, in the early 1990s there were attempts to form a monolithic Turkic-speaking Karachay-Balkar Republic as well as a Circassian Cherkessia-Kabardino Republic to which Adygea would be joined. These plans came to nothing. In addition the claim laid by Kabardino-Balkaria to a part of the Mozdok District in the north of today's North Ossetia–Alania, which had belonged until 1944 to the Kabardino-Balkarian ASSR, bore no fruit, since Moscow was reluctant to redraw borders and risk further unrest. In the 1990s the republic was seriously affected by the wars in Chechnya and Georgia which provoked not only a sharp economic decline and high levels of unemployment but also a radicalization of the younger Muslim segments of society, which was also fuelled by the brutality and corruption of the police forces. This Islamic radicalization manifested itself on 13–14 October 2005 when some 150 to 220 Islamist militants attacked buildings in the capital Nalchik related to public security and tax authority, as well as the city's airport. The attack was planned and organized by the Chechen Shamil Basayev who had been responsible for the Budyonnovsk hospital siege of 1995 and in 2004 had masterminded the terrorist attack on a school in Beslan (see below). It was led by the Ingush Ilyas Gorchkhanov who was killed during the attack. About two-thirds of the attackers on Nalchik were locals with only a few Chechens involved. According to official figures, about 35 security service members, 12 civilians and 89 insurgents were killed, while 36 were captured.[16]

East of Kabardino-Balkaria is the small **Republic of North Ossetia–Alania** whose area measures 8,000 square kilometres. About 65 per cent of the 702,000 inhabitants (estimate, 2018) are Ossetians who speak an East Iranian language, and 21 per cent are Russian. Unlike their Ingush and Chechen Muslim neighbours, the Ossetians are predominantly Christians (62 per cent, at least nominally), mainly Russian Orthodox; about 15 per cent are Muslims. As of the later 1980s a striking kind of neo-pagan 'religion' has been propagated by a group of nationalist intellectuals and religious activists under the name of Ætsæg Din or Uatsdin (True Faith). This neo-religious movement claims heritage from the ancient, pre-Christian religion of the Alans and even of the Scythians. Such 'nation-building ideologies' which seek their origins in pre-Christian traditions also emerged in other non-Slavic regions of Russia, in the Baltics and Ukraine.[17] Uatsdin bases itself on the ancient mythology embodied in the North Caucasian Nart sagas whose Ossetian version is considered a central element of the Ossetian identity. Among the deities of Uatsdin, Uastyrdzhi, the role model of the perfect man, is the most venerated. The underlying conception of Uastyrdzhi might be the ancient Alan god of war who was worshipped in the shape of a sword.[18] He is considered to be the protector of travellers and soldiers.[19] His popularity is based on the fact that Uastyrdzhi is also the local name for St George, the conqueror of all evil (fig. 148). According to the scholar of Iranian religions Richard Foltz, the main festival held in July in honour of Uastyrdzhi draws 'thousands of participants every year'.[20] Being a nationalist ideology, Uatsdin strives to distance itself from Christianity which is perceived as an alien, international and colonizing religion, a tool of Russian cultural imperialism. In this sense, Uatsdin is a 'protest against cultural colonialism'.[21] Since advocates of Uatsdin, such as its best-known spokesman Daurbek Makayev, define Christianity and Islam as Semitic religions, they do not hold back from anti-Semitic propaganda:

There are no words about Honesty in the Jewish religion, but there is a description how to achieve one's self-interested goals. ...[M]aking profits through corruption of other nations and their moral depravation is crucial for Judaism. It is the basic religion for Christians and Muslims.[22]

For Makayev, the decline of the Ossetian nation was caused by the Judeo-Christian missionization of Ossetia. In the wake of rising nationalism, the name Alania was added in 1994 to the republic's official designation as a reference to the glorious warlike Alan ancestors.

In contrast to other North Caucasian republics, there was very little in the way of an independence movement in North Ossetia–Alania. The majority of Ossetians were traditionally pro-Russian and they were aware of their dependence on Russia in economic and security matters. The republic quickly found itself engulfed in neighbouring conflicts, first of all in 1991, when the brief Georgian–South Ossetian war erupted and tens of thousands of South Ossetians fled to North Ossetia where they were resettled, many of them in the Prigorodny Rayon. While the government in Vladikavkaz (in Ossetian, Dzæwdžyqæw) supported the South Ossetians in their conflict against Georgia, it declined to discuss unification with the South and thus avoided being dragged into this dispute. One year later, war broke out with neighbouring Ingushetia, which had been established on 4 June 1992 when the Chechen-Ingush ASSR was split into two without a precise determination of the Ingush–Ossetian borders. Immediately the old ethno-territorial conflicts, going back to the deportation of the Ingush in World War II, broke out

148. Equestrian statue of Uastyrdzhi. In North Ossetia, Uastyrdzhi is not only the North Ossetian name for St George, but also embodies the warlike perfect man within Uatsdin, the recent attempt to form a new popular religion based on ancient mythology. He is depicted as horseman riding a white horse. Alagirsky District, North Ossetia–Alania, Russian Federation. Photo 2018.

again. Whereas in 1944 Ossetia had been assigned the formerly Chechen-Ingush territories of Malgobek, Mozdok and the eastern Prigorodny Rayon, it had to return some of these territories in 1957 to the Chechen-Ingush ASSR, but was allowed to keep the Mozdok and eastern Prigorodny districts.[23] When the Ingush returned from exile in 1957, they also resettled, in parts illegally, in the eastern Prigorodny Rayon in the east of the North Ossetian ASSR. As soon as the Ingush Republic had been established in 1992, Ingush nationalists demanded the reattachment of eastern Prigorodny to Ingushetia as well as a partition of Vladikavkaz, a demand that led to a flare-up of violence by Ossetians against the Ingush settlers. On 30 October 1992 Ingush militias overran the disputed district and advanced as far as the outskirts of Vladikavkaz. One day later, North Ossetian security forces and local militias including South Ossetian refugees counterattacked with the support of Russian MVD forces and paratroopers, and by 6 November the attackers had been expelled. President Yeltsin confirmed that Prigorodny would remain part of North Ossetia. As a result of this brief Prigorodny War about 6,000 Ossetians and between 40,000 and 65,000 Ingush were forced to flee, the latter mainly from the Prigorodny Rayon.[24]

Proximity to Chechnya brought several terror attacks to Ossetia–Alania. In 1999, 52 people were killed in an attack in Vladikavkaz, and 50 more in 2003 in Mozdok. In 2008, so-called 'black widows', female Chechen suicide bombers, murdered 12 people in Vladikavkaz and wounded another 40. Another suicide bomber killed 12 people in Vladikavkaz and injured 80 more during Ramadan 2010. The worst terrorist attack occurred on 1–3 September 2004 when 32 Ingush and Chechen gunmen and a number of 'black widows' attacked a school in Beslan located at the eastern edge of Ossetia, only 30 kilometres away from Ingushetia's capital of Nazran. The attack was again masterminded by Shamil Basayev who probably aimed to provoke an Ossetian retaliation that would set the whole North Caucasus aflame. The terrorists took about 1,100 hostages of which 800 were children. The hostages were locked under appalling conditions and after three days of siege, Russian special units from MVD, OMON and GRU stormed the school. After several explosions the roof of the hall where the hostages were packed collapsed and at least 331 civilians including 186 children were killed, with about 700 civilians wounded. Thirty-one terrorists and ten Russian commando soldiers were also killed. It remains unclear whether the roof collapsed due to rockets fired by the besiegers or bombs placed by the terrorists.[25] In spite of the shock and outcry in North Ossetia–Alania, the act of terror failed to provoke a new Caucasian war.

The **Republic of Ingushetia** is, at 3,628 square kilometres, the smallest republic of the Russian Federation. As per the census of 2010, the republic counts 413,000 inhabitants, of which more than 90 per cent are Ingush and 5 per cent Chechens.[26] In their own language the name for Ingush is 'Ghalghai' which means inhabitants (*ghai*) of a fortress (*ghala*). After their return from exile in 1957 the Ingush lived in the Chechen-Ingush ASSR whose capital was Grozny. However, in the last months of the USSR it became obvious that Chechnya was heading towards full independence. After President Dzhokhar Dudayev had unilaterally proclaimed on 2 November 1991 the Chechen Republic of Ichkeria without agreement from its Ingush constituency, the Ingush decided in a referendum with a 68 per cent majority to secede from Chechnya and form an Ingush republic within Russia, which included the Prigorodny Rayon. The two peoples separated peacefully and the Republic of Ingushetia was declared on 4 June 1992.[27] However, as noted by Svante Cornell, 'this republic had no capital, no fixed boundaries, no administration, and no power structures of its own'.[28] In Prigorodny, armed Ingush militia had already attempted to seize the former homes of their forefathers in March and April 1991. As described above, the ensuing short Prigorodny War in November 1992 ended in an Ingush defeat, not least because Chechnya avoided getting involved. To end the chaos, Yeltsin nominated the Ingush general Ruslan Aushev as president of Ingushetia (in office 1993–2001), who managed to restore order and keep Ingushetia out of both Chechen wars. Nevertheless Ingushetia faced the enormous task of sheltering and feeding about 65,000 refugees from North Ossetia–Alania and up to 200,000 from Chechnya. In 2004, the Second Chechen War briefly spilled into Ingushetia when on 21–22 June a Chechen-Ingush terror commando attacked security forces buildings in the former capital Nazran killing about 90 people. The new capital of Magas, founded by Aushev in 1995 as an administrative centre, had replaced Nazran in 2002. In 2008, President Medvedev appointed Yunus-bek Yevkurov as third president of Ingushetia (in office 2008–2019). Under his government, a fragile calm was restored but Ingushetia remains one of the poorest Russian republics with high unemployment and low investment. President Yevkurov resigned in June 2019 after ongoing protests over a highly unfavourable land swap with Chechnya signed in September 2018.[29] The Chechen president Ramzan Kadyrov had probably applied intense pressure to 'convince' Yevkurov to cede 9 per cent of Ingushetia's territory and the Kremlin shied away from opposing the unpredictable Kadyrov.

149. Painted portrait of Ramzan Kadyrov on a house in Grozny. Chechnya, Russian Federation.

3. The eastern region: Chechnya and Dagestan

The **Chechen Republic** is the only former Soviet ASSR to have, radically, sought full independence from Russia, even at the cost of war. Two factors set the course early for the drive for independence. First, the narrative of a two- or even three-centuries-long fight by Chechens against Russian imperialism fuelled a deep mistrust of central government in Moscow and of Russians in general which was easily instrumentalized by separatist forces to legitimize armed resistance against Russia. The second factor has similarities to the social conditions in Baku at the turn of the twentieth century. Although Chechen industry was thriving, the Chechens hardly benefited from it since they accounted for only 2 to 3 per cent of the oil industry's workforce. Most Chechens were employed in low-salary jobs and in agriculture and in the 1980s tens of thousands of young Chechen men were unemployed, which provided an ideal recruiting ground for armed insurgents in the 1990s.[30] Chechnya's first steps towards sovereignty were nonetheless modest, since when the first All-National Congress of the Chechen People declared Chechnya's withdrawal from the Russian SFSR on 27 November 1990, it basically demanded a status equal to the fifteen republics of the Soviet Union. The driving force behind this demand was the air force major general Dzhokhar Dudayev (1944–1996), the newly elected chairman of the All-National Congress who shortly thereafter resigned from the armed forces.[31]

When in August 1991 the Chechen Communist Soviet government failed to condemn the anti-Gorbachev putsch, Dudayev took it as a pretext to send a commando of armed militants to assault the Supreme Chechen Soviet and topple the government. Dudayev was elected president on 27 October 1991 in a controversial vote and six days later on 2 November proclaimed the independence of the **Chechen Republic of Ichkeria**, which was not recognized by any UN member states.[32] In November 1991, Dudayev's militia blockaded the airport of Grozny and prevented incoming Russian MVD troops from deploying.[33] Yeltsin responded by imposing an economic embargo but afterwards took little interest in Chechnya since he was absorbed in a power struggle with the Duma. Yet Chechnya wasted this golden opportunity to establish itself as a stable state. Having no economic education, Dudayev was unable to cope with the economic problems. When public employees went unpaid, civil services stopped working. Dudayev aggravated the situation with his anti-Russian rhetoric, which led the *ca.* 150,000 Russian nationals working in Chechnya to leave the republic. Within months, Ichkeria lost most of its engineers, skilled labour and doctors. As a result, the Russian share of Chechnya's population dropped from 25 per cent in 1989 to 4 per cent in 2002; today, 95 per cent of around 1.1 million inhabitants are Chechens.[34] The mismanagement of the economy and the Russian exodus led to a sharp decline in industrial output, of 30 per cent in 1992 and a staggering 61 per cent in 1993. In its place, a black market boomed including a flourishing arms trade; Chechnya developed into a smugglers' paradise. The republic's revenues stemmed mainly from the illegal importation of commodities into Russia, arms sales and oil theft from the BGN pipeline or illegal drilling. Also highly profitable was the re-export of cheap Russian oil to other Russian republics. At the same time, the Chechen mafia based in Moscow laundered its illegal earnings in Chechnya.[35] According to an official summary, Chechnya 'inherited' from the withdrawing Soviet/Russian troops 226 aircraft, 42 tanks and 29,000 machine guns, though probably in reality much more. Some of this Dudayev sold to the Bosniaks for the war in the former Yugoslavia.[36] Dudayev's erratic behaviour and hostility towards Russia was mirrored by Yeltsin's refusal to enter direct and official negotiations. The successful negotiation between Tatarstan and Moscow in February 1994 shows that an alternative to war could have been found.[37] Moscow's intransigence towards Chechnya was also related to the fear of a domino effect, in other words that other autonomous republics would demand independence. When in 1993 the Chechen parliament challenged Dudayev's rule, he dissolved it, and by summer 1994 Chechnya stood at the brink of civil war. In the meantime, Moscow supplied Dudayev's political opponents with heavy weapons, but the latter mostly sold them on the black market.

Ironically, Dudayev's regime was saved by his own worst enemy – Russia, which launched the **First Chechen War** (11 December 1994–31 August 1996). After an attack by the Chechen opposition, reinforced by a Russian tank unit, had failed on 26 November 1994, Russian defence minister Pavel Grachev launched a badly coordinated attack on 11 December 1994, although veteran Russian commanders had warned against starting an offensive in winter when it would be barely possible to deploy helicopters and aviation. Furthermore they stressed that the invading troops would meet similar conditions as in Afghanistan, namely highly motivated Muslim guerrilla fighters in a mountainous environment. And indeed, the badly trained Russian troops met disaster when they entered Grozny with their tanks. Grachev ignored the lessons from Stalingrad whereby a large city had to be first cut off from its supplies and that advancing tanks without strong infantry support were highly vulnerable to portable armour-piercing weapons such as rocket-propelled grenades; the unprotected tanks were like 'moving coffins'.[38] Directed by the chief of staff Aslan Maskhadov and the battle-hardened leader of the National Guard Shamil Basayev, Chechen fighters inflicted heavy losses on the Russians. It took the Russians more than two months to take Grozny at the cost of thousands of their own casualties, more than 20,000 civilians killed and the total destruction of the city. With hindsight, the carpet bombing executed by the Russian air force in Grozny anticipated the systematic destruction of Syrian cities such as Raqqa and Idlib or Ukrainian cities like Mariupol and Kharkiv during the 2022 Russian invasion. But the Chechen fighters remained undefeated and took to the mountains. Their war was funded by the widespread Chechen diaspora and so-called 'Islamic charity organizations'. Furthermore, agents forcefully collected a 'war tax' among Chechen expats.[39] The Chechens also enjoyed the support of the Saudi Arabian Wahhabi Samir al-Suwailim, aka Ibn al-Khattab (d. 2002), an Afghanistan veteran, and his fellow Arab fighters whose aim was to establish a strict Islamic emirate.[40]

With spring, Russian helicopters and planes could be deployed which gave Russia control over the Chechen lowlands. Maskhadov and Basayev now decided to export the war to Russia by launching terror attacks and taking hostages by the hundreds. Their first target was Budyonnovsk which came under attack on 14–19 June 1995 (see above).[41] The taking of up to 1,800 hostages not only demonstrated Russia to be incapable of protecting its own citizens but also enabled the Russian government to brand the Chechens as terrorists. On January 1996, a 200-strong Chechen commando attacked Kizlyar in Dagestan and seized up to 3,000 hostages. Most of them were soon released but in an ensuing battle 26 hostages were killed, as well as about 200 fighters on both sides. Since most of the hostages were Dagestanis, local public opinion became strongly hostile to Chechens.[42] Russia retaliated by killing Dudayev on 21 April 1996; he was succeeded by Zelimkhan Yandarbiyev (in office 1996–1997), but Maskhadov was the strongman. Having exploited a ceasefire arranged by the OSCE to regroup and rearm, Basayev recaptured Grozny in August 1996, which led President Yeltsin to acknowledge defeat and, in the Khasavyurt peace agreement of 30 August, approve the end of hostilities – which however left the core question of Chechnya's status aside. By the end of 1996 all Russian troops had left Chechnya. About 30,000–40,000 civilians had lost their lives.[43]

Having been elected president in January 1997, Maskhadov (in office 1997–2000) nominated Basayev as vice prime minister. Although the war had ended, law and order collapsed and the industry of kidnapping for ransom boomed. However, the illegal earnings from ransoming and smuggling never reached the state treasury, but went to the warlords and criminal gangs. Unemployment among young men, other than those engaged in farming, soared to 80 per cent. In short, Chechnya had 'won the war but lost the peace'.[44] In the course of 1998, Maskhadov gradually lost authority over the field commanders who behaved like autonomous warlords and accused the president of being willing to compromise with Moscow for the sake of peace. According to Ware and Kisriev, about 160 armed groups operated more or less independently of government control to illegally collect revenues.[45] In order to sabotage Maskhadov's authority his vice president Vakha Arsanov introduced a State Shura (Council) mainly composed of warlords who were to oversee the activities of government. In an effort to regain control Maskhadov declared a state of emergency; nevertheless armed clashes occurred between National Guards and militias.[46] Maskhadov then decreed the dissolution of the militias and the expulsion of non-Chechen Islamist fighters, but without effect. Finally, to reduce pressure, Maskhadov dissolved parliament on 3 February 1999 and introduced *sharia* law.[47] But when Moscow's special envoy for Chechnya, General Gennady Shpigun arrived in early March, he was kidnapped, ending any prospect for negotiations.[48]

The high unemployment rate among young men was an ideal breeding ground for radical Islamism, specifically for Wahhabi Salafism. Sunni *Salafiyyah* propagates a return to the strict teachings of the ancestors, called in Arabic *salāf*; the exonym 'Wahhabism' designates Saudi Arabian Salafism.[49] It was *glasnost* that allowed Salafism to spread unhindered in Soviet Central Asia and the northern Caucasus where it was propagated by the Avar Dagestani Akhmad Akhtayev (d. 1998), a chairman of the Islamic Party of Revival (IRP) based in Tajikistan.[50] Akhtayev's relative and successor, Sirajuddin Ramazanov radicalized Dagestani Salafism and aligned it with Wahhabism, which aimed at the establishment of a pan-North Caucasian Islamic state and rejected both secular state structures and legitimate political activities. Similar to the nineteenth century, when the fight against local despots and Tsarist domination demanded the introduction of *sharia* law, in the 1990s a segment of the younger generation, finding themselves without prospects, fought the established order under the banner of Wahhabism. The only economy these young unemployed men knew was the economy of war. Salafist fundamentalism replaced Marxism as the ideology that promised a better future. Generous funding from Gulf states greatly helped the Salafist cause. However, as observed by the scholar Walter Richmond, Salafism also appealed to criminals. Since Salafism considers non-Muslims, specifically Christian Russians and also Sufi Muslims, as *kuffār*, unbelievers, they stand 'outside the law and it is therefore permissible to kill them … in the name of Allah'.[51] In December 1997, the Chechen field commander Salman Raduyev, who had organized the hostage-taking at Kizlyar, and representatives of the extremist organization Islamic Jamaat of Dagestan, led by Bagaudtin Kebedov, sealed an alliance to jointly fight for the establishment of an Islamic state in the Caucasus.[52] Militant Dagestanis were integrated into al-Khattab's International Islamic Battalion. Dagestan, which hitherto had been the ideological stronghold of Salafism, became the starting point for building an Islamic state while Chechnya took over the leadership, based on its guerrilla forces. To be precise, it was not President Maskhadov who was the leader of this project, but the warlord Shamil Basayev and the Saudi Ibn al-Khattab who held operational command over the Islamic Army.

Supported by al-Khattab's fighters, in May 1998 the Jamaat established the nucleus of its future statelet in the villages of Karamakhi, Chabanmakhi and Kadar located in central Dagestan; the government was forced to yield control. One year later, on 2 August 1999, the Islamic Army, consisting of *ca.* 2,000 Chechen and Dagestani fighters as well as Ibn Khattab's Arab Battalion and Muslim mercenaries,[53] invaded Dagestan from Chechnya and seized the Avar and Andi districts of Tsumadi and Botlikh, some 80 kilometres west of Karamakhi.[54] On 10 August they declared the **Independent Islamic Republic of Dagestan** and installed Sirajuddin Ramazanov as prime minister. The Islamic Republic was obviously inspired by the Islamic Emirate of Afghanistan (1996–2001). However, if Basayev and al-Khattab expected to be welcomed by the locals, they soon learnt better, for the villagers considered the jihadists as invaders and religious fanatics. The jihad turned into the 1999 **Chechen–Dagestan War**. The local Dagestanis, Laks, Avars and Andis did not flock to the Islamic

State, but overwhelmingly formed armed militias reinforced by local and Russian (OMON) police forces who stubbornly resisted the jihadists and forced them to withdraw.[55] Russian federal forces being slow to react, the first three weeks of this war were a real people's war. Salafist forces retaliated with a bomb attack in the nearby town of Buynaksk that killed 64 people, and on 5 September launched a second attack. On 9 September, 94 Russian civilians were murdered in Moscow when a bomb exploded in their apartment building, and on the 13th another apartment bomb explosion killed 118 persons, again in Moscow. In typical terrorist fashion, the jihadists, defeated in battle, now turned against unarmed civilians.[56] At the same time, Russian troops and local militias had by 16 September together driven the Islamists out of Dagestan and crushed the Islamic Republic.[57] For the first time, the vast majority of Dagestanis welcomed Russian troops not as invaders but as allies. Although the homes of *ca.* 32,000 Dagestanis were destroyed in the brief war, in the words of Dagestan specialists Robert Bruce Ware and Enver Kisriev, 'the conflict was nearly as cathartic for Dagestan as it was catastrophic for Chechnya, … and it stimulated a dramatic improvement in relations between Makhachkala [Dagestan's capital] and Moscow.'[58] The successful defence against the invaders turned out to be a major nation-building experience since a large majority of the people now identified themselves with Dagestan rather than with their ethnicity.

The Chechen invasion of Dagestan and the apartment bombings in Moscow prompted (or, according to Moscow's critics, gave the pretext for) the start of the **Second Chechen War** (1999–2000, with military anti-insurgency operations lasting till 2002). Russian aircraft bombed the airport of Grozny on 23 September and on 30 September Russian troops crossed the border. Ten days later, President Maskhadov proposed a peace plan including the suppression of the rebellious warlords, but the Kremlin refused, since the prime minister, Vladimir Putin had decided to put a stop to Chechnya's defection. Furthermore, in Putin's view, the export of armed Chechen–Wahhabi Islamism to Dagestan threatened the cohesion of the Russian Federation.[59] Furthermore, a civil war in Dagestan would carry the risk of disrupting the Baku–Novorossiysk pipeline. The Russian defence minister Igor Sergeyev had learnt from Grachev's previous mistakes in the First Chechen War and ordered the ground troops to advance slowly only after massive air strikes and artillery preparation.

150. The Akhmad Kadyrov Mosque in Grozny, Chechnya, was completed in 2008. It is named after President Akhmad Kadyrov, the father of the current head of republic Ramzan Kadyrov.

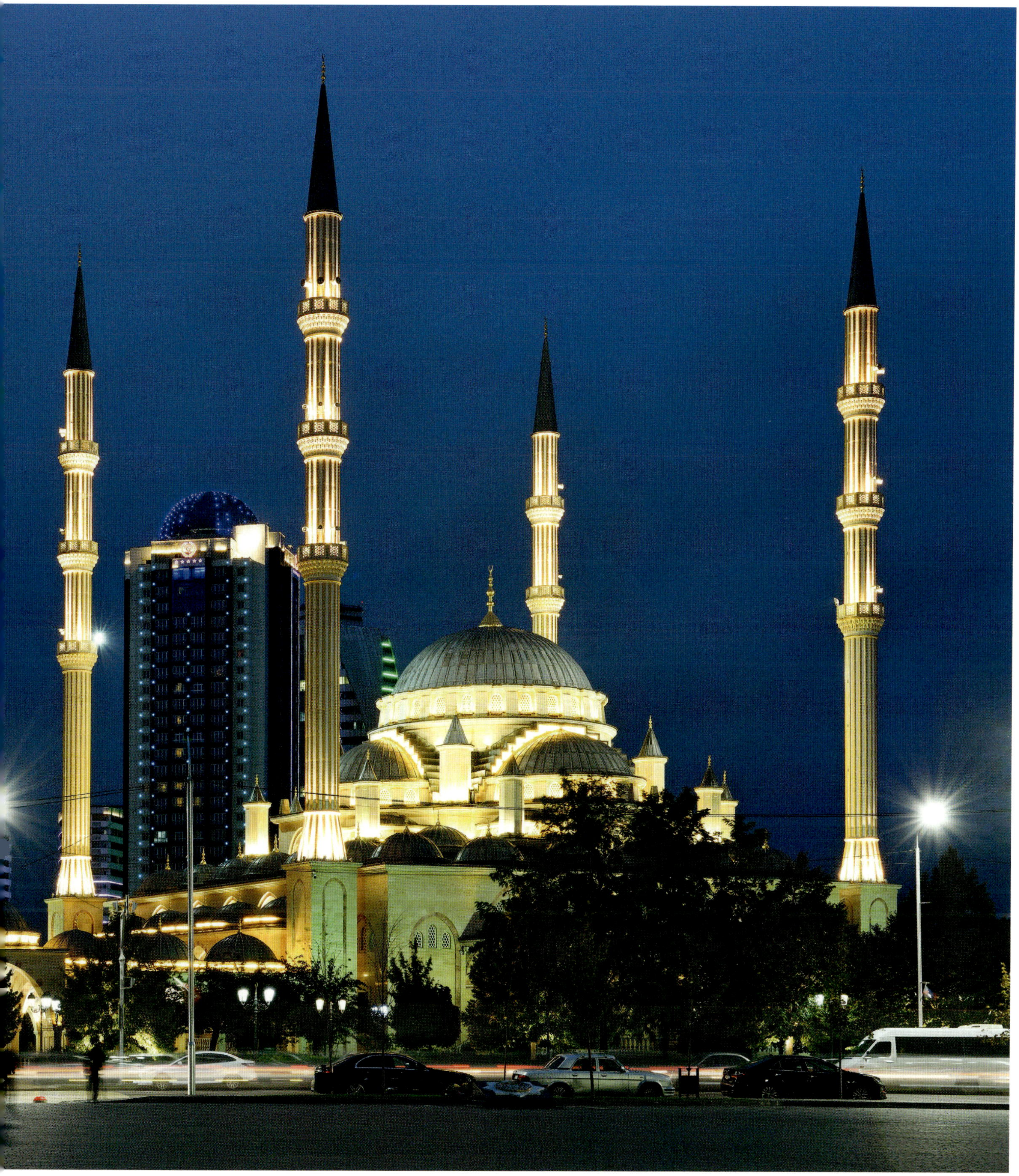

This strategy led to the displacement of some 100,000 people at the least. Instead of the troops rushing into Grozny, the city was tightly blockaded. On 2 February 2000 Russian troops controlled the once more totally devastated city, and the Islamist regime of Ichkeria collapsed. As for Maskhadov, he resumed guerrilla warfare and was involved in the infamous Moscow theatre hostage-taking in 2002 (see below) before being killed in 2005. He was succeeded as underground 'president' of Ichkeria by Abdul-Halim Sadulayev who was also killed one year later. Ichkeria's next 'president' was Dokka Umarov (Abu Umar) who in 2007 switched from Chechen nationalism to pan-Caucasian Islamism and proclaimed himself emir of a virtual Caucasus emirate. He was most probably killed in 2013.[60]

The Kremlin put Chechnya under direct rule but soon transferred governmental and some military responsibilities to the pro-Russian former chief mufti of Ichkeria, Akhmad Kadyrov, as a first step towards the 'Chechenization' of the conflict and of its solution. Kadyrov had been a leading militia commander during the First Chechen War, but became suspicious of the increasingly high numbers of Arab Wahhabis. Concerned that the Wahhabis would hijack the leadership of the Chechen Republic, Kadyrov switched sides in autumn 1999 and offered to collaborate with Moscow. He advocated issuing an amnesty for most insurgents, excluding those involved in terror acts such as bombing and hostage-taking. Kadyrov's U-turn exemplified the fact that in general, Chechens sought freedom in a secular state whereas the Salafists wanted a religious Islamic state.[61] For most Chechens, the Saudi Wahhabis remained foreigners. After al-Qaeda's 9/11 terror attack, the Russian counter-insurgency operation became part of the war against terrorism. In spite of their military defeat, the insurgents hiding in the mountains had still strength enough to launch terrorist attacks outside Chechnya, such as the hostage-taking on 23 October 2002 of more than 900 persons in a Moscow theatre. When Russian Special Forces stormed the theatre, not only were the 42 Chechen terrorists killed, but also 130 hostages.[62] There followed two plane crashes killing 89 passengers caused by two female Chechen suicide bombers (2004); three bombings in the Moscow subway and one at a market (2004, 2006, 2010) that murdered 104 people in total;[63] the bomb attack on the Moscow–Saint Petersburg Express killing 27 passengers (2009);[64] a suicide bomb attack at Moscow's Domodedovo airport (2011); and the Volgograd suicide bombing (2013), as well as the hostage siege at Beslan (2004) and the attack on Nalchik (2005) already discussed.

In March 2003, a new constitution guaranteeing Chechnya significant autonomy within the Russian Federation was accepted by referendum. In October Akhmad Kadyrov was elected President of Chechnya but was assassinated on 9 May 2004. According to *The New York Times* of 17 June 2006, Shamil Basayev claimed responsibility for Kadyrov's murder.[65] Kadyrov was succeeded *ad interim* by the Russians Sergey Abramov and Alu Alkhanov until Akhmad Kadyrov's son, Prime Minister Ramzan Kadyrov was elected President in February 2007 with Putin's endorsement. By spring 2002, military anti-insurgency action had ended, and in April 2009 the 'counter-terrorism operation' was officially terminated and the federal army withdrawn. By then, several key Chechen and Arab commanders such as al-Khattab (2002), Maskhadov (2005) and Basayev (2006) had been liquidated. The second war cost about 5,000 to 7,000 Russian, and between 3,000 and 16,000 Chechen deaths in battle, as well as up to 15,000 or 20,000 civilians killed.[66] Due to considerable efforts at reconstruction, Grozny was quickly rebuilt, but political power remained closely associated with the Kadyrov family and its 4,000-strong armed militia, nicknamed the Kadyrovtsy.[67] Although Ramzan Kadyrov is a Chechen nationalist and not pro-Russian minded, his regime may also be viewed as Moscow's proxy. From Putin's perspective, the 'Chechenization' of state power and administration was a success, and it probably was too for many Chechen citizens. Chechen Islam was partly de-radicalized in favour of traditional Sufi Islam and the Chechens were granted a far-reaching autonomy without the drawbacks of independence, that is the cessation of financial support from Moscow. The main losers were the warlords and the groups involved in criminal activities. However, Kadyrov used his almost unlimited powers to gradually establish a brutal, repressive regime, correctly assessing that Putin would want to avoid another conflict with Chechnya at all costs. To put it bluntly, Putin neutralized Chechen terrorism by installing a loyal terrorist in power whom he has to keep satisfied in terms of financial support and complete freedom of action within Chechnya, which if he fails to do, risks provoking a resurgence of unrest. In this respect, Putin is not only Kadyrov's superior but also his hostage.

The **Republic of Dagestan** differs from the other North Caucasian republics in its distinctively multi-ethnic character. For in a state of 50,300 square kilometres with 2.9 million inhabitants (2010 census) live no fewer than 34 ethnolinguistic groups of which 14 are considered to be titular ethnicities, many of them are mutually unintelligible. The largest ethnicities are the Avars (29%), Dargins (17%), (Kumyks (15%), Lezgins (13%) and Laks (5%).[68] During the Soviet period, Marxist ideology managed somehow to function as a supra-ethnic umbrella and the three or four largest ethnicities usually shared the major governmental appointments in order to secure balanced relations among them. When the Soviet Union dissolved, Dagestan's prospects looked bleak: the central authority and organizer of the economy had disappeared, more than half of the workforce was unemployed, the country was flooded by Chechen refugees, war and civil conflicts were raging on its borders and it was the target of military attacks by Chechen–Wahhabi militias, which in 1999 drove *ca.* 32,000 people from their homes to become internal refugees. Industrial production fell between 1991 and 1998 by an enormous 80 per cent and agricultural output by 65 per cent.[69] And as described the population was highly fragmented along ethnolinguistic lines. Yet Dagestan neither fell apart nor did it suffer a major civil war; as shown above, most of the acts of war and terrorism in Dagestan were not perpetrated by Dagestanis. Clearly Dagestan and its people managed to secure a minimum of stability. Among the small minority of Dagestani terrorists was the Lak Rappani Khalilov (d. 2007) who took part in the 1999 Chechen–Dagestani War and claimed responsibility for several murders. Nevertheless, assassinations of government and police officials continued for

151. The offshore Yury Korchagin oilfield is located 240 km east of Makhachkala in the Dagestani/Russian sector of the North Caspian Sea. It is owned and operated by Lukoil.

years.[70] Dagestan's internal security only improved after the Second Chechen War had fully ended and the country had been cleared of foreign fighters. The last major military mopping-up operation took place in 2012.

In such a multi-linguistic environment as Dagestan, the question of a common or official language is a major challenge. Today, the language of each of the 14 titular ethnicities is recognized as an official language (with the exception of the tiny minority (0.03 per cent) of Mountain Jews): Aghul, Avar, Azerbaijani, Chechen, Dargwa, Kumyk, Lezgin, Lak, Nogai, Rutul, Tabasaran, Tat and Tsakhur; in addition, Russian is an official language, as throughout the whole Russian Federation. This tolerance towards minority languages has contributed significantly to the containment of separatist aspirations. Another helpful element has been the fact that most of the leading groups and politicians, as well as the population as a whole, were aware of the delicate balance between the numerous ethnicities and also of the poor economic situation. It was also Dagestan's luck that no leader emerged who was interested in radical and intolerant nationalism in the way that Gamsakhurdia had used it in Georgia to promote his political ascent. Dagestanis understood that an inter-ethnic struggle would only create losers. The leaders refrained from declaring full sovereignty but accepted wide-ranging autonomy within the Russian Federation, which in the long run guaranteed financial support from Moscow. At the collapse of the USSR, the Nogai, the Kumyks and the Lezgins demanded their own territories without success. Whereas the Kumyks aspired to a kind of federation with other Turkic-speaking nations, the Lezgin organization Savdal (Unity) wanted an independent Lezgistan in order to unite the Dagestani and Azerbaijani Lezgins who were sundered by the collapse of the USSR. The terror attack on the Baku subway on 19 March 1994 which killed 14 people and wounded another 42 has been attributed to Savdal, allegedly in cooperation with the Armenian Secret Service.[71] In an interesting survey conducted in 2000 among Dagestan's population, it appeared that overall a high 74 per cent identified with Dagestan, 64 per cent with Russia but only 15 per cent with their ethnicity and 11 per cent with their religion. Only the Dagestani Chechens deviated significantly since they identified primarily with religion (51 per cent), then with Dagestan (47 per cent) and 40 per cent identified with their ethnicity, while a large majority (77 per cent) rejected Russia.[72] Obviously the recent events had changed the sense of affiliation of the Dagestani population. As mentioned above, the joint Dagestani–Russian military defence against the Chechen–Wahhabi attackers in 1999 greatly strengthened the trust of the Dagestanis in Russia and their distrust of Chechnya.[73]

Unlike in Chechnya, in Dagestan Islam contributed to the stability of the new republic where about 83 per cent of people claim to be Muslim. Under Soviet rule Islam was suppressed in the cities and lowlands, but it survived in the northern and western foothills in underground mosques inside private houses. The importance of these hidden mountain mosques was magnified by the fact that pilgrimages to places associated with a venerated Sufi holy man served as substitutes for the *haj* to Mecca, which was forbidden. As soon as state suppression waned, mosques emerged; their number rose from 27 in 1988 to 5,000 in 1994.[74] While the Spiritual Administration of the Muslims of Dagestan based in Makhachkala is an official, moderate institution regulating the affairs of all Muslim communities within Dagestan, with the exception of the Salafists, there were other associations that were critical of the state. One was the initially relatively moderate movement of Akhmad Akhtayev (see above), another the Islamic Democratic Party of Dagestan which rejected the secular character of the republic. In addition there were Salafist preachers maintaining close contacts with al-Khattab's militia and the Independent Islamic Republic of Dagestan. Extremist Islamic organizations, including Wahhabism, were prohibited on 16 September 1999, the last day of the war.[75] However, the vast majority of Dagestani Muslims disapprove of the extremist 'Wahhabis' and support the traditional imams embedded in the Spiritual Administration. This body also plays an important, nation-building role as a supra-ethnic umbrella uniting all Dagestani Muslims.

To avoid ethnic and territorial conflicts, the model recommended by the Kumyk party Tenglik (Unity) by which the country would be divided into autonomous ethno-regional units similar to Swiss cantons was rejected, as it would have opened the door to a plethora of conflicts over ethnically mixed cities, villages and regions.[76] Instead, the country was divided into ten multi-ethnic city districts and 42 non-urban rayons (districts). Dagestan's first constitution, from 1994, provided for a special State Council composed of one member of each titular ethnicity, which chose the head of state. In 2003 the State Council was abolished and, as in all other Russian Federal republics, as of 2005 the president, or rather the governor, was nominated by Russia's president.[77] Immediately following the 1999 Chechen–Dagestani War, Russia had already not only increased its financial support towards Dagestan's budget but also invested in its economy, for example in developing Makhachkala into an oil terminal linked to the Baku–Novorossiysk Pipeline.

The Caucasus in the Twenty-First Century

XI

1. Republics and regions of the North Caucasus

After the end of the Second Chechen War and the ensuing counter-terrorism operations that lasted till 2009, the northern Caucasus came back under Moscow's control. However, as a result of the jihadist defeat in Chechnya, the focal points of terror and insurgency shifted from Chechnya to Dagestan, Ingushetia, North Ossetia–Alania and Kabardino-Balkaria. The number of casualties due to terrorism rose after 2009 for three years before decreasing significantly from the mid 2010s.[1] With the decline of terrorist attacks and deadly confrontations, the northern Caucasus more or less disappeared from international headlines and thus partially from historical records. The region returned to its former status as Russia's backyard. According to Article 73 of the Russian Constitution, the eleven North Caucasian semi-sovereign federal subjects, namely (in alphabetical order) Adygea, Chechnya, Dagestan, Ingushetia, Kabardino-Balkaria, Kalmykia, Karachay-Cherkessia, Krasnodar, North Ossetia–Alania, Rostov and Stavropol Krai have retained all those competences and powers which are not explicitly attributed to the federal government.[2] This division of competences grants the regional governments relatively wide powers which in practice are exercised very differently. In some North Caucasian republics or krais regional governments remain under the close scrutiny of the Kremlin and governors may find themselves swiftly removed by the Russian president if they are underperforming or widely unpopular. On the other hand, Chechnya's head of state Ramzan Kadyrov rules the republic like an independent autocrat and may be compared to a powerful medieval vassal whom the Russian president cannot dismiss without seriously jeopardizing Chechnya's internal stability. Following an electoral reform in 2012, governors are no longer nominated by the president but are elected by popular vote for a term of five years.[3] All governors of the North Caucasian federal subjects belong to the United Russia party which controls 57 governorates and supports President Putin.

As mentioned above, the successful 'pacification' of Chechnya had the undesired side-effect of squeezing out the insurgents into the other Muslim republics of Ingushetia, North Ossetia and Kabardino-Balkaria, which led to a proliferation of terrorist cells controlled by the **Caucasus Emirate**. This network and virtual state was proclaimed on 7 October 2007 by the Chechen jihadist Dokka Umarov whose goal was not to build another small North Caucasian state but to unite all Muslims of Russia under his authority. In the North Caucasus, Umarov divided the virtual emirate into provinces called *vilayat*, namely the Vilayat of Nokhchicho – as successor of the Chechen Republic of Ichkeria – Dagestan (the former Shariat Jamaat), Galgaycho (Ingushetia) and the United Vilayat of Kabarda, Balkaria and Karachay which emerged from a mainly Balkar jihadist group called Yarmuk. The latter's name alluded to the decisive victory of the Muslim Arabs led by their legendary commander Khalid ibn al-Walid over numerically far superior Byzantine forces in August 636. It was the Yarmuk group which raided Nalchik in 2005. Although Umarov managed to mastermind several terrorist acts in Russia such as the suicide bombings at Domodedovo airport (2011) and Volgograd (2013) as well as some other attacks, the jihadist network of the Caucasus Emirate disintegrated in 2014–2015. Several factors led to this: first, the Islamist insurgency had lost the wider backing of the local Chechen population since its goal was no longer an independent Chechnya but the imposition of a religious state. Also, the jihadists had long since lost the financial support of certain circles in Saudi Arabia and the Gulf States since extreme Wahhabism also threatened the regimes of the Gulf. As a consequence the jihadists financed themselves by hijacking, extortion of so-called 'jihad taxes', theft and drug trafficking. Furthermore, Umarov's authority did not remain unchallenged and, most importantly, Russian security forces succeeded in tracking down and eliminating many of the emirate's leading commanders.[4] Finally, according to several press reports, in the run-up to the 2014 Winter Olympics (held at Sochi in Krasnodar Krai), Russia not only encouraged but even helped North Caucasian jihadists to leave the country. Most of the *ca.* 3,000–5,000 militant Islamists who left the Caucasus (mainly Dagestanis and Chechens) joined Abu Bakr al-Baghdadi's Islamic State and the Jabhat al-Nusra (al-Nusra Front, or 'Front of the Liberators') affiliated to al-Qaeda, in order to fight in Iraq and Syria. In return, al-Baghdadi nominated the Dagestani Rustam Aselderov, aka Abu Muhammad al-Kadari, emir of the North Caucasus Vilayat of his recently proclaimed Caliphate, which gave the IS an offshoot in Russia.[5] According to the Turkish newspaper *Daily Sabah*, Emir al-Kadari was killed by Russian Federal Security Forces (FSB) on 3 December 2016 in Dagestan's capital Makhachkala.[6] At that time, Russia had already been fighting Caucasian jihadists based in the Levant for a year, as it had begun its military intervention in the Syrian civil war in September 2015.

The poorer North Caucasian republics were badly impacted by the global financial crisis of 2007–2008 which in Russia triggered the Great Recession of 2008–2009, with the

152. The Irganskaya hydroelectric station located on the Avarskoye Koisu River near Gimry. Dagestan, Russian Federation. Photo 2021.

economy contracting by 7.9 per cent in 2009 due to a fall in energy and mineral prices.[7] As a consequence of the domestic recession, remittances from North Caucasian nationals working in Russia outside their homelands declined as well, and subsidies from central government to the North Caucasian republics were also reduced. A few years earlier, one month after the terror attack in Beslan, President Putin had sought ways to tighten federal control over the Northern Caucasus and to remedy its chronic economic insufficiencies by nominating Dmitry Kozak (b. 1958) as Presidential Plenipotentiary Representative in the Southern Federal District (that is, the North Caucasus and southern European Russia).[8] Concerning **Dagestan**, Kozak's report, submitted in summer 2005, highlighted a dangerously dwindling popular support for the local government, a profound distrust toward the legal system, an abysmal public health service, a record-high 44–49 per cent share of the economy taken up by a shadow economy that bypassed legal and fiscal regulations, very high unemployment and rampant corruption at all governmental sectors and levels, resulting in a per capita income half the Russian average.[9] Furthermore, federal financial aid seeped away, 'disaster relief funds did not reach victims … and large agricultural enterprises that remained under state control were being intentionally bankrupted so that they could be acquired cheaply when they were subsequently privatized.'[10] Kozak's report warned that the social disintegration which resulted from the dysfunctional government and civil services would result in a renewed fragmentation of Dagestan into Islamic enclaves and autonomous statelets. In conclusion, Kozak recommended complementing the efforts of the security forces with robust socio-economic measures and reforms. President Putin reacted by forcing the head of Dagestan's State Council, the Dargin Magomedali Magomedov (in office 1994–2006)[11] to resign and replaced him with the Avar Mukhu Aliyev (in office 2006–2010) who became head of the Republic. After four years, Aliyev was in turn forced to resign and was succeeded by Magomedsalam Magomedov, son of Aliyev's predecessor, which highlighted the Kremlin's wariness about upsetting the local power structures in an unstable territory such as Dagestan. As described by Ware and Kisriev, 'Magomedali Magomedov had proven himself the master of political manoeuvre … [H]e was both the principal architect of, and the central player in, that system of dynamic balancing among pluralistic political forces.[12] But whereas Magomedov ensured Dagestan's stability by preserving his own power, he utterly failed in terms of developing the Dagestani economy and addressing its numerous problems. Putin's intervention was part of his general recentralization efforts of the Russian bureaucracy in order to achieve a coherent political system throughout the federation. In Dagestan the results of this process of recentralization were an example to those achieved in other less developed regions of Russia. While the officials appointed by Moscow remained independent of corrupt local networks and did not hesitate to implement necessary and sometimes painful economic and social reforms, they relied on the cooperation of only a small number of local power-holders and were immune to local sensitivities and public opinion. As a result, ordinary people not only became disillusioned with such officials parachuted in from Moscow but also turned away from the ruling party, United Russia.

The party's heavy losses in the parliamentary elections of 2011 prompted the Kremlin to reintroduce direct gubernatorial elections in order to shift accountability for bad provincial administration back to the federal subjects themselves. But in October 2017 the pendulum swung once more in the direction of recentralization as the Avar head of the Republic of Dagestan, Ramazan Abdulatipov (in office 2013–2017) resigned and President Putin installed the ethnic Russian Vladimir Vasilyev (in office

153. The Georgian Military Highway linking Tbilisi, Georgia, with Vladikavkaz, North Ossetia-Alania, Russian Federation. Photo 2016.

2017–2020), a former police colonel general. Then, in January 2018, FSB security forces arrested Makhachkala's mayor, Musa Musayev on charges of corruption and the formation of a criminal organization, whereupon Prime Minister Abdusamad Gamidov and his two deputies were also arrested on the same charges and were brought to Moscow. Ironically, five years earlier, in another major political clean-up, the then head of republic Abdulatipov had deposed and arrested Makhachkala's mayor, Dagestan's 'strongman' Said Amirov (in office 1998–2013). He was sentenced to life imprisonment for commissioning a contract assassination.[13]

Unlike in Dagestan, the Kremlin has so far avoided interfering in the politics of **Chechnya**, which is ruled with an iron fist by Ramzan Kadyrov (prime minister 2005–2007, head of republic 2007–). Having established his power base in his own clan and his several thousand-strong paramilitary private army, nicknamed the Kadyrovtsy and made up of former insurgents,[14] Kadyrov succeeded in greatly reducing violence and stabilizing Chechnya while rapidly reconstructing the capital Grozny and the republic's infrastructure thanks to large federal subsidies.[15] But Kadyrov not only cracked down rigorously on jihadists and extremists, he also refused to tolerate any activity of federal security forces and services within Chechnya unless his government had approved them beforehand. As a consequence, Chechnya has been described as an 'FSB-free zone'. The use of collective punishment towards family members of alleged terrorists, targeted contract killings of opponents and violations of human rights has been repeatedly rebuked by both Russian and international NGOs. Kadyrov's autocratic rule is grounded on a strange mixture of Chechen nationalism, Islamic devoutness and bombastic loyalty to President Putin. More than once Kadyrov declared in Grozny's football stadium in front of thousands of armed uniformed men: 'We are Vladimir Putin's foot soldiers' and 'we will execute his orders'.[16] However, such statements of loyalty are ambiguous as they seem to be at the same time *bona fide* and a disguised warning, by displaying Chechnya's potential for a renewed insurgency.

That Kadyrov's statements of loyalty were not empty words was highlighted by the dispatch of Chechen units on Russia's side in the Georgian–Russian War of 2008 and to Eastern Ukraine in 2014–2015.[17] Then, in 2022, Kadyrovtsy forces joined in the Russian invasion of Ukraine starting on 24 February. A few days later, the Ukrainian Defence Ministry announced the destruction of a unit of Chechen special troops and the death of its commander Major General Magomed Tushayev.[18] Regardless of the military relevance of the Chechen Kadyrovtsy engaged in Ukraine, it remains a strange turn of history that the former Islamic enemy Chechnya, once branded by the Kremlin as a terrorist rebellious state, now acts as an apparently ultra-loyal ally of Russia in the fight against the former Ukrainian brother nation whose democratically elected leadership is being labelled by the Kremlin as Nazi. Not all Chechens approve of Kadyrov's participation in the Russian aggression, however. Other Chechen fighters living in exile joined battalions named after Dzhokhar Dudayev and Sheikh Mansur to fight on the Ukrainian side against the Russian aggressors. For these fighters, the war in the Ukraine represents a continuation of the wars against Russia in Chechnya.[19] As the Ingush head of republic Yevkurov had already confirmed in July 2014, Ingush soldiers too were fighting on both sides in Ukraine, both for the Russian-supported separatists and for the Ukrainian defenders.[20] Kadyrov can be expected to remain loyal to the Kremlin as long as Moscow continues to finance Chechnya's deficit-ridden budget. In that sense, the Chechen Kadyrovtsy serving in Ukraine can be labelled as 'Putin's mercenaries'.[21] In general, one can assume that Moscow's war in Ukraine is unpopular among most North Caucasian natives, with the exception of mercenaries who seek employment in the Russian army as *kontraktniki*.[22]

The jihadist spill-over from Chechnya was especially explosive in **Ingushetia**. Civil unrest and terrorist attacks against police officers and politicians increased after 2003 as President Murat Zyazikov (in office 2002–2008) was unable to master the situation despite implementing brutal repressive measures. When in August 2008 Magomed Yevloyev, a vocal critic of Zyazikov and leading opposition politician, was shot while in police custody, the Kremlin forced Zyazikov to resign and nominated Major General Yunus-bek Yevkurov (in office 2008–2019) in his place; the following year in June 2009, Yevkurov was hit by a suicide bomb attack which he only just survived. As in Chechnya, security forces succeeded in time in decapitating the local insurgent jihadist network by eliminating their leading commanders such as Said Buryatsky (born Aleksandr Tikhomirov, killed 2010), Ali 'Maghas' Taziyev (surrendered June 2010) and Artur Getagazhev (killed May 2014). To Yevkurov's credit, he not only relied on repressive measures to bring the insurgency under control, but also addressed Ingushetia's socio-economic problems and reduced the level of corruption. In contrast to Ramzan Kadyrov, Yevkurov did not build up a private army but rather called on lower-ranking insurgents to lay down arms, and left the 'dirty work' of hunting down jihadist commanders to FSB forces.[23] As already mentioned Yevkurov stumbled politically over the unfavourable land exchange with Chechnya and was replaced by the ethnic

Kazakh Mahmud-Ali Kalimatov (in office 2019–). A somewhat similar development took place in **Kabardino-Balkaria** where an upsurge of terrorist violence in 2010/11 was brought under control after the liquidation of leading jihadist commanders.[24] Despite the plan announced in 2011 by President Dmitry Medvedev (in office 2008–2012) to exploit Kabardino-Balkaria's natural beauty by constructing a huge ski resort in the region of Mt Elbrus, at the time of writing the project has not yet taken off due to persistently unsatisfactory levels of public security, tensions within the republic between Balkars and Kabardians, and more recently the Covid-19 pandemic. Until well into the 2010s, the eastern half of the Trans-Caucasus Highway leading from Pyatigorsk via Nalchik, Vladikavkaz and Grozny to Makhachkala on the Caspian Sea deserved its nickname of the 'European Kidnapping Highway'.

Like Chechnya, Dagestan, Ingushetia and Kabardino-Balkaria, **North Ossetia–Alania** too is dependent on federal subsidies and like the other three republics it suffered badly from terrorist spill-over from Chechnya, such as the jihadist attacks in Beslan (2004) and Vladikavkaz (2008, 2010). North Ossetia's politics and history remains affected today (2022) by the 1992 Ossetian–Ingush conflict over the eastern Prigorodny Rayon. Although this frozen conflict has been defused by the return of some 23,000 (as per October 2016) expelled Ingush to North Ossetia, a slightly higher number remain living in exile in Ingushetia.[25] The mutual hostility between Ossetians and Ingush has persisted to the present day. Another factor affecting North Ossetia is the question of a potential unification with South Ossetia which would mean the latter's annexation by Russia. The question flared up in the wake of the Russian invasion of Ukraine in February 2022, raising the prospect of an additional Russian land grab. The de facto South Ossetian president Anatoly Bibilov declared on 30 March 2022 that

unification with Russia is our strategic goal, our path, the hope of our people, and we will move on this path. We will take the corresponding legal steps in the near future. The Republic of South Ossetia will be part of its historical homeland – Russia.[26]

Bibilov promised a referendum on the question of unification with Russian North Ossetia should he win the forthcoming presidential elections. Whereas Georgia vehemently condemned Bibilov's statement as a provocation, President Putin's press secretary and spokesman Dmitry Peskov indicated that Russia would 'treat the expression of the opinion of the South Ossetian people with respect' and North Ossetia's head of republic, Sergey Menyaylo, promptly signalled consent to the proposed unification.[27]

2. The independent republics in the South Caucasus

Of the three South Caucasian independent states, only Azerbaijan managed to distance itself from the Russian zone of influence. Armenia has remained economically and militarily dependent on Russia, and Georgia suffered the loss of two provinces supported by Moscow. All three republics were concerned about the Russian invasion of Ukraine in February 2022, albeit for different reasons. Azerbaijan and especially Georgia were reminded of the fact that the present Russian regime would not hesitate to question and even shift boundaries by military means should the opportunity arise, while Armenia was forced to evaluate the value of Russian military protection in view of the poor performance of the Russian army against the much smaller Ukrainian forces. In any case, Russia's aggression against Ukraine signals that states which once belonged to the Soviet Union and want to leave the Russian sphere of influence must expect hostile reactions from Moscow.

2.1 Azerbaijan

Political and military developments in the Caucasus and Eastern Europe have confirmed President Aliyev's strategic positioning of minimizing Azerbaijan's economic dependence on Russia without provoking harsh retaliatory measures from Moscow. In this delicate balancing act between Russia and the Western powers, Aliyev's alignment in general tilted towards the USA, Turkey and, albeit somewhat covertly, Israel. Both Heydar and Ilham Aliyev quickly realized the attractive advantages of entering into the US-sponsored partnership with Israel. Azerbaijan not only secured a reliable customer of fossil fuels, but above all obtained a supplier of state-of-the-art military hardware such as UAVs (drones) and air defence missile systems. Turkey, for its part, remains of paramount importance for landlocked[28] Azerbaijan not only as the only viable transit route for its oil and gas exports, but also as a reliable military ally in its conflict with Armenia and Nagorno-Karabakh and as a protective power for Nakhchivan. The brief Russian–Georgian war in August 2008 had shown clearly that Moscow was prepared and willing to use military means to achieve its political goals. The war had also highlighted the relative passivity of the Western powers, which were unwilling to interfere in conflicts within Russia's Caucasian Near Abroad. Although Baku strove to signal its neutrality in the 2022 Russian–Ukrainian war, there is no doubt that the Russian aggression must have once again sent shockwaves to Baku (and Tbilisi) and confirmed President Aliyev in his view of the necessity to invest

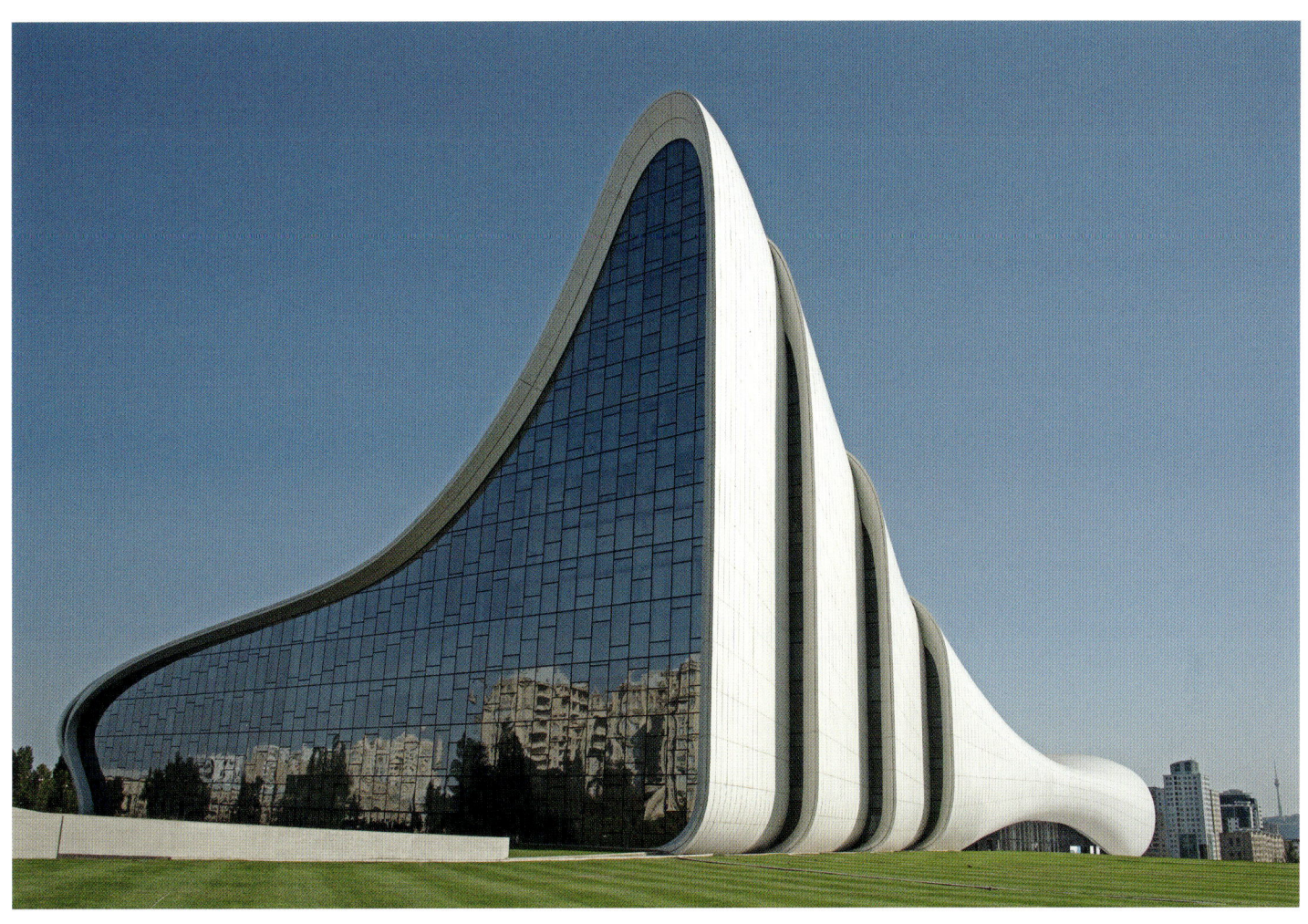

154. The Heydar Aliyev Center (Heydər Əliyev Mərkəzi) in Baku. It was designed by the architect Zaha Hadid and opened in 2012. Baku, Azerbaijan. Photo 2016.

in modern military defence systems. Aliyev's general orientation towards the USA and Turkey did not of course prevent his tactical use of the Russian trump card, by letting one of his ministers think aloud about Azerbaijan joining the Russian-led Collective Security Treaty Organization (CSTO), or by evaluating an Azerbaijani investment in Russia's pipeline system. The Azerbaijani government also regularly expressed resentment at Western, mainly European admonitions concerning the observance of human rights or the orderly conduct of elections. For example, in 2009, Aliyev's adviser for foreign affairs Novruz Mammadov (Məmmədov) snarkily remarked 'that the West cared more about the jailing of two bloggers than about hundreds of thousands of refugees who had yet to return to their homes'.[29] Nevertheless, the axis of Azerbaijan–Turkey–USA and Israel remains for Baku a vital counterweight to the Russia–Armenia–Iran alliance. Azerbaijan's strategy of a non-aligned foreign policy is underscored by its leading role in the Non-Aligned Movement of which it has been a member since 2011 and whose chair for the period 2019–2023 is President Aliyev.

Overall, Azerbaijan has achieved the highest degree of political independence of the three South Caucasian republics and may claim the strongest economy. The greatest threats for Azerbaijan remain the uneasy *modus vivendi* with Russia, economic dependence on price-volatile fossil fuels which account for *ca.* 90 per cent of exports, leaving the currency (the *manat*) highly vulnerable to falls in oil price. For example, when oil prices sharply declined in 2015–2016, the country's Central Bank had to twice devalue the *manat* by first 25 and then 30 per cent, which caused existing state and private loans previously taken out in foreign currencies to be subject to galloping inflation.[30] Furthermore, the State Oil Company SOCAR has been rather slow in modernizing its largest oil refinery and in investing in petro-chemical production projects. And while Azerbaijan has huge proven gas reserves, about half of its proven oil reserves have already been exploited; moreover, the country's landlocked position adds substantial transit costs to the price of Azerbaijan's fossil fuels.

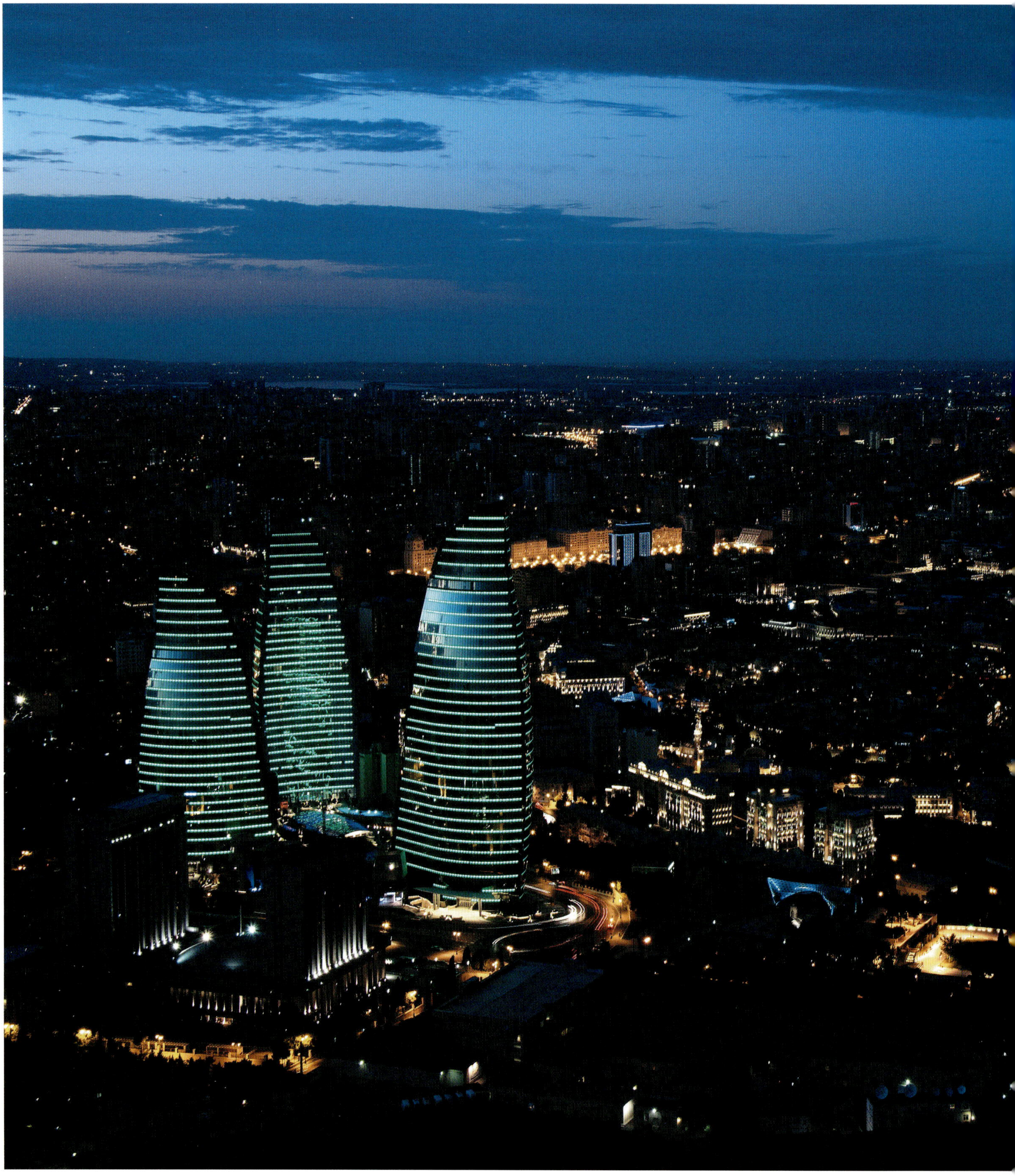

Concerning Azerbaijan's disputes with Iran and Turkmenistan over the exploitation rights of fossil fuels in the southern part of the Caspian Sea, an intermediary compromise was achieved in November 2021. With the dissolution of the Soviet Union the question had quickly arisen as to whether the landlocked Caspian was to be defined as a lake or a sea. If it was treated as a lake, its seabed and fossil fuel reserves would be in common ownership and would have to be equally divided among the five adjacent states. But if the Caspian was considered a sea, the distribution of its submarine resources among the five states would be proportional to the length of their coastline. Furthermore, the River Volga and its canal systems could then be considered as part of the same body of water, which would place the Volga–Don and Volga–Baltic canal systems under international law, thus severely curtailing Russian sovereignty.[31] Russia understandably denied that the Caspian had any natural connection with the world oceans, as canals are not natural bodies of water; Iran, too, advocated for the Caspian to be defined as a lake since an equal-sharing scheme is more advantageous for Tehran than a division according to its coastline, which would allow Iran only *ca.* 12 per cent of the sea's ownership. Contrariwise Azerbaijan and Kazakhstan argued, based on their long coastlines, that the Caspian was a sea. Turkmenistan, finally, claimed co-ownership or even exclusive ownership of the Azeri, Chirag and Kyapaz (Serdar) fossil fuel fields.[32] While a partial solution had been achieved between Azerbaijan, Russia and Kazakhstan in 2003, a further step was taken on 12 August 2018 when the five states signed a convention defining the Caspian Sea as 'the body of water surrounded by the land territories of the Parties'.[33] This neutral understanding took notice of Russia's strong opposition to a definition of the Caspian as a sea, but failed to solve the problem of partitioning its natural resources, leaving it up to bilateral and multilateral negotiations to settle those issues.

The next step was taken on 21 January 2021 when Azerbaijan and Turkmenistan agreed to jointly develop the Kyapaz gas field which at the occasion was renamed Dostluq (Dostluk), meaning 'friendship'.[34] In the wake of this compromise, Iran, Azerbaijan and Turkmenistan signed ten months later, on 28 November 2021, a trilateral gas-swap deal for up to 2 billion cubic metres per year. The agreement specifies that Turkmenistan, which owns the

---

155. Baku and the three Flame Towers. The towers, which range in height from 161 to 182 m, were built between 2007 and 2013. The Flame Towers are completely covered with LED screens; they display various motifs: static red, blue and green flames which are the colours of the Azerbaijani flag, blazing flames and a figure waving the national flag. Baku, Azerbaijan. Photo 2016.

fourth-largest proven gas reserves in the world, will supply Iran with gas and Iran will separately deliver an equivalent amount of gas to Azerbaijan.[35] This agreement was a twofold success for Azerbaijan. First, it unblocked an impasse two decades old, and second it defused political tensions with Iran, Armenia's traditional ally and Azerbaijan's indirect adversary. In all these treaties, Azerbaijan managed to cleverly use its few trump cards in a poker game against stronger parties. In view of the 2022 Ukrainian–Russian War and the European Union's declared will to end as fast as possible its dependency on Russian gas, the two agreements may have paved the way for re-evaluating the project of a Trans-Caspian Gas pipeline (TCG) since the EU will need alternative gas suppliers.[36] Because the US would veto the 'easiest' solution, namely a gas pipeline leading to Turkey via Iran, and Russia would block the construction of a submarine Trans-Caspian pipeline, a more modest project has emerged. The Florida-based TransCaspian US Resources Company proposes to link Turkmenistan's Banka Livanova gas field with Azerbaijan's Azeri–Chirag–Guneshli gas field with a 78-kilometre connecting pipeline. By way of this Trans-Caspian Interconnector Turkmen gas would be fed into the Southern Gas Corridor.[37]

Azerbaijan will furthermore gain in importance for the EU as Brussels has to find ways to compensate for the shortfall in Russian natural gas provoked by the war in Ukraine. Baku's significance as an energy transit hub will also continue to grow as a result of Kazakhstan's efforts to export crude oil to Europe via the Caspian Sea and the BTC pipeline instead of the traditional export route via the Aktau–Novorossiysk pipeline which passes through Russia. Kazakhstan is highly dependent on this alternative route as Russia closed the Aktau–Novorossiysk pipeline to Kazakh oil exports three times in 2022 alone, each time on a spurious pretext after the Kazakhstani authorities had either confirmed Kazakhstan's independence or had offered the EU an increase in the supply of fossil fuels.[38]

A potentially explosive weakness of Azerbaijan is the highly unequal distribution of wealth; that is, the poverty of the rural regions. Other issues, such as corruption and earthquake hazards, are common to all three South Caucasian republics. An additional threat to Azerbaijan's economy, and one that is hard to control, is a possible rise of the Caspian's water level due to an increased inflow from the River Volga caused by climate change. A temporary or permanent inundation of industrial facilities, oil fields, infrastructure and agricultural land would cause losses of billions of dollars.[39] Finally, Azerbaijan managed in autumn 2020 to partially redress another major weakness, namely the loss of 10 per cent of its territory in the First Nagorno-Karabakh War of 1992–1994.

2.2 The Second Nagorno-Karabakh War 27 September–10 November 2020

The situation along the Azerbaijani–Armenian ceasefire line had been tense since the agreement of May 1994, yet it remained in place despite two significant border skirmishes in March 2008 and April 2016 when Azerbaijan reoccupied the village of Talish. As mentioned above, after the shooting in the Armenian parliament of 27 October 1999, Armenia and Nagorno-Karabakh/Artsakh consistently refused to consider territorial exchanges or 'land-for-peace' arrangements. Convinced that only military action could restore Azerbaijan's territorial integrity, Ilham Aliyev patiently and systematically built up, with Turkish and Israeli help, an army fit for war and deepened his country's military cooperation with Turkey. Tensions rose in 2020 when the Armenian prime minister declared that the capital of Nagorno-Karabakh would be moved from Stepanakert (Azerbaijani Khankendi) to the neighbouring historic city of Shushi (Şuşa). Following skirmishes at the border, Azerbaijan and Turkey undertook major military manoeuvres involving artillery, armoured vehicles and aeroplanes in Azerbaijan and Nakhchivan from 29 July to 10 August.[40] Six weeks later, on 27 September 2020, the Azerbaijani attack began with the use of missiles, combat UAVs and aircraft followed by howitzers and finally tanks and infantry. The governments of Artsakh and Armenia ordered a general mobilization, and Azerbaijan a partial call to arms. According to Armenian sources, Azerbaijani forces were supported by Turkish military advisers and mercenaries redeployed from Syria.[41] Although the Armenian side offered spirited resistance, its lack of modern air defence systems led to heavy losses of materiel and to relatively rapid territorial retreats from the occupied districts.[42] Armenia then retaliated by attacking the Azerbaijani city of Ganja with missiles, causing civilian casualties.

This war was from the start not only a local affair, but carried a substantial risk of a military wildfire insofar as Armenia is a member of CSTO and Turkey of NATO. However, Moscow remained passive, arguing that CSTO's (that is Russia's) obligation to intervene applied only in case of an attack on Armenia proper. Since Nagorno-Karabakh was not part of Armenia, this obligation was not applicable. The course of the war gave rise to high hopes among the *ca*. 750,000 Azerbaijanis who had become refugees in the 1992–1994 war for a return to their homeland, while about 70,000 inhabitants of Nagorno-Karabakh and Armenian settlers fled to Armenia proper. Those Armenians who had been settled in the seven occupied districts preferred to burn down their houses rather than to leave them to their previous owners, the returning refugees.

Map 11. The Second Karabakh War 27 September–10 November 2020

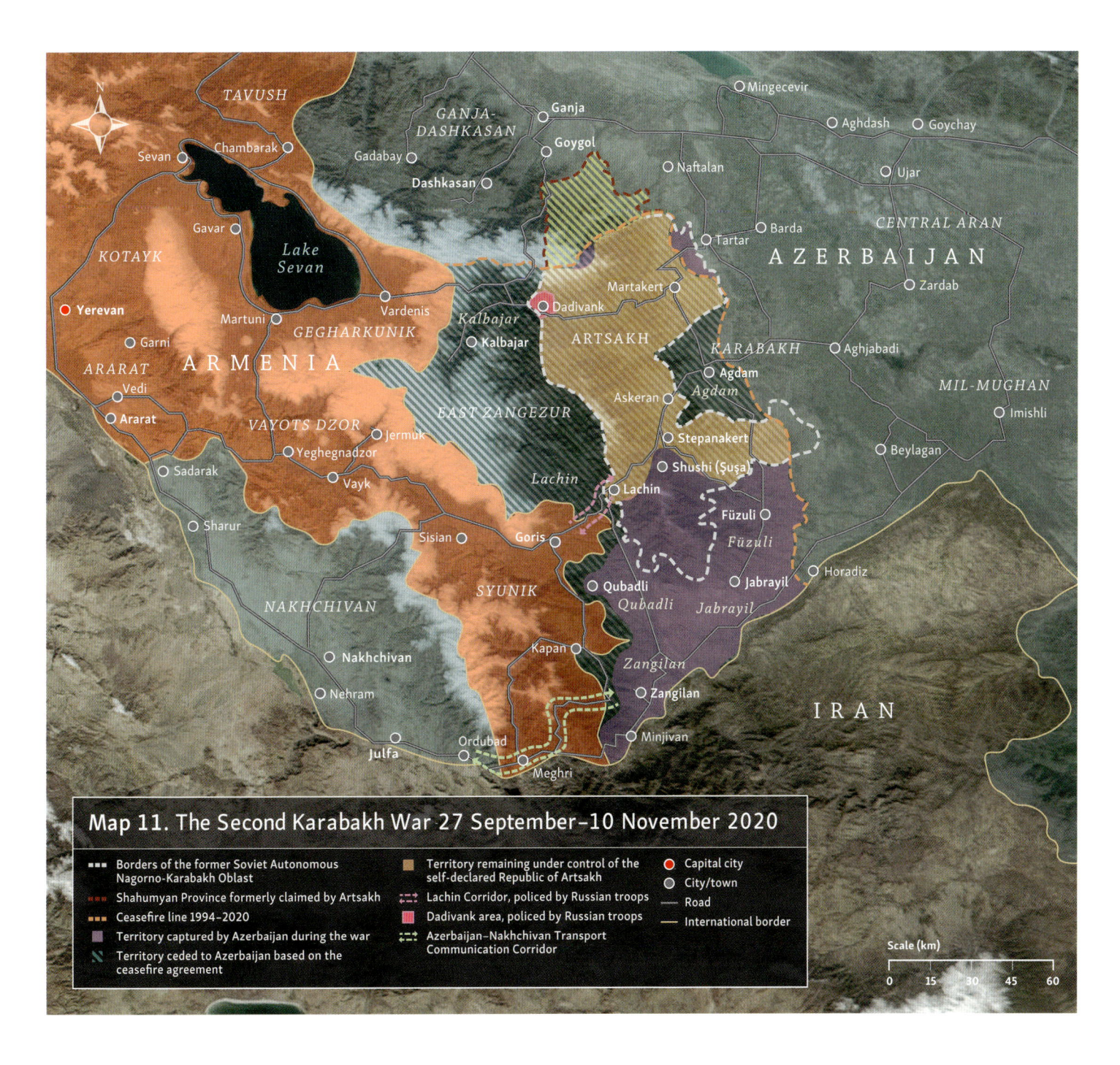

- Borders of the former Soviet Autonomous Nagorno-Karabakh Oblast
- Shahumyan Province formerly claimed by Artsakh
- Ceasefire line 1994–2020
- Territory captured by Azerbaijan during the war
- Territory ceded to Azerbaijan based on the ceasefire agreement
- Territory remaining under control of the self-declared Republic of Artsakh
- Lachin Corridor, policed by Russian troops
- Dadivank area, policed by Russian troops
- Azerbaijan–Nakhchivan Transport Communication Corridor
- Capital city
- City/town
- Road
- International border

Azerbaijani forces next isolated Nagorno-Karabakh from the Iranian border and on 23 October reached the Lachin Corridor, Nagorno-Karabakh's lifeline with Armenia, whereupon they captured the strategically vital city of Shushi on 6 November, which opened the way to Stepanakert. Whoever controls Shushi, perched high on a rocky plateau, controls all of Nagorno-Karabakh, including the lower-lying city of Stepanakert, and the vital connecting road to Armenia via the Lachin Corridor. In the aftermath of Shushi's fall the Armenian army evacuated Stepanakert and within hours Yerevan sued for peace. Finally Moscow mediated a ceasefire which came into force on 10 November.[43] Decisive for the course of the war were the systematic build-up of the Azerbaijani army as well as Israeli and Turkish combat drones as compared to the obsolete Armenian air defence supplied by Russia. According to the ceasefire agreement, Azerbaijan recovered the seven districts of Agdam, Füzuli, Jabrayil, Zangilan, Qubadli, Lachin and Kalbajar plus the city of Shushi, which are in international law an intrinsic part of Azerbaijan. Baku thus reconquered the full length of its border with Iran, and the Azerbaijani refugees were allowed to return to their (destroyed) homeland. Furthermore, Azerbaijan obtained the long-awaited access by road through Armenian territory to its exclave of Nakhchivan. On the other hand it failed to reoccupy the main disputed part of Nagorno-Karabakh, and the agreement imposed on Azerbaijan for at least five years an almost 2,000-strong Russian peace-keeping force deployed along the Armenian–Azerbaijani border and in the Lachin Corridor in order to secure a land connection between Nagorno-Karabakh and Armenia that bypasses Shushi and to guarantee the security of the gas pipeline running parallel to the Lachin passage. Basically the armistice saved Armenia from an even bigger defeat. According to official data, Azerbaijan lost 2,783 of its own soldiers as well as some 540 mercenaries; and Armenia and Artsakh lost 3,773 troops.[44] The real numbers were most probably quite a lot higher on both sides.

After Azerbaijan, Turkey was the second winner as it consolidated its position as a regional power although it was not able to force Russia to accept the stationing of Turkish peace-keeping troops. But the possibility of a direct land connection from Turkey to Baku and the Caspian Sea via Nakhchivan represents a major strategic asset and Turkish construction companies can expect to obtain a large share in the reconstruction of the seven devastated districts. The third winner was Israel which witnessed the superior performance of its UAV systems. Israel's cooperation with Shiite Azerbaijan is not contradictory at all, since Baku secures Israel's fossil-fuel supply and both partners are opposed to Iran's religious zealotry.

Conversely, Armenia and Nagorno-Karabakh/Artsakh were the key losers since they lost all territorial gains from the 1992–1994 war and thus most of their bargaining heft plus a third of Nagorno-Karabakh's territory and half of Armenia's military hardware. Armenia had been lulled into a false sense of security by overestimating its strength and underestimating its adversary. It was

156. Armenian soldiers of the Artsakh Defence Army pose with Father Hovhannes Hovhannisyan, abbot of the Armenian Dadivank Monastery during the Second Nagorno-Karabakh War. Photo before 10 November 2020.

punished for its diplomatic passivity and its belief that the conflict with Azerbaijan could be frozen indefinitely. Possibly the Kremlin's relative passivity during the war was also meant as a lesson for Armenia's prime minister Nikol Pashinyan (in office 2018–) because of his pro-Western sympathies. Moscow let him flounder in the face of impending defeat and intervened only to prevent Baku from seizing all of Nagorno-Karabakh, whereby Moscow replaced Armenia as Nagorno-Karabakh's protector. Although Russia gained a military foothold in Nagorno-Karabakh, it was at the same time the second loser since its weaponry used by the Armenian army, above all its surface-to-air missiles, proved outdated and it had to acknowledge Turkey's position as a strong player in the Caucasus, as well as in northern Syria. The Kremlin's annoyance over Turkey's interference in Syria and the Caucasus was expressed by President Putin's de facto chief propagandist, Margarita Simonyan, the editor-in-chief of the Russian state media group RT, when she stated in October 2021 that Russia should annex the Turkish provinces of Kars and Ağrı (Ararat).[45] The third loser was Iran which played no role either during the war or in its mediation, and the fourth the EU which remained a powerless spectator tolerated solely as a supplier of humanitarian goods.

Following the war, pride and joy prevailed in Azerbaijan, mixed with annoyance over the Russian mediation which stopped the Azerbaijani offensive short of its final goal. But in Yerevan, consternation about the defeat which had annihilated all previous gains and fury over the 'treachery' of the ruling politicians erupted in violent mass demonstrations. In the medium and long term, the defeated Armenia would be well advised to find a definite, negotiated solution to the conflict since the present armistice failed to address the thorny question of the political status of Nagorno-Karabakh – leading at best to a 'status of controlled instability'.[46] A normalization of relations with Azerbaijan and Turkey would also have the welcome side-effect of a strong economic upswing, not only for Armenia but also for eastern Turkey and Nakhchivan. But such a compromise would have to bury forever the nationalistic ambition of unifying Armenia proper with Nagorno-Karabakh. An additional handicap for Armenia is the fact that it has only limited political scope. As Russia's wars in Georgia (2008) and Ukraine (2022) showed, Moscow will never allow Armenia to move towards the EU and will maintain it within its zone of influence. Russia's military base in Gyumri, Armenia's second largest city, gives Moscow a strong lever for 'convincing' Yerevan to stay within its orbit.[47] It also remains to be seen how Moscow will utilize its peace-keeping force in Nagorno-Karabakh – will it limit its task to securing the cease-fire or will it instrumentalize these troops to create another pseudo-independent client statelet like South Ossetia or Abkhazia? Victorious Baku, on the other hand, might decide to remain uncompromising and wait for the opportunity for a renewed attack should Russia be decisively weakened in the Ukrainian War. President Aliyev's public claims, made during the victory parade held on 10 December 2020 in the presence of the Turkish president Recep Tayyip Erdoğan, to the territories of Zangezur (Syunik), Goycha (Sevan) and even Iravan (Yerevan) do not bode well for Armenia.[48]

A recent development concerning the agreed road access for Azerbaijan to its exclave of Nakhchivan through Armenian Zangezur foreshadows new tensions: whereas Baku insists that this road connection must be internationally controlled without the involvement of Armenian border control, Yerevan refuses to compromise on the exercise of its rights of sovereignty. In view of Armenia's intransigence, Azerbaijan repeatedly threatened that 'if there is no Zangezur Corridor, then there will be no Lachin Corridor'. As a consequence, Baku agreed with Iran in March 2022 to build a road and rail transport corridor passing through the Islamic Republic in order to connect Azerbaijan with Nakhchivan. The road is planned to run only five kilometres from the Armenian border. This agreement will nullify Armenia's trump card of a Zangezur Corridor and create an economic junction for Azerbaijan, Iran and Turkey while further isolating Armenia from the flow of international trade.[49] At the same time, it will give Iran a lever vis-à-vis Baku and will also undermine Georgia's virtual monopoly on an efficient land transit route from Azerbaijan to Turkey. Since in 2022 Armenia continued its stalling policy concerning the implementation of the Zangezur Corridor as defined in the cease-fire agreement of 10 November 2020, in March and August 2022 Azerbaijan provoked skirmishes against Nagorno-Karabakh and on 13–14 September even against Armenia proper.[50] The fact that Baku dared to shell targets within Armenia despite the Armenian–Russian defence alliance reveals that the Russian military setbacks in the Ukrainian war have damaged Russia's reputation as a powerful force of order.

Finally, as Thomas de Waal correctly observed, unless the mind-sets change in Armenia and Azerbaijan, no peace will prevail.

The [ultra-nationalist] *ideas expanded inside the ideological vacuum created by the end of the Soviet Union were given fresh oxygen by warfare. The darkest of these convictions, the 'hate narratives', have taken such deep root that unless they are addressed, nothing can change in Armenia and Azerbaijan.*[51]

2.3 Armenia

During the 1990s and early 2000s Armenia underwent a period of economic difficulties, corruption and commodity-based cartels as well as a 'brain drain' resulting in a steady population decline. Between 1991 and 2008 the total population fell by 17 per cent from 3,505,258 to 2,907,618.[52] At the same time the political agenda remained dominated by the conflict with Azerbaijan over the issue of Nagorno-Karabakh. When President Kocharyan's successor Serzh Sargsyan (in office 2008–2018) came to power, he and his government tried to unblock the foreign policy deadlock and to carefully loosen Russia's grip on Armenia. Both projects failed, which once again demonstrated Armenia's limited political leeway. Sargsyan's first initiative was a protocol on the normalization of relations with Turkey signed in Switzerland on 10 October 2009 in the presence of the US and Russian foreign ministers Hillary Clinton and Sergei Lavrov.[53] However, on 12 January 2010 the Constitutional Court of Armenia torpedoed the agreement by ruling that the planned 'mutual recognition of existing borders' between Armenia and Turkey as defined in the preamble could neither apply to Nagorno-Karabakh nor to 'the existing Turkish-Armenian border established by the 1921 treaty of Kars'. At the same time, the Armenian diaspora communities in the USA, France and Lebanon vehemently rejected the protocol and branded President Sargsyan as a 'traitor'.[54] As a result, the process of parliamentary ratification was halted in Armenia, and Turkey lost interest; the agreement remained a dead letter. President Sargsyan's attempt to establish closer ties with the European Union was also shipwrecked. His aim was to achieve a Free Trade Association Agreement with the EU, yet shortly before concluding such an agreement with the EU president, Sargsyan announced in Moscow on 3 September 2013 that Armenia would join the Moscow-led Eurasian Economic Union.[55] This ended Armenia's negotiation with the EU since the two economic unions are mutually exclusive. Because Armenia is a member of the Moscow-led military alliance CSTO and also economically heavily dependent on Russia, it had no other option than to yield to the Kremlin's pressure.[56]

Since Armenia's constitution allows the president a maximum of two terms and Sargsyan's term would end in spring 2018, he attempted to copy the ploy of President Putin who had in 2008 switched positions with Dmitry Medvedev for four years in order to remain in power. First, in December 2015, Sargsyan arranged a constitutional amendment which altered Armenia's political system from a semi-presidential (or dual executive) to a parliamentary, whereby the executive power shifted from the president to the prime minister, with the presidential office to be reduced to mainly ceremonial functions following the next general election. Next, Sargsyan's Republican Party, which had dominated national politics since 1999, won an absolute majority in the April 2017 parliamentary elections which meant that it would form the new government independently of any other party a year later. Third, the Republican Party declared on 11 April 2018 that it would nominate the outgoing president Serzh Sargsyan, whose term had ended two days before, as the new prime minister. By this manoeuvre, Sargsyan would remain in full power.[57] But at this point the anger that had long built up over the mismanagement and corruption of the ruling Republican Party erupted in peaceful mass demonstrations and strikes led by the opposition politician Nikol Pashinyan, who was a long-term adversary of ex-presidents Kocharyan and Sargsyan. When parliament nevertheless elected Sargsyan as the new prime minister on 17 April, Pashinyan proclaimed the 'Velvet Revolution'. Sargsyan tried to cling to his new position but when army units began to join the demonstrators he resigned on 23 April and Pashinyan (in office 2018–) was elected prime minister two weeks later. To break the power of the Republican Party for certain, Pashinyan caused the dissolution of parliament and subsequently won a ruling majority with his My Step Alliance in December 2018.[58] Pashinyan's victory ended both the dominance of the Republican Party and the supremacy of Nagorno-Karabakh politicians. Following the anti-Sargsyan protests, demonstrators demanded without success the resignation of Catholicos Garegin II because of his close association with Sargsyan as well as with Russian business circles.

Pashinyan kept his word to fight corruption by having former president Kocharyan and the high-ranking general Mavel Grigoryan arrested and charged with bribery.[59] But he failed to explore a possible restart of negotiations with Azerbaijan and even advocated re-evaluating the option of unifying Nagorno-Karabakh with Armenia. The crushing defeat in the war of autumn 2020 was a brutal awakening to reality, and protesters quickly blamed Prime Minister Pashinyan for his lack of preparation for the event of war. Nevertheless, Pashinyan consolidated his position by winning early parliamentary elections in summer 2021. He agreed to meet President Aliyev in a discussion mediated by the EU in April 2022 after a renewed border clash on 25 March. After it became public that both presidents had decided to prepare peace negotiations, protests and mass rallies erupted in Yerevan and Pashinyan was vilified as a traitor by opposition politicians close to ex-president Kocharyan.[60] Two months before, in January 2022, a minor crisis occurred when Armenia's president Armen

157. Government Building No. 1 in Yerevan is the official residence of the prime minister of Armenia. It stands on the eastern side of Republic Square. Yerevan, Armenia. Photo 2015.

Sarkissian (in office 2018–2022) stepped down three years before his term was due to expire. As a reason, Sarkissian cited a lack of sufficient power to influence politics, yet the true cause was that it had become public that he held a passport of the tiny Caribbean state St Kitts and Nevis after investing half a million dollars in a hotel some years earlier. Sarkissian resigned because such a purchase of a passport raised questions and dual nationality is forbidden for a president.[61] In Armenia, not only does the issue of Nagorno-Karabakh remain highly emotional, but the people in the south-eastern province of Syunik fear the establishment of an Azerbaijani transit corridor through their territory, while the population of Kapan, the provincial capital which became a border town after the Azerbaijani reconquest of the Zangilan district, feels threatened because the expressway from Yerevan to Kapan runs for long stretches south of the town of Goris directly along the new border, and in part even on Azerbaijani soil, which means it is closed to Armenians. In order to avoid the isolation of Kapan, and of Meghri on the border with Iran, the narrow mountain road from Goris to Kapan via the Tatev monastery is being hastily enlarged.

In the early 2020s, Armenia faced several almost insoluble dilemmas. On the international level, its only military protector is Russia which at the same time attacked Ukraine in spring 2022 and seriously threatens peace in Europe. On the other hand Armenia is dependent on the goodwill of the EU and the US for obtaining further financial support, but the Western powers are involved in a proxy war against Russia in Ukraine and are likely to perceive Armenia as a Russian satellite.[62] Furthermore, the EU will court Armenia's adversary Azerbaijan to increase its gas supply in order to help compensate for the loss of boycotted Russian gas. Finally, Armenia counts on Russian and, to a lesser degree, Iranian support while at the same time being financially dependent on the US-based Armenian diaspora, which means that it banks on incompatible interests. Pashinyan is also under tremendous domestic pressure. He is well aware that Azerbaijan may start a third war to fully recover Nagorno-Karabakh, which Armenia would most probably again lose. Therefore he must enter negotiations with Azerbaijan while securing the rights of the Nagorno-Karabakh Armenians. Yet the very possibility of Armenia considering Azerbaijani sovereignty over

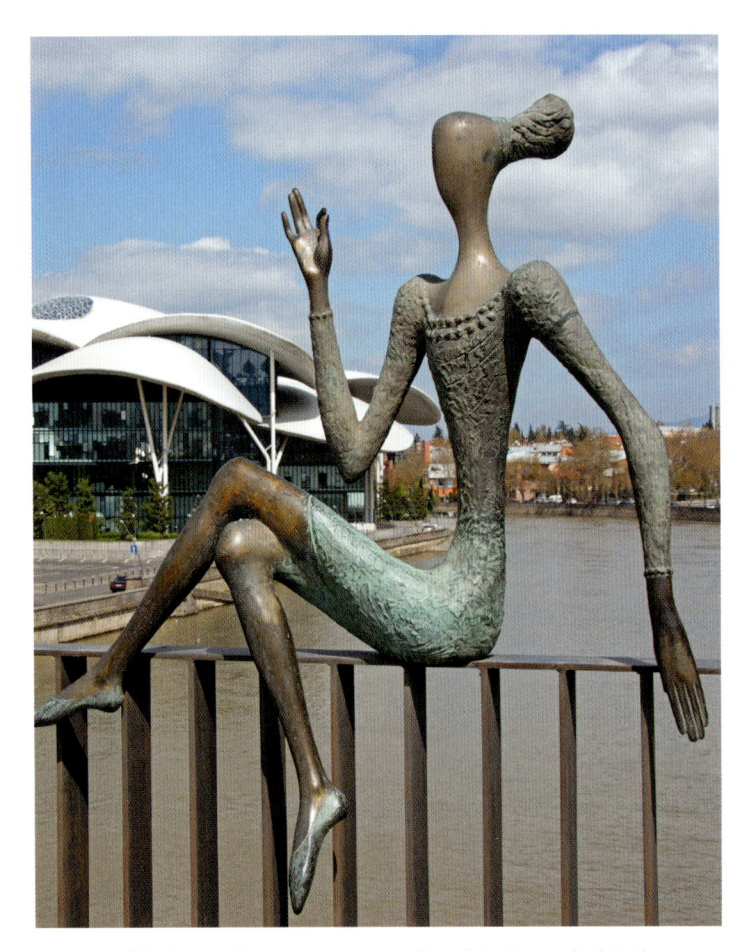

158. One of the bronze figures sitting on a railing of the Baratashvili Bridge which stretches over the Mtkvari (Kura) river in Tbilisi. The bridge is named after the Georgian poet Nikoloz Baratashvili (1817–1845). In the background is the Public Service Hall, designed by the Italian architects Studio Fuksas and built in 2011. Tbilisi, Georgia. Photo 2018.

Nagorno-Karabakh, in whatever form, would be treason to the Moscow-aligned opposition and the diaspora. Should Armenia refuse a negotiated compromise, whether Pashinyan hardens his position or the opposition comes to power, a renewed military confrontation may well take place.

2.4 Georgia

When Mikheil Saakashvili was elected president on 4 January 2004, he set himself the task of aligning Georgia with Western democracies and relaunching the stagnating economy by enforcing far-reaching reforms to end corruption, curb crime, and improve government efficiency and public services. Corrupt officials in administration, police and public services were fired while the salaries of government employees were raised to such a level that they no longer needed to take bribes to survive. Law and order were restored by strictly applying laws and passing severe judgements, which led to an increase in the prison population. In order to quickly raise funds, break the oligarchs' corrupt cartels and put a stop to tax evasion, Saakashvili had many of the oligarchs arrested and then let them buy their freedom with the payment of heavy fines – a manoeuvre that the Saudi crown prince Mohammed bin Salman repeated in much grander style in 2017. The president also strove to attract foreign investments by radically reducing the bureaucracy required to open and transact business in Georgia and by streamlining tax and customs regulations.[63] Within a few years Saakashvili managed to catapult Georgia from post-Soviet staleness and stagnation to economic growth and a liberal environment. The economic reforms quickly brought annual growth rates totalling 70 per cent from 2002 to 2013; however this economic boom did not significantly reduce poverty.[64] Since Saakashvili's reform programme was a top-down exercise, it met with resistance and lost some momentum as a result.

Saakashvili's agenda went beyond transforming an almost failed state into a functioning market economy. He wanted to restore state sovereignty over all Georgian territories and to decisively leave the Russian political orbit by integrating Georgia into the EU and NATO. The latter project ended in disaster due to Russian military intervention, which highlighted the limits of Georgian sovereignty. One of Saakashvili's first initiatives was to reimpose central authority on the renegade province of Adjara where Aslan Abashidze ruled de facto independently from Tbilisi thanks to Russian backing. When Saakashvili attempted in mid March 2004 to enter Adjara for a pre-election rally he was stopped by Abashidze's paramilitary forces, whereupon he imposed an economic blockade on the province. Abashidze resigned on 5 May after failing to obtain Russian military support and with his paramilitary forces starting to defect to the Georgian troops. Adjara returned under central control while retaining a narrowly defined autonomous status. But to reintegrate Abkhazia and South Ossetia into Georgia's central authority was a much more difficult and dangerous task since their separatist governments enjoyed robust Russian support. In this respect, Georgia shares the same problem as Azerbaijan and Moldova, namely the presence of separatist quasi- and pseudo-states (respectively Nagorno-Karabakh and Transnistria) that are militarily and economically backed by Russia. The presence of Russian troops transformed these renegade political entities, figuratively speaking, into dormant hostile cells which might emerge at any moment to threaten the legitimate central governments. Saakashvili now gambled that a strong rapprochement with EU and NATO, ideally a full membership, would allow Georgia to leave the Russian zone of influence and to reassert central authority throughout Georgia.

Even before Saakashvili's election, in November 2002, President Shevardnadze had already declared Georgia's determination to join NATO.[65] Shevardnadze's decision came after Russian-backed South Ossetia had begun preparations in summer 2002 to distribute Russian passports to its population (that is, to de jure Georgian nationals) and after President Putin had threatened Georgia with a military operation should it fail to evict the Chechen refugees from the Pankisi Gorge.[66] Clearly Moscow's distribution of Russian passports to non-Russian citizens in its self-declared 'Near Abroad' is nothing other than a pseudo-legal trick to obtain a pretended right for extra-territorial authority and military intervention. The tense situation escalated in 2006 when Russia not only started the construction of a third military base in South Ossetia but also strongly upgraded the latter's armed forces. Shortly thereafter, Moscow announced a ban on the import of Georgian wine and bottled mineral water, whereupon Tbilisi attempted to block Russia's entry into the World Trade Organization (WTO). Russia retaliated by announcing that 90 per cent of the Abkhazian and South Ossetian population held Russian passports and that Russia would protect its new nationals against Georgian aggression according to Article 51 of the UN Charter.[67] Such 'passportization'-programmes brought severely into question the alleged impartiality of the so-called Russian 'peace-keeping' forces stationed in South Ossetia and Abkhazia. The Kremlin also closed all transport and postal links with Georgia, stopped granting visas to Georgian nationals and began deporting Georgian immigrants from Russia.[68] In autumn 2006, Saakashvili attempted to regain control of South Ossetia by organizing parallel 'presidential' elections to the re-election of the Moscow-backed separatist leader Eduard Kokoity. Saakashvili's candidate Dmitry Sanakoyev won the election within the Georgian-controlled half of South Ossetia, and installed his government in Kurta, less than 10 kilometres away from the separatist capital Tskhinvali.[69]

159. Mural of Christ Pantocrator in the cupola of the seventeenth-century castle church of Samtsevrisi. The murals were executed in the years 2008–2010 in the traditional style of the late sixteenth–early seventeenth century. Shida Kartli, Georgia. Photo 2013.

2.4.1 The Georgian–Russian War 7–12 August 2008

The situation came to a head after Putin's speech on 10 February 2007 at the Munich Security Conference in which he castigated NATO's eastward expansion.[70] Two days later, President Saakashvili asserted Georgia's will to join NATO which was unanimously confirmed by the Georgian parliament on 13 March.[71] In parallel, Georgia launched an ambitious programme to modernize its army. Russia countered that a Georgian NATO membership would represent a direct threat to Russian security,[72] in other words a *casus belli*. In fact, as of October 2022, Russia refuses to recognize full domestic and foreign policy sovereignty in all states belonging to the CIS (Commonwealth of Independent States), regardless of whether they are full members or not.[73] Russia's next move, to close its remaining Georgian military bases by November 2007, might have seemed surprising. However, this withdrawal was not in fact a conciliatory gesture, but a preventative measure: the Kremlin wanted to ensure that no Russian garrison could be captured in case of war, which it considered an option should Georgia join NATO. Relations between Russia and the Western powers worsened when major Western states recognized the independence of Kosovo which broke away from Serbia on 17 February 2008. Three weeks later, South Ossetia and Abkhazia requested Russia's recognition of their self-declared independence. The next step on the path to war was taken in April. Although at the NATO summit of 3 April 2008 Germany vetoed the granting of a Membership Action Plan (MAP) to Georgia and Ukraine, since both applicants were currently involved in territorial conflicts,[74] the final communiqué was intended to sound encouraging:

NATO welcomes Ukraine's and Georgia's Euro-Atlantic aspirations for membership in NATO. We agreed today that these countries will become members of NATO. … MAP is the next step for Ukraine and Georgia on their direct way to membership. Today we make clear that we support these countries' applications for MAP.[75]

160. The Bridge of Peace, opened in 2010, is a pedestrian bridge over the River Kura. Tbilisi, Georgia. Photo 2018.

161. A column of Russian tanks in North Ossetia–Alania on its way to join the war against Georgia. Photo 9 August 2008.

Russia's foreign minister Sergei Lavrov warned bluntly five days later: 'We will do everything possible to prevent the accession of Ukraine and Georgia to NATO.'[76] Both wars against Georgia (2008) and Ukraine (2022) show unequivocally that Russia has no qualms about putting words into action when it judges the moment opportune. The Kremlin correctly interpreted NATO's refusal to grant Tbilisi a MAP to mean that the alliance was not prepared to defend Georgia in case of a Russian attack. In the next three months, first the US president George W. Bush and then the secretary of state Condoleezza Rice visited Georgia, where both tried to restrain President Saakashvili from letting himself be provoked by Russia, but without success.[77] The fact that joint US–Georgian military exercises were held near Tbilisi in mid July while Russia had started large-scale manoeuvres near the Russian–Georgian border further fuelled tensions. The US–Georgian manoeuvres obviously lulled Saakashvili into a false sense of security.

Whereas it remains debatable which side actually started the war, there seems little doubt that Moscow set a trap and Saakashvili fell into it. Following an attack on Georgian policemen by South Ossetian separatists on 1 August 2008, an intense exchange of fire began between Georgian and South Ossetian forces. By the evening of 5 August, 11,700 Russian troops, 891 armoured vehicles and 138 artillery pieces were concentrated a few kilometres north of the Roki Tunnel which links Russian North Ossetia with separatist South Ossetia. The next day, civilians were evacuated from Tskhinvali to Russia while Russian 'volunteers' (that is, mercenaries) arrived from the north. In the early evening of 7 August President Saakashvili announced a unilateral ceasefire but a few hours later issued a counter-command after hearing of a deployment of Russian troops in the Lower Kodori Gorge in separatist Abkhazia, and that Russian troops were passing through the Roki Tunnel. In addition, the Russian Foreign Ministry had refused to connect Saakashvili by telephone to President Medvedev.[78] Subsequently, just before midnight, Saakashvili ordered an attack on the separatist capital, Tskhinvali. After some initial successes by the advancing Georgian forces, Russian troops and tanks supported by aircraft poured into South Ossetia on 8 August – Georgia having neglected to block or sabotage the southern exit of the Roki Tunnel. Despite their modern US-supplied equipment the Georgian forces were forced to evacuate Tskhinvali and retreat to Gori which they also had to abandon on 11 August. The road

162. Georgian citizens stand at the border with South Ossetia, protesting against the Russian occupation of South Ossetia. The text on the board at the far right of the image, PUTIN KHUILO, can be translated as 'Putin is a prick'. The slogan is part of a Ukrainian protest song created in 2014 during the Russian attack on Crimea and eastern Ukraine. It is used by Ukrainian and Georgian nationals to assert their countries' sovereignty. Photo 2015.

to Tbilisi was now open. In the west, Abkhaz and Russian troops opened a second front by sweeping through the Kodori Valley after heavy bombing while Russian warships in the Black Sea repelled a Georgian naval counterattack. On 10 and 11 August Abkhaz and Russian troops invaded western Georgia and occupied Zugdidi and the military base at Senaki, while Russian forces captured the Black Sea harbour of Poti. At the same time, Russian aircraft bombed the Georgian military bases of Bolnisi, Marneuli and Rustavi, located south of Tbilisi, which were within Russian artillery range. Finally in Moscow on 12 August, the French president Nicolas Sarkozy negotiated a truce including a retreat of both armies to their starting positions, which Saakashvili had to accept in view of the wholesale Georgian defeat.[79] Georgia lost control over the Upper Kodori Valley and of territories east of South Ossetia which pushed the eastern South Ossetian border to as close as 2 kilometres from the Georgian Military Highway.[80] As a next step, on 26 August 2008 Russia recognized the breakaway, self-proclaimed republics of South Ossetia and Abkhazia as independent sovereign states. Yielding to Russian economic pressure, Venezuela, Nicaragua, Nauru, Vanuatu and Tuvalu followed.[81] Russia furthermore violated the truce by maintaining thousands of troops in Abkhazia and South Ossetia.[82] Tbilisi considers that Abkhazia and South Ossetia, which account for 20 per cent of Georgia's territory, are occupied territories.[83] This position is shared by most UN member states and was confirmed by the Parliamentary Assembly of the OSCE (Organization for Security and Co-operation in Europe) on 9 July 2012.[84]

Immediately after the war began, the question arose as to which side was responsible for its start. Ominous evidence for it being a Russian initiative is the above-mentioned concentration of Russian offensive forces on 5 August close to the Roki Tunnel. Several first-hand witnesses indicate that the Russian column entered the tunnel at the same time as the Georgian attack on Tskhinvali began, or even some hours before.[85] The International Crisis Group based in Brussels concluded on 22 August,

at approximately 1:30 am [on 8 August]*, tank columns of the Russian 58th Army started crossing into Georgia from the Roki tunnel separating North and South Ossetia. Apparently, the Russians had anticipated, if they did not actually entice, the Georgian move* [to attack Tskhinvali].[86]

This conclusion strongly suggests that President Saakashvili fell head first into a Russian trap. The Crisis Group then summarized that Saakashvili had been the victim of his 'disastrous miscalculation' which allowed for 'Russia's disproportionate counterattack'. Already in 2008 the Crisis Group was warning that Ukraine could be the next Russian target. Its report also blamed the Western powers:

The crisis also reflects serious mistakes by the U.S. and the European Union (EU) in Georgia since 2004, most significantly failing to adequately press President Saakashvili to abandon a quick-fix approach toward restoring Georgian control over South Ossetia and Abkhazia.[87]

Later, the *Report of the Independent International Fact-Finding Mission on the Conflict in Georgia* (the so-called *Tagliavini Report*) commissioned by the EU Council of Foreign Ministers, which was published on 30 September 2009, identified Georgia as the main culprit in starting the war but at the same time blamed all four participants involved.[88] The report was well received by Russia although it criticized the excessive size of the Russian response. Its major flaws were that it downplayed the extent of Russian preparations for war, omitted to question the role of the Russian 'peacekeeping' forces and neglected to address the failure of the US administration to restrain the Saakashvili government.

The Georgian defeat had grave consequences for the South Caucasian republic. Not only was reintegration of Abkhazia and South Ossetia an extremely distant prospect, but Georgia's aspired NATO membership was put off and there was no further discussion about granting Georgia a MAP.[89] With hindsight it was a costly mistake on Tbilisi's part to have refused after independence to seriously consider a federal model as a solution to the aspirations of Abkhazia and South Ossetia. The war also scared off private investors. Finally, the Obama and Trump administrations that succeeded Bush had no interest in the South Caucasus. In terms of the lessons of this brief 'Five Days' War', both the Western powers and Russia drew the wrong conclusions.

The former underestimated Russia's determination to annex parts of Ukraine and to keep the rest within its political orbit; the latter erroneously assumed in February 2022 that it could crush the Ukrainian army as it had done in Georgia in 2008. Both wars of 2008 and 2022 also showed that it remains dangerous for a country neighbouring Russia to seek NATO membership.[90] On the other hand, the NATO accession of Finland and Sweden decided on 5 July 2022[91] will probably take place without Russian military intervention, as the Kremlin will be reluctant to open a second war front in parallel with the difficult war in Ukraine. However, Russian pinpricks and provocations against Finland and Sweden are to be expected.

2.4.2 Georgia, Abkhazia and South Ossetia since the 2008 war

Since Saakashvili's second and last presidential term was due to end in late 2013, he attempted to emulate President Putin and initiated in 2009 a constitutional change from a presidential to a parliamentary state system in order to retain power as prime minister.[92] The constitutional change was implemented as planned, but Saakashvili's United National Movement unexpectedly lost the October 2012 parliamentary elections to a coalition led by Georgian Dream, the party founded and financed by Georgia's wealthiest individual Bidzina Ivanishvili. Ivanishvili at first had vigorously supported Saakashvili but prior to the elections made a U-turn, styling himself as saviour of Georgia from the claws of Saakashvili and his coterie. Saakashvili acknowledged defeat and submitted to an awkward cohabitation with Prime Minister Ivanishvili.[93] In October 2013, Ivanishvili's candidate for the now ceremonial presidency, Giorgi Margvelashvili, won the elections whereupon Ivanishvili stepped down as prime minister, installing in his stead his business associate Irakli Garibashvili (in office 2013–2015, 2021–) while continuing to pull the political strings in the background. But when President Margvelashvili warned that the constitutional majority won by Georgian Dream in the 2016 parliamentary elections represented a hazardous concentration of power, he lost the endorsement of Ivanishvili who in the next presidential election switched political and financial support to Salome Zourabichvili (in office 2018–). Already in the course of 2013, the judicial authorities had initiated legal proceedings against Saakashvili's associates and, as soon as the ex-president had left Georgia, against him too. When in summer 2014 various criminal charges were filed against Saakashvili on dubious grounds, the US and the EU voiced concern, emphasizing that the legal system should not be misused for purposes of political retaliation.[94] The mercurial Saakashvili later followed an unusual career: he took Ukrainian nationality and in May 2015 was appointed by the Ukrainian president Petro Poroshenko to be governor of Odessa, but one year later resigned whereupon he was stripped of his Ukrainian nationality. In autumn 2017 he re-entered Ukraine as a stateless person, from where he was deported to Poland in February 2018. He finally returned to Georgia on 1 October 2021 where he was arrested and imprisoned to serve a six-year sentence pronounced in 2018.[95]

The changes in government did not alter Georgia's strategic orientation towards the EU, the US and NATO.[96] The small country continued to put its soldiers at the disposal of ISAF in Afghanistan, which was also a way to associate with and secure training by NATO troops. However, the doors to NATO have so far remained closed and the Association Agreement with the EU which came into preliminary effect on 1 September 2014 and fully on 1 July 2016 has not yet brought about any real improvement in Georgia's economic situation. Nevertheless, Georgian Dream defended its absolute majority in the 2020 parliamentary elections by winning 48 per cent of the vote, and 90 of 150 seats.[97] Despite Georgia's Western alignment, it remained till early 2022 in a kind of waiting mode. However, the full-scale Russian invasion of Ukraine that began on 24 February 2022 prompted Georgia, along with Moldova, to formally apply for EU membership on 3 March 2022.[98] The Russian aggression also triggered a wave of solidarity with Ukraine among Georgians.

In **Abkhazia**, the presidential elections held on 3 October 2004 produced a surprising result insofar as Moscow's minion, Prime Minister Raul Khadjimba, who enjoyed the strong support of Putin, was beaten by opposition leader Sergei Bagapsh (in office 2005–2011). The result was interpreted as a backlash against the massive Russian support for Khadjimba as it expressed an underlying distrust of Russia's dominant influence. Following two months of protests and unrest in which both candidates claimed victory, they struck a compromise whereby they would run as a joint ticket in a repeat election. Together they won in December an overwhelming majority exceeding 90 per cent, confirming Bagapsh as president and Khadjimba as vice president.[99] Less than two months before the Russian–Georgian War of 2008, Khadjimba attacked President Bagapsh for his 'multivector foreign policy', that is his efforts to start a dialogue with Georgia and establish contacts with Western diplomats at the expense of stronger ties with Russia. He then added that only a Russian military intervention would be able to chase the remaining Georgians out of the Upper Kodori Valley.[100] Two years earlier, in May 2006, Bagapsh had offered comprehensive peace proposals to Georgia which were turned down by Saakashvili since they implied a recognition of Abkhazia's independence.[101] Following the war and its recognition by Moscow as a sovereign state, Abkhazia transferred the key tasks of securing borders and managing the railways and airport to Russia.[102] The increased integration of Abkhazia into Russia left many Abkhazians wondering whether they had not exchanged rule by one foreign power, Georgian for dominance by another, Russia. In December 2009, Bagapsh won a second term in presidential elections over Khadjimba. When he died in May 2011, he was succeeded by Aleksandr Ankvab (in office 2011–2014).[103]

The questions of 'multivectoral' versus 'univectoral' foreign policy and how to deal with ethnic Georgians in Abkhazia became President Ankvab's undoing too.[104] In May 2014, thousands of protesters mobilized by the pro-Russia opposition leader Khadjimba paralyzed public life in the capital, Sukhumi and stormed Ankvab's offices, which amounted to a *coup d'état*. The protesters' anger was directed as Ankvab's relatively tolerant policy towards the remaining ethnic Georgians. The president was forced to flee to the Russian military base at Gudauta, and resigned after parliament had declared him 'unable to assume his responsibilities'.[105] In the ensuing elections Khadjimba became the fourth president of Abkhazia. In November, two months after taking office, Khadjimba signed a treaty with Putin which stipulated a close alignment of Abkhaz foreign, defence and economic policy with Russia and a Russian-led 'joint Russian–Abkhaz military unit' as well as 'a joint coordination centre of the organs of internal affairs'.[106] Tbilisi condemned the treaty as a further step towards annexing occupied Georgian territory. The Moscow-orchestrated putsch of May 2014 and the treaty with Russia brought previous efforts to find Abkhazia a place within the community of international states to a standstill. In 2019, Khadjimba won re-election as president while his rival Aslan Bzhania had to drop out due to alleged poisoning. But Khadjimba was forced to resign and Bzhania won the March 2020 elections.[107] As of 2022, any reunification of Abkhazia with Georgia was further away than ever before, not least because the return of *ca.* 250,000 former Georgian refugees to their homeland would turn the 125,000 ethnic Abkhazians once more into a minority within their own territory.[108] For Abkhazia, the question of Georgians returning to their homeland is taboo, whereas for Georgia it is a condition *sine qua non* of any solution. Finally, a strong Russia will never voluntarily abandon this foothold in South Caucasus.

In **South Ossetia**, the presidential elections of April–May 2022 turned out to be a referendum on how far the self-declared republic should defer to the Kremlin. In the run-up to the elections, the incumbent Anatoly Bibilov had expressed enthusiasm for the

163. Bronze figure at the bottom of the Yerevan Cascade, a huge stairway built out of limestone. Yerevan, Armenia. Photo 2018.

unification of South Ossetia with North Ossetia, that is for joining Russia: he had also called for a referendum on the issue. Interestingly, Bibilov lost to the opposition leader Alan Gagloyev in the second round of the presidential elections on 8 May 2022, for being too close to Moscow.[109] During his election campaign, the challenger Gagloyev had rejected Bibilov's idea of a referendum and had instead emphasized the importance of South Ossetia's own statehood and institutions. Bibilov also lost popularity when he supported the deployment of South Ossetian soldiers to fight for Russia in Ukraine; he lost further ground when about 300 of these South Ossetian soldiers drafted to fight in Ukraine deserted in late March and returned to Tskhinvali complaining of poor leadership and bad logistics.[110] Three weeks after having won the presidential elections, on 30 May 2022, president Gagloyev shelved the planned referendum on joining Russia which his predecessor had scheduled for 17 June.[111]

3. Outlook

The Second Nagorno-Karabakh War and the Russian invasion of Ukraine have transmitted threatening messages throughout the Caucasus and deepened its historic divisions. In the South Caucasus, Georgia seeks EU membership and an even closer alignment to NATO, and Azerbaijan strives to strengthen its independence from Russia without provoking a hostile reaction from the Kremlin. The North Caucasus, on the other hand, is fully within Russia's grip and contributes disproportionally in manpower to the Russian war effort in Ukraine. Whereas in Soviet times the Caucasus was united within the USSR, the divide runs now along the main crest of the Great Caucasus mountain range. Within the South Caucasus, the existing divisions have increased. Georgia continues to gravitate towards the West while fearing to share the fate of Ukraine should President Putin prevail there. This concern is also reflected in a slight apprehension about the thousands of Russian migrants entering Georgia since February 2022. For should they stay, so the concern goes, that may induce Moscow to assert the need to 'protect' these expats, in spite of the fact that these people left Russia in protest against Putin's regime.[112] Azerbaijan for its part strengthened its strategic and military cooperation with Turkey in the Second Nagorno-Karabakh War. Yet Baku had to accept Russian peace-keeping troops on its territory. It is forced to apply a seesaw policy towards Russia and Turkey, two regional powers with often conflicting interests, for example in Syria or Libya.

Azerbaijan also faces the challenge of facilitating the return of the hundreds of thousands of internal refugees to their destroyed homes in the seven western districts – assuming that these people want to return at all. Finally, Armenia is more than ever dependent on Russian protection and, to a lesser degree, Iranian goodwill. Armenia's position vis-à-vis its protector has become weaker since Moscow has replaced Yerevan as defender of Nagorno-Karabakh. Armenia's position could be further weakened by the Russian setbacks in the Ukrainian war, as Russia's perceived military clout as an efficient protector has diminished. Nevertheless, Armenia remains locked within the Russian sphere of influence since its only chance to escape Moscow's grip would be to conclude peace with Azerbaijan by more or less sacrificing Nagorno-Karabakh's quasi-independence.

In any case, the prospects of any South Caucasian state joining the EU in the foreseeable future are very slim to zero. For Brussels will be absorbed in the coming decade with the membership application of Ukraine and Moldova and their eventual integration. Furthermore, the extension of the EU to include non-contiguous countries separated by a non-member state (Turkey) is illusory. The Caucasus will remain at the European Union's periphery. Likewise NATO membership for a South Caucasian state is for the time being out of reach, unless NATO should decide in favour of an active confrontational strategy towards Russia. The EU and NATO have an interest in stable conditions in the Caucasus that do not give Russia an excuse to intervene militarily, but their interest goes no further than this. If Russia emerges from the war against Ukraine severely weakened, it is to be expected that Turkey will gain further political influence in the Caucasus and China in Central Asia.

Even if the Russian presence and interference in South Caucasus were to dwindle or vanish, the political positions of the three sovereign states and the three, internationally hardly recognized, quasi-states are so disparate, their objectives so divergent and their mind-sets so entrenched that conflict-free cooperation, let alone unity, can hardly be expected in the foreseeable future. A similar observation applies to an even greater extent to the North Caucasus, whose states, left to their own devices, would hardly be economically viable. In the North Caucasus, anger over a disproportionate recruitment of soldiers for the casualty-ridden Ukrainian war could act as a destabilizing factor, especially in Chechnya and Dagestan. To conclude, any vision of a politically united Caucasus or a Caucasian Union remains an unrealistic dream. As it is, achieving a long-term *modus vivendi* with functioning mechanisms to defuse and resolve conflicts will be challenge enough.

Appendix

Appendix: Chronology of the most important Caucasian dynasties

Bagrationi kings of Georgia, 1014–1491

Giorgi (George) I (r. 1014–1027)

Bagrat IV (r. 1027–1072)

Giorgi II (r. 1072–1089)

Davit (David) IV (r. 1089–1125)

Demetre I (first reign 1125–1154)

Davit V (r. 1055–1056)

Demetre I (probable second reign 1155–1156)

Giorgi III (r. 1156–1184)

Tamar (co-ruler 1178–1184, r. 1184–1213)

Giorgi IV Lasha (co-ruler 1207–1213, r. 1213–1223)

Rusudan (r. 1223–1245)

Davit VI Narin (r. 1247–1293, from 1258/59 in Imereti and Abkhazia)

Davit VII Ulu (r. 1247–1270, from 1259/62 in east Georgia)

Demetre II (r. 1270–1289 in east Georgia),

Vakhtang II (r. 1289–1292)

Davit VIII (r. 1292–1299, d. 1308)

Konstantine (r. 1293–1327 in Imereti)

Mikel (Michael) I (anti-king in west Georgia 1293–1327, r. 1327–1329)

Giorgi V (first reign 1299–1302)

Vakhtang III (r. 1302–1311)

Giorgi VI (r. 1311–1313)

Giorgi V (as regent 1311–1313, r. 1314–1346)

Davit IX (r. 1346–1360)

Bagrat V (co-ruler from 1355, r. 1360–1393)

Giorgi VII (from 1369 co-ruler, r. 1393–1405 or 1407)

Konstantine I (r. 1405 or 1407–1412)

Aleksandre (Alexander) I (r. 1412–1442, d. *ca.* 1446)

Vakhtang IV (r. 1442–1446)

Demetre III (co-ruler 1442–1446)

Giorgi VIII (r. 1446–1465, as **Giorgi I of Kakheti** r. 1466–1476)

Bagrat VI (r. 1466–1478; previously as **Bagrat II of Imereti** r. 1463–1466)

Konstantine II (r. 1478–1491, as **Konstantine II of Kartli** 1491–1505)

Barons and kings of Cilician Armenia, 1080–1375

Rubenid barons

Ruben I (r. 1080–1095)

Kostantin (Constantine) I (r. 1095–1099)

Thoros I (r. 1099–1129)

Kostantin II (r. 1129)

Levon (Leo, Leon) I (r. 1129–1137, d. 1140)

Thoros II (r. 1145–1169, d. 1170)

Ruben II (r. 1169–1170)

Mleh I (r. 1170–1175)

Ruben III (r. 1175–1187)

Levon II (r. as prince 1187–1198)

Kings

Levon (Leo, Leon) I (r. 1198–1219)

Zabel (queen 1219–1252)

Philip (r. 1222–1224, d. 1225)

Hethum I (r. 1226–1269, d. 1270)

Levon II (r. 1269–1289)

Hethum II (first reign 1289–1293)

Thoros III (r. 1293–1295, co-ruler 1295–1296).

Hethum II and **Thoros III** (co-rulers 1295–1296)

Smbat (r. 1296–1298)

Kostantin I (r. 1298–1299)

Hethum II (third reign 1299–1303)

Hethum II (regent 1303–1307)

Levon III (r. 1303–1307)

Oshin (r. 1307–1320),

Levon IV (r. 1320–1341),

Kostantin II (1342–1344)

Kostantin III (r. 1344–1363)

Kostantin IV (r. 1365–1373)

Levon V (r. 1374–1375, d. 1393)

Kings of unified Kartli and Kakheti

Teimuraz II of Kartli (r. 1744–1762) and his son **Erekle II of Kakheti** (r. 1744–1762)

Erekle II of Kartli and Kakheti (r. 1762–1798)

Giorgi XII (r. 1798–1800)

Georgia annexed by Imperial Russia on 18 January 1801

Notes

I. A Fragmented Identity: An Introduction to Contemporary Ethnic and Political Conditions in the Caucasus

1. Kissinger, Henry, *A World Restored: Metternich, Castlereagh and the Problems of Peace, 1812–22* (1957; Brattleboro, VT: Echo Point Books & Media, 2013), p. 331.
2. For an overview of the plethora of ethnicities and languages within the Caucasus, see: Baumer, Christoph, *History of the Caucasus*, vol. 1: *At the Crossroads of Empires* (London: I.B.Tauris/Bloomsbury, 2021), pp. 7, 300–304.
3. Kissinger, *A World Restored* (2013), p. 331.
4. Status as per 31 August 2022.
5. In the text, dates are given according to the Gregorian calendar, but in quotations from Russian sources they are according to the Julian calendar, which was valid until 31 January 1918. The Julian calendar lagged behind the Gregorian calendar by 11 days in the eighteenth century, by 12 days in the nineteenth century and by 13 days in the twentieth. The date of the October Revolution is by the Julian calendar 25 October, but according to the Gregorian, 7 November 1917. In Islamic documents, the year is given according to the Muslim lunar calendar; it has the abbreviation AH, which stands for *Anno Hegirae*, whose beginning corresponds to the year 622 CE.
6. All states and republics include minorities to a greater or lesser degree.

II. In the Wake of International Great-Power Politics

1. Baumer, *History of the Caucasus*, vol. 1 (2021), pp. 249–51.
2. Baumer, *History of the Caucasus*, vol. 1 (2021), pp. 249f.
3. Baumer, *History of the Caucasus*, vol. 1 (2021), pp. 281–83.
4. Rapp, Stephen H. Jr., *Studies in Medieval Georgian Historiography: Early Texts and Eurasian Contexts* (Leuven: Peeters, 2003), pp. 337–9.
5. Rapp, *Studies in Medieval Georgian Historiography* (2003), pp. 363–6; Thomson, Robert W., *Rewriting Caucasian History: The Medieval Armenian Adaptation of the Georgian Chronicles. The Original Georgian Texts and the Armenian Adaptation*, 284–290 (Oxford: Clarendon, 1996), pp. 281–6.
6. In was not until 1074 that Giorgi II was able to reconquer Anakopia after the devastating Byzantine defeat of Manzikert (1071). Thomson, *Rewriting Caucasian History*, 291–5, 317 (1996), pp. 286–88, 308.
7. The reconstruction of the chronology of the events is uncertain. Thomson, *Rewriting Caucasian History*, 295–303 (1996), pp. 288–95.
8. Skylitzes, John, *A Synopsis of Byzantine History 811–1057*, 21.14–15 (Cambridge: Cambridge University Press, 2010), pp. 425f. See also: [Matthew of Edessa,] *Armenia and the Crusades, 10th to 12th Centuries: The Chronicle of Matthew of Edessa*, I. 94 (Belmont, MA: Armenian Heritage Press, 2013), pp. 78f.
9. Athir, Izz ad-Din ibn al-, *The Annals of the Saljuq Turks: Selections from al-Kamil fi'l-Tarikh of Izz ad-Din ibn al-Athir* (London: Routledge Curzon, 2002), pp. 67f.
10. Thomson dates Bagrat's captivity in Constantinople from 1054 to 1057 which seems somewhat late. Thomson, *Rewriting Caucasian History* (1996), p. 295, n19.
11. Thomson, *Rewriting Caucasian History*, 303–4 (1996), pp. 295f.
12. For an excellent presentation of Bagrat's complicated reign see also: Rayfield, Donald, *Edge of Empires: A History of Georgia* (London: Reaktion Books, 2012), pp. 76–82.
13. Baumer, *History of the Caucasus*, vol. 1 (2021), p. 283, fig. 205.
14. Al-Athir, *The Annals of the Saljuq Turks* (2002), p. 153.
15. Al-Athir, *The Annals of the Saljuq Turks* (2002), pp. 152–5.
16. See below p. 16
17. Thomson, *Rewriting Caucasian History*, 309 (1996), p. 300.
18. According to Minorsky, the name Sitlarabi is a corruption of the title *Sayyid al Arab*. Minorsky, V[ladimir], *Studies in Caucasian History* (London: Taylor's Foreign Press, 1953), p. 67 n2.
19. Minorsky, *Studies in Caucasian History* (1953), pp. 23, 29, 66f; Thomson, *Rewriting Caucasian History*, 311–13 (1996), pp. 302–4. See also: Baumer, *History of the Caucasus*, vol. 1 (2021), p. 270.
20. Baumer, *History of the Caucasus*, vol. 1 (2021), p. 286.
21. Al-Athir, *The Annals of the Saljuq Turks* (2002), pp. 172, 197f; Runciman, Steven, *A History of the Crusades*, vol. 1 (1954; London: The Folio Society, 1994), pp. 62–5.
22. Baumer, *History of the Caucasus*, vol. 1 (2021), p. 287; Thomson, *Rewriting Caucasian History*, 315–18 (1996), p. 306–9.
23. Thomson, *Rewriting Caucasian History*, 320 (1996), p. 311. The last part of Thomson's *Rewriting Caucasian History*, from which this quote is taken, begins under the title *The History of David, King of Kings*. This *History* also builds the first section of a later compilation called by Toumanoff *The History of the Five Reigns* which was translated by Katharine Vivian under the title *The Period of Giorgi Lasha*. Rapp, *Studies in Medieval Georgian Historiography* (2003), p. 346; *The Georgian Chronicle: The Period of Giorgi Lasha*, trans. Katharine Vivian and ed. S. Qaukhchishvili (Amsterdam: Adolf M. Hakkert, 1991).
24. Thomson, *Rewriting Caucasian History*, 324 (1996), p. 315.
25. In the literature King Davit is also denoted as II or III, depending on how many previous rulers called Davit are counted as kings of Georgia or of Kartli.
26. Thomson, *Rewriting Caucasian History*, 324 (1996), p. 316.
27. Thomson, *Rewriting Caucasian History*, 329 (1996), p. 320.
28. Both the sultan and his vizier were murdered: Baumer, Christoph, *The History of Central Asia*, vol. 3: *The Age of Islam and the Mongols* (London: I.B.Tauris, 2016), pp. 88f, 98.
29. Thomson, *Rewriting Caucasian History*, 324–29 (1996), pp. 315–21. See also: Rayfield, *Edge of Empires* (2012), pp. 85–9.
30. Thomson, *Rewriting Caucasian History*, 327 (1996), p. 318.
31. For an image of Ikalto see: Baumer, *History of the Caucasus*, vol. 1 (2021), p. 242, fig. 173.
32. Thomson, *Rewriting Caucasian History*, 330f (1996), p. 322.
33. Thomson, *Rewriting Caucasian History*, 348 (1996), p. 339.
34. Baumer, *History of the Caucasus*, vol. 1 (2021), p. 273.
35. It remains unclear whether King Davit married Äträk's daughter Gurandukht before or after the immigration of the Kipchaks; in any case, this marriage was connected with Davit's efforts to form an alliance with the bellicose Kipchaks. Peter B. Golden, 'Nomads in the sedentary world: The case of Pre-Chinggisid Rus' and Georgia', in Anatoly Khazanov and André Wink (eds), *Nomads in the Sedentary World* (Richmond: Curzon, 2001), p. 46; Rayfield, *Edge of Empires* (2012), pp. 90f.
36. Thomson, *Rewriting Caucasian History*, 335–337 (1996), pp. 326–8.

37 Athir, 'Izz ad-Din ibn al-, *The Chronicle of Ibn al-Athir for the Crusading Period* from *al-Kamil fi'l-Ta'rikh*, part 1, 555, trans. D.S. Richards (Aldershot: Ashgate, 2006), p. 204; Runciman, *A History of the Crusades*, vol. 2 (1994), pp. 120f.

38 Athir, *The Chronicle of Ibn al-Athir*, part 1, 567f (2006), p. 213.

39 Richard, Jean (ed.), *Au-delà de la Perse et de l'Arménie. L'Orient latin et la découverte de l'Asie intérieure. Quelques textes inégalement connus aux origines de l'alliance entre Francs et Mongols (1145–1262)* (Turnhout: Brepols, 2005), pp. 30, 41–56.

40 Athir, *The Chronicle of Ibn al-Athir*, part 1, 567f (2006), pp. 213f.

41 Peacock, A.C.S., 'Identity, culture and religion on medieval Islam's Caucasian frontiers', *Bulletin of the Royal Institute for Inter-Faith Studies*, vol. 13 (Amman: 2011), pp. 78–80.

42 Minorsky, *Studies in Caucasian History* (1953), p. 136; id., *A History of Sharvān and Darband in the 10th–11th Centuries* (Cambridge: W. Heffer and Sons, 1958), p. 85, n2; Thomson, *Rewriting Caucasian History*, 343f (1996), pp. 335f.

43 Minorsky, *Studies in Caucasian History* (1953), pp. 83f; Thomson, *Rewriting Caucasian History*, 344f (1996), p. 337.

44 Thomson, *Rewriting Caucasian History*, 356–7 (1996), pp. 346–8.

45 *The Georgian Chronicle* (1991), p. 42.

46 *The Georgian Chronicle* (1991), p. 49. A suspicious testament from 1125 which is probably a much later forgery names Demetre only as regent for his half-brother Vakhtang, Davit's son by his second wife Gurandukht. Rayfield, *Edge of Empires* (2012), p. 96.

47 Baumer, *History of the Caucasus*, vol. 1 (2021), pp. 288f.

48 Rayfield, *Edge of Empires* (2012), p. 99.

49 Bosworth, C.E., 'The political and dynastic history of the Iranian world (A.D. 1000–1227)', in: *The Cambridge History of Iran*, vol. 5: *The Saljuq and Mongol Periods*, ed. J.A. Boyle (Cambridge: Cambridge University Press, 1968), pp. 169f.

50 The Orbeli or Orbeliani were a branch of the Liparitids whose existence dates from the year 1177.

51 Eastmond, Antony, *Royal Imagery in Medieval Georgia* (Philadelphia: University of Pennsylvania Press, 2008), 107.

52 Rayfield, *Edge of Empires* (2012), pp. 100f.

53 Orbélian, Stéphannos, *Histoire de la Siounie*, trans. M.-F. Brosset (1864; repr. New Delhi: Facsimile Publisher, 2019), p. 217.

54 Minorsky, *A History of Sharvān and Darband in the 10th–11th centuries* (Cambridge: W. Heffer & Sons, 1958), p. 140; Rayfield, *Edge of Empires* (2012), p. 102.

55 Athir, *The Chronicle of Ibn al-Athir*, part 2, 278 (2007), p. 129.

56 Baumer, *History of the Caucasus*, vol. 1 (2021), p. 288.

57 *The Georgian Chronicle* (1991), p. 162.

58 Orbélian, *Histoire de la Siounie* (2019), pp. 218–21.

59 *Geschichten und Lobpreisungen der Könige*, in *Chroniken der georgischen Königin Tamar*, trans. Surab Sardshweladse and Heinz Fähnrich (Aachen: Shaker Verlag, 2004), pp. 16, 26, 45.

60 Baumer, *History of the Caucasus*, vol. 1 (2021), p. 177.

61 *Geschichten und Lobpreisungen der Könige* (2004), p. 31.

62 The sequence of commanders differs depending on the editions of the Chronicles. The present author follows the older version: Gamrekeli Toreli is followed by Sargis Mkhargrdzeli who is followed by Zakare Mkhargrdzeli; in later editions Gamrekeli follows Sargis. *The Georgian Chronicle* (1991), pp. 62f, 114; *Chroniken der georgischen Königin Tamar* (2004), p. 32.

63 *Chroniken der georgischen Königin Tamar*, Foreword (2004), p. 7; Fähnrich, Heinz, *Geschichte Georgiens* (Leiden: Brill, 2010), pp. 210; Limper, Bernhard, *Die Mongolen und die christlichen Völker des Kaukasus* (Cologne: University of Cologne, 1980), pp. 39f.

64 Ezosmodzghvari, Basil, *Life of the Queen of Queens, Tamar*, in: *The Georgian Chronicle: The Period of Giorgi Lasha* (1991), p. 60. Ezosmodzghvari was the title of the royal household's controller.

65 Fähnrich, *Geschichte Georgiens* (2010), p. 211; Gambashidze, Irina, Hauptmann, Andreas, et al. (eds), *Georgien. Schätze aus dem Land des Goldenen Vlies* (Bochum: Deutsches Bergbau-Museum Bochum, 2001), p. 206.

66 Ezosmodzghvari, *Life of the Queen of Queens* (1991), p. 115.

67 Ezosmodzghvari, *Life of the Queen of Queens* (1991), pp. 62, 115–22; Rayfield, *Edge of Empires* (2012), pp. 111f.

68 Ezosmodzghvari, *Life of the Queen of Queens* (1991), pp. 63, 141f; Conrad, Heiko, *Geschichte und Wundergeschichten im Werk des Kirakos Ganjakec'i (13. Jh.). Armenien zwischen Chasaren und Arabern, Franken und Mongolen* (Bern: Peter Lang, 2018), pp. 173, 184.

69 *Geschichten und Lobpreisungen der Könige* (2004), pp. 59–64. See also: Ezosmodzghvari, *Life of the Queen of Queens, Tamar* (1991), p. 63; Eastmond, Antony, *Tamta's World: The Life and Encounters of a Medieval Noblewoman from the Middle East to Mongolia* (Cambridge: Cambridge University Press, 2017), p. 4.

70 Conrad, *Geschichte und Wundergeschichten* (2018), p. 189.

71 Conrad, *Geschichte und Wundergeschichten* (2018), p. 317.

72 Conrad, *Geschichte und Wundergeschichten* (2018), p. 317; translation from: Eastmond, *Tamta's World* (2017), p. 57.

73 Conrad, *Geschichte und Wundergeschichten* (2018), pp. 317–18; translation from: Eastmond, *Tamta's World* (2017), p. 59. It remains unknown whether in Akhtala in the early thirteenth century holy mass was celebrated according to the Armenian or Georgian rite.

74 Athir, *The Chronicle of Ibn al-Athir*, part 3, 183f, 255f (2008), pp. 70, 123f; Ezosmodzghvari, *Life of the Queen of Queens* (1991), pp. 65–72; Rayfield, *Edge of Empires* (2012), pp. 112f.

75 Ezosmodzghvari, *Life of the Queen of Queens* (1991), pp. 74, 88.

76 Lake Sevan is called Gegham in Armenian, in Turkish Gokcha.

77 Conrad, *Geschichte und Wundergeschichten* (2018), p. 191; Limper, *Die Mongolen und die christlichen Völker des Kaukasus* (1980), pp. 60–63.

78 Conrad, *Geschichte und Wundergeschichten* (2018), pp. 174, 177, 185f, 195.

79 Eastmond, *Tamta's World* (2017), pp. 4, 26f, 51.

80 Eastmond, *Tamta's World* (2017), p. 85; Ezosmodzghvari, *Life of the Queen of Queens* (1991), p. 84. Peacock and Yildiz name the captured Mangujakid emir of Erzincan Fakhr al-Din Bahramshah. Peacock, A.C.S and Yildiz, Sara Nur, *The Seljuks of Anatolia* (London: I.B.Tauris, 2013); no pagination in online e-book: google.co.uk/books/edition/The_Seljuks_of_Anatolia/dp-LDwAAQBAJ?hl=en&gbpv=1&dq=Fakhr+al-Din+in+Peacock+vahramshah&pg=PT282&printsec=frontcover.

81 Ezosmodzghvari, *Life of the Queen of Queens* (1991), pp. 86f, 163.

82 Al-Athir dates Tamar's death to 1207. Athir, *The Chronicle of Ibn al-Athir*, part 3, 256 (2008), p. 124.

83 Ezosmodzghvari, *Life of the Queen of Queens* (1991), pp. 131–4; Conrad, *Geschichte und Wundergeschichten* (2018), p. 174f.

84 Ezosmodzghvari, *Life of the Queen of Queens* (1991), pp. 134–40.

85 Eastmond, *Tamta's World* (2017), p. 79; see also pp. 1, 5, 82.

86 Eastmond, *Tamta's World* (2017), pp. 8–14, 327f, 343, 368f.

87 Kirakos Gandzakets'i, *History of the Armenians*, trans. Robert Bedrosian, 149 (New York: Sources of the Armenian Tradition, 1986); no pagination in online e-book.

88 The greatest expansion was achieved in 1219–20 with the occupation of Syunik. Limper, *Die Mongolen und die christlichen Völker des Kaukasus* (1980), p. 56.

89 'Life of King Giorgi Lasha', part of *History of the Five Reigns*, in: *The Georgian Chronicle. The Period of Giorgi Lasha* (1991), pp. 97–100.

90 'Life of King Giorgi Lasha', pp. 101f.

91 'Life of King Giorgi Lasha', pp. 101, 103.

92 Nasawi, Muhammad ibn Ahmad, *Histoire du sultan Djelâl ed-Dîn Mankobirti, prince du Kharezm*, trans. O. Houdas, VII–VIII (Paris: E. Leroux, 1895; reprint, 2014), pp. 26–33.

93 Tvaradze, Aleksandre, '"Hunderjährige Chronik" — Georgien in der Mongolenzeit', in: Hubert Kaufhold and Manfred Kropp (eds), *Oriens Christianus. Hefte für die Kunde des christlichen Orients*, vol. 91 (Wiesbaden: Harrassowitz, 2007), pp. 96f.

94 Allen, W.E.D., *A History of the Georgian People from the Beginning down to the Russian Conquest in the Nineteenth Century* (London: Routledge and Kegan Paul, 1971), p. 110.

95 The Shah died on a small island in the south-western Caspian Sea at the turn of the years 1220 to 1221. Baumer, *The History of Central Asia*, vol. 3 (2016), pp. 136, 188f.

96 It remains disputed if two or three battles between the Georgians and the Mongol invaders took place. In addition, the last, decisive battle is dated to either 1221 or 1222. According to al-Athir, there were three separate battles between late autumn 1220 and autumn 1221. The main primary sources are: Athir, *The Chronicle of Ibn al-Athir*, part 3, 373–84 (2008), pp. 213–21; Kirakos, *History of the Armenians*, 166–71 (1986); Rasiduddin Fazlullah [Rashid ad-Din Fadhlallah Hamdani], *Jami'u't-Tawarikh: Compendium of Chronicles (Tome 1)*, Classical Writings of the Medieval Islamic World, vol. 3, trans. Wheeler M. Thackston, 532–535 (London: I.B.Tauris, 2012), pp. 184f. Secondary sources: Conrad, *Geschichte und Wundergeschichten* (2018), pp. 197f, 212f; Dashdondog, Bayarsaikhan,

The Mongols and the Armenians (1220–1335) (Leiden: Brill, 2011), pp. 48–50; Gabriel, Richard A., *Subotai the Valiant: Genghis Khan's Greatest General* (Westport: Praeger, 2004), pp. 90–95; Limper, *Die Mongolen und die christlichen Völker des Kaukasus* (1980), pp. 80–87; Rayfield, *Edge of Empires* (2012), pp. 120f; Tvaradze, '"Hunderjährige Chronik"' (2007), p. 98; id., 'Der Westfeldzug von 1219–1221: Die "Mongolenerwartung" im Kreuzfahrerlager von Damiette und im christlichen Kaukasus', in: Jürgen Tubach, Sophia G. Vashalomidze and Manfred Zimmer (eds), *Caucasus during the Mongol Period / Der Kaukasus in der Mongolenzeit* (Wiesbaden: Reichert, 2012), pp. 254–64.

97 Athir, *The Chronicle of Ibn al-Athir*, part 3, 385f (2008), pp. 222f; Baumer, *History of the Caucasus*, vol. 1 (2021), pp. 260f; Rasiduddin, *Jami'u't-Tawarikh*, 534–6 (2012), p. 185.

98 Athir, *The Chronicle of Ibn al-Athir*, part 3, 386f (2008), p. 223.

99 Athir, *The Chronicle of Ibn al-Athir*, part 3, 416f (2008), p. 244; Eastmond, *Tamta's World* (2017), p. 91; Peacock, 'Identity, culture and religion' (2011), p. 83. According to other authors, Rusudan was betrothed to the Shirvanshah: Rayfield, *Edge of Empires* (2012), p. 121.

100 Athir, *The Chronicle of Ibn al-Athir*, part 3, 416f (2008), pp. 244f.

101 Athir, *The Chronicle of Ibn al-Athir*, part 3, 406–19 (2008), pp. 237–9.

102 Limper, *Die Mongolen und die christlichen Völker des Kaukasus* (1980), pp. 90f.

103 Rayfield, *Edge of Empires* (2012), p. 121. The *Darbazi* accepted Rusudan as queen since Giorgi's son Davit was an infant bastard.

104 It was only with the Mongol campaign into Eastern Europe masterminded by Sübotai in 1241 that the eyes of Western powers were definitively opened.

105 Tvaradze, '"Hunderjährige Chronik"' (2007), p. 99; 'Der Westfeldzug von 1219–1221' (2012), pp. 293f.

106 Baumer, *The History of Central Asia*, vol. 3 (2016), p. 136. Jalal al-Din behaved in Iran and the Caucasus more like a warlord than a statesman.

107 Juvaini, 'Ala-ud-Din 'Ata-Malik, [*Tarikh-e Jahan-gusha:*] *The History of the World-Conqueror*, trans. John Andrew Boyle, II.XVII (Manchester: Manchester University Press, 1958), p. 426; Nasawi, *Histoire du sultan Djelâl ed-Dîn Mankobirti*, XLVIII (2014), p. 185.

108 Athir, *The Chronicle of Ibn al-Athir*, part 3, 435 (2008), p. 258; Nasawi, *Histoire du sultan Djelâl ed-Dîn Mankobirti*, XLVIII (2014), pp. 185f.

109 *The Hundred Years' Chronicle*, in: Stephen Jones (ed.), *Kartlis Tskhovreba: A History of Georgia* (Tbilisi: Artanuji Publishing, 2014), pp. 323f.

110 Kirakos, *History of the Armenians*, 187–190 (1986).

111 *The Hundred Years' Chronicle* (2014), p. 325.

112 Athir, *The Chronicle of Ibn al-Athir*, part 3, 451 (2008), p. 270.

113 Juvaini, [*Tarikh-e Jahan-gusha,*] II.XVIIf (1958), pp. 426–42; Nasawi, *Histoire du sultan Djelâl ed-Dîn Mankobirti*, LXXX (2014), pp. 293f ; Rasiduddin, *Jami'u't-Tawarikh*, 552 (2012), p. 191. See also: Boyle, J.A., 'Dynastic and political history of the Il-Khans', in: Boyle, *The Cambridge History of Iran*, vol. 5 (1968), pp. 327–35; Tvaradze, '"Hunderjährige Chronik"' (2007), pp. 100f.

114 Athir, *The Chronicle of Ibn al-Athir*, part 3, 487–91 (2008), pp. 298–300; Nasawi, *Histoire du sultan Djelâl ed-Dîn Mankobirti*, LXXXIX (2014), pp. 342–6. See also: Eastmond, *Tamta's World* (2017), p. 327.

115 Juvaini, [*Tarikh-e Jahan-gusha,*] II. XX (1958), pp. 453–9 ; Nasawi, *Histoire du sultan Djelâl ed-Dîn Mankobirti*, CVI (2014), pp. 405–11.

116 Kirakos, *History of the Armenians*, 263 (1986). According to *The Hundred Years' Chronicle* Rusudan wanted her son-in-law to kill her nephew, but the Sultan spared him: (2014), pp. 327f.

117 *The Hundred Years' Chronicle* (2014), pp. 330f.

118 Dashdondog, Bayarsaikhan, 'The Mongol conquerors of Armenia', in: Tubach et al., *Caucasus during the Mongol Period* (2012), p. 68.

119 Kirakos, *History of the Armenians*, 217–20 (1986).

120 Kirakos, *History of the Armenians*, 215 (1986).

121 Kirakos, *History of the Armenians*, 224–6 (1986).

122 Dashdondog, 'The Mongol conquerors of Armenia' (2012), p. 71.

123 Hewsen, Robert H., *Armenia: A Historical Atlas* (Chicago: The University of Chicago Press, 2001), pp. 119f, 163.

124 Orbélian, *Histoire de la Siounie* (2019), pp. 228–30.

125 Dashdondog, 'The Mongol conquerors of Armenia' (2012), pp. 72f.

126 Baumer, *History of the Caucasus*, vol. 1 (2021), p. 261.

127 Simon of Saint-Quentin, *History of the Tartars*, in: Vincent of Beauvais, *Speculum Historiale* (1264), XXX.89, XXXII.42, transl. and ed. Stephen Pow et al. (2019).

128 In 1247 the Great Khan Güyük replaced Baiju with Eljigidai who was never able to assert himself; he was executed by Möngke Khan in winter 1251/52.

129 Kirakos, *History of the Armenians*, 264 (1986); *The Hundred Years' Chronicle* (2014), pp. 338f, 343–6.

130 Juvaini, [*Tarikh-e Jahan-gusha,*] I.XXXVI (1958), p. 257.

131 Kirakos, *History of the Armenians*, 265 (1986).

132 Juvaini, [*Tarikh-e Jahan-gusha,*] II.XXX (1958), p. 507.

133 Conrad, *Geschichte und Wundergeschichten* (2018), pp. 224–30; May, Timothy, 'The conquest and rule of Transcaucasia: The era of Chormaqan', in: Tubach, et al., *Caucasus during the Mongol Period* (2012), pp. 146f.

134 Rubruck, William of, *The Mission of Friar William of Rubruck: His Journey to the Court of the Great Khan Möngke, 1253–1255*, trans. Peter Jackson (Indianapolis: Hackett, 2009), p. 265.

135 Hethum von Korykos, [*La Flor des estoires d'Orient.*] *Geschichte der Mongolen*, trans. Raimund Senoner, ed. Wilhelm Baum (Klagenfurt: Kitab, 2006), pp. 9f, 75. For the Nestorians, see Baumer, Christoph, *The Church of the East: An Illustrated History of Assyrian Christianity* (London: I.B.Tauris, 2016).

136 Rubruck, *The Mission of Friar William of Rubruck* (2009), pp. 270f.

137 Simon of Saint-Quentin, *History of the Tartars*, XXXII.42–4 (2019).

138 Batu Khan's and the Golden Horde's claim to Georgia derived from the fact that Batu had the nominal command over the first pan-Mongol westward campaign of 1236–42. He also claimed that Genghis Khan had granted to his son Jochi, that is Berke's father, the territories west of Qayaliq and Chorasmia 'as far in that [western] direction as the hoof of Tatar horse had penetrated'. Juvaini, [*Tarikh-e Jahan-gusha,*] I.IV (1958) p. 42.

139 Baumer, *The History of Central Asia*, vol. 3 (2016), pp. 249–58. The title *Il-Khan* means 'subordinate Khan', that is subordinate to the Great Khan in Karakorum.

140 Kirakos, *History of the Armenians*, 311 (1986).

141 Dashdondog, *The Mongols and the Armenians* (2011), p. 67.

142 Arawelts'i, Vardan, *Compilation of History*, transl. Robert Bedrosian (New York: Sources of the Armenian Tradition, 2007), p. 88.

143 Limper, *Die Mongolen und die christlichen Völker des Kaukasus* (1980), pp. 163, 190; Rayfield, *Edge of Empires* (2012), p. 140.

144 Kirakos, *History of the Armenians*, 321–4 (1986).

145 Arawelts'i, *Compilation of History* (2007), p. 93.

146 The principality of the Mkhargrdzeli finally fell apart in the later 1350s. Limper, *Die Mongolen und die christlichen Völker des Kaukasus* (1980), pp. 184, 188.

147 *The Hundred Years' Chronicle* (2014), pp. 352–4.

148 Concerning the war in Palestine and Syria between Mongols, Mamelukes and Cilician Armenians, see the next chapter.

149 The four sons of Genghis Khan – Jochi, Chagatai, Ögödei and Tolui – each founded a dynasty of rulers and princes named after their ancestor.

150 Kirakos, *History of the Armenians*, 330f (1986); Rasiduddin, *Jami'u't-Tawarikh,* 738, 1034, 1044 (2012), pp. 256, 360, 363.

151 Wassaf al-Hadrat (Shihab al-Din Abd'Allah ibn Fadl-Allah Shirazi), *Tajziyat al-amsar wa taziyat al-a'sar (Geschichte Wassafs),* trans. and ed. Josef von Hammer-Purgstall (Vienna: K.-K. Hof- und Staatsdruckerei, 1856), p. 94.

152 Baumer, *The History of Central Asia*, vol. 3 (2016), p. 250. As mentioned by Rubruck, Berke had already converted to Islam by 1252: Rubruck, *The Mission of Friar William of Rubruck* (2009), p. 127.

153 Möngke and later Kublai Khan were Great Khans and directly controlled Mongolia and China, Hülegü and his successors ruled over Iran. They formed the Toluid axis as opposed to the rather weak Chagataids ruling in Central Asia and the Jochids of the Golden Horde. Batu and Berke were sons of Genghis Khan's oldest son Jochi.

154 *The Hundred Years' Chronicle* (2014), pp. 361; Limper, *Die Mongolen und die christlichen Völker des Kaukasus* (1980), pp. 168f; Peacock, A.C.S., 'Between Georgia and the Islamic world: The atabegs of Samc'xe and the Turks', in: Deniz Beyazit (ed.), *At the Crossroads of Empires: 14th–15th Century Eastern Anatolia* (Istanbul: Varia Anatolica, 2012), p. 52.

155 Hage, Wolfgang, *Das orientalische Christentum* (Stuttgart: Kohlhammer, 2007), p. 120.

156 Orbélian, *Histoire de la Siounie* (2019), pp. 234f.

157 Rasiduddin, *Jami'u't-Tawarikh*, 1044–7 (2012), pp. 363f.

158 Armenia, John, *Armenian Cilicia XII–XV Century: Dawn, Splendor and Twilight of a Christian Kingdom in the Near East during the Crusades* (Charleston: CreateSpace, 2010), p. 109.

159 Orbélian, *Histoire de la Siounie* (2019), pp. 248–64; Stopka, Krzysztof, *Armenia Christiana: Armenian Religious Identity and the Churches of Constantinople and Rome (4th–15th Century)* (Kraków: Jagiellonian University Press, 2017), pp. 180f, 280f.

160 *The Hundred Years' Chronicle* (2014), p. 369.

161 Rasiduddin, *Jami'u't-Tawarikh,* 1116f (2012), pp. 386f; *The Hundred Years' Chronicle* (2014), pp. 373f.
162 Hethum, [*La Flor des estoires d'Orient*] (2006), p. 73.
163 *The Hundred Years' Chronicle* (2014), p. 376–9; Khwandamir, Ghiyas ad-Din Muhammad, *Habibu's-Siyar: The History of the Mongols and Genghis Khan,* 128–30, Classical Writings of the Medieval Islamic World, vol. 2, trans. Wheeler M. Thackston (London: I.B.Tauris, 2012), pp. 71–3.
164 *The Hundred Years' Chronicle* (2014), pp. 382–8.
165 Peacock, 'Between Georgia and the Islamic world' (2012), pp. 49, 54.
166 *The Hundred Years' Chronicle* (2014), pp. 390–92.
167 *The Hundred Years' Chronicle* (2014), pp. 391–3.
168 Rapp, Stephen H., Jr. 'Georgian Christianity', in: Ken Parry (ed.), *The Blackwell Companion to Eastern Christianity* (Malden, MA: Blackwell Publishing, 2007), p. 148.
169 The Mongols were not really tolerant in religious matters, merely indifferent. But this indifference ended sharply as soon as taboos of the steppe were transgressed.
170 Peratoner, Alberto, *From Ararat to San Lazzaro: A Cradle of Armenian Spirituality and Culture in the Venice Lagoon* (Venice: Armenian Mekhitarist Congregation, 2015), p. 57; Stopka, *Armenia Christiana* (2017), pp. 204f, 219–22, 273–7.
171 The monastery of St Thaddeus was returned to the Orthodox Armenian Church after Iskander, ruler of the Qara Qoyunlu (r. 1421–1436) had expelled the Armenian Catholics. Hage, *Das orientalische Christentum* (2007), p. 245; Stopka, *Armenia Christiana* (2017), pp. 207, 212, 266, 289.
172 Stopka, *Armenia Christiana* (2017), pp. 290, 306f.
173 Rayfield, *Edge of Empires* (2012), pp. 141–5.
174 Ciocîltan, Virgil, *The Mongols and the Black Sea Trade in the Thirteenth to Fourteenth Centuries*, trans. Samuel Willcocks (Leiden: Brill, 2012), pp. 79, 94, 132.
175 Jani Beg's attacks on Genoese traders and siege of Caffa from 1343 to 1346 were a total failure: Ciocîltan, *The Mongols and the Black Sea Trade* (2012), pp. 199–212.
176 Allen, *A History of the Georgian People* (1971), p. 122 n2.
177 Ciocîltan, *The Mongols and the Black Sea Trade* (2012), pp. 218f; Spuler, Bertold, *Die Goldene Horde. Die Mongolen in Russland 1223–1502* (Leipzig: Harrassowitz, 1943), pp. 102, 108–10.

III. The Armenian Kingdom of Cilicia

1 Baumer, *History of the Caucasus*, vol. 1 (2021), pp. 281–8.
2 Matthew of Edessa, *Armenia and the Crusades* (2013), p. 137.
3 Dadoyan, Seta B., *The Fatimid Armenians: Cultural and Political Interaction in the Near East* (Leiden: Brill, 1997), pp. 75–8; id., *The Armenians in the Medieval Islamic World*, vol. 2: *Armenian Realpolitik in the Islamic World and Diverging Paradigms – Case of Cilicia, Eleventh to Fourteenth Centuries* (New Brunswick, NJ: Transaction Publishers, 2013), pp. 35, 56f; Ghazarian, Jacob G., *The Armenian Kingdom in Cilicia during the Crusades: The Integration of Cilician Armenians with the Latins, 1080–1393* (London: Routledge, 2000), p. 100.
4 Dadoyan, *The Armenians in the Medieval Islamic World*, vol. 1 (New Brunswick, NJ: Transaction Publishers, 2011), pp. 133f.; vol. 2 (2013), pp. 3, 43f, 50–56, 59f. The origin of Hrahad is contested; other authors attribute to him an Arsacid, Turcoman or Seljuk origin.
5 It was forbidden to enslave Muslims.
6 Dadoyan, *The Armenians in the Medieval Islamic World*, vol. 2 (2013), pp. 78–84.
7 Dadoyan, *The Fatimid Armenians* (1997), pp. 127–30.
8 Athir, *The Chronicle of Ibn al-Athir*, part 1, 283–6 (2006), pp. 21f.
9 Athir, *The Chronicle of Ibn al-Athir*, part 1, 394f, 480f (2006), pp. 93, 152f.
10 Athir, *The Chronicle of Ibn al-Athir*, part 1, 589–91 (2006), pp. 229–31.
11 Dadoyan, *The Fatimid Armenians* (1997), pp. 127–43.
12 The Greek and Armenian Mamelukes were often called *rumis*.
13 Dadoyan, *The Armenians in the Medieval Islamic World*, vol. 2 (2013), pp. 70–72.
14 Dadoyan, *The Fatimid Armenians* (1997), p. 155.
15 Athir, *The Chronicle of Ibn al-Athir*, part 2, 188f (2007), pp. 64f.
16 Athir, *The Chronicle of Ibn al-Athir*, part 2, 274f (2007), p. 126.
17 Athir, *The Chronicle of Ibn al-Athir*, part 2, 290 (2007), p. 138.
18 The only time Lampron was captured was by treacherous subterfuge. While most of the Armenian churches and monasteries of Cilicia have been destroyed, many Armenian fortresses have survived to this day, since they were taken over by subsequent occupiers following the demise of the Armenian kingdom.
19 Runciman, *A History of the Crusades*, vol. 1 (1994), p. 163.
20 Baumer, *History of the Caucasus*, vol. 1 (2021), pp. 283f.
21 Armenia, *Armenian Cilicia* (2010), p. 89.
22 Boase, T.S.R. (ed.), *The Cilician Kingdom of Armenia* (Edinburgh and London: Scottish Academic Press, 1978), p. 3; Ghazarian, *The Armenian Kingdom in Cilicia* (2000), pp. 46f; Runciman, *A History of the Crusades*, vol. 1 (1994), pp. 62, 162. The traditional claims that Ruben was of royal Bagratid descent are unsubstantiated.
23 Ghazarian, *The Armenian Kingdom in Cilicia* (2000), pp. 82f; Runciman, *A History of the Crusades*, vol. 1 (1994), pp. 125f.
24 Matthew of Edessa, *Armenia and the Crusades*, II.118 (2013), p. 169. See also: Ghazarian, *The Armenian Kingdom in Cilicia* (2000), pp. 101f; Runciman, *A History of the Crusades*, vol. 1 (1994), pp. 164–73.
25 Runciman, *A History of the Crusades*, vol. 1 (1994), pp. 180–207. The last two Crusader States to be founded were the Kingdom of Jerusalem (1099) and the County of Tripoli (1102/9).
26 Matthew of Edessa, *Armenia and the Crusades*, II.63 (2013), p. 140.
27 Ormanian, Malachia, *The Church of Armenia: Her History, Doctrine, Rule, Discipline, Liturgy, Literature, and Existing Condition* (London: A.R. Mowbray, 1912), pp. 54–6, 234; Stopka, *Armenia Christiana* (2017), pp. 112–17.
28 Dashdondog, 'The Mongol conquerors of Armenia' (2012), pp. 73f n32.
29 *Vahram's Chronicle of the Armenian Kingdom in Cilicia, during the Time of the Crusades*, transl. Charles Fried. Neumann (London: Oriental Translation Fund, 1831), p. 30. Ghazarian states that Thoros had no male heir: Ghazarian, *The Armenian Kingdom in Cilicia* (2000), p. 115.
30 Runciman, *A History of the Crusades*, vol. 2 (1994), pp. 147, 161f.
31 Ghazarian, *The Armenian Kingdom in Cilicia* (2000), pp. 115f; Runciman, *A History of the Crusades*, vol. 2 (1994), pp. 147, 166–73; *Vahram's Chronicle* (1831), pp. 31f.
32 Translation from the French by the author. *La chronique attribuée au connétable Smbat*, vol. 3, trans. Gérard Dédéyan (Paris: Paul Geuthner, 1980), pp. 47f. The translator believed that Smbat's brother Barsegh, archbishop of Sis, was the author: p. 26.
33 Ghazarian, *The Armenian Kingdom in Cilicia* (2000), pp. 118–21; Runciman, *A History of the Crusades*, vol. 2 (1994), pp. 282–8, 297; *Vahram's Chronicle* (1831), pp. 37–40.
34 Dadoyan, *The Armenians in the Medieval Islamic World*, vol. 2 (2013), p. 167.
35 *La chronique attribuée au connétable Smbat*, 6–13 (1980), pp. 49–55.
36 Conrad, *Geschichte und Wundergeschichten* (2018), p. 160; Runciman, *A History of the Crusades*, vol. 2 (1994), pp. 336f.
37 Ghazarian, *The Armenian Kingdom in Cilicia* (2000), pp. 121f.
38 Athir, *The Chronicle of Ibn al-Athir*, part 2, 534–53 (2007), pp. 322–35; *La chronique attribuée au connétable Smbat*, 19–23 (1980), pp. 59–63.
39 *La chronique attribuée au connétable Smbat*, 24 (1980), pp. 63f.
40 Armenia, *Armenian Cilicia XII–XV Century* (2010), pp. 74f; Boase, *The Cilician Kingdom of Armenia* (1978), p. 15.
41 Runciman, *A History of the Crusades*, vol. 3 (1994), pp. 12–14, 37–43.
42 Boase, *The Cilician Kingdom of Armenia* (1978), p. 99.
43 Levon returned Baghras to the Templars in 1216. Armenia, *Armenian Cilicia XII–XV Century* (2010), pp. 67f, 76f; Runciman, *A History of the Crusades*, vol. 3 (1994), pp. 73f, 83f, 117, 144.
44 Hage, *Das orientalische Christentum* (2007), pp. 243f; Stopka, *Armenia Christiana* (2017), pp.115–17, 123f, 134–6. The pallium is an ecclesiastical insignia bestowed by the pope on patriarchs and metropolitans confirming their jurisdictional authority.
45 Mutafian, Claude, *Le Royaume arménien de Cilicie, XIIe–XIVe siècle* (Paris: CNRS Éditions, 1993), p. 149.
46 Hewsen, Robert H., *Armenia: A Historical Atlas* (Chicago: The University of Chicago Press, 2001), p. 129.
47 Baumer, *History of the Caucasus*, vol. 1 (2021), p. 288.
48 Kirakos, *History of the Armenians* (1986), 3; *La chronique attribuée au connétable Smbat*, 34 (1980), p. 73. See also: Conrad, *Geschichte und Wundergeschichten* (2018), pp. 161, 164, 289, 315; Stopka, *Armenia Christiana* (2017), pp. 128–30. The alternative date mentioned of 6 January 1199 is less likely. Conrad, *supra*, p. 161, n281.
49 Hage, *Das orientalische Christentum* (2007), pp. 244–6 ; Stopka, *Armenia Christiana* (2017), p. 268.

50 *La chronique attribuée au connétable Smbat*, 36 (1980), p. 82.
51 Athir, *The Chronicle of Ibn al-Athir*, part 3, 464–6 (2008), pp. 279f.
52 *La chronique attribuée au connétable Smbat*, 49–54 (1980), pp. 91–6; Runciman, *A History of the Crusades*, vol. 3 (1994), pp. 138, 144–6.
53 Ghazarian, *The Armenian Kingdom in Cilicia* (2000), pp. 55, 58.
54 *Het'um the Historian's History of the Tartars* [The Flower of Histories of the East], trans. Robert Bedrosian (New York: Sources of the Armenian Tradition, 1986), Chapter 28.
55 Kirakos, *History of the Armenians* (1986), 246.
56 The Franciscan Pian del Carpine who attended Güyük's enthronement in 1246 had already reported about the Nestorian communities in Central Asia and Mongolia.
57 Mutafian, *Le Royaume arménien de Cilicie* (1993), p. 55.
58 Osipian, Alexandr, 'Baptised Mongol rulers, Prester John and the Magi: Armenian image of the Mongols produced for the Western readers in the mid-thirteenth–early fourteenth centuries', in: Tubach et al., *Caucasus during the Mongol Period* (2012), pp. 157–60.
59 Baumer, *The History of Central Asia*, vol. 3 (2016), pp. 204f.
60 *Het'um the Historian's History of the Tartars* (1986), Chapter 23; Runciman, *A History of the Crusades*, vol. 3 (1994), pp. 246f.
61 Kirakos, *History of the Armenians* (1986), 301.
62 Bar Hebraeus, *The Chronography of Gregory Abû'l Faraj … Being the First Part of his Political History of the World*, trans. Ernest A. Wallis Budge (London: Oxford University Press, 1932), pp. 418f.
63 Kirakos, *History of the Armenians* (1986), 303.
64 Kirakos, *History of the Armenians* (1986), 308.
65 Jackson, Peter, *The Mongols and the West* (Harlow: Pearson, 2005), p. 121.
66 The family of Genghis Khan and his descendants counted many Nestorians, mainly women, since several major tribes were Christians. Baumer, Christoph, *The Church of the East: An Illustrated History of Assyrian Christianity* (London: I.B.Tauris, 2016), pp. 195–228.
67 Bar Hebraeus, *The Chronography of Gregory Abû'l Faraj* (1932), p. 436.
68 Runciman, *A History of the Crusades*, vol. 3 (1994), p. 257.
69 Rashid al-Din, *Jamia al-Tawarikh* 1024–27 (2012), pp. 356f; Jackson, *The Mongols and the West* (2005), p. 116.
70 See Hülegü's letter to King Louis IX of 10 April 1262: Richard, Jean (ed.), *Au-delà de la Perse et de l'Arménie. L'Orient latin et la découverte de l'Asie intérieure. Quelques textes inégalement connus aux origines de l'alliance entre Francs et Mongols (1145–1262)* (Turnhout: Brepols, 2005), p. 181.
71 Hethum von Korykos, [*La Flor des estoires d'Orient*] (2006), p. 67.
72 *La chronique attribuée au connétable Smbat*, 49–54 (1980), pp. 106 f ; Rasiduddin Fazlullah, *Jami'u't-Tawarikh*, 1028–31 (2012), pp. 358f.
73 Jackson, *The Mongols and the West* (2005), pp. 166–72.

74 Di Cosmo, Nicola, 'Mongols and merchants on the Black Sea frontier in the thirteenth and fourteenth centuries: convergences and conflicts', in: Reuven Amitai and Michal Biran (eds), *Mongols, Turks and Others: Eurasian Nomads and the Sedentary World* (Leiden: Brill, 2005), pp. 407f.
75 *La chronique attribuée au connétable Smbat*, 79 (1980), p. 115.
76 Athir, *The Chronicle of Ibn al-Athir*, part 3, 238, 464 (2008), pp. 111, 279.
77 *La chronique attribuée au connétable Smbat*, 81 (1980), p. 117.
78 Runciman, *A History of the Crusades*, vol. 3 (1994), p. 269.
79 Polo, Marco, *The Book of Ser Marco Polo the Venetian Concerning the Kingdoms and Marvels of the East*, trans. and ed. Sir Henry Yule, vol. I (London: J. Murray, 1903), p. 41.
80 *La chronique attribuée au connétable Smbat*, 87 (1980), pp. 121f.
81 See above p. 44f.
82 Bar Hebraeus, *The Chronography of Gregory Abû'l Faraj* (1932), pp. 506f.
83 Rabban Ṣâwmâ [Bar Sauma], *The Monks of Ḳûblai Khân, Emperor of China*, trans. E. A. Wallis Budge (London: The Religious Tract Society, 1928), pp. 213f.
84 Armenia, *Armenian Cilicia XII–XV Century* (2010), pp. 97–100; Ghazarian, *The Armenian Kingdom in Cilicia* (2000), pp. 66–9.
85 The tales whereby the Mongols occupied Jerusalem and King Hethum even entered the holy city are gross exaggeration or simply false. Also, the reasons for Ghazan's hasty retreat remain unknown since at the moment of his withdrawal in February temperatures were still mild. Possibly an attack by the Chagataids from the east was threatening.
86 Jackson, *The Mongols and the West* (2005), pp. 171, 185.
87 Armenia, *Armenian Cilicia XII–XV Century* (2010), p. 98.
88 Stopka, *Armenia Christiana* (2017), pp.177f, 184–8.
89 Dashdondog, The *Mongols and the Armenians* (2011), p. 206.
90 Stopka, *Armenia Christiana* (2017), p. 192.
91 Translation by the author from the French. Mutafian, *Le Royaume arménien de Cilicie* (1993), p. 81.
92 Armenia, *Armenian Cilicia XII–XV Century* (2010), pp. 109f, 113; Stewart, Angus Donal, *The Armenian Kingdom and the Mamluks: War and Diplomacy during the Reigns of Het'um II (1289–1307)* (Leiden: Brill, 2001), pp. 176–80, 185.
93 Dashdondog, *The Mongols and the Armenians* (2011), p. 212.
94 Dashdondog, *The Mongols and the Armenians* (2011), p. 212.
95 Boase, *The Cilician Kingdom of Armenia* (1978), pp. 155, 166; Mutafian, *Le Royaume arménien de Cilicie* (1993), pp. 87f, 123.
96 Stopka, *Armenia Christiana* (2017), p. 231.
97 Stopka, *Armenia Christiana* (2017), pp. 225–32, 237–42.
98 Stopka, *Armenia Christiana* (2017), p. 243.
99 Ghazarian, *The Armenian Kingdom in Cilicia* (2000), pp. 158f; Stopka, *Armenia Christiana* (2017), pp. 246f.
100 Stopka, *Armenia Christiana* (2017), pp. 251–8.
101 Hage, *Das orientalische Christentum* (2007), p. 246; Stopka, *Armenia Christiana* (2017), p. 268.

102 Armenia, *Armenian Cilicia XII–XV Century* (2010), p. 117; Boase, *The Cilician Kingdom of Armenia* (1978), p. 186.
103 Dadoyan, *The Armenians in the Medieval Islamic World*, vol. 2 (2013), p. 191.
104 It is unclear whether Levon V capitulated in Sis or whether he had previously fled to the castle of Geben north of Sis and surrendered there. Armenia, *Armenian Cilicia XII–XV Century* (2010), pp. 120–23; Boase, *The Cilician Kingdom of Armenia* (1978), pp. 30, 131; Ghazarian, *The Armenian Kingdom in Cilicia* (2000), pp. 162f; Mutafian, *Le Royaume arménien de Cilicie* (1993), pp. 89f.
105 Stopka, *Armenia Christiana* (2017), pp. 282f.
106 The Principality of Khachen and the four other principalities of the Five Melikdoms of Karabakh (until 1822) were autonomous, only semi-independent entities under Muslim sovereignty. They were subjugated by the Khanate of Karabakh after 1750 and became its vassals. Also the few tiny principalities in mountainous Cilicia were at best only semi-independent. Armenia, *Armenian Cilicia* (2010), pp. 182, 187.
107 Nersessian, Vrej, *The Bible in the Armenian Tradition* (London: British Library, 2001), p. 49.
108 Stewart, *The Armenian Kingdom and the Mamluks* (2001), pp. 185–7.

IV. The South Caucasus under Turkmen, Ottoman and Iranian Safavid Domination

1 Georgian history of the fifteenth century is characterized by a lack of historiographical sources and a dearth of numismatic evidence, which is partially compensated for by numerous charters, certificates and diplomas. Toumanoff, Cyril, 'The fifteenth century Bagratids and the institution of collegial sovereignty in Georgia' in: *Traditio*, vol. 7 (New York: Fordham University Press, 1949–51), p. 170.
2 documentacatholicaomnia.eu/03d/1378-1446,_T'ovma_Metsobets'i,_History_Of_Tamerlane_And_His_Successors,_EN.pdf, [p. 4].
3 Bakikhanov, Abbas Qoli Aqa, *The Heavenly Rose-Garden: A History of Shirvan and Dagestan* (Washington DC: Mage Publishers, 2009), p. 69; Fähnrich, *Geschichte Georgiens* (2010), pp. 252–4; Rayfield, *Edge of Empires* (2012), pp. 146–8.
4 Khwandamir, Ghiyas ad-Din Muhammad, *Habibu's-Siyar: The History of the Mongols and Genghis Khan*, Classical Writings of the Medieval Islamic World, vol. 2, trans. Wheeler M. Thackston, III, 463–6 (London: I.B.Tauris, 2012), pp. 255f.
5 Bakikhanov, *The Heavenly Rose-Garden* (2009), pp. 71f.
6 Minorsky, Vladimir, *A History of Sharvan and Darband* (1958), p. 130.
7 Allen, *A History of the Georgian People* (1971), p. 124; Roemer, H. R., 'Timur in Iran', in: Peter Jackson and Lawrence Lockhart (eds), *The Cambridge History of Iran*, vol. 6: *The Timurid and Safavid Periods* (Cambridge: Cambridge University Press, 1986), p. 74f.
8 Clavijo, Ruy Gonzalez de, *Clavijo: Embassy to Tamerlane 1403–1406*, trans. Guy Le Strange

9 Toumanoff, 'The fifteenth century Bagratids' (1949–51), pp. 173f.
10 Khwandamir, *Habibu's-Siyar*, vol. 2, III, 517f (2012), p. 281 n2. According to Khwandamir's translator Wheeler M. Thackston, Kurtin is the same as the fortress of Bintvisi.
11 Fähnrich, *Geschichte Georgiens* (2010), pp. 255f; Rayfield, *Edge of Empires* (2012), pp. 151f.
12 Bakikhanov, *The Heavenly Rose-Garden* (2009), p. 73.
13 Baumer, Christoph, *The History of Central Asia*, vol. 3: *The Age of Islam and the Mongols* (London: I.B.Tauris, 2016), pp. 292f.
14 Clavijo, *Clavijo: Embassy to Tamerlane 1403–1406* (1928), p. 323.
15 Baumer, *History of the Caucasus*, vol. 1 (2021), pp. 227f, 262ff.
16 Minorsky, *A History of Sharvan and Darband* (1958), p. 131; Roemer, H. R., 'The successors of Timur', in: Jackson and Lockhart, *The Cambridge History of Iran*, vol. 6 (1986), p. 102.
17 Shah Rukh led three campaigns into Azerbaijan in 1420–21, 1429 and 1434–6. Baumer, *The History of Central Asia*, vol. 3 (2016), p. 293.
18 Toumanoff, 'The fifteenth century Bagratids' (1949–51), pp. 179, 182; Rayfield, *Edge of Empires* (2012), pp. 154f.
19 Toumanoff, 'The fifteenth century Bagratids' (1949–51), pp. 171f.
20 documentacatholicaomnia.eu/03d/1378-1446,_T'ovma_Metsobets'i,_History_Of_Tamerlane_And_His_Successors,_EN.pdf, [p. 21].
21 Rayfield, *Edge of Empires* (2012), p. 155.
22 Stopka, *Armenia Christiana* (2017), pp. 291–304.
23 Ghazarian, *The Armenian Kingdom in Cilicia* (2000), pp. 205f; Hage, *Das orientalische Christentum* (2007), p. 248; Hewsen, *Armenia: A Historical Atlas* (2001), pp. 141, 144; Stopka, *Armenia Christiana* (2017), p. 303f.
24 The see of the Great House of Cilicia has been located since 1930 at Antelias, Lebanon.; it counts *ca.* 200,000 members.
25 Hage, *Das orientalische Christentum* (2007), pp. 227f, 246–50, 425–31; Hewsen, *Armenia: A Historical Atlas* (2001), pp. 141, 144; Kouymjian, Dickran, 'Armenia from the fall of the Cilician kingdom (1375) to the forced emigration under Shah Abbas (1604)', in: Richard G. Hovannisian, *The Armenian People from Ancient to Modern Times*, vol. 2 (New York: Palgrave Macmillan, 1997), pp. 36–40. In 1409, an agreement was also reached between Sis and Aghtamar.
26 Hewsen, *Armenia: A Historical Atlas* (2001), pp. 158, 179.
27 Further south-west, Jahan Shah also controlled the regions of Ani, Lake Van and Erzurum. Hewsen, *Armenia: A Historical Atlas* (2001), pp. 142f.
28 Hewsen, *Armenia: A Historical Atlas* (2001), p. 163. Concerning the issue of the Hasan-Jalalids controlling the catholicosate of Albania see: Baumer, *History of the Caucasus*, vol. 1 (2021), pp. 206f.
29 The identity of catholicoi Davit II, III and IV is debated. The Georgian Church lists three different prelates named Davit for the period 1426–1457 and two further intermediate catholicoi, Theodore III (1427–35) and Shio II (1440–1446), while Toumanoff argues that Davit was officially catholicos from 1426 to 1457, but that his rule was interrupted by the *locum tenentes* Theodore and Shio. Toumanoff, 'The fifteenth century Bagratids' (1949–51), pp. 189f.
30 Fähnrich, *Geschichte Georgiens* (2010), p. 259f; Rayfield, *Edge of Empires* (2012), pp. 157f.
31 Feuerstein, Wolfgang, 'Die Eroberung und Islamisierung Südgeorgiens', in: Motika and Ursinus, *Caucasia between the Ottoman Empire and Iran, 1555–1914* (Wiesbaden: Reichert, 2000), p. 24.
32 Rayfield, *Edge of Empires* (2012), p. 158f; Toumanoff, 'The fifteenth century Bagratids' (1949–51), pp. 187, 190–92, 214.
33 Mehmet II was victorious thanks to the use of modern technologies: handguns and cannons.
34 Earlier, in autumn 1467 Uzun Hasan had crushed Jahan Shah of the Qara Qoyunlu who fell in battle. Two years later, in 1469, he also annihilated the small Timurid army of the grandson of Miran Shah, Abu Said. Abu Said controlled Khorasan and Herat, and had hoped to reconquer the western part of Shah Rukh's realm. At the climax of his reign, Uzun Hasan's empire roughly enclosed today's Iran, Iraq and Eastern Turkey. Baumer, *The History of Central Asia*, vol. 3 (2016), p. 295. Under Uzun's rule, Armenian Christians suffered discrimination since they were required to wear a blue mark identifying them as Christians. Kouymjian, 'Armenia from the fall of the Cilician kingdom' (1997), p. 7.
35 Forsyth, James, *The Caucasus: A History* (Cambridge: Cambridge University Press, 2013), p. 205; Hewsen, *Armenia: A Historical Atlas* (2001), p. 144.
36 The history of the individual kingdoms and principalities is not given individually for this period, but that of the southern Caucasus as a whole.
37 Richmond, Walter, *The Northwest Caucasus: Past, Present, Future* (London: Routledge, 2011), p. 16.
38 Possibly only Haydar or Isma'il were avowed Shiites. Roemer, H. R., 'The Safavid period', in: Jackson and Lockhart, *The Cambridge History of Iran*, vol. 6 (1986), p. 194f.
39 Minorsky, *A History of Sharvan and Darband* (1958), pp. 131f; Roemer, 'The Safavid period' (1986), pp. 182–207.
40 Roemer, 'The Safavid period' (1986), pp. 209–14, 229f.
41 Minorsky, *A History of Sharvan and Darband* (1958), pp. 132f.
42 W.E.D. Allen, *Russian Embassies to the Georgian Kings 1589–1605* (London: Hakluyt Society, 1970), vol. 1, p. 54.
43 Feuerstein, 'Die Eroberung und Islamisierung Südgeorgiens' (2000), p. 26.
44 Hewsen, *Armenia: A Historical Atlas* (2001), p. 151; Roemer, 'The Safavid period' (1986), pp. 218–25.
45 Fähnrich, *Geschichte Georgiens* (2010), pp. 265–8; Peacock, 'Between Georgia and the Islamic world' (2012), p. 57.
46 Roemer, 'The Safavid period' (1986), pp. 238f, 242.
47 Minorsky, *A History of Sharvan and Darband* (1958), p. 133.
48 Bakikhanov, *The Heavenly Rose-Garden* (2009), p. 89.
49 Bournoutian, George A., *From the Kur to the Aras: A Military History of Russia's Move into the South Caucasus and the First Russo-Iranian War, 1801–1813* (Leiden: Brill, 2021), p. 256.
50 Rayfield, *Edge of Empires* (2012), pp. 167–70.
51 Bakikhanov, *The Heavenly Rose-Garden* (2009), p. 249; Roemer, 'The Safavid period' (1986), pp. 242f.
52 Moscow paid tribute to the Crimean Tatars, with interruptions, till Tsar Peter I took power.
53 Allen, *Russian Embassies* (1970), vol. 1, pp. 52f; Hewsen, *Armenia: A Historical Atlas* (2001), p. 151; Kortepeter, Carl Max, *Ottoman Imperialism during the Reformation* (London: University of London Press, 1973), pp. 8f, 17; Rayfield, *Edge of Empires* (2012), pp. 167–71, 214.
54 Translation from the French by the author. Toumarkine, Alexandre, 'L'Abkhazie et la Circassie dans le Cihān-nümā de Kātib Çelebi: Un regard ottoman sur le Caucase du Nord-Ouest', in: Motika and Ursinus, *Caucasia between the Ottoman Empire and Iran* (2000), p. 38.
55 Allen, *Russian Embassies* (1970), vol. 2, p. 415 n1.
56 Rayfield, *Edge of Empires* (2012), pp. 177–9.
57 Allen, *Russian Embassies* (1970), vol. 2, p. 529.
58 Baddeley, John F., *The Russian Conquest of the Caucasus* (London: Longmans, Green and Co., 1908), p. 198; Feuerstein, 'Die Eroberung und Islamisierung Südgeorgiens' (2000), pp. 24f; Peacock, 'Between Georgia and the Islamic world' (2012), p. 57.
59 Baumer, *History of the Caucasus*, vol. 1 (2021), pp. 140–42, 166–72.
60 Translated from the French by the author. Chardin, Jean, *Journal du voyage du chevalier Chardin en Perse et aux Indes Orientales, par la Mer Noire et par la Colchide* (Amsterdam: Jean Wolters et Ysbrand Haring, 1686), p. 240.
61 Baumer, *The History of Central Asia*, vol. 4 (2018), pp. 39, 43.
62 Allen, *Russian Embassies* (1970), vol. 1, pp. 24, 281f.
63 Allen, *Russian Embassies* (1970), vol. 1, pp. 59f; Rayfield, *Edge of Empires* (2012), p. 173.
64 Allen, *Russian Embassies* (1970), vol. 1, p. 363; vol. 2, pp. 464, 539f.
65 This Ottoman commander Lala Mustafa Pasha is not identical with Manuchihr Jaqeli II who was also called Mustafa Pasha.
66 Kortepeter, *Ottoman Imperialism* (1973), pp. 51–9.
67 Allen, *Russian Embassies* (1970), vol. 1, p. 21; Kortepeter, *Ottoman Imperialism* (1973), pp. 74–92, 107; Roemer, 'The Safavid period' (1986), p. 266f.
68 Baumer, *History of the Caucasus*, vol. 1 (2021), pp. 240, 252.
69 Allen, *Russian Embassies* (1970), vol. 1, pp. 21f, 60–62, 80, 88, 201.
70 Allen, *Russian Embassies* (1970), vol. 2, pp. 371, 374.
71 Roemer, 'The Safavid period' (1986), p. 265. *Ghilmān* is an Arabic plural, the singular being *ghulām*.
72 Allen, *Russian Embassies* (1970), vol. 2, pp. 446–60.
73 Allen, *Russian Embassies* (1970), vol. 2, pp. 481–512.
74 Allen gives as name for this son of the *shamkal* also Saltan Magmut and Sultan Mahmut. Allen, *Russian Embassies* (1970), vol. 2, pp. 421, 446, 451 n1, 528, 549f.
75 Allen, *Russian Embassies* (1970), vol. 2, p. 549f.
76 Chardin, *Journal du voyage du chevalier Chardin* (1686), pp. 244–53 ; Rayfield, *Edge of Empires* (2012), p. 190.
77 Allen, *A History of the Georgian People* (1971), p. 167.
78 Of course the accuracy of such huge numbers remains questionable. Allen, *A History of the Georgian People* (1971), p. 167 n2; Rayfield, *Edge of Empires* (2012), p. 191.

79 Kouymjian, 'Armenia from the fall of the Cilician kingdom' (1997), p. 20.
80 Chardin, *Journal du voyage du chevalier Chardin* (1686), pp. 348f.
81 Rayfield, *Edge of Empires* (2012), p. 192.
82 Beradze, Grigol and Kutsia, Karlo, 'Towards the interrelations of Iran and Georgia in the 16th–18th centuries', in: Motika and Ursinus, *Caucasia between the Ottoman Empire and Iran* (2000), pp. 123f.
83 Sidorko, Clemens P., '"Kampf den ketzerischen Qizilbāš!" Die Revolte des Ḥāǧǧī Dāʾūd (1718–1728)', in: Motika and Ursinus, *Caucasia between the Ottoman Empire and Iran* (2000), p. 134.
84 Hewsen, *Armenia: A Historical Atlas* (2001), pp. 154f. See below p. 111.
85 Aliev, Ayaz A., Ibrahimov, A. Sh., and Khalilova, Iradna S. 'Evaluation of Y-DNA diversity of Azerbaijanis', in: *Bulletin of Moscow State University*, Series XXIII, Anthropology, No. 4 (Moscow: Moscow State University, 2018), p. 49–55; Forsyth, *The Caucasus* (2013), pp. 95–8, 308. For further sources, see also: en.wikipedia.org/wiki/Origin_of_the_Azerbaijanis.
86 Baumer, *History of the Caucasus*, vol. 1 (2021), pp. 140–229.
87 Beradze and Kutsia, 'Towards the interrelations of Iran and Georgia' (2000), pp. 123f; Fähnrich, *Geschichte Georgiens* (2010), pp. 281–4; Rayfield, *Edge of Empires* (2012), p. 196–210.
88 Rayfield, *Edge of Empires* (2012), p. 196.
89 Fähnrich, *Geschichte Georgiens* (2010), pp. 309f.
90 Darejan was a daughter of King Teimuraz.
91 Translation from the French by the author. Chardin, *Journal du voyage du chevalier Chardin* (1686), pp. 183f.
92 Chardin, *Journal du voyage du chevalier Chardin* (1686), pp. 117–23.
93 Baumer, *The History of Central Asia*, vol. 3 (2016), pp. 103f.
94 Boeck, Brian J., *Imperial Boundaries: Cossack Communities and Empire-Building in the Age of Peter the Great* (Cambridge: Cambridge University Press, 2009), pp. 207, 216f, 247.
95 Rayfield, *Edge of Empires* (2012), pp. 223f.
96 The alleged murder of Russian traders in Shamakhi by Lezgian tribal warriors led by the Sunni Hajji Daud on 15 August 1721 was simply a pretext for Tsar Peter to attack. The Sunni Lezgins murdered thousands of Shiites living in Shamakhi, but not the Russian merchants, 'merely' stealing all their goods. Sidorko, '"Kampf den ketzerischen Qizilbāš!"' (2000), pp. 133, 137f.
97 Baumer, *The History of Central Asia*, vol. 3 (2016), p. 24.
98 Sidorko, Clemens P., *Dschihad im Kaukasus. Antikolonialer Widerstand der Dagestaner und Tschetschenen gegen das Zarenreich (18. Jahrhundert bis 1859)* (Wiesbaden: Reichert 2007), p. 67.
99 Tsar Peter's campaign to Derbent was described in 1763 by Voltaire who stressed the Russian interest in diverting part of the Western European trade via Russia. Voltaire (François Marie d'Arouet), *Histoire de l'empire de Russie sous Pierre le Grand* (no publisher given, 1763), vol. 2, pp. 218–34.
100 Villari, Luigi, *Fire and Sword in the Caucasus* (London: T. Fisher Unwin, 1906), p. 30.

101 Jenkinson, Anthony, *Early Voyages and Travels to Russia and Persia*, ed. E. Delmar Morgan and C.H. Cote, 2 vols (London: Hakluyt Society, 1886), pp. i–ii; Mayers, Kit, *The First English Explorer: The Life of Anthony Jenkinson (1529–1611) and his Adventures en route to the Orient* (Kibworth Beauchamp: Matador, 2017), pp. 10–16, 36f, 188.
102 For the concept of the Great Game see: Baumer, *The History of Central Asia*, vol. 4 (2018), pp. 124ff.
103 Axworthy, Michael, *The Sword of Persia: Nader Shah, from Tribal Warrior to Conquering Tyrant* (London: I.B.Tauris, 2006), pp. 63f; Bakikhanov, *The Heavenly Rose-Garden* (2009), p. 119; Sidorko, '"Kampf den ketzerischen Qizilbāš!"' (2000), pp. 140, 143.
104 Bournoutian, *From the Kur to the Aras* (2021), pp. 60, 88; Hewsen, *Armenia: A Historical Atlas* (2001), p. 165.
105 Suny, Ronald Grigor, *The Making of the Georgian Nation* (Bloomington: Indiana University Press, 1994), p. 55.
106 Axworthy, *The Sword of Persia* (2006), pp. 115–17.
107 Tsutsiev, Arthur, *Atlas of the Ethno-Political History of the Caucasus* (New Haven: Yale University Press, 2014), p. 5.
108 Kazemdazeh, F., 'Iranian relations with Russia and the Soviet Union', in: Avery, Hambly and Melville, *The Cambridge History of Iran*, vol. 7 (1991), p. 324; Kemper, Michael, *Herrschaft, Recht und Islam in Dagestan. Von den Khanaten und geheimbünden zum ǧihād-Staat* (Wiesbaden: Reichert, 2005), pp. 143, 150, 167.
109 Kemper, *Herrschaft, Recht und Islam in Dagestan* (2005), p. 150.
110 Axworthy, *The Sword of Persia* (2006), pp. 146–54.
111 The Ottoman sultans had claimed title and function of caliph since Sultan Selim's conquest of Egypt in 1517.
112 Ja'afar al-Sadiq was the sixth imam according to the Twelver Shia.
113 Axworthy, *The Sword of Persia* (2006), pp. 161, 164–8, 248, 252.
114 Kemper, *Herrschaft, Recht und Islam in Dagestan* (2005), pp. 151–63.
115 Beradze and Kutsia, 'Towards the interrelations of Iran and Georgia' (2000), p. 128.
116 Arat, Mari Kristin, *Die Wiener Mechitharisten* (Vienna: Böhlau, 1990), pp. 20–23.
117 Within the Armenian Church, there is no division into different congregations.
118 Matfunian, Vartan Gerges, 'Der Orden der Mechitaristen', in: Friedrich Heyer (ed.), *Die Kirche Armeniens* (Stuttgart: Evangelisches Verlagswerk, 1987), pp. 35, 108f, 177; Peratoner, Alberto, *From Ararat to San Lazzaro: A Cradle of Armenian Spirituality and Culture in the Venice Lagoon* (Venice: Armenian Mekhitarist Congregation, 2015), pp. 110–17.
119 Even today, intercommunion is only allowed under special circumstances.
120 Peratoner, *From Ararat to San Lazzaro* (2015), p. 128.
121 Arat, *Die Wiener Mechitharisten* (1990), pp. 25–7; Peratoner, *From Ararat to San Lazzaro* (2015), pp. 59f, 124.
122 Hage, *Das orientalische Christentum* (2007), p. 433; Peratoner, *From Ararat to San Lazzaro* (2015), p. 135–8, 150–56, 165–9, 194.
123 Bournoutian, *From the Kur to the Aras* (2021), pp. 251f.

124 Bournoutian, *From the Kur to the Aras* (2021), p. 260.
125 Bournoutian, *From the Kur to the Aras* (2021), map 7; for a history of these khanates see pp. 249–64.
126 Forsyth, *The Caucasus* (2013), pp. 168, 253.
127 Perry, John, 'The Zand dynasty', in: Avery, Hambly and Melville, *The Cambridge History of Iran*, vol. 7 (1991), p. 96.
128 Rayfield, *Edge of Empires* (2012), pp. 238f.
129 Allen, *A History of the Georgian People* (1971), pp. 206–9; Rayfield, *Edge of Empires* (2012), pp. 239–47.
130 Allen, *A History of the Georgian People* (1971), p. 208.

V. First Russian Advances into the North Caucasus

1 Towards the end of the eighteenth century, other, more blatantly imperialistic goals came to the fore as was seen in the territorial gains in Poland, the South Caucasus and Central Asia.
2 Khodarkovsky, Michael, *Russia's Steppe Frontier: The Making of a Colonial Empire, 1500–1800* (Bloomington: Indiana University Press, 2002), pp. 22, 223.
3 Ware, Robert Bruce, and Kisriev, Enver, *Dagestan: Russian Hegemony and Islamic Resistance in the North Caucasus* (Armonk, NY: M.E. Sharpe, 2010), pp. 4, 9, 16.
4 See below pp. 152f.
5 The first, pre-tsarist Russian advance into the North Caucasus took place in the tenth century when the Kievan Rus occupied the Taman Peninsula, and in the eleventh century part of Adygea. Baumer, *History of the Caucasus,* vol. 1 (2021), pp. 254f.
6 Baumer, *The History of Central Asia*, vol. 4 (2018), p. 39.
7 Kortepeter, Ottoman Imperialism (1973), pp. 17, 27; Sidorko, *Dschihad im Kaukasus* (2007), pp. 33f.
8 As noted by the British adventurer and covert agent James Bell (1797–1858), the Circassians called themselves Adyghe and rejected the ethnonym Cherkess as being a Tatar word. Bell, James Stanislaus, *Journal of a Residence in Circassia during the Years 1837, 1838 and 1839* (London: Edward Moxon, 1840), vol. 2, p. 53.
9 Although the Kabardians speak an autochthonous north-west Caucasian language, some authors including W.E.D. Allen stick to the legend whereby the Kabardians emigrated from Crimea around the year 1475 to Circassia and Kabardia. Allen, *Russian Embassies* (1970), vol. 1, pp. 270, 279f. It would be more correct to state that some Kabardians left their homeland under Mongol pressure and settled in Crimea in the late 1230s and that their descendants returned in the later fifteenth century.
10 Lemercier-Quelquejay, Chantal, 'Co-optation of the elites of Kabarda and Daghestan in the sixteenth century', in: Broxup, Marie Bennigsen (ed.), *The North Caucasus Barrier: The Russian Advance towards the Muslim World* (London: Hurst & Co., 1992), pp. 25f; Richmond, *The Northwest Caucasus* (2011), p. 20f.
11 Taitbout de Marigny was employed in Russian service to establish trade relations between Russia and the Western Circassians. Russia wanted to break the Turkish trade monopoly at Anapa and

12 Taitbout de Marigny, [Edouard] Chevalier, *Three Voyages in the Black Sea to the Coast of Circassia* (London: John Murray, 1837), pp. 56f.
13 Wagner, Moritz, *Der Kaukasus und das Land der Kosaken in den Jahren 1843 bis 1846* (Dresden: Arnoldsche, 1848), pp. 233f.
14 Baddeley, John F., *The Rugged Flanks of Caucasus* (London: Humphrey Milford, 1940), vol. 2, p. 211.
15 The modern ethnonyms 'Nakh' and 'Vainakh' as unifying terms for Chechen and Ingush people and the earlier ethnonym 'Nakhchi' were coined in the nineteenth and twentieth centuries. Perović, Jeronim, *Der Nordkaukasus unter russischer Herrschaft. Geschichte einer Vielvölkerregion zwischen Rebellion und Anpassung* (Köln: Böhlau, 2015), p. 69.
16 Forsyth, *The Caucasus* (2013), pp. 201–4.
17 His descendants and those of his two brothers bore the name Cherkessky (Cherkassky).
18 Jaimoukha, Amjad, 'A brief history of Kabarda [from the seventh century ad]' (n. d., circassianworld.com/pdf/Kabardian_History.pdf), p. 22 n20.
19 Jaimoukha, 'A brief history of Kabarda' (n.d.), pp. 1–3, 9.
20 Richmond, *The Northwest Caucasus* (2011), p. 46.
21 Khodarkovsky, *Russia's Steppe Frontier* (2002), p. 56.
22 Lemercier-Quelquejay, 'Co-optation of the elites of Kabarda and Daghestan' (1992), pp. 29f.
23 Richmond, *The Northwest Caucasus* (2011), p. 38.
24 Richmond, *The Northwest Caucasus* (2011), pp. 41f.
25 W.E.D. Allen believes that the Russians built an even earlier fort in 1563 somewhere at the border between Semryuk's and Kaitukin's realms. Allen, *Russian Embassies* (1970), vol. 1, pp. 20f.
26 Jaimoukha, 'A brief history of Kabarda' (n.d.), p. 24.
27 Jaimoukha, 'A brief history of Kabarda' (n.d.), p. 24.
28 Kemper, *Herrschaft, Recht und Islam in Dagestan* (2005), pp. 95–7, 118–21.
29 The beginning of the Time of Troubles is also set at the death of Tsar Feodor I in 1598. Since Feodor was weak and disabled, the power was held by the boyar Boris Godunov who seized the throne at Feodor's death.
30 Richmond, *The Northwest Caucasus* (2011), pp. 44f.
31 Boeck, *Imperial Boundaries* (2009), pp. 23f.
32 Forsyth, *The Caucasus* (2013), p. 221.
33 Boeck, *Imperial Boundaries* (2009), p. 114.
34 Boeck, *Imperial Boundaries* (2009), pp. 103–16.
35 Boeck, *Imperial Boundaries* (2009), pp. 137, 145.
36 Boeck, *Imperial Boundaries* (2009), pp. 200–204, 224, 242–6.
37 Wagner, *Der Kaukasus und das Land der Kosaken* (1848), pp. 83–5.
38 Between the sixteenth century and the 1860s, dozens of military lines were erected. Some of them had mainly defensive purposes, others served as a starting point for attacks.
39 Boeck, *Imperial Boundaries* (2009), pp. 231f; Khodarkovsky, Michael, *Where Two Worlds Met: The Russian State and the Kalmyk Nomads, 1600–1771* (Ithaca: Cornell University Press, 1992), pp. 148–53.
40 See below pp. 152f.
41 Boeck, *Imperial Boundaries* (2009), p. 239. See also: Baumer, *The History of Central Asia*, vol. 4 (2018), p. 125.
42 Burnaby, Captain Fred, *On Horseback through Asia Minor* (London: Sampson Low, Martson, Searle and Rivington, 1877), pp. 90f.
43 Sidorko, *Dschihad im Kaukasus* (2007), p. 171. At the same time, Gmelin's colleague Johann Anton Güldenstädt was held prisoner for a month before he was freed by Russian troops. Güldenstädt, Johann Anton, *Reisen durch Russland und im Caucasischen Gebürge* (St Petersburg: Kayserliche Akademie der Wissenschaften, 1787), vol. 1, pp. 324, 430.
44 Sidorko, *Dschihad im Kaukasus* (2007), p. 40; Tsutsiev, *Atlas of the Ethno-Political History of the Caucasus* (2014), maps 2, 3, 6.
45 Baumer, *History of the Caucasus,* vol. 1 (2021), p. 255.
46 Allen, *A History of the Georgian People* (1971), p. 209.
47 Grassi, Fabio L., *A New Homeland: The Massacre of the Circassians, their Exodus to the Ottoman Empire and their Role in the making of Modern Turkey* (Istanbul: Istanbul Aydin University Press, 2014), pp. 38f, 44; Khodarkovsky, *Where Two Worlds Met* (1992), pp. 84, 163, 218, 230; Richmond, *The Northwest Caucasus* (2011), p. 53; Ware and Kisriev, *Dagestan* (2010), pp. 14f.
48 Unlike in the older Russian literature, where the ethnonym 'Kalmyks' means all western Mongolian Oirats, today it is only applied to the Volga Oirats. As the only western Mongols, they referred to themselves as 'Kalmyks' (Kalimag, Khal'mag). Atwood, Christopher, *Encyclopedia of Mongolia and the Mongol Empire* (New York: Facts on File, 2004), p. 288.
49 For the Kalmyks see: Baumer, *The History of Central Asia*, vol. 4 (2018), pp. 96–100.
50 *Tayishi* is a Chinese honorific title meaning 'great master'.
51 Khodarkovsky, *Where Two Worlds Met* (1992), pp. 66f, 90–95.
52 Khodarkovsky, *Where Two Worlds Met* (1992), pp. 95–9.
53 Khodarkovsky, *Where Two Worlds Met* (1992), pp. 27, 48f.
54 John Bell of Antermony, *Travels from St. Petersburg in Russia, to Diverse Parts of Asia in Two Volumes* (Glasgow: Robert and Andrew Foulis, 1763), vol. 2, pp. 331–3.
55 Khodarkovsky, *Where Two Worlds Met* (1992), pp. 212–30.
56 Pelliot, Paul, *Notes critiques d'histoires Kalmouke* (Paris: Adrien-Maisonneuve, 1960), vol. 1, p. 38.

VI. The Caucasus under Russian Rule

1 Two senior advisers to Tsar Alexander warned in 1801 that the project to substantially increase trade with Asia via the western Caspian coast was an illusion. Atkin, Muriel, *Russia and Iran 1780–1828* (Minneapolis: University of Minneapolis, 1980), p. 61.
2 Atkin, *Russia and Iran* (1980), pp. 33f; Bournoutian, George A., *From the Kur to the Aras: A Military History of Russia's Move into the South Caucasus and the First Russo-Iranian War, 1801–1813* (Leiden: Brill, 2021), p. 15.
3 Treuttel, Johann Georg, *Anecdoten zur Lebensgeschichte des Ritters und Reichs-Fürsten Potemkin* (Freistadt am Rhein [Strasbourg], Treuttel, 1792), p. 210.
4 Baddeley, John F., The Russian Conquest of the Caucasus (London: Longmans, Green and Co., 1908), p. 59. John F. Baddeley's description of the Russian conquest of the Caucasus is still, more than a century after its publication, an excellent overview.
5 Sidorko, *Dschihad im Kaukasus* (2007), p. 24.
6 'The Treaty of Georgievsk, 1783', translated from the Russian by Russell E. Martin, www.russianlegitimist.org/the-treaty-of-georgievsk-1783.
7 Hambly, Gavin, and Hambly, R.G., 'Āghā Muhammad Khān and the establishment of the Qājār dynasty', in: Avery, Hambly and Melville, *The Cambridge History of Iran*, vol. 7 (1991), pp. 126–9; Kazemdzadeh, F., 'Iranian relations with Russia and the Soviet Union', in: Avery, Hambly and Melville, *The Cambridge History of Iran*, vol. 7 (1991), p. 329.
8 Rayfield, *Edge of Empires* (2012), p. 256.
9 Atkin, *Russia and Iran 1780–1828* (1980), p. 55.
10 Allen, *A History of the Georgian People* (1971), pp. 214–16; Bournoutian, *From the Kur to the Aras* (2021), pp. 21–7; Kazemdzadeh, 'Iranian relations with Russia' (1991), pp. 329–31.
11 Baumer, *History of the Caucasus,* vol. 1 (2021), p. 247.
12 Baddeley, *The Russian Conquest of the Caucasus* (1908), p. 61.
13 An exarch is, in the context of Orthodox churches, a bishop representing a patriarch to another patriarch. In the case of the exarch for Georgia, he represented a nonexistent patriarch.
14 Hage, *Das orientalische Christentum* (2007), p. 122; Rapp, Stephen H. Jr., 'Georgian Christianity', in: Ken Parry (ed.), *The Blackwell Companion to Eastern Christianity* (Malden, MA: Blackwell Publishing, 2007), p. 148.
15 Hewsen, *Armenia: A Historical Atlas* (2001), pp. 173, 179, 213.
16 Hewsen, *Armenia: A Historical Atlas* (2001), p. 179.
17 According to the administrative divisions around 1865. Hewsen, *Armenia: A Historical Atlas* (2001), pp. 184–212.
18 Barsoumian, Hagop, 'The Eastern Question and the Tanzimat era', in: Richard G. Hovannisian, *The Armenian People from Ancient to Modern Times*, vol 2 (New York: Palgrave Macmillan, 1997), pp. 188, 191f.
19 *Encyclopaedia Britannica*, 9th ed., vol. 2 (Edinburgh: Adam and Charles Black, 1875), p. 548.
20 Rayfield, *Edge of Empires* (2012), pp. 251f, 265, 269–71.
21 George Hewitt believes that the Russian falsely accused the pro-Ottoman Aslan Bey of patricide and that the conspirators were in fact Sefer Ali-Bey and Nino Dadiani, regent-dowager of Mingrelia

22 Baddeley, *The Russian Conquest of the Caucasus* (1908), p. 79.
23 Barsoumian, 'The Eastern Question and the Tanzimat era' (1997), p. 176; Rayfield, *Edge of Empires* (2012), p. 274.
24 Atkin, *Russia and Iran 1780–1828* (1980), pp. 76f, 86, 105–10, 113, 120f; Hewsen, *Armenia: A Historical Atlas* (2001), p. 169.
25 Greaves, Rose, 'Iranian relations with Great Britain and British India', in: Avery, Hambly and Melville, *The Cambridge History of Iran*, vol. 7 (1991), pp. 379f.
26 Hambly and Hambly, 'Āghā Muhammad Khān and the establishment of the Qājār Dynasty' (1991), p. 129.
27 France and Turkey had concluded peace in 1802: Amini, Iradj, *Napoleon and Iran: Franco-Iranian Relations under the First Empire* (Richmond: Curzon, 1999), p. 47. But France underestimated the deep hostility between the Ottomans and Iran.
28 Amini, *Napoleon and Iran* (1999), pp. 65–72.
29 Jaubert, Amédée P., *Voyage en Arménie et en Perse fait dans les années 1806 et 1806* (Paris: Pélicier et Nepveu, 1821), pp. 27–218.
30 Amini, *Napoleon and Iran* (1999), pp. 91–102, 205–8.
31 Amini, *Napoleon and Iran* (1999), p. 148.
32 'Preliminary Treaty concluded by Sir Harford Jones with the Shah of Persia in 1809', in: *A collection of treaties, engagements and sanads relating to India and neighbouring countries* [53–55] (70/578 (London: British Library, 1933), Ref: IOR/L/PS/20/G3/14: www.qdl.qa/en/archive/81055/vdc_100023947390.0x000047; Amini, *Napoleon and Iran* (1999), pp. 159, 173–82; Greaves, 'Iranian relations with Great Britain and British India' (1991), pp. 384f; Kazemdazeh, F., 'Anglo-Iranian relations, ii: Qajar period', in: *Encyclopaedia Iranica*, vol. 2I, fasc. 1, pp. 46–51 (1994): www.iranicaonline.org/articles/anglo-iranian-relations-ii.
33 The training of Iranian troops by British instructors began in 1811 and bore fruit in February 1812 at the Iranian victory in the Battle of Soltanabad. Eslami, Kambiz, 'D'Arcy, Joseph', in: *Encyclopaedia Iranica* (1994). www.iranicaonline.org/articles/darcy-joseph.
34 Atkin, *Russia and Iran 1780–1828* (1980), pp. 135–9.
35 Rayfield, *Edge of Empires* (2012), pp. 272f.
36 Translation from the German by the author. Radde, Gustav, *Die Chews'uren und ihr Land untersucht im Sommer 1876* (Cassel: Theodor Fischer, 1878), pp. 115–17, 150f.
37 Phillipps-Wolley, Clive, *Savage Svanetia* (London: Richard Bentley and Son, 1883), vol. 2, pp. 19, 90f.
38 Neither the Definitive Treaty between Britain and Iran of 1812 nor its revision in 1814 altered Britain's position towards Iran.
39 Daniel, Elton L., 'Golestān Treaty', in: *Encyclopaedia Iranica*, vol. 11, fsc. 1 (2012), pp. 86–90: www.iranicaonline.org/articles/golestan-treaty; Kazemdazeh, 'Iranian relations with Russia' (1991), p. 334.
40 Baddeley, *The Russian Conquest of the Caucasus* (1908), p. 90.
41 Baddeley, *The Russian Conquest of the Caucasus* (1908), pp. 153–60.
42 Treaty of Turkmenchay, 1828, Russian text, www.hist.msu.ru/ER/Etext/FOREIGN/turkman.htm.
43 Greaves, 'Iranian relations with Great Britain and British India' (1991), p. 390.
44 Baumer, *The History of Central Asia*, vol. 4 (2018), pp. 129f.
45 Curzon, George N., *Russia in Central Asia in 1889 and the Anglo-Russian Question* (London: Longmans, Green, and Co., 1889), p. 321.
46 Wagner, *Der Kaukasus und das Land der Kosaken* (1848), vol. 1, p. 175.
47 Sidorko, *Dschihad im Kaukasus* (2007), p. 142.
48 Baddeley, *The Russian Conquest of the Caucasus* (1908), pp. 185–224. Bournoutian gives, with 25,000 Turkish Armenian migrants, a significantly lower figure than Baddeley. Bournoutian, George A., 'Eastern Armenia from the seventeenth Century to the Russian annexation', in: Hovannisian, *The Armenian People from Ancient to Modern Times*, vol. 2 (1997), p. 105.
49 Bournoutian, 'Eastern Armenia from the seventeenth Century to the Russian annexation' (1997), p. 105; Suny, 'Eastern Armenia under Tsarist Rule', in Hovannisian, *The Armenian People from Ancient to Modern Times*, vol. 2 (1997), pp. 112, 126.
50 Russia's religious policy was much less tolerant towards Orthodox dissenters.
51 The Arabic word *ghazawat* is the plural form of *ghazwa* meaning 'religiously motivated raiding'.
52 Henze, Paul B., 'Circassian resistance to Russia', in: Broxup, *The North Caucasus Barrier* (1992), pp. 75f; Kemper, Michael, *Herrschaft, Recht und Islam in Daghestan. Von den Khanaten und Geheimbünden zum ğihād-Staat* (Wiesbaden: Reichert, 2005), pp. 174–82; Sidorko, *Dschihad im Kaukasus* (2007), pp. 70–84.
53 Although there existed no political entity of Dagestan in the period under discussion, we use this ethnonym as a collective term of reference for the peoples living within Dagestan's borders.
54 Baddeley, *The Russian Conquest of the Caucasus* (1908), p. 112.
55 Gammer, Moshe, *Muslim Resistance to the Tsar: Shamil and the Conquest of Chechnia and Daghestan* (Abingdon: Frank Cass, 1994), pp. 12–17, 23–5, 30.
56 Baddeley, *The Russian Conquest of the Caucasus* (1908), p. 97.
57 Khodarkovsky, Michael, *Bitter Choices: Loyalty and Betrayal in the Russian Conquest of the North Caucasus* (Ithaca: Cornell University Press, 2011), p. 71.
58 Baddeley, *The Russian Conquest of the Caucasus* (1908), pp. 130–37.
59 Sidorko, *Dschihad im Kaukasus* (2007), pp. 98–103; Ware and Kisriev, *Dagestan* (2010), p. 17.
60 Baddeley, *The Russian Conquest of the Caucasus* (1908), pp. 144f; Sidorko, *Dschihad im Kaukasus* (2007), pp. 99, 103.
61 Baddeley, *The Russian Conquest of the Caucasus* (1908), pp. 149ff.
62 Wagner, *Der Kaukasus und das Land der Kosaken* (1848), vol. 2, pp. 118ff.
63 Richmond, *The Northwest Caucasus* (2011), pp. 60f.
64 Henze, 'Circassian resistance to Russia' (1992), pp. 81f; Richmond, *The Northwest Caucasus* (2011), p. 61.
65 Wagner, *Der Kaukasus und das Land der Kosaken* (1848), vol. 1, p. 23ff.
66 Bell, *Journal of a Residence in Circassia* (1840), vol. 2, p. 426.
67 Bell, *Journal of a Residence in Circassia* (1840), vol. 1, pp. 29–101, 173, 235, 267, 334; vol. 2, p. 308ff, 332f.
68 Richmond, *The Northwest Caucasus* (2011), p. 62.
69 Wagner, *Der Kaukasus und das Land der Kosaken* (1848), vol. 2, p. 121ff.
70 Sidorko, *Dschihad im Kaukasus* (2007), pp. 111–14.
71 Sidorko, *Dschihad im Kaukasus* (2007), p. 135.
72 The Arabic name Ghazi means 'victorious Muslim warrior'.
73 Baddeley, *The Russian Conquest of the Caucasus* (1908), pp. 261ff.
74 Baddeley, *The Russian Conquest of the Caucasus* (1908), pp. 240–81; Fadeev, Rostislav Andreeviç and Miljutin, Dimitrij Alekseeviç, *Sechzig Jahre des kaukasischen Krieges mit besonderer Berücksichtigung des Feldzuges im nördlichen Daghestan im Jahre 1839*, ed. and trans. Gustav Baumgarten (Leipzig: Berhard Schlicke, 1861), pp. 25, 127; Gammer, *Muslim Resistance to the Tsar* (1994), pp. 49–59; Sidorko, *Dschihad im Kaukasus* (2007), pp. 121–56.
75 Baddeley, *The Russian Conquest of the Caucasus* (1908), pp. 283–8.
76 Kemper, *Herrschaft, Recht und Islam in Daghestan* (2005), p. 370; Sidorko, *Dschihad im Kaukasus* (2007), pp. 180, 268f.
77 Gammer, Moshe, 'Was General Klüge-von-Klugenau Shamil's Desmichels?', in: *Cahiers du Monde Russe et Soviétique*, vol. 33, nos. 2–3 (Paris: EHESS, 1992), pp. 207–10.
78 Wagner, *Der Kaukasus und das Land der Kosaken* (1848), vol. 2, p. 126.
79 Gammer, *Muslim Resistance to the Tsar* (1994), pp. 86–8, 337 n41.
80 Fadeev and Miljutin, *Sechzig Jahre des kaukasischen Krieges* (1861), pp. 77–109.
81 Baddeley, *The Russian Conquest of the Caucasus* (1908), pp. 323–42; Sidorko, *Dschihad im Kaukasus* (2007), p. 208; Wagner, *Der Kaukasus und das Land der Kosaken* (1848), vol. 2, pp. 144f.
82 Gammer, *Muslim Resistance to the Tsar* (1994), pp. 122–5.
83 Sidorko, *Dschihad im Kaukasus* (2007), p. 264.
84 It is noteworthy that about half of the Russian generals fighting in the Caucasus were of German, Austrian or Swiss descent.
85 Kemper, *Herrschaft, Recht und Islam in Daghestan* (2005), pp. 307f.
86 Baddeley, *The Russian Conquest of the Caucasus* (1908), p. 386.
87 Baddeley, *The Russian Conquest of the Caucasus* (1908), pp. 385–410; Gammer, *Muslim Resistance to the Tsar* (1994), pp. 152–61, 169; Sidorko, *Dschihad im Kaukasus* (2007), pp. 232–7; Wagner, *Der Kaukasus und das Land der Kosaken* (1848), vol. 2, pp. 156–65.
88 Wagner, *Der Kaukasus und das Land der Kosaken* (1848), vol. 2, pp. 174–8.
89 Baddeley, *The Russian Conquest of the Caucasus* (1908), pp. 412–24.
90 Baddeley, *The Russian Conquest of the Caucasus* (1908), pp. 439–43.
91 Khodarkovsky, *Bitter Choices* (2011), pp. 137f, 148; Richmond, *The Northwest Caucasus* (2011), pp. 69–73.
92 Erkan, Aydin Osman, *Turn My Head to the Caucasus: The Biography of Osman Ferid Pasha* (Istanbul: Çitlembik Publications, 2009), p. 56. To mollify Amin,

93 General Nikolai Nikolayevich Muravyov-Karsky (1787–1866) who gained his additional name after he captured Kars in 1855, is not to be confused with General Nikolai Nikolayevich Muravyov-Amursky (1809–1881), governor general of Eastern Siberia.

94 Jamal al-Din had been thoroughly Russified. He was estranged from his father and could not adapt to the roughness of life in Chechnya where he died in 1858.

95 Prince Ivane Bagration-Mukhransky (1812–1895) was the head of the Mukhrani branch of the former Gorgian royal house of the Bagrationi dynasty of Georgia.

96 Allen, W.E.D., and Muratoff, Paul, *Caucasian Battlefields: A History of the Wars on the Turco-Caucasian Border 1828–1921* (Cambridge: Cambridge University Press, 1953), pp. 66–102; Baddeley, *The Russian Conquest of the Caucasus* (1908), pp. 447–54; Gammer, *Muslim Resistance to the Tsar* (1994), pp. 267–74; Henze, 'Circassian resistance to Russia' (1992), pp. 90–96; Rayfield, *Edge of Empires* (2012), pp. 291–3; Sidorko, *Dschihad im Kaukasus* (2007), pp. 405–10.

97 Albrecht Prinz von Preussen, Friedrich Heinrich, *Im Kaukasus 1862* (Berlin: Privatdruck bei Hayn, 1865), pp. 291–6.

98 Troops marching in the middle of a road with a width double the range of a rifle were safe from enemies shooting from forest edges.

99 Fadeev and Miljutin, *Sechzig Jahre des kaukasischen Krieges* (1861), p. 139.

100 Baddeley, *The Russian Conquest of the Caucasus* (1908), p. 471.

101 Baddeley, *The Russian Conquest of the Caucasus* (1908), pp. 458–82; Fadeev, and Miljutin, *Sechzig Jahre des kaukasischen Krieges* (1861), p. 135–87; Gammer, *Muslim Resistance to the Tsar* (1994), pp. 277–91.

102 Translation from the German by the author. Perović, *Der Nordkaukasus unter russischer Herrschaft* (2015), p. 94.

103 For this view see: Natho, Kadir I., *Circassian History* (Bloomington: Xlibris, 2009), pp. 354–97. Also: Jaimoukha, Amjad, *The Circassians* (London: Routledge, 2014), p. 69.

104 Richmond, *The Northwest Caucasus* (2011), pp. 75–8. See also: Perović, *Der Nordkaukasus unter russischer Herrschaft* (2015), p. 96.

105 Grassi, *A New Homeland* (2014), pp. 63, 79; Perović, *Der Nordkaukasus unter russischer Herrschaft* (2015), pp. 98f.

106 Grassi, A New Homeland (2014), pp. 75–7; Perović, *Der Nordkaukasus unter russischer Herrschaft* (2015), p. 98; Tsutsiev, *Atlas of the Ethno-Political History of the Caucasus* (2014), p. 25.

107 Hewitt, George, *The Abkhazians* (2014), p. 83.

108 Hewitt, George, *The Abkhazians* (2014), pp. 81, 83.

109 Grassi, *A New Homeland* (2014), pp. 82, 85, 95–9, 105f.

110 Grassi, *A New Homeland* (2014), p. 124.

111 Erkan, *Turn My Head to the Caucasus* (2009).

112 Grassi, *A New Homeland* (2014), p. 109.

113 Grassi, *A New Homeland* (2014), p. 130.

114 Perović, *Der Nordkaukasus unter russischer Herrschaft* (2015), pp. 101–18.

115 Status in the 1860s–80s. Tsutsiev, *Atlas of the Ethno-Political History of the Caucasus* (2014), maps 10, 14.

116 Barry, Quintin, *War in the East: A Military History of the Russo-Turkish War 1877–78* (Solihull: Helion, 2011), p. 26. For Stalin's comments on the liberation of the serfs see: Beria, Lavrenti, *On the History of the Bolshevik Organizations in Transcaucasia* (Moscow: Foreign Languages Publishing House, 1949), pp. 144–8.

117 Önol, Onur, *The Tsar's Armenians: A Minority in Late Imperial Russia* (London: I.B.Tauris, 2017), p. 110.

118 Richmond, *The Northwest Caucasus* (2011), pp. 92f, 97.

119 Perović, *Der Nordkaukasus unter russischer Herrschaft* (2015), p. 126.

120 In a tax-farming system, the highest bidder pays the state the taxes due from a defined province for a certain period upfront, and then obtains the right to collect as much tax as he can. The difference between the total tax collected, usually forcefully, and the lump sum paid upfront is his profit.

121 Barsoumian, 'The Eastern Question and the Tanzimat era' (1997), pp. 182f, 192–4.

122 Barsoumian, 'The Eastern Question and the Tanzimat era' (1997), pp. 182–8.

123 Barsoumian, 'The Eastern Question and the Tanzimat era' (1997), p. 199.

124 Reynolds, Michael A., *Shattering Empires: The Clash and Collapse of the Ottoman and Russian Empires 1908–1918* (Cambridge: Cambridge University Press, 2011), pp. 11–17.

125 Tsutsiev, *Atlas of the Ethno-Political History of the Caucasus* (2014), p. 51.

126 The ethnonym Azeri became widely used towards the end of the twentieth century for Azerbaijani persons. Both terms, Azerbaijani and Azeri, replaced at the end of the nineteenth century the previous misnomer Tatar.

127 Berberian, Houri, *Roving Revolutionaries: Armenians and the Connected Revolutions in the Russian, Iranian and Ottoman Worlds* (Oakland: University of California Press, 2019), p. 8. For the SDHP and ARF see below.

128 Contrary to numerous statements in the literature, Armenian Church properties were not confiscated, but the revenues deriving from them were administered by the Russian authorities. See: Önol, *The Tsar's Armenians* (2017), p. 21.

129 Villari, Luigi, *Fire and Sword in the Caucasus* (London: T. Fisher Unwin, 1906), p. 156.

130 Önol, *The Tsar's Armenians* (2017), pp. 6, 18.

131 Önol, *The Tsar's Armenians* (2017), pp. 129, 234 n136.

132 Önol, *The Tsar's Armenians* (2017), p. 25.

133 Prior to the population exchanges during World War I and following the collapse of the Soviet Union, all the major ethnicities were spread throughout the whole South Caucasus.

134 Villari, *Fire and Sword in the Caucasus* (1906), p. 157.

135 Villari, *Fire and Sword in the Caucasus* (1906), pp. 157f.

136 Villari, *Fire and Sword in the Caucasus* (1906), p. 73f.

137 Önol, *The Tsar's Armenians* (2017), p. 32.

138 See below.

139 Barry, *War in the East* (2011), pp. 68, 117.

140 The Ottoman fleet was commanded by the Englishman Augustus Charles Hobart-Hampden, who held the rank of an admiral and was known as Hobart Pasha. Barry, *War in the East* (2011), pp. 97ff, 191.

141 Allen and Muratoff, *Caucasian Battlefields* (1953), pp. 116–31.

142 Perović, *Der Nordkaukasus unter russischer Herrschaft* (2015), pp. 132–8.

143 Allen and Muratoff, *Caucasian Battlefields* (1953), pp. 172, 179–210; Barry, *War in the East* (2011), pp. 309–30.

144 Allen and Muratoff, *Caucasian Battlefields* (1953), pp. 211–24; Barry, *War in the East* (2011), pp. 421–39; Hovannisian, Richard G., 'The Armenian Question in the Ottoman Empire 1876–1914', in: Hovannisian, *The Armenian People from Ancient to Modern Times*, vol. 2 (1997), pp. 206–12.

145 Reisner, Oliver, 'Integrationsversuche der muslimischen Adscharer in die georgische Nationalbewegung', in: Motika and Ursinus (eds), *Caucasia between the Ottoman Empire and Iran* (2000), p. 217.

146 Allen and Muratoff, *Caucasian Battlefields* (1953), p. 225.

147 The Crimean War was almost a global war, being fought in the Baltic, the Danube region, Crimea, south-western Caucasus and the Pacific.

148 Huseinova, Azada et al., *Nobel. Nobellər və Bakı Nefti = The Nobels and Baku Oil* (Baku: Nobel Family Society, 2009), p. 55; Tolf, Robert W., *The Russian Rockefellers: The Saga of the Nobel Family and the Russian Oil Industry* (Stanford: Hoover Institution Press, 1976), pp. 9–20.

149 Tolf, *The Russian Rockefellers* (1976), pp. 85f, 160.

150 Tolf, *The Russian Rockefellers* (1976), p. 61.

151 Huseinova, *Nobel* (2009), pp. 109f.

152 Tolf, *The Russian Rockefellers* (1976), pp. 61–144.

153 Suny, Ronald Grigor, 'Eastern Armenia under Tsarist rule, in: Hovannisian, *The Armenian People from Ancient to Modern Times*, vol. 2 (1997), p. 125.

154 The Russian Social Democratic Workers' Party split in 1903 into the slightly more moderate Mensheviks and the more radical Bolsheviks.

155 Hingley, Ronald, *Joseph Stalin: Man and Legend* (New York: McGraw Hill, 1974), pp. 24, 27f.

156 Stalin was jailed for 18 months in Georgia and then deported to Irkutsk in eastern Siberia from where he quickly escaped and returned to Tbilisi in early 1904. Lang, David Marshall, *A Modern History of Georgia* (London: Weidenfeld and Nicolson, 1962), p. 140.

157 Villari, *Fire and Sword in the Caucasus* (1906), p. 189.

158 The Nobel plants and wells suffered less since Emanuel Nobel was a Russian citizen and had been rather responsive to workers' specific demands.

159 Tolf, *The Russian Rockefellers* (1976), pp. 152–62.

160 In the war against Japan of 1904–5 Russia suffered a humiliating defeat.

161 Royal Dutch Petroleum and Shell Transport and Trading Company merged in 1907.

162 Concerning the White Armies of the Russian Civil Wars 1917–1920 see pp. 217f.

163 Suny, 'Eastern Armenia under Tsarist rule' (1997), pp. 131f; Reynolds, *Shattering Empires* (2011), p. 54.

164 Reynolds, *Shattering Empires* (2011), p. 16.

165 Barsoumian, 'The Eastern Question and the Tanzimat era' (1997), p. 200.

166 Dadrian, Vahakn N., *The History of the Armenian Genocide* (Providence: Berghahn Books, 1995), pp. 127–30.

167 Hovannisian, 'The Armenian Question in the Ottoman Empire 1876–1914' (1997), pp. 219–35.

168 See below pp. 176f.

169 Berberian, *Roving Revolutionaries* (2019), p. 32.

170 Önol, *The Tsar's Armenians* (2017), pp. 56f.
171 Önol, *The Tsar's Armenians* (2017), pp. 65–70.
172 Önol, *The Tsar's Armenians* (2017), pp. 71–99.
173 Önol, *The Tsar's Armenians* (2017), p. 59.
174 en.wikipedia.org/wiki/1908_Ottoman_general_election, accessed 11 January 2022. A-Do gives other numbers and omits the Greek. A-Do [Hovhannes Ter Martirosian], *Van 1915: The Great Events of Vashbouragan* (1917; reprint and translation London: Gomidas Institute, 2017), p. 25.
175 Baumgart, Winfried (ed.), *Friedrich Freiherr Kress von Kressenstein. Bayerischer General und Orientkenner. Lebenserinnerungen, Tagebücher und Berichte 1914–1946* (Leiden: Brill, 2020), pp. 107, 652.
176 After the end of World War I, the victorious colonial empires France and Great Britain legitimated their quasi-colonial acquisition of parts of the defeated Ottoman Empire by defining them as 'mandates' assigned by the League of Nations.
177 Berberian, *Roving Revolutionaries* (2019), pp. 120, 132; Hovannisian, 'The Armenian Question in the Ottoman Empire 1876–1914' (1997), pp. 231f; Önol, *The Tsar's Armenians* (2017), p. 60.
178 Reynolds, *Shattering Empires* (2011), pp. 72, 77.
179 A-Do, *Van 1915* (2017), pp. 33–6, 46; Hovannisian, 'The Republic of Armenia' (1997), pp. 335–8.
180 Through the Ottoman Public Debt Administration European lenders controlled the income from some taxes, and through the 'capitulations' they enjoyed extraterritorial rights.
181 Baumer, *The History of Central Asia*, vol. 4 (2018), pp. 171f. Shared concern about the rapidly growing military and industrial power of Germany was the main motivation behind the Anglo-Russian Convention.
182 The Iranian Cossack Brigade, formed in 1879, consisted of Caucasian and Russian cavalry commanded by Russian officers.
183 Ter Minassian, Anahide, 'Le rôle des Arméniens du Caucase dans la révolution constitutionnaliste de la Perse (1905–1912)', in: Motika and Ursinus, *Caucasia between the Ottoman Empire and Iran* (2000), pp. 150f, 169f.
184 Ter Minassian, 'Le rôle des Arméniens du Caucase' (2000), pp. 170–73.
185 241,000 roubles in 1907 would correspond to *ca.* 3.51 million USD in comparable purchasing power in 2015. historicalstatistics.org/Currencyconverter.html.
186 Hingley, *Joseph Stalin* (1974), 51f; Lang, *A Modern History of Georgia* (1962), p. 176.
187 Sebag Montefiori, Simon, *Young Stalin* (New York: Vintage, 2008), pp. 4–11, 14, 87, 127, 165, 178; Rayfield, *Edge of Empires* (2012), p. 316.
188 Beria, *On the History of the Bolshevik Organizations in Transcaucasia* (1949), pp. 18f.
189 Villari, *Fire and Sword in the Caucasus* (1906), p. 122.
190 Villari, *Fire and Sword in the Caucasus* (1906), p. 77.
191 Lang, *A Modern History of Georgia* (1962), pp. 120f.
192 Villari, *Fire and Sword in the Caucasus* (1906), p. 79.
193 Lang, *A Modern History of Georgia* (1962), pp. 119f, 172.
194 Villari, *Fire and Sword in the Caucasus* (1906), pp. 74–9.
195 Lang, *A Modern History of Georgia* (1962), p. 132.
196 Villari, *Fire and Sword in the Caucasus* (1906), p. 95.

197 Lee, Eric, *The Experiment: Georgia's Forgotten Revolution 1918–1921* (London: Bloomsbury, 2017), p. 11.
198 Jones, S.F., *Socialism in Georgian Colors* (Cambridge, MA: Harvard University Press, 2005), p. 142; Lang, *A Modern History of Georgia* (1962), pp. 113ff, 123, 131.
199 Lang, *A Modern History of Georgia* (1962), pp. 142f, 150f.
200 Lang, *A Modern History of Georgia* (1962), pp. 162–8; Suny, Ronald Grigor, *The Making of the Georgian Nation*, 2nd ed. (Bloomington: Indiana University Press, 1994), pp. 168–72.
201 Hingley, *Joseph Stalin* (1974), p. 54; Lang, *A Modern History of Georgia* (1962), p. 176; Rayfield, *Edge of Empires* (2012), p. 316.
202 Lang, *A Modern History of Georgia* (1962), pp. 154f, 178; Rayfield, *Edge of Empires* (2012), p. 317.
203 en.wikipedia.org/wiki/January_1907_Russian_legislative_election (accessed 5 December 2021).
204 Suny, 'Eastern Armenia under Tsarist rule' (1997), p. 135; Lang, *A Modern History of Georgia* (1962), pp. 169–75.
205 The toponym Azerbaijan is derived from the ancient toponym Atropatene which in turn derives from the Iranian satrap Atropates. Baumer, *History of the Caucasus,* vol. 1 (2021), p. 327 n75. It has been widely used in Arabic since the tenth century, but in the modern sense only since the 1860s. Rayfield, *Edge of Empires* (2012), p. 311.
206 See above, note 126. For simplicity's sake we use the ethnonym Azeri also for Azerbaijanis of the early twentieth century.
207 Around 1914 there were about 300 million Muslims (of all denominations) worldwide, of which 13.4 million lived in what was left of the Ottoman Empire, whose population additionally included officially 1.2 million Armenians and 1.6 million Greeks: en.wikipedia.org/wiki/Demographics_of_the_Ottoman_Empire#1914_Ottoman_census. The real Armenian population figure was significantly higher, around 2 or even 2.4 million: en.wikipedia.org/wiki/Ottoman_Armenian_population; see above, notes 18 and 19.
208 The jadidist movement took its name from the phrase *usul ul-jadid* meaning 'new method' of education.
209 Forsyth, *The Caucasus* (2013), pp. 325f.
210 Bolukbasi, Suha, *Azerbaijan: A Political History* (London: I.B.Tauris, 2011), pp. 26–30.
211 Suny, Ronald Grigor, *The Baku Commune, 1917–1918: Class and Nationality in the Russian Revolution* (Princeton: Princeton University Press, 2019), pp. 28f.
212 Suny, *The Baku Commune* (2019), p. 34.
213 Suny, *The Baku Commune* (2019), p. 53.
214 Beria, *On the History of the Bolshevik Organizations in Transcaucasia* (1949), p. 80.
215 Önol, *The Tsar's Armenians* (2017), p. 112.

VII. A Short-Lived Independence and Foreign Interventions

1 Egypt belonged nominally to the Ottoman Empire, but it had been ruled by Great Britain since 1882.
2 Imperial Germany aimed with its five Naval Laws from 1898 to 1912 to match the British Royal Navy.
3 Reynolds, *Shattering Empires* (2011), p. 38.
4 avalon.law.yale.edu/20th_century/turkgerm.asp; Reynolds, *Shattering Empires* (2011), p. 109.
5 Churchill had already given orders not to let the two dreadnoughts leave England on 29 July 1914. Richter, Heinz, 'The impact of the confiscation of the Turkish dreadnoughts and of the transfer of Goeben and Breslau to Constantinople upon the Turkish Entry into WWI', in: *Çanakkale Araştırmaları Türk Yıllığı*, Year 11, no. 15 (Çanakkale: 2013), pp. 3f: dergipark.org.tr/tr/download/article-file/45128 (accessed 14 July 2022).
6 The Entente consisted in August 1914 of France, Great Britain and Russia.
7 Morgenthau, Henry, *Ambassador Morgenthau's Story: A Personal Account of the Armenian Genocide* (1918; repr. New York: Cosimo Classics, 2010), pp. 48–56; Reynolds, *Shattering Empires* (2011), pp. 109–11.
8 Capitulations are unilateral treaties by which a state cedes within its own borders its jurisdiction over the subjects of the beneficiary foreign state which therefore enjoys extraterritorial rights. Several European states and the USA had forced the Ottomans to grant them such capitulations.
9 Allen and Muratoff, *Caucasian Battlefields* (1953), p. 239; Morgenthau, *Ambassador Morgenthau's Story* (2010), pp. 48–56; Reynolds, *Shattering Empires* (2011), pp. 109–14.
10 The Russian attack on Prussia led to the catastrophic defeat of Tannenberg on 26–30 August 1914 with *ca.* 70,000 dead and 93,000 Russian POWs.
11 Ailsby, Christopher, *Hitler's Renegades: Foreign Nationals in the Service of the Third Reich* (Dulles, VA: Brown Reference Group, 2004), p. 124; Chalabian, Antranig, *Dro (Drastamat Kanayan): Armenia's First Defense Minister of the Modern Era* (Los Angeles: Indo-European Publishing, 2009).
12 A-Do, *Van 1915* (2017), p. 48f, 62f.; Walker, Christopher J., 'World War I and the Armenian Genocide', in: Hovannisian, Richard G., *The Armenian People from Ancient to Modern Times*, vol. 2 (1997), pp. 245f.
13 Allen and Muratoff, *Caucasian Battlefields* (1953), p. 242.
14 Allen and Muratoff, *Caucasian Battlefields* (1953), pp. 249–85.
15 The majority of Assyrians, like the Armenians, lived in eastern Anatolia and were mainly peasants. Their strongholds were the mountainous Hakkâri Province in today's south-eastern Turkey and the regions of Salmas and Urmia in today's Iranian Azerbaijan.
16 Allen and Muratoff, *Caucasian Battlefields* (1953), pp. 295–9.
17 Reynolds, *Shattering Empires* (2011), pp. 143f.
18 Allen and Muratoff believed that Russia had no real interest in the Gallipoli attack, but other historians such as Johnson think that Britain rejected Russian participation because it might motivate the so-far neutral Bulgarians to enter the war on the Central Powers' side. Allen and Muratoff, *Caucasian*

Battlefields (1953), p. 288; Johnson, Rob, *The Great War in the Middle East: A Strategic Study* (Oxford: Oxford University Press, 2016), p. 95. Perhaps the two German warships in Ottoman service operating in the Black Sea were a strong deterrent for Russia.

19. Keddie, Nikki and Amanat, Mehrdad, 'Iran under the later Qajars', in: Avery, Hambly and Melville, *The Cambridge History of Iran*, vol. 7 (1991), p. 208; Kazemdazeh, 'Iranian relations with Russia' (1991), p. 343.
20. A-Do, *Van 1915* (2017), pp. 48f; Morgenthau, *Ambassador Morgenthau's Story* (2010), p. 211.
21. Morgenthau, *Ambassador Morgenthau's Story* (2010), pp. 231f, 241.
22. Morgenthau, *Ambassador Morgenthau's Story* (2010), p. 241.
23. Walker, 'World War I and the Armenian Genocide' (1997), p. 249.
24. Walker, 'World War I and the Armenian Genocide' (1997), p. 253f; Reynolds, *Shattering Empires* (2011), pp. 119, 121.
25. Since the German consuls and army officers were allies of the Ottomans, they had no reason to exaggerate the facts; there is also abundant photographic evidence of the genocide. Akçam, Taner, *A Shameful Act: The Armenian Genocide and the Question of Turkish Responsibility* (New York: Metropolitan Books, 2006), pp. 149–204; Walker, 'World War I and the Armenian Genocide' (1997), pp. 246–65; Robertson, Geoffrey, *An Inconvenient Genocide: Who Now Remembers the Armenians?* (London: Biteback Publishing, 2015), pp. 59–90.
26. Pattie, Susan Paul, *The Armenian Legionnaires: Sacrifice and Betrayal in World War I* (London: I.B.Tauris, 2018), pp. 7, 9.
27. One of the most exhaustive sources for the Armenian Genocide is: Kévorkian, Raymond, *Le Génocide des Arméniens* (Paris: Odile Jacob, 2006). See also: Akçam, *A Shameful Act* (2006), p. 183; Reynolds, *Shattering Empires* (2011), pp. 119, 121; Robertson, *An Inconvenient Genocide* (2015), pp. 50–57; Toynbee, Arnold Joseph, *The Treatment of Armenians in the Ottoman Empire: Documents Presented to Viscount Grey of Fallodon* (London: Hodder and Stoughton, 1916); Walker, 'World War I and the Armenian Genocide' (1997), pp. 246–65.
28. This interior minister Cemal (Jemal) Bey in 1919 is not to be confused with Jemal Pasha, one of the CUP triumvirate ruling the Ottoman Empire during WWI.
29. Akçam, *A Shameful Act* (2006), p. 183. For further post-war Turkish acknowledgements see: Robertson, *An Inconvenient Genocide* (2015), pp. 81f.
30. Robertson, *An Inconvenient Genocide* (2015), pp. 81f.
31. https://digitallibrary.un.org record/209873?ln=en#record-files-collapse-header.
32. en.wikipedia.org/wiki/Armenian_genocide_recognition#United_Kingdom (accessed 9 December 2021).
33. *Case of Perinçek v. Switzerland* (Application no. 27510/08). Judgment, Strasburg 15 October 2015: https://hudoc.echr.coe.int/eng#_Toc516647594; *Neue Zürcher Zeitung*, Zurich, 16 October 2015, p. 13; Reuters, 17 December 2013, reuters.com/article/us-switzerland-turkey-genocide-idUSBRE9BG11J20131217 (accessed 1 May 2022).
34. Derogy, Jacques, *Resistance and Revenge: The Armenian Assassination of Turkish Leaders Responsible for the 1915 Massacres and Deportations* (New Brunswick: Transaction Publishers, 2016), pp. xvii–xx, 1, 84f, 188, 190f; Robertson, *An Inconvenient Genocide* (2015), p. 83. The Dashnaks also assassinated Fatali Khan Khoyski, former prime minister, and Behbud Khan Javanshir, former interior minister of the first Republic of Azerbaijan, whom they held responsible for the Armenian massacres of September 1918 in Baku.
35. 3,000 Armenians and 1,000 Muslims lived in Van city, and in the neighbouring region 23,000 Armenians and 18,000 Muslims. A-Do, *Van 1915* (2017), p. 135.
36. A-Do, *Van 1915* (2017), pp. 95f, 99, 101, 103, 115f, 147.
37. Allen and Muratoff, *Caucasian Battlefields* (1953), pp. 299–310; A-Do, *Van 1915* (2017), pp. 147ff, 198f, 220–23, 283–90, 293, 296.
38. Hewsen, *Armenia: A Historical Atlas* (2001), map 225; Hovannisian, 'Armenia's road to independence', in: Hovannisian, Richard G., *The Armenian People from Ancient to Modern Times*, vol. 2 (1997), pp. 281f.
39. Reynolds, *Shattering Empires* (2011), p. 160.
40. It has been a constant in Russian warfare and general staff planning since the 1860s to accept without demur high losses of their own soldiers, in view of the country's exceptionally large population.
41. Allen and Muratoff, *Caucasian Battlefields* (1953), pp. 326–83; Hewsen, *Armenia: A Historical Atlas* (2001), p. 228.
42. In the war, Russia lost almost two million killed, five million wounded and more than two million prisoners. Ullman, Richard H., *Intervention and the War: Anglo-Soviet Relations, 1917–1921* (Princeton: Princeton University Press, 1961), p.4.
43. The tsarist government had renamed St Petersburg (in Russian, Sankt-Peterburg) as Petrograd in 1914 to remove the German elements of the city's name.
44. Forsyth, *The Caucasus* (2013), p. 330.
45. Reynolds, *Shattering Empires* (2011), p. 168.
46. Allen and Muratoff, *Caucasian Battlefields* (1953), pp. 448f.
47. Hovannisian, 'Armenia's road to independence' (1997), pp. 283f.
48. Forsyth, *The Caucasus* (2013), p. 367.
49. Reynolds, *Shattering Empires* (2011), p. 193.
50. Forsyth, *The Caucasus* (2013), p. 345.
51. Smele, Jonathan D., *The 'Russian' Civil Wars 1916–1926* (London: C. Hurst & Co., 2016), pp. 30f. To compare the very similar counts of Svyatitsky and Lenin: en.wikipedia.org/wiki/1917_Russian_Constituent_Assembly_election#Dissolution_of_Constituent_Assembly_by_Bolsheviks (accessed 12 December 2021).
52. avalon.law.yale.edu/20th_century/bl34.asp#treatytext (accessed 12 December 2021).
53. Hovannisian, 'Armenia's road to independence' (1997), pp. 288f; avalon.law.yale.edu/20th_century/bl34.asp#treatytext (accessed 12 December 2021).
54. Reynolds, *Shattering Empires* (2011), p. 196.
55. Reynolds, *Shattering Empires* (2011), p. 197.
56. Allen and Muratoff, *Caucasian Battlefields* (1953), pp. 460–67; Reynolds, *Shattering Empires* (2011), pp. 196–200, 206.
57. Baumgart, *Friedrich Freiherr Kress von Kressenstein* (2020), p. 110. Translation by the author.
58. Cornell, Svante E., *Azerbaijan since Independence* (Armonk: M.E. Sharpe, 2011), p. 21; Reynolds, *Shattering Empires* (2011), p. 200.
59. Fischer, Fritz, *Germany's Aims in the First World War* (New York: W.W. Norton, 1968), pp. 556f.
60. Fischer, *Germany's Aims in the First World War* (1968), p. 578; Forsyth, *The Caucasus* (2013), p. 376. See also: Baumgart, *Friedrich Freiherr Kress von Kressenstein* (2020), pp. 143–6, 678f; Ellis, Charles Howard, *The Transcaspian Episode 1918–1919* (London: Hutchinson, 1963), pp. 35, 37; Hovannisian, Richard G., *The Republic of Armenia*, vol. 1: *The First Year, 1918–1919* (Berkeley: University of California Press, 1971), p. 29; Teague-Jones, Reginald, *The Spy Who Disappeared: Diary of a Secret Mission to Russian Central Asia in 1918* (London: Victor Gollancz, 1990), pp. 52, 62f, 82.
61. Teague-Jones, *The Spy Who Disappeared* (1990), pp. 62–9.
62. On the strategic importance of cotton, see also: Blacker, L.V.S., *On Secret Patrol in High Asia* (London: John Murray, 1922), pp. 6, 20f.
63. Forsyth, *The Caucasus* (2013), p. 373.
64. Charles Howard Ellis, 'The Transcaspian episode', *Royal Central Asian Journal*, vol. XLVI, No. 2, April 1959 (London: Royal Central Asian Society, 1959), p. 107; Rayfield, *Edge of Empires* (2012), pp. 326–30.
65. Reynolds, *Shattering Empires* (2011), p. 213f; Waal, Thomas de, *Black Garden: Armenia and Azerbaijan through Peace and War* (New York: New York University Press, 2003), p. 63.
66. Baumgart, *Friedrich Freiherr Kress von Kressenstein* (2020), pp.120f.
67. De Waal, Thomas, *The Caucasus: An Introduction* (Oxford: Oxford University Press, 2010), pp. 65, 137; Saparov, Arsène, *From Conflict to Autonomy in the Caucasus: The Soviet Union and the Making of Abkhazia, South Ossetia and Nagorno Karabakh* (London: Routledge, 2015), pp. 66–70.
68. Saparov, *From Conflict to Autonomy in the Caucasus* (2015), pp. 81f.
69. Andersen, Andrew, *Abkhazia and Sochi: The Roots of the Conflict 1918–1921* (n.p.: Asteroid Publishing, 2014), p. 13.
70. Andersen, *Abkhazia and Sochi* (2014), pp. 30–36, 55; Baumgart, *Friedrich Freiherr Kress von Kressenstein* (2020), pp. 123, 664, 705f; Saparov, *From Conflict to Autonomy in the Caucasus* (2015), p. 48.
71. Andersen, *Abkhazia and Sochi* (2014), pp. 28–43.
72. Contrary to the opinion expressed by some authors, Abkhazia never joined the United Mountain Peoples UMP; Andersen, *Abkhazia and Sochi* (2014), p. 18; Andersen, Andrew and Partskhaladze, George, *Armeno-Georgian War of 1918 and Armeno-Georgian Territorial Issue in the 20th Century* (2015), p. 34; Saparov, *From Conflict to Autonomy in the Caucasus* (2015), p. 43.
73. Andersen, *Abkhazia and Sochi* (2014), p. 57; Baumgart, *Friedrich Freiherr Kress von Kressenstein* (2020), pp. 122, 143, 664.
74. The term 'White' was introduced by the Bolsheviks to vilify their conservative adversaries. It referred to the white standard of French monarchists. Kopisto, Lauri, 'The British intervention in South Russia 1918–1920' (dissertation, University of Helsinki, 2011), p. 23.
75. Andersen, *Abkhazia and Sochi* (2014), p. 86.

76 Saparov, *From Conflict to Autonomy in the Caucasus* (2015), pp. 45f.
77 Andersen, *Abkhazia and Sochi* (2014), pp. 73f, 80–82.
78 Andersen, *Abkhazia and Sochi* (2014), p. 150, 153f.
79 Within the Soviet Union, the main administrative units were, in decreasing degree of status: Soviet Socialist Republic (SSR), Autonomous Soviet Socialist Republic (ASSR), Autonomous Oblast (AO) and Autonomous Okrug.
80 The Kavbyuro was the Caucasian Bureau of the Central Committee of the Russian, later Soviet Communist Party, that is its executive leadership.
81 Saparov, *From Conflict to Autonomy in the Caucasus* (2015), pp. 48–62.
82 Baumgart, *Friedrich Freiherr Kress von Kressenstein* (2020), p. 634; see also pp. 36, 132, 648, 656, 710. Translation by the author.
83 Fischer, *Germany's Aims in the First World War* (1968), p. 557.
84 Hovannisian, *The Republic of Armenia*, vol. I (1971), pp. 40, 147.
85 Hewsen, *Armenia: A Historical Atlas* (2001), p. 230; Hovannisian, 'Armenia's road to independence' (1997), pp 299f.
86 Hovannisian, Richard, 'The Republic of Armenia', in: Hovannisian, Richard G., *The Armenian People from Ancient to Modern Times*, vol. 2 (1997),pp. 308, 318f.
87 According to the Russian census of 1897, Akhalkalaki's population was 71 per cent Armenian and Lori's 32 per cent. In addition, thousands of Armenian refugees from Anatolia settled in these two districts in 1915–18. Andersen and Partskhaladze, *Armeno-Georgian War of 1918* (2015), p. 13.
88 Shortly after the Treaty of Batumi in 4 June 1918, the Ottomans had requested this strategically important transit zone for themselves. Andersen and Partskhaladze, *Armeno-Georgian War of 1918* (2015), pp. 4–7, 9.
89 Lee, *The Experiment* (2017), pp. 63–6, 72.
90 Andersen and Partskhaladze, *Armeno-Georgian War of 1918* (2015), p. 34.
91 Lee, *The Experiment* (2017), p. 69.
92 Suny, Ronald Grigor, 'Soviet Armenia', in: Hovannisian, Richard G., *The Armenian People from Ancient to Modern Times*, vol. 2 (1997), p. 368. The British general Forestier-Walker was also convinced that such a secret agreement between Armenia and Denikin existed. Andersen and Partskhaladze, *Armeno-Georgian War of 1918* (2015), p. 38.
93 Andersen and Partskhaladze, *Armeno-Georgian War of 1918* (2015), p. 40.
94 Hewsen, *Armenia: A Historical Atlas* (2001), p. 228.
95 Baumgart, *Friedrich Freiherr Kress von Kressenstein* (2020), pp. 125, 153, 703; Hovannisian, *The Republic of Armenia*, vol. 1 (1971), pp. 73–8, 93–124.
96 Maksoudian, Krikor, 'Armenian communities in Eastern Europe', in: Hovannisian, Richard G., *The Armenian People from Ancient to Modern Times*, vol. 2 (1997.), p. 73.
97 Andersen and Partskhaladze, *Armeno-Georgian War of 1918* (2015), p. 55.
98 Hovannisian, *The Republic of Armenia*, vol. 1 (1971), pp. 360, 380f.
99 Hovannisian, 'The Republic of Armenia' (1997), p. 317.
100 Hovannisian, 'The Republic of Armenia' (1997), pp. 311, 313.
101 Fischer, *Germany's Aims in the First World War* (1968), pp. 535–49; Kopisto, *The British Intervention in South Russia* (2011), pp. 48, 53; Smele, *The 'Russian' Civil Wars 1916–1926* (2016), p. 61.
102 By September the Army of Islam had grown to 30,000 men.
103 Reynolds, *Shattering Empires* (2011), pp. 217–34.
104 Reynolds, *Shattering Empires* (2011), p. 223.
105 Smele, *The 'Russian' Civil Wars 1916–1926* (2016), p. 64.
106 Baumgart, *Friedrich Freiherr Kress von Kressenstein* (2020), pp. 142f, 676–82.
107 Hingley, *Joseph Stalin* (1974), pp. 338, 56, 119f.
108 Marshall, Alex, *The Caucasus under Soviet Rule* (London: Routledge, 2012), pp. 96f.
109 Allen and Muratoff, *Caucasian Battlefields* (1953), pp. 489–92; Dunsterville, Lionel C., *The Adventures of Dunsterforce* (London: Edward Arnold, 1920), pp. 207f; Reynolds, *Shattering Empires* (2011), pp. 224–31.
110 Dunsterville, *The Adventures of Dunsterforce* (1920), pp. 3f, 140f.
111 Rawlinson, Alfred, *Adventures in the Near East 1918–1922* (London: Andrew Melrose, 1924), pp. 79–81.
112 Dunsterville, *The Adventures of Dunsterforce* (1920), pp. 265–9, 276–8, 293–317; Ellis, *The Transcaspian Episode* (1963), pp. 34, 36, 39.
113 Seidt, Hans-Ulrich, *Berlin, Kabul, Moskau. Oskar Ritter von Niedermayer und Deutschlands Geopolitik* (München: Universitas, 2002), pp. 116f.
114 Andersen and Partskhaladze, *Armeno-Georgian War of 1918* (2015), p. 55.
115 Teague-Jones was a member of the British Malleson Mission which supported anti-Bolshevik forces in today's Turkmenistan. In fact, Stalin benefited from Shahumyan's execution since it eliminated an old internal Party rival. Suny, Ronald Grigor, *The Baku Commune, 1917–1918: Class and Nationality in the Russian Revolution* (Princeton: Princeton University Press, 1972), pp. 338–43.
116 Sinclair continued to work for British intelligence, and his true identity was only discovered and made public after his death in 1988. Ellis, *The Transcaspian Episode* (1963), pp. 59–62; Ter Minassian, *Most Secret Agent of Empire* (2014), pp. 5, 10, 105–39, 174; Teague-Jones, *The Spy Who Disappeared* (1990), pp. 12, 119–22, 211–16.
117 Chorbajian, Levon, Donabédian, Patrick and Mutafian, Claude, *The Caucasian Knot: The History and Geo-Politics of Nagorno-Karabagh* (London: Zed Books, 1994), p. 114
118 Baumgart, *Friedrich Freiherr Kress von Kressenstein* (2020), pp. 651f; Perović, *Der Nordkaukasus unter russischer Herrschaft* (2015), pp. 218f; Reynolds, *Shattering Empires* (2011), pp. 249–51.
119 Armistice of Mudros, 30 October 1918: germanhistorydocs.ghi-dc.org/pdf/eng/armistice_turk_eng.pdf. See also: Hovannisian, *The Republic of Armenia*, vol. 1. (1971), pp. 55–7, 199, 300.
120 Andersen and Partskhaladze, *Armeno-Georgian War of 1918* (2015), p. 21.
121 Kazemdazeh, Firuz, *The Struggle of Transcaucasia (1917–1921)* (New York: Philosophical Library, 1951), p. 169.
122 Lee, *The Experiment* (2017), p. 74.
123 Forsyth, *The Caucasus* (2013), pp. 378f.
124 Andersen, *Abkhazia and Sochi* (2014), pp. 101–3; Lee, *The Experiment* (2017), p. 76.
125 Hovannisian, *The Republic of Armenia*, vol. 2 (1982), pp. 501, 512; vol. 3 (1996), p. 410f.
126 Andersen and Partskhaladze, *Armeno-Georgian War of 1918* (2015), p. 33.
127 Chorbajian et al., *The Caucasian Knot* (1994), p. 119; Hovannisian, *The Republic of Armenia*, vol. 1 (1971), pp. 159–62.
128 Hovannisian, *The Republic of Armenia*, vol. 1 (1971), pp. 167, 170.
129 Hovannisian, *The Republic of Armenia*, vol. 1 (1971), p. 191.
130 Hovannisian, *The Republic of Armenia*, vol. 1 (1971), pp. 192-95.
131 Hovannisian, *The Republic of Armenia*, vol. 2 (1982), pp. 206–12, 216–19, 234–9.
132 Due to the infrastructural situation, all food and supplies imported into Karabakh came from Azerbaijan.
133 Hovannisian, *The Republic of Armenia*, vol. 1 (1971), pp. 175–88; vol. 2 (1982), p. 135.
134 Hovannisian, *The Republic of Armenia*, vol. 1 (1971), pp. 229–47.
135 Hovannisian, *The Republic of Armenia*, vol. 1 (1971), pp. 207, 416–33.
136 Poidebard was a Jesuit and pioneer in aerial archaeology in the Middle East.
137 Hovannisian, *The Republic of Armenia*, vol. 2 (1982), pp. 64–75.
138 Hovannisian, *The Republic of Armenia*, vol. 2 (1982), pp. 134–200.
139 Hovannisian, *The Republic of Armenia*, vol. 4 (1996), pp. 76, 83, 182.
140 The Kars Shura (Council) was formed as early as 5 November 1918. Andersen and Partskhaladze, *Armeno-Georgian War of 1918* (2015), p. 32.
141 Hovannisian, *The Republic of Armenia*, vol. 1 (1971), pp. 199–225.
142 Hovannisian, *The Republic of Armenia*, vol. 1 (1971), p. 480.
143 A serious stroke incapacitated President Wilson as of 2 October 1919, and an inner circle of aides including Wilson's wife took over in the background.
144 Hewsen, *Armenia: A Historical Atlas* (2001), map 231; Tsutsiev, *Atlas of the Ethno-Political History of the Caucasus* (2014), pp. 77, 79.
145 Hewsen, *Armenia: A Historical Atlas* (2001), map 232; Hovannisian, *The Republic of Armenia*, vol. 1 (1971), p. 288; vol. 2 (1982), pp. 191–5.
146 Ahmadi, Hamid, 'The clash of nationalisms: Iranian response to Baku's irredentism', in: Mehran Kamrava (ed.), *The Great Game in West Asia* (Oxford: Oxford University Press, 2017), pp. 108f.
147 In fact, two different Armenian delegations lobbied in Paris. The first one, headed by Avetis Aharonian, represented the Armenian parliament which was dominated by the Dashnaktsutiun Party. It demanded the unification of Russian and Ottoman Armenia plus a Black Sea harbour. The second delegation was headed by Boghos Nubar, political leader of the Armenian volunteer corps, the Légion d'Orient, and self-appointed spokesman of the Armenian diaspora. His claims were much more aggressive, as he demanded an Armenia stretching from the Black to the Mediterranean Sea. Given his forceful personality, Nubar prevailed over the

148 Hewsen, *Armenia: A Historical Atlas* (2001), map 227; Hovannisian, *The Republic of Armenia*, vol. 1 (1971), p. 259f, 274, 278; vol. 2 (1982), pp. 191–5.
149 en.wikipedia.org/wiki/Historical_Armenian_ population#1922 (accessed 20 December 2021).
150 Hovannisian, *The Republic of Armenia*, vol. 1 (1971), p. 283f.
151 Hovannisian, *The Republic of Armenia*, vol. 2 (1982), p. 454.
152 Hovannisian, *The Republic of Armenia*, vol. 2 (1982), p. 83.
153 Hovannisian, *The Republic of Armenia*, vol. 2 (1982), p. 332.
154 Hovannisian, *The Republic of Armenia*, vol. 2 (1982), p. 418; see also pp. 125, 127, 411–17.
155 Pattie, *The Armenian Legionnaires* (2018), pp. xxi, 136.
156 On 29 October 1923, the Republic of Turkey replaced the Ottoman Sultanate.
157 Hovannisian, *The Republic of Armenia*, vol. 4 (1996), p. 139
158 Hovannisian, *The Republic of Armenia*, vol. 3 (1996), pp. 216-53); vol. 4 (1996), pp. 139–42.
159 Hovannisian, *The Republic of Armenia*, vol. 3 (1996), p. 79.
160 The French Army, which had borne the brunt of the war in the West, had by 1919 become unreliable as demonstrated by its abysmally poor performance, including mutinies of French troops and marines in the Ukraine and Crimea during the December 1918–April 1919 intervention. France and Britain had already divided South Russia into zones of operation in late December 1917. The Caucasus was allocated to Britain, the Ukraine and Crimea to France. Kopisto, *The British Intervention in South Russia* (2011), pp. 83f; Lehovich, Dimitry V., *White against Red: The Life of General Anton Denikin* (New York: W.W. Norton, 1974), pp. 257–67; Smele, *The 'Russian' Civil Wars 1916–1926* (2016), p. 100.
161 Hovannisian, *The Republic of Armenia*, vol. 3 (1996), p. 80.
162 Hovannisian, *The Republic of Armenia*, vol. 3 (1996), p. 81.
163 Hovannisian, *The Republic of Armenia*, vol. 3 (1996), pp. 86–90.
164 Hovannisian, *The Republic of Armenia*, vol. 2 (1982), p. 371; vol. 3 (1996), p. 73.
165 Hovannisian, *The Republic of Armenia*, vol. 2 (1982), p. 389.
166 Hovannisian, *The Republic of Armenia*, vol. 4 (1996), p. 23.
167 Hovannisian, *The Republic of Armenia*, vol. 3 (1996), pp. 326–52.
168 'Treaty of Sèvres, 10 August 1920': wwi.lib.byu.edu/ index.php/Section_I,_Articles_1_-_260.
169 Hovannisian, *The Republic of Armenia*, vol. 4 (1996), pp. 94f.
170 Hovannisian, *The Republic of Armenia*, vol. 1 (1971), p. 444.
171 Hovannisian, *The Republic of Armenia*, vol. 4 (1996), pp. 158–64; id., *The Armenian People from Ancient to Modern Times*, vol. 2 (1997), p. 340.
172 Colonel Rawlinson was held prisoner by Kemal's nationalists from 16 March 1920 till 5 November 1921 as hostage. Rawlinson, *Adventures in the Near East* (1924), pp. 286–359.
173 Hovannisian, *The Republic of Armenia*, vol. 4 (1996), pp. 213f.
174 Hovannisian, *The Republic of Armenia*, vol. 4 (1996), pp. 188–96, 256–91.
175 'The Arbitral Award of the President of the United States of America Woodrow Wilson. Full Report of the Committee upon the Arbitration of the Boundary between Turkey and Armenia. Washington, November 22nd,1920': ararat-heritage.org.uk/PDF/ WoodrawWilsonArbitrationText.pdf.
176 Treaty of Alexandropol, 2–3 December, 1920: genocide.ru/lib/treaties/17.htm; www. deutscharmenischegesellschaft.de/wp-content/ uploads/2011/01/Vertrag-von-Alexandropol-2.- Dezember-1920.pdf
177 Treaty of Moscow, 16 March 1921, amsi.ge/istoria/ sab/moskovi.html.
178 Treaty of Kars, 13 October 1920, amsi.ge/istoria/sab/ yarsi.html.
179 Hovannisian, *The Republic of Armenia*, vol. 2 (1982), pp. 350f.
180 Chorbajian et al., *The Caucasian Knot* (1994), pp. 133f; Saparov, *From Conflict to Autonomy in the Caucasus* (2015), pp.104–6.
181 Lowland Karabakh was populated by Muslim Azeris.
182 Hovannisian, *The Republic of Armenia*, vol. 4 (1996), pp. 380–82.
183 Montainous (Nagorno-) Karabakh was not only supplied from Azerbaijan, but it also possessed the summer pastures of the semi-mobile pastoralists of Lowland Karabakh, who had a keen interest in keeping unimpeded access to those pastures: a thorn in the side of the Armenian farmers.
184 Bolukbasi, *Azerbaijan* (2011), p. 42; Chorbajian et al., *The Caucasian Knot* (1994), pp. 135–8, 178f.
185 Hewsen, *Armenia: A Historical Atlas* (2001), p. 266.
186 Pattie, *The Armenian Legionnaires* (2018), pp. xix– xxii, 110–24, 135.
187 Up to 12,000 Armenians lost their lives at Maraş. Hovannisian, *The Republic of Armenia*, vol. 3 (1996), pp. 36–42, Pattie, *The Armenian Legionnaires* (2018), pp. 154–84.
188 Treaty of Angora [Ankara], 20 October 1921, hri. org/docs/FT1921/Franco-Turkish_Pact_1921.pdf; Hovannisian, *The Republic of Armenia*, vol. 3 (1996), pp. 375–85; Pattie, *The Armenian Legionnaires* (2018), pp. 191–207.
189 Treaty of Moscow, 7 May 1920, soviethistory.msu. edu/1921-2/transcaucasia/transcaucasia-texts/ georgian-independence.
190 Lee, *The Experiment* (2017), pp. 195–215; Rayfield, *Edge of Empires* (2012), pp. 334–8.
191 The entity The United Mountain Peoples (UMP) of the North Caucasus is also called in the literature Mountainous Republic of the Northern Caucasus, United Republics of the North Caucasus, Mountain Republic or the Republic of the Mountaineers.
192 Forsyth, *The Caucasus* (2013), pp. 356–62; Marshall, *The Caucasus under Soviet Rule* (2012), pp. 58–61, 66f; Perović, *Der Nordkaukasus unter russischer Herrschaft* (2015), pp. 194–203; Tsutsiev, *Atlas of the Ethno-Political History of the Caucasus* (2014), p. 67.
193 Lehovich, *White against Red* (1974), p. 228; Tsutsiev, *Atlas of the Ethno-Political History of the Caucasus* (2014), maps 22f.
194 Marshall, *The Caucasus under Soviet Rule* (2012), p. 99.
195 Marshall, *The Caucasus under Soviet Rule* (2012), pp. 75–80; Perović, *Der Nordkaukasus unter russischer Herrschaft* (2015), pp. 219f.
196 Kort, Michael, *The Soviet Colossus: History and Aftermath* (Armonk, NY: M.E. Sharpe, 2001), p. 144.
197 Forsyth, *The Caucasus* (2013), p. 365; Marshall, *The Caucasus under Soviet Rule* (2012), p. 84; Perović, *Der Nordkaukasus unter russischer Herrschaft* (2015), p. 217; Tsutsiev, *Atlas of the Ethno-Political History of the Caucasus* (2014), p. 68.
198 Reynolds, *Shattering Empires* (2011), p. 237.
199 Smele, *The 'Russian' Civil Wars 1916–1926* (2016), pp. 40f.
200 Kopisto, *The British Intervention in South Russia* (2011), pp. 52, 86; Lehovich, *White against Red* (1974), pp.171–89; Marshall, *The Caucasus under Soviet Rule* (2012), pp. 55–7; Mueggenberg, Brent, *The Cossack Struggle against Communism, 1917–1945* (Jefferson: McFarland & Co., 2019), pp. 34–55.
201 Lehovich, *White against Red* (1974), pp. 200–204; Smele, *The 'Russian' Civil Wars 1916–1926* (2016), pp. 56f; When Alekseyev died in October 1918, Denikin also became political leader of the Volunteer Army.
202 The pro-German Don ataman Krasnov was replaced by General Bogayevsky. Kopisto, *The British Intervention in South Russia* (2011), p. 75.
203 Forsyth, *The Caucasus* (2013), pp. 413–19; Perović, *Der Nordkaukasus unter russischer Herrschaft* (2015), pp. 190–92, 228; Smele, *The 'Russian' Civil Wars 1916–1926* (2016), p. 120.
204 Kolchak was as determined as Denikin neither to recognize the independence of 'renegade' republics nor to compromise on territories.
205 There was also no coordination with White General Yudenich whose forces in October stood before Petrograd.
206 Smele, *The 'Russian' Civil Wars 1916–1926* (2016), p. 112–15.
207 Harris, John (ed.), *Farewell to the Don: The Journal of Brigadier H.N.H. Williamson* (London: Collins, 1970), pp. 158–62.
208 Lehovich, *White against Red* (1974), p. 351; Smele, *The 'Russian' Civil Wars 1916–1926* (2016), p. 122–6.
209 Denikin refused to recreate a strong cavalry when the Don Cossacks returned home after their attack on Voronezh. Harris, *Farewell to the Don* (1970), pp. 145, 158.
210 Forsyth, *The Caucasus* (2013), p. 449; Kopisto, *The British Intervention in South Russia* (2011), p. 150; Smele, *The 'Russian' Civil Wars 1916–1926* (2016), pp. 134.
211 Lehovich, *White against Red* (1974), pp. 347–50.
212 Mueggenberg, *The Cossack Struggle against Communism* (2019), p. 136.
213 Lehovich, *White against Red* (1974), p. 140; Smele, *The 'Russian' Civil Wars 1916–1926* (2016), pp. 385–8. General Wrangel and the evacuated Whites managed to hold Crimea till November 1920 only because of the Polish–Soviet War. His attempt to reconquer the Kuban in August 1920 failed miserably. Mueggenberg, *The Cossack Struggle against Communism* (2019), p. 161

VIII. Under Soviet Rule

1. Tsutsiev, *Atlas of the Ethno-Political History of the Caucasus* (2014), pp. 80, 82, map 29.
2. Translation by the author. Perović, *Der Nordkaukasus unter russischer Herrschaft* (2015), pp. 243f.
3. The 1926 census listed 190 ethnicities within the Soviet Union.
4. The AOs of Kabardino-Balkaria and Karachay-Cherkessia each combined two different ethnicities, for overriding economic reasons. Tsutsiev, *Atlas of the Ethno-Political History of the Caucasus* (2014), map 29.
5. Perović, *Der Nordkaukasus unter russischer Herrschaft* (2015), pp. 315–18.
6. Perović, *Der Nordkaukasus unter russischer Herrschaft* (2015), pp. 239f, 246, 268, 275f, 288–99; Ware and Kisriev, *Dagestan* (2010), pp. 28f.
7. Lee, *The Experiment* (2017), p. 230. There were several loose anti-Bolshevik and anti-Russian organisations of Caucasian political expatriates, one of which was the Prometheus League supported by Turkey and Poland. Copeaux, Étienne, 'Le mouvement «prométhéen»', in: *CEMOTI, Cahiers d'Études sur la Méditerranée Orientale et le monde Turco-Iranien*, vol. 16 (Paris: AFEMOTI, 1993) pp. 9–46.
8. Lee, *The Experiment* (2017), pp. 219–28.
9. Suny, Ronald Grigor, *The Making of the Georgian Nation*, 2nd ed. (Bloomington: Indiana University Press, 1994), p. 285.
10. Beria's book *On the History of the Bolshevik Organizations in Transcaucasia* is a sycophantic adulation of Stalin. Lang, *A Modern History of Georgia* (1962), p. 254.
11. Suny, 'Soviet Armenia' (1997), pp. 362, 366.
12. Exceptionially, the Baltic States were allowed to keep the Latin script.
13. Forsyth, *The Caucasus* (2013), pp. 451–3, 491–500.
14. Hewsen, *Armenia: A Historical Atlas* (2001), p. 242.
15. Bolukbasi, *Azerbaijan* (2011), p. 41; Hewsen, *Armenia: A Historical Atlas* (2001), p. 266.
16. Lang, *A Modern History of Georgia* (1962), p. 248; Perović, *Der Nordkaukasus unter russischer Herrschaft* (2015), pp. 354f.
17. Fisher, *The Crimean Tatars* (1978), pp. 136f; Mueggenberg, *The Cossack Struggle against Communism* (2019), pp. 211f.
18. Suny, 'Soviet Armenia' (1997), p. 359; Rayfield, *Edge of Empires* (2012), p. 350.
19. The Ukrainians call this famine 'Holodomor' which is derived from мориты голодом meaning 'to kill by hunger' in order to stress the manmade, intentional character of this catastrophe. en.wikipedia.org/wiki/Holodomor (accessed 21 April 2022).
20. Mueggenberg, *The Cossack Struggle against Communism* (2019), p. 218.
21. *Neue Zürcher Zeitung*, Zurich, dated 16 May 2022, p. 3.
22. Marshall, *The Caucasus under Soviet Rule* (2012), p. 214.
23. Perović, *Der Nordkaukasus unter russischer Herrschaft* (2015), pp. 354–6, 369f; Richmond, *The Northwest Caucasus* (2011), pp. 112f.
24. Suny, *The Making of the Georgian Nation* (1994), p. 262.
25. Many kulaks deported in the 1920s had escaped and returned home to the Don and the North Caucasus.
26. Tucker, Robert C., *Stalin in Power: The Revolution from Above* (New York: Norton & Company, 1990), pp. 418–20.
27. Avalishvili, Levan, 'The Great Terror of 1937–1938 in Georgia', in: *Caucasus Analytical Digest: Stalinist Terror in the South Caucasus*, No. 22 (Zurich: ETH Center for Security Studies, December 2010), pp. 2–6; Ismailov, Eldar, 'Great Terror in Azerbaijan', ibid., pp. 9–12; Melkonian, Eduard, 'Repressions in 1930s Soviet Armenia', ibid., pp. 6–9; Perović, *Der Nordkaukasus unter russischer Herrschaft* (2015), p. 411. The figures given by Forsyth are much too high. Forsyth, *The Caucasus* (2013), pp. 509–17.
28. Marshall, *The Caucasus under Soviet Rule* (2012), pp. 241, 254. The enormous contribution of the Baku oilfields to the war effort led to their almost total depletion until new gas and oilfields were found, mainly offshore.
29. Most of the Luftwaffe's aviation fuel was produced in hydrogenation plants, where, for example, lignite and coal tar were liquefied at high pressure and processed into aviation fuel. In the peak year 1943, German synthetic oil plants produced a total of 5,748 million tons of synthetic fuel. The other arms, above all the tank units, needed conventional fuels. It remains a mystery why the Allies did not attempt more decisively to destroy the Romanian oilfields which accounted for almost 90 per cent of the Axis Powers' oil production. Koppensteiner, Bruno W. and Häusler, Hermann, 'Das Kaukasus-Öl – Ziel der Deutschen Wehrmacht im Zweiten Weltkrieg', in: *Festschrift Brigadier i.R. Prof. Dr. Gerhard L. Fasching. Berichte der Geologischen Bundesanstalt*, vol. 140 (Vienna: Geologische Bundesanstalt, 2021), p. 80. Matthews, Owen, *An Impeccable Spy: Richard Sorge, Stalin's Master Agent* (London: Bloomsbury, 2019), p. 241.
30. The Oberkommando Wehrmacht was the High Command of the German armed forces (Wehrmacht).
31. Forczyk, Robert, *The Caucasus 1942–43: Kleist's Race for Oil* (Oxford: Osprey Publishing, 2015), pp. 25, 28, 45–9.
32. Matthews, *An Impeccable Spy* (2019), pp. 13, 15.
33. The Communist International propagated worldwide communism.
34. NSDAP: Nationalsozialistische Deutsche Arbeiterpartei.
35. Matthews, *An Impeccable Spy* (2019), pp. 59–131.
36. Matthews, *An Impeccable Spy* (2019), pp. 208-12.
37. Matthews, *An Impeccable Spy* (2019), pp. 257–9, 274–6, 280f.
38. Matthews, *An Impeccable Spy* (2019), pp. 295f.
39. Matthews, *An Impeccable Spy* 2019), pp. 314–16.
40. Translation by the author. Hitler, Adolf, *Weisungen für die Kriegsführung. Dokumente des Oberkommandos der Wehrmacht*, ed. Walter Hubatsch (1964), pp. 202f.
41. Hitler, *Weisungen für die Kriegsführung* (1964), pp. 212f.
42. Marshall, *The Caucasus under Soviet Rule* (2012), pp. 257f.
43. Kaltenegger, Roland, *Gebirgsjäger im Kaukasus. Die Operation „Edelweiss" 1942/43* (Graz: Leopold Stocker, 1997), pp. 53f.
44. Hitler, Adolf, *Weisungen für die Kriegsführung* (1964), pp. 218f. See also: Kaltenegger, *Gebirgsjäger im Kaukasus* (1997), pp. 30–39.
45. Liddell Hart, Basil H., *The Other Side of the Hill: Germany's Generals, their Rise and Fall, with their Own Account of Military Events 1939–1945* (London: Cassell, 1948), pp. 306f.
46. Forczyk, *The Caucasus 1942–43* (2015), pp. 11, 62, 73, 79.
47. Kaltenegger, *Gebirgsjäger im Kaukasus* (1997), pp. 78–80. See also Grechko, Andrei, *Battle for the Caucasus* (Honululu: University Press of the Pacific, 2001), pp. 87–90, 96–8.
48. Forczyk, *The Caucasus 1942–43* (2015), pp. 45, 47, 49. The Germans reached the most productive oilfields west of Maikop only in early October, seven weeks after the capture of the city. Koppensteiner and Häusler 'Das Kaukasus-Öl' (2021), p. 92.
49. Liddell Hart, *The Other Side of the Hill* (1948), pp. 303, 305; Hoffmann, Joachim, *Kaukasien 1942/43. Das deutsche Heer und die Orientvölker der Sowjetunion* (Freiburg: Rombach, 1991), pp. 65f; Kaltenegger, *Gebirgsjäger im Kaukasus* (1997), pp. 66f, 158.
50. The Germans failed to cut the Baku–Astrakhan railway line. Oil from Baku was also shipped over the Caspian Sea and the oilfields in the Urals compensated for the temporary shortfall from the Caucasus.
51. Officially, Hitler took personal command of Group A but de facto von Kleist ran the group; Kleist's official nomination was on 23 November. Forczyk, *The Caucasus 1942–43* (2015), p. 79.
52. Grozny was only bombed by the Luftwaffe on 10 and 12 October. Forczyk, *The Caucasus 1942–43* (2015), pp. 81–5.
53. Liddell Hart, *The Other Side of the Hill* (1948), pp. 303.
54. Local Chechen revolts had already broken out in 1940 and 1941. Forsyth, *The Caucasus* (2013), pp. 536f.
55. Hoffmann, *Kaukasien 1942/43* (1991), pp. 102–16.
56. Forczyk, *The Caucasus 1942–43* (2015), pp. 49, 87.
57. Feferman, Kiril, 'Nazi Germany and the Mountain Jews: Was there a policy?', in: *Holocaust and Genocide Studies* vol. 21, no. 1 (Oxford: Oxford Academic, 2007), pp. 96, 105–7.
58. Forsyth, *The Caucasus* (2013), pp. 522f, 529; Hoffmann, *Kaukasien 1942/43* (1991), pp. 38, 117.
59. Liddell Hart, *The Other Side of the Hill* (1948), p. 305.
60. Grechko, *Battle for the Caucasus* (2001), p. 137.
61. Hoffmann, *Kaukasien 1942/43* (1991), p. 69; Kaltenegger, *Gebirgsjäger im Kaukasus* (1997), pp. 75–111; Statiev, Alexander, *At War's Summit: The Red Army and the Struggle for the Caucasian Mountains in World War II* (Cambridge: Cambridge University Press, 2018), pp. 115–29, 148–201.
62. Grechko, *Battle for the Caucasus* (2001), pp. 148–69.
63. Glantz, David M., *Operation Don's Left Wing: The Trans-Caucasus Front's Pursuit of the First Panzer Army, November 1942–February 1943* (Lawrence: University Press of Kansas, 2019), pp. 63–103.
64. Glantz, *Operation Don's Left Wing* (2019), pp. 134–40.
65. Liddell Hart, *The Other Side of the Hill* (1948), pp. 316f; Seaton, Albert, *Stalin as Warlord* (London: B.T. Batsford, 1976), p. 173.
66. Forczyk, *The Caucasus 1942–43* (2015), pp. 88f; Hoffmann, *Kaukasien 1942/43* (1991), p. 77; Kaltenegger, *Gebirgsjäger im Kaukasus* (1997), pp. 146f.
67. Forczyk, *The Caucasus 1942–43* (2015), p. 91; Kaltenegger, *Gebirgsjäger im Kaukasus* (1997), pp. 247–59.

68 Hoffmann, *Kaukasien 1942/43* (1991), pp. 47–58, 133; Jurado, Carlos Caballero, *Von Niedermayer und die Ostlegionen der Wehrmacht* (Zweibrücken: Schild Verlag, 2017), pp. 25–53; Seidt, *Berlin, Kabul, Moskau* (2002), pp. 329–31; Thomassian, Levon, *Summer of '42. A Study of German–Armenian Relations during the Second World War* (Atglen, PA: Schiffer Publishing, 2012), pp. 146–54.

69 Ailsby, Christopher, *Hitler's Renegades: Foreign Nationals in the Service of the Third Reich* (Dulles: Brown Reference Group, 2004), p. 129; Thomassian, *Summer of '42* (2012), pp. 115–17.

70 Excluding Cossacks. Other sources name 28,000 North Caucasian collaborators. Richmond, *The Northwest Caucasus* (2011), pp. 114.

71 It was mainly Don Cossacks that fought on the German side; the Kuban and Terek Cossacks remained loyal to the Red Army. Ailsby, *Hitler's Renegades* (2004), p. 124, 130; Forsyth, *The Caucasus* (2013), pp. 533f; Hoffmann, *Kaukasien 1942/43* (1991), pp. 184–365. According to Ailsby, as many as 250,000 Cossacks fought for Germany, which is much too high a figure.

72 Hoffmann, *Kaukasien 1942/43* (1991), pp. 315–18; Thomassian, *Summer of '42* (2012), pp. 33–9.

73 Jurado, *Von Niedermayer und die Ostlegionen der Wehrmacht* (2017), pp.36f.

74 Thomassian, *Summer of '42* (2012), pp. 82, 150.

75 Mueggenberg, *The Cossack Struggle against Communism* (2019), pp. 267–89.

76 Erlikhman, Vadim, Потери народонаселения в XX веке: справочник *(Poteri narodonaseleniya v XX veke: spravochnik = Human Losses in the Twentieth Century: A Handbook)* (Moscow: Russkaia Panorama, 2004), pp. 23–35; Forsyth, *The Caucasus* (2013), pp. 531f; Rayfield, *Edge of Empires* (2012), pp. 358, 363.

77 Thomassian, *Summer of '42* (2012), pp. 157.

78 Marshall, *The Caucasus under Soviet Rule* (2012), pp. 263–5.

79 Hoffmann, *Kaukasien 1942/43* (1991), pp. 456–8.

80 Forsyth, *The Caucasus* (2013), pp. 534–42; Marshall, *The Caucasus under Soviet Rule* (2012), pp. 265–71; Perović, *Der Nordkaukasus unter russischer Herrschaft* (2015), pp. 443–7; Richmond, *The Northwest Caucasus* (2011), pp. 115–25; sciencespo.fr/mass-violence-war-massacre-resistance/fr/document/soviet-massive-deportations-chronology.html; en.wikipedia.org/wiki/Population_transfer_in_the_Soviet_Union#Post-war_expulsion_and_deportation (accessed 3 January 2022). The fate of the Cherkess and Adygeans is not well documented.

81 Tsutsiev, *Atlas of the Ethno-Political History of the Caucasus* (2014), map 39.

82 Suny, 'Soviet Armenia' (1997), pp. 367.

83 Hasanli, Jamil, *At the Dawn of the Cold War: The Soviet–American Crisis over Iranian Azerbaijan, 1941–1946* (Lanham: Rowman & Littlefield, 2006), pp. 133, 166.

84 Hasanli, *At the Dawn of the Cold War* (2006); pp. 3–7.

85 Saikal, Amin, 'Iranian foreign policy, 1921–1979', in: Avery, Hambly and Melville, *The Cambridge History of Iran*, vol. 7 (1991), p. 436.

86 These provinces were Iranian Azerbaijan, Gilan, Mazandaran, Gorgan and Khorassan. Hasanli, *At the Dawn of the Cold War* (2006); pp. 26, 66, 151.

87 Hasanli, *At the Dawn of the Cold War* (2006); pp. 225–44.

88 Hasanli, *At the Dawn of the Cold War* (2006); pp. 363–73.

89 en.wikipedia.org/wiki/Population_transfer_in_the_Soviet_Union.

90 Forsyth, *The Caucasus* (2013), pp. 593–7; Tsutsiev, *Atlas of the Ethno-Political History of the Caucasus* (2014), p. 101.

91 The KGB, the Committee for State Security, succeeded the NKVD in 1954.

92 Bolukbasi, *Azerbaijan* (2011), pp. 51f.

93 De Waal, *The Caucasus* (2010), p. 92.

94 Forsyth, *The Caucasus* (2013), p. 568.

95 Lang, *A Modern History of Georgia* (1962), p. 265; Suny, *The Making of the Georgian Nation* (1994), pp. 302f.

96 oikoumene.org/resources/documents/country-profile-georgia.

97 orthodoxinfo.com/ecumenism/georgia_wcc.aspx.

98 Gamsakhurdia was released in 1979. Suny, *The Making of the Georgian Nation* (1994), pp. 308f.

99 Suny, *The Making of the Georgian Nation* (1994), pp. 306–8.

100 Suny, 'Soviet Armenia' (1997), p. 377.

101 Forsyth, *The Caucasus* (2013), p. 563.

102 On the question of Karabakh's state affiliation see: Baumer, *History of the Caucasus,* vol. 1 (2021), pp. 139, 158.

103 For the Caucasian Albanians see: Baumer, *History of the Caucasus,* vol. 1 (2021), pp. 156–66.

104 Bolukbasi, *Azerbaijan* (2011), pp. 63f; Waal, *Black Garden* (2003), pp. 152f.

105 Mammadova, Gulchohra, *Architecture of Caucasian Albania* (Saarbrücken: Lambert Academic Publishing, 2011). Dozens of Armenian churches are reinterpreted as Albanian.

106 Mammadova, *Architecture of Caucasian Albania* (2011), p. 45.

107 Forsyth, *The Caucasus* (2013), pp. 466, 599–601.

108 Richmond, *The Northwest Caucasus* (2011), p. 128.

IX. Independence in the South Caucasus

1 Marx, Karl, 'The Eighteenth Brumaire of Louis Bonaparte', *Die Revolution*, vol. 1 (New York: Deutsche Vereins-Buchhandlung von Schmidt u. Helmich, 1852), ch. 1: marxists.org/archive/marx/works/1852/18th-brumaire/ch01.htm.

2 Walo, Ellen A., *Saudi Inc.: The Arabian Kingdom's Pursuit of Profit and Power* (New York: Pegasus Books, 2019), p. 217.

3 Forsyth, *The Caucasus* (2013), pp. 641–5; Ware and Kisriev, *Dagestan* (2010), pp. 33f.

4 Ethnicity may be defined by language, social structures, history and prejudices.

5 Today, there are no Armenians left in Nakhchivan. Cornell, *Small Nations and Great Powers* (2001), p. 78; De Waal, *The Caucasus* (2010), p. 104; Walker, Christopher J., *Armenia and Karabakh: The Struggle for Unity* (London: Minority Rights Group, 1991), pp. 64f.

6 Cornell, *Small Nations and Great Powers* (2001), pp. 85, 94; Hewsen, *Armenia: A Historical Atlas* (2001), p. 283; Tsutsiev, *Atlas of the Ethno-Political History of the Caucasus* (2014), p. 113.

7 Chorbajian et al., *The Caucasian Knot* (1994), pp. 151, 182.

8 Bolukbasi, *Azerbaijan* (2011), pp. 101f.

9 Bolukbasi, *Azerbaijan* (2011), pp. 115–21; Suny, 'Soviet Armenia' (1997), pp. 381f.

10 Bolukbasi, *Azerbaijan* (2011), pp. 123–9.

11 Bolukbasi, *Azerbaijan* (2011), p. 150; Suny, 'Soviet Armenia' (1997), pp. 383–5.

12 Suny, 'Soviet Armenia' (1997), pp. 384f.

13 A single GRAD ('hailstorm') multiple launcher can fire forty rockets over a wide area within less than twenty seconds.

14 For example, the Armenians acquired the weaponry of the 366th Soviet Regiment and the Azeris that of the 23rd Division stationed in Ganja. Bolukbasi, *Azerbaijan* (2011), p. 14; De Waal, *The Caucasus* (2010), pp. 115f; Taarnby, Michael, 'The Mujahedin in Nagorno-Karabakh: A case study in the evolution of global jihad' (Madrid: Real Instituto Elcano, 2008), p. 6.

15 82 per cent of registered voters participated while the Azerbaijanis, accounting for 18 per cent, boycotted the election. De Waal, *The Caucasus* (2010), pp. 114f; nkr.am/en/independence-referendum-in-karabakh (accessed 18 January 2022).

16 Kosovo became independent in 2008; it is recognized by 115 UN member states.

17 Minority Rights Group International, London, May 2020: minorityrights.org/country/lebanon (accessed 1 May 2022).

18 Bolukbasi, *Azerbaijan* (2011), pp. 111, 126f, 140.

19 Bolukbasi, *Azerbaijan* (2011), pp.131–8; Cornell, *Small Nations and Great Powers* (2001), p. 89; Cornell, Svante E., *Azerbaijan since Independence* (Armonk, NY: M.E. Sharpe, 2011), pp. 54–6.

20 Bolukbasi, *Azerbaijan* (2011), pp. 138, 159, 172.

21 In Armenia too Soviet toponyms changed back to traditional Armenian ones, for example Leninakan reverted to Gyumri.

22 Cornell, *Azerbaijan since Independence* (2011), pp. 58f.

23 Bolukbasi, *Azerbaijan* (2011), pp. 145, 155.

24 Bolukbasi, *Azerbaijan* (2011), p. 182. Cornell, *Azerbaijan since Independence* (2011), pp. 62.

25 Bolukbasi, *Azerbaijan* (2011), pp. 185–95; Cornell, *Azerbaijan since Independence* (2011), pp. 64f.

26 Ahmadi, 'The clash of nationalisms' (2017), pp. 119–21; Cornell, *Azerbaijan since Independence* (2011), p. 328.

27 Quoted from: Cornell, *Azerbaijan since Independence* (2011), p. 78.

28 Bolukbasi, *Azerbaijan* (2011), pp. 185–208; Cornell, *Small Nations and Great Powers* (2001), pp. 99–107; id., *Azerbaijan since Independence* (2011), pp. 70–78.

29 Cornell, *Small Nations and Great Powers* (2001), pp. 108, 300f.; id., *Azerbaijan since Independence* (2011), pp. 86f, 372.

30 Dekmejian, R. Hrair and Simonian, Hovann H., *Troubled Waters: The Geopolitics of the Caspian Region* (London: I.B.Tauris, 2001), p. 62.

31 Mehdiyeva, Nazrin, *Power Games in the Caucasus: Azerbaijan's Foreign and Energy Policy towards the West, Russia and the Middle East* (London: I.B.Tauris, 2011), pp. 168f.

32 In Russian foreign policy, the fourteen Soviet successor states other than Russia form its 'Near Abroad', that is a claimed zone of influence that is closed to NATO. So far, the three Baltic States are

33 members of NATO. But when two other so-called 'Near Abroad' states, namely Georgia and Ukraine, actively sought a rapprochement to NATO, Russia retaliated with war in 2008 and 2022 respectively.

33 The Azerbaijani sector of the Caspian Sea holds proven oil reserves of at least four billion barrels, the total Caspian Sea area *ca.* twenty billion barrels. Petersen, Alexandros, *Integration in Energy and Transport. Azerbaijan, Georgia and Turkey* (Lanham, MD: Lexington Books, 2016), p. 104.

34 The offshore ACG fields are located 120 km east of the Azerbaijani Absheron Peninsula at water depths of 119–175 m. Mehdiyeva, *Power Games in the Caucasus* (2011), p. 189.

35 This was probably an overestimate. Itochu (Japan) and Exxon joined later.

36 president.az/en/pages/view/azerbaijan/contract; azerbaijans.com/content_775_en.html (accessed 20 January 2022); Cornell, *Azerbaijan since Independence* (2011), pp. 91f; Mehdiyeva, *Power Games in the Caucasus* (2011), p. 214.

37 Mehdiyeva, *Power Games in the Caucasus* (2011), pp. 120–26.

38 Mehdiyeva, *Power Games in the Caucasus* (2011), pp. 138f; Temnikov, Roman, 'Caspian pipeline geopolitics: Competition between Western and Northern oil and gas transport routes to Europe', in: *Central Asia and the Caucasus: Journal of Social and Political Studies*, vol. 20, no. 4 (Luleå: Institute for Central Asian and Caucasian Studies, 2019), pp. 72, 74: researchgate.net/publication/338209306_CASPIAN_PIPELINE_GEOPOLITICS_Competition_between_Western_and_Northern_Oil_and_Gas_Transport_Routes_to_Europe.

39 Mehdiyeva, *Power Games in the Caucasus* (2011), p. 216; Petersen, *Integration in Energy and Transport* (2016), p. 108.

40 Dekmejian and Simonian, *Troubled Waters* (2001), p. 82.

41 Cornell, *Azerbaijan since Independence* (2011), pp. 345.

42 Mehdiyeva, *Power Games in the Caucasus* (2011), p. 145.

43 Cornell, *Azerbaijan since Independence* (2011), p. 76.

44 The US presidents had to waive section 907a of the 1992 Freedom Support Act which prohibited US governments from assisting Azerbaijan. Congress had accepted Section 907a based on a draft introduced by Senator John Kerry following strong Armenian lobbying. Cornell, *Azerbaijan since Independence* (2011), pp. 71, 100, 405–7. Despite several waivers, Section 907a has at the time of writing not been repealed; on 23 April 2021, Secretary of State Antony Blinken renewed the waiver. federalregister.gov/documents/2021/05/04/2021-09259/extension-of-waiver-of-section-907-of-the-freedom-support-act-with-respect-to-assistance-to-the (accessed 23 January 2022). US policy towards Azerbaijan was handicapped by conflicting interests: whereas government wanted to support Azerbaijan in order to contain Russia and to satisfy demands from the big oil companies, the powerful Armenian ethnic lobby representing at least 500,000, possibly 800,000 Armenian Americans strictly opposed such support.

45 Having no access to the world's oceans also means that the cost of bringing oil to a seaport via pipelines amounts to some $10 a barrel for Caspian oil compared to $2–3 for Saudi oil. Cornell, *Azerbaijan since Independence* (2011), p. 213.

46 The alternative transport to Novorossiysk by rail was more expensive and vulnerable to terrorism; Russia also blocked crude oil transport via the Don–Volga Canal which anyway had a low capacity. Mehdiyeva, *Power Games in the Caucasus* (2011), pp. 141, 146.

47 Bluth, Christoph, *US Foreign Policy in the Caucasus and Central Asia: Politics, Energy and Security* (London: I.B.Tauris, 2014), p. 182.

48 Dekmejian and Simonian, *Troubled Waters* (2001), pp. 110, 137. See also: Sokolsky, Richard and Charlik-Paley, Tanya, *NATO and Caspian Security: A Mission Too Far?* (Santa Monica, CA: RAND Corp., 1999), ch. 6, 7.

49 Petersen, *Integration in Energy and Transport* (2016), p. 107.

50 The Azerbaijani International Gas Consortium was established in 1996, and in 1999 the Shah Deniz field was discovered 70 km south-east of Baku. Its reserves are estimated at 1.2 trillion cubic metres of gas; president.az/en/pages/view/azerbaijan/contract; azerbaijans.com/content_775_en.html (accessed 23 January 2022).

51 As a consequence of the BP-led Shah Deniz II Consortium's decision to ship all its gas through the Southern Corridor, the alternative Nabucco pipeline project supported by the EU was aborted in 2013. Nabucco should have brought gas to Austria via Bulgaria, Romania and Hungary, but Azerbaijan and the EU failed to agree who would carry the cost if the pipeline was not operating at full capacity. Winrow, Gareth, 'Turkey's energy policy in the Middle East and South Caucasus', in: Kamrava, *The Great Game in West Asia* (2017), p. 96; Mehdiyeva, *Power Games in the Caucasus* (2011), pp. 248f. Without a guaranteed ceiling for the transportation costs of Azerbaijani gas to Europe, the price of Azerbaijani gas would have been dependent on the degree of pipeline use, which was unacceptable for Baku.

52 Dekmejian and Simonian, *Troubled Waters* (2001), p. 94.

53 Temnikov, 'Caspian pipeline geopolitics' (2019), pp. 78, 80.

54 Mehdiyeva, *Power Games in the Caucasus* (2011), pp. 243–7.

55 president.az/en/pages/view/azerbaijan/contract; www.gratanet.com/news/extension-of-psa-for-azeri-chirag-gunashli-oil-field (accessed 4 February 2023).

56 Although construction had already started, the alternative Russian 'South Stream' gas pipeline project was stopped by Russia in December 2014 following obstructions by the EU. It was planned to transport Russian gas via the Black Sea to Bulgaria to Austria. For the network of pipelines see: eurodialogue.org/Caspian-Pipelines-Map; globalenergymonitor.org/projects/global-fossil-infrastructure-tracker/tracker-map.

57 jpost.com/Israel-News/Jewish-state-sends-Christian-envoy-to-Muslim-country-572001 (accessed 23 January 2022).

58 web.archive.org/web/20190331103641/https://news.am/eng/news/504144.html (accessed 23 January 2022).

59 Kamrava, Mehran (ed.), *The Great Game in West Asia* (Oxford: Oxford University Press, 2017), pp. 19–20.

60 iHLS, Israel Homeland Security, 15 October 2014, i-hls.com/archives/40876 (accessed 27 April 2022).

61 Global Defence Corp., globaldefensecorp.com/2021/05/21/azerbaijan-bought-israeli-iron-dome-missile-system (accessed 29. April 2022).

62 haaretz.com/1.5209546 (accessed 23 January 2022); *Neue Zürcher Zeitung*, Zurich, 11 July 2018, p. 7.

63 Petersen, *Integration in Energy and Transport* (2016), p. 95.

64 Halbach, Uwe, *Religion und Nation. Kirche und Staat im Südkaukasus* (Berlin: Stiftung Wissenschaft und Politik, 2016), p. 15.

65 Cornell, *Azerbaijan since Independence* (2011), pp. 173, 276.

66 Chorbajian et al., *The Caucasian Knot* (1994), p. 33.

67 Armenia's population counted 550,000 men in the age bracket 17–32 years and Azerbaijan 1,300,000. Chorbajian et al., *The Caucasian Knot* (1994), p. 14f; *SIPRI Yearbook 1994* (Oxford: Oxford University Press, 1994), p. 88; *SIPRI Yearbook 1995* (Oxford: Oxford University Press, 1995), p. 28.

68 An Azerbaijani delegation visited Chechnya in 1992 to obtain Chechen aid against Armenian Karabakh, but President Dzhokhar Dudayev refused to intervene in the Karabakh War. He only allowed Azerbaijan to recruit Chechen mercenaries. Demoyan, Hayk, *The Islamic Mercenaries in the Karabakh War: The Way International Terrorist Networks Penetrated Azerbaijan* (Yerevan: no pub., 2004), pp. 6f; http://ermeni.hayem.org/english/chechen-terrorists-azerbaijan.htm (accessed 24 January 2022, link expired, 9 August 2022); Bolukbasi, *Azerbaijan* (2011), p. 190; Charalampidis, Ioannis, *Sponsored to Kill: Mercenaries and Terrorist Networks in Azerbaijan* (Moscow: MIA Publishers, 2013), pp. 20f.

69 Bolukbasi, *Azerbaijan* (2011), p. 192–6; Chorbajian et al., *The Caucasian Knot* (1994), pp. xiv, 17, 40.

70 The Minsk Group is responsible for trying to find a peaceful solution to the Karabakh conflict. It is co-chaired by Russia, the USA and France and incorporates Sweden, Germany, Turkey, Belarus, Hungary, Italy, Armenia, Azerbaijan and Karabakh. It was dead in the water from the very beginning, given its cumbersome co-chairmanship.

71 De Waal, *Black Garden* (2003), p. 254.

72 Badalyan, Lusine, 'Interlinked energy supply and security challenge in the South Caucasus' in: *Caucasus Analytical Digest*, no. 33 (Bremen: Heinrich Böll Foundation, 2011), pp. 2–5, 8. See also: tert.am/en/news/2010/08/09/pipeline/171952; caspiannews.com/news-detail/azerbaijan-helps-russia-with-natural-gas-supplies-to-armenia-2021-3-20-0 (accessed 25 January 2022).

73 Petersen, *Integration in Energy and Transport* (2016), p. 106.

74 De Waal, *Black Garden* (2003), p. 215.

75 Cornell, *Azerbaijan since Independence* (2011), pp. 88f.

76 Charalampidis, *Sponsored to Kill* (2013), pp. 6–8; Demoyan, *The Islamic Mercenaries in the Karabakh War* (2004), pp. 5, 9; Taarnby, 'The Mujahedin in Nagorno-Karabakh' (2008), p. 9.

77 Demoyan, *The Islamic Mercenaries in the Karabakh War* (2004), pp. 13f.

78 De Waal, *The Caucasus* (2010), pp. 238f, 253.

79 Cornell, *Azerbaijan since Independence* (2011), p. 73.

80 Paul B. Henze, 'The demography of the Caucasus according to 1989 Soviet census data', in: *Central*

81. Dekmejian and Simonian, *Troubled Waters* (2001), p. 104.
82. Ter-Petrosyan had won re-election in 1996 under dubious circumstances. De Waal, *Black Garden* (2003), p. 257.
83. Cornell, *Azerbaijan since Independence* (2011), pp. 139–47; the Armenian daily newspaper *Azg* dated 9 November 2008: http://www.freezepage.com/1270569339JOFECUAZJM?url=http://www.azg.am/EN/2005050307 (accessed 25 January 2022).
84. Cornell, *Azerbaijan since Independence* (2011), p. 148.
85. The wholesale market of Sadakhlo located in southern Georgia close to the Armenian and Azerbaijani borders was from *ca.* 1990 till 2007 a rare place where Azerbaijanis and Armenians could trade with each other. Similar, albeit smaller tri-national frontier markets exist at the border between Turkish Ardahan Province and Georgian Samtskhe–Javakheti. The Turkish–Armenian trade blockade is also detrimental to the economics of eastern Turkey.
86. Giragosian, Richard, 'The Armenian imperative: Confronting and containing oligarchs' in: Kamrava, *The Great Game in West Asia* (2017), pp. 206–21.
87. As remarked by Svante Cornell, the Adjara ASSR was a Soviet exception since 'it was the only autonomy granted on a religious and not on an ethnic basis'; the Adjarians were basically Muslim Georgians. Cornell, *Small Nations and Great Powers* (2001), p. 175.
88. The Meskhetians were not allowed to return from their exile to Georgia. Cornell, *Small Nations and Great Powers* (2001), pp. 142f.
89. Most of the Abkhaz had emigrated to Turkey in the second half of the nineteenth century.
90. Abkhazia had already requested in 1978 to be made part of the Russian Soviet Republic instead of Georgia. Suny, *The Making of the Georgian Nation* (1994), p. 321.
91. Forsyth, *The Caucasus* (2013), pp. 673–82; Suny, *The Making of the Georgian Nation* (1994), pp. 318–26.
92. Cornell, *Small Nations and Great Powers* (2001), pp. 164–6; Forsyth, *The Caucasus* (2013), pp. 685–8.
93. Suny, *The Making of the Georgian Nation* (1994), p. 325.
94. Cornell, *Small Nations and Great Powers* (2001), p. 180.
95. Nilson, Nijkas, 'Georgia's Rose Revolution: The break with the past', in: Cornell, Svante E. and Starr, S. Frederick (eds), *The Guns of August 2008: Russia's War in Georgia* (Armonk, NY: M.E. Sharpe, 2011), p. 91.
96. reuters.com/article/us-georgia-russia-bases-idUSL1387605220071113 (accessed 28 January 2022).
97. Suny, *The Making of the Georgian Nation* (1994), p. 328.
98. In fact the JCC consisted of four groups, namely Russian, North Ossetian, South Ossetian and Georgian which represented an outnumbering for Georgia of 1:3. Gordadze, Thornike, 'Georgian–Russian relations in the 1990s', in: Cornell and Starr, *The Guns of August 2008* (2011), p. 31.
99. Cornell, *Small Nations and Great Powers* (2001), p. 183; De Waal, *The Caucasus* (2010), pp. 141–5; Tsutsiev, *Atlas of the Ethno-Political History of the Caucasus* (2014), p. 117.
100. These fighter planes could only be Russian since Abkhazia had none. In March 1993 the Georgians shot down such a Su-27 plane whose pilot was a Russian air force major. Cornell, *Small Nations and Great Powers* (2001), pp. 349f.
101. Chervonnaya, Svetlana, 'Абхазия-1992: Посткоммунистическая вандея/Abkhaziya-1992: Postkommunisticheskaya vandeya = Abkhazia 1992: The Post-Communist Vendetta', in: *Nasha Abkhazia*, 26 January 2006: abkhazeti.info/war/20060126255768833783764.php (accessed 10 February 2020).
102. McGregor, Andrew, 'Military jamaats in the North Caucasus: A continuing threat', in: Howard, Glen E. (ed.), *Volatile Borderland: Russia and the North Caucasus* (Washington, DC: The Jamestown Foundation, 2012), pp. 238f
103. Cornell, *Small Nations and Great Powers* (2001), pp. 170–74, 191, 348–51; De Waal, *The Caucasus* (2010), pp. 153–64; Gordadze, 'Georgian–Russian Relations in the 1990s' (2011), p. 35.
104. Rayfield, *Edge of Empires* (2012), p. 387.
105. According to a former Georgian member of parliament, in autumn 2003 Soros put up $42 million towards Saakashvili's putsch. fdd.org/analysis/2004/05/24/georgia-on-his-mind-george-soross-potemkin-revolution (accessed 30 January 2022). The private investor and speculator George Soros also contributed to financing the Orange Revolution of 2004–5 in the Ukraine, and possibly also the Kyrgyz Tulip Revolution of 2005.
106. De Waal, *The Caucasus* (2010), p. 190; Gordadze, 'Georgian–Russian Relations in the 1990s' (2011), p. 42–7; Nilson, 'Georgia's Rose Revolution' (2011), pp. 88f, 102; Rayfield, *Edge of Empires* (2012), p. 387–92; Tsutsiev, *Atlas of the Ethno-Political History of the Caucasus* (2014), p. 122.

X. Autonomy and Failed Independence in the North Caucasus

1. 'What we may be witnessing is not just the end of the Cold War, or the passing of a particular period of post-war history, but the end of history as such; that is, the end-point of mankind's ideological evolution and the universalization of Western liberal democracy as the final form of human government.' Fukuyama, Francis, 'The end of history?', in: *The National Interest*, Summer 1989 (Washington: Centre for the National Interest, 1989), p. 4.
2. The Yugoslav Wars of 1991–2001 had already falsified Fukuyama's thesis by exemplifying that the end of an autocratic regime by no means necessarily leads to democratic liberalism, but often to cruel, ethnically based wars.
3. The privatization of Soviet industry was carried out recklessly and international aid was too small and ineffective. As in Central Asia, in the early 1990s Russia received a lot of credit but very little private investment, which led Russia's debt to grow rapidly.
4. In 2005, 88 per cent of the Ingush state budget was still met by federal subsidies, in Dagestan 81 per cent, Chechnya 79 per cent and Kabardino-Balkaria 73 per cent.
5. Oblast and krai are regional federal administrative entities of Russia.
6. Federal State Statistics Service ROSSTAT, Moscow, '26. Численность постоянного населения Российской Федерации по муниципальным образованиям на 1 января 2018 года': rosstat.gov.ru/compendium/document/13282 (accessed 3 February 2022). All the population estimates for 2018 are taken from this source. For the percentage of a titular minority within a republic see also: Gammer, Moshe, 'Separatism in the North Caucasus', in: Howard, *Volatile Borderland* (2012), pp. 89–91.
7. As mentioned in vol. I of the present work, the Adyghe are a subgroup of the Circassians/Cherkess.
8. rosstat.gov.ru/compendium/document/13282.
9. Smirnov, Andrei, 'The Republic of Adygea: An overview', in: Howard, *Volatile Borderland* (2012), pp. 364–85; Light, Matthew A., 'A survey of political trends of the Northwest Caucasus: Krasnodar, Adygea, and Stavropol,' in: Howard, *Volatile Borderland* (2012), pp. 386–404; Tsutsiev, *Atlas of the Ethno-Political History of the Caucasus* (2014), p. 107.
10. Zürcher, Christoph, *The Post-Soviet Wars: Rebellion, Ethnic Conflict, and Nationhood in the Caucasus* (New York: New York University Press, 2009), p. 83. See also: en.wikipedia.org/wiki/Budyonnovsk_hospital_hostage_crisis.
11. en.chessbase.com/post/the-rock-star-and-the-ajin-lama (accessed 6 February 2022).
12. Forsyth, *The Caucasus* (2013), p. 722.
13. Corfield, Justin J., *The History of Kalmykia: From Ancient Times to Kirsan Ilyumzhinov and Aleksey Orlov* (Victoria: Gentext Publications, 2015); Guchinova, Elza-Bair, *The Kalmyks* (London: Routledge, 2014).
14. Kazenin, Konstantin, 'Село вместо города: как сохранили мир в Карачаево-Черкесии', Moscow Carnegie Center, 3 February 2016: carnegie.ru/commentary/62652 (accessed 3 February 2022).
15. Tlisova, Fatima, 'An inside look at Karachevo-Cherkassia', in: Howard, *Volatile Borderland* (2012), pp. 294–308; Tsutsiev, *Atlas of the Ethno-Political History of the Caucasus* (2014), pp. 107f.
16. Tlisova, Fatima, 'Kabardino-Balkaria: Sleeping Beauty and the awakening of the Circassian heartland', in: Howard, *Volatile Borderland* (2012), p. 339; CNN, 14 October 2005: web.archive.org/web/20071226230511/http://edition.cnn.com/2005/WORLD/europe/10/14/russia.attack/index.html (accessed 3 February 2022).
17. Foltz, Richard, 'Scythian neo-paganism in the Caucasus: The Ossetian Uatsdin as a "Nature religion"', in: *Journal for the Study of Religion, Nature and Culture* (Sheffield: Equinox Publishing, 2020), pp. 314, 317; Shtyrkov, Sergei, 'Religious nationalism in contemporary Russia: The case of the Ossetian ethnic religion project', in: Alapuro, Risto, Mustajoki, Arto and Pesonen, Pekka (eds), *Understanding Russianness* (London: Routledge, 2012), p. 236: eusp.org/sites/default/files/archive/et_dep/Shtyrkov/Shtyrkov_Understandig_Russianness_Text.pdf (accessed 5 February 2022).
18. Baumer, Christoph, *The History of Central Asia*: vol. 1, *The Age of the Steppe Warriors* (London: I.B.Tauris, 2012), pp. 196f.
19. Foltz, 'Scythian neo-paganism in the Caucasus' (2020), pp. 319, 321.

20 Foltz, 'Scythian neo-paganism in the Caucasus' (2020), p. 328.
21 Shtyrkov, Sergei, 'Ritual feasts and transpersonal experience: Ossetian religious traditionalists in search of legitimization', in: *Hypotheses: New Age in Russia – Ideologies, Networks, Discourses* (Mainz: Mainz University, 2021), p. 3: newageru.hypotheses.org/1589 (accessed 5 February 2022).
22 Shtyrkov, 'Religious nationalism in contemporary Russia' (2012), p. 240.
23 Tsutsiev, *Atlas of the Ethno-Political History of the Caucasus* (2014), maps 34, 36, 37, 38.
24 Cornell, *Small Nations and Great Powers* (2001), pp. 220f, 253, 256–62; Gall, Carlotta and de Waal, Thomas, *Chechnya: Calamity in the Caucasus* (New York: New York University Press, 1998), pp. 116f; Tsutsiev, *Atlas of the Ethno-Political History of the Caucasus* (2014), p. 110.
25 Forsyth, *The Caucasus* (2013), pp. 784f; Ware and Kisriev, *Dagestan* (2010), pp. 33f.
26 gks.ru/free_doc/new_site/perepis2010/croc/perepis_itogi1612.htm (accessed 6 February 2022; link out of service 14 August 2022).
27 Forsyth, *The Caucasus* (2013), pp. 713f.
28 Cornell, *Small Nations and Great Powers* (2001), p. 255; see also pp. 210, 256–9.
29 Radio Free Europe, 10 October 2018, rferl.org/a/explainer-ingush-chechen-land-swap/29536507.html; Geo History, 8 December 2018, geohistory.today/chechen-ingush-land-dispute (accessed 6 February 2022).
30 Perović, *Der Nordkaukasus unter russischer Herrschaft* (2015), pp. 478, 482.
31 Zürcher, *The Post-Soviet Wars* (2009), pp. 77f.
32 Cornell, *Small Nations and Great Powers* (2001), pp. 206–10.
33 Zürcher, *The Post-Soviet Wars* (2009), p. 80.
34 The number of inhabitants is possibly inflated. Gammer, 'Separatism in the North Caucasus' (2012), p. 90.
35 Zürcher, *The Post-Soviet Wars* (2009), pp. 103f.
36 Gall and de Waal, *Chechnya* (1998), p. 113.
37 Gall and de Waal, *Chechnya* (1998), pp. 143, 370.
38 Gall and de Waal, *Chechnya* (1998), pp. 3, 191.
39 Zürcher, *The Post-Soviet War* (2009), p. 106.
40 Bluth, *US Foreign Policy in the Caucasus* (2014), p. 144; Cornell, *Small Nations and Great Powers* (2001), p. 226; Gall and de Waal, *Chechnya* (1998), pp. 159–227.
41 For a list of the major Chechen and Ingush terrorist acts outside Chechnya see: Baev, Pavel K., 'The Russian military campaign in the North Caucassus: Is a victory in sight?', in: Howard, *Volatile Borderland* (2012), pp. 130f.
42 Gall and de Waal, *Chechnya* (1998), pp. 289–304.
43 Cherkasov, Aleksandr, 'Книга чисел. Книга утрат. Книга страшного суда', polit.ru, 19 February 2014: polit.ru/article/2004/02/19/kniga_chisel (accessed 7 February 2022).
44 Cornell, *Small Nations and Great Powers* (2001), pp. 248f.
45 Many of these more or less criminal groups were related to specific clans. They reflected the fragmentation of Chechen society into more than 150 clans. Marshall, *The Caucasus under Soviet Rule* (2012), p. 290.

46 Jaimoukha, Amjad, *The Chechens: A Handbook* (London: Routledge, 2005), p. 68.
47 Zürcher, *The Post-Soviet War* (2009), pp. 81–92.
48 Shpigun's mortal remains were found in 2000. Howard, 'Timeline', in: id., *Volatile Borderland* (2012), p. 15.
49 In the context of the North Caucasus, non-Saudi radical Islamists are sometimes also called 'Wahhabis'.
50 Ware and Kisriev, *Dagestan* (2010), p. 96.
51 From: Ware and Kisriev, *Dagestan* (2010), p. 95.
52 Ware and Kisriev, *Dagestan* (2010), p. 103.
53 Of the Arab fighters in Chechnya, 59 per cent were Saudis and 14 per cent Yemenis. Al-Shishani, Murad Batal, 'The rise and fall of Arab fighters in Chechnya', in: Howard, *Volatile Borderland* (2012), p. 268.
54 The co-organizers of the attack on Dagestan were the Chechen Wahhabi Zelimkhan Yandarbiyev (1952–2004) and Movladi Udugov (b. 1962). Aksoy, Metin and Karaağaçli, Abbas, 'Fundamentalist movements in the northern region of the Caucasus: Chechnya and Dagestan at the end of the 20th century and the beginning of the 21st century' (Gümüşhane: Gümüşhane University, 2021): dergipark.org.tr/en/download/article-file/1417491 (accessed 8 February 2022).
55 In Dagestan, only the Akkins, a Chechen subgroup, joined the invaders. Ware and Kisriev, *Dagestan* (2010), p. 151.
56 Although hard evidence of Chechen responsibility for the Moscow apartment bombings is lacking, a Chechen origin remains probable.
57 Ware and Kisriev, *Dagestan* (2010), pp. 105–28.
58 The exception was the Akkins, who identified mainly with their religion. Ware and Kisriev, *Dagestan* (2010), p. 128–30; Roshchin, Mikhail, 'Islam in the North Caucasus', in: Howard, *Volatile Borderland* (2012), pp. 174.f
59 Sakwa, Richard, 'Great powers and small wars in the Caucasus', in: Sussex, Matthew (ed.), *Conflict in the Former USSR* (Cambridge: Cambridge University Press, 2012), p. 74.
60 BBC News, 18 March 2014, 'Profile: Chechen rebel leader Doku Umarov': bbc.co.uk/news/world-europe-12269155 ; Radio Free Europe, 1 April 2010, rferl.org/a/News_Profile_Who_Is_Doku_Umarov/1999886.html (both accessed 12 February 2022).
61 Al-Shishani, 'The rise and fall of Arab fighters in Chechnya' (2012), pp. 271, 285, 289; Zürcher, *The Post-Soviet War* (2009), pp. 92–6.
62 Zürcher, *The Post-Soviet War* (2009), p. 96.
63 Howard, 'Timeline' (2012), p. 22.
64 BBC News, 28 November 2009, news.bbc.co.uk/2/hi/europe/8383960.stm (accessed 15 April 2022).
65 *New York Times*, 17 June 2006, nytimes.com/2006/06/17/world/europe/17briefs-002.html (accessed 9 February 2022).
66 Forsyth, *The Caucasus* (2013), p. 766; Howard, 'Timeline' (2012), pp. 15–26; Zürcher, *The Post-Soviet War* (2009), p. 100f. Zürcher gives the lower number of casualties, the sources mentioned by Wikipedia higher ones. en.wikipedia.org/wiki/Second_Chechen_War (accessed 9 February 2022).
67 Zürcher, *The Post-Soviet War* (2009), p. 98.
68 gks.ru/free_doc/new_site/perepis2010/croc/perepis_itogi1612.htm (accessed 11 February 2022, link no longer in service); Coene, Frederik, *The Caucasus: An Introduction* (London: Routledge, 2010),

pp. 70–73, 214–16; Ware and Kisriev, *Dagestan* (2010), pp. 41f, 165.
69 Marshall, *The Caucasus under Soviet Rule* (2012), p. 291.
70 Ware and Kisriev, *Dagestan* (2010), pp. 185–90.
71 Coene, Frederik, *The Caucasus: An Introduction* (London: Routledge, 2010), pp. 160f.
72 Ware, Robert Bruce, 'Ethnicity and democracy in Dagestan', in: NCEEER, 28 November 2001 (Washington: The National Council for Eurasian and East European Research), p. 5: ucis.pitt.edu/nceeer/2001_814-30f_Ware.pdf (accessed 13 August 2022).
73 Ware, 'Ethnicity and democracy in Dagestan' (2001), pp. 25f.
74 Bobrovnikov, Vladimir, 'The Islamic revival and the national question in Post-Soviet Dagestan', in: *Religion, State & Society*, vol. 24, nos 2/3 (Taylor & Francis Online, September 1996), p. 233: tandfonline.com/doi/abs/10.1080/09637499608431741 (accessed 12 February 2022).
75 Ware and Kisriev, *Dagestan* (2010), p. 152.
76 Cornell, *Small Nations and Great Powers* (2001), pp. 278–80.
77 Ware and Kisriev, *Dagestan* (2010), pp. 180, 211.

XI. The Caucasus in the Twenty-First Century

1 Numbers of individuals killed due to insurgency and terror in the following years (mainly) according to the online news network *Caucasian Knot*: 2009: 508; 2010: 754; 2011: 750; 2012: 700; 2013: 529; 2014: 341; 2015: 209; 2016: 202; 2017: 134; 2018: 83; 2019: 32; 2020: 49. eng.kavkaz-uzel.eu; jamestown.org/program/is-political-conflict-supplanting-insurgency-as-the-main-challenge-in-the-north-caucasus (accessed 22 April 2022).
2 constitution.ru/en/10003000-04.htm (accessed 22 April 2022).
3 Governors head the highest executive body in a federal subject. With the exception of Krasnodar, Rostov and Stavropol, the North Caucasian governors have the title of 'head of the republic'. Teague, Elizabeth, 'Russia's return to the direct election of governors: Re-shaping the power vertical?', in: *Region*, vol. 3, no. 1 (Bloomington: Slavica Publications, 2014), pp. 37–57; en.wikipedia.org/wiki/List_of_heads_of_federal_subjects_of_Russia#Current (accessed 23 April 2022).
4 *Neue Zürcher Zeitung*, 27 May 2009, p. 5; 14 April 2016, p. 9; rferl.org/a/insurgency-north-caucasus-terrorism-isis/26840778.html (accessed 23 April 2022).
5 Al-Baghdadi proclaimed the caliphate on 29 June 2014. *Neue Zürcher Zeitung*, 11 June 2015, p. 7; 14 April 2016, p. 9; Reuters, 13 May 2016: reuters.com/investigates/special-report/russia-militants (accessed 23 April 2022); The Atlantic Council (Washington), 19 January 2018, atlanticcouncil.org/blogs/syriasource/chechen-and-north-caucasian-militants-in-syria (accessed 24 April 2022).
6 dailysabah.com/deutsch/welt/2016/12/04/russischer-geheimdienst-toetet-emir-der-daesh-im-nordkaukasus (accessed 23 April 2022).

7. tradingeconomics.com/articles/02012010104734.htm (accessed 23 April 2022); Hermann, Werner and Linn, Johannes F. (eds), *Central Asia and The Caucasus: At the Crossroads of Eurasia in the 21st Century* (Los Angeles: Sage, 2011), pp. 3, 147ff.
8. Federal districts are clusters of Russian federal subjects. They have no competences of their own and serve only to ensure federal control over the civil service as well as judiciary and federal agencies operating in the provinces.
9. Ware and Kisriev, *Dagestan* (2010), pp. 190–93.
10. Ware and Kisriev, *Dagestan* (2010), p. 194.
11. Magomedov had previously been, since 1990, chairman of the Supreme Soviet of Dagestan.
12. Ware and Kisriev, *Dagestan* (2010), p. 200.
13. *Neue Zürcher Zeitung*, 12 February 2018, p. 6. In November 2018, the acting mayor of the capital, Abusupyan Gasanov, was also arrested on corruption charges. Open Caucasus Media, Tbilisi, 8 November 2018: oc-media.org/acting-mayor-of-makhachkala-detained-over-missing-40-million (accessed 24 April 2022). OCM is an independent, Tbilisi-based online news platform. Radio Free Europe, 22 January 2018, rferl.org/a/daghestan-mayor-arrested-corruption-crackdown/28990306.html (accessed 24 April 2022).
14. According to the *Financial Times*, 15 March 2022, the Kadyrovtsy number 25,000 men, which seems a high estimate. ft.com/content/a3d1a964-ad3c-4924-a563-5729e8c93bc2 (accessed 24 April 2022).
15. In the mid 2010s, 82 per cent of Chechnya's expenditure was met by the federal budget.
16. *Neue Zürcher Zeitung*, 4 April 2015, p. 7.
17. Ouvaroff, Nathalie, 'The role of Chechens in the Georgian–South Ossetian conflict', in: *Russian Analytical Digest*, vol. 45, no. 8 (Zurich: ETH, 2008), pp. 27–30: css.ethz.ch/content/dam/ethz/special-interest/gess/cis/center-for-securities-studies/pdfs/RAD-45-27-29.pdf; *Neue Zürcher Zeitung*, 4 June 2014, p. 5.
18. United Press, 3 March 2022: upi.com/Top_News/World-News/2022/03/03/ukraine-russia-invasion-chechen-magomed-tushayev-killed/9981646322278; ntv/RTL-Germany, 27 February 2022, n-tv.de/politik/Tschetschenische-Sondereinheit-in-Ukraine-zerschlagen-article23158727.html (accessed 24 April 2022).
19. *The Globe and Mail*, 13 February 2022: theglobeandmail.com/world/article-chechens-and-georgians-in-ukraine-preparing-to-continue-fight-against; *Deutsche Welle*, 24 March 2022: dw.com/en/chechen-and-tatar-muslims-take-up-arms-to-fight-for-ukraine/a-61174375.
20. Newsru.com, 2 July 2014, updated 6 December 2017: newsru.com/russia/02jul2014/ukraine.html (accessed 25 April 2022). Newsru.com was an independent online news site which was forced to shut down on 31 May 2021.
21. The Kadyrovtsy cannot be compared with the paramilitary Wagner Group which is de facto President Putin's private mercenary army, since the latter has neither an ethnic nor a territorial basis and no state-like frame.
22. The *kontraktniki* are paid professional soldiers who sign a contract for certain duration of service. Paid professional military service is a way out of poverty for young unemployed men. In the Russia–Ukraine War, the majority of Russian soldiers are recruits conscripts, criminals released early from prison, a minority are professional *kontraktniki*.
23. *Neue Zürcher Zeitung*, 29 March 2009, p. 7; 29 June 2019, p. 6.
24. Reuters, 29 April 2011: reuters.com/article/topNews/idCATRE73S5IQ20110429?edition-redirect=ca (accessed 25 April 2022).
25. Radio Free Europe, 6 February 2018: rferl.org/a/russia-ingushetia-north-ossetia-prigorodny-dispute-poisons-relations/29023492.html (accessed 25 April 2022).
26. Eurasianet, New York, 31 March 2022, eurasianet.org/south-ossetia-says-it-will-seek-to-join-russia (accessed 25 April 2022). Euronews, 31 March 2022: euronews.com/2022/03/31/unacceptable-georgia-condemns-proposed-separatist-referendum-on-joining-russia (accessed 25 April 2022).
27. *Vedomosti*, Moscow, dated 31 March 2022, vedomosti.ru/politics/articles/2022/03/31/916143-prisoedinenii-osetii-rossii (accessed 25 April 2022).
28. The Caspian Sea is considered landlocked because it is only linked to the Mediterranean via the narrow Volga–Don Canal.
29. Cornell, *Azerbaijan since Independence* (2011), p. 401; *Eurasianet*, 4 December 2009: eurasianet.org/azerbaijan-baku-upset-over-lack-of-karabakh-progress-steps-up-anti-western-rhetoric (accessed 27 April 2022).
30. *Neue Zürcher Zeitung*, 22 December 2016, p. 27.
31. Dekmejian and Simonian, *Troubled Waters* (2001), pp. 22f; Mehdiyeva, *Power Games in the Caucasus* (2011), pp. 125–9.
32. Pietkiewicz, Michal, 'Legal status of Caspian Sea – problem solved?', in: *Marine Policy*, no. 123 (Amsterdam: Elsevier, 2021), pp. 3–5; Temnikov, 'Caspian pipeline geopolitics' (2019), p. 78.
33. Pietkiewicz, 'Legal status of Caspian Sea' (2021), p. 5.
34. Eurasianet, 22 January 2021: eurasianet.org/azerbaijan-and-turkmenistan-agreement-advances-caspian-gas-cooperation (accessed 28 April 2022).
35. The Turkmen gas will be used in north-eastern Iran while Iran will ship gas to Azerbaijan from its southern fields. Argus Media, London, 29 November 2021: argusmedia.com/en/news/2278061-iran-signs-gas-swap-deal-with-turkmenistan-azerbaijan; Eurasianet, 29 November 2012: eurasianet.org/azerbaijan-turkmenistan-and-iran-reach-gas-trade-deal (accessed 28 April 2022).
36. Importing LNG from the USA is expensive and the EU will strive to avoid becoming too dependent on gas from Qatar.
37. Trans Caspian Resources, Inc., transcaspianresources.us (accessed 4 May 2022); *Neue Zürcher Zeitung*, 4 May 2022, p. 21.
38. *Neue Zürcher Zeitung*, 8 July 2022, p. 9.
39. Dekmejian and Simonian, *Troubled Waters* (2001), p. 26.
40. Ahval News, Cyprus (Emirates-funded), 11 August 2020, ahvalnews.com/nagorno-karabakh/turkey-azerbaijan-cooperation-nakhchivan-destabilise-region-analyst (accessed 28 April 2022); Miarka, Agnieszka, 'Autumn war in Nagorno-Karabakh (2020) – course and implications for the strategic balance of power in the South Caucasus region', in: *Asian Affairs*, vol. 52, no. 4 (London: Royal Society for Asian Affairs, 2021), p. 828.
41. Miarka, 'Autumn war in Nagorno-Karabakh' (2021), p. 829.
42. In the first three weeks of the war Armenia lost hundreds of tanks and pieces of artillery.
43. *Neue Zürcher Zeitung*, 28 September 2022, p. 4; 9 October, p. 4; 19 October, p. 2; 11 November, pp. 2f.
44. Radio Free Europe, 24 August 2021, rferl.org/a/armenian-deaths-karabakh-war/31425644.html (accessed 30 April 2022).
45. *Yeni Şafak*, Istanbul, 7 October 2021: yenisafak.com/dunya/sputnik-yoneticisi-margarita-simonyandan-skandal-sozler-kars-ve-agri-daginin-rusyaya-geri-donmesini-istiyorum-3705848 (accessed 1 May 2022).
46. *Zenith*, Berlin, 9 November 2021: magazin.zenith.me/de/politik/interview-zum-waffenstillstand-zwischen-armenien-und-aserbaidschan (accessed 1 May 2022).
47. The 2010 revision of the 1995 agreement between Russia and Armenia guarantees the presence of a *ca*. 4,000-strong Russian force in Gyumri until 2044. *Eurasia Review*, 25 February 2021: eurasiareview.com/25022021-armenian-defense-minister-says-yerevan-would-like-russia-expand-gyumri-base-oped (accessed 1 May 2022).
48. Azerbaijan State news Agency AZERTAG, 10 December 2020: azertag.az/en/xeber/A_Victory_parade_dedicated_to_Victory_in_the_Patriotic_war_was_held_at_Azadlig_Square_Baku_Azerbaijani_President_Ilham_Aliyev_and_Turkish_President_Recep_Tayyip_Erdogan_attended_the_parade_VIDEO-1662787 (accessed 1 May 2022).
49. JAMnews, 12 March 2022 (Tbilisi: Go Group Media): jam-news.net/azerbaijan-to-build-road-to-nakhichevan-bypassing-armenia (accessed 17 August 2022).
50. CNN, 13 and 14 September 2002: edition.cnn.com/2022/09/13/middleeast/azerbaijan-armenia-artillery-strikes-intl-hnk/index.html
51. De Waal, *Black Garden* (2003), p. 273.
52. macrotrends.net/countries/ARM/armenia/population-growth-rate#:~:text=The%20current%20population%20of%20Armenia,a%200.2%25%20increase%20from%202018 accessed 1 May 2022.
53. Press release of the Swiss Foreign Ministry, 9 October 2009: admin.ch/gov/de/start/dokumentation/medienmitteilungen.msg-id-29446.html (accessed 2 May 2022).
54. Mikhelidze Nona, 'The Turkish-Armenian rapprochement at the deadlock', in: *Istituto Affari Internazionali*, vol. 10, no. 5 (Rome: IAI, 2015), pp. 1, 6.
55. Radio Fre e Europe, 3 September 2013: rferl.org/a/armenia-customs-union/25094560.html (accessed 2 May 2022).
56. Moscow had drastically increased prices for energy supplies a few months earlier and lowered them again after Armenia's entry into the EEU. *Neue Zürcher Zeitung*, 16 May 2014, p. 7.
57. Miarka, Agnieszka, 'Velvet Revolution in Armenia and its influence on state policy: Selected aspects', in: *Central Asia and the Caucasus: Journal of Social and Political Studies*, vol. 20, no. 4, 2019 (Lulea: Institute for Central Asian and Caucasian Studies, 2019), pp. 42–4.
58. Miarka, 'Velvet Revolution in Armenia' (2019), pp. 45–7.
59. *Neue Zürcher Zeitung*, 4 August 2018, p. 6; 7 December, p. 6; Miarka, 'Velvet Revolution in Armenia' (2019), pp. 47f.

60 Arab News, 1 and 3 May 2022: arabnews.com/node/2074116/world; arabnews.com/node/2074556/world (accessed 3 May 2022).

61 Organized Crime and Corruption Reporting Project OCCRP, Maryland, 18 March 2022: occrp.org/en/daily/16088-armenia-investigates-ex-president-s-second-passport-discovered-by-occrp (accessed 3 May 2022).

62 At the vote of the UN General Assembly on March 27, 2014, Armenia was already on the wrong side from the Western perspective when it voted against resolution 68/262 condemning Russia's annexation of Crimea. news.un.org/en/story/2014/03/464812-backing-ukraines-territorial-integrity-un-assembly-declares-crimea-referendum. In the vote on resolution ES-11/2 held on 24 March 2022 demanding the withdrawal of Russian troops, Georgia voted for it, Armenia abstained and Azerbaijan was absent. en.wikipedia.org/wiki/United_Nations_General_Assembly_Resolution_ES-11/2#Voting (accessed 3 May 2022).

63 Radio Free Europe, 24 October 2014, rferl.org/a/saakashvili-mixed-legacy/25146918.html; World Bank, *Fighting Corruption in Public Services. Chronicling Georgia's Reforms* (Washington, DC: The World Bank, 2012): www-wds.worldbank.org/external/default/WDSContentServer/WDSP/IB/2012/01/20/000356161_20120120010932/Rendered/PDF/664490PUB0EPI0065774B09780821394755.pdf (accessed 4 May 2022).

64 *World Bank Indicator*, data.worldbank.org/indicator/NY.GDP.MKTP.KD.ZG?locations=GE (accessed 4 May 2022).

65 Radio Free Europe, 22 November 2002, rferl.org/a/1101463.html (accessed 4 May 2022).

66 *New York Times*, 12 September 2002: nytimes.com/2002/09/12/us/vigilance-memory-russia-putin-warns-georgia-root-chechen-rebels-within-its.html (accessed 4 May 2022).

67 Bescotti, Elia et al., 'Passportization: Russia's "humanitarian" tool for foreign policy, extra-territorial governance, and military intervention', in: *EUI, Global Citizenship Observatory* (Florence: R. Schuman Centre, 25 March 2022); *Charter of the United Nations*, Art. 51, legal.un.org/repertory/art51.shtml (accessed 5 May 2022); Illarionov, Andrei, 'The Russian leadership's preparation for war, 1999–2008', in: Cornell and Starr, *The Guns of August 2008* (2011), pp. 56, 59f, 62; Rayfield, *Edge of Empires* (2012), pp. 395f.

68 De Waal, *The Caucasus* (2010), p. 205.

69 De Waal, *The Caucasus* (2010), p. 206.

70 Text of President Putin's speech on 10 February 2007, is.muni.cz/th/xlghl/DP_Fillinger_Speeches.pdf (accessed 5 May 2022).

71 Malek, Martin, 'NATO and the South Caucasus: Armenia, Azerbaijan, and Georgia on different tracks', in: *Connections*, vol. 7, no. 3 (Garmisch: Partnership for Peace Consortium of Defense Academies and Security Studies Institutes, 2008), pp. 35f. Georgia has long participated in NATO's involvement in Afghanistan (in ISAF) and Kosovo (in KFOR) as well as in Iraq.

72 De Waal, *The Caucasus* (2010), pp. 206f, 221.

73 Ukraine refused to ratify the CIS charter and Georgia withdrew in August 2008. Malek, 'NATO and the South Caucasus' (2008), p. 44, n49.

74 Chancellor Merkel's argument was hypocritical since it should also have applied to West Germany when it joined NATO in 1955.

75 'Bucharest Summit Declaration', dated 3 April 2008: nato.int/cps/en/natolive/official_texts_8443.htm (accessed 15 August 2022).

76 *NATO Off the Wire*, 9 April 2008, nato.int/multi/video/now/now080409.htm (accessed 5 May 2022).

77 Blank, Stephen, 'From neglect to duress: The West and the Georgian crisis before the 2008 war', in: Cornell and Starr, *The Guns of August 2008* (2011), p. 117; De Waal, *The Caucasus* (2010), p. 203; *New York Times*, 12 August 2008: nytimes.com/2008/08/13/washington/13diplo.html (accessed 5 May 2022). Rice later claimed in her memoirs that she had privately warned Saakashvili : 'Mr. President, whatever you do, don't let the Russians provoke you. You remember when President Bush said that Moscow would try to get you to do something stupid. And don't engage Russian military forces. No one will come to your aid, and you will lose.' Quoted from: *The Atlantic*, 16 November 2011: theatlantic.com/international/archive/2011/11/condoleezza-rice-warned-georgian-leader-on-war-with-russia/248560 (accessed 16 August 2022).

78 Illarionov, 'The Russian leadership's preparation for war' (2011), pp. 75f; Popjanevski, Johanna, 'From Sukhumi to Tskhinvali: The path to war in Georgia', in: Cornell and Starr, *The Guns of August 2008* (2011), pp. 151f.

79 De Waal, *The Caucasus* (2010), pp. 210–15; Popjanevski, 'From Sukhumi to Tskhinvali' (2011), pp. 149–53; Rayfield, *Edge of Empires* (2012), pp. 397f.

80 Despite its clear victory, Russia abstained from demanding a land transit route through Georgia to its base in Gyumri, Armenia.

81 Tuvalu and Vanuatu retracted their recognition of Abkhazia and South Ossetia in 2014. Radio Free Europe, 31 March 2014: rferl.org/a/tuvalu-georgia-retracts-abkhazia-ossetia-recognition/25315720.html (accessed 8 May 2022).

82 *Neue Zürcher Zeitung*, 25 February 2014, p. 7.

83 *Civil Georgia*, Tbilisi, 28 August 2008, old.civil.ge/eng/article.php?id=19330 accessed (6 May 2022).

84 OSCE, 9 July 2012: oscepa.org/en/news-a-media/press-releases/press-2012/osce-parliamentary-assembly-passes-resolution-on-georgia (accessed 7 May 2022).

85 *Washington Post*, 17 August 2008: alt.religion.christian.east-orthodox.narkive.com/fZaqx6xw/a-two-sided-descent-into-full-scale-war (accessed 6 May 2022); Felgenhauer, Pavel, 'The escalation of the Russia–Georgia war', in: Cornell and Starr, *The Guns of August 2008* (2011), p. 169; Popjanevski, 'From Sukhumi to Tskhinvali' (2011), p. 156.

86 International Crisis Group, 'Russia vs Georgia: The fallout', 22 August 2008, p. 1: crisisgroup.org/europe-central-asia/caucasus/georgia/russia-vs-georgia-fallout.

87 International Crisis Group, 'Russia vs Georgia: The fallout', 22 August 2008, pp. i–ii: crisisgroup.org/europe-central-asia/caucasus/georgia/russia-vs-georgia-fallout.

88 Independent International Fact-Finding Mission on the Conflict in Georgia, *Report* ('Tagliavini Report'), September 2009, pp. 10–32, especially 3, 14, 19, 20 and 36. www.echr.coe.int/Documents/HUDOC_38263_08_Annexes_ENG.pdf

89 Georgia has cooperated with NATO within the framework of the Substantial NATO–Georgia Package (SNGP) since 2014. Statement updated on 12 April 2022, nato.int/cps/en/natohq/topics_38988.htm (accessed 6 May 2022).

90 Apart from Norway and Poland, the three Baltic States, Estonia, Latvia and Lithuania are the only NATO member states (since 29 March 2004) with common borders with Russia, as per August 2022.

91 At the time of writing the protocol of admission of Finland and Sweden still has to be ratified by all 30 member states of which 23, including the USA, had done so by early August 2022. CNBC, New York, 9 August 2022: cnbc.com/2022/08/09/biden-to-ratify-finland-and-swedens-nato-membership-bids.html (accessed 18 August 2022).

92 International Crisis Group, 1 March 2012. crisisgroup.org/europe-central-asia/caucasus/georgia/georgia-s-constitutional-changes (accessed 7 May 2022).

93 Eurasianet, 8 February 2013, eurasianet.org/georgia-conflict-rather-than-cohabitation (accessed 7 May 2022); *Neue Zürcher Zeitung*, 16 November 2013, p. 8.

94 Embassy of the United States in Georgia, 29 July 2014: georgia.usembassy.gov/news-events/dc2014t/29072014saak.html; *Civil Georgia*, 31 July 2014: web.archive.org/web/20140810204420/http://civil.ge/eng/article.php?id=27540 (accessed 7 May 2022).

95 Radio Free Europe, 29 June 2018: rferl.org/a/saakashvili-convicted-of-abuse-of-power-sentenced-in-absentia/29327555.html?ltflags=mailer (accessed 7 May 2022).

96 The present author has never seen in any European capital so many EU flags as in Tbilisi during his stays in 2013 and 2018.

97 archiveresults.cec.gov.ge/results/20201031/#/en-us/election_43;path=election_43/dashboard (accessed 7 May 2022).

98 Government of Georgia, 3 March 2022: gov.ge/index.php?lang_id=ENG&sec_id=574&info_id=81399 (accessed 7 May 2022). Ukraine applied for EU membership on 28 February 2022.

99 Beacháin, Donnacha, 'The dynamics of electoral politics in Abkhazia', in: *Communist and Post-Communist Studies,* vol. 45, no. 1/2 (Oakland: University of California, March/June 2012), pp. 168f.

100 REGNUM News Agency, Moscow, 20 June 2008, regnum.ru/news/1017559.html (accessed 8 May 2022).

101 Radio Free Europe, 12 May 2006, rferl.org/a/1341678.html; 29 May 2011: rferl.org/a/abkhazia_leader_sergei_bagapsh_dies/24208717.html (accessed 8 May 2022).

102 *Neue Zürcher Zeitung*, 13 October 2010, p. 9.

103 There remain questions whether Bagapsh really died from natural causes in a Moscow clinic where he had undergone surgery. *GeoHistory*, Moscow, 24 January 2015: geohistory.today/abkhazia (accessed 8 May 2022).

104 In foreign policy the terms 'multivectoral' and 'univectoral' refer mainly to medium and smaller states. A multivectoral policy as applied by Azerbaijan seeks close cooperation with several more powerful states, which often compete with each other. A univectoral policy as followed by Armenia is oriented

(voluntarily or involuntarily) towards a single great power.

105 *The Economist*, 4 June 2014: economist.com/eastern-approaches/2014/06/04/exit-alexander-ankvab; IPI *Global Observatory*, New York, 13 June 2014: theglobalobservatory.org/2014/06/what-happens-when-unrecognized-country-experiences-revolution (accessed 8 May 2022).

106 *Financial Times*, 24 November 2014: web.archive.org/web/20141230131736/http://www.ft.com/cms/s/0/24239f90-73e8-11e4-82a6-00144feabdc0.html#axzz3OO6EwaPi; *The Guardian*, 25 November 2014: theguardian.com/world/2014/nov/25/georgia-russia-abkhazia-military-agreement-putin (accessed 8 May 2022).

107 Eurasianet, 3 March 2020: eurasianet.org/candidates-illness-casts-doubt-on-abkhazias-elections; Radio Free Europe, 22 March 2020, rferl.org/a/abkhazia-pushes-forward-with-presidential-vote-amid-coronavirus-anxiety/30502139.html (accessed 8 May 2022).

108 In total, 245,000 people live in Abkhazia of whom 51 per cent are ethnic Abkhazians.

109 Gagloyev obtained 54 per cent of the vote, Bibilov 43 per cent. Open Caucasus Media, Tbilisi, 9 May 2022: oc-media.org/opposition-leader-wins-south-ossetia-presidential-election (accessed 10 May 2022).

110 Echo of the Caucasus/Radio Free Europe, 31 March 2022: ekhokavkazacom/a/31780166html?fbclid=IwTISToj1Ed4bZI9AfGXsrXFOVHaeSc74kMKrYHWsVM8rMhRFpZ8oVISQU; Eurasianet, 9 May 2022: eurasianet.org/south-ossetias-incumbent-leader-loses-reelection (accessed 10 May 2022).

111 Reuters, 30 May 2022: reuters.com/world/europe/georgian-breakaway-territory-suspends-announced-referendum-joining-russia-decree-2022-05-30/ (accessed 18 August 2022).

112 International Politics and Society (IPS), Brussels, 18 March 2022: ips-journal.eu/topics/foreign-and-security-policy/the-south-caucasus-russia-quagmire-5802 (accessed 7 May 2022); Neue Zürcher Zeitung, 20 April 2022, p. 5.

Bibliography

Abich, Hermann, *Aus kaukasischen Ländern*, 2 vols (Vienna: Alfred Hölder, 1896).

A-Do [Hovhannes Ter Martirosian], *Van 1915: The Great Events of Vashbouragan* (1917; reprint and translation, London: Gomidas Institute, 2017).

Agathangelos, *History of the Armenians*, trans. with commentary R.W. Thomson (Albany: State University of New York Press, 1976).

Ahmadi, Hamid, 'The clash of nationalisms: Iranian response to Baku's irredentism', in: Kamrava, *The Great Game in West Asia* (2017, q.v.), pp. 105–37.

Ailsby, Christopher, *Hitler's Renegades: Foreign Nationals in the Service of the Third Reich* (Dulles, VA: Brown Reference Group, 2004).

Akçam, Taner, *A Shameful Act: The Armenian Genocide and the Question of Turkish Responsibility* (New York: Metropolitan Books, 2006).

Aksoy, Metin and Karaağaçli, Abbas, 'Fundamentalist movements in the northern region of the Caucasus: Chechnya and Dagestan at the end of the 20th century and the beginning of the 21st century' (Gümüşhane: Gümüşhane University, 2021); dergipark.org.tr/en/download/article-file/1417491 (accessed 8 February 2022).

[Friedrich Heinrich] Albrecht, Prinz von Preussen, *Im Kaukasus 1862* (Berlin: Privatdruck bei Hayn, 1865).

Alemany, Agusti, *Sources on the Alans: A Critical Compilation* (Leiden: Brill, 2000).

Aliev, Ayaz A., Ibrahimov, A.Sh. and Khalilova, Iradna S. 'Evaluation of Y-DNA diversity of Azerbaijanis', in: *Bulletin of Moscow State University*, Series XXIII, Anthropology, No. 4 (Moscow: Moscow State University, 2018), p. 49–55.

Allen, W.E.D. (ed.), *Russian Embassies to the Georgian Kings 1589–1605* (London: Hakluyt Society, 1970).

— *A History of the Georgian People from the Beginning down to the Russian Conquest in the Nineteenth Century* (London: Routledge and Kegan Paul, 1971).

Allen, W.E.D. and Muratoff, Paul, *Caucasian Battlefields: A History of the Wars on the Turco-Caucasian Border 1828–1921* (Cambridge: Cambridge University Press, 1953).

Allsen, Thomas T., 'Mongols and North Caucasia', *Archivum Eurasiae Medii Aevi*, vol. 7 (Wiesbaden: Harrassowitz, 1992).

Alpago-Novello, Adriano et al., *Les Arméniens* (Milan: Jaca Book, 1986).

Amini, Iradj, *Napoleon and Persia: Franco-Persian Relations under the First Empire* (Richmond: Curzon, 1999).

Amitai, Reuven and Biran, Michal (eds), *Mongols, Turks and Others: Eurasian Nomads and the Sedentary World* (Leiden: Brill, 2005).

Andersen, Andrew, *Abkhazia and Sochi: The Roots of the Conflict 1918–1921* (no place of publication given: Asteroid Publishing, 2014).

Andersen, Andrew and Partskhaladze, George, *Armeno-Georgian War of 1918 and Armeno-Georgian Territorial Issue in the 20th Century* (2015); academia.edu/10176756/Armeno_Georgian_War_of_1918_and_Armeno_Georgian_Territorial_Issue_in_the_20th_Century (accessed 19 December 2021).

Anet, Claude, *Through Persia in a Motor Car* (London: Hodder and Stoughton, 1907).

Angold, Michael, 'Belle époque or crisis? 1025–1118', in: *The Cambridge History of the Byzantine Empire* (2008, q.v.), pp. 583–626.

Arabshah, ibn Ahmad, *Tamerlane or Timur the Great Amir*, trans. from the Arabic by J. H. Sanders (1936; reprint, London: Martino Publishing, 2007).

Arat, Mari Kristin, *Die Wiener Mechitharisten* (Vienna: Böhlau, 1990).

Arawelts'i, Vardan, *Compilation of History*, transl. Robert Bedrosian (New York: Sources of the Armenian Tradition, 2007); attalus.org/armenian/vaint.htm.

The Arbitral Award of the President of the United States of America Woodrow Wilson. Full Report of the Committee upon the Arbitration of the Boundary between Turkey and Armenia. Washington, November 22nd.1920: ararat-heritage.org.uk/PDF/WoodrawWilsonArbitrationText.pdf (accessed 21 December 2021).

Armenia, John, *Armenian Cilicia XII–XV Century: Dawn, Splendor and Twilight of a Christian Kingdom in the Near East during the Crusades* (Charleston: CreateSpace, 2010).

Armenian Historical Sources of the 5th–15th Centuries, Selected Works: attalus.org/armenian.

Armistice of Mudros 30 Octobre 1918, germanhistorydocs.ghi-dc.org/pdf/eng/armistice_turk_eng.pdf (accessed 17 December 2021).

Athir, Izz ad-Din ibn al-, *The Annals of the Saljuq Turks: Selections from al-Kamil fi'l-Tarikh of Izz ad-Din ibn al-Athir*, trans. and annotated D. S. Richards (London: Routledge Curzon, 2002).

— *The Chronicle of Ibn al-Athir for the Crusading Period from al-Kamil fi'l-Tarikh*, Part 1: *The Years 491–541/1097–1146: The Coming of the Franks and the Muslim Response*, trans. D.S. Richards (Aldershot: Ashgate, 2006).

— *The Chronicle of Ibn al-Athir for the Crusading Period from al-Kamil fi'l-Tarikh*, Part 2: *The Years 541–589/1146–1193: The Age of Nur al-Din and Saladin*, trans. D.S. Richards (Aldershot: Ashgate, 2007).

— *The Chronicle of Ibn al-Athir for the Crusading Period from al-Kamil fi'l-Tarikh*, Part 3: *The Years 589–629/1193–1231: The Ayyubids after Saladin and the Mongol Menace*, trans. D.S. Richards (Aldershot: Ashgate, 2008).

Atkin, Muriel, *Russia and Iran 1780–1828* (Minneapolis: University of Minneapolis, 1980).

Atwood, Christopher, *Encyclopedia of Mongolia and the Mongol Empire* (New York: Facts on File, 2004).

Auch, Eva-Maria, *Muslim-Untertan-Bürger. Identitätswandel in gesellschaftlichen Transformationsprozessen der muslimischen Ostprovinzen Südkaukasiens (Ende 18.–20. Jh.). Ein Beitrag zur vergleichenden Nationalismusforschung* (Wiesbaden: Reichert, 2004).

Avalisshvili, Levan, 'The Great Terror of 1937–1938 in Georgia: Between the two reports of Lavrentiy Beria', in: *Caucasus Analytical Digest*, no. 22: *Stalinist Terror in the South Caucasus* (Zurich: ETH Center for Security Studies, December 2010), pp. 2–6.

Avery, Peter, 'Nadir Shah and the Afsharid Legacy', in: *The Cambridge History of Iran*, vol. 7 (1991, q.v.), pp. 3–62.

Avtorkhanov, Abdurahman, 'The Chechens and the Ingush during the Soviet period and its antecedents', in: Broxup, *The North Caucasus Barrier* (1992, q.v.), pp. 146–94.

Axworthy, Michael, *The Sword of Persia: Nader Shah, from Tribal Warrior to Conquering Tyrant* (London: I.B.Tauris, 2006).

Bacci, Michele, 'Echoes of Golgotha: On the iconization of monumental crosses in medieval Svanet'i', in: Foletti and Thunø, *Medieval South Caucasus* (2016, q.v.), pp. 206–25.

Bacci, Michele, Kaffenberger, Thomas and Studer-Karlen, Manuela (eds), *Cultural Interactions in Medieval Georgia* (Wiesbaden: Ludwig Reichert, 2018).

Bachmann, Walter, *Kirchen und Moscheen in Armenien und Kurdistan* (Leipzig: J.C. Hinrichs'sche Buchhandlung, 1913).

Badalyan, Lusine, 'Interlinked energy supply and security challenge in the South Caucasus', in: *Caucasus Analytical Digest*, no. 33 (Bremen: Heinrich Böll Foundation, 2011), pp. 2–9; files.ethz.ch/isn/135318/CaucasusAnalyticalDigest33.pdf (accessed 25 January 2022).

Baddeley, John F., *The Russian Conquest of the Caucasus* (London: Longmans, Green and Co., 1908).

— *The Rugged Flanks of Caucasus*, 2 vols. (London: Humphrey Milford, 1940).

Baev, Pavel K., 'The Russian military campaign in the North Caucassus: Is a victory in sight?', in: Howard, *Volatile Borderland* (2012, q.v.), pp. 114–31.

— 'The targets of terrorism and the aims of counter-terrorism in Moscow, Chechnya and the North Caucasus', in: Howard, *Volatile Borderland* (2012, q.v.), pp. 132–58.

Bakikhanov, Abbas Qoli Aqa, *The Heavenly Rose-Garden: A History of Shirvan and Daghestan*, trans. Willem M. Floor and Hasan Javadi (Washington DC: Mage Publishers, 2009).

Baladhuri, Abu-I Abbas Ahmad ibn-Jabir al-, *Kitab Futuh al-Buldan*, trans. Philip Khuri Hitti (vol. 1) and Francis Clark Murgotten (vol. 2) (New York: Columbia University, 1916, 1924).

Balci, Bayram, 'The Gülen movement and Turkish soft power in the South Caucasus and the Middle East', in: Kamrava, *The Great Game in West Asia* (2017, q.v.), pp. 183–201.

Baratov, Boris, *The Chronicles of Karabakh 1989–2009* (Moscow: Linguist Publishers, 2010).

Bar Hebraeus, *The Chronography of Gregory Abû'l Faraj … Being the First Part of his Political History of the World*, trans. Ernest A. Wallis Budge (London: Oxford University Press, 1932).

Barry, Quintin, *War in the East: A Military History of the Russo-Turkish War 1877–78* (Solihull: Helion, 2011).

Barsoumian, Hagop, 'The Eastern Question and the Tanzimat era', in: Hovannisian, *The Armenian People*, vol. 2 (1997, q.v.), pp. 175–202.

Baum, Wilhelm, 'Die Mongolen und das Christentum', in: Tubach et al., *Caucasus during the Mongol Period* (2012, q.v.), pp. 13–51.

Baumer, Christoph, *The History of Central Asia*, vol. 1: *The Age of the Steppe Warriors* (London: I.B.Tauris, 2012).

— *The History of Central Asia*, vol. 2: *The Age of the Silk Roads* (London: I.B.Tauris: 2014).

— *The History of Central Asia*, vol. 3: *The Age of Islam and the Mongols* (London: I.B.Tauris, 2016).

— *The Church of the East: An Illustrated History of Assyrian Christianity* (London: I.B.Tauris, 2016).

— *The History of Central Asia*, vol. 4: *The Age of Decline and Revival* (London: I.B.Tauris, 2018).

— *History of the Caucasus*, vol. 1: *At the Crossroads of Empires* (London: I.B.Tauris/Bloomsbury, 2021).

Baumgart, Winfried (ed.), *Friedrich Freiherr Kress von Kressenstein. Bayerischer General und Orientkenner. Lebenserinnerungen, Tagebücher und Berichte 1914–1946* (Leiden: Brill, 2020).

Beacháin, Donnacha, 'The dynamics of electoral politics in Abkhazia', in: *Communist and Post-Communist Studies*, vol. 45, nos 1/2 (Oakland: University of California, March/June 2012), pp. 165–74.

Bedrosian, Robert, *Armenia in Ancient and Medieval Times* (New York: Armenian National Education Committee, 1985).

— 'Armenia during the Seljuk and Mongol periods', in: Hovannisian, *The Armenian People*, vol. 1 (1997, q.v.), pp. 241–71.

Bell, James Stanislaus, *Journal of a Residence in Circassia during the Years 1837, 1838 and 1839*, 2 vols (London: Edward Moxon, 1840).

Bell, John of Antermony, *Travels from St. Petersburg in Russia, to Diverse Parts of Asia*, 2 vols (Glasgow: Printed for the author by Robert and Andrew Foulis, 1763).

Beradze, Grigol and Kutsia, Karlo, 'Towards the interrelations of Iran and Georgia in the 16th–18th centuries', in: Motika and Ursinus, *Caucasia between the Ottoman Empire and Iran* (2000, q.v.), pp. 121–32.

Berberian, Houri, *Roving Revolutionaries: Armenians and the Connected Revolutions in the Russian, Iranian and Ottoman Worlds* (Oakland: University of California Press, 2019).

Bergmann, Benjamin, *Nomadische Streifereien unter den Kalmücken in den Jahren 1802 und 1803*, 4 vols (Riga: Hartmann'sche Buchhandlung, 1804–5).

Beria, Lavrenti, *On the History of the Bolshevik Organizations in Transcaucasia* (Moscow: Foreign Languages Publishing House, 1949).

Bescotti, Elia et al, 'Passportization: Russia's "humanitarian" tool for foreign policy, extra-territorial governance, and military intervention', in: *EUI, Global Citizenship Observatory* (Florence: R. Schuman Centre, 25 March 2022); globalcit.eu/passportization-russias-humanitarian-tool-for-foreign-policy-extra-territorial-governance-and-military-intervention (accessed 5 May 2022).

Blacker, L.V.S., *On Secret Patrol in High Asia* (London: John Murray, 1922).

Blank, Stephen, 'From neglect to duress: The West and the Georgian Crisis before the 2008 war', in: Cornell and Starr, *The Guns of August 2008* (2011, q.v.), pp. 104–21.

Blessing, Patricia, 'Medieval monuments from empire to nation state: Beyond Armenian and Islamic architecture in the South Caucasus (1180–1300)', in: Foletti and Thunø, *Medieval South Caucasus* (2016, q.v.), pp. 52–69.

Bluth, Christoph, *US Foreign Policy in the Caucasus and Central Asia: Politics, Energy and Security* (London: I.B.Tauris, 2014).

Boase, T.S.R. (ed.), *The Cilician Kingdom of Armenia* (Edinburgh and London: Scottish Academic Press, 1978).

— 'The history of the kingdom', in: Boase, *The Cilician Kingdom of Armenia* (1978, q.v.), pp. 1–33.

— 'Gazetteer' [of Armenian Cilician fortresses], in: Boase, *The Cilician Kingdom of Armenia* (1978, q.v.), pp. 145–85.

Bobrovnikov, Vladimir, 'The Islamic revival and the national question in post-Soviet Dagestan', in: *Religion, State & Society*, vol. 24, nos 2/3 (Taylor & Francis Online, Sept. 1996), pp. 233–8; tandfonline.com/doi/abs/10.1080/09637499608431741 (accessed 12 February 2022).

Bodenstedt, Friedrich, *Völker des Kaukasus und ihre Freiheitskämpfe gegen die Russen* (Frankfurt am Main: Hermann Johann Kessler, 1848).

Boeck, Brian J., *Imperial Boundaries: Cossack Communities and Empire-Building in the Age of Peter the Great* (Cambridge: Cambridge University Press, 2009).

Bolukbasi, Suha, *Azerbaijan: A Political History* (London: I.B.Tauris, 2011).

Bosworth, C. E., *The Islamic Dynasties* (Edinburgh: Edinburgh University Press, 1967).

— 'The political and dynastic history of the Iranian World (A.D. 1000–1227)', in: *The Cambridge History of Iran*, vol. 5 (1968, q.v.), pp. 1–202.

— *The History of the Seljuk Turks: From the Jamia al-Tawārīkh – An Ilkhanid Adaptation of the Saljūk-Nāma of Zahīr ad-Dīn Nīshāpūri* (London: Routledge, 2001).

Bosworth, C.E. et al., 'Azerbaijan', *Encyclopaedia Iranica*, vol. 3, fasc. 2–3 (1987), pp. 205–57; iranicaonline.org/articles/azerbaijan-index.

Bournoutian, George A., 'Eastern Armenia from the seventeenth century to the Russian annexation', in: Hovannisian, Richard G., *The Armenian People*, vol. 2 (1997, q.v.), pp.81–108.

— *Armenians and Russia 1626–1796: A Documentary Record* (Costa Mesa, CA: Mazda Publications, 2001).

— *Armenia and Imperial Decline: The Yerevan Province, 1900–1914* (Abingdon: Routledge, 2018).

— *From the Kur to the Aras: A Military History of Russia's Move into the South Caucasus and the First Russo-Iranian War, 1801–1813* (Leiden: Brill, 2021).

Boyle, John Andrew, 'The journey of Hethum I, king of Little Armenia, to the court of the Great Khan Möngke', in: *Central Asiatic Journal*, vol. 9, no. 3 (Wiesbaden: Harrassowitz, 1964), pp. 175–89; ia801201.us.archive.org/0/items/Boyle1964Hetum/Boyle_1964_Hetum.pdf.

— 'Dynastic and political history of the Il-Khans', in: *The Cambridge History of Iran*, vol. 5 (1968, q.v.), pp. 303–421.

Bregel, Yuri, *An Historical Atlas of Central Asia* (Leiden and Boston: Brill, 2003).

Bretanitski, L[eonid] S. and Veimarn, B.V., Искусство Азербайджана IV–XVIII веков = *Iskusstvo Azerbaydzhana IV–XVIII vekov* (Moscow: Izdatelstvo Iskusstvo, 1976).

Brosset, Marie Félicité, *Deux historiens arméniens. Kirakos de Gantzac, XIIIe s., Histoire d'Arménie; Oukhtanès d'Ourha, Xe s., Histoire en trois parties* (St Petersburg: 1870; reprint, Delhi: Pranava Books, 2021).

Broxup, Marie Bennigsen (ed.), *The North Caucasus Barrier: The Russian Advance towards the Muslim World* (London: Hurst & Co., 1992).

— 'The last Ghaznavat: The 1920–1921 uprising', in: Broxup, *The North Caucasus Barrier* (1992, q.v.) pp. 112–45.

— 'After the putsch, 1991', in Broxup, *The North Caucasus Barrier* (1992, q.v.) pp. 219–40.

Bryan, Fanny E.B., 'Internationalism, nationalism and Islam before 1990', in: Broxup, *The North Caucasus Barrier* (1992, q.v.), pp. 195–218.

Bryer, Anthony, 'The Roman Orthodox world (1393–1492)', in: *The Cambridge History of the Byzantine Empire* (2008, q.v.), pp. 852–80.

Bulia, Marina and Janjalia, Mzia, *Mc'xeta (Mtskheta)* (Tbilisi: Eka Publishing Centre Betania, 2006).

— 'Medieval art and modern approaches: A new look at the Akhtala paintings', in: Foletti and Thunø, *Medieval South Caucasus* (2016, q.v.), pp. 106–23.

Burchuladze, Nana (ed.), *Šua saukuneebis k'art'uli saeklesio xelovneba sak'art'velos erovnul muzeumši / Medieval Georgian Ecclesiastical Art in Georgian National Museum* (Tbilisi: Georgian National Museum, 2012).

Burnaby, Captain Fred, *On Horseback through Asia Minor*, 2 vols (London: Sampson Low, Martson, Searle and Rivington, 1877).

Cahen, Claude, *Pre-Ottoman Turkey: A General Survey of the Material and Spiritual Culture and History c. 1071–1330* (London: Sidgwick and Jackson, 1968).

The Cambridge History of the Byzantine Empire, c. 500–1492, ed. Jonathan Shepard (Cambridge: Cambridge University Press, 2008).

The Cambridge History of Inner Asia: The Chinggisid Age, ed. Nicola Di Cosmo, Allen J. Frank, and Peter B. Golden (Cambridge: Cambridge University Press, 2009).

The Cambridge History of Iran, vol. 5: *The Saljuq and Mongol Periods*, ed. J. A. Boyle (Cambridge: Cambridge University Press, 1968).

The Cambridge History of Iran, vol. 6: *The Timurid and Safavid Periods*, ed. Peter Jackson and Lawrence Lockhart (Cambridge: Cambridge University Press, 1986).

Cambridge History of Iran, vol. 7: *From Nadir Shah to the Islamic Republic*, ed. Peter Avery, Gavin Hambly, Charles Melville (Cambridge: Cambridge University Press, 1991).

The Cambridge Medieval History, vol. 4: *The Byzantine Empire. Part I: Byzantium and its Neighbours*, ed. J.M. Hussey (Cambridge: Cambridge University Press, 1966).

Carpini, Giovanni di Plano, *The Story of the Mongols whom we call the Tartars*, trans. Erik Hildinger (Boston: Branden 1996).

Castelli, Don Christophoro, *C'nobebi da albomi Sak'art'velos šesaxeb / Relazione e album dei schizzi sulla Georgia del secolo XVII* (Tbilisi: Scienza, 1976).

Chahin, Mack, *The Kingdom of Armenia* (Abingdon: RoutledgeCurzon, 2001).

Chalabian, Antranig, *Dro (Drastamat Kanayan): Armenia's First Defense Minister of the Modern Era* (Los Angeles: Indo-European Publishing, 2009).

Charalampidis, Ioannis, *Sponsored to Kill: Mercenaries and Terrorist Networks in Azerbaijan* (Moscow: MIA Publishers, 2013); karabakhfacts.com/wp-content/uploads/2013/02/Ioannis-Charalampidis-Sponsored-to-Kill-ENG.pdf (accessed 25 January 2022).

Chardin, Jean, *Journal du voyage du chevalier Chardin en Perse et aux Indes Orientales, par la Mer Noire et par la Colchide* (Amsterdam: Jean Wolters et Ysbrand Haring, 1686).

Chatwin, Mary Ellen, *Svaneti Museum* (Tbilisi: Georgian National Museum, 2014).

Chelebi, Evliya, *Travels in Iran and the Caucasus, 1647 and 1654*, trans. Hasan Javadi and Willem Floor (Washington DC: Mage Publishers, 2011).

Cherkasov, Aleksandr A. et al., Книга чисел. Книга утрат. Книга страшного суда = *Book of Numbers, Casualties and Doomsday* (2014); polit.ru/article/2004/02/19/kniga_chisel (accessed 7 February 2022).

— 'The destruction of the Christian historical-cultural heritage of the Black Sea area: Trends and characteristics (The late 18th and first half of the 19th centuries)', in: *Annales: Annals for Istrian and Mediterranean Studies. Series Historia et Sociologia*, 26, no.1 (Koper: Zgodovinsko društvo za južno Primorsko, 2016).

Chkhikvadze, Nestan (ed.), *Georgian Manuscript Book, 5th–19th Centuries* (Tbilisi: National Centre of Manuscripts, 2014).

Chorbajian, Levon, Donabédian, Patrick and Mutafian, Claude, *The Caucasian Knot: The History and Geo-Politics of Nagorno-Karabagh* (London: Zed Books, 1994).

Christian, David, *A History of Russia, Central Asia and Mongolia*, vol. 1: *Inner Eurasia from Prehistory to the Mongol Empire* (Cambridge, MA and Oxford: Blackwell, 1998).

Chroniken der georgischen Königin Tamar, trans. Surab Sardshweladse and Heinz Fähnrich (Aachen: Shaker Verlag, 2004).

La chronique attribuée au connétable Smbat, trans. Gérard Dédéyan (Paris: Paul Geuthner, 1980).

Ciocîltan, Virgil, *The Mongols and the Black Sea Trade in the Thirteenth to Fourteenth Centuries* (Leiden: Brill, 2012).

Clarke, Eduard [Edward] Daniel, *Reise durch Russland und die Tartarei in den Jahren 1800–1801* (Weimar: Landes-Industrie-Comptoir, 1817).

Clavijo, Ruy Gonzalez de, *Narrative of the Embassy of Ruy Gonzalez de Clavijo to the Court of Timour at Samarcand, A.D. 1403–06*, ed. and trans. Clements R. Markham (London: Hakluyt Society, 1859).

— *Clavijo: Embassy to Tamerlane 1403–1406*, trans. Guy Le Strange (New York and London: Routledge, 1928).

Coene, Frederik, *The Caucasus: An Introduction* (London: Routledge, 2010).

Cohen, Ariel, *Russia's counterinsurgency in North Caucasus: Performance and consequences* (Carlisle, PA: United States Army War College SSI, 2014); files.ethz.ch/isn/178554/pub1189.pdf (accessed 02 January 2022).

Conrad, Heiko, 'Beobachtungen und Notizen zur Situation der armenischen Fürsten unter der Mongolenherrschaft', in: Tubach et al., *Caucasus during the Mongol Period* (2012, q.v.), pp. 83–105.

— *Geschichte und Wundergeschichten im Werk des Kirakos Ganjakec'i (13. Jh.). Armenien zwischen Chasaren und Arabern, Franken und Mongolen* (Bern: Peter Lang, 2018).

Cooley, Alexander, *Great Games, Local Rules: The New Great Power Contest in Central Asia* (Oxford: Oxford University Press, 2012).

Copeaux, Étienne, 'Le mouvement «prométhéen»', in: *CEMOTI, Cahiers d'Études sur la Méditerranée Orientale et le monde Turco-Iranien*, no. 16 (Paris: AFEMOTI, 1993) pp. 9–46 ; journals.openedition.org/cemoti/79.

Corfield, Justin J., *The History of Kalmykia: From Ancient Times to Kirsan Ilyumzhinov and Aleksey Orlov* (Lara, Victoria: Gentext Publications, 2015).

Cornell, Svante E., *Small Nations and Great Powers* (Richmond: Curzon, 2001).

— *Azerbaijan since Independence* (Armonk, NY: M.E. Sharpe, 2011).

Cornell, Svante E. and Starr, S. Frederick (eds), *The Guns of August 2008: Russia's War in Georgia* (Armonk, NY: M.E. Sharpe, 2011).

Crozat, Régis, *Châteaux oubliés et cites disparues. Sur les routes de l'Orient*, 2 vols (Paris: no publisher given, 2016, 2020).

Curzon, George N., *Russia in Central Asia in 1889 and the Anglo-Russian Question* (London: Longmans, Green, and Co., 1889).

Dadoyan, Seta B., *The Fatimid Armenians: Cultural and Political Interaction in the Near East* (Leiden: Brill, 1997).

— *The Armenians in the Medieval Islamic World*, vol. 1: *The Arab Period in Arminyah, Seventh to Eleventh Centuries* (New Brunswick, NJ: Transaction Publishers, 2011).

— *The Armenians in the Medieval Islamic World*, vol. 2: *Armenian Realpolitik in the Islamic World and Diverging Paradigms – Case of Cilicia, Eleventh to Fourteenth Centuries* (New Brunswick: Transaction Publishers, 2013).

— *The Armenians in the Medieval Islamic World*, vol. 3: *Medieval Cosmopolitanism and Images of Islam, Thirteenth to Fourteenth Centuries* (New Brunswick: Transaction Publishers, 2014).

Dadrian, Vahakn N., *The History of the Armenian Genocide* (Providence: Berghahn Books, 1995).

Daniel, Elton L., 'Golestān Treaty', in: *Encyclopaedia Iranica*, vol. 11, fasc. 1 (2012), pp. 86–90; iranicaonline.org/articles/golestan-treaty.

Dashdondog, Bayarsaikhan, *The Mongols and the Armenians (1220–1335)* (Leiden: Brill, 2011).

— 'The Mongol conquerors of Armenia', in: Tubach, et al., *Caucasus during the Mongol Period* (2012, q.v.), pp. 53–82.

Davies, Brian L., *Warfare, State and Society on the Black Sea Steppe,1500–1700* (London: Routledge, 2007).

Déchy, Moritz von, *Kaukasus. Reisen und Forschungen im kaukasischen Hochgebirge*, 3 vols (Berlin: Dietrich Reimer (Ernst Vohsen), 1905).

Dekmajian, R. Hrair, 'The Armenian Diaspora', in: Hovannisian, Richard G., *The Armenian People*, vol. 2 (1997, q.v.), pp. 413–44.

Dekmejian, R. Hrair and Simonian, Hovann H., *Troubled Waters: The Geopolitics of the Caspian Region* (London: I.B.Tauris, 2001).

Demoyan, Hayk, *The Islamic Mercenaries in the Karabakh War: The Way International Terrorist Networks Penetrated Azerbaijan* (Yerevan: no publisher given, 2004).

Der Nersessian, Sirarpie and Mekhitarian, Arpag, *Armenian Miniatures from Isfahan* (Brussels: Éditeurs d'Arts Associés, 1986).

Derogy, Jacques, *Resistance and Revenge: The Armenian Assassination of Turkish Leaders Responsible for the 1915 Massacres and Deportations* (New Brunswick: Transaction Publishers, 2016).

De Waal, Thomas, *Black Garden: Armenia and Azerbaijan through Peace and War* (New York: New York University Press, 2003).

— *The Caucasus: An Introduction* (Oxford: Oxford University Press, 2010).

Di Cosmo, Nicola, 'Mongols and merchants on the Black Sea frontier in the thirteenth and fourteenth centuries: convergences and conflicts', in: Amitai and Biran, *Mongols, Turks and Others* (2005, q.v.), pp. 391–424.

Donabédian, Patrick, *L'âge d'or de l'architecture arménienne, VIIe siècle* (Marseille: Éditions Parenthèses, 2008)

Donabédian, Patrick and Mutafian, Claude (eds), *Les douze capitales d'Arménie* (Paris: Somogy, 2010).

Donabédian, Patrick and Thierry, Jean-Michel, *Armenische Kunst* (Freiburg im Breisgau: Herder, 1989).

Donohoe, M.H., *With the Persian Expedition* (1919; reprint, Uckfield: The Naval & Military Press, 2009)

Dörner, Friedrich Karl (ed.), *Vom Bosporus zum Ararat* (Mainz: Philipp von Zabern, 1984).

Drasxanakertc'i, Yovhannes, *History of Armenia*, trans. Krikor H. Maksoudian (Atlanta: Scholars Press, 1987).

DuBois de Montpéreux, Frédéric, *Voyage autour du Caucase, chez les Tscherkesses et les Abkhases, en Colchide, en Géorgie, en Arménie et en Crimée*, 6 vols with atlas (Paris: Librairie de Gide, 1839–49).

Dumézil, Georges, 'Mythologie der Kaukasischen Völker', in: H.W. Haussig (ed.), *Wörterbuch der Mythologie*, part I: *Die alten Kulturvölker*, 11–12 (Stuttgart: Klett-Cotta, 1986).

Dunlop, John, 'Putin, Kozak and Russian policy toward the North Caucasus', in: Howard, *Volatile Borderland* (2012), pp. 44–69.

Dunsterville, Lionel C., *The Adventures of Dunsterforce* (London: Edward Arnold, 1920).

Eastmond, Antony, *Royal Imagery in Medieval Georgia* (Philadelphia: University of Pennsylvania Press, 2008).

— *Tamta's World: The Life and Encounters of a Medieval Noblewoman from the Middle East to Mongolia* (Cambridge: Cambridge University Press, 2017).

Eichwald, Eduard, *Reise auf dem Caspischen Meere und in den Kaukasus*, 2 vols (Stuttgart: Cotta, 1837).

Eid, Volker, *Im Land des Ararat. Völker und Kulturen im Osten Anatoliens* (Stuttgart: Theiss, 2006).

Ellis, Charles Howard, *The Transcaspian Episode 1918–1919* (London: Hutchinson, 1963).

Erckert, R. von, *Der Kaukasus und seine Völker* (Leipzig: Eduard Baldamus, 1888).

Erkan, Aydin Osman, *Turn My Head to the Caucasus: The Biography of Osman Ferid Pasha* (Istanbul: Çitlembik Yayınları, 2009).

Erlikman, Vadim, Потери народонаселения в XX веке: справочник = *Poteri narodonaseleniia v XX veke: spravochnik* (Moscow: Russkaia panorama, 2004).

Erman, Georg Adolf (ed.), *Archiv für wissenschaftliche Kunde von Russland*, vol. 12 (Berlin: Reimer, 1852).

Evans, Helen C., 'Imperial aspirations: Armenian Cilicia and Byzantium in the thirteenth century', in: Eastmond, *Eastern Approaches* (2001, q.v.), pp. 243–53.

— (ed.), *Armenia: Art, Religion and Trade in the Middle Ages* (New York: The Metropolitan Museum of Art, 2018).

Ezosmodzghvari, Basil (attrib.), *Life of the Queen of Queens, Tamar, ca.* 13th century, in: *The Georgian Chronicle: The Period of Giorgi Lasha* (1991, q.v.), pp. 55–96, with additionally an extract from an earlier edition or from another, unknown earlier historian: *Life of Queen Tamar*, ibid., pp. 113–42. See also (for a German translation): *Chroniken der georgischen Königin Tamar* (2004, q.v.), pp. 79–101.

Fadeev, Rostislav Andreeviç and Miljutin, Dimitrij Alekseeviç, *Sechzig Jahre des kaukasischen Krieges mit besonderer Berücksichtigung des Feldzuges im nördlichen Daghestan im Jahre 1839*, ed.. and trans Gustav Baumgarten (Leipzig: Berhard Schlicke, 1861).

Fähnrich, Heinz, *Geschichte Georgiens* (Leyden: Brill, 2010).

Fatullaev-Figarov, Shamil, *Architecture of Absheron* (Baku: Shar-Qarb Publishing House, 2013).

Feferman, Kiril, 'Nazi Germany and the Mountain Jews: Was there a policy?', in: *Holocaust and Genocide Studies*, vol. 21, no. 1 (Oxford: Oxford Academic, 2007), pp. 96–114; doi.org/10.1093/hgs/dcm005.

Felgenhauer, Pavel, 'The escalation of the Russia–Georgia war ', in: Cornell and Starr, *The Guns of August 2008* (2011), pp.162–80.

Feuerstein, Wolfgang, 'Die Eroberung und Islamisierung Südgeorgiens', in: Motika and Ursinus, *Caucasia between the Ottoman Empire and Iran* (2000, q.v.), pp. 21–30.

Feyzullayev, A. et al., 'Oil source rocks and geochemistry of hydrocarbons in South Caspian Basin', in: Akif S. Ali-Zadeh, *South-Caspian Basin: Geology, Geophysics, Oil and Gas Content* (Baku: Nafta-Press, 2004), pp. 286–321.

Fischel, Walter J., *Ibn Khaldun and Tamerlane: Their Historic Meeting in Damascus, 1401 A.D. (803 A.H.): A Study Based on Arabic Manuscripts of Ibn Khaldun's 'Autobiography', with a Translation into English and a Commentary* (Berkeley: University of California Press, 1952).

Fischer, Fritz, *Germany's Aims in the First World War* (New York: W.W. Norton, 1968).

Fisher, Alan W., *The Crimean Tatars* (Stanford: Hoover Institution Press, 1978).

Foletti, Ivan and Thunø, Erik (eds), *The Medieval South Caucasus: Artistic Cultures of Albania, Armenia and Georgia* (Turnhout: Brepols, 2016).

Foltz, Richard, 'Scythian neo-paganism in the Caucasus. The Ossetian Uatsdin as a 'Nature religion', in: *Journal for the Study of Religion, Nature and Culture*, vol. 13, no. 3 (Sheffield: Equinox Publishing, 2020), pp. 314–32.

— 'The Rekom shrine in North Ossetia-Alania and its annual ceremony', in: *Iran and the Caucasus*, no. 24 (Leiden: Brill, 2020), pp. 38–52.

— *The Ossetes: Modern-Day Scythians of the Caucasus* (London: I.B.Tauris/Bloomsbury, 2022).

Forbes Manz, Beatrice, *The Rise and Rule of Tamerlane* (Cambridge: Cambridge University Press, 1991).

Forczyk, Robert, *The Caucasus 1942–43: Kleist's Race for Oil* (Oxford: Osprey Publishing, 2015).

Forsyth, James, *The Caucasus: A History* (Cambridge: Cambridge University Press, 2013).

Freshfield, Douglas W., *Travels in the Central Caucasus and Bashan Including Visits to Ararat and Tabreez and Ascents of Kazbek and Elbruz* (London: Longmans, Green and Co., 1869).

— 'Journey in the Caucasus and ascent of Kasbek and Elbruz', *Proceedings of the Royal Geographical Society*, vols 13–14 (London: RGS, 1869), pp. 66–73.

— *The Exploration of the Caucasus*, 2 vols (London: Arnold, 1902).

Fukuyama, Francis, 'The end of history?', in: *The National Interest*, Summer 1989 (Washington: Center for the National Interest, 1989), pp. 3–18.

— *The End of History and the Last Man* (Don Mills, Ontario: Maxwell Macmillan, 1992).

Gabriel, Richard A., *Subotai the Valiant: Genghis Khan's Greatest General* (Westport: Praeger, 2004).

Galichian, Rouben, *Clash of Histories in the South Caucasus: Redrawing the Map of Azerbaijan, Armenia and Iran* (London: Bennett & Bloom, 2012).

Gall, Carlotta and de Waal, Thomas, *Chechnya: Calamity in the Caucasus* (New York: New York University Press, 1998).

Gamakharia, Jemal et al. (eds), *Assays from the History of Georgia: Abkhazia from Ancient Times till the Present Days* (Tbilisi: Ministry of Education and Culture of Abkhazia, 2011).

Gambashidze, Irina, Hauptmann, Andreas et al. (eds), *Georgien. Schätze aus dem Land des Goldenen Vlies* (Bochum: Deutsches Bergbau-Museum Bochum, 2001).

Gammer, Moshe, 'Russian strategies in the conquest of Chechnia and Daghestan, 1825–1859', in: Broxup, *The North Caucasus Barrier* (1992, q.v.), pp. 45–61.

— 'Was General Klüge-von-Klugenau Shamil's Desmichels?', in: *Cahiers du Monde Russe et Soviétique*, vol. 33, nr. 2-3 (Paris: EHESS, 1992), pp. 207–21; persee.fr/issue/cmr_0008-0160_1992_num_33_2?sectionId=cmr_0008-0160_1992_num_33_2_2317.

— 'The conqueror of Napoleon in the Caucasus', in: *Central Asian Survey*, vol. 12 (St. Louis Park, MN: CESS, Central Eurasian Studies Society, 1993), pp. 253–67; tandfonline.com/doi/abs/10.1080/02634939308400818.

— *Muslim Resistance to the Tsar: Shamil and the Conquest of Chechnia and Daghestan* (Abingdon: Frank Cass, 1994).

— 'Šāmil and the Muslim Powers: The Ottomans, the Qāǧārs and Muhammad 'Ali of Egypt', in: Motika and Ursinus, *Caucasia between the Ottoman Empire and Iran* (2000, q.v.), pp. 11–20.

— 'Separatism inn the North Caucasus', in: Howard, *Volatile Borderland* (2012, q.v.), pp. 70–91.

Garsoïan, Nina, 'The independent kingdoms of medieval Armenia', in: Hovannisian, *The Armenian People*, vol. 1 (1997, q.v.), pp. 143–85.

— *Church and Culture in Early Medieval Armenia* (Aldershot: Ashgate Variorum, 1999).

Gedevanishvili, Ekaterine, 'Cult and image of St George in medieval Georgian art', in: Bacci, Kaffenberger and Studer-Karlen, *Cultural Interactions* (2018, q.v.), pp. 143–68.

Gelenava, Irakli (ed.), *Cultural Heritage in Abkhazia* (Tbilisi: Ministry of Education and Culture of the Autonomous Republic of Abkhazia, 2015).

Georgi, Johann Gottlieb, *Beschreibung aller Nationen des Russischen Reichs, ihrer Lebensart, Religion, Gebräuche, Wohnungen, Kleidungen und übrigen Merkwürdigkeiten*, 2 vols (St Petersburg: Carl Müller, 1776).

The Georgian Chronicle: The Period of Giorgi Lasha, translated by Katharine Vivian and edited by S. Qaukhchishvili (Amsterdam: Adolf M. Hakkert, 1991).

Geschichten und Lobpreisungen der Könige = Histories and Eulogies of the Sovereigns (anon., 13th century), in: *Chroniken der georgischen Königin Tamar* (2004, q.v.), pp. 15–78.

Ghani, Cyrus, *Iran and the Rise of Reza Shah: From Qajar Collapse to Pahlavi Power* (London: I.B.Tauris, 1998).

Ghazarian, Jacob G., *The Armenian Kingdom in Cilicia during the Crusades: The Integration of Cilician Armenians with the Latins 1080–1393* (London: Routledge, 2000).

Gippert, Jost, *Georgische Handschriften* (Wiesbaden: Ludwig Reichert, 2018).

Giragosian, Richard, 'The Armenian imperative: Confronting and containing oligarchs', in: Kamrava, *The Great Game in West Asia* (2017, q.v.), pp. 205–28.

Glantz, David M., *Operation Don's Left Wing: The Trans-Caucasus Front's Pursuit of the First Panzer Army, November 1942–February 1943* (Lawrence: University Press of Kansas, 2019).

Goiladze, Vakhtang (ed.), *Caucasus in Georgian Sources: Foreign States, Tribes, Historical Figures. Encyclopedical Dictionary* (Tbilisi: Favorite, 2012).

Golden, Peter, 'Nomads in the sedentary world: the case of the pre-Chinggisid Rus' and Georgia', in Khazanov and Wink, *Nomads in the Sedentary World* (2001, q.v.), pp. 24–75.

Goltz, Thomas, 'The paradox of living in a paradise: Georgia's descent into chaos', in: Cornell and Starr, *The Guns of August 2008* (2011, q.v.), pp. 10–27.

Goltz, Hermann and Göltz, Klaus E., *Rescued Armenian Treasures from Cilicia* (Wiesbaden: Ludwig Reichert, 2000).

Gordadze, Thornike, 'Georgian–Russian relations in the 1990s', in: Cornell and Starr, *The Guns of August 2008* (2011, q.v.), pp. 29–48.

Grassi, Fabio L., *A New Homeland: The Massacre of the Circassians, their Exodus to the Ottoman Empire and their Role in the making of Modern Turkey* (Istanbul: Istanbul Aydin University Press, 2014).

Greaves, Rose, 'Iranian relations with Great Britain and British India', in: *The Cambridge History of Iran*, vol. 7 (1991, q.v.), pp. 374–425.

Grechko, Andrei, *Battle for the Caucasus* (Honululu: University Press of the Pacific, 2001).

Griffin, Nicholas, *Caucasus: In the Wake of Warriors* (London: Headline Book, 2001).

Guchinova, Elza-Bair, *The Kalmyks* (London: Routledge, 2014).

Güldenstädt, Johann Anton, *Reisen durch Russland und im Caucasischen Gebürge*, 2 vols (St Petersburg: Kayserliche Akademie der Wissenschaften, 1787–91).

Gumppenberg, Marie-Carin von and Steinbach, Udo (eds), *Der Kaukasus. Geschichte – Kultur – Politik* (Munich: Beck, 2018).

Haarmann, Harald, *Universalgeschichte der Schrift* (Frankfurt am Main: Campus, 1998).

Hage, Wolfgang, *Das orientalische Christentum* (Stuttgart: Kohlhammer, 2007).

Haghnazarian, Armen, *Julfa: The Annihilation of the Armenian Cemetery by Nakhijevan's Azerbaijani Authorities* (Yerevan: RAA, Research on Armenian Architecture, 2006).

Hahn, C[arl] von, *Kaukasische Reisen und Studien* (Leipzig: Duncker und Humblot, 1896).

— *Bilder aus dem Kaukasus. Neue Studien zur Kenntnis Kaukasiens* (Leipzig: Duncker und Humblot, 1900).

Halbach, Uwe, *Religion und Nation. Kirche und Staat im Südkaukasus* (Berlin: Stiftung Wissenschaft und Politik, 2016).

Halperin, Charles J., *Russia and the Golden Horde: The Mongol Impact on Russian History* (London: I.B.Tauris, 1985).

Hambly, Gavin and Hambly R.G., ''Āghā Muhammad Khān and the establishment of the Qājār dynasty', in: *The Cambridge History of Iran*, vol. 7 (1991, q.v.), pp. 104–43.

— 'Iran during the reigns of Fath 'Alī Shāh and Muhammad Shāh', in: *The Cambridge History of Iran*, vol. 7 (1991, q.v.), pp. 144–73.

— 'The Pahlavī autocracy: Rizā Shāh, 1921–1941', in: *The Cambridge History of Iran*, vol. 7 (1991, q.v.), pp. 244–93.

Harris, John (ed.), *Farewell to the Don: The Journal of Brigadier H.N.H. Williamson* (London: Collins, 1970).

Harris, Walter B., *From Batum to Baghdad via Tiflis, Tabriz and Persian Kurdistan* (Edinburgh: William Blackwood, 1896).

Hasan-Jalaliants, Archbishop Sergius [Sargis], *A History of the Land of Artsakh*, ed. Robert H. Hewson and trans. Ka'ren Ketendjian (Costa Mesa, CA: Mazda Publishers, 2013).

Hasanli, Jamil, *At the Dawn of the Cold War: The Soviet–American Crisis over Iranian Azerbaijan, 1941–1946* (Lanham: Rowman & Littlefield, 2006).

— *Foreign Policy of the Republic of Azerbaijan: The Difficult Road to Western Integration, 1918–1920* (London: Routledge, 2016).

Haxthausen, Baron August von, *The Tribes of the Caucasus: With an Account of Schamyl and the Murids* (London: Chapman and Hall, 1855).

Henze, Paul B., 'Circassian resistance to Russia', in: Broxup, *The North Caucasus Barrier* (1992, q.v.), pp. 62–111.

Hermann, Werner and Linn, Johannes F. (eds), *Central Asia and The Caucasus: At the Crossroads of Eurasia in the 21st Century* (Los Angeles: Sage, 2011).

Hethum von Korykos, *La Flor des Estoires d'Orient. Geschichte der Mongolen*, trans. Raimund Senoner, ed. Wilhelm Baum (Klagenfurt: Kitab, 2006).

Het'um the Historian's History of the Tartars [The Flower of Histories of the East], trans. Robert Bedrosian (New York: Sources of the Armenian Tradition, 1986); attalus.org/armenian/hetumtoc.html.

Hewitt, George, *The Abkhazians: A Handbook* (London: Routledge, 2014).

Hewsen, Robert H., *Armenia: A Historical Atlas* (Chicago: The University of Chicago Press, 2001).

Heyer, Friedrich (ed.), *Die Kirche Armeniens* (Stuttgart: Evangelisches Verlagswerk, 1987).

Hingley, Ronald, *Joseph Stalin: Man and Legend* (New York: McGraw Hill, 1974).

Hitler, Adolf, *Weisungen für die Kriegsführung. Dokumente des Oberkommandos der Wehrmacht*, ed. Walter Hubatsch (1964) docplayer.org/44050472-Hitlers-weisungen-fuer-die-kriegfuehrung.html.

Hoffmann, Joachim, *Kaukasien 1942/43. Das deutsche Heer und die Orientvölker der Sowjetunion* (Freiburg: Rombach, 1991).

Hommaire de Hell, Xavier, *Travels in the Steppes of the Caspian Sea, the Crimea, the Caucasus, etc.* (London: Chapman and Hall, 1847).

Hopkirk, Peter, *On Secret Service East of Constantinople* (Oxford: Oxford University Press, 1994).

Hovannisian, Richard G., *Armenia on the Road to Independence 1918* (Berkeley: University of California Press, 1967).

— *The Republic of Armenia*, vol. 1: *The First Year, 1918–1919* (Berkeley: University of California Press, 1971).

— *The Republic of Armenia*, vol. 2: *From Versailles to London, 1919–1920* (Berkeley: University of California Press, 1982).

— *The Republic of Armenia*, vol. 3: *From London to Sèvres, February–August 1920* (Berkeley: University of California Press, 1996).

— *The Republic of Armenia*, vol. 4: *Between Crescent and Sickle: Partition and Sovietization* (Berkeley: University of California Press, 1996).

— (ed.), *The Armenian People from Ancient to Modern Times*, 2 vols (New York: Palgrave Macmillan, 1997).

— 'The Armenian Question in the Ottoman Empire 1876–1914', in: Hovannisian, Richard G., *The Armenian People*, vol. 2 (1997, q.v.), pp. 203–38.

— 'Armenia's road to independence', in: Hovannisian, Richard G., *The Armenian People*, vol. 2 (1997, q.v.), pp. 275–302.

— 'The Republic of Armenia', in: Hovannisian, Richard G., *The Armenian People*, vol. 2 (1997, q.v.), pp. 303–46.

— *Armenian Kars and Ani* (Costa Mesa, CA: Mazda Publishers, 2011).

Howard, Glen E. (ed.), *Volatile Borderland: Russia and the North Caucasus* (Washington DC: The Jamestown Foundation, 2012).

Hubbard, Gilbert Ernest, *From the Gulf to the Ararat: Imperial Boundary Making in the Late Ottoman Empire* (London: I.B.Tauris, 2016).

Hughes, James, *Chechnya: From Nationalism to Jihad* (Philadelphia: University of Pennsylvania Press, 2007).

The Hundred Years' Chronicle, in: Jones, Stephen (ed.), *Kartlis Tskhovreba: A History of Georgia* (Tbilisi: Artanuji Publishing, 2014), pp. 315–99.

Hunter, Shireen T., *Islam and Russia: The Politics of Identity and Security* (Armonk, NY: M.E. Sharpe, 2004).

Huseinova, Azada et al., *Nobel. Nobellər və Baki Nefti = The Nobels and Baku Oil* (Baku: Nobel Family Society, 2009).

Illarionov, Andrei, 'The Russian leadership's preparation for war, 1999–2008', in: Cornell and Starr, *The Guns of August 2008* (2011, q.v.), pp. 49–85.

Imanidzé, Nina, *Saints cavaliers. Culte et images en Géorgie aux IVe–XIe siècles* (Wiesbaden: Ludwig Reichert, 2016).

Independent International Fact-Finding Mission on the Conflict in Georgia. Report (=Tagliavini Report), September 2009: echr.coe.int/Documents/HUDOC_38263_08_Annexes_ENG.pdf (accessed 6 May 2022).

Ingram, Edward, *The Beginning of the Great Game in Asia 1828–1834* (Oxford: Oxford University Press, 1979).

International Crisis Group, *Russia vs Georgia: The Fallout*, 22 August 2008, crisisgroup.org/europe-central-asia/caucasus/georgia/russia-vs-georgia-fallout (accessed 6 May 2022).

Ironside, Edmund, *High Road to Command: The Diaries of Major General Sir Edmund Ironside 1920–22*, ed. Lord Ironside (London: Leo Cooper, 1972).

Isgenderli Anar, *Realities of Azerbaijan: 1917–1920* (self-published at Bloomington: Xlibris Corporation, 2011).

Ismailov, Eldar, 'Great Terror in Azerbaijan', in: *Caucasus Analytical Digest*, no. 22: *Stalinist Terror in the South Caucasus* (Zurich: ETH Center for Security Studies, December 2010), pp. 9-12.

Jackson, Peter, *The Mongols and the West* (Harlow: Pearson, 2005).

Jaimoukha, Amjad, *The Chechens: A Handbook* (London: Routledge, 2005).

— *The Circassians* (London: Routledge, 2014).

— *A Brief History of Kabarda [from the Seventh Century AD]* (n.d.): circassianworld.com/pdf/Kabardian_History.pdf (accessed 2 November 2021)

Janberidze, Nodar and Tsitsishvili, Irakly, *Architectural Monuments of Georgia* (Moscow: Stroyizdat, 1996).

Jaubert, Amédée P., *Voyage en Arménie et en Perse fait dans les années 1806 et 1806* (Paris: Pélicier et Nepveu, 1821).

Javakhishvili, Alexander and Abramishvili, Guram, *Jewellery and Metalwork in the Museums of Georgia* (Leningrad: Aurora, 1986).

Jenkinson, Anthony, *Early Voyages and Travels to Russia and Persia*, ed. E. Delmar Morgan and C.H. Cote, 2 vols (London: Hakluyt Society, 1886).

Johnson, Rob, *The Great War in the Middle East: A Strategic Study* (Oxford: Oxford University Press, 2016).

Jones, S.F., 'Marxism and peasant Revolt in the Russian Empire: The case of the Gurian Republic', in: *The Slavonic and East European Review*, vol. 67. no. 3 (Cambridge: Modern Humanities Research Association MHRA, 1989), pp. 403–34.

— *Socialism in Georgian Colors: The European Road to Social Democracy 1883–1917* (Cambridge MA: Harvard University Press, 2005).

Jones, Stephen (ed.), *Kartlis Tskhovreba: A History of Georgia* (Tbilisi: Artanuji Publishing, 2014).

Jonson, Lena, *Vladimir Putin and Central Asia: The Shaping of Russian Foreign Policy* (London: I.B.Tauris 2004).

Jurado, Carlos Caballero, *Von Niedermayer und die Ostlegionen der Wehrmacht* (Zweibrücken: Schild Verlag, 2017).

Juvaini, 'Ala-ad-Din 'Ata-Malik, [*Tarikh-e Jahan-gusha:*] *The History of the World-Conqueror*, trans. John Andrew Boyle, 2 vols (Manchester: Manchester University Press, 1958).

Kaltenegger, Roland, *Gebirgsjäger im Kaukasus. Die Operation „Edelweiss" 1942/43* (Graz: Leopold Stocker, 1997).

Kamrava, Mehran (ed.), *The Great Game in West Asia* (Oxford: Oxford University Press, 2017).

— 'The Great Game in West Asia', in: Kamrava, *The Great Game in West Asia* (2017, q.v.), pp. 1–28.

Kanet, Roger E., 'The return of imperial Russia,' in: Sussex, *Conflict in the Former USSR* (2012, q.v.), pp. 15–34.

Kappeler, Andreas, *Rußland als Vielvölkerreich. Entstehung, Geschichte, Zerfall* (Frankfurt am Main: Büchergilde Gutenberg, 1992).

Kármán, Gábor, *Tributaries and Peripheries of the Ottoman Empire* (Leyden: Brill, 2020).

Kartlis Tskhovreba (K'art'lis C'xovreba), The Life of Kartli: see (in English): Thomson, *Rewriting Caucasian History* (1996, q.v.); Jones, *Kartlis Tskhovreba: A History of Georgia* (2014, q.v.); and (in German): Pätsch, *Das Leben Kartlis* (1985).

Kaufhold, Hubert and Kropp, Manfred (eds.), *Oriens Christianus. Heft für die Kunde des christlichen Orients*, vol. 91 (Wiesbaden: Harrassowitz, 2007), pp. 87–123.

Kausen, Ernst, *Die Sprachfamilien der Welt*, part I: *Europa und Asien* (Hamburg: Buske, 2010).

Kazemdazeh, Firuz, *The struggle of Transcaucasia (1917–1921)* (New York: Philosophical Library, 1951).

— 'Iranian relations with Russia and the Soviet Union', in: *The Cambridge History of Iran*, vol. 7 (1991, q.v.), pp. 314–49.

— 'Anglo-Iranian relations ii. Qajar period', in: *Encyclopaedia Iranica*, vol. 2, fasc. 1, pp. 46–51 (1994); iranicaonline.org/articles/anglo-iranian-relations-ii.

Kazenin, Konstantin, 'Село вместо города: как сохранили мир в Карачаево-Черкесии', Moscow Carnegie Center, 3 February 2016: carnegie.ru/commentary/62652 (accessed 3 February 2022).

Keddie, Nikki and Amanat, Mehrdad, 'Iran under the later Qajars', in: *The Cambridge History of Iran*, vol. 7 (1991, q.v.), pp. 213–43.

Kemper, Michael, *Herrschaft, Recht und Islam in Daghestan. Von den Khanaten und Geheimbünden zum ğihād-Staat* (Wiesbaden: Reichert, 2005).

Kent, Neil, *Crimea: A History* (London: Hurst, 2016).

Kernen, Beat and Sussex, Matthew, 'The Russo-Georgian war: identity, intervention and norm adaptation', in: Sussex, *Conflict in the Former USSR* (2012, q.v.), pp. 91–117.

Keshishian, Vahakn, Löker, Koray and Polatel, Mehmet (eds), *Adana with its Armenian Cultural Heritage* (Istanbul: HDV Yayınları, 2018).

Kévorkian, Raymond, *Le Génocide des Arméniens* (Paris: Odile Jacob, 2006).

Khachikyan, Armen, *History of Armenia* (Yerevan: Edit Print, 2010).

Khazanov, Anatoly M. and Wink, André (eds), *Nomads in the Sedentary World* (Richmond: Curzon, 2001).

Khodarkovsky, Michael, *Where Two Worlds Met: The Russian State and the Kalmyk Nomads, 1600–1771* (Ithaca: Cornell University Press, 1992).

— *Russia's Steppe Frontier: The Making of a Colonial Empire, 1500–1800* (Bloomington: Indiana University Press, 2002).

— *Bitter Choices: Loyalty and Betrayal in the Russian Conquest of the North Caucasus* (Ithaca: Cornell University Press, 2011).

Khroushkova, Liudmila, *Les monuments chrétiens de la côte orientale de la mer noire. Abkhazie IVe–XIVe siècles* (Turnhout: Brepols, 2006).

Khwandamir, Ghiyas ad-Din Muhammad, *Habibu's-Siyar: The History of the Mongols and Genghis Khan*, Classical Writings of the Medieval Islamic World, vol. 2, trans. Wheeler M. Thackston (London: I.B.Tauris, 2012).

Kieser, Hans-Lukas, *Talaat Pasha: Father of Modern Turkey, Architect of Genocide* (Princeton: Princeton University Press, 2018).

King, Charles, *The Ghost of Freedom: A History of the Caucasus* (Oxford: Oxford University Press, 2008)

Kirakos Gandzakets'i, *History of the Armenians*, trans. Robert Bedrosian (New York: Sources of the Armenian Tradition, 1986); attalus.org/armenian/kgtoc.html.

Kissinger, Henry, *A World Restored: Metternich, Castlereagh and the Problems of Peace, 1812–22* (1957; Brattleboro, VT: Echo Point Books & Media, 2013).

Klaproth, Julius von, *Reise in den Kaukasus und nach Georgien unternommen in den Jahren 1807 und 1808*, 3 vols (1812; repr. Leipzig: Zentralantiquariat der DDR, 1970).

Klein, Janet, *The Margins of Empire: Kurdish Militias in the Ottoman Tribal Zone* (Stanford: Stanford University Press, 2011).

Koch, Karl, *Wanderungen im Oriente, während der Jahre 1843 und 1844*, 3 vols (Weimar: Druck und Verlag des Landes-Industrie-Comptoirs).

Kolodziejczyk, Dariousz, 'Daghestan during the Long Ottoman–Safavid War (1578–1639): The Shamkhals' Relations with Ottoman Pashas', in: Kármán, *Tributaries and Peripheries of the Ottoman Empire* (2020, q.v.), pp. 117–33.

Kondakof N[ikodim], Tolstoï, J. and Reinach, S. *Antiquités de la Russie méridionale* (Paris: Ernest Leroux, 1891).

Kopisto, Lauri, 'The British Intervention in South Russia 1918–1920' (dissertation, University of Helsinki, 2011); helda.helsinki.fi/bitstream/handle/10138/26041/thebriti.pdf?sequence=1.

Koppensteiner, Bruno W. and Häusler, Hermann, 'Das Kaukasus-Öl. – Ziel der Deutschen Wehrmacht im Zweiten Weltkrieg', in: *Festschrift Brigadier i.R. Prof. Dr. Gerhard L. Fasching. Berichte der Geologischen Bundesanstalt*, vol. 140 (Vienna: Geologische Bundesanstalt, 2021), pp. 77–102.

Korkhmazyan, Emma, Крымская Армянская миниатюра = *Krymskaja armjanskaja miniatjura / Grimi haykakan manrankarc'owt'yowne / Armenian Miniatures of the Crimea* (Yerevan: Matenadaran, 2008).

Korobeinikov, D.A., 'Raiders and neighbours: The Turks (1040–1304)', in: *The Cambridge History of the Byzantine Empire* (2008, q.v.), pp. 692–727.

Kort, Michael (2001), *The Soviet Colossus: History and Aftermath* (Armonk, NY: M.E. Sharpe, 2001).

Kortepeter, Carl Max, *Ottoman Imperialism during the Reformation* (London: University of London Press, 1973).

Kouymjian, Dickran, 'Armenia from the fall of the Cilician kingdom (1375) to the forced emigration under Shah Abbas (1604)', in: Hovannisian, *The Armenian People*, vol. 2 (1997, q.v.), pp. 1–50.

Kouznetsow [Kuznetsov], Vladimir and Lebedynsky, Iaroslav, *Les chrétiens disparus du Caucase. Histoire et archéologie du christianisme au Caucase du Nord et en Crimée* (Paris: Errance, 1999).

— *Les Alains* (Paris: Errance, 2005).

Kraft, Ekkehard, 'Die griechische Emigration aus dem Osmanischen Reich in den Kaukasus', in: Motika and Ursinus, *Caucasia between the Ottoman Empire and Iran* (2000, q.v.), pp. 69–86.

Kupatadze, Alexander, 'Understanding variation in corruption and white-collar crime: Georgia and Armenia', in: Kamrava, *The Great Game in West Asia* (2017, q.v.), pp. 239–41.

Kusnezow, Alexander, *Swanetien. In Bergen und Tälern des Kaukasus* (Leipzig: VEB F.A. Brockhaus, 1977).

Lane, George, *Early Mongol Rule in Thirteenth-Century Iran: A Persian Renaissance* (Abingdon: RoutledgeCurzon, 2003).

Lang, David Marshall (ed. and trans.), *A Modern History of Georgia* (London: Weidenfeld and Nicolson, 1962).

Langer, Jacob, 'Corruption and the Counterrevolution: The Rise and Fall of the Black Hundreds' (dissertation, Duke University, 2007).

Lapinsky, Theophil, *Die Bergvölker des Kaukasus und ihr Freiheitskampf gegen die Russen*, 2 vols. (1863; reprint, no place of publication given: Elibron Classic, 2005).

Lawrence, A.W., 'The castle of Baghras', in: Boase, *Cilician Kingdom* (1978, q.v.), pp. 34–84.

Lebedynsky, Iaroslav, *Armes et guerriers du Caucase. Les traditiones guerrières des peuples caucasiens* (Paris : L'Harmattan, 2008).

— *Les Cosaques. Une société guerreère entre libertés et pouvoirs, Ukraine 1490–1790* (Paris : Errance, 2004).

— *La Horde d'Or. Conquête mongole et 'Joug tatar' en Europe 1236–1502* (Arles: Éditions Errance, 2013).

Lee, Eric, *The Experiment: Georgia's Forgotten Revolution 1918–1921* (London: Bloomsbury, 2017).

Lee, James R., *Climate Change and Armed Conflict: Hot and Cold Wars* (Oxford: Routledge, 2009).

Lehmann-Haupt, C.F., *Armenien. Einst und Jetzt*, 3 vols (Berlin: Behr's Verlag, 1910, 1926, 1931).

Lehovich, Dimitry V., *White against Red: The Life of General Anton Denikin* (New York: W.W. Norton, 1974).

Lemercier-Quelquejay, Chantal, 'Co-optation of the Elites of Kabarda and Daghestan in the sixteenth century', in: Broxup, *The North Caucasus Barrier* (1992, q.v.), pp. 18–44.

Liddell Hart, Basil H., *The Other Side of the Hill. Germany's Generals, their Rise and Fall, with their own Account of Military Events 1939–1945* (London: Cassell, 1948).

Lieven, Anatol, 'West Asia since 1900: Living through the wreck of empires', in: Kamrava, *The Great Game in West Asia* (2017, q.v.), pp. 31–55.

'Life of King Giorgi Lasha', part of *History of the Five Reigns*, 13th century, in: *The Georgian Chronicle. The Period of Giorgi Lasha* (1991, q.v.), pp. 97–103.

Light, Matthew A., 'A survey of political trends of the Northwest Caucasus: Krasnodar, Adygea, and Stavropol', in: Howard, *Volatile Borderland* (2012, q.v.), pp. 386–404.

Limper, Bernhard, *Die Mongolen und die christlichen Völker des Kaukasus* (Cologne: University of Cologne, 1980).

Luther, K.A., 'Atābakān-e Ādarbāyjān', in: *Encyclopaedia Iranica*, vol. 2, fasc. 8, pp. 890–94 (1987); iranicaonline.org/articles/atabakan-e-adarbayjan.

Luttrell, A.T., 'The Hospitallers' intervention in Cilician Armenia: 1291–1375', in: Boase, *Cilician Kingdom of Armenia* (1978, q.v.), pp. 118–44.

Lynch, H.F.B., *Armenia: Travels and Studies*, 2 vols (London: Longmans, Green and Co., 1901).

McGregor, Andrew, 'Military jamaats in the North Caucasus: A continuing threat', in: Howard, *Volatile Borderland* (2012, q.v.), pp. 237–64.

McMeekin, Sean, *The Berlin–Baghdad Express: The Ottoman Empire and Germany's Bid for World Power 1898–1918* (London: Penguin, 2011).

— *The Ottoman Endgame* (London: Penguin, 2015).

Maksoudian, Krikor, 'Armenian communities in Eastern Europe', in: Hovannisian, *The Armenian People*, vol. 2 (1997, q.v.), pp. 51–80.

Malek, Martin, 'NATO and the South Caucasus: Armenia, Azerbaijan, and Georgia on different Tracks', in: *Connections*, vol. 7, no. 3 (Garmisch: Partnership for Peace Consortium of Defense Academies and Security Studies Institutes, 2008), pp. 30–51; jstor.org/stable/pdf/26323347.pdf?refreqid=excelsior%3A2c8e28de0651d3d48fd49fd3f139eb81&ab_segments=&origin=.

Mammadova, Gulchohra, *Architecture of Caucasian Albania: Natural Investigation and Measurement of Christian Monuments of Caucasian Albania, Ways of their Preservation* (Saarbrücken: Lambert Academic Publishing, 2011).

Mankoff, Jeffrey, '"Un-civil society" and the sources of Russian influence in West Asia: The South Caucasus', in: Kamrava, *The Great Game in West Asia* (2017, q.v.), pp. 141–60.

Marozzi, Justin, *Tamerlane: Sword of Islam, Conqueror of the World* (London: HarperCollins, 2004).

Matfunian, Vartan Gerges, 'Der Orden der Mechitaristen', in: Heyer, *Die Kirche Armeniens* (1987, q.v.), pp. 175–93.

Marshall, Alex, *The Caucasus under Soviet Rule* (London: Routledge, 2012).

Материалы по археологии Кавказа = *Materialy po archeologii Kavkaza*, vol. 10 (Moscow: Voronovim, 1904).

[Matthew of Edessa / Matt'eos Urhayets'i,] *Chronique de Matthieu d'Édesse (962–1136) avec la continuation de Grégoire le Prêtre jusqu'en 1162*, trans. Édouard Dulaurier (1858; repr., no publisher given, *ca.* 2017).

— *Armenia and the Crusades, 10th to 12th Centuries: The Chronicle of Matthew of Edessa*, trans. with commentary Ara Edmond Dostourian (Belmont, MA: Armenian Heritage Press, 2013).

Matthews, Owen, *An Impeccable Spy: Richard Sorge, Stalin's Master Agent* (London: Bloomsbury, 2019).

May, Timothy, 'The conquest and rule of Transcaucasia: The era of Chormaqan', in: Tubach, et al., *Caucasus during the Mongol Period* (2012, q.v.), pp. 129–51.

Mayers, Kit, *The First English Explorer: The Life of Anthony Jenkinson (1529–1611) and his Adventures on the Route to the Orient* (Kibworth Beauchamp: Matador, 2017).

Mazaewa, Tamara and Tamrasjan, Hratschja (eds), *Armenische Miniatur* (Yerevan: Nairi, 2013).

Mehdiyeva, Nazrin, *Power Games in the Caucasus: Azerbaijan's Foreign and Energy Policy towards the West, Russia and the Middle East* (London: I.B.Tauris, 2011).

Melville, Charles (ed.), *Safavid Persia in the Age of Empires*: The Idea of Iran, vol. 10 (London: Bloomsbury, 2021).

Melkonian, Eduard, 'Repressions in 1930s Soviet Armenia', in: *Caucasus Analytical Digest*, No. 22: *Stalinist Terror in the South Caucasus* (Zurich: ETH Center for Security Studies, December 2010), pp. 6–9.

Merzbacher, Gottfried, *Aus den Hochregionen des Kaukasus*, 2 vols (Leipzig: Duncker und Humblot, 1901).

Metsobets'i, T'ovma, *History of Tamerlane and His Successors*, ed. and trans. Robert Bedrosian (New York: 1987); attalus.org/armenian/tm1.htm.

Meyer, James H., *Turks across Empires: Marketing Muslim Identity in the Russian–Ottoman Borderlands, 1856–1914* (Oxford: Oxford University Press, 2019).

Miarka, Agnieszka, 'Velvet Revolution in Armenia and its influence on state policy: Selected aspects', in: *Central Asia and the Caucasus. Journal of Social and Political Studies*, vol. 20, no. 4 (Lulea: Institute for Central Asian and Caucasian Studies, 2019), pp. 41–50; researchgate.net/publication/338445018_VELVET_REVOLUTION_IN_ARMENIA_AND_ITS_INFLUENCE_ON_STATE_POLICY_SELECTED_ASPECTS.

— 'Autumn war in Nagorno-Karabakh (2020) – Course and implications for the strategic balance of power in the South Caucasus region', in: *Asian Affairs*, vol. 52, no. 4 (London: Royal Society for Asian Affairs, 2021), pp. 826–51; tandfonline.com/doi/abs/10.1080/03068374.2021.1993050 (accessed 12 November 2022).

Mignan, Robert, *A Winter Journey through Russia, the Caucasian Alps, and Georgia* (1839; repr. London: British Library, 2011).

Mikaberidze, Alexander (ed.), *Conflict and Conquest in the Islamic World*, 2 vols (Santa Barbara: ABC-Clio, 2011).

Mikhelidze Nona, 'The Turkish–Armenian rapprochement at the deadlock', in: *Istituto Affari Internazionali*, vol. 10, no. 5 (Rome: IAI, 2015), pp. 1–9.

Minassian, Anahide, Ter, 'Le rôle des Arméniens du Caucase dans la révolution constitutionnaliste de la Perse (1905–1912)', in: Motika and Ursinus, *Caucasia between the Ottoman Empire and Iran* (2000, q.v.), pp. 147–76.

Minassian, Gaïdz, *The Armenian Experience: From Ancient Times to Independence* (London: I.B.Tauris/Bloomsbury, 2020).

Minassian, Taline Ter, *Most Secret Agent of Empire: Reginald Teague-Jones, Master Spy of the Great Game* (London: Hurst, 2014).

Minez, Roland P., *At the Limit of Complexity: British Military Operations in North Persia and the Caucasus 1918* (Fort Leavenworth, KS: US Army Command and General Staff College Press, 2018);

https://www.armyupress.army.mil/Portals/7/combat-studies-institute/csi-books/ArtOfWar-At-the-limit-of-complexity-british-military-operations-in-nort-persia-and-the-caucasus-1918.pdf (accessed 26 December 2021).

Minorsky, V[ladimir], *Studies in Caucasian History*: I. *New Light on the Shaddādids of Ganja*; II. *The Shaddādids of Ani*; III. *Prehistory of Saladin* (London: Taylor's Foreign Press, 1953).

— *A History of Sharvan and Darband in the 10th–11th Centuries* (Cambridge: W. Heffer and Sons, 1958).

Mirak, Robert, 'The Armenians in America', in: Hovannisian, Richard G., *The Armenian People*, vol. 2 (1997, q.v.), pp. 389–412.

Mirfendereski, Guive, *A Diplomatic History of the Caspian Sea: Treaties, Diaries, and Other Stories* (New York: Palgrave, 2001).

Mitrokhin, Leonid, *Failure of Three Missions* (Moscow: Progress Publishers, 1987).

Moberly, Frederick James (ed.), *Operation in Persia, 1914–1919. Compiled by Arrangement with the Government of India, under the Direction of the Historical Section of the Committee of Imperial Defence* (1929; reprint, London: Imperial War Museum, 1987).

Monshipouri, Mahmood, 'Pipeline politics in Iran, Turkey, and the South Caucasus', in: Kamrava, *The Great Game in West Asia* (2017, q.v.), pp. 57–81.

Montgomery Hyde, H., *Stalin: The History of a Dictator* (London: Rupert Hart-Davis, 1971).

Morgenthau, Henry, *Ambassador Morgenthau's Story: A Personal Account of the Armenian Genocide* (1918, reprint, New York: Cosimo Classics, 2010).

Mostashari, Firouzeh, *On the Religious Frontier: Tsarist Russia and Islam in the Caucasus* (London: I.B.Tauris, 2006).

Motika, Raoul and Ursinus, Michael (eds), *Caucasia between the Ottoman Empire and Iran, 1555–1914* (Wiesbaden: Reichert, 2000).

Mueggenberg, Brent, *The Cossack Struggle against Communism, 1917–1945* (Jefferson, NC: McFarland & Co., 2019).

Mutafian, Claude, *Le Royaume Arménien de Cilicie, XIIe–XIVe siècle* (Paris: CNRS Éditions, 1993).

— 'Ani after Ani, eleventh to seventeenth century', in: Hovannisian, *Armenian Kars and Ani* (2011, q.v.), pp. 155–70.

Nasawi, Muhammad ibn Ahmad, *Histoire du sultan Djelâl ed-Dîn Mankobirti, prince du Kharezm*, trans. O. Houdas (Paris: E. Leroux, 1895; reprint, 2014).

Natho, Kadir I., *Circassian History* (Bloomington: Xlibris, 2009).

Nersessian, Vrej, *Treasures from the Ark: 1700 Years of Armenian Christian Art* (London: British Library, 2001).

— *The Bible in the Armenian Tradition* (London: British Library, 2001).

Neubauer, Edith, *Altgeorgische Baukunst. Felsenstädte, Kirchen, Höhlenklöster* (Leipzig: Koehler und Amelang, 1976).

Neumann, Karl Friedrich, *Russland und die Tscherkessen* (Stuttgart: J.G. Cotta'sche Buchhandlung, 1840).

Nilsson, Niklas, 'Georgia's Rose Revolution: The break with the past', in: Cornell and Starr, *The Guns of August 2008* (2011, q.v.), pp. 85–103.

Nuriyev, Elkhan, *The South Caucasus at the Crossroads: Conflicts, Caspian Oil and Great Power Politics* (Piscataway, NJ: Transaction Publishers, 2000).

O'Ballance, Edgar, *Wars in the Caucasus, 1990–95* (Houndmills: Macmillan, 1997).

Oliphant, Laurence, *The Transcaucasian Campaign of the the Turkish Army under Omer Pasha* (1856; reprint, no place of publication given: Sagwan Press, 2020).

Önol, Onur, *The Tsar's Armenians: A Minority in Late Imperial Russia* (London: I.B.Tauris, 2017).

Orbélian, Stéphannos, *Histoire de la Siounie*, trans. M.-F. Brosset (1864; repr. New Delhi: Facsimile Publisher, 2019).

Ormanian, Malachia, *The Church of Armenia: Her History, Doctrine, Rule, Discipline, Liturgy, Literature, and Existing Condition* (London: A.R. Mowbray, 1912).

Osipian, Alexandr, 'Baptised Mongol rulers, Prester John and the Magi: Armenian image of the Mongols produced for the Western readers in the mid-thirteenth-early fourteenth centuries', in: Tubach, et al., *Caucasus during the Mongol Period* (2012, q.v.), pp. 153–67.

Ouvaroff, Nathalie, 'The role of Chechens in the Georgian–South Ossetian conflict', in: *Russian Analytical Digest*, vol. 45, no. 8 (Zurich: ETH, 2008); css.ethz.ch/content/dam/ethz/special-interest/gess/cis/center-for-securities-studies/pdfs/RAD-45-27-29.pdf.

Pallas, Peter Simon, *D. Johann Anton Güldenstädts Reisen durch Russland und im Caucasischen Gebürge*, 2 vols (1787, 1791; repr. Saarbrücken: Fines Mundi, 2018).

— *Bemerkungen auf einer Reise in die südlichen Statthalterschaften des Russischen Reichs in den Jahren 1793–1794*, 3 vols (Leipzig: G. Martini, 1799–1801).

Pätsch, Gertrud (ed.), *Das Leben Kartlis. Eine Chronik aus Georgien, 300–1200* (Leipzig: Dieterich'sche Verlagsbuchhandlung, 1985).

Pattie, Susan Paul, *The Armenian Legionnaires: Sacrifice and Betrayal in World War I* (London: I.B.Tauris, 2018).

Payaslian, Simon, *The History of Armenia* (New York: Palgave Macmillan, 2007).

Peacock, A.C.S., 'Identity, culture and religion on medieval Islam's Caucasian frontiers', in: *Bulletin of the Royal Institute for Inter-Faith Studies*, no. 13 (Amman: 2011), pp. 69–90; academia.edu/15642825/Identity_Culture_and_Religion_on_Medieval_Islams_Caucasian_Frontier.

— 'Between Georgia and the Islamic world: The atabegs of Samc'xe and the Turks', in: *At the Crossroads of Empires: 14th–15th Century Eastern Anatolia*. Proceedings of the International Symposium held in Istanbul, 4th–6th May 2007 (Istanbul: Varia Anatolica, 2012), pp. 49–70; academia.edu/17203351/

Between_Georgia_and_the_Islamic_World_The_Atabegs_of_Samcxe_and_the_Turks.

Peacock, A.C.S and Yıldız, Sara Nur, *The Seljuks of Anatolia* (London: I.B.Tauris, 2013).

Pelliot, Paul, *Notes critiques d'histoires Kalmouke*, 2 vols (Paris: Adrien-Maisonneuve, 1960).

Peratoner, Alberto, *From Ararat to San Lazzaro: A Cradle of Armenian Spirituality and Culture in the Venice Lagoon* (Venice: Armenian Mekhitarist Congregation, 2015).

Perović, Jeronim, *Der Nordkaukasus unter russischer Herrschaft. Geschichte einer Vielvölkerregion zwischen Rebellion und Anpassung* (Köln: Böhlau, 2015).

Perry, John, 'The Zand Dynasty', in: *The Cambridge History of Iran*, vol. 7 (1991, q.v.), pp. 63–103.

Petersen, Alexandros, *Integration in Energy and Transport: Azerbaijan, Georgia and Turkey* (Lanham, MD: Lexington Books, 2016).

Phillipps-Wolley, Clive, *Savage Svanetia*, 2 vols (London: Richard Bentley and Son, 1883).

Pietkiewicz, Michal, 'Legal status of Caspian Sea – problem solved?', in: *Marine Policy*, no. 123 (Amsterdam: Elsevier, 2021), pp. 1–9; doi.org/10.1016/j.marpol.2020.104321.

Podbolotov, Sergei, '"… And the entire mass of loyal people lept up": The attitude of Nicholas II towards the pogroms', in: *Cahiers du Monde Russe et Soviétique*, vol. 45, no. 1–2 (Paris: EHESS, 1992), pp. 193–207; cairn.info/revue-cahiers-du-monde-russe-2004-1.htm.

Pogossian, Zaroui, 'Armenians, Mongols and the end of times: An overview of 13th century sources', in: Tubach, et al., *Caucasus during the Mongol Period* (2012, q.v.), pp. 169–98.

Polo, Marco, *The Book of Ser Marco Polo the Venetian Concerning the Kingdoms and Marvels of the East*, ed. and trans. Sir Henry Yule, 3rd ed. revised by Henri Cordier (London: J. Murray, 1903).

Popjanevski, Johanna, 'From Sukhumi to Tskhinvali: The path to war in Georgia', in: Cornell and Starr, *The Guns of August 2008* (2011, q.v.), pp. 143–61.

Preiser-Kapeller, Johannes, 'Zwischen Konstantinopel und Goldener Horde: Die byzantinischen Kirchenprovinzen der Alanen und Zichen im mongolischen Machtbereich im 13. und 14. Jahrhundert', in: Tubach, et al., *Caucasus during the Mongol Period* (2012, q.v.), pp. 199–216.

Prüfer, Curt, *Germany's Covert War in the Middle East. Espionage, Propaganda and Diplomacy in World War I*, ed. and trans. Kevin Morrow (London: I.B.Tauris, 2018).

Rabban Ṣâwmâ [Bar Sauma], *The Monks of Ḳûblai Khân, Emperor of China*, trans. E. A. Wallis Budge (London: The Religious Tract Society, 1928).

Radde, Gustav, *Die Chews'uren und ihr Land untersucht im Sommer 1876* (Cassel: Theodor Fischer, 1878).

Radzinsky, Edvard, *Stalin* (London: Hodder & Staughton, 1996).

Rahimov, Rahim, 'Azerbaijan, Iran reach breakthrough on disputed fields in the Caspian Sea', in: *Eurasia Daily Monitor*, vol. 15, no. 52 (Washington DC: The Jamestown Foundation, 5 April 2018), pp. 1–4; https://jamestown.org/program/azerbaijan-iran-reach-breakthrough-on-disputed-fields-in-the-caspian-sea (accessed 12 November 2022).

Rapp, Stephen H. Jr. *Studies in Medieval Georgian Historiography: Early Texts and Eurasian Contexts* (Leuven: Peeters, 2003).

— 'Georgian Christianity', in: Parry, Ken (ed.), *The Blackwell Companion to Eastern Christianity* (Malden, MA: Blackwell Publishing, 2007), pp. 137–55.

Rasiduddin Fazlullah [Rashid ad-Din Fadhlallah Hamdani], *Jami'u't-Tawarikh: Compendium of Chronicles (Tome 1)*, Classical Writings of the Medieval Islamic World, vol. 3, trans. Wheeler M. Thackston (London: I.B.Tauris, 2012).

Rauch, Karl, *Seidenstrasse über Moskau. Die grosse Reise des Adam Olearius nach Moskau und Ispahan zwischen 1633 und 39* (München: J. Pfeiffer, 1960).

Rawlinson, Alfred, *Adventures in the Near East 1918–1922* (London: Andrew Melrose, 1924).

Rayeva, G.I., Альбом видовъ Кавказа = *Album of views of the Caucasus* (Kislovodsk: Kislovodsk Publishing, ca. 1905).

Rayfield, Donald, *Edge of Empires: A History of Georgia* (London: Reaktion Books, 2012).

Redgate, A.E., *The Armenians* (Oxford: Blackwell, 1998).

Reisner, Oliver, 'Integrationsversuche der muslimischen Adscharer in die georgische Nationalbewegung', in: Motika and Ursinus, *Caucasia between the Ottoman Empire and Iran* (2000, q.v.), pp. 207–22.

Reynolds, Michael A., *Shattering Empires: The Clash and Collapse of the Ottoman and Russian Empires 1908–1918* (Cambridge: Cambridge University Press, 2011).

Richard, Jean (ed.), *Au-delà de la Perse et de l'Arménie. L'Orient latin et la découverte de l'Asie intérieure. Quelques textes inégalement connus aux origines de l'alliance entre Francs et Mongols (1145–1262)* (Turnhout: Brepols, 2005).

Richmond, Walter, *The Northwest Caucasus: Past, Present, Future* (London: Routledge, 2011).

Richter, Heinz, 'The impact of the confiscation of the Turkish dreadnoughts and of the transfer of Goeben and Breslau to Constantinople upon the Turkish entry into WWI', in: Çanakkale *Araştırmaları Türk Yıllığı*, year 11, no.15 (Çanakkale: 2013), pp. 1–16; dergipark.org.tr/tr/download/article-file/45128.

Riley-Smith. J.S.C., 'The Templars and the Teutonic Knights in Cilician Armenia', in: Boase, *Cilician Kingdom* (1978, q.v.), pp. 92–117.

Robertson, Geoffrey, *An Inconvenient Genocide: Who Now Remembers the Armenians?* (London: Biteback Publishing, 2015).

Robinson, Neil, 'Why not more conflict in the former USSR? Russia and Central Asia as a zone of relative peace', in: Sussex, *Conflict in the Former USSR* (2012, q.v.), pp. 118–46.

Roemer, H. R., 'Timur in Iran', in: *The Cambridge History of Iran*, vol. 6 (1986, q.v.), pp. 42–97.

— 'The Successors of Timur', in: *The Cambridge History of Iran*, vol. 6 (1986, q.v.), pp. 98–146.

— 'The Türkmen dynasties', in: *The Cambridge History of Iran*, vol. 6 (1986, q.v.), pp. 147–88.

— 'The Safavid period', in: *The Cambridge History of Iran*, vol. 6 (1986, q.v.), pp. 189–350.

Roshchin, Mikhail, 'Dagestan and the war next door', in: *Perspective*, vol. 11, no. 1 (Boston: Boston University, September–October 2000); https://open.bu.edu/bitstream/handle/2144/3580/perspective_11_1_roshchin.pdf?sequence=1&isAllowed=y (accessed 8 February 2022).

— 'Islam in the North Caucasus', in: Howard, *Volatile Borderland* (2012, q.v.), pp. 159–79.

Rota, Giorgio, 'Caucasians in Safavid service in the 17th century', in: Motika and Ursinus, *Caucasia between the Ottoman Empire and Iran* (2000, q.v.), pp. 107–20.

Rubel, Paula G., *The Kalmyk Mongols: A Study in Continuity and Change* (Bloomington: Indiana University, 1967).

Rubruck, William of, *The Mission of Friar William of Rubruck: His Journey to the Court of the Great Khan Möngke, 1253–1255*, trans. Peter Jackson (Indianapolis: Hackett, 2009).

Rucevska, Ieva, *Vital Caspian Graphics: Challenges beyond Caviar* (Arendal: UNEP/GRID-Arendal, 2006).

Runciman, Steven, *A History of the Crusades*, 3 vols (1951–4; reprint, London: The Folio Society, 1994).

Saikal, Amin, 'Iranian foreign policy, 1921–1979', in: *The Cambridge History of Iran*, vol. 7 (1991, q.v.), pp. 426–56.

Sakwa, Richard, 'Great powers and small wars in the Caucasus', in: Sussex, *Conflict in the Former USSR* (2012, q.v.), pp. 64–90.

Sanders, Thomas et al. (eds), *Russian–Muslim Confrontation in the Caucasus: Alternative Visions of the Conflict between Imam Shamil and the Russians, 1830–1859* (London: Routledge, 2004).

Saparov, Arsène, *From Conflict to Autonomy in the Caucasus: The Soviet Union and the Making of Abkhazia, South Ossetia and Nagorno Karabakh* (London: Routledge, 2015).

Schiltberger, Hans, *The Bondage and Travels of Johann Schiltberger in Europe, Asia and Africa, 1396–1427*, trans. J.B. Telfer (London: Hakluyt Society, 1879).

Seaton, Albert, *Stalin as Warlord* (London: B.T. Batsford, 1976).

Sebag Montefiori, Simon, *Young Stalin* (New York: Vintage, 2008).

Seibt, Werner, (ed.), *Die Christianisierung des Kaukasus* (Vienna: Österreichische Akademie der Wissenschaften, 2002).

— 'Die orthodoxe Metropolis "Kaukasos"', in: Tubach, et al., *Caucasus during the Mongol Period* (2012, q.v.), pp. 239–50.

Seidt, Hans-Ulrich, *Berlin, Kabul, Moskau. Oskar Ritter von Niedermayer und Deutschlands Geopolitik* (München: Universitas, 2002).

Shafiyev, Farid, *Resettling the Borderlands: State Relocations and Ethnic Conflict in the South Caucasus* (Montreal & Kingston: McGill-Queen's University Press, 2018).

Shaw, Stanford, 'Iranian relations with the Ottoman Empire in the eighteenth and nineteenth centuries', in: *The Cambridge History of Iran*, vol. 7 (1991, q.v.), pp. 297–313.

Sherr, James, 'The implications of the Russia-Georgia War for European security', in: Cornell and Starr, *The Guns of August 2008* (2011, q.v.), pp. 196–224.

al-Shishani, Murad Batal, 'The rise and fall of Arab fighters in Chechnya', in: Howard, *Volatile Borderland* (2012, q.v.), pp. 265–93.

Shtyrkov, Sergei, 'Religious nationalism in contemporary Russia: The case of the Ossetian ethnic religion project', in: Alapuro, Risto, Mustajoki, Arto and Pesonen, Pekka (eds), *Understanding Russianness* (London: Routledge, 2012), pp. 232–44; eusp.org/sites/default/files/archive/et_dep/Shtyrkov/Shtyrkov_Understandig_Russianness_Text.pdf [*sic*] (accessed 5 February 2022).

— 'Ritual feasts and transpersonal experience: Ossetian religious traditionalists in search of legitimization', in: *New Age in Russia – Ideologies, Networks, Discourses* (hypotheses.org/Mainz: Mainz University, 2021); newageru.hypotheses.org/1589 (accessed 5 February 2022).

Sidorko, Clemens P., 'Kampf den ketzerischen Qizilbāš! Die Revolte des Ḥāǧǧī Dā'ūd (1718–1728)', in: Motika and Ursinus, *Caucasia between the Ottoman Empire and Iran* (2000, q.v.), pp. 133–46.

— *Dschihad im Kaukasus. Antikolonialer Widerstand der Dagestaner und Tschetschenen gegen das Zarenreich (18. Jahrhundert bis 1859)* (Wiesbaden: Reichert 2007).

Simon of Saint-Quentin, *History of the Tartars*, in: Vincent of Beauvais, *Speculum historiale* (1264), ed. and trans. Stephen Pow et al. (2019); simonofstquentin.org/index.html.

Sipri Yearbook 1994, Stockholm International Peace Research Institute (Oxford: Oxford University Press, 1994), sipri.org/sites/default/files/SIPRI%20Yearbook%201994.pdf (accessed 24 January 2022).

Skylitzes, John, *A Synopsis of Byzantine History 811–1057*, trans. John Wortley (Cambridge: Cambridge University Press, 2010).

Smele, Jonathan D., *The 'Russian' Civil Wars 1916–1926* (London: C. Hurst & Co., 2016).

Smirnov, Andrei, 'The Republic of Adygea: An overview', in: Howard, *Volatile Borderland* (2012, q.v.), pp. 346–85.

Smith, David J., 'The Saakashvili administration's reaction to Russian policies before the 2008 war', in: Cornell and Starr, *The Guns of August 2008* (2011, q.v.), pp. 122–42.

Sokolsky, Richard and Charlik-Paley, Tanya, *NATO and Caspian Security: A Mission too Far?* (Santa Monica, CA: RAND Corp., 1999).

Soltes, Ori Z. (ed.), *National Treasures of Georgia* (London: Philip Wilson, 1999).

Spuler, Bertold, *Die Goldene Horde. Die Mongolen in Russland 1223–1502* (Leipzig: Harrassowitz, 1943).

— *Die Mongolen in Iran. Politik, Verwaltung und Kultur der Ilchanzeit 1220–1350* (Berlin: Akademie-Verlag, 1955).

Statiev, Alexander, *At War's Summit: The Red Army and the Struggle for the Caucasian Mountains in World War II* (Cambridge: Cambridge University Press, 2018).

Stewart, Angus Donald, *The Armenian Kingdom and the Mamluks: War and Diplomacy during the Reigns of Het'um II (1289–1307)* (Leiden: Brill, 2001).

Stewart, George, *The White Armies of Russia: A Chronicle of Counter-Revolution and Allied Intervention* (Uckfield: The Naval & Military Press, 2009).

Stopka, Krzysztof, *Armenia Christiana: Armenian Religious Identity and the Churches of Constantinople and Rome (4th–15th Century)* (Kraków: Jagiellonian University Press, 2017).

Strahlenberg, Philipp Johann von, *Das Nord- und Östliche Theil von Europa und Asia, in so weit solches das gantze russische Reich mit Siberien und der grossen Tartarey in sich begreiffet* (Stockholm: published by the author, 1730).

Strzygowski, Josef, *Die Baukunst der Armenier und Europa*, 2 vols (1918; reprint, London: Forgotten Books, 2015).

Suny, Ronald Grigor, *The Making of the Georgian Nation*, 2nd ed. (Bloomington: Indiana University Press, 1994).

— 'Eastern Armenia under tsarist rule' in: Hovannisian, *The Armenian People*, vol. 2 (1997, q.v.), pp. 109–34.

— 'Soviet Armenia', in: Hovannisian, *The Armenian People*, vol. 2 (1997, q.v.), pp. 347–88.

— *The Baku Commune, 1917–1918: Class and Nationality in the Russian Revolution* (Princeton: Princeton University Press, 1972).

Sussex, Matthew (ed.), *Conflict in the Former USSR* (Cambridge: Cambridge University Press, 2012).

Taarnby, Michael, 'The Mujahedin in Nagorno-Karabakh: A case study in the evolution of global Jihad' (Madrid: Real Instituto Elcano, 2008); realinstitutoelcano.org/en/work-document/the-mujahedin-in-nagorno-karabakh-a-case-study-in-the-evolution-of-global-jihad-wp (accessed 12 November 2022).

Taitbout de Marigny, Chevalier [Edouard], *Three Voyages in the Black Sea to the Coast of Circassia* (London: John Murray, 1837).

Taki, Victor, *Tsar and Sultan: Russian Encounters with the Ottoman Empire* (London: I.B.Tauris, 2016).

Talibov, Vasif et al. (eds), *The Encyclopaedia of Nakhchivan Monuments* (Nakhchivan: Academy of Sciences, Nakhchivan Branch, 2008).

Teague, Elizabeth, 'Russia's return to the direct election of governors: Re-shaping the power vertical?', in: *Region*, vol. 3, no. 1 (Bloomington: Slavica Publications, 2014), pp. 37–57.

Teague-Jones, Reginald, *The Spy Who Disappeared: Diary of a Secret Mission to Russian Central Asia in 1918*, with introduction and epilogue by Peter Hopkirk (London: Victor Gollancz, 1990).

Teissier, Beatrice (ed), *Russian Frontiers: Eighteenth-Century British Travellers in the Caspian, Caucasus and Central Asia* (Oxford: Signal Books, 2011).

Temnikov, Roman, 'Caspian pipeline geopolitics: Competition between western and northern oil and gas transport routes to Europe', in: *Central Asia and the Caucasus. Journal of Social and Political Studies*, vol. 20, no. 4 (Luleå: Institute for Central Asian and Caucasian Studies, 2019), pp. 70–81; researchgate.net/publication/338209306_CASPIAN_PIPELINE_GEOPOLITICS_Competition_between_Western_and_Northern_Oil_and_Gas_Transport_Routes_to_Europe.

Ter Minassian, Anahide, *La Question Arménienne* (Roquevaire: Éditions Parenthèses, 1983).

Tielke, Wilhelm, *The Caucasus and the Oil: The German–Soviet War in the Caucasus 1942/43* (Winnipeg, Manitoba: J.J. Fedorowicz Publishing, 1995).

Thierry, Michel, *Répertoire des monastères Arméniens* (Turnhout: Brepols, 1993).

— *Armenien im Mittelalter* (Regensburg: Schnell und Steiner, 2002).

Thierry, Nicole, 'Sur le culte de Sainte Nino', in: Seibt, *Christianisierung* (2002, q.v.), pp. 151–8.

Thomassian, Levon, *Summer of '42: A Study of German–Armenian Relations during the Second World War* (Atglen, PA: Schiffer Publishing, 2012).

Thomson, Robert W., *Rewriting Caucasian History: The Medieval Armenian Adaptation of the Georgian Chronicles. The Original Georgian Texts and the Armenian Adaptation* (Oxford: Clarendon, 1996).

Thunø, Erik, 'Cross-cultural dressing: The medieval South Caucasus and art history', in: Foletti and Thunø, *Medieval South Caucasus* (2016, q.v.), pp. 144–59.

Tlisova, Fatima, 'An inside look at Karachevo-Cherkassia', in: Howard, *Volatile Borderland* (2012, q.v.), pp. 294–308.

— 'Kabardino-Balkaria: Sleeping Beauty and the awakening of the Circassian heartland', in: Howard, *Volatile Borderland* (2012, q.v.), pp. 309–45.

Tolf, Robert W., *The Russian Rockefellers: The Saga of the Nobel Family and the Russian Oil Industry* (Stanford, CA: Hoover Institution Press, 1976).

Toumanoff, Cyril, 'The fifteenth-century Bagratids and the institution of collegial sovereignty in Georgia', in: *Traditio*, vol. 7 (New York: Fordham University Press, 1949–51), pp. 169–221.

— *Studies in Christian Caucasian History* (Washington DC: Georgetown University Press, 1963).

— (Cyrille,) *Manuel de généalogie et de chronologie pour l'histoire de la Caucasie chrétienne (Arménie – Géorgie – Albanie)* (Rome: Edizione Aquila, 1976).

Toumarkine, Alexandre, 'L'Abkhazie et la Circassie dans le *Cihān-nümā* de Kātib Çelebi: Un regard ottoman sur le Caucase du Nord-Ouest', in: Motika and Ursinus, *Caucasia between the Ottoman Empire and Iran* (2000, q.v.), pp. 31–40.

Toynbee, Arnold Joseph, *The Treatment of Armenians in the Ottoman Empire: Documents Presented to Viscount Grey of Fallodon* (London: Hodder and Stoughton, 1916).

Treaty of Alexandropol, 2–3 December, 1920: genocide.ru/lib/treaties/17.htm (accessed 22 December 2021).

Treaty of Angora [Ankara], 20 October 1921: hri.org/docs/FT1921/Franco-Turkish_Pact_1921.pdf accessed 23.12.1921.

Treaty of Brest-Litovsk, 1918: avalon.law.yale.edu/20th_century/bl34.asp#treatytext (accessed 12 November 2022).

Treaty of Georgievsk, 1783, translated from the Russian by Russell E. Martin: russianlegitimist.org/the-treaty-of-georgievsk-1783 (accessed 8 November 2021).

Treaty of Golestan [Gulistan] 12 [24] October, 1813, in: Bournoutian, George A., *From the Kur to the Aras* (2021, q.v.), pp. 274–77.

Treaty of Kars, 13 October 1920: amsi.ge/istoria/sab/yarsi.html (accessed 22 December 2021).

Treaty of Moscow, 7 May 1920: soviethistory.msu.edu/1921-2/transcaucasia/transcaucasia-texts/georgian-independence (accessed 23 December 2021).

Treaty of Moscow, 16 March 1921: amsi.ge/istoria/sab/moskovi.html (accessed 22 December 2021).

Treaty of Sèvres, 10 August 1920: wwi.lib.byu.edu/index.php/Section_I,_Articles_1_-_260 (accessed 21 December 2021).

Treaty of Turkmenchay, 1828, Russian text: hist.msu.ru/ER/Etext/FOREIGN/turkman.htm (accessed 15 November 2021).

Treuttel, Johann Georg, *Anecdoten zur Lebensgeschichte des Ritters und Reichs-Fürsten Potemkin* (Freistadt am Rhein [Strasbourg]: Treuttel, 1792).

Tsitlanadze, Tea, Karchava, Tea and Kavtaradze, Giorgi, 'Towards the clarification of the identity and sphere of activities of the missionaries who visited the Orient and Georgia in the 14th century', in: *Bulletin of the Georgian National Academy of Sciences*, vol. 3, no. 3 (Tbilisi, 2009), pp. 185–9.

Tsutsiev, Arthur, *Atlas of the Ethno-Political History of the Caucasus* (New Haven: Yale University Press, 2014).

Tubach, Jürgen, Vashalomidze, Sophia G. and Zimmer, Manfred (eds), *Caucasus during the Mongol Period / Der Kaukasus in der Mongolenzeit* (Wiesbaden: Reichert, 2012).

Tucker, Robert C., *Stalin in Power: The Revolution from Above* (New York: Norton & Company, 1990).

Tucker-Jones, Anthony, *Images of War: The Battle for the Caucasus 1942–1943* (Barnsley: Pen & Sword Military, 2018).

Tumanishvili, Dimitri, *Sak'art'velos kulturuli memkvidreobis jeglebi = Monuments of Georgia's Cultural Heritage* (Tbilisi: National Agency for Cultural Heritage Preservation, 2010).

Tvaradze, Aleksandre, '«Hunderjährige Chronik» – Georgien in der Mongolenzeit', in: Kaufhold and Kropp, *Oriens Christianus* (2007, q.v.), pp. 87–123.

— 'Der Westfeldzug von 1219–1221: Die "Mongolenerwartung" im Kreuzfahrerlager von Damiette und im christlichen Kaukasus', in: Tubach, et al., *Caucasus during the Mongol Period* (2012, q.v.), pp. 251–307.

Ullman, Richard H. *Intervention and the War: Anglo-Soviet Relations, 1917–1921* (Princeton: Princeton University Press, 1961).

Ulrichsen, Kristian Coates, *The First World War in the Middle East* (London: Hurst, 2019).

United Nations General Assembly Resolution 96 from 11 December 1946: digitallibrary.un.org/record/209873?ln=en#record-files-collapse-header (accessed 12 November 2022).

Usscher, John, *A Journey from London to Persepolis; including Wanderings in Daghestan, Georgia, Armenia, Kurdistan, Mesopotamia, and Persia* (London: Hurst and Blackett, 1865).

Vahram's Chronicle of the Armenian Kingdom in Cilicia, during the Time of the Crusades, transl. Charles Fried. Neumann (London: Oriental Translation Fund, 1831); archive.org/details/vahramschronicleoovahrrich/mode/2up.

Valiyev, Anar, 'Baku: Creating a Persian Gulf Paradise on the Caspian Sea', in: Kamrava, *The Great Game in West Asia* (2017, q.v.), pp. 243–60.

Vásáry, István, *Cumans and Tatars: Oriental Military in the Pre-Ottoman Balkans, 1185–1365* (Cambridge: Cambridge University Press, 2005).

— 'The Jochid realm: The western steppe and Eastern Europe', in: *The Cambridge History of Inner Asia: The Chinggisid Age* (2009, q.v.), pp. 67–85.

Vashalomidze, Sophia, 'Mongol invasions in the Caucasus and the Georgian source *Kartlis cxovreba*', in: Tubach, et al., *Caucasus during the Mongol Period* (2012, q.v.), pp. 309–319.

Vashalomidze, Sophia and Greisiger, Lutz (eds), *Der Christliche Orient und seine Umwelt* (Wiesbaden: Harrassowitz, 2007).

Vereschaguine, Basile [Vereshchagin, Vasilii], *Voyage dans les provinces du Caucase, 1864–1865*, trans. Ernest le Barbier and his wife, in *Le Tour du monde*, vols 17 & 19 (Paris: L. Hachette, 1868–9), vol. 17, pp. 162208 ; vol. 19, pp. 241–336.

Vigo, Graziella, *Karabakh: The Secret Garden of Armenia* (Venice: Marsilio Editori, 2013).

Villari, Luigi, *Fire and Sword in the Caucasus* (London: T. Fisher Unwin, 1906).

Vivien [de Saint-Martin], Louis, 'Die geographischen Kenntnisse der Europäer von Cirkassien', *Zeitschrift für vergleichende Erdkunde*, vol. 1, no. 3 (Magdeburg: Emil Baensch, 1842), pp. 214–47.

Voltaire (François Marie d'Arouet), *Histoire de l'empire de Russie sous Pierre le Grand*, 2 vols (no publisher given, 1763).

Wagner, Friedrich, *Schamyl als Feldherr, Sultan und Prophet und der Kaukasus* (Leipzig: Gustav Remmelmann, 1854).

Wagner, Moritz, *Der Kaukasus und das Land der Kosaken in den Jahren 1843 bis 1846* (Dresden: Arnoldsche, 1848).

— *Reise nach dem Ararat und dem Hochland Armeniens* (Stuttgart: Cotta'sche Buchhandlung, 1848).

— *Reise nach Kolchis und nach den deutschen Colonien jenseits des Kaukasus* (Leipzig: Arnoldsche, 1850).

Wakhoucht, le Tsarévitch [Vakhushti Bagration], *Description géographique de la Géorgie*, trans. Marie-Félicité Brosset (St Petersburg: Typographie de l'Académie, 1842).

Walker, Christopher J., *Armenia and Karabakh: The Struggle for Unity* (London: Minority Rights Group, 1991).

— 'World War I and the Armenian genocide', in: Hovannisian, *The Armenian People*, vol. 2 (1997, q.v.), pp. 239–74.

Walo, Ellen A., *Saudi Inc.: The Arabian Kingdom's Pursuit of Profit and Power* (New York: Pegasus Books, 2019).

Wanderer, the [Walter Tschudi Lyall], *Notes on the Caucasus* (London: Macmillan, 1883).

Ware, Robert Bruce, 'Ethnicity and democracy in Dagestan', in: NCEEER, 28 November 2001 (Washington DC: The National Council for Eurasian and East European Research,2001); ucis.pitt.edu/nceeer/2001_814-30f_Ware.pdf (accessed 12 February 2022).

Ware, Robert Bruce and Kisriev, Enver, *Dagestan: Russian Hegemony and Islamic Resistance in the North Caucasus* (Armonk, NY: M.E. Sharpe, 2010).

Wassaf al-Hadrat (Shihab al-Din Abd'Allah ibn Fadl-Allah Shirazi), *Tajziyat al-amsar wa taziyat al-a'sar (Geschichte Wassafs)*, ed. and trans. Josef von Hammer-Purgstall (Vienna: K.-K. Hof- und Staatsdruckerei, 1856).

Wilson, Robert, *A Sketch of the Military and Political Power of Russia in the Year 1817*, published as *The Great Game: Britain and Russia in Central Asia*, ed. Martin Ewans, vol. 4 (1817; reprint, London: RoutledgeCurzon, 2004).

Winrow, Gareth, 'Turkey's energy policy in the Middle East and South Caucasus', in: Kamrava, *The Great Game in West Asia* (2017, q.v.), pp. 83–103.

Zardabli, Ismail bey, *The History of Azerbaijan from Ancient Times to the Present Day* (London: Rossendale Books, 2004).

Zürcher, Christoph, *The Post-Soviet Wars: Rebellion, Ethnic Conflict, and Nationhood in the Caucasus* (New York: New York University Press, 2009).

Zürrer, Werner, *Kaukasien 1918–1921. Der Kampf der Grossmächte um die Landbrücke zwischen Schwarzrm und kaspischem Meer* (Düsseldorf: Verlag, 1978).

List of Maps

1. The major historical sites in the Caucasus after ca. 1000 CE (inner front endpaper). Satellite imagery © NASA; visibleearth.nasa.gov.

2. Georgia's expansion under King Davit IV (r. 1089–1125) and Queen Tamar (r. 1184–1213) (p. 19). Adapted from: commons.wikimedia.org/wiki/File:David_IV_map_de.png, authors Don-kun, Bourrichon.

3. The Armenian Kingdom of Cilicia, 1198–1375 (p. 59). Adapted from: de.wikipedia.org/wiki/K%C3%B6nigreich_Kleinarmenien#/media/Datei:Cilician_Armenia-en.svg, no author given.

4. The partition of Georgia in 1491 CE (p. 83). Adapted from: commons.wikimedia.org/wiki/File:Caucasus_topographic_map-fr.svg, author Bourrichon.

5. The Russian conquest of the Caucasus by late 1829 and the foundation of Russian forts to 1838 (pp. 124–25). Adapted from: Tsutsiev, Arthur, *Atlas of the Ethno-Political History of the Caucasus* (New Haven: Yale University Press, 2014), maps 5, 6.

6. Territorial claims of Azerbaijan and Georgia at the Paris Peace Conference, June 1919 (p. 208). Adapted from: Hewsen, Robert H., *Armenia: A Historical Atlas* (Chicago: The University of Chicago Press, 2001), maps 231, 232.

7. Territorial claims of Armenia at the Paris Peace Conference, June 1919 and US President Wilson's arbitration, November 1920 (p. 209). Adapted from: Hewsen, Robert H., *Armenia: A Historical Atlas* (Chicago: The University of Chicago Press, 2001), maps. 227, 229; commons.wikimedia.org/wiki/File:Treaty_of_S%C3%A8vres_%26Soviet_Republics_of_Transcaucasia.jpg.

8. Greatest extent of advance of the Armed Forces of South Russia, early October 1919 (p. 219). Adapted from: Lehovich, Dimitry V., *White against Red: The Life of General Anton Denikin* (New York: W.W. Norton, 1974), p. 355.

9. Operation Edelweiss, 25 July 1942–9 October 1943 with the key army commanders (p. 235). Adapted from: commons.wikimedia.org/wiki/File:Ww2_map23_july42_Nov_42.jpg. Source: public domain. Department of History, United States Military Academy.

10. Main gas and oil pipelines in the Caucasus (pp. 256–57). Adapted from: Baumer, Christoph, *The History of Central Asia*, vol. 4: *The Age of Decline and Revival* (London: I.B.Tauris, 2018), pp. 264f.

11. The Second Karabakh War, 27 September–10 November 2020 (p. 299). Adapted from: commons.wikimedia.org/wiki/File:2020_Nagorno-Karabakh_war.svg, author Kalj, based on commons.wikimedia.org/wiki/File:2020_Nagorno-Karabakh_war_map.png, author Golden.

12. The Caucasus in the twenty-first century (inner back endpaper). Adapted from: Baumer, Christoph, *History of the Caucasus,* vol. 1: *At the Crossroads of Empires* (London: I.B.Tauris/Bloomsbury, 2021), inner back endpaper.

Photo Credits

All photos are by the author with the exception of the following:

AKG Images, Berlin, Germany: figs. 13, 28, 40, 82, 119–121.

Alamy Ltd, Abingdon, Great Britain: figs. 5, 64, 76, 87, 88, 95, 96, 98, 100, 101, 104, 105, 113, 114, 117, 122, 123, 125–127, 133, 135, 140, 149–151, 153, 156.

Alexxx, via Wikipedia: commons.wikimedia.org/wiki/File:North Ossetia. Alagirsky District. Monument Uastyrdzhi PB060319 2200.jpg. Licensed under Creative Commons 2.0 Generic license: fig. 148.

Baku Nobel Heritage Fund, Azerbaijan: fig. 92.

British Museum, London, Great Britain: fig. 10.

Cathedral Museum, Holy Etchmiadzin, Etchmiadzin, Armenia: fig. 94.

Getty Images, Seattle, USA: figs. 161, 162.

Getty Museum, Los Angeles, USA: figs. 54, 55.

Hormann, Christoph, Freiburg, GermanyIImagico.de: fig. 1

iStock, Huntington Beach, USA: fig. 81.

Masis, via Wikipedia: commons.wikimedia.org/wiki/File:8.1.8.1 Ամրոց Հալիձոր (Հալիձորի բերդ),.jpg. Licensed under Creative Commons 2.0 Generic license: fig. 62.

Mesrop Mashtots Institute of Ancient Manuscripts Matenadaran, Yerevan, Armenia: fig. 35.

Ourishian, Serouji, via Wikipedia: commons.wikimedia.org/wiki/File:Yerevan 2012 February.jpg. Licensed under Creative Commons 2.0 Generic license: fig. 105.

Planet of Hotels, planetofhotels.com/guide/de/tuerkei/erzurum: fig. 107.

Roinashvili, Alexander, via Wikipedia: commons.wikimedia.org/wiki/ File: იმამი შამილი შვილებთან ერთად. ალექსანდრე როინაშვილი.jpg. Licensed under Creative Commons 2.0 Generic license: fig. 89.

Svirkin, Alexander, Nalchik, Russian Federation: front jacket, figs. 24, 65–71, 75, 83, 84, 86, 90, 102, 112, 116, 138, 146, 147, 152.

Vahanyan, Armand, Yerevan: fig. 103

Weber, Therese, Arlesheim, Switzerland: back inner jacket flap.

Witt, Travis K, via Wikipedia: commons.wikimedia.org/wiki/File:Haghartsin_Patron_Relief_Zakaryan_Brothers.JPG. Licensed under Creative Commons 2.0 Generic license: fig. 17

All efforts have been made to name or identify copyright holders. We will endeavour to rectify any unintended omissions in future editions of this work, upon receipt of evidence of relevant intellectual property rights.

Acknowledgements

This book is based on ten journeys undertaken between 2001 and 2019. My research was successful only thanks to dozens of kind people in Armenia, Azerbaijan, Crimea (Ukraine), Dagestan (Russian Federation), Georgia, Iran, Kalmykia (Russian Federation) and Turkey; to all of them I remain grateful. The book itself was produced with the help of several people. Most preferred to remain anonymous; others are briefly acknowledged here, in alphabetical order:

Nijat Azimzade, Baku, Azerbaijan, who kindly gave me references concerning the ethnogenesis of Azerbaijani people.

Jay Mens, University of Cambridge, Great Britain, who pointed me in the direction of a quote from Henry Kissinger's *A World Restored* (2013 [1957]).

Alexander Svirkin, Nalchik, Kabardino-Balkaria, who photographed on my account in Dagestan, Chechnya, North Ossetia and Kabardino-Balkaria (all in the Russian Federation) and in Abkhazia (de jure Georgia). Alexander Svirkin also gathered interesting information about the places he photographed.

Natia Tavadze, Tbilisi, Georgia, who very kindly translated several ancient Georgian inscriptions and who was in 2018 an excellent guide during my last photo journey through Georgia.

Armand Vahanyan, Yerevan, Armenia, who photographed for me the Sardarapat Memorial located in the Armenian Province of Armavir.

Therese Weber, Arlesheim, Switzerland, who accompanied me on most of these journeys to the Caucasus and contributed to the research.

Indexes

Index: Concepts

Page locators in *italic* refer to captions and those in **bold** refer to maps. 'n' after a locator indicates the endnote number.

A

Abbasids 50, *71*, 130
Abkhazians 147, 164, 270, 310, 338n108
    Russian passport for 272
    see also Abkhazia
the Abzakh 115–16, 119
adat (customary laws) 148, 149, 152–3, 160, 166
Adyghe people 276, 323n8, 334n7
Afghans
    Abdali Afghans 107
    Sunni Afghan Pashtuns 102
    see also Afghanistan
Alans (Ossetians) 15, 37
Albanian Church 246
alphabets 103
    Batumi Alphabetic Tower, Georgia *267*
    Cyrillic alphabet 226
    Latin alphabet 226, 331n12
    see also languages
Aq Qoyunlu 76, 81, *82*, 84, *168*
Armen-Shahs of Akhlat 20–1
Armenian Catholic Church 110
    Armenian Catholic patriarchate of Cilicia 110
    Armenian Catholics 47, 320n171
    autocephaly 137
    Catholic Armenian *millet* 166
    Russian Empire and 137
Armenian Genocide (1915–1917) 72, 178, 185, 186–9, 328n25
    1915 escape of Armenians from Musa Dagh 188
    1918 Armistice of Mudros 188
    Armenian Genocide Memorial, Tsitsernakaberd *188*, *244*, 245
    Armenian refugees 190, 194, 329n87
    Armenians of Bitlis, Muş and Sasun 189–90
    culprits condemned to death 189
    Dashnaks: Operation Nemesis 189, 328n34
    death marches to the Syrian Desert 187–8
    deportations of Armenians 186–7, 189
    Doğu Perinçek v. Switzerland 189
    ethnic cleansing 187
    forced conversion to Islam 188
    Hamidiye and 176, 187
    official recognition of 189
    Ottoman CUP triumvirate 187, 188
    public denial of 189
    Sardarapat war memorial *198*, 245
    as state-organized genocide 188
    survivors 188
    Teşkilat-ı Mahsusa (Special Organization) 165, 187–8, 189
    Young Turks 175
    Van, siege of 189–90, *189*
    see also Armenians and the Ottoman Empire
Armenian Mekhitarist congregation 109–10
    monastery of San Lazzaro, Venice *109*
    schism 110
Armenian nationalism 167, 175–8, 200, 245
    see also Dashnaks; Hunchaks
Armenian Orthodox Church 3, 72
    Armenian Creed 60
    Armenian identity and 72, 80
    autocephaly 80
    Azerbaijan and Armenian churches 246
    Catholic Church, union with 44, 47, 60, 67, 68, 69, 71–2, 80, 109–10, 320n171
    Catholicosate 44, 54, *57*, 60, *61*, 71, 80, 138, *215*
    Catholicosate in Etchmiadzin 44, 80
    Cilicia 53, 60–1, 67, 68, 69, 71–2, 80, *215*
    confiscation of revenues by Russians 167, 169, 175, 180, 326n128
    crozier (staff) *177*
    Dashnaks and 167, 169, 175–6, 180
    Decretum pro Armenis 80
    icons 24–5
    intellectual isolation 109
    Latinization of 60–1, 69
    liturgy and rites 24–6, 60–1, 68, 72, 109
    Miaphysite Armenian Orthodox Church 44, 68
    papacy and 44, 60, 67, 68, 69, 71, 72
    Patriarch of Constantinople 80
    pentarchy 80
    revival of 245
    Rubenids of Cilicia and 53
    Russian Empire and 166, 167
    schism 54, 80
    Soviet Union and 226
    synods 25, 60, 61, 69, 71–2, 80
    tax exemption 107
Armenian Socialist Democrat Hunchakian Revolutionary Party (SDHP) *see* Hunchaks
Armenian Revolutionary Federation (ARF/Dashnaktsutyun) *see* Dashnaks
Armenians
    anti-Armenian pogroms 173, 175, 186, *250*, 251, 252, 253
    Armenian Americans 333n44
    Armenian Fatimid vizierates in Egypt 50–3, 57
    Armenian refugees 190, 194, 209, 215, 329n87
    in Azerbaijan 203, 251
    Azeris/Armenians ethnic strife 180, 181, 182, 251
    under Byzantium 11, 50
    in Cilicia 209, 215
    Crimean Armenians 80
    in Cyprus 72
    deportations of 96, 98, 186–7, 189, 251, 252
    diaspora 72, 98, 147, 252, 264, 302, 303–4, 325n48
    discrimination against Christian Armenians 98, 107, 166, 174, 322n34
    in Georgia 18, 24–5, 200, 203, 329n87
    Georgians/Armenians antagonism 179
    in India 98
    in Iran 96, *96*, 98, *98*, *99*, 138, 176
    in Lebanon 252
    Miaphysite Armenians 18, 23
    Muslim Armenians 50
    Russian Armenians 167, 169, 185, 186
    in the Russian Empire 138, 147, 167, 164, 174, 190, 325n48
    in Tbilisi 174
    World War II 185, 239, 240
    see also Armenian Genocide; Armenians and the Ottoman Empire
Armenians and the Ottoman Empire 4, 87, 147, 166, 167, 169, 174, 199–200, 325n48
    1878 Berlin Congress 175
    1909 Adana massacre 175, 176
    1918 May battles *198*, 200
    Armenian Orthodox Church 138
    'Armenian Question' 178, 209–10
    Christianity 4
    equalization of status for Christian Armenians and Assyrians 176
    Hamidiye and 175, 176
    massacres 146, 175, 176, 186, 328n34
    millets 166
    Patriarch of Constantinople 4, 138, 166
    persecution 175
    Sardarapat victory *198*, 200, 245
    taxes 166, 175
    Zeitun blockade 175
    see also Armenian Genocide; Armenians
Armeno-Tatar War (1905–1906) 182
armistices
    1917 Armistice of Erzincan 194, 195
    1918 Armistice of Mudros 188, 196, 200, 203–4
Army of Islam 201–2, 329n102
Artuqids of Diyarbakır 20–1
the Assassins (the Nizariyya) 42, 51–2, 53, 61
Avars 93, 111, 118, 180, 240, 242, 283–4, 286
    Avar royal family 153, 156
Ayyubids 30, 35, 53
    Cilicia and 50, 57
    Mongols and 65
Azerbaijani Popular Front Party (APF) 252–4
Azerbaijanis 144, 312
    1990 'Black January' (Soviet military intervention, Baku) *250*, 251, 252, 253
    Azeris (Muslim Azerbaijanis) 167, 181, 195, 326n126, 327n206
    Azeris/Armenians ethnic strife 180, 181, 182, 251
    ethnicity of 4, 100, 181
    Hummet (Muslim Social Democratic Party) 182
    in Iran 144
    as peasants or low-skilled workers 174, 181
    see also Azerbaijan

B

Bagrationi dynasty 22, 26, 83, 96, 101, 104, 107, 136, 137, 326n95
    end of 136
Bagratuni dynasty 26
Balkan League 187
Balkan Wars
    1912–1913 First Balkan War 178, 184, 187
    Balkan refugees and deportation of Armenians 187
Baltic War (1854–1855) 171
Battle of 'Ain Jalut 42–3, 65
Battle at Aladja Dagh (Alacadağ) 170
Battle of Aradeti 81
Battle of Aslanduz 142–3
Battle of Baghavard (Yeghevard) 107
Battle of Başgedikler 160
Battle of Basiani 27
Battle of Bazaleti Teimuraz 98
Battle for the Caucasus 238
Battle of Çeşme 135
Battle of Chalagan 76
Battle of Chaldiran 85, 87
Battle of Chikhori 81, 83
Battle of Didgori 10, 16–17, *16*
Battle of Dighomi 89
Battle of Ertsukhi 14
Battle of Garisi 89
Battle of Germenchuk (Kermenchik) 153
Battle of Hattin 57
Battle of Homs, First 65
Battle of Homs, Second 44–5
Battle of Homs, Third 68
Battle of the Kalka River 33
Battle of Kapetron 10
Battle of Khalkhin Gol 231
Battle of Khresili 111
Battle of the Kondurcha River 75
Battle of Köprüköy 191
Battle of Köse Dağ 40, 62
Battle of Krtsanisi 135
Battle of Kurijan 107
Battle of Manzikert 11, 20, 50, 317n6
Battle of Marabda 98
Battle of Mari (Disaster of Mari) 65, 66, *66*
Battle of Marj al-Saffar (Battle of Shaqhab) 46
Battle of Martqopi 98
Battle of Myriokephalon 57
Battle of Nakhchivan 76
Battle of Otlukbeli 82, 322n33
Battle of Partskhisi 90
Battle of Samadlo 89
Battle of Sardrud 76
Battle of Sarmeda (Battle of the Field of Blood) 16
Battle of Shamkor 25
Battle of Soltanabad 325n33
Battle of Tashiskari 96
Battle of the Terek River 43–4
Battle of Torches 92
Battle of Tsitsamuri 96
Battle of Yassıçemen 35
Bene Boghusaks 50
Berlin Congress (1878) 166, 167, 170, 175, 177, 184
Bible 177
    Gospel of 1211, Haghpat monastery 23
    illuminated gospels 57, *96*, *98*
Black Death 48, 74, 76
Black Hundreds 173, 180
blood debt/feuds 143, 152, 156, 165
blood money 47, 103
Bolsheviks 173, 179, 189, 326n154
    1907 Tbilisi bank robbery 173, 179
    1917–1920 Russian Civil Wars 217, 218–19, 222
    in Baku 180
    famine 218
    raiding banks and money transports 173, 179
    strikes and violence as political tool 182
    'War Communism' 218
    World War I as armed class struggle 193
    see also Bolshevik Russia; Russian Civil Wars
Buddhism 64, 67
    Burkhan Bakshin Altan Sume *131*
    Kalmykia 130, *131*, 276, *276*
    Russian Empire and 148
    Tibetan Buddhism 225, 276
Bulgarian April Revolt (1876) 165

C

calendars
    Gregorian calendar 191, 317n5
    Julian calendar 317n5
    Muslim lunar calendar 317n5
capitalism 179, 181
castles 36, 50, 66
    Baghras (castle of Gaston) 58–9, 320n43
    Finckenstein castle 141
    Korykos sea castle *56*
    Kveshi castle *34*
    Mansau castle *128*
    Pardzerpert castle *51*
    Samtsevrisi castle church *305*
    Vahka castle 53, *55*
    see also fortresses; palaces
Catholicism
    1141 Synod of Jerusalem 60
    Armenian Orthodox Church, union with 44, 47, 60, 67, 68, 69, 71–2, 80, 109–10, 320n171
    Cilicia 47, 110
    conversion from Orthodox Churches 89, 109, 110
    Georgia 46–7
    Georgian Orthodox Church and 80, 260
    Khanbaliq Archbishopric 47
    missionaries 46–7, 166
    Nakhchivan Armeno-Catholic bishopric 47
    Ottoman Empire, special protection of Catholics 89
    proselytism 47
    Sultaniyeh Archbishopric 47
    see also Armenian Catholic Church; papacy
Catholicosate 24, 43
    Abkhazia 43, 82
    Abraham III 107
    Albania 81, 137
    Ambrosi, Catholicos-Patriarch 226
    Anton II 137
    Armenian Orthodox Church 44, 54, 57, 60, *61*, 71, 80, 138, 215
    Barsegh I 54
    'Catholicosate of the Great House of Cilicia' 80, 322n24
    Davit 79
    Davit II 322n29
    Davit III 81, 322n29
    Davit IV 322n29
    Davit V 243
    Eprem II 243
    in Etchmiadzin 44, 80
    Garegin II 302
    Georgia and 30–1
    Gevorg V Surenian, Patriarch-Catholicos 176
    Grigor II Vkayaser 52, 54
    Grigor III 54
    Grigor IV Tgha 60
    Grigor V 60
    Grigor VI Apirat 60
    Grigor VII 67, 68
    Grigor IX 80
    Ilia II 243
    Ioane IV 15
    Ioane VI 24–5
    Ioane VII 23–4
    Jacob of Tarsus 69
    Kevork (Gevorg) V 226
    Kevork VI 245
    Khoren I 226
    Khrimian, Mkrtich, Patriarch-Catholicos 176
    Kirakos I of Khor Virap 80
    Kostantin I 57
    Kostantin III 69
    Kostantin VI of Vahka 80
    Mar Yahballaha III, Nestorian Catholicos 67
    Matteos II Izmirlian, Patriarch-Catholicos 176
    Mesrop I of Cilicia 71–2
    Mukhitar I 69, 71
    Nerses IV Shnorhali 57
    Poghos (Paul) I 72
    Shio II 322n29
    Stephen IV 67
    Theodore III 322n29
    Vazken I 245
Celali rebellions 96
cemeteries
    Armenia 5, 94
    Dargavs, medieval graveyard *116*
    funeral stele *266*
    funerary chapels 5, 94
    khachkars 5, 94
    seven türbe (tombs), Yeddi Gumbaz *142*
    tombstones 94
    see also necropolis
Central Caspian Dictatorship 202
Chagataids 43, 319n153, 321n85
    Mongol Chagatai Khanate 44
Chalcedonian Creed 60, 68, 109, 110
Chechen Wars 262
    1994–1996 First Chechen War 255, 276, 282, 284, 286
    1995 Chechen terrorist attack, Budyonnovsk 276, 278, 282
    1996 Chechen terrorist attack, Kizlyar 282
    1996 Khasavyurt Peace Agreement 283
    1999–2000 Second Chechen War 272, 280, 284, 286, 288, 290
    2002 Chechen Moscow theatre hostage-taking 286
    2004 Chechen-Ingush terrorist attack, Nazran 280, 286
    2004 Chechen terrorist attack, Beslan school 278, 280, 286, 294
    2005 terrorist attack, Nalchik 278, 286
    Grozny 282, 283, 284, 286
    'Islamic charity organizations' 282
    Russian Federation and 6, 255, 282–4, 286
    Wahhabism 282, 284, 286, 335n54
Chechens 118, 324n15
    2008 'black widows' terrorist attack, Vladikavkaz 280
    2008 Georgian–Russian War and 293
    2008, 2010 terrorist attack, Vladikavkaz 280, 294
    2014–2015 Eastern Ukraine 293
    2022–present Russian invasion of Ukraine and 293
    Caucasian jihadists 290
    Chechen refugees 272, 287, 305
    Chechens/Russians clashes 276
    deportation in World War II 240, 242
    kidnapping by 276, 283
    Nagorno-Karabakh conflict, Chechen mercenaries 261, 333n68
    Russian Empire and 129, 150, 162, 165
    terrorism 276, 278, 280, 282, 286, 293, 294
    in Turkey 165
    see also Chechen Wars; Chechnya; the Kadyrovtsy
Christianity 279
    conversion from Islam to 17, 33
    Ottoman Christians 166
    see also Catholicism; Orthodox Church; Protestantism
churches
    apses 30, 85
    Astvatsatsin Cathedral, Harichavank, Armenia *24*
    Astvatsatsin Church, Akhtala Monastery, Armenia 25, *30*
    Astvatsatsin Church, Goshavank Monastery, Armenia *25*
    Astvatsatsin Church, Haghartsin Monastery, Armenia *26*, *27*
    Astvatsatsin Church, Noravank, Armenia *40*
    Astvatsatsin Church, Sevanavank Monastery, Armenia *144*
    Astvatsatsin Church, Tegher Monastery, Armenia *37*
    Azerbaijan and Armenian churches 246
    bell towers 20, 85
    burial vaults 33
    Cathedral of Nikortsminda, Georgia *103*
    Cathedral of Our Lady, Gelati Monastery (founded by King Davit IV) *12*, *13*
    Cathedral of St Grigor the Illuminator, Yerevan *263*
    Church of the Apostles, Sevanavank Monastery, Armenia *144*
    Church of the Archangels, Gremi *86*, *88*
    Church dedicated to the Blessed Virgin Mary, South Ossetia *266*
    Church of the Dormition, Ananuri, Georgia *104*
    Church of the Dormition, Cave Monastery, Georgia *21*
    Church of the Holy Cross, Haghpat Monastery *20*
    Church of the Redeemer, Ananuri, Georgia *104*

Church of Saints Quiricus and Julitta, Zarati, Georgia *102*
Church of St Gregory, Haghpat Monastery *20*
Church of St Grigor, Goshavank Monastery, Armenia *25*
Church of St Grigor, Haghartsin Monastery, Armenia *26*
Church of St Grigor the Enlightener, Harichavank, Armenia *24*
Cilicia 320n18
dedicated to Maximus the Confessor, Katskhi *11*
destruction of 35
funerary chapels *5*, *94*
Gandzasar Cathedral *36*
gavit 26, *33*, *37*
Holy Saviour Cathedral, Armenia *214*
Holy Trinity Cathedral or Tsminda Sameba, Tbilisi *271*
Khobayr Monastery Church, Armenia *43*
Kutaisi Cathedral *101*
Martyrs' Monastery Church, Martvili, Georgia *14*
Mother of God Church, Pitareti Monastery, Georgia *31*, *32*
Monastery of the Nativity, Katskhi *9*
reconstruction of 100
rock church, Geghard Monastery, Armenia *33*
Samtavisi Cathedral, Shida Kartli *8*
Samtsevrisi Castle Church, Georgia *305*
'soldiers' church' of Zorats, Armenia *46*
St Gayane Church, Etchmiadzin, Armenia *79*
St George Monastery, Alaverdi, Georgia *93*, *96*
St Grigori Church, Ubisa, Georgia *74*, *77*
St Mary Magdalene Church, Nalchik *278*
Tanahativank, monastery church, Armenia *45*
turned into mosques *93*, *96*
Circassians
as Adyghe 323n8
Circassian language 116
Circassian–Russian defensive pacts 119
displacement of 164–5
Great Britain and 152
Islamization of 149
konak 116, 118
Ottomans and 4, 119, 147, 149, 163, 164
Russian Empire and 147, 148, 149, 150–2
Shamil, Imam and 159–60
slavery 89, 116, 89, 116, 119, 151, 163, 164
social structures 115–16
taxes 89
Turkey, emigration to 164
coinage 87
Armenia 100
Azerbaijan 100
Georgia *17*, 81, 321n1
Cold War 240
Iran 240–1
militarization of South Caucasian border states 242
oil and gas 240–1

Soviet Union 240–1
US 241
Collective Security Treaty Organization (CSTO) 295, 298, 302
Commonwealth of Independent States (CIS) 252, 254, 260, 270, 306, 337n73
communism 169
War Communism 218, 226–7
see also Soviet Union
Cossacks 122, 180
anti-Bolsheviks Cossack uprising 218
Circassia and 164
as commissioned pirates of the steppes 122
economic model 128, 129
first Russian military lines and 122–30
hereditary membership 129
as 'irregulars' 114, 129, *151*
Old Believers 122–3
Ottomans and 122
Raskolnik Cossacks 123, 126
Russian Empire and 126–9, 131, 145, 166
Russian 'outer' frontiers and 114, 122
as Slav-Tatar ethnic hybrid 122
Soviet 'de-Cossackization' policy 218, 224
Soviet deportation and massacre of 218
stanitsas (military settlements) 122, 126, 129, 130, 166
taxes 129
weaponry 129, 131
White armies and 218–19, 222
Cossacks: hosts 122, 126, 224
ataman 126, 129
Black Sea Host 122, 129
Don Cossacks 122–3, 128, 129, 131, 132, 218, 222, 238, *241*, 330n209, 332n71
Greben (Ridge) Host 122, 123
krug 126, 129
Kuban Host 122, 129, 130, *151*, 166, 218–19
Terek Host 122–3, 126, 128, 129, 166
Ukrainian hosts 122
Yaik (Ural) Cossacks 132
Zaporizhzhian Cossacks 119, 122, 130–1
Covid-19 pandemic 294
Crimean Tatars 96, 98, 129
1562–1563 Russian–Crimean war 121
campaign to Dagestan 108
Crimean Tatar dynasty of the Genghisid Giray 84
Georgia and 88
North Caucasus and 114, 115, 121
Ottomans and 92, 108, 115, 121, 122
Russia and 92, 119, 130–1
slavery/slave trade 88–9, 92, 119, 122
tribute payments to 88–9, 322n52
Crimean War (1853–1856) 138, 160–1, 165, 166, *168*
almost a global war 326n147
Treaty of Paris 161, 169, 170, 171
Crusaders 15, 22, 51, 52–3, *62*
1099 Jerusalem, capture by 14, 51
Byzantium and 14, 27, 53–4
Cilicia and 53–4, 57–8, 63, 64
Crusader Latin Empire 27
Latin Crusaders 53
Mamelukes and 64, 66

see also Crusader States; Knights Hospitaller; Templars; Teutonic Knights
Crusades
First Crusade 12, 53
Third Crusade 57, 58
Fourth Crusade 27
Fifth Crusade 31
Seventh Crusade 63, 64
anti-Ottoman Crusade 81
Georgia and 31–2, 35
papacy and 67, 81, 99
the Seljuks and 12, 53
culture
cultural diversity 4
Leitkultur (guiding culture) 4
Cyprus Convention (1878) 170

D

the Dadianis 83
Dagestanis 118, 240
Caucasian jihadists 290
Dagestani Avar imams: jihad of 149, 152–63
Lezgian Dagestanis 96
relocated to Chechnya and returned to Dagestan 242, 246
Russia and 104
Russian Empire and 150, 162
Danishmendid dynasty 50, 55
Dargans 118, 240, 242
Dashnaks (Dashnaktsutyun, Armenian Revolutionary Federation—ARF) 167, 175, 181, 182, 194
Armenian Genocide: Operation Nemesis 189, 328n34
Armenian Orthodox Church and 167, 169, 175–6, 180
attacks against high authorities 175, 176
Baku unrest and 173, 175, 176, 178
Central Committee for Armenian Self-Defence 169
CUP and 176, 178
guerrilla war and *fedayi* 175, 176, 178
in Iran 178
mafia-like methods 167, 176
nationalism 175
objective 175, 176
Plan of Action for the Caucasus 169
Russian strategies against 176
six Armenian *vilayets* 175, 176, 204, 207
socialism 175, 176
Soviet dissolution of 225
terrorism 175
World War I 185, 202, 205
World War II 239
Young Turks and 176
defence towers 118
Egikal *115*
Erzi *121*
Galiata, *118*
Goor *148*
Nij *37*
Targim *147*
Definitive Treaty between Britain and Iran 325n38
deities
'old wise man' *276*
Uastyrdzhi *278*, *279*

democracy 274
as retreating 274
Western liberal democracy 334n1
deportations
of Armenians 96, 98, 186–7, 189, 251, 252
of Georgians *86*, 135, 136
Ingush, deportation and return after World War II 240, 242, 246, 279–80
Safavid deportations *86*, 96, 98, 99
Soviet deportations 218, 225, 227, 239, 240, 242, 276
Dominican Order 40, 42, 46–7, 69
drug trafficking 262, 272, 290
Dzungars 132

E

earthquakes
Armenia *25*, 245, 251
Ganja 18
Georgia *93*
Tmogvi *13*
East India Company 105, 141
see also British Empire; Great Britain
Ecumenical Councils
1438 Ferrara 80
1439 Florence 80
ethnicity 332n4
Abkhazia, ethnic and social conflicts 197–8, 199, 265
Azerbaijanis 4, 100, 181
conflict and 173
Dagestan, ethnic diversity 275, 286–7, 288
empire and ethnic diversity 4, 178
ethnic cleansing 167, 182, 187, 267
ethnic displacement 101, 130, 163–4, 167
ethnic diversity 4, 100
ethnic engineering 130
ethnic identities 3, 4
ethnic Russians 4, 137, 167
ethnically based wars 274, 334n2
Georgia, ethnic and social conflicts 4, 196–9, 265
nationalism and 166–7, 175, 182, 274
North Caucasus, ethnic diversity 246, 274
power and 53
Russian Empire: ethno-religious diversity 4, 148, 167
smaller ethnicities defined as minorities 167
South Caucasus, ethnic and territorial conflicts 249
Soviet deportations of ethnic groups 218
Soviet Union, ethnic diversity 224, 227, 248, 331n3
state and ethnic homogeneity 4, 178, 203
Turkic peoples 100
European Bank for Reconstruction and Development (EBRD) 272

F

Fatimids 8, 12
    Armenian Fatimid vizierates in Egypt 50–3, 57
    Ismailism 53
fortresses
    Agarani 11
    Akhaltsikhe *90*, 146
    Amberd 26
    Anahşa, Pozantı *51*
    Anamur (Mamure Kalesi) *62*, *63*
    Ananuri *104*
    Anazarbos (Anavarza Kalesi) 54, *58*, 68
    Ayas (Laiazzo, Yumurtalık) *62*
    Azov 119, 122
    Bayburt *193*
    Burnaya 149
    Byzantine fortresses 12, *51*, *56*, *58*, *63*, *71*
    Chokh 162
    Crac des Chevaliers 66
    Dmanisi 18
    Gori 85
    Gremi Royal Fortress *86*
    Gunib 162
    Halidzor 106, *106*
    Hromkla 54–5, 57, *57*, *61*, 67
    Kars *168*
    Khertvisi *78*
    Korykos *56*
    Kurtin *76*
    Kveshi *34*
    Lampron *52*, 53, 61, 320n18
    Nazran 149
    Oltisni 18
    Russian forts **124**, 126, 134, 151–2
    Samshvilde 12
    Shlisselburg (Schlüsselburg) 149
    Sis *71*
    Svyatoi Krest (Holy Cross) fortress 126
    Tell Hamdun (Toprak Kale) *66*, 67
    Terskaya Krepost 92, 121, 122
    Vladikavkaz fortification 134
    Vnezapnaya 149
    Yernjak (Alinja) 35
    see also castles
Franciscan Order 47
Fratres Unitores, Armeno-Catholic Order 47, 69, 72

G

the Gelovanis 83
Georgian Dream Party 309, 310
Georgian Orthodox Church 3, 11, 37, 43, 47
    abolition of the patriarchate 137
    autocephaly 68, 80, 135, 137, 180, 194
    Catholicism and 80, 260
    Chalcedonian Dyophysites 23
    conversion to Catholicism 89
    corruption 14, 15, 101
    divisions within 43
    as exarchate of the Russian Orthodox Church 137, 324n13
    liturgy 24–5, 137
    Mkhargrdzeli, Ivane: conversion to 23–4
    reform 15
    revival of 243
    Russian liturgy 137
    Russification of 137
    Second Church Council 18
    Soviet persecution of 225, 226
    subordination to the state 15
    Synod of Ruisi–Urbnisi 15
    Treaty of Georgiyevsk and 135
    World Council of Churches (WCC) and 243
Georgians
    in Abkhazia 310
    Anarchists 179
    deportation of *86*, 135, 136
    Federalists 179
    Georgian Mensheviks 181, 195, 196–7, 198
    Georgian opposition 179
    Georgian refugees 270, 310
    Georgians/Armenians antagonism 179
    in Kutaisi 174
    nationalism 167, 179, 243–4, 265
    in the Ottoman Empire 170
    Party of Independence 179
    Progressive Democrats 179
    rural aspect of 174
    in the Russian Federation 305
    Social Democrats 179, 181
    socialism 179–81
Ghilman cavalry 94–5
Ghilzai tribal federation 102
glasnost 248, 249, 265, 283
Golden Horde 36, 42, 43, 46, 48, 74, 114, 319n138
    Blue Horde 74
    Timur-e Lang and 75
    White Horde 74
graves *see* cemeteries; necropolis
Great Game 106
Great Northern War (1700–1721) 105
'Green Russian' guerrillas 199

H

Hamidiye Alayları ('Hamid's Regiments') 175
    Armenian Genocide 175, 187
Hasan-Jalalids 81
heresy 47, 50, 53, 108, 110
Hethumids of Cilicia 50, 53, 55, 56, 57
    Anamur fortress *63*
    Greek Orthodoxy 53
    Lampron fortress, ancestral seat of *52*, 53, 61, 320n18
Hohenstaufen dynasty 60
Hotaki dynasty 102
Hunchaks (Armenian Socialist Democrat Hunchakian Revolutionary Party—SDHP) 167, 169, 175, 181
    mass demonstrations and strikes 175
    Zeitun 175
Hundred Years War 69, 72
Hussite anti-papal reform movement 80

I

identity
    Armenia 4, 72, 80, 169
    Azerbaijan 4, 181
    collective identity 3
    ethnic identities 3, 4
    Georgia 4
    Ossetian identity 278
    religion and 3
    secular identity 169
    South Ossetian identity 197
    state and 4
industrialization 174, 227
    industrial workers 174
    Russian Empire 165, 174
    Soviet Union 226, 227
Ingush 118, 324n15
    2022–present Russian invasion of Ukraine and 293
    deportation and return after World War II 240, 242, 246, 279–80
International Crisis Group 309
International Monetary Fund (IMF) 272, 274
International Security Assistance Force (ISAF) 310, 337n71
Iranian Cossack Brigade 178, 327n182
Islam 279
    circumcision 10, 13, 35
    conversion from Christianity to 10, 13, 27, 35, 43, 50, 57, 75, 87, 89, 94–5, 101, 104, 119, 319n152
    Dagestan 288
    fundamentalism 246
    ghazawat 149, 150, 153, 156, 325n51
    Great Mufti *100*
    hajj 157, 162, 288
    imam, imamate 152
    Islamization 149, 163
    lunar calendar 317n5
    pan-Islamism 167, 181, 182
    political Islam 115
    radical Islamism 278, 283
    Ramadan 280
    revival of 246
    sharia law 148, 149, 153, 156, 160, 224, 283
    slavery and 89, 164
    Soviet Union, suppression of Islam 224–5, 288
    underground prayer rooms and madrasas 246, 288
    see also jihad/jihadism; Ismailism; Muslims; Salafism; Shia Islam; Sufism; Sunni Islam; Wahhabism
Islamic Democratic Party of Dagestan 288
Islamic Jamaat of Dagestan 283
Islamic Party, Nardaran 260
Islamic Party of Revival (IRP) 283
Islamic State
    al-Baghdadi, Abu Bakr 290, 335n5
    in the Caucasus 283, 286
    Chechnya 283
    Dagestan 283
    Islamic Army 283, 335n53
    pan-Caucasian Islamism 286
    pan-North Caucasian Islamic State 283
    in Russia 290
Ismailism 51, 53
Ittifaq (Union of the Muslims of Russia) 181

J

the Ja'afariya 108, 323n112
jadidist movement 181, 327n208
jamaats 116, 118, 152–3, 156, 224
Janissaries 95
the Jaqelis 83
Jews
    anti-Semitism 173, 279
    Nazi *Einsatzgruppen*: massacres of Jews 236
    see also Judaism
jihad/jihadism 25, 185, 274, 283–4, 290
    anti-Soviet jihad 224
    Caucasian jihadists 290
    Dagestani Avar imams: jihad of 149, 152–63
    Ingushetia 293
    'jihad taxes' 290
    jihadist network of the Caucasus Emirate 290
    Kabardino-Balkaria 294
    North Ossetia–Alania 294
Jochids 43, 319n153
Judaism 67
    see also Jews

K

Kabardians 6, 92, 116, 132, 323n9
    ataliq educational system 116
    Kabardian–Russian defensive pacts 119, 121
    Ottomans and 139
    Russian Empire and 148
    social structures 116
Kadets (Russian Constitutional Democrats) 181
the Kadyrovtsy 286, 293, 336n14, 336n21
Kalmyks 324n48
    forced exile of 274, 276
    Mongol Kalmyks in the north-eastern Caucasus 130–2
    return to Kalmykia 276
    Russian Empire and 131
    Russian–Kalmyk treaties 130–1, 132
    Soviet Union and 225
    see also Kalmykia
Kartlis Tskhovreba 8, 10, 13, 15
khachkar 5, 94
Khevsurs 101, 118, 143, *143*, 153
Khwarazmians
    Georgian invasion by 35, 36, 41
    Mongols and 35–6
    see also Khwarazmia
kidnapping 89, 111, 114, 119, 129, 150, 272, 276
    by Chechens 276, 283
    'European Kidnapping Highway' 294
Kievan Rus 15, 323n5
Kipchaks
    Christianity 15
    Georgia and 15–16, 17, 18, 21, 34, 35, 317n35
    Mongols and 33
    slavery 33
Knights Hospitaller 60, 71
Knights Templar *see* Templars
Kumyks 75, 93, 96, 118, 121–2, 150, 286, 288
Kurdistan Workers' Party (PKK) 254

L

Laks 118, 240, 242, 283–4, 286
languages 118
    Armenian 109, 226, 242
    Azerbaijan 84, 226, 242
    Circassian 116
    Dagestan, official languages 288
    Georgian language 103, 167, 197, 226, 242
    Kalmyks 226
    Russian language 167, 288
    Soviet Union and 226
    see also alphabets
League of Nations 209, 210, 327n176
Lezgian War 108
Lezgians 118, 288
libraries: Goshavank Monastery 25

M

Mamelukes 42, 43, 44, 46, 53
    Ayas fortress 62
    Cilicia and 50, *58*, 62, 65–7, 68, 69, 71, *71*, 72
    Crusaders and 64, 66
    as leading power in the Near East 65
    Mongols and 64
    slavery 33, 43, 67
    Syria and 65–6, 68
Marxism 5, 180, 242, 283
Mensheviks 173, 179, 326n154
    Georgian Mensheviks 181, 195, 196–7, 198
    nationalism 179
    Soviet dissolution of 225
Meskhetian Turks 89, 240, 242
miniatures (illuminated manuscripts)
    Battle of Mari, *Livre des Merveilles* 65
    Levon II, gospel 57
    Prophet Jonah, by Toros Roslin, lectionary 44
    St John Evangelist and Prokhoros, by Mesrop of Khizan, gospel 96
    St Luke, by Mesrop of Khizan, gospel 98
monasteries
    Akhtala Monastery, Armenia 25, *30*
    Cilicia 320n18
    Dadivank Monastery, Azerbaijan *261*, *300*
    Geghard Monastery, Armenia *33*, 44
    Gelati Monastery, Georgia *12*, *13*, 15, 18, 85
    Goshavank Monastery, Armenia 25
    Haghartsin monastery, Armenia 26, *26*, *27*
    Haghpat Monastery, Armenia 20, *23*, 25
    Harichavank Monastery, Armenia *24*
    Horomos Monastery, Ani *23*
    Khobayr Monastery, Armenia *43*
    Maghardavank Monastery/St Stepanos Monastery, Iranian Azerbaijan *99*
    Martyrs' Monastery of Martvili, Georgia *14*
    Monastery of the Dormition, Nojikhevi, Georgia *136*
    Monastery of the Nativity, Katskhi, Georgia *9*
    New Athos Monastery, Abkhazia *197*
    Ninotsminda Nunnery, Georgia *85*
    Noravank Monastery, Armenia *40*
    Pitareti Monastery, Georgia *31*, *32*
    reconstruction of 25
    San Lazzaro Monastery, Armenian Mekhitarist congregation, Venice *109*, 110
    Sevanavank Monastery, Armenia *144*
    St George Monastery, Alaverdi, Georgia *93*
    St Thaddeus Monastery, Azerbaijan 47, *99*, 320n171
    Tanahativank Monastery, Armenia 44, *45*
    Tatev Monastery, Armenia 44
    Tegher Monastery, Armenia *37*
    Vardzia Monastery, Georgia *21*, 88
Mongols
    Anatolia and 36
    Armenia and 32, 36, 42, 62
    Azerbaijan and 36, 42
    battle tactics, military logistics and intelligence 30, 33
    Chagatai Khanate 44
    Cilicia and 50, 62–4, 68
    Georgia, invasion and occupation of 30, 31, 32–3, 35, 36–7, 40, 42, 43–6, 47, 62, 318–19n96, 319n138
    Great Khan 36, 63, 319n139
    Heavenly Mandate 43
    incursions and supremacy 30–48, 63, 64
    inter-Mongol war 43–4
    Iran and 36, 41, 42, 46, 64, 319n153
    Khwarazmians and 35–6
    Kipchaks and 33
    Mamelukes and 64
    Mongol Kalmyks in the north-eastern Caucasus 130–2
    as 'nation of the archers' 32
    Nestorianism 43, 63, 64, 321n56, 321n66
    noyans 32, 36, 37, 40, 47
    religious indifference 41, 43, 46, 320n169
    Russia and 130
    Syria and 42, 46, 64
    Tamta, Ivane's daughter and 30
    taxes 40–1
    Tbilisi and 32, 40, 43
    tümen 32
    see also Golden Horde; Il-Khanate; Mongol Empire
Montreux Convention (1936) 240
mosques
    Akhmad Kadyrov Mosque, Grozny *284*
    Blue Mosque, Yerevan *145*
    central mosque, Nalchik, Kabardino-Balkaria *277*
    churches turned into mosques 93
    Nardaran Mosque, Absheron Peninsula *258*
    Soviet suppression of Islam and 224–5
mountains 3
    Greater Caucasus Mountains *3*, 45, 114, 118, 148, 160, *234*, *236*, 272, 312
    Lak Mountains 121
    Likhi (Surami) mountain range 88
    Mount Elbrus *237*, *237*
    Nur Mountains 66
    Taurus Mountains *51*, 53
    Tsorey-Loam Mountains *37*
murals
    Astvatsatsin Church, Akhtala Monastery, Armenia 25
    Cathedral of Our Lady, Gelati Monastery *13*
    Church of the Archangels, Gremi *86*, *88*
    Church of the Dormition, Cave Monastery *21*
    Church of Saints Quiricus and Julitta, Zarati, Georgia *102*
    Georgian Orthodox Church, whitewashing of murals 137
    Monastery of the Dormition, Nojikhevi, Georgia *136*
    St Grigori Church, Ubisa, Georgia *74*
murals: Christ Pantocrator
    Cathedral of Nikortsminda, Georgia *103*
    Khobayr Monastery Church, Armenia *43*
    Mother of God Church, Pitareti Monastery, Georgia *32*
    Samtsevrisi Castle Church, Georgia *305*
    St Grigori Church, Ubisa, Georgia *77*
Muridism 152–3
Müsavat Party 182, 195, 196, 201, 205, 206, 216
    Soviet dissolution of 225
    Stalinist purges 226
Muscovy Company 105
Muslims
    anti-Muslim pogroms 195
    Georgia, Muslim population in 17
    Muslim nationalism 182
    Russian Empire and 148
    worldwide population 327n207
    see also Islam
the Mustalawiyya 51

N

Nagorno-Karabakh conflict 4, 205–6, 246, 249, 251–2, 253, 255, 312
    1988 Sumgait massacre by Azerbaijanis 249, 251, 254
    1992–1994 First Nagorno-Karabakh War *250*, 252, 260–5, *261*, 298
    1992 Khojaly occupation/massacre by Armenians 253–4, 260, 261
    1994 ceasefire agreement 262, 298
    1999 Armenian Parliament killings 264–5, 298
    1999 negotiations 264
    2020 Second Nagorno-Karabakh War *261*, 262, 298–301, **299**, *300*, 302, 312
    2020 ceasefire agreement 299–301
    Afghanistan 262
    Armenian army 260–1, 298–9, 300, *300*
    Azerbaijani army 260, 261, 298–9, 300
    Azerbaijani refugees 263, 298, 299–300
    commodity-based cartels and 265
    current challenges 301, 302, 303–4
    EU 301, 302
    Iran 262, 264, 300, 301
    Israel/Azerbaijan cooperation 298, 299, 300
    Kalbajar 262
    Karabakh Committee 251
    Lachin 261–2
    mercenaries 261, 262, 298, 300, 333n68
    Minsk Group (OSCE) 262, 263, 333n70
    Nakhchivan, Azerbaijani road access to 300, 301
    Operation Ring 251, 260
    Pan-Armenian National Movement 251
    Republic of Artsakh 252, 260, *261*, 265, 332n15
    Russian Federation 262, 264, 265, 299, 300, 301, 312
    Saudi Arabia 262
    Shushi 205–6, 261–2, 298, 299, 300
    State Defence Committee 262
    'status of controlled instability' 301
    Sunni/Shia clashes 262
    territorial exchanges as solution 263, 264–5, 298
    Turkey/Azerbaijan cooperation 254, 260, 262, 294, 298, 299, 300, 301, 312
    US 264
    US/Russia rivalry and 262, 264
    weaponry 260–1, 265, 298, 299
    see also Nagorno-Karabakh
Napoleonic Wars 13–41
    1803–1806 Third Coalition 141
    see also Napoleon I
National United Party (NUP), Armenia 245
nationalism 174
    Abkhazia 265
    Azerbaijan 167, 246, 253
    Black Hundreds 173
    Caucasian nationalisms 6
    ethnicity and 166–7, 175, 182, 274
    Georgian nationalism 167, 179, 243–4, 265
    glasnost and 248, 265
    Mensheviks 179
    Muslim nationalism 182
    North Caucasian national consciousness 246
    populist nationalism 265
    Russian nationalism 5, 166–9
    Russification and nationalism 167, 196
    Serbian nationalism 170
    South Ossetian nationalism 197
    Soviet Caucasian republics and ASSRs 243
    Soviet Union 224, 242, 248–9, 301
    Turkey/Turkish nationalism 4, 176, 184, 207, 210, 211, 212, *212*, 215, *215*, 330n172
    see also Armenian nationalism; pan-Turkism
the Natukhai 115–16, 119, 151, 160
Nawiqis (Awaqis) 50
'Near Abroad' (Russian Federation) 6, 255, 264, 272, 294, 305, 332–3n32
    see also Russian Federation
necropolis 147
    burial houses *116*, *147*
    see also cemeteries
nepotism 13–14, 15, 244
Nestorianism 41, 47
    among Mongols 43, 63, 64, 321n56, 321n66
    Nestorian Catholicos Mar Yahballaha III 67
    Nestorian Church of the East 67
the Nizariyya *see* the Assassins
Nogai Horde 115, 122, 129, 130
Non-Aligned Movement 295

North Atlantic Treaty Organization (NATO)
  Armenia and 212
  Azerbaijan and 255, 259
  the Caucasus 312
  Estonia 337n90
  Finland 309, 337n91
  Georgia and 272, 304–7, 309, 310, 333n32, 337n71, 337n89
  Latvia 337n90
  Lithuania 337n90
  Norway 337n90
  Poland 337n90
  Putin on NATO's eastward expansion 306
  rapprochement of Caucasus states to 6, 333n32
  Russia's 'Near Abroad' and 309, 333n32
  South Caucasus 272, 312
  Sweden 309, 337n91
  Turkey and 214, 240, 254, 260, 298
  Ukraine and 306–7, 333n32
nuclear power
  1986 Chernobyl catastrophe 245
  Armenia, nuclear power plant at Medzamor 245
al-Nusra Front (Jabhat al-Nusra) 290

O

the Oghuz 76
oil and gas 171
  Azerbaijan 171, 174, 245–6, 253, 255, 259–60, 295, 297–8, 303, 333nn33–4, 333n50
  Azeri–Chirag–Gunashvili (ACG) Agreement 260
  Baku 171–4, 196, 201–3, 230, 235, 245, 331n28, 331n50
  Batumi, oil terminal and port 172–3, 195
  Branobel company 171, 173–4
  Caspian ACG fields 255, 259, 333n34
  Cold War 240–1
  'Contract of the Century' 255
  Dashnaks and Baku unrest 173, 175, 176, 178
  Dashnaks and Iran unrest 178
  diesel-powered oil barge 174
  diesel submarines 174
  EU 298, 303, 333n51, 336n36
  gasoline refinery 173
  Gazprom, Russia 262, 277
  Georgia 259
  Grozny 173, 230, 232, 235, 237, 331n52
  Iran 178, 240–1, 255, 297–8
  Iran–Azerbaijan–Turkmenistan trilateral gas-swap deal 297–8
  Iraq 241
  Israel 300
  Kazakhstan 259
  Kyapaz/Dostluq (Dostluk) gas field 297
  Lukoil, Russia 255, 277, 287
  Maikop 230, 232, 331n48
  Nagorno-Karabakh 215
  Nazi Germany 230, 232, 235, 237, 331n29, 331n48
  Nobel brothers 171–4
  oil burners 173
  oil storage 172
  OPEC 248, 255
  price wars and rivalries 173
  propeller-driven oil tanker 173–4
  railway oil-tank wagons 172
  Romanian oilfields 230, 331n29
  Royal Dutch Shell 174
  Russian Empire 171–4
  Russian Federation 255, 260, 333n46
  Russian General Oil Corporation (RGO) 174
  Saudi Arabia 248
  Shah Deniz II Consortium 333n51
  Shah Deniz Caspian Sea field 259, 333n50
  Siberia 245
  SOCAR, Azerbaijan 255, 260, 295
  Soviet sabotage of own oilfields 230, 233, 235
  Soviet Union 174, 230
  Standard Oil 172, 173
  strikes and attacks against oil industry 173, 178, 182, 326n158
  TransCaspian US Resources Company (Florida-based) 298
  Turkey 259–60
  Turkmenistan 259, 297–8, 336n35
  the Urals 255, 259, 331n50
  US 255, 259, 298, 336n36
  World War I 195, 196, 201–3, 204
  World War II 230, 232, 245, 331n29, 331n48
  Yury Korchagin offshore oilfield 287
  Zoroaster, oil tanker 172
oil and gas pipelines 172, 202, 230, 255, **256–7**, 259, 333n45
  Baku–Batumi pipeline 173, 230, 259
  Baku–Grozny–Novorossiysk pipeline (BGN) 255, 259, 282
  Baku–Novo Filya pipeline (BNF) 259–60
  Baku–Novorossiysk oil pipeline 255, 284, 288
  Baku–Tbilisi–Ceyhan pipeline (BTC) 259, 260, 272, 298
  Baku–Tbilisi–Erzurum pipeline (BTE) 259
  Baku–Tbilisi–Supsa pipeline (BTS) 259, 272
  the Caucasus: main gas and oil pipelines in **256–7**
  Mozdok–Tbilisi–Yerevan gas pipeline (MTY) 260, 262
  Nabucco pipeline project 333n51
  'South Stream' gas pipeline 333n56
  Southern Gas Corridor 259, 298
  Tengiz–Atyrau–Novorossiysk oil pipeline 277
  Trans-Adriatic Pipeline (TAP) 259
  Trans-Anatolian Pipeline (TANAP) 259
  Trans-Caspian Gas pipeline (TCG) 259, 298
  Trans-Caspian Interconnector pipeline 298
  TurkStream 260
Order of St John of Jerusalem 44
Organization for Security and Co-operation in Europe (OSCE) 262, 263, 283, 308
Orthodox Church
  exarch 324n13
  Greek Orthodox Church 47, 60
  icons 24–5, 72
  union of Orthodox and Roman Catholic churches 80
  Syriac Orthodox Church 47, 82
  see also Armenian Orthodox Church; Georgian Orthodox Church; Russian Orthodox Church
Ossetians 15, 47, 118
  Christians 278
  Ossetian–Georgian clashes 197
  Ossetian identity 278
  relocation and return of territories 242, 246
  serfdom 118
  slavery 118
  social structures 118
  South Ossetian identity 197
Ottoman–Safavid Wars 84–100
  First Ottoman–Iranian War 85, 87
  Second Ottoman–Iranian War 87
  Third Ottoman–Iranian War 87–8
  Fourth Ottoman–Iranian War 88–92
  Fifth Ottoman–Iranian War 92–5
  Sixth Ottoman–Iranian War 95–8
  Seventh Ottoman–Iranian War 98–9
  Eighth Ottoman–Iranian War 99–100
  Ninth Ottoman–Iranian War 107–8
  Tenth Ottoman–Iranian War 108
  Treaty of Amasya 88, 89, 96, 99
  Treaty of Constantinople (Peace of Istanbul) 92
  Treaty of Kordan (Kerden) 108
  Treaty of Nasuh Pasha 96, 98
  Treaty of Serav 98
  Treaty of Zuhab/Treaty of Qasr-e Shirin 99, 101, 108

P

Palaiologos dynasty 74
paganism 3, 119
  neo-paganism 278
palaces
  Ishak Palace, Doğubayazıt, Turkey *140*, 141
  Palace of Finckenstein, Poland *139*, 141
  Palace of the khans of Nakhchivan *204*
  Shervashidze family's Palace, Likhny *137*
  see also castles
pan-Islamism 167, 181, 182
pan-Turkism 167, 176, 181–2, 205, 246
  modern education and modernization in Muslim societies 181
  Ottoman Empire 182, 185, 195
  Turkey 201
papacy
  anti-Mameluke coalition with 46
  Armenian Orthodox Church and 44, 60, 67, 68, 69, 71, 72
  Benedict XII 69
  Callixtus III 81
  Celestine III 60
  Clement III 58
  Clement VI 71
  Clement XI 58
  Crusades and 67, 81, 99
  Eugene III 60
  Eugene IV 80
  Francis 260
  Gregory IX 37, 40
  Honorius III 35
  Hussite anti-papal reform movement 80
  Innocent XI 101
  John XXII 46
  John Paul II 260
  Lucius III 60
  papal supremacy 60
  Pius II 81
  Urban II 53
  Urban VIII 98–9
  see also Catholicism
Paris Peace Conference (1919–1920) 200, 205, 207–16
  Armenia 207, 208–13, **209**, 329–30n147
  Azerbaijan 207, **208**
  Bolsheviks and the Whites as Russian contenders for supremacy 207
  Georgia 207, **208**
  Iran 207–8
  Nakhchivan 207
  pre-war status quo of Russian sovereignty over the South Caucasus 207
  South Caucasian delegations 207
  Turkey 207, 210, 211–12
  US 210
patriarchate
  abolition of patriarchates of Georgia, Abkhazia and Imereti 137
  Abraham Petros I Ardzivian 110
  Armenians and the Patriarch of Constantinople 4, 80, 138, 166
  Gevorg V Surenian, Patriarch-Catholicos 176
  Khrimian, Mkrtich, Patriarch-Catholicos 176
  Matteos II Izmirlian, Patriarch-Catholicos 176
  Nikon 122–3
  Sargis I of Jerusalem 68
Peace of Istanbul 92
Peace of Nystad 105
People's Militia 180
Polish–Soviet War 211, 213, 216, 330nn213
Preliminary Treaty between Britain and Iran 142
printing 103, 110
Prometheus League 331n7
Protestantism 166
  Protestant Armenian *millet* 166
Pshavs 101, 118

Q

al-Qaeda 272, 286, 290
Qara Qoyunlu 76, 78, 79, 81, *168*, 320n171, 322n34

R

railways 184, 196, 216
  Baku–Astrakhan Railway 331n50
  Baku–Batumi Railway 172, 202
  Baku–Nakhchivan Railway 251
  Baku–Tbilisi–Batumi Railway 180
  Baku–Tbilisi–Kars (BTK) Railway line 260
  Berlin–Baghdad Railway 184
  Kars–Alexandropol–Julfa Railway 196
  World War I 196
  World War II 233

Yerevan–Nakhchivan–Julfa Railway 211
Ramazanids 72
Red Army 174, 194, 206, 210, 214, 222, 227
    1991–1992 disintegration of 252
    Armenians in 240
    Battle for the Caucasus 238
    disintegration of the Army and sale of weaponry 252, 282, 332n14
    Khulkhuta memorial *238*
    as occupying force 224
    Soviet flag over the German Reichstag, Berlin *239*
    'War Communism' 218
    Warsaw Uprising and 136
    World War II and Caucasians 239–40, *239*, *241*
    see also Soviet Union
reliefs
    Astvatsatsin Church, Haghartsin Monastery, Armenia *27*
    Astvatsatsin Church of Noravank, Armenia *40*
    Geghard Monastery, Armenia *33*
religion
    ethno-religious diversity 4, 148, 167
    identity and 3
    see also Buddhism; Christianity; Islam; Judaism
remittances 264, 272, 291
Republican Party, Armenia 302
Rubenids of Cilicia 50, *51*, 53–60
    Pardzerpert, ancestral seat of *51*, 53
    Seljuks and 54
    Vahka, seat of 53, *55*
Russian Civil Wars (1917–1920) 207, 217–22
    Armed Forces of South Russia (AFSR) **219**, 220–2
    Bolsheviks/Red Army 217, 218–19, 222
    North Caucasus 217
    'wars within the main Civil War' 218
    White army/Volunteer Army 217, 218–22, *220*, *221*
    see also Bolsheviks; White armies/Whites
Russian–Iranian Wars
    1804–1813 Russian–Iranian War 138, 140
    1826–1828 Russian–Iranian War 142–4
    Treaty of Turkmenchay 144, 145, 146, *146*
Russian military lines **124**, 129, 324n38
    Abatis Line 126
    Aras–Kura Line 143, 144, 148
    Asov–Mozdok Line 129, 130
    Belgorod Line 122, 126, 128, 129
    Black Sea–Kuban–Terek Line 130, 148
    Caspian Terek Line 136
    Cossacks and first Russian military lines 122–30
    Dnieper Line 129, 132
    foundation of new Cossack and Russian cities and 130
    Kizlyar–Mozdok Line 129, 149
    Kuban Line 130, 151
    Mozdok Line 132
    Orenburg Line 129, 132
    Simbirsk Line 126, 128
    Sunzha Line 150
    Trans-Kama Line 126, 128
    Tsaritsyn Line 129, 132

Russian nationalism 5, 166–9
    Russian Empire and 166
    Russification and 167
Russian Orthodox Church 3, 72, 90, 119, 167
    Georgian Orthodox Church as exarchate of 137, 324n13
    proselytism 4, 166
    schism (*Raskol*) 122–3
    synod 123
Russian–Ottoman clashes 92, 104, 105, 106, 108, 119, 130
    1735–1739 Russian–Ottoman War 108
    1768–1774 Russian–Ottoman War 111, 135
    1787–1792 Russian–Ottoman War 135
    1806–1812 Russian–Ottoman War 138, 141, 142
    1828–1829 Russian–Ottoman War 90, 146
    1877–1878 Russian–Ottoman War *168*, 169
    1914–1915 Ottoman attack on Russian fortifications at Sarıkamış *184*, 186
    Treaty of Adrianople 90, 147, 151, 152
    Treaty of Bucharest 138
    Treaty of Constantinople 128–9
    Treaty of Küçük Kaynarca (Kainarji) 112, 119, 130
    Treaty of San Stefano 170
Russian Social Democratic Workers' Party 179, 326n154
Russification programmes
    education and schools 167
    Georgian Orthodox Church 137
    nationalism and 167, 196
    Russian Empire 4–5, 166, 167, 196, 326n94
    Russian language 167

S

Safavids (Safavid dynasty of Iran) 81, 84
    1511 Anatolian Qizilbash revolt 85
    1736 fall of the Safavid dynasty 96
    Anatolia and 178
    Armenia and 100
    army/Qizilbash (red-heads) 84, 85, 87, 88, 92, 96
    Azerbaijan and 87, 92, 96, 100, 181
    deportation of conquered peoples 86, 96, 98, 99
    end of the Safavid dynasty 102, 107
    expansion 84, 87
    foundation of independent khanates after end of Safavid rule 111
    Kakheti and 96, 98, 101
    Kars and *168*
    Kartli and 87, 88, 92, 95, 96, 98
    Nakhchivan and 96, 98
    Ottomans/Iran/Russia rivalry 92, 107
    Qazvin 88
    Safaviyya 84, 85
    Safavid Empire 87
    Shia Islam 84, 87
    Shirvan and 84, 87
    slavery 88
    South Caucasus and 101–8
    Tabriz and 84, 88, 95

taxes 107
    theocracy 84
    trade 92
    Turkification of 76, 101
    zamburak 107–8, *108*
    see also Iran; Ottoman–Safavid Wars
Sakartvelo Mkhedrioni ('Georgia's Knights'/Ioseliani's Knights) 265–6, 268, 270
Salafism 283–4, 286, 288
    terrorist attack, Buynaksk 284
Saltukids of Erzurum 20–1
San Remo Conference (1920) 210
Savdal (Unity, Lezgin organization) 288
self-determination 4, 114, 128, 198, 203, 205, 206, 248
Seljuks 10
    Cilicia and 50, 54, 62
    Crusades and 12, 53
    Georgia/Seljuks conflict 10, 12–13, 15–17, *16*, 18, 22, 27
    Rum Seljuks 27, 35, 50, 54, 62
    Seljuk Empire 14
    slavery 13
    Turkification of the South Caucasus 76
serfdom 165–6
    Kartli 102–3
    Ossetians 118
    Russian Empire 103, 128, 129, 150, 165–6
    Soviet collectivization of agriculture 226
Shaddadids 9
Shapsugs 115–16, 119, 151, 160, 276
Sharia Army of Highlanders 224
Sharvashidzes 83
Shia Islam
    Azerbaijan 87, 246, *258*, 260
    'hidden Imam' 52
    Iran 260
    Persia 3
    proselytism 85, 102
    Safavids 84, 87
    Sunni/Shia clashes 262
    Sunni/Shia religious disagreements 108
    Twelver Shiism 52, 84, 323n112
    see also Islam
Silk Road 43
slavery/slave trade
    abolition of 165, 166
    Akhaltsikhe 89, *90*
    Anapa 150, 151
    children 101, 103
    Circassians 89, 116, 89, 116, 119, 151, 163, 164
    Crimean Tatars 88–9, 92, 119, 122
    Il-Khanate 42
    Islam and 89, 164
    Janissaries 95
    Kabardians 116
    Kipchaks 33
    Mamelukes 33, 43, 67
    nobility and upper clergy 101, 112
    Ossetians 118
    Ottomans 88, 112, 119, 164
    Safavids 88
    Seljuks 13
    Russia 89
smuggling 269, 282, 283
    arms smuggling 152, 282
    drug smuggling 272
socialism 169, 175, 176
    Georgian socialism 179–81
    industrialization and 174

international socialism 230
pan-Turkism and socialism in the South Caucasian Muslim provinces 181–2
People's Militia 180
Soviet socialism 224, 227
see also Dashnaks; Hunchaks
Somkhiti, Armenian–Georgian marches 76
South Caucasian Commissariat 195
Soviet–Turkish Friendship Treaty 211
state
    1878 Berlin Congress 166, 167
    concept of 3, 166, 224
    ethnic homogeneity and 4, 178, 203
    history as the memory of states 3–4
    identity and 4
    imperial state model 4
    multinational state 4, 6, 207
    nation-state building 4, 278, 288
    nation states 4, 6, 178
    state borders, drawing of 170
    state-within-the-state 26
Studio Fuksas *269*, *304*
Sufism 149, 286, 288
    Naqshbandi Sufism 152
    see also Islam
Sunni Islam 53, 57, 119
    Nader Shah's rapprochement with 108
    Ottoman Empire 3, 84
    Sunni Afghan Pashtuns 102
    Sunni Lezgins 323n96
    Sunni *Salafiyyah* 283
    Sunni/Shia clashes 262
    Sunni/Shia religious disagreements 108
    ulama 149
    see also Islam
Svans 118, 143
Sykes–Picot Agreement (1916) 190, 207, 209

T

Taliban 152, 153
Tagliavini Report (Report of the Independent International Fact-Finding Mission on the Conflict in Georgia) 309
taxes
    Armenians and the Ottoman Empire 166, 175
    Circassians 89
    Cossacks 129
    darughachi/basqaq 41
    fiscal discrimination 166
    Georgia 15, 17, 20, 25, 40–1, 46, 76, 81, 180, 304
    Il-Khanate 42
    'jihad taxes' 290
    jizia/poll tax 76, 89, 166
    Mongols 40–1
    Russian Empire 128
    Safavids 107
    tax exemption 107, 129, 164
    tax-farming system 166, 326n120
Templars (Knights Templar) 56, 57, 58, 59, 60, 68, 320n43
Tenglik Party (Unity) 288
terrorism 176
    9/11 attacks 272, 286
    1994 Savdal attack 288

1999 apartment bombings, Moscow 284
2002 Moscow theatre hostage-taking 286
Chechen terrorism 276, 278, 280, 282, 286, 293, 294
counter-terrorism 286, 290
Dagestan and 287
Dashnak activities 175
Ingushetia 293
North Caucasus 290, 335n1
North Ossetia–Alania 280, 294
al-Qaeda 272, 286
Russian social-revolutionaries 166, 169
Salafist attacks 284
Umarov, Dokka (Abu Umar) 290
Wahhabism 261
war against terrorism 286
Yarmuk group 290
Teşkilat-ı Mahsusa (Special Organization) 165, 187–8, 189
Teutonic Knights 60
Timurids 75–6, 322n34
Toluids 43, 319n153
Trans-Caucasus Highway 294
Transcaspian Provisional Government (Ashgabat Executive Committee) 202
Transcaucasian Commissariat 194
Transcaucasian Committee (Ozakom) 194
Transcaucasian Democratic Federative Republic 5
Treaty of Adrianople 90, 147, 151, 152
Treaty of Alexandropol 213
Treaty of Amasya 88, 89, 96, 99
Treaty of Batumi 200, 329n88
Treaty of Brest-Litovsk 194, 196
Treaty of Bucharest 138
Treaty of Constantinople (1700) 128–9
Treaty of Constantinople (Peace of Istanbul, 1590) 92
Treaty of Finckenstein 139, 141–2
Treaty of Ganja 107
Treaty of Georgiyevsk 111, 135–6, 149
Treaty of Gulistan 143, 145
Treaty of Istanbul (1736) 108
Treaty of Kars 170, 214, 302
Treaty of Kordan (Kerden) 108
Treaty of Küçük Kaynarca (Kainarji) 112, 119, 130
Treaty of Lausanne 211
Treaty of Moscow 213–14
Treaty of Nasuh Pasha 96, 98
Treaty of Nymphaion 48
Treaty of Paris 161, 169, 170, 171
Treaty of Poti 196
Treaty of Resht 107
Treaty of San Stefano 170
Treaty of Serav 98
Treaty of Sèvres 210–11, 212, 263
Treaty of Tilsit 141–2
Treaty of Turkmenchay 144, 145, 146, 146
Treaty of Versailles 210
Treaty of Zuhab/Treaty of Qasr-e Shirin 99, 101, 108
Tripartite Agreement (1942) 240, 241
Truce of Shamkor 76
Turkification policy 76, 101, 177, 255
Turkmen
  Aq Qoyunlu 76, 81, 82, 84, 168
  Qara Qoyunlu 76, 78, 79, 81, 168, 320n171, 322n34
Turkification of the South Caucasus 76
Tushetians 101, 118

U

United National Movement 309
United Nations (UN) 252, 265, 281, 308, 332n16
  UN Charter 305
  UN General Assembly Resolution 68/262 337n62
  UN General Assembly Resolution 96 (on Genocide) 188–9
United Russia Party 290, 292
Unmanned Aerial Vehicles (UAVs, drones) 260, 294, 298, 299, 300
Uzbek Khanate of Bukhara 92

V

Vienna Congress (1814–1815) 170
volcanoes
  Greater Ararat 3, 203
  Lesser Ararat 3, 203

W

Wagner Group 336n21
Wahhabism 152, 261, 283, 286, 288, 290, 335n49
  Chechen Wars/Chechnya 282, 283, 286, 335n54
  Dagestan 284, 287, 288
  Wahhabi Salafism 283, 286
  see also Islam
war/warfare
  war of motion 170
  war of position 170
weaponry 210
  1919 British Military Mission 219
  ammunition 129, 131, 151, 152, 153, 156, 159, 195, 196, 199, 202, 210, 213
  Armenians 212, 213
  Azerbaijan 260
  arms smuggling 152, 282
  arms trade 260
  bows and arrows 131, 132
  cannons 108, 130, 131, 175, 221, 322n33
  Cossacks 129, 131
  cotton and 196
  factory of 171
  firearms 87, 92, 131
  German troops 234
  gunpowder 131, 152
  Kalmyks 131, 132
  machine-guns 186, 234
  missiles 253, 260, 294, 298, 301
  muskets 95, 130, 131
  Nagorno-Karabakh conflict 260–1, 265, 298, 299
  nuclear weapons 226
  Red Army disintegration and 252, 282, 332n14
  rifles 161, 171, 180, 326n98
  Russian 95, 131, 159
  Safavids: zamburak 107–8, 108
Soviet Union 227
  tanks 170, 227
Wehrmacht 136, 185, 227, 227, 231, 238, 331n30
  Armenians in 185, 239
  Battle for the Caucasus 238
  German troops in the Caucasus 233, 234, 236, 236, 237
  High Command (OKW) 230, 232, 331n30
  Luftwaffe 232, 237, 331n29, 331n52
  military alpinism 237
  North Caucasian small minorities and 235–7, 238–9, 332nn70–71
  Operation Edelweiss 232–8, 235
  Sonderkommando Dromedar 239
  Sonderverband Bergmann 236, 238
  Sonderverband Tamara 239
  Soviets serving in 238–9
  Unternehmen Wintergewitter ('Operation Winter Storm') 238
  Warsaw Uprising 238
  see also Nazi Germany; World War II
White armies/Whites 199, 207, 218–22, 220, 221, 328n74, 330n213
  Cossacks and 218–19, 222
  Denikin, Anton Ivanovich, General 199, 201, 204, 207, 210, 217, 218–22, 224, 330n201, 330n209
  'Ice March' through the Kuban 218
  Kolchak, Aleksandr, Admiral 220–1, 330n204
  'Moscow Directive' 221
  Volunteer Army 199, 201, 218–22, 224, 225, 330n201
  see also Russian Civil Wars
World Council of Churches (WCC) 243
World Trade Organization (WTO) 305
World War I 170
  1914 assassination of Franz Ferdinand of Austria 170, 185
  1914–1915 Ottoman attack on Russian fortifications at Sarıkamış 184, 186
  1916 Sykes–Picot Agreement 190, 207, 209
  1917 Armistice of Erzincan 194, 195
  1918 Armistice of Mudros 188, 196, 200, 203–4
  1919–1920 Paris Peace Conference 200, 205, 207–16
  Allied Supreme War Council 206
  Armenian and Assyrian villages 186, 327n15
  Bolsheviks/Bolshevik Russia 193–4, 201, 207
  cotton industry and 196, 201
  Dashnaks 185, 202, 205
  the Entente 185, 195, 327n6
  France 185, 186, 191, 203
  Gallipoli campaign 186, 191, 327n18
  Germany 185, 191, 194, 196, 200, 201, 202
  Great Britain 185, 186, 191, 196, 201, 202, 203–5, 206
  oil production and 195, 196, 201–3, 204
  Ottoman Empire 178, 185–6, 190–1, 196, 201–4
  population displacement 163–4
  post-war partition of Ottoman Empire/'mandates' 190–1, 210–11, 327n176
  POWs 199, 327n10
  railways 196
Russian Empire 174, 185–6, 187, 190–1, 193–4, 328n42
Treaty of Batumi 200, 329n88
Treaty of Brest-Litovsk 194, 196
Treaty of Lausanne 211
Treaty of Sèvres 210–11, 212, 263
Treaty of Versailles 210
see also Paris Peace Conference
World War II 170
  1941 Japanese attack on Pearl Harbour 239
  1942 Tripartite Agreement 240, 241
  1945 Yalta Agreements 239, 240
  Armenians in 185, 239, 240
  Azerbaijan 245
  Battle for the Caucasus 238
  Dashnaks 239
  Nazi Germany 232–8
  oil and gas 230, 232, 245, 331n29, 331n48
  population displacement 163–4
  POWs 238, 240
  railways 233
  Red Army and Caucasians 239–40, 239, 241
  Soviet Union 221, 237–8
  see also Nazi Germany; Wehrmacht

X

xenophobia 173

Y

Yalta Agreements (1945) 239, 240
Yarmuk group 290
Yeni Azərbaycan Partiyası (New Azerbaijan Party) 260
Yerkrapah 263
Yernjak 35, 75, 76
Young Turks 176
  1878 Berlin Congress 177
  Armenian Genocide 175
  Committee of Union and Progress (CUP) 164, 176
  Dashnaks and 176
  triumvirate dictatorship 176, 328n28
Yugoslav Wars (1991–2001) 334n2

Z

Zviadists 270, 272

Index: People

Page locators in *italic* refer to captions; 'n' after a locator indicates the endnote number.

A

Abaqa, Il-Khan 43, 44, 66, 67
Abashidze, Aslan 267–8, 304
Abashidze, Ivan 112
Abbas I, Shah 86, 92, 94–5, 96, 98, 99, *99*
Abbas II, Shah 100, 101
Abbas Mirza, Crown Prince 143, 150
'Abd al-Kadr, *qadi* 150
Abdul Hamid II, Sultan-Caliph 175, 181
Abdulatipov, Ramazan 292–3
Abdulaziz, Sultan 164
Abdullah Beg, King 107, 111
Abdulmejid, Sultan 160, 166, 325–6n92
Abraham III, Catholicos 107
Abraham Petros I Ardzivian, Patriarch 110
Abramov, Sergey 286
Abu'l-Aswar Shavur, Emir 17, 18
Abu Bakr, Nusrat al-Din, *atabeg* 22, 25, 30
Abu Bakr, Miran Shah's son 76
Abu Sa'id, Il-Khan 47
Abu Said, Miran Shah's grandson, 322n34
Abuletisdze, Dzagan, Duke 14
Adam of Gaston, Baron and Regent 61
al-Adid, Caliph 53
al-Adil I Ayyub, Emir 30
al-Afdal Shahanshah, Vizier 50, 51–2
Afridun, Shirvanshah 15, 16
Agha Muhammad Khan Qajar 135, 136
Aghbugha II, *atabeg* 81
Aghsartan I (Akhsitan), King 10–11
Aghsartan I (Akhsitan) ibn Manuchihr, King 20
Aghsartan II, King 15
Aharonian, Avetis 329n147
Ahmad, Il-Khan 41
Ahmad Jalayir, Sultan 75
Ahmad Khan Usmi of the Kaitag 129
Ahmad Shah Qajar, Shah 178
Ahmed III, Sultan 109
Akhtayev, Akhmad 283, 288
Akhundov, Vali (Vəli Axundov) 243, 246
'Ala al-Din Muhammad II, Shah 31, 35
Albrecht, Prince of Prussia 161
Alda, Alanian Princess 8–9
Aleksandre I, *eristavi* 75
Aleksandre (Alexander) I, King 76, 78–9, 80, 81

Aleksandre I of Kakheti, King 82, 84
Aleksandre II of Imereti, King 82, 84
Aleksandre II of Kakheti, King 92, 93–4, 95
Aleksandre III of Imereti, King 100, 101
Aleksandre III of Kakheti, King 107
Aleksandre IV of Imereti, King 101
Aleksandre, Prince (Vakhtang VI's grandson) 111
Aleksandre of Imereti, Prince 103
Alekseyev, Mikhail Vasilyevich 218, 330n201
Alexander I, Tsar 136, 137, 138, 141–2, 143, 324n1
Alexander II, Tsar 129, 161, 164, 165, 166
Alexander III, Tsar 166, 170, *225*
Alexander, Prince 143
Alexander Gagarin, Prince 161
Alexei I, Tsar 100, 130
Alexios I Komnenos, Emperor 27, 53–4
Alexios III Angelos, Emperor 60
'Ali, Caliph 84
Ali-Bey, Sefer 324n21
'Ali ibn Musa al-Rida, eighth Shiite Imam *258*
Alibek Haji (Khadzhi) 169–70
Alice of Armenia, Levon I's niece 59
Alikhanov-Avarsky, Maksud, General 180
Aliyev, Heydar (Heydər Əliyev), General and President 243, 246, 252–3, 254–5, 259, 260, 262, 264, 265, 294
Aliyev, Ilham, President 260, 265, 294–5, 298, 301, 302
Aliyev, Mukhu 292
Alkhanov, Alu 286
Allaverdi II Hasan Jalalyan, melik 36
Allen, W.E.D. 89, 92, 112, 324n25, 327n18
Alp Arslan, Sultan 10, 11, 12
Alqas Mirza, Governor 87–8
Amak Bek 150
Amaury I (Amalric) of Jerusalem 53, 56–7
Amaury de Lusignan 60, 71
Ambrosi, Catholicos-Patriarch 226
al-Amir, Caliph 52
Amirov, Said 293
Ananias, Archbishop 60
Andranik Ozanian, General 185, 189, 195, 200, 205, *263*
Andronikos Komnenos, Emperor 27
Andropov, Yuri 246
Ankvab, Aleksandr 310
Anna, Empress 48

Anton II, Catholicos 137
Apraksin, Fyodor Matveyevich, General Admiral 129, 132
Apridon 22
Archil (Nazar Khan), King 101, 103
Ardzinba, Vladislav 269–70
Areveltsi, Vardan 18, 42
Arghun, Il-Khan 45
Arghun Aqa, Emir 40–1, 42
Argutinsky-Dolgorukov, Prince *157*
Arsanov, Vakha 283
Arslan-Shah, Prince 18
Artsruni, Abul Gharib 53
Artsruni family 26, 37, 54
Ascelin of Cremona 42
Ashot I Bagrationi, *kouropalates* 136
Ashraf Hotaki Ghilzai, Shah 107
al-Ashraf Musa, Emir 35
al-Ashraf Sha'ban, Sultan 72
Atatürk *see* Kemal Pasha, Mustafa
al-Athir, Izz ad-Din ibn 10, 33, 35, 51, 62, 66, 318n82
Athon, King 15
Äträk, Prince 15
Atsiz ibn Uvaq 12
Aushev, Ruslan, General 280
Avar royal family 153, 156
al-Awhad Ayyub, Emir 30, 35
Ayuka Khan 131–2

B

Babadzhanian, Hamazasp, Chief Marshal 240
Babikian, Astvatzatur, Abbot 110
Baddeley, John F. 118, 324n4
Badr al-Jamali, Vizier 50, 52, 54, 57
Bagapsh, Sergei 310, 337n103
al-Baghdadi, Abu Bakr 290, 335n5
al-Baghdadi, Khalid, Sheikh 152
Baghirov, Kamran 252
Baghirov, Mir Jafar (Mircəfər Bağırov) 226, 240–1, 243
Baghvashi family 14
Bagramyan, Ivan, Marshal 240
Bagrat I, Prince of Mukhrani 85
Bagrat III, King 8, 46
Bagrat III of Imereti, King *13*, 87
Bagrat IV, King 8, 9–11, 12, 317n10
Bagrat IV of Imereti, King 101
Bagrat V, Prince and King *13*, 48, 74–5
Bagrat VI/Bagrat II of Imeret 81–2
Bagrat VII (Bagrat Khan) 96
Bahaeddin Şakir 189
Baibars I, Sultan 43, 44, 46, 65–6, 67

Baiju Noyan, General 40, 42, 63, 64
Bairam Beg 84
Bakar, Regent 104
Bakikhanov, Abbas Qoli 87
Balagai, Prince 43
Baldwin I of Jerusalem (Baldwin of Boulogne), King 51, 54
Baldwin III of Jerusalem, King 56
Baldwin of Marash 55
Balfour, Arthur 205
Bamatov, Haydar 196
Bar Hebraeus 64, 67
Baraq Khan 4
Baratashvili, Nikoloz *304*
Barsama, Philaretos' son 53
Barsegh I, Catholicos 54
Bartolomeo of Bologna 47
Baryatinsky, Alexander Ivanovich, General and Viceroy 161, 162, 164, 165
Barzani, Mustafa, Mullah 241
Basayev, Shamil 261, 270, 276, 278, 280, 282, 283, 286
Basil, Emperor 48
Basil II, Emperor 8
Batu Khan 36, 40, 42, 43, 64, 319n138, 319n153
Baydu, Il-Khan 45
Bayezid I, Sultan 76
Bayezid II, Sultan 85
Bebutov, Vasily Ossipovich, General 160
Behbud Khan Javanshir 328n34
Beka Jaqeli of Samtskhe 46, 48
Bell, James Stanislaus 132, 152, 160, 323n8
Benedict XII, Pope 69
Berdi Beg, Governor 48
Bergmann, Georgy, General 185–6
Beria, Lavrenti 179, 182, 225–6, 233, 240, 241, 242, 331n10
Berke, Khan 43, 44, 65, 319n138, 319n152, 319n153
Berkyaruq, Sultan 14
Berthelot, Philippe 208
Beybulat Taymazoğlu (Taymi Bibolt) 150
Bibilov, Anatoly 294, 310, 312, 338n109
Bicherakhov, Georgy 218
Bicherakhov, Lazar, Colonel 202, 218
Bierkamp, Walther 236
Bilarghu, Emir 58, 68, 69
Birkin, Rodion Petrovich 93, 94
Bismarck, Otto von 4, 170
Blinken, Antony 333n34
Bohemond II of Antioch, King 55
Bohemond III of Antioch, King 57, 59, 60
Bohemond IV of Antioch, King 61–2, 64
Bohemond of Taranto, Prince 54

Borena, Princess 10
Boris Godunov, Tsar 94, 122, 324n29
Boschayev, Akhmet 275
Bournoutian, George A. 325n48
Brezhnev, Leonid 244, 246
Budyonny, Semyon, General 222
Bugha, Emir 45
Bulakh Khan 153
Burdukhan, Giorgi III's wife 22
Burjanadze, Nino 272
Buryatsky, Said (Aleksandr Tikhomirov) 293
Bush, George W. 307
Buturlin, Ivan, General 96, 122, 126
Bzhania, Aslan 310

C

Callixtus III, Pope 81
Carpine, Giovanni da Pian del 63, 64, 321n56
Catherine II, Tsarina 105, 111, 135–6
Celestine III, Pope 60
Cemal Azmi 189
Cemal (Jemal) Bey 188, 328n28
Chagatai Khan 319n149
Chancellor, Richard, Captain 105
Chardin, Jean 90, 96, 101
Charles V, Emperor 87
Chavchavadze, Ilia 180
Cherevichenko, Yakov, General 233
Cherkezov, Varlam 179
Chermoyev, Abdul Mejid (Tapa) 217, 218
Chernomyrdin, Viktor 275, 276
Chkheidze, Nikolai (Karlo) 180, 194
Chkhenkeli, Akaki 195
Chkhetidze, Yevdemon, Catholicos 13
Choban, Emir 47
Chormaghun (Chormaqan), General 35, 36, 40, 62
Chqondideli, Giorgi, Archbishop 13, 15, 17
Christie, Charles, Captain 143
Churchill, Winston 185, 186, 327n5
Çiller, Tansu 214, 254, 262
Clement III, Pope 58
Clement VI, Pope 71
Clement XI, Pope 58
Clinton, Bill 255
Clinton, Hillary 302
Conrad of Hildesheim, Bishop 60
Conrad von Wittelsbach, Cardinal 60
Constantine I, Emperor 43
Constantine IX, Emperor 10
Cornell, Svante 255, 280, 334n87
Curzon, George Nathaniel, Lord 145, 205

D

Dadiani, Nino, regent-dowager 324n21
Dadiani family 78, 83, 87, *136*, 138
Dadishkeliani, Konstantine 161
Dadoyan, Seta 50, 52
Daichin Tayishi, King 130, 131
Dalai Lama 276
Damadian, Mihran 216
Damat Ferid Pasha, Grand Vizier 188, 189
Daniyal, Sultan 159
Darbinyan, Armen 264
D'Arcy, Joseph, Major 143
Dardel, Jean 72

Darejan, Queen consort 101, 323n90
Darma Bala 132
Davit, Catholicos 79
Davit, Prince 136
Davit I of Kakheti, King 94
Davit II, Catholicos 322n29
Davit II of Imereti, King 138
Davit III, Catholicos 81, 322n29
Davit III Kouropalates of Tao 8
Davit IV (David), King 10, 12, *12*, 13–18, *13*, *16*, *17*, **19**, 34, 46
Davit IV, Catholicos 322n29
Davit V, Catholicos 243
Davit V, Prince and King 18, 21
Davit VI Narin, King 34, 36, 37, 40, 42, 47
Davit VII Ulu, Prince and King 30, 36, 40, 42, 43–4, 319n103, 319n116
Davit VIII, King 45–6, 47
Davit IX, King 48
Davit X, King 85, 87
Davit XI (Daud Khan), King 89, 90, 92, 99
Davit of Kakheti, Prince 8
Davit Soslan, Prince and Consort King 22, 23, 25, 27, 30
De Castelli, Teramo Christoforo 100
De Waal, Thomas 301
Değmer, Mustafa Arif 188
Demetre I, Prince and King 9–10, *12*, 18, 20
Demetre II, Prince and King 15, 16, 44–5
Demetre III, co-ruler King 79, 81
Demetre of Kakheti 84–5
Demirchyan, Karen 245, 251, 252, 264
Demirel, Süleyman 254–5
Demna (Demetre), Prince 20, 21
Denikin, Anton Ivanovich, General 199, 200, 203, 204, 205, 206, 211, 329n92
  White army 199, 201, 204, 207, 210, 217, 218–22, *220*, 224, 330n201, 330n209
Derev, Stanislav 278
Devlet Giray, Crimean Tatar Khan 90, 119, 121
Disraeli, Benjamin 170
Div Sultan Rumlu, General 87
Dmitry Svyatopolk-Mirsky, Prince 169
Doihara, Kenji, Colonel 230
Dokuz Khatun, Hülegü's wife 43, 64
Donduk Dashi Khan 132
Donduk Ombo Khan 132
Dondukov-Korsakov, Alexander 166, 167
Doukas family 27
Dro (Drastamat Kanayan), General 185, 189, 200, 206, 214, 239
Dubois de Montpéreux, Frédéric 151–2
Dudayev, Dzhokhar 268, 280, 281–2, 293, 333n68
Dunsterville, Lionel, Major General 202
Durgulel, King 10, 11
D'Usson, Jean-Louis, Marquis 106

E

Eastmond, Antony 26, 30
Edward I of England, King 65
Elchibey (Elçibəy, 'the messenger', Abulfaz Aliyev) 246, 252, 253–5, 259
Eldigüz, Shams al-Din, *atabeg* 18, 21

Elena of Imereti *13*
Elizabeth I, Queen 122
Eljigidei, General 64
Emmanuel, Georgy Arsenyevich, General 153
Enver Pasha, İsmail 4, 176, 185–7, 189, 193, 195, 196, 199, 201–3
Eprem II, Catholicos 243
Erdoğan, Recep Tayyip 301
Erekle I of Kakheti, King 100, 101
Erekle I of Kartli (Nazar Ali Khan) 101–1
Erekle II of Kakheti and Kartli, King 107, 108, 111–12, *134*, 135, 136
Eugene III, Pope 60
Eugene IV, Pope 80

F

Fadhl II of Ganja, Emir 10–11
Fadhl IV, Emir 18
Fadhlallah Hamdani, Rashid al-Din, Grand Vizier 43
Fakhr al-Din Bahramshah, Emir 318n80
Farrukh Yasar, Shirvanshah 84
Fäsi, Johann Kaspar, Major General 156, 158
Fath-'Ali, Shah 141–2, 143–4
Fath-'Ali Khan Quba'i 111
Fath-'Ali Shah Qajar 136
Feodor I, Tsar 93, 94, 324n29
Ferhad Pasha 89
Filimonov, Ataman Alexander Petrovich 218–19, 222
Foch, Ferdinand, Field Marshal 210
Francis, Pope 260
Franz Ferdinand of Austria, Crown Prince Archduke 170, 185
Frederick I Barbarossa, Emperor 17, 22, 58
Frederick II, Emperor 35
Frederick III, Emperor 81
Frederick VI, Duke of Swabia 22
Freytag, Robert Karlovich, General 159
Fukuyama, Francis 274, 334n2

G

Gabriel de Luetz, Baron 87
Gabriel of Melitene 50
Gagetsi, Vahram 36
Gagik II, King 53
Gagloyev, Alan 312, 338n109
Gaidar, Yegor 275
Galafiyev, General 158
Galvani, Pelagio 31
Gamidov, Abdusamad 293
Gamrekeli Toreli 22
Gamsakhurdia, Konstantine 244
Gamsakhurdia, Zviad 244, 265–6, 267–8, 269, 270, 272, 288, 332n98
Gardane, Claude Matthieu de 141
Garegin II, Catholicos 302
Garsevan Chavchavadze, Prince 135
Gasanov, Abusupyan 336n13
Gaspıralı (Gasprinsky), Ismail 181
Gayane, Abbess 79
Gaykhatu, Il-Khan 45
Genghis Khan 31, 32, 43, 65, 75–6, 319n138, 319n149
Getagazhev, Artur 293
Gevorg V Surenian, Patriarch-Catholicos 176, 184–5

Ghazan, Il-Khan 41, 45–6, 67, 68, 321n85
Ghazi, Emir 55
Ghazi, Prince 121
Ghazi Muhammad, Dagestani Avar Imam 149, 152, 153
Ghazi Muhammad Pasha (Shamil's son) 157, 159, *161*, 164, 169
Ghiyath ad-Din, Prince 33–4
Ghiyath al-Din Masud, Sultan 18
Gilbert de Bois 31
Giorgi I, King 8–9, 317n6
Giorgi I Dadiani, *eristavi* 136
Giorgi I, Prince and King of Georgia (r. 1072–1089) 10, 11, 12–13, 14
Giorgi II of Imereti, King (r. 1565–1585) *13*
Giorgi II of Kakheti, King (r. 1511–1513) 84–5
Giorgi III, Prince and King 18, 20, 21–2, *21*
Giorgi III of Imereti 96
Giorgi IV Lasha, co-ruler King 22, 27, 30–3, 34, 40
Giorgi V 'the Magnificent', King 46, 47–8
Giorgi VI, Prince and King 46
Giorgi VII, Prince and King 75, 76
Giorgi VIII/Giorgi I of Kakheti, King 79, 81–2
Giorgi IX, King 87
Giorgi X of Kartli, King 93, 95, 96
Giorgi XI of Kartli (Shah Nawaz II), King 101–2
  Gurgin Khan 102, 104
Giorgi XII, King 136
Giray, Adil, *shamkhal* 104
Glonistavisdze, Anton, Archbishop 27
Gmelin, Samuel Gottlieb 129
Godfrey of Bouillon 51
Golikov, Filipp, General 231
Golitsyn, Grigory Sergeyevich 167, 169, 179
Golovin, Yevgeny Alexandrovich, General 156, 158
Goltz, Thomas 254
González de Clavijo, Ruy 76
Gorbachev, Mikhail 244, 246, 248, 251–2, 253, 265, 266, 281
Gorchkhanov, Ilyas 278
Göring, Hermann 230
Gosh, Mkhitar 24, 25, *25*
Gotsinsky, Najmuddin 217, 218, 224
Grabbe, Pavel Khristoforovich, General 152, 156–7, 158
Grachev, Pavel 282, 284
Grechko, Andrei, General 237
Gregory IX, Pope 37, 40
Grekov, Nikolai Vasilyevich, General 150
Grigor II, Catholicos 54
Grigor II Vkayaser, Catholicos 52, 54
Grigor III, Catholicos 54
Grigor IV Tgha, Catholicos 60
Grigor V, Catholicos 60
Grigor VI Apirat, Catholicos 60
Grigor VII, Catholicos 67, 68
Grigor IX, Catholicos 80
Grigores, Abbot 25
Grigoryan, Mavel, General 302
Gryznov, General 180
Gudovich, General 135, 141, 142, 149
Güldenstädt, Johann Anton 324n43
Gumbaridze, Givi 265–6
Gumbatov, Alikram (Hummatov), Colonel 255
Gurandukht (Äträk's daughter) 317n35
Gurandukht (Bagrat IV's sister) 10

Gurandukht (Davit IV's wife) 18, 318n46
Gurieli, Sophia, Regent-Dowager 138
Guy de Lusignan *see* Kostantin II of Cilician Armenia
Guy de Lusignan of Jerusalem, King 57, 58
Güyük, Great Khan 40, 43, 63, 64, 321n56
Gvantsa, Davit Ulu's wife 42

H

Hadid, Zaha 295
al-Hafiz, Caliph 52
Hagelin, Karl Wilhelm 173–4
Hagop, scribe 23
Hajinsky, Isabey, Baron 172
Hajji Bakr 160
Hajji Daud 105, 323n96
Hajji Muhammad 160
Hajji Murad 153, 156, 157, 159
al-Hakim bin-Amr Allah, Fatimid caliph 8
Hamazasp (Srvandztian) 189
Hamidov, Iskender (İsgəndər Həmidov) 254, 261
Hamza Bek, Dagestani Avar Imam 149, 152, 153, 156
al-Harakani, Said, *alim* 150
Hart, Liddell 235
Harutyunyan, Grigor (Grigory Arutinov) 242
Harutyunyan, Suren 251
Hasan-i Buzurg, Jalayirid ruler 48
Hasan-i Kuchik, Prince 48
Hasan Jalal Dawla of Khachen 36, 42, 63, 81
Haydar, Sheikh 84
Hekmatyar, Gulbuddin 262
Helena (Emperor Constantine's mother) 43
Helena Argyros, Princess 9
Henry I of Jerusalem, King 59
Henry VI, Emperor 60
Henry of Cyprus, King 63
Hethum I, King 62–4, 66, 67
Hethum II, King 46, 67–8
Hethum II, Regent 58
Hethum III, Baron 61
Hethum of Korykos 45, 62
Hewitt, George 324n21
Hewsen, Robert 81
Heygendorff, Ralph von, Colonel 238
Himmler, Heinrich 236
Hitler, Adolf 134, 230, 232, 237, 238, 331n51
see also Nazi Germany
Hobart Pasha (Augustus Charles Hobart-Hampden) 326n140
Hoff, Nicolai 178
Honorius III, Pope 35
Hovannisian, Richard G. 175, 209
Hovhannes Krnetsi 47
Hovhannes-Smbat III, Armenian ruler 8
Hovhannisyan, Hovhannes, Abbot 300
Hovsepian, General 207
Hrahad 50, 320n4
Hülegü, Il-Khan 42–4, 62, 64–5, 66, 319n153
Husayn, Shah 98, 102, 104
Husayn ibn al-Afdal 51
Huseynov, Surat (Surət Hüseynov) 254, 260, 262

I

Ibrahim I, Shirvanshah 75, 76
Ibrahim II, Sheikh 84
Ibrahim Inal 10
Ibrahim Khalil Khan Javanshir, King 111
Ibrahim Pasha, Ottoman General 61
Ibrahim Pasha Milli 176
Iese (Ali Quli Khan/Mustapha Pasha) 104, 106–7
Ilia II, Catholicos 243
Ilyumzhinov, Kirsan 277
Imad al-Din Zengi, *atabeg* 55
Inauri, Aleksi, General 242
Innocent XI, Pope 101
Ioane IV, Catholicos 15
Ioane VI, Catholicos 24–5
Ioane VII, Catholicos 23
Ioseliani, Jaba 265–6, 268, 270, 272
Irene Palaiologina (Emperor Basil's wife) 48
Isa Khan of Kakheti 96
Isakov, Ivan, Admiral 240
Iskander, ruler of the Qara Qoyunlu 320n171
Isma'il, Shah 84, 85, 87
Isma'il Mirza, Governor 87, 88
Ismailov, Abdulkhakim 239
Iulon, Prince 136
Ivan III of Moscow, Grand Duke 84
Ivan IV 'Grozny', Tsar 90, 95, 105, 115, 118–19, 121, 122
Ivane II Jaqeli of Samtskhe, *atabeg* 76, 78
Ivane Abazasdze, Duke 8
Ivane Baghvashi 12
Ivane Bagration-Mukhransky, Prince 160, 326n95
Ivane Mukhrani, Prince 135
Ivanishvili, Bidzina 271, 309
Ivelich, Major General 156
Izzet Pasha, Yusuf, Major General 203

J

Ja'afar al-Sadiq 323n112
Jacob of Tarsus, Catholicos 69
Jadaros, Prince 15
Jafar Pasha, 93
Jaffar III Ali, Emir 9
Jahan Shah, Muzaffar al-Din, Sultan 79, 80, 81, 322n27, 322n34
Jalal al-Din Manguberti, Sultan 30, 35–6, 319n106
Jamal al-Din 156, 160, 326n94
Jani Beg, Khan 48, 320n175
Jaqeli family 89, 90
Jaubert, Pierre Amédée 140, 141
Javadov, Rovshan (Rövşən Cavadov), Colonel 254–5, 262
Jebe, Mongol General 32, 33
Jemal Pasha, Ahmed 176, 189, 328n28
Jevdet (Cevdet) Bey 186, 189
Jochi Khan 319n138, 319n149, 319n153
John, Prester 17
John II Komnenos, Emperor 55, 71
John XXII, Pope 46
John Armenia 53
John de Brienne, King of Jerusalem 61
John of Castile, King 72
John of Florence, 46–7
John of Montecorvino, Archbishop 68
John Paul II, Pope 260

Jones, Harford, Sir 141, 142
Joscelin II, Count of Edessa 55
Junaid, Sheikh 84
Juvaini, 'Ala al-Din Ata-Malik 35, 40, 42, 319n138
Juvaini, Shams al-Din, Vizier 42

K

al-Kadari, Abu Muhammad (Rustam Aselderov) 290
Kadyrov, Akhmad 284, 286
Kadyrov, Ramzan 280, 281, 286, 290, 293
Kadyrov family 286
Kai-Khosrow II, Sultan 36, 40, 319n116
Kaikhosro II Jaqeli, *atabeg* 87
Kaikhosro Bagrationi, King 102
Kaitukin, Sheapshoko (Qeitiqwe) 121
Kajaznuni, Hovhannes 200
Kalamanos, Governor 57
Kaledin, Ataman Aleksei 218
Kalimatov, Mahmud-Ali 294
Kamenev, Lev 173
Kamkov, Fyodor, Major General 237
Kanbulat, Prince 121
Kantaria, Meliton Varlamis dze, Sergeant 239
Karabekir Pasha, Kâzım, General 195, 206, 211, 211–13
Karachaqay Khan 98
Kay-Qubad I, Sultan 35, 62, 63
Kebedov, Bagaudin 283
Ked Buqa, Commander 64, 65
Kekaumenos, General 10
Kelesh Ahmed Bey 138
Kemal Pasha, Mustafa (Atatürk) 191, 206, 207, 210, 211–12
Kerbogha, *atabeg* 54
Kerensky, Aleksandr 193, 218
Kerry, John 333n44
Keshishian, Gabriel ('Mihran') 176
Ketevan, Dowager Queen 96, 98
Kevork V, Catholicos 226
Kevork VI, Catholicos 245
Khadjimba, Raul 310
Khalil, Sultan (al-Ashraf Khalil) 66, 67
Khalil Bey, General 196, 206
Khalid ibn al-Walid 290
Khalil Pasha, General 201
Khalilov, Rappani 287
Khalilullah II, Sheikh 84
Khanjian, Aghasi 226
Khatisyan, Alexander 213
al-Khattab (Samir al-Suwailim) 261, 282, 283, 286, 288
Kheren Donduk Khan 132
Khodarkovsky, Michael 114, 119
Khoo-Örlög Tayishi, King 130
Khoren I, Catholicos 226
Khosia Lashkhishvili, Vizier 101
Khoyski, Fatali Khan (Fətəli xan Xoyski) 205, 328n34
Khrimian, Mkrtich, Patriarch-Catholicos 176
Khrushchev, Nikita 226, 242–3, 246, 248, 277
'Secret Speech' 242, 276
Khudabanda, Shah 92
Khudyakov, Sergei, Marshal 240
Khutlu Bugha, *amirspasalar* 44, 45
Khwandamir, Ghiyas ad-Din Muhammad 75
Kilaghbian, Yeghia, General Abbot 110

Kilij Arslan II, Sultan 57
Kirakos I of Khor Virap, Catholicos 80
Kirakos Gandzaketsi 24, 36, 40, 42, 60, 63, 64
Kirichenko, Nikolai, General 237
Kirov, Sergei 214, 216, 218
Kisriev, Enver 114, 283, 284, 292
Kissinger, Henry 3–4
Kitovani, Tengiz 265, 268, 270, 272
Kleist, Ewald von, Field Marshal 232, 233, 235, 237, 238
Klugenau, Franz Klüge von, Major General 156, 158
Knorring, Carl Heinrich von, General 136
Kocharyan, Robert 262, 263–4, 265, 302
Kochinyan, Anton 242–3, 245
Kogh Vasil, 'Basil the Bandit' 50, 55
Kokoity, Eduard 305
Kolchak, Aleksandr, Admiral 220–1, 330n204
Komnenos, Andronikos 56
Komnenos, David 27
Komnenos, Manuel 21, 27
Komnenos family 27
Kondratyev, Veniamin, Governor 276
Konrad, Rudolf, General 237
Konstantine, King (r. 1293–1327 in Imereti) 47
Konstantine I of Georgia, King (Giorgi VII's half-brother, r. 1405–1412) 76
Konstantine I of Kakheti 92, 95–6
Konstantine I of Vahka, Baron 53, 54
Konstantine II of Georgia, King 82–3
Konstantine II of Kakheti (Muhammad Quli Khan), King 106–7
Korganian, Stepan 207
Kornilov, Lavr, General 218, 219
Kostantin I, Catholicos 57
Kostantin I of Cilician Armenia, King 68
Kostantin II of Cilician Armenia, Baron 53
Kostantin II of Cilician Armenia (Guy de Lusignan), King 71
Kostantin III, Catholicos 69
Kostantin III of Cilician Armenia, King 63, 71–2
Kostantin IV of Cilician Armenia, King 72
Kostantin VI, Catholicos of Vahka 80
Kostantin of Barbaron 61–2
Kostantin *sparapet* 69
Kotlyarevsky, Pyotr, Major General 143
Kovalensky, Pyotr Ivanovich 136
Kozak, Dmitry 291
Krasin, Leonid 173, 179
Krasnov, Pyotr, General 219, 330n202
Kravchenko, General 169
Kress von Kressenstein, Friedrich Freiherr, General 176, 195, 196, 199, 200, 201–2
Krimetsi, Malachia 72
Kublai Khan, Great Khan 43, 44, 319n153
Kuchenei (Gueshchenei/Maria Cherkasskaya) 90, 119
Kunduchov, Musa, General 165
Kutateladze, Vakhtang 272
Kutayfat ibn al-Afdal, Vizier and Caliph 52
Kvirike III of Kakheti, Prince 8, 93
Kymineianos, Eustathios, Admiral 56

L

Lakoba, Nestor 226
Lala Mustafa Pasha 92
Lavrov, Sergei 302, 307
Lazarev, Ivan, General 136, 137
Lenin 173, 179, 194, 198, 211, 212, 216, 224, 240
Levan I Dadiani of Mingrelia, King 87
Levan I of Kakheti, King 86, 87, *88*, 89, 90, 92
Levan, Prince 135
Levon I, Baron (Leon, Leo, r. 1129–1137) 55
Levon I, King (Leon, Leo, r. 1198–1219) 24, *52*, 57–61, *57*
Prince Levon II (1187–1198) 60
Levon II, Prince and King 65, 66, 67
Levon III, King *58*, 68
Levon IV, King 69
Levon V, King 72, 321n104
Lindsay, Henry, Lieutenant 143
Liparit IV Baghvashi, Duke 8, 9–10
Liparit V Baghvashi, Duke 12, 14
Liparit family 9
Lissanevich, General 150
List, Field Marshal 233, 235, 237
Litvinenko, Aleksandr 264–5
Lloyd George, David 210
Longworth, John 152
Loris-Melikov, Mikhail, Lieutenant General 169
Lossow, Otto von, General 196, 199
Louis IX, King of France 41, 63–4, 81
Luarsab I of Kartli, King 87, 89
Luarsab II Kartli, King 96
Lucius III, Pope 60
Ludovico da Bologna 81
Lyakhov, Vladimir, General 186

M

MacDonell, Ranald, Major 202
Madatov, Major General 150
Magomedov, Magomedali 292, 336n11
Magomedov, Magomedsalam 292
Mahmud I, Sultan-Caliph 108
Mahmud II bin Muhammad, Sultan 16, 17, 18
Mai-Mayevsky, Vladimir, General 221
Makayev, Daurbek 279
Malcolm, John, Captain 141
Malenkov, Georgy 226
Malik Shah, Sultan 10, 12, 13, 14, 317n28
Malik Shah of Iconium 54
Mamia I of Guria, King 87
Mammadov, Novruz (Məmmədov) 295
Mammadov, Yagub (Yaqub Məmmədov) 254
Mammadova, Gulchohra (Gülçöhrə Məmmədova) 246
Mamontov, Konstantin, General 221
Mamstruk, Prince 121
Mankaberdeli family 44
Manstein, Erich von, Field Marshal 238
Mansur, Sheikh (Ushurma) 149, 152, 293
Mantashev, Alexander 173
Manuchihr (Manuchar) I 87
Manuchihr II Jaqeli (Mustafa Pasha), Prince 89
Manuchihr III ibn Kasran, Shirvanshah 15, 17, 18
Manuel I Komnenos, Emperor 17, 56, 57

Manukian, Aram 200
Mao Zedong 226
Mar Yahballaha III, Nestorian Catholicos 67
Marco Polo 62, 66–7
Margvelashvili, Giorgi 309
Mariam Artsruni of Vashpurakan, Queen Dowager 8, 9, 10
Markare of Ani 23
Marshall, Alex 227
Marta, Princess 10
Marutha, St 42
Marx, Karl 248
Maskhadov, Aslan 282–3, 284, 286
Mas'ud I, Sultan 56
Matteos II Izmirlian, Patriarch-Catholicos 176
Matthew of Edessa 50, 54
Mazniashvili, Giorgi, General 198–9, 200
Medvedev, Dmitry 280, 294, 302, 307
Mehmet II, Sultan 82, 119, 322n33
Mehmet III, Sultan 93
Mehmet V, Sultan 185
Melkhonian, Stephanos, Abbot 110
Menyaylo, Sergey 294
Merkel, Angela 337n74
Mesrop I of Cilicia, Catholicos 71–2
Mesrop of Khizan 96, *98*
Metsobetsi, Tovma 75
Michael II Doukas, Prince and Emperor 10
Michael IX Palaiologos, Emperor 67
Michael Romanov, Tsar 99
Mikaelian, Arsen 206
Mikel (Michael) I, King 47
Mikhail Nikolayevich, Grand Duke 165, 166, 171
Mikoyan, Anastas 202
Miles, Richard 272
Milne, George, Major General 199, 200, 206–7
Milyutin, Dmitry Alekseyevich, General 156, 161, 163, 164, 169, 170
Minas, Bishop 25
Minorsky, Vladimir 20
Mir Mahmud 102
Mir Ways 102, 107
Miran Shah, Governor 75, 76
Mirtskhulava, Aleksandre 242
Mirza Muhammad Reza Qazvini *139*, 141
Mitayev, Ali, Sheikh 224
Mkhargrdzeli, Avag, *amirspalasar* 35, 36–7, 40, 42, 62
Mkhargrdzeli, Ivane, *msakhurtukhutsesi* and *atabeg* 23–4, 25, 26, *27*, 30, 31, 32, 34, 35, *43*
Mkhargrdzeli, Sargis, *amirspalasar* 21, 23, 318n62
Mkhargrdzeli, Shanshe 30, 36, 41, *43*
Mkhargrdzeli, Vahram 31, 32
Mkhargrdzeli, Zakare, *amirspalasar* 23, 24–5, 26, *27*, 30, 318n62
Mkhargrdzeli, Zakare II 41, 42
Mkhargrdzeli brothers 22, 23–7, *24*, 30
see also Mkhargrdzeli, Ivane; Mkhargrdzeli, Zakare
Mkhargrdzeli family 26, 37, 42, *157*
Mkhetsidze family *102*
Mkhitar (Mekhitar) Sebastatsi 109–10
Mkhitar Sparapet 106
Mleh I, Baron 57
Mohammad, Qazi 241
Mohammad Reza, Shah 240

Mohammed bin Salman, Crown Prince 304
Molotov, Vyacheslav 226, 240
Momine Khatun 18
Monck-Mason, Major 205
Möngke, Great Khan 37, 41, 42, 43, 64–5, 319n153
Möngke-Temür Khan 44–5
Morgenthau, Henry 186–7
Mshetsi, Nerses 44
Mugith al-Din Tughril Shah, Emir 33
Muhammad, Prophet 84, 149, 164
Muhammad I Tapar, Sultan 15
Muhammad 'Ali Mirza 141
Muhammad 'Ali Shah Qajar, Shah 178
Muhammad Amin 160, 325–6n92
Muhammad Asiyalav 160
Muhammad Hasan Khan 111
Muhammad Şefi (Shafi), Shamil's son 161
Mukhitar I, Catholicos 69, 71
Mukhrani family 85, 191, 135
Mukhrani-Bagrationi family 107, 326n95
Mulard, François Henri *139*
Münejjimbashi, Ahmad ibn Lütfullah 75
Münnich, von, Field Marshal 129, 134
Murad III, Sultan 89
Muratoff, Paul 327n18
Muravyov-Amursky, Nikolai Nikolayevich, General 326n93
Muravyov-Karsky, Nikolai Nikolayevich, General 160, *168*, 326n93
Musayev, Musa 293
Mustafayev, Imam 243
al-Mustali (Ahmad ibn al-Mustansir), Caliph 50–1
al-Mustansir, Caliph 50, 51
Mutallibov, Ayaz (Mütəllibov) 253–4
Muzaffar al-Din Qajar, Shah 178
Myshlayevsky, Aleksandr, General 185, 186
Mzetchabuk Jaqeli of Samtskhe-Saatabago, *atabeg* 87
Mzhavanadze, Vasil, General 242, 244

N

Nader Shah (Tahmasp-Quli Khan) 107–8, 111, *168*
Najm al-Din Ilghazi ibn Artuq, ruler of Aleppo 16, 51
Napoleon I, Emperor 110, 129, 138, *139*, 141
1798 Egyptian campaign 140
1812 invasion of Russia 142
see also Napoleonic Wars
Narimanov, Nariman 215
al-Nasawi, Muhammad 35, 36
al-Nasir, Caliph 25
Nasir al-Din Vahram Shah, Emir 27
Nazarbekian, Tovmas, General 194, 195, 200, 212
Nauruz, Emir 67
Nefiset (Shamil's grand-daughter) 164
Neidhardt, Alexander Ivanovich, General 158, 159
Nepokoychitsky, Arthur, General 169
Nerses IV Shnorhali, Catholicos 57
Neumann, Karl Friedrich 116
Nicholas I, Tsar 129, 143, 152, 156, 159, 160, 161, 165
Nicholas II, Tsar 167, 169, 176, 180–1, 193

Niedermayer, Oskar von, Major General 238
Nikephoros II Phokas, Emperor *58*, 71
Nikolai, Grand Duke 169, 190, *191*, 194
Nikolayevich de Giers, Mikhail 178
Nikon, Patriarch 122–3
Nizam al-Mulk, Vizier 10, 14, 317n28
Nizar ibn al-Mustansir 51, 52
Nobel, Alfred 171, 172, 173
Nobel, Emil 171
Nobel, Immanuel 171
Nobel, Immanuel (Ludwig's son) 173, 174, 326n158
Nobel brothers (Ludwig and Robert) 171–4, *171*
Nogai Noyan 43, 44
Norris, David, Commodore 202
Nubar, Boghos 329–30n147
Nur al-Din Zengi, *atabeg* 56
Nur al-Din Zengi, ruler of Syria 52–3, 57
Nuri Pasha (Nuri Killigil) 202, 205
Nzhdeh, Garegin (Ter-Harutyunyan), General 185, 205, 206, *213*, 214

O

Obama, Barack 309
Obruchev, Nikolay, General 170
Ögödei Great Khan 36, 40, 319n149
Oljeitu, Il-Khan 69
Omar, Caliph 108
Omar, Miran Shah's son 76
Omar Khan 135, 137
Omar Pasha 160
Orbelian, Abuleth, Governor 17, 18
Orbelian, Elikum 36
Orbelian, Ivane, Governor 18, 20, 21
Orbelian, Smbat 18, 36–7
Orbelian, Stepanos, Bishop and Archbishop 20, 21, 43, 44, *46*, 69, 80
Orbelian, Tarsaich, *atabeg* 44
Orbeliani, Grigol 165
Orbeliani family 20, 37, *40*, 44, *45*, 318n50
Ordzhonikidze, Sergo Konstantinovich 179, 180, 199, 214, 216, 218, 227
Oscar II, King 173
Oshin (founder of the Hethumid dynasty) 53, 54
Oshin, King 68–9
Oshin III, Baron 61
Oshin of Korykos, Regent 69, 71
Osman Ferid Pasha (Sheikh al-Haram) 164
Osman Pasha 92, 121
Othman Murad 156
Ott, Eugen, Colonel 230
Otto of Freising 17
Ouseley, Gore 143
Ozaki, Hotsumi 230, 231
Özbek Khan 46

P

Paata Bagrationi, Prince 111
Pakhu-Bike, regent 153
Pakourianos, Gregory 12
Palmerston, Lord 151
Pannwitz, Helmuth von, General 238
Pashinyan, Nikol 301, 302, 303, 304

Paskevich, Ivan Fyodorovich, General 90, 143–3, 146–7, 153, *168*, *193*
Patiashvili, Jumber 265
Paul I, Tsar 136
Paykar Khan, chieftain 98
Peratoner, Alberto 110
Peskov, Dmitry 294
Peter I, Tsar 96, 103, 104–5, 119, 126, 129, 132, 323n96, 323n99
Peter I of Cyprus, King 72
Philaretos Brachamios 50, 53
Philip, King 61–2
Philip IV, King of Spain 98–9
Philip VI, King of France 69
Philippa, Levon I's niece 61
Philippe II Augustus, French King 58
Philippe of Burgundy, Duke 81
Phokas, Nikephoros Barytrachelos 8
Pirumian, General 207
Pishevari, Sayyed Ja'far 241
Pius II, Pope 81
Platon Zubov, Prince 135
Plehve, Vyacheslav von 167, 169
Poghos (Paul) I, Catholicos 72
Poidebard, Antoine, Captain 206
Poroshenko, Petro 310
Potemkin, Grigory, Prince 135
Potemkin, Pavel, Lieutenant General 135
Proshian family *33*, *44*, *45*
Przhevalsky, Mikhail, General 193
Puntsuk Tayishi 131
Putin, Vladimir 272, 274, 276, 290, 302, 309, 312
   Chechnya and 274, 284, 286, 305
   on NATO's eastward expansion 306
   North Caucasus economy 291–2
   recentralization of Russian bureaucracy 292
   Wagner Group and 336n21

Q

Qalawun, Sultan 44, 46, 65, *65*, 66, 67
Qara Yusuf, Sultan 76
Qavam, Ahmad 241
Qizil Arslan, *atabeg* 22
Qubasar 21, 22
Quli, Prince 43
Qutlu Arslan 22
Qutlugh Shah, General 46, 68
Qvarqvare I Jaqeli, King 47
Qvarqvare II Jaqeli, King 81–2
Qvarqvare II of Samtskhe 82
Qvarqvare III of Samtskhe 87
Qvarqvare IV, *atabeg* 89

R

Rabban Bar Sauma 67
Radde, Gustav 143
Raduyev, Salman 283
Rahima Khanim *258*
Rainald of Dassel 22
Ramazanov, Sirajuddin 283
Ramishvili, Noe 225
Rasulzade, Mahammad Amin 182
Rawlinson, Alfred, Colonel 202, 208, 212, 330n172
Rayevsky, Nikolai, General 152
Rayfield, Donald 35, 135–6, 272
Raymond, Prince 59

Raymond I of Antioch, King 55
Raymond-Ruben, Prince 59, 60, 61
Raynald of Châtillon, Prince 56
Read, Nikolai Andreyevich, General 160
Reynolds, Michael 195
Reza Shah 240
Rice, Condoleezza 307, 337n77
Richard I of England, 'the Lionheart' 58
Richmond, Walter 119, 152, 283
Roger of Salerno 16
Roinashvili, Alexander *161*
Romanos III, Emperor 9
Romanos IV, Emperor 11
Romanov, Michael 122
Romieu, Antoine-Alexandre 141
Rosen, Grigory Vladimirovich, General 153
Rosenberg, Alfred 236
Roslin, Toros *44*
Rostom of Guria, Prince 87
Rostom Khan (Khosro Mirza), King 99, 100, 101
Rostom of Racha, *eristavi* 112
the Rothschilds 172, 173, 174
Roubaud, Franz 157
Ruben I, Baron 53
Ruben II, Baron 57
Ruben III, Baron 57
Rubruck, William of 41–2, 64
Ruoff, Richard, General 232, 237
Rukn al-Din Süleyman II, Sultan 27
Runciman, Steven 64
Rusudan (Davit IV's daughter) 15
Rusudan (Demetre I's daughter) 18
Rusudan (Giorgi III's daughter) 21, 27
Rusudan, (Davit IV's first wife) 15
Rusudan, Georgian Queen *13*, 22, 30, 33–5, 36, 37, 40, 62, 319n103, 319n116
Ruzzik ibn Tala'i, Vizier 53
Rycroft, William, Major General 200

S

Saakadze, Giorgi 96, 98
Saakashvili, Mikheil 272, 304–10, 334n105, 337n77
Sadulayev, Abdul-Halim 286
Sadun Mankaberdeli 44
Safi, Shah 99, 100
Safi al-Din Ishaq, Sheikh 84
Safonov, General 251
Saif ad-Din Qutuz, Sultan 64, 65
Saladin, Sultan (Salah al-Din Yusuf ibn Ayyub) 30, 53, 57, 58
Saltan Mahmut 96
Saltanuk (Sultanuko/Mikhail Temryukovich), Prince 119, 121
Sam Mirza 87
Samaghar, General 65
Sanakoyev, Dmitry 305
Sanders, Liman von, General 184
Sanuto the Elder, Marino 68
Sargis I of Jerusalem, Patriarch 68
Sargis Jaqeli, Prince 42, 43, 44
Sargsyan, Serzh 262, 263–4, 302
Sargsyan, Vazgen 264
Sarkissian, Armen 302–3
Sarkozy, Nicolas 308
Sartaq Khan 36, 64
Sattar Khan 178
Sayid Ahmed Orlat, lord of Shaki 76

Schellendorf, Friedrich Bronssart von, General 184
Schulenburg, Friedrich-Werner von der 196, 236
Sefer Bey Zaneqo 160
Selim I, Sultan 72, 85, 87
Selim Khan, ruler of Ganja 101
Semyon Zvenigorodsky, Prince 94
Semyonov, Vladimir 277–8
Senekerim-Hovhannes, Armenian ruler 8
Serebryakov, Lazar Markosovich, Admiral 152
Sergeyev, Igor 284
Şevki, Yakub, General 206
Shadjin Lama 276
Shah Nawaz II (Giorgi XI), King 101
Shah Rukh (Timur's son, 1409–1447) 78, 79, 322n17
Shah Rukh, Shirvanshah (r. 1535–1538) 87
Shahmazian, Arsen, Lieutenant Colonel 205
Shahumyan (Shaumian), Stepan 180, 182, 194, 195, 202, 329n115
Shahverdi Khan Ziyadoghlu Qajar, King 111
Shahverdi Sultan, Governor 89
Shamil, Dagestani Avar Imam 115, 149, 151, 152, 153, 156–60, 161–3, *161*, *162*, 165, 218
Shams al-Khilafa, Governor 51
Shaposhnikov, Yevgeny, Marshal 260
Sharaf al-Ma'ali ibn al-Afdal, Vizier 52
Sharukhan, Khan 15
Shendrikovtsy/Shendrikov brothers (Lev and Ilia) 182
Shevardnadze, Eduard 244, 248, 265, 268, 269, 270, 272, 305
Shervashidze, Aslan Bey 138
Shervashidze, Mikhail 138
Shervashidze, Sefer Ali-Bey 138
Shervashidze family *137*, 138
Shihab al-Din Toghrul, *atabeg* 62
Shio II, Catholicos 322n29
Shuttleworth, Digby, Colonel 205
Sidorin, Vladimir, General 221
Sigua, Tengiz 268
al-Simirumi, Kamal al-Din, Vizier 18
Simon, bishop of Bedia and Alaverdi 17
Simon I of Kartli (r. 1556–1569, 1578–1599) 89–90, 92, 93
Simon II Khan 98, 99
Simon of Kartli (r. 1712–1714) 104
Simon of Saint-Quentin 40
Simonyan, Margarita 301
Sitlarabi (*Sayyid al Arab*) 11, 317n18
Skoropadskyi, Hetman Pavel Petrovich 201
Skylitzes, John 10
Smbat, King 67–8
Smbat Sparapet 56, 57, 63–4, 66
Smele, Jonathan 218
Sofiysky, Nikon, Archbishop 180
Solomon I, King 101
Solomon I Bagrationi of Imereti, King 111–12, 138
Solomon II of Imereti, King 138
Sorge, Richard 230–1, *231*
Sorkaktani Beki, Hülegü's mother 64
Soros, George 272, 334n105
Spencer, Edmund 152
Stalin, Joseph (Ioseb Jughashvili) 134, 136, 137, 179, 202, 207, 214, 215, 216, *224*, *242*, 326n156
   1907 Tbilisi bank robbery 173, 179
   Cold War 241

   crimes committed/ordered by 173, 179, 180, 242, 243
   dacha (country house), Abkhazia *225*
   death 226, 240, 242
   definition of nation 224
   mass deportations of Caucasians 240
   Order No. 227 233
   personality cult 226
   Stalinist purges 216, 225–6, 227, 230
   'Workers of the Caucasus, the hour of revenge has struck' 173
   see also Soviet Union
Stanyan, Abraham 105
Stauffenberg, Claus Schenk von, Colonel 236
Stenka Razin 122
Stephanie (Rita), Levon I's daughter 61
Stephen (Thoros II's brother) 56, 57
Stephen IV, Catholicos 67
Stokes, Claude, Colonel 202
Stolypin, Pyotr 181
Stopka, Krzysztof 68
Sübotai, Mongol General 32, 33, 319n104
Sufi Khalil Beg Mawsilu 82
Sukhotin, Major General 112
Suleiman, Shah 101
Suleiman Efendi 160
Süleyman, Sultan 87–8
Süleyman ibn Qutalmïsh, Sultan 53
Sultan-Galiev, Mirsaid 226
Sultan ibn Mahmud (Shahanshah ibn Mahmud) 21, 60
Sultanov, Khosrov bey (Xosrov bəy Sultanov) 205–6
Sumbat Davitis-dze 8
Suslov, Mikhail 240

T

Talbot, Strobe 264
Tahir, Prince 75, 76
Tahmasp I, Shah 87, 88, 89
Tahmasp II, Shah 106, 107
Tahmasp-Quli Khan (Nader Shah) 107–8, 111
Taitbout de Marigny, Chevalier 116, 323n11
Talaat Pasha, Mehmet 176, 178, 186–7, 189
Tala'i ibn Ruzzik al-Armani, Vizier 52–3
Talleyrand-Périgord, Charles-Maurice de 141
Tamar (Bagrat IV's wife) 101
Tamar (Davit IV's daughter) 15
Tamar (Queen Rusudan's daughter) 34, 36
Tamar, Queen (Giorgi III's daughter) 18, **19**, 21–3, *21*, 26, 27, 30, 31, 35, 47, 318n82
Tamar, heiress to Imereti 76
Tamta, Ivane Mkhargrdzeli's daughter 30, 35
Tancred of Hauteville 54
Targamadze, Kakha 272
Tatishchev, Mikhail Ignatyevich 95–6
Tatoul 50
Taziyev, Ali 'Maghas' 293
Teague-Jones, Reginald 196, 202, 329n115
   as Ronald Sinclair 202, 329n116
Teimuraz (Solomon I's nephew) 112
Teimuraz I of Kakheti, King 96, 98–9, 100

Teimuraz II of Kakheti and Kartli, King 107, 108, 111
Temryuk, Prince 90, 118–19, 121
Ter-Petrosian ('Kamo') 179
Ter-Petrosyan, Levon 251–2, 262, 264, 334n82
Theodore III, Catholicos 322n29
Thomas, Regent 57
Thomson, Robert W. 13, 15, 317n10, 317n23
Thomson, William Montgomerie, General 204–5
Thoros (Hethum I's son) *65*, 66
Thoros I, Baron 54, 55, *58*, 71, 320n29
Thoros II, Baron 55–7, *56*
Thoros III, King 67
Thoros of Edessa 50, 54
Tigranes II, King 207
Timur e-Lang, Emir 48, 72, 74–6, *168*
Tolf, Robert 173
Tolui Khan 43, 319n149
Toqtamish, Prince 74, 75
Töregene, Ögödei's widow 40
Toreli, Gamrekeli 318n62
Toreli-Akhaltsikheli, Ivane, General 35
Toreli-Akhaltsikheli, Shalva, General 35
Tormasov, Alexander, viceroy 138
Tornikian, Davit, Archbishop 54
Tottleben, Gottlob Curt Heinrich von, General 112
Toumanoff, Cyril 317n23, 322n29
Trdat IV, King 79
Trotsky, Leon 179, 202, 222
Truman, Harry 241
Trump, Donald 309
Tsereteli, Irakli 181
Tsitsianov, Pavel, General 136–7, 138, 140–1
Tughril (Doğlubeg), Sultan 10
Tughril, ruler of Nakhchivan 16
Tushayev, Magomed, Major General 293
Tutar, Prince 43
Tyulenev, Ivan, General 233

U

Ubashi Khan 132
Umarov, Dokka (Abu Umar) 286, 290
Urban II, Pope 53
Urban VIII, Pope 98–9
Urquhart, David 151, 152, 160
Uthman, Caliph 108
Uzbek, Muzaffar al-Din, *atabeg* 30, 35
Uzun Hajji (Saltinsky) 217, 220
Uzun Hasan, Sultan 81, 82, *82*, 322n34

V

Vahram, chronicler 55
Vahram, Vizier 52
Vakhtang (Davit IV's son) 18, 318n46
Vakhtang (Simon I's son) 89
Vakhtang I of Imereti, King 101
Vakhtang II, King 45
Vakhtang III, King 46
Vakhtang IV, King 79, 81
Vakhtang V of Kartli (Shah Nawaz), King 100, 101
Vakhtang VI of Kartli 102–5, 106–7, 111

Vasilyev, Vladimir 292–3
Vazirov, Abdurrahman (Əbdürrəhman Vəzirov) 252, 253
Vazken I, Catholicos 245
Velyaminov, Aleksei 149–50, 152, 153, 159, 161
Veradzin, Minas 216
Verkovsky, Colonel 150
Villari, Luigi 167, 169, 179, 180
Vivian, Katharine 317n23
Vladimir Monomakh 15
Vladislav, Aaron 10
Vladislav, Ivan 10
Volsky, Arkady 251
Volynsky, Artemy, Governor 104
Vorontsov, Mikhail Semyonovich, General 159, 160
Vorontsov-Dashkov, Ilarion 169, 176, 180, 185, 186, 190
Voroshilov, Kliment 226
Vyshnevetsky, Dmytro, *ataman* 119

W

Wagner, Moritz 145, 151–2, 156
Wangenheim, Hans von, Baron 178, 185
Ware, Robert 114, 283, 284, 292
Wehib Pasha, Mehmed, General 194, 195, 196, 199, 200, 210
Westenenk, Louis 178
Wilhelm II, Emperor 182
Williams, William Fenwick, General 160–1, *168*
Wilson, Henry, Sir 210
Wilson, Woodrow 4, 203, 206, 207, 208, 210, 213, 329n143
Witsen, Nicolaas 103
Wrangel, Pyotr Nikolayevich, General 211, 213, 221, 225, 330n213

X

Xiphias, Nikephoros 8

Y

Yandarbiyev, Zelimkhan 283, 335n54
Yanis al-Rumi al-Armani, Vizier 52
Yaqub Beg, Emir 80
Yaqub Beg, Sultan 82, 84
Yegorov, Mikhail *239*
Yemelyan Pugachev 132
Yeprem Khan 178
Yermolov, Alexei Petrovich, Commander-in-Chief 143, 149–52
Yeltsin, Boris 248, 269, 270, 280, 282, 283
Yevdokimov, Nikolai, General 161–2, 164
Yevkurov, Yunus-bek, General 280, 293–4
Yevloyev, Magomed 293
Yudenich, General 186, 189, 190–1, *191*, 193, 202
Yuri, Kipchak Prince 33
Yuri Bogolyubsky, Prince 22, 25
Yusifbeyli, Nasib bey 206

Z

Zabel (Isabella), Queen 60, 61–2, 64
Zal (Aleksandre I's son) 79
Zaleski, Marcin *146*
Zarobyan, Yakov 245
Zass, Grigory Khristoforovich von, General 152
Zavriev, Hakob 194
Zeitzler, Kurt, General 238
Zhordania, Noe 179, 180, 181, 194, 200, 204, 216
Zhukov, Georgy, Marshal 226
Zhvania, Zurab 272
Zourabichvili, Salome 309
Zubov, Valeriyan, General 136
Zurab I, *eristavi* 98, 99
Zyazikov, Murat 293

Index: Places

Page locators in *italic* refer to captions and those in **bold** refer to maps; 'n' after a locator indicates the endnote number.

A

Abkhazeti principality 83
Abkhazia 12, **13**
    1992–1993 Abkhaz–Georgian War 268, *268*, 270
    2008 Georgian–Russian War 307–8
    Abkhaz Autonomous Soviet Socialist Republic (ASSR) 199, 265
    Abkhaz National Guard 269, 270
    Abkhaz People's Council 197, 198–9
    Abkhaz Revolutionary Committee (Revkom) 199
    Abkhaz Supreme Council 266
    abolition of autonomous princedom 164
    Bolshevik Russia and 198, 199
    Catholicosate of 43, 82
    Chechen fighters 270, 272
    Confederation of Mountain Peoples of the Caucasus and 270
    ethnic and social conflicts 197–8, 199, 265
    Georgia and 42, 197–9, 310
    independence from Georgia 4, 83, 199, 265, 266, 269, 270, 306, 308, 334n90, 337n81
    as internationally isolated republic 270, 272
    military interventions 198
    'multivectoral' vs 'univectoral' foreign policy 310, 337n104
    nationalism 265
    New Athos Monastery *197*
    Ottomans and 138
    reintegration into Georgia's central authority 304, 310
    Russian Empire and 138, 163, 197
    Russian Federation and 270, 304, 305, 306, 308, 310
    Russian 'peace-keeping force' *268*, 270, 305
    Russophobia 265
    Stalin's dacha (country house) in *225*
    see also Abkhazians; Georgia
Absheron Peninsula 173, 259, 333n34
    Nardaran Mosque *258*
    oil derricks of the Branobel Company *171*
    Ramana medieval fortress *41*

Adjara
    Adjarian Autonomous Soviet Socialist Republic (ASSR) 265, 334n87
    independence from Georgia 267–8
    reintegration into Georgia's central authority 304
Adygea/Republic of Adygea 276, **290**
Afghanistan
    1979–1989 war 246
    1996–2001 Islamic Emirate of Afghanistan 283
    Afghan Taliban 152, 153
    heroin exports 262
    Iran and 144–5
    Kandahar province 102
    Nagorno-Karabakh conflict and 262
    Soviet Union and 246
    US operations in 152
    see also Afghans
Agarani fortress 11
Ahlat 30, 35
Akhalkalaki 10, 138, 196, 200, 203, 207, 267
    population 329n87
    Russian military base at 270
Akhaltsikhe
    1828–1829 Russian–Turkish War 90
    fortress (Lomsia) *90*, 146
    Ottomans and 89
    Russian Empire and 138, 147
    slave trade 89, *90*
Akhulgo: Russian siege and capture of 156–7
Akka, siege of 58
Alagir ruins *123*
Albania 81, 137, 246
Amberd 25
    Amberd fortress *26*
Anahşa fortress, Pozantı *51*
Anakopia 9, 12, 81, 317n6
Anamur fortress (Mamure Kalesi) 62, *63*
Ananuri
    Church of the Dormition *104*
    Church of the Redeemer *104*
    fortress *104*
Anapa 130, 147, 160, 237
    slavery 150, *151*
Anatolia
    1511 Qizilbash revolt 85
    Circassians in 164
    Georgia and 11, 25
    Mongols and 36
    Ottomans and 87, 93
    Russian Empire and 178

Anazarbos 55, *58*
    Anazarbos fortress (Anavarza Kalesi) 54, *58*, 68
    Justinopolis, Justinianopolis *58*
Ani 10
    Georgia and 8, 17, 18, 20–1, 25, 26–7, 41–2, 60, 76
    Horomos Monastery *23*
    Mongol invasions 36
    Muslim plunder of 30
Antioch 50, 53, 54, 55
    fall of 66, 67
    Syriac Orthodox Church 82
Antioch, Principality of 54, 58–60, *58*
Ararat
    Ararat plain 25, 80
    Mount Ararat 213
Aras plain 3
Ardabil 30
Armenia 72
    1828 Russian annexation of Iranian Armenia 80
    1877–1878 Russian conquest of former western Armenia 169–70
    1919–1920 Paris Peace Conference 207, 208–13, **209**, 329–30n147
    1921 anti-Soviet uprising 214
    1991 Alma-Ata Protocol 252
    twenty-first century 302–4, 312
    2018 'Velvet Revolution' 302
    2022–present Russian invasion of Ukraine 294, 303, 312
    'Armenian Question' 178, 209–10
    Armenian Soviet Socialist Republic 213, 214, 224, 242–3, 244
    Azerbaijan/Armenia population exchange 251
    Azerbaijan/Armenia relations 4, 251, 333n44
    Byzantium and 20
    cemeteries *5*, *94*
    churches 20, *24*, 25, *26*, *27*, *30*, *33*, *37*, *40*, 41, *43*, *45*, *46*, *79*, *144*
    coinage 100
    Collective Security Treaty Organization (CSTO) 298, 302
    Constitutional Court of Armenia 302
    corruption 302
    current dilemmas 302, 303–4, 312
    de-Russification of names 332n21
    earthquakes 25, 245, 251
    energy issues 244–5
    EU and 301, 302, 303, 336n56, 337n62
    Evangelical Church in 80

Georgia–Armenia war 200, 205
Gladzor university 44, *45*
identity 4, 72, 80, 169
independence 196, 213, 248, 249, 251, 252
Iran and 312
as landlocked country 216, 249, 265
language 109, 226, 242
monasteries 20, *23*, *24*, 25, *25*, *26*, *27*, *33*, *37*, *40*, *43*, 44, *45*, *144*, *261*
Mongol invasions 32, 36, 42, 62
mosques *145*
NATO 212
Nazi Germany and 239
population decline 302
reconquest of former Armenian territories 25–6
Republic of Armenia 199–200, 206, 252
Republic of Mountainous Armenia 185, 214
Russian Federation and 195, 294, 301, 302, 303, 312, 336n56
Safavids and 100
six Armenian *vilayets* 175, 176, 178, 204, 207
Soviet collectivization of agriculture 227
Soviet Union and 213, 214, 216, 224, 227
Treaty of Batumi 200
Turkey/Armenia relations 4, 212–14, 302
Turkish Western Armenia 166, 245
univectoral foreign policy 337–8n104
US and 303, 333n44
see also Armenian Catholic Church; Armenian Genocide; Armenian nationalism; Armenian Orthodox Church; Armenians; Armenians and the Ottoman Empire; Cilicia; Nagorno-Karabakh conflict; Yerevan
Armenian Cilicia *see* Cilicia
Armenian Genocide Memorial, Tsitsernakaberd *188*, *244*, 245
Arran 18, 31
    Georgia and 20
    Mongols and 33, 42
Ascalon 51, 52, 64
Astvatsatsin Church, Monastery of Tegher, Armenia *37*
Austro-Hungarian Empire 4, 167, 191, 207
    1878 Berlin Congress 170
Autonomous Gorskaya (Mountainous) SSR 224

Ayas 67, 69
    Ayas fortress (Laiazzo, Yumurtalık) 62, 66
Azerbaijan 18, 75
    1918 partition 196, 205
    1919–1920 Paris Peace Conference 207, **208**
    twenty-first century 294–8, 312
    2022–present Russian invasion of Ukraine 294, 298
    annexation by Russia 181
    anti-Armenian nationalism 246
    anti-Armenian pogroms 251
    Armenia/Azerbaijan population exchange 251
    Armenia/Azerbaijan relations 4, 251, 333n44
    Atropatene/Azerbaijan toponyms 327n205
    Azerbaijan Democratic Republic 205
    Azerbaijan People's Republic 240, 241
    Azerbaijan Soviet Socialist Republic 206, 224, 242–3, 245–6
    cemeteries *142*
    coinage 100
    Collective Security Treaty Organization (CSTO) 295
    Commonwealth of Independent States (CIS) 252, 254
    current challenges 298, 312
    de-Russification of names 253
    economy 295, 298
    EU and 303
    identity 4, 181
    independence 196, 246, 248, 253
    Iran and 254, 260, 297, 301
    Israel/Azerbaijan relations 260, 294, 295
    as landlocked country 259, 294, 295
    language 84, 226, 242
    monasteries 47, *99*, *261*, 320n171
    Mongols and 36, 42
    multivectoral foreign policy 337n104
    nationalism 167, 246, 253
    NATO and 255, 259
    oil and gas industry *171*, 174, 245–6, 253, 255, 259–60, 295, 297–8, 303, 333nn33–4, 333n50
    Ottoman–Iranian wars 92
    Ottoman–Russian clashes 105
    pan-Islamism 181, 182
    Russia Empire and 181
    Russian Federation and 255, 294–5, 312
    Russification and nationalism 167
    Safavids and 87, 92, 96, 100, 181
    as secular state 260
    Shia Islam 87, 246, *258*, 260
    social order 181
    Soviet Union and 206, 224
    Timur e-Lang and 75
    Turkey/Azerbaijan relations 6, 254–5, 294–5, 312
    Turkification policy 255
    Turkmenistan and 297
    US and 255, 259, 294–5, 333n44
    World War II 245
    see also Azerbaijanis; Baku; Nagorno-Karabakh conflict
Azerbaijan Autonomous Republic of Nakhchivan 6
Azov fortress 119, 122, 130, 201

B

Baghdad
    caliphate in 14
    Mongols and 64
    Safavids and 107
Baghras fortress (castle of Gaston) 58–9, 320n43
Baku 84, 181
    1905 Baku unrest and Dashnaks 173, 175, 176, 178
    1918 Armenian massacres 328n34
    1990 'Black January' (Soviet military intervention) *250*, 251, 252, 253
    Azeris/Armenians ethnic strife 182
    Bolsheviks/Bolshevik Russia 180, 206
    city wall *105*
    'Dunsterforce' mission 202
    Eternal Flame Monument, Martyr's Cemetery *250*, 252
    ethnic nationalism 182
    Flame Towers *250*, 297
    Heydar Aliyev Center 295
    'Norperforce' in 204, 205
    oil production at 171–4, 196, 201–3, 230, 235, 245, 331n28, 331n50
    Ottomans and 92
    revolutionaries from 173
    Russia and 105, 107
    Russian Empire and 140–1
    Safavids and 87, 96
    Social Democratic Party 182
    Soviet Union and 230
    World War I 201–3, 204
    World War II 230, 331n28
    see also Azerbaijan
Baku Commune 195, 201
the Balkans 4, 166
    Circassians in 164
    Ottomans and 170
Batumi 48, 138, 169, 205, 216
    Alphabetic Tower 267
    oil terminal and port 172–3, 195
    Porta Tower 267
    Russian Empire and 170
    Russian base at 267–8, 270
Bayburt 191, *193*, 195
Black Sea 13, 17, 27, 196
    1918 Armistice of Mudros 203
    2008 Georgian–Russian War 308
    Ottomans and 80, 84, 134
    Russian Empire and 134, 147, 148, 151, 160, 161, 170
    Treaty of Nymphaion 48
    Venice and 48
Black Sea Soviet Republic 218
Bolshevik Russia 196, 197, 210
    Abkhazia and 198, 199
    Turkish–Russian alliance 210
    World War I 193–4, 201, 207
    see also Bolsheviks; Russian Empire; Soviet Union
Bosnia and Herzegovina 170
British Empire 105, 166
    India and 145
    Russian Empire and 145
    trade 105–6
    see also Great Britain
Bukhara 92
Bulgaria 146
    1876 Bulgarian April Revolt 165, 169
Bulgarian Empire 8
Byzantium
    Armenia and 20
    Cilicia and 50, 53, 54, 55, 56–7

    crisis in 11
    Crusaders and 14, 27, 53–4
    Georgia and 8, 9–10, 11, 27
    fortresses 12, *51*, *56*, *58*, *63*, 71
    see also Byzantine Empire; Constantinople
Byzantine Empire 81, 84, 130
    Roman–Byzantine Empire 114
    see also Byzantium

C

Calicadnus (Göksu) River 58
Caspian Sea 6, 27, 134
    Caspian ACG fields 255, 259, 333n34
    fossil fuels in 6, 297
    as landlocked 297, 336n28
    as lake or sea? 297
    Russian Empire and 143
    Russian Federation and 297
    Shirvan and 20
    Volga–Baltic Canal system 297
    Volga–Don Canal system 297, 336n28
the Caucasus
    Caucasian Union 312
    EU and 312
    geography 3
    German troops in *233*, *234*, 236, *236*, *237*
    Islamic State 283, 286
    main gas and oil pipelines in **256–7**
    nationalisms 6
    NATO and 312
    present states and republics of 3–4, 6
    Russian conquest of the Caucasus by late 1829 and foundation of forts to 1818 **124**
    Soviet Union 4, 5, 312
    state-building process 4
    Turkey and 6, 301
    volatility 6
    see also North Caucasus; South Caucasus
Caucasus Emirate 290
Chechen-Ingush ASSR 240, 246, 279–80
Chechnya 153, 240
    1999 Chechen–Dagestan War 283–4, 287, 288
    2022–present Russian invasion of Ukraine 312
    All-National Congress of the Chechen People 281
    Chechen Republic 281–3
    Chechen Republic of Ichkeria 280, 281, 290
    'Chechenization' of state power and administration 286
    Cossacks and 165
    as destabilizing neighbour 275, 276
    federal subsidies 293, 294, 336n15
    as 'FSB-free zone' 293
    imamate 169–70
    independence from Russia 281–2
    Islamic State 283
    'pacification' of 290
    Putin, Vladimir and 274, 284, 286, 305
    radical Islamism 283
    religious self-awareness 246
    Russian Empire and 148, 149, 150, 157, 158–9, 161–2, 165, 281
    Russian Federation and 275, 281–2, 290, 293

    Shamil, Imam and 157–9, 162
    sharia law 283
    smuggling 282, 283
    Soviet repression in 224–5
    State Shura (Council) 283
    Wahhabi Salafism 283, 286
    see also Chechen Wars; Chechens; Grozny
China 48, 132, 319n153
    2022–present Russian invasion of Ukraine 312
    Cultural Revolution 226
    economic reform 248
    Great Walls of 128
Chokh fortified village 162
Cilicia (Armenian Cilicia) 44, 45, 47
    1895 and 1909 massacres 72
    1915 genocide 72
    Armenian Catholic patriarchate of Cilicia 110
    Armenian Legion 215–16
    Armenian refugees in 209, 215
    Armenian Orthodox Church 53, 60–1, 67, 68, 69, 71–2, 80, *215*
    Armenian warlords and Muslim Armenian viziers 50–3
    Ayyubids and 50, 57
    Byzantium and 50, 53, 54, 55, 56–7
    'Catholicosate of the Great House of Cilicia' 80, 322n24
    churches 320n18
    Crusader States and 50, 52–3, 55, 57
    Crusaders and 53–4, 57–8, 63, 64
    Cyprus and 50, 58, 60, 69, 72
    Danishmendid dynasty and 50, 55
    fortresses 53, 320n18
    France and 207, 209
    fratricidal wars 67–9
    Holy Roman Empire and 60
    Il-Khanate and 67, 69
    infighting 50, 68, 69, 71
    kingdom of Cilician Armenia *58*, **59**, 60–72, *71*
    as kingdom in exile 50
    Mamelukes and 50, *58*, 62, 65–7, 68, 69, 71, *71*, 72
    monasteries 320n18
    Mongols and 50, 62–4, 68
    principalities 50, 53–60, *63*
    Republic of Cilicia 216
    Rubenids of Cilicia 50, *51*, 53–60
    Rum Seljuks and 50, 54, 62
    trade 58, 66, 67, 69
    Turkey and 72, 216
    see also Armenia; Sis
Cilician Gates *51*, 53, 54, 66
Circassia
    Cossacks and 164
    Crimean Tatars and 115, 122
    Ottoman–Crimean Tatar slave-hunting raids into 119
    Russian Empire and 115, 149, 150–1, 161, 163–5
    see also Circassians
Confederation of Mountain Peoples of the Caucasus 270
Constantinople 9, 10, 14
    1204 Sack of Constantinople 27
    1453 fall of Constantinople 27, 48, 80, 81
    Kostantiniyye/Istanbul (Ottoman era) 84
    Patriarch of Constantinople 4
    Russian Empire and 129, 134, 135, 145, 170, 184, 186

INDEX: PLACES

Crimea 48
  1562–1563 Russian–Crimean war 121
  Crimean Tatar dynasty of Giray 84
  famine 226–7
  the Nogai and 130
  Ottoman–Crimean campaign against Astrakhan 90
  Ottoman era 84
  Russian annexation of 129, 135, 161, 337n62
  Soviet Union and 226–7
  vilayet (province) of Kefe (Caffa) 84
  see also Crimean Tatars; Crimean War
Crusader States 12
  Cilicia and 50, 52–3, 55, 57
  County of Tripoli 320n25
  Edessa 54
  infighting 55
  Kingdom of Jerusalem 320n25
  see also Crusaders; Crusades
Cyprus 50, 56, *56*, 69
  1878 Cyprus Convention 170
  Cilicia and 50, 58, 60, 69, 72
  emigration of Armenians to 72
  Great Britain and 184
  Holy Roman Empire and 60

D

Dadivank Monastery, Azerbaijan *261*, *300*
Dagestan 75, 134, 246, 274
  1999 Chechen–Dagestan War 283–4, 287, 288
  2022–present Russian invasion of Ukraine 312
  Chechen refugees in 287
  Crimean campaign to 108
  Dagestan SR 224
  ethnic diversity 275, 286–7, 288
  federal subsidies 294
  Independent Islamic Republic of Dagestan 283–4, 288
  Iranian–Russian military alliance 107
  Irganskaya hydroelectric station *291*
  Islam 288
  Islamic State 283
  official languages 288
  principalities emerged after Nader Shah's death 111
  recentralization of Russian bureaucracy 292–3
  religious self-awareness 246
  Republic of Dagestan 286–8, 291, 292
  Russian Empire and 148, 149, 150, 165, 169–70, 325n53
  Russian Federation and 288, 290, 291–3
  Salafism 283–4, 288
  Soviet Union 224–5, 286–7, 288
  Spiritual Administration of the Muslims of Dagestan 288
  State Council 288, 292
  terrorism 287
  Wahhabism 284, 287, 288
  Yury Korchagin offshore oilfield 287
  see also Dagestanis
the Dardanelles 112, 129, 170, 184, 186
  1917 Bolshevik Revolution 185
  1918 Armistice of Mudros 203
Dargavs, medieval graveyard *116*

Darial Pass/Gorge 15, 75, 112, 119, 134, 135, 159
Debet Valley 21
Derbent
  Georgia and 18, 20, 21, 36
  Mongol invasions 37
  Ottomans and 92
  Russia and 105, 107, 323n99
Dmanisi 17, 21, 96
  fortress 8
Don Cossack Host (Don Republic) 219
Dvin 25, 26
Dzungaria 132

E

Edessa 17, 54
Egrisi 13
Egypt
  1798 Napoleon's Egyptian campaign 140
  Armenian Fatimid vizierates in 50–3, 57
  Great Britain and 184, 327n1
Erzurum 170, 178, *211*
  Georgia and 27, 76
  Russian Empire and 191, *191*
Estonia 337n90
Etchmiadzin
  Armenian Catholicosate in 44, 80
  complex of 79
Euphrates River *61*, 65
European Union (EU)
  2022–present Russian invasion of Ukraine 298
  Armenia and 301, 302, 303, 336n56, 337n62
  Azerbaijan and 303
  Georgia and 195, 304–5, 309, 310, 312, 337n96
  Moldova and 310, 312
  Nagorno-Karabakh conflict 301, 302
  oil and gas 298, 303, 333n51, 336n36
  South Caucasian states and 312
  Ukraine and 312

F

Federative Union of Socialist Soviet Republics of Transcaucasia 224
Finland 134
  NATO 309, 337n91
  Soviet–Finnish Wars 134
France
  1795–1799 French Directory 139, 141
  1799–1804 Consulate 139
  1804–1815 First Empire 139
  1921 withdrawal from Turkey 216
  Cilicia and 207, 209
  French Army 210, 330n160
  Iran and *139*, 140, 141–2, 144
  Napoleonic Wars 139
  post-war partition of the Ottoman Empire/'mandates' 190, 216, 327n176, 330n160
  Russian Empire and 139–40
  Syria and 209
  World War I 185, 186, 191, 203
Free Peoples of the Steppe 217

G

Galiata, defence tower *118*
Gamsutl: ruined mountain village *126*, *158*
Ganja (Gəncə)
  earthquake 18
  Georgia and 9, 11, 20, 25, 30, 34, 36, 76, 111
  Kipchaks and 34
  Mongols and 36
  see also Yelisavetpol
Geghard Monastery, Armenia *33*, 44
Gelati 18
Gelati Monastery, Georgia *12*, *13*, 15, 18, 85
Genoa 48, 58
  Treaty of Nymphaion 48
  treaty with Sultan Qalawun 66
Georgia 321n1
  1088 Tmogvi earthquake 13
  1919–1920 Paris Peace Conference 207, **208**
  1992–1993 Abkhaz–Georgian War 268, *268*, 270
  twenty-first century 304–12
  2003 'Rose Revolution' (*coup d'état*) 272
  2008 Georgian–Russian War 293, 294, 301, 306–9, *307*, 337n80
  2022–present Russian invasion of Ukraine 294, 310, 312
  2022–present Russian migrants in 312
  Anatolia and 11, 25
  Ani and 8, 17, 18, 20–1, 25, 26–7, 41–2, 60, 76
  Armenia–Georgia war 200, 205
  army 13, 14, 15–16, 18, 24–5, 27, 32, 33, 34, 35, 36, 46, 111, 306, 318n62
  Black Death 48, 74, 76
  Bolshevik Russia and 198
  British occupation of 204–5
  Byzantium and 8, 9–10, 11, 27
  Catholicism in 46–7
  Catholicosate and 30–1
  churches 8, *11*, *14*, *21*, *31*, *32*, *74*, 77, *93*, *103*
  coinage 17, 81, 321n1
  Commonwealth of Independent States (CIS) 252, 270, 337n73
  Court of Appeal 15
  corruption 272, 304
  cronyism and nepotism 13–14, 15
  Crusades and 31–2, 35
  Darbazi council 22, 31, 47, 82–3, 319n103
  Didgori Monument *16*
  disintegration of state unity 81–3, 90, 138
  dzeglis dadeba 47
  earthquakes *93*
  economy 304
  education centres and cultural revival 15
  enemies 30, 31
  ethnic and social conflicts 4, 196–9, 265
  ethnic territories 265
  EU and 195, 304–5, 309, 310, 312, 337n96
  expansion 16–18, **19**, 26, 27, 30, 318n88
  foreign domination 90, 100
  Ganja and 9, 11, 20, 25, 30, 34, 36, 76, 111

Georgian alphabets/language 103, 167, 197, 226, 242
Georgian Soviet Socialist Republic 216, 224, 242–4, 265
'Georgification' 196–7
German troops on the march in Georgia (1918) *201*
Golden Age 8–30
government reorganization 15, 47
identities and internal tensions 4
independence of 196, 197, 205, 248, 265–6, 269
infighting and rebellions 42, 81, 100
Iran and 141–2
Karavi council 22
Khwarazmian invasion 35, 36, 41
Kipchaks and 15–16, 17, 18, 21, 34, 35, 317n35
law enforcement 21
Military Council 268, 269, 270
monasteries *9*, *12*, *13*, *14*, 15, 18, *21*, *31*, *32*, 85, *85*, *93*, *136*
Mongol invasion and occupation 30, 31, 32–3, 35, 36–7, 40, 42, 43–6, 47, 62, 318–19n96, 319n138
Muslim population 17
Nakhchivan and 25, 48, 76
NATO and 272, 304–7, 309, 310, 333n32, 337n71, 337n89
nobles 15, 18, 21, 22, 36–7, 40, 42, 47, 79, 81
oil and gas 259
Ossetian–Georgian clashes 197
Ottomans and 81, 82, 85, 87, 88, 90, 135
partition of 78–9, 82–3, **83**
peasant revolts 179–80
'Regulations of the Monarch's Court' 47
renaissance after 1744 111
reunification of 46, 47, 88, 138
Russian annexation of 136
Russian Empire and 104–5, 111–12, 135–6, 138, 180
Russian Federation and 4, 272, 294, 304, 305, 333n32
Russification and nationalism 167, 196
Safavids and 81, 88, 90
Seljuks, conflict with 10, 12–13, 15–17, *16*, 18, 22, 27
Shirvan and 15, 17, 18, 20, 25, 36
Soviet Union and 216, 224
state-within-the-state 26
tanmas/tamma 40, 41
taxes 15, 17, 20, 25, 40–1, 46, 76, 81, 180, 304
Timur e-Lang's devastation of 48, 74–6
UN membership 268
US and 195, 272, 307, 309, 310
Western democracies and 304
women high roles in 22
see also Abkhazia; Adjara; Georgian Orthodox Church; Georgians; Imereti; Kakheti; Kartli; South Ossetian; Tbilisi
Georgian Military Highway 119, **124**, 135, 149, 159, 232, *292*, 308
Germany 306, 337n74
  1878 Berlin Congress 170
  1907 Anglo-Russian Convention 327n181
  1918 German troops on the march in Georgia *201*
  Imperial Germany 207, 327n2

Ottoman–German
    cooperation 184–5
  training of foreign troops by German
    instructors 184
  Turkic pan-Islamism and 182
  World War I 185, 191, 194, 196, 200,
    201, 202
  see also World War I; Nazi Germany
Gilan 46, 106, 107, 134, 141, 241
  Soviet Republic of Gilan 216
Gladzor University, Armenia 44, 45
Goor, medieval defence towers 148
Gori 22
  Gori fortress 85
  Safavids and 87
Goshavank Monastery, Armenia 25
  Astvatsatsin Church 25
  St Grigor Church 25
Great Britain
  1878 Berlin Congress 170, 184
  1907 Anglo-Russian Convention 145,
    178, 327n181
  1915 Anglo-Russian agreement 184
  1919 British Military Mission 219
  1921 Anglo-Soviet Trade
    Agreement 216
  anti-Russian covert operations 151–2
  'Armenian Question' 209–10
  British Royal Navy 140, 141, 145, 146,
    170, 185, 230, 327n2
  Cyprus and 184
  Egypt and 184, 327n1
  Georgia, British occupation of 204–5
  Iran and 140, 141, 142, 143, 144, 145,
    241, 325n38
  Napoleonic Wars 139–40
  Ottomans and 106, 139, 170
  post-war partition of the Ottoman
    Empire/'mandates' 190, 327n176,
    330n160
  Russian Empire and 105–6, 138,
    139–40, 143, 145
  training of foreign troops by British
    instructors 143, 152, 325n33
  'war for cotton' 196
  World War I 185, 186, 191, 196, 201,
    202, 203–5, 206
  see also British Empire; East India
    Company
Greater Caucasus Mountains 3, 45, 114,
  118, 148, 160, 234, 272, 312
  German troops in 234, 236
Greece 4
Gremi 94, 96
  Church of the Archangels 86, 88
  Royal Fortress 86
Grozny 130, 149, 280, 281, 293, 294,
  331n52
  Akhmad Kadyrov Mosque 284
  Chechen Wars 282, 283, 284, 286
  oil and gas production 173, 230, 232,
    235, 237, 331n52
  see also Chechnya
Gunib 153, 218
  fortress 162
Guria 81, 82, 83, 88, 199
  'Gurian Republic' 180
  peasant revolts 179–80
  as Russian protectorate 138
Gyumri (Alexandropol) 196, 199, 213,
  332n21
  Russian military base in 301, 336n47,
    337n80

H

Haghartsin Monastery, Armenia 26, 26
  Astvatsatsin Church 26, 27
  St Grigor Church 26
Haghpat Monastery, Armenia 20, 23, 25
Halidzor fortress, Armenia 106, 106
Harichavank Monastery, Armenia 24
  Astvatsatsin Cathedral 24
  St Grigor the Enlightener Church 24
Herat
  1833 Iranian war against 145
  1837–1838 Iranian–Russian siege
    of 145
Hereti 8, 10, 14, 75
Holy Roman Empire 60
Hromkla fortress 54–5, 57, 57, 61, 67

I

Ikalto academy, Georgia 15
Il-Khanate 42, 43, 65, 74, 319n139
  anti-Mameluke coalition with
    Western European powers 46
  Cilicia and 67, 69
  slavery 42
  struggles within 45, 46
  taxes 42
Imereti 46, 76, 101
  Georgia and 37, 42, 47, 75, 82
  as kingdom 83
  Ottomans and 111–12, 135, 138
  peasant revolts 179–80
  Russia and 100
  Russian Empire, annexation by 138
  Saints Quiricus and Julitta
    Church 102
  St Grigori Church, Ubisa 74, 77
  union of Kartli and Imereti 101
  see also Georgia
India 107
  Armenian diaspora in 98
  British Empire and 145
  Russian Empire and 104, 105
  trade with 48, 98, 104
Indian Ocean 105, 134
Ingushetia 148, 279, 290
  1992 Ossetian–Ingush conflict over
    Prigorodny Rayon 280, 294
  defence towers, Nij 37
  federal subsidies 294
  Ingushetia AO 224
  jihadism 293
  medieval defence and residential
    towers, Egikal 115
  medieval defence and residential
    towers, Erzi 121
  medieval defence and residential
    towers, Targim 147
  Republic of Ingushetia 280
  Russian Federation and 290, 293
  secession from Chechnya 280
  Second Chechen War 280
  terrorism 293
Iran 74, 130
  1828 Russian annexation of Iranian
    Armenia 80
  1833 Iranian war against the emirate
    of Herat 145
  1907 Anglo-Russian Convention 145,
    178
  1919–1920 Paris Peace
    Conference 207–8
  Afghanistan and 144–5
  architecture, influence on 85, 86
  Armenia and 312
  Azerbaijan and 254, 260, 297, 301
  Cold War and 240–1
  Dashnaks and Iran unrest 178
  France and 139, 140, 141–2, 144
  Georgia and 141–2
  Great Britain and 140, 141, 142, 143,
    144, 145, 241, 325n38
  Iranian Cossack Brigade 178,
    327n182
  Iranian–Russian treaties 107, 144,
    145, 146, 146
  Israel/Iran relations 300
  majlis (national parliament) 178
  Mongols and 36, 41, 42, 46, 64,
    319n153
  Nagorno-Karabakh conflict 262, 264,
    300, 301
  New Julfa 96, 98, 98
  oil production/oilfields 178, 240–1,
    255, 297–8
  Russian Empire and 107, 140–1,
    143–5, 146
  Safavids 81, 84
  Shia Islam 260
  Soviet Union and 216, 240–1
  Sultaniyeh Archbishopric 47
  trade routes 74, 134
  training of Iranian troops by British
    instructors 143, 325n33
  US and 241, 242
  see also Ottoman–Safavid Wars;
    Russian–Iranian Wars; Safavids
Iranian Azerbaijan 47, 48, 92, 100, 144,
  176, 254
  Maghardavank Monastery/St
    Stepanos Monastery 99
  Soviet Union and 240, 252
  St Thaddeus Monastery 99
  unification of Soviet and Iranian
    Azerbaijan 246, 252, 253
Iraq
  oil production/oilfields 241
  Ottomans and 88
Ishak Palace, Doğubayazıt, Turkey 140
Israel
  Azerbaijan/Israel relations 260, 294,
    295
  Iran/Israel relations 300
  Nagorno-Karabakh conflict: Israel/
    Azerbaijan cooperation 298, 299,
    300
  oil and gas 300

J

Jaffa, Crusader victory at 58
Japan
  1904–5 Russia–Japan War 173, 180,
    326n160
  1931 invasion and occupation of
    Manchuria 230, 231
  1938 Russo–Japanese clashes over
    the Changkufeng Heights 230
  1941 attack on Pearl Harbour 239
  Germany–Japan Anti-Comintern
    Pact 230
  Hiroshima and Nagasaki, atomic
    explosions at 226
  Sorge, Richard and 230–1

Jerusalem
  1071 capture by Atsiz ibn Uvaq 12
  1099 capture by the Crusaders 14, 51
  Latin Kingdom of Jerusalem 52,
    320n25
  Saladin/Richard I truce 58

K

Kabarda 112, 129
  1557 defence pact between Kabarda
    and Russia 114–22
  Crimean Tatars and 122, 129
  Russian Empire and 150
Kabardino-Balkaria 6, 246
  federal subsidies 294
  Islamic radicalization 278
  jihadism 294
  Republic of Kabardino-Balkaria 278
  Russian Federation and 290
  see also Nalchik
Kakheti 10, 14–15, 82
  as kingdom 83
  Ottomans and 106
  revolt by Khevsurs, Pshavs and
    Tushetians 101
  Russia and 92, 93–4, 95–6, 98, 100
  Safavids and 96, 98, 101
  Seljuk Empire and 14
  St George Monastery, Alaverdi 93, 96
  Turkification of 101
  see also Georgia
Kakheti–Kartli unified kingdom 98, 107,
  108, 111–12, 134
Kakhib 153
Kalmyk Autonomous Region 224
Kalmykia 240
  Buddhism 130, 131, 276, 276
  Burkhan Bakshin Altan Sume, Golden
    Temple, Elista 131, 276
  chess 277
  'Exile and Return' monument,
    Elista 274
  Kalmykian AO 276
  Kalmykian ASSR 276–7
  Kalmyks' return to 276
  Khulkhuta memorial 238
  Office Building, Elista 275
  Republic of Kalmykia 276–7
  Russian Federation and 290
  Seven Days Pagoda, Elista 275
  see also Kalmyks
Kapan (Safavid vassal state) 106
Karabakh 75, 76
  Armenian National Council of
    Karabakh 206
  blockade of 206
  Five Melikdoms of 81, 111, 321n106
  Khanate of 321n106
  Nagorno-Karabakh conflict 4, 205
  war in 206
  see also Nagorno-Karabakh
Karachay-Cherkessia (Republic of
  Karachay-Cherkessia) 6, 224, 237,
  246, 277–8, 290
Karaman Emirate 63
Kars 195
  citadel of Kars 212, 213
  fortress 168
  Georgia and 25, 26, 27
  Kars Republic 206–7
  Kars Shura 206
  Mongol invasions 36

Ottoman Empire and 147, 161, *168*
Russian Empire and 146, 147, 160–1, *168*
Safavids *168*
Turkey and 212–13
war in 206–7
Kartli 10, 13, 82, 84–5, 160
dasturlamali (law code) 102–3
as kingdom 83
Ottomans and 106–7
Russia and 95, 96, 104–5, 106
Safavids and 87, 88, 92, 95, 96, 98
serfdom 102–3
Shida Kartli *8*, *14*, *224*, *305*
trade 103
union of Kartli and Imereti 101
see also Georgia; Kakheti–Kartli unified kingdom
Khachen 36
Principality of Khachen 321n106
Khakheti 85
Khertvisi fortress *78*
Khwarazmia 74, 75
see also Khwarazmians
Khwarazmian Empire 31
Klukhor Pass 236
Korykos fortress *56*
Kosovo 252, 306, 332n16
Kozan 53, *71*
Krasnodar Krai 275–6, 290
Kuban-Black Sea Oblast 224
Kuban Cossack Host (Kuban People's Republic) 218
Kuban Soviet Republic 218
Kurdish Republic of Mahabad 240, 241
Kurdistan Uyezd (district) 226
Kurtin fortress *76*
Kutaisi
Georgians in 174
Kutaisi Cathedral 101
Kveshi fortress, Georgia *34*
Kyrgyz: 2005 Tulip Revolution 334n105

L

Lachin Corridor 226, 262, 263, 299, 300, 301
Lak Mountains 121
Lake Sevan *5*, *26*, *94*, 143, *144*, 244, 318n76
Lake Van 30, 189, 322n27
Lampron fortress *52*, 53, 61, 320n18
Latvia 337n90
Libya 312
Likhi (Surami) mountain range 88
Lithuania 337n90
Lori 207, 329n87
Akhtala Monastery 25, *30*
Church synod 25
Haghpat Monastery *20*, *23*
Holy Cross Church *20*
Holy Mother of God Church, 25, *30*
Georgia and 21, 26, 78, 200, 216
Khobayr Monastery *43*
St Gregory Church *20*

M

Maraş, siege of 216, 330n187
Marmashen (Miryam Nashin) 10, 81
Martyropolis 37, 42
Martyrs' Monastery of Martvili, Georgia *14*
Mesopotamia 43, 87, 92, 99
Mingrelia 81, 82, 83, 88–9
peasant revolts 179–80
as Russian protectorate 138, 143
Moldova 304, 310, 312
Mongol Empire 42, 319n153
dissolution of 43
expansion of 31, 46
Pax Mongolica 43
see also Mongols
Mongolia 36, 319n153
Karakorum 36, 37, 40, 41, 63, 319n139
Mount Elbrus 237, *237*
Mughan
Mughan Steppe 32, 201
Provisional Dictatorship of Mughan 216
Soviet Republic of Mughan 216

N

Nagorno-Karabakh 214–15, 245, 330n183
Armenian population in 249
as Autonomous Oblast 215, 251
oil and gas 215
Republic of Artsakh 252, 260, *261*, 332n15
Soviet Autonomous Region of Nagorno-Karabakh 251
Soviet Union and 215, 226, 251
see also Karabakh; Nagorno-Karabakh conflict
Nakhchivan 18, 246, 294
1919–1920 Paris Peace Conference 207
Armenian population in 249, 332n5
Armeno-Catholic bishopric 47
as Autonomous Soviet Socialist Republic 215, 252
Georgia and 25, 48, 76
Julfa 96, 98
Mongols and Khwarazmians 41
Nagorno-Karabakh conflict 300, 301
Palace of the khans of Nakhchivan 204
Russian Empire and 143, 144
Safavids and 96, 98
Soviet Union and 215, 252
war in 206
Nalchik 130, 149, 235, 236
2005 terrorist attack 278, 286, 290
central mosque 277
St Mary Magdalene Church 278
Nativity Monastery, Katskhi, Georgia *9*
Nauru 272, 308
Nazi Germany
Armenia and 239
Germany–Japan Anti-Comintern Pact 230
Hitler's initial war directive 232
invasion of Soviet Union by 231
Ministry for Occupied Eastern Territories 236
Nazi Party (NSDAP) 230

oil and gas 230, 232, 235, 237, 331n29, 331n48
Russian and Asiatic people as *Untermenschen* (sub-humans) 236
Soviet flag over the Reichstag, Berlin *239*
SS death squads/*Einsatzgruppen* 236
World War II 232–8
see also Germany; Hitler, Adolf; Wehrmacht; World War II
Nicaragua 272, 308
Nikortsminda Cathedral, Georgia 103
Ninotsminda Nunnery, Georgia 85
Nojikhevi: Monastery of the Dormition 136
Noratus cemetery, Armenia *94*
North Caucasian Emirate 220
North Caucasian Imamate 218
North Caucasus 3
2007–2008 global financial crisis 290–1
2022–present manpower in Russian war against Ukraine 312
abolition of slavery and serfdom 166
Circassians: conquest, resettlement and expulsion of the 163–5
corruption 291
Cossacks and 122
Dagestani Avar Imams: jihad of 149, 152–63
economic vulnerability and insufficiencies 274–5, 291–2
ethnic diversity 246, 274
famine 227
governors 290, 335n3
insurgencies 290, 335n1
Kozak's report on 291
land use conflicts 115, 130, 132, 165
mass deportations 246
national consciousness 246
North/South Caucasus differences 274
pan-North Caucasian Islamic State 283
'political Islam' 115
Republics and regions of 290–4
Russian advance into 114, 323n5
Russian Civil Wars 217
Russian Empire and 115, 129
Russian Empire and resistance of North Caucasian mountain peoples 148–65, 169–70
Russian political domination 3, 290–1, 312
social structures of 114–15
Soviet collectivization of agriculture 227
subsidies from Moscow 274, 275, 334n4
terrorism 290, 335n1
unification of 218
Yermolov's first offensives north of the Greater Caucasus 149–52
North Caucasus Soviet Republic 218
North Ossetia–Alania
1992 Ossetian–Ingush conflict over Prigorodny Rayon 280, 294
2004 terrorist attack, Beslan school 278, 280, 286, 294
2008, 2010 terrorist attacks, Vladikavkaz 280, 294
federal subsidies 294
jihadism 294
Mansan castle *128*
Republic of North Ossetia–Alania 278–80

Russian Federation and 290, *307*
terrorism 280, 294
Uatsdin (True Faith) 278–9, *279*
unification with South Ossetia 294, 312
North Ossetian ASSR 280
Norway 337n90
Novorossiysk 130, 160, 185, *221*
Admiral Kutuzov, Russian warship *221*
British Military Mission 219
Nazi Germany and 237, 238
Whites at *221*, 222
Nur Mountains 66

O

Oltisni fortress 18
Ottoman Empire
1714–1715 Seventh Venetian–Ottoman War 110
1833 Ottoman–Russian Mutual Defence Treaty of Hünkâr İskelesi 151
1878 Berlin Congress 170, 184
1908 Parliament 176
Anamur fortress *63*
Anatolia and 87, 93
army 92–3, 164, 186, 190, 191, 194
beylerbeys 89
Black Sea and 80, 84, 134
Catholics' special protection in 89
covert agents 182
CUP triumvirate 176, 178, 185, 187, 188, 328n28
dismemberment and end of 4, 167, 184, 207
ethno-religious diversity 4
expansion of 80, 84, 92–3
Georgia and 81, 82, 85, 87, 88, 90, 135
Great Britain and 106, 139, 170
as Greater Turkish nation state 4, 176, 178
Iraq and 88
Kars and 147, 161, *168*
Kartli 106–7
Khertvisi fortress *78*
millets 4, 166
modern technologies 322n33
as multinational state 4
Ottoman Christians 166
Ottoman–Crimean campaign against Astrakhan 90
Ottoman–German cooperation 184–5
Ottoman 'irregulars' 92, 164–5
Ottoman Public Debt Administration 327n180
Ottomans/Iran/Russia rivalry 92, 107
pan-Turkism 182, 185, 195
post-war partition/'mandates' 190–1, 210–11, 327n176
slavery 88, 112, 119, 164
South Caucasus and 3
Sultan-Caliphs 323n111
Sunni Islam 3, 84
trade 84
World War I 178, 185–6, 190–1, 196, 201–4
see also Armenians and the Ottoman Empire; Ottoman–Safavid Wars; Russian–Ottoman clashes; Young Turks

P

Palestine 42–3, 57, 64, 66, 68, 215
Pankisi Gorge 272, 305
Pera: 1453 fall 80
Persia 18
    looting by Zakare Mkhargrdzeli 30
    Shia Islam 3
    see also Il-Khan dynasty; Iran
Persian Gulf 87, 88, 134, 139, 240, 259
Petrograd 193
    St Petersburg 328n43
Pitareti Monastery: Mother of God Church, Georgia 31, *32*
Poland
    1772 First Partition of 134
    1795 Third Partition of 134
    1939 Fourth Partition of 134
    Finckenstein, Palace *139*, 141
    NATO and 337n90
    Polish–Soviet War 211, 213, 216, 330nn213
    Warsaw Uprising 136, 238
Pontic Steppe Belt 114
Prigorodny Rayon: 1992 Ossetian–Ingush conflict over 280, 294
Prussia 114, 138, 139, 141, 185, 327n10

Q

Qabala (Qəbələ) 16

R

Republic of Aras 203, 206
Republic of the Union of Mountain Peoples of the North Caucasus (UMPR) 218, 220, 222
Roki Tunnel 197, 269, 307, 308–9
Rostov Oblast *241*, 275, 290
Rostov-on-Don, Kremlin of *227*
Russia (pre-imperial Russia)
    1557 defence pact between Kabarda and Russia 114–22
    1562–1563 Russian–Crimean war 121
    1571 burning of Moscow 121
    1649 Law Code 103
    1719 'passport decree' 103
    1717 expedition to Khiva 104
    Caspian Sea 90
    ethnic Russians 4, 137, 167
    expansion 90, 92, 114
    Kakheti and 92, 93–4, 95–6, 98, 100
    Kartli and 95, 96, 104–5, 106
    Mongols and 130
    Ottomans and 90, 92, 105
    Ottomans/Iran/Russia rivalry 92, 107
    Russian–Kalmyk treaties 130–1
    Samtskhe, conquest of 89
    slavery 89
    'Time of Troubles'/*Smuta* 122, 126, 218, 324n29
    trade 90, 92, 104, 105, 114
    see also Russian Empire; Russian Orthodox Church
Russian Empire (1721–1917)
    1812 Napoleon's invasion of Russia 142
    1828 Russian annexation of Iranian Armenia 80
    1833 Ottoman–Russian Mutual Defence Treaty of Hünkâr İskelesi 151
    1877–1878 conquest of former western Armenia 169–70
    1878 Berlin Congress 170
    1904–1905 Russia–Japan War 173, 180, 326n160
    1906 First Duma 181
    1907 Anglo-Russian Convention 145, 178, 327n181
    1907 Second Duma 181
    1907 Third Duma 181
    1915 Anglo-Russian agreement 184
    1917 Bolshevik Revolutions 4, 185, 191, 193, 194, 317n5
    1917 tsar's abdication 193
    abduction of Russians 114
    agriculture and land use issues 114, 126, 128, 130, 132, 164
    Armenian Catholic Church and 137
    army 129, 149, 164, 185, 186, *187*, 190, 191, *191*, 193, 194
    Black Sea and 134, 147, 148, 151, 160, 161, 170
    British Empire and 145
    the Caucasus: conquest by late 1829 and foundation of forts to 1818 **124**
    Chechnya and 148, 149, 150, 157, 158–9, 161–2, 165, 281
    Circassia and 115, 149, 150–1, 161, 163–5
    Constantinople and 129, 134, 135, 145, 170, 184, 186
    Dagestan and 148, 149, 150, 165, 169–70, 325n53
    end of 167, 207
    ethnic displacement 130
    ethno-religious diversity 4, 148, 167
    expansion of 129, 134, 136, 138, 151, 323n1
    forts **124**, 126, 134, 151–2
    frontier demarcation 114
    Georgia 104–5, 111–12, 135–6, 138, 180
    Great Britain and 105–6, 138, 139–40, 143, 145
    India and 104, 105
    industrialization 165, 174
    Iran and 107, 140–1, 143–5, *146*
    Iranian–Russian treaties 107, 144, 145, *146*, *146*
    Kars and *146*, 147, 160–1, *168*
    as multinational state 4, 207
    Nakhchivan and 143, 144
    Napoleonic Wars 139
    non-Christian ethnic minorities 148
    North Caucasian mountain peoples, resistance of 148–65, 169–70
    North Caucasus and 115, 129
    oil and gas industry 171–4
    Ottoman Empire, policy towards 178
    Ottomans/Iran/Russia rivalry 92, 107
    Pax Russica 146
    post-war partition of the Ottoman Empire/'mandates' 190–1
    Provisional Government 193, 194, 217
    Russification programmes 4–5, 166, 167, 196, 326n94
    serfdom 103, 128, 129, 150, 165–6
    South Caucasus and 134, 142, 145–6
    state administration 163, 165–9, 175
    State Duma 181
    taxes 128
    trade 134, 324n1
    tsar/tsarist system 4, 180–1, 193
    World War I 174, 185–6, *187*, 190–1, 193–4, 328n42
    see also Bolshevik Russia, Cossacks; Russia; Russian–Iranian Wars; Russian military lines; Russian Orthodox Church; Russian–Ottoman clashes
Russian Federation 248
    2008 Georgian–Russian War 293, 294, 301, 306–9, *307*, 337n80
    2008–2009 Great Recession 290–1
    2014 annexation of Crimea 129, 135, 161, 337n62
    2014 Winter Olympics 290
    2022–present invasion of Ukraine 227, 282, 293, 294, 298, 301, 303, 309, 310, 312, 336n22
    Abkhazia and *268*, 270, 304, 305, 306, 308, 310
    'Atlanticist' strategy 275
    Armenia and 195, 294, 301, 302, 303, 312, 336n56
    Azerbaijan and 255, 294–5, 312
    as bellicose superpower 249
    Chechen Wars and 6, 255, 282–4, 286
    Chechnya and 275, 281–2, 290, 293
    Dagestan and 288, 290, 291–3
    debt 334n3
    Georgia and 4, 272, 294, 304, 305, 333n32
    Eurasianism 275
    Federal Security Service (FSB) 264, 290, 293
    Foreign Military Intelligence (GRU) 264, 280
    Ingushetia and 290, 293
    Islamic State in 290
    Kabardino-Balkaria and 290
    Kalmykia and 290
    kontraktniki 293, 336n22
    Kremlin 290, 292, 293
    Nagorno-Karabakh conflict 262, 264, 265, 299, 300, 301, 312
    'Near Abroad' 6, 255, 264, 272, 294, 305, 332–3n32
    North Caucasus: political domination of 3, 290–1, 312
    North Ossetia-Alania and 290, *307*
    oil and gas industry 174, 255, 260, 262, 277, *287*, 333n46
    'passportization'-programmes 269, 272, 305
    political domination in Northern Caucasus 3, 290
    recentralization of bureaucracy 292–3
    Russian Constitution 290
    Russian police forces (OMON) 281, 284
    South Caucasus and 312
    South Ossetia and 294, 304, 305, 306, 308, 312
    Syrian civil war 282, 290
    Turkish–Russian alliance 210
    war against terrorism 286
    Western powers and 306, 309
    see also Putin, Vladimir; Soviet Union

S

Samarkand 63, 75, 76
Samegrelo principality 83
Samshvilde 15, 79
    Samshvilde fortress 12
Samtavisi Cathedral, Shida Kartli *8*
Samtsevrisi Castle Church, Georgia *305*
Samtskhe-Saatabago 47, 81, 82, 83
    Islamization of 89
    Ottomans and 87, 89, 92
    Russian conquest of 89
Sardarapat war memorial, Armenia *198*, 245
Sarıkamış *184*, 186, 195, 210, 212
Saudi Arabia 304
    Nagorno-Karabakh conflict 262
    oil and gas 248
    'Wahhabism'/Saudi Arabian Salafism 283, 290
Serbia 169
    Serbian nationalism 170
Sevanavank Monastery, Armenia
    Astvatsatsin Church *144*
    Church of the Apostles *144*
Shamakhi 323n96
Shamkhalate 93–4, 96, 99, 107, 121–2, 150
Shapsug National District 276
Shervashidze family's palace, Likhny *137*
Shirvan
    Caspian Sea and 20
    Georgia and 15, 17, 18, 20, 25, 36
    Iranians and 135
    Safavids and 84, 87
Shushi (Shusha) 143, 182, 202
    Holy Saviour Cathedral *214*
    Nagorno-Karabakh conflict 205–6, 261–2, 298, 299, 300
Siberia 114, 230, 276
    concentration camps 225
    deportations to 225, 227, 239, 240, 276
    oilfields 245
Sis 54, 71, 72
    'Catholicosate of the Great House of Cilicia' 80
    fortified complex of 71
    Mamelukes and 67, 71
    Timur-e Lang and 72
South Caucasus 3, *3*, 6
    ethnic and territorial conflicts 249
    EU and 312
    independent republics in 294–312
    NATO and 272, 312
    North/South Caucasus differences 274
    Ottoman Empire 3
    Ottoman–Safavid satellite states 88
    Ottoman–Safavid Wars 84–100
    Pax Russica 146
    Persian influence 3
    Russian Empire and 134, 142, 145–6
    Russian Federation and 312
    Safavid rule in 101–8
    South Caucasian unity 195
    sovereignty of South Caucasian states 5
    Soviet Union and 214, 216
    Turkification of 76, 101
    see also Ottoman–Safavid Wars
South-Eastern Union of Cossack Hosts 217
South Ossetia
    2008 Georgian–Russian War 307–8

INDEX: PLACES | 375

2022 presidential elections 310, 312, 338n109
2022–present Russian invasion of Ukraine 312
Autonomous Oblast (AO) 197, 265, 269
Church dedicated to the Blessed Virgin Mary 266
ethnic cleansing 267
Georgia/South Ossetia clashes 266–7, 268, 269, 279
independence from Georgia 4, 266, 269, 306, 308, 337n81
nationalism 197
reintegration into Georgia's central authority 304, 305
Republic of South Ossetia 269, 294
Russian Federation and 304, 305, 306, 308
Russian 'peace-keeping' forces stationed in 305
as smuggling hub 269
South Ossetian identity 197
unification with North Ossetia 294, 312
unification with Russia 294, 312
see also Georgia
Soviet Union (USSR)
1917 Bolshevik Revolutions 4, 185, 191, 193, 194, 317n5
1921 Anglo-Soviet Trade Agreement 216
1938 Russo–Japanese clashes over the Changkufeng Heights 230
Afghanistan and 246
Armenia and 213, 214, 216, 224, 227
autonomy concept 224
Azerbaijan and 206, 224
the Caucasus and 4, 5, 312
Cold War 240–1
collectivization of agriculture 225, 226–7
control of population's speech and thoughts 148
corruption 243, 244
Dagestan and 224–5, 286–7, 288
deportations by 218, 225, 227, 239, 240, 242, 276
dissolution and fall of 3, 5–6, 199, 246, 248–9, 251, 288, 297, 301
ethnic diversity 224, 227, 248, 331n3
expansion of the Soviet Empire 240
famines caused by 226–7
Georgia and 216, 224
glasnost 248, 249, 265, 283
Gulag prisoners 242
as imperial in character 5
industrialization 226, 227
Iran and 216, 240–1
Iranian Azerbaijan and 240, 252
Islam, suppression of 224–5, 288
language 226
Marxism 5, 242
military interventions by 198
Nagorno-Karabakh and 215, 226, 251
Nakhchivan and 215, 252
national borders 215, 248
nationalism 224, 242, 248–9, 301
New Economic Policy (NEP) 226
oil and gas industry 174, 230, 233, 235
passport regime 227, 242
Pax Sovietica 248
perestroika and *demokratizatsiya* 248, 249
Polish–Soviet War 211, 213, 216, 330nn213

post–World War II crisis and stagnation 242
reconquest of the Caucasus 4, 5
social policy 148
socialism 224, 227
South Caucasus and 214, 216
Soviet–Finnish Wars 134
Soviet–Turkish Friendship Treaty 211
Sovietization of Armenia and Georgia 211
Stalinism 242
Stalinist purges/Great Terror 216, 225–6, 227, 230
Transcaucasian Commissariat/ Sovnarkom rift 194
Ukraine and 226–7
War Communism 218, 226–7
World War II 221, 237–8
see also Bolshevik Russia; Russian Empire; Russian Federation; Siberia; Soviet Union: administrative units and institutions; Stalin, Joseph
Soviet Union: administrative units and institutions 329n79
army 206, 211, 213
Autonomous Oblast (AO) 215, 329n79
Autonomous Okrug 329n79
Autonomous Soviet Socialist Republic (ASSR) 5, 282, 329n79
the Cheka/GPU (Soviet secret police) 224, 225, 226, 227
Committee for State Security (KGB) 242, 243, 265, 332n91
Kavbyuro 199, 214, 215, 329n80
Kremlin 227
People's Commissariat for Internal Affairs (NKVD) 226, 227, 240, 332n91
Petrograd Soviet (Council of Workers and Soldiers' Deputies) 193
Politburo of the Communist Party of the Soviet Union (CPSU) 5, 202, 244, 246, 251
Provisional Government 193, 194, 217
Soviet Army Intelligence (GRU) 230, 231
Soviet Communist Party 148, 243, 329n80
Soviet MVD (Ministry of Interior) troops 252, 265, 267, 268, 280, 282
Soviet Socialist Republic (SSR) 329n79
Sovnarkom 194
STAVKA 233, 237
see also Red Army; Soviet Union
St Gayane Church, Armenia 79
St Petersburg 328n43
1905 Bloody Sunday massacre 173, 180
see also Petrograd
St Thaddeus Monastery, Azerbaijan 47, 320n171
Stalingrad 172, 220, 232, 235, 237, 238, 282
Stavropol Autonomous Region 224
Stavropol Krai 276, 290
Stavropol Soviet Republic 218
Sukhum Military Sector 164
Svaneti 36, 37, 40, 82, 165, 225, 227
principality 83
Upper Svaneti 161
Svyatoi Krest (Holy Cross) fortress 126

Sweden 114, 134, 139, 173, 174
1700–1721 Great Northern War 105
Minsk Group 333n70
NATO 309, 337n91
Syria 312
France and 209
Mamelukes and 65–6, 68
as middleman in Russian sale of stolen Ukrainian wheat 227
Mongols and 42, 46, 64
Ottomans and 72
Russia Federation and Syrian civil war 282, 290
Turkey and 301, 312
Syrian Gates 66
Syunik 185
Georgia and 37, 318n88
Ottomans and 106, 106
see also Zangezur

T

Tabriz 31, 32, 35, 48, 74
Ottomans and 87–8
Russian Empire and 144
Safavids and 84, 88, 95
Talysh-Mughan Autonomous Republic 255
Taman Peninsula 232, 237, 239, 323n5
Tanahativank Monastery, Armenia 44, 45
Tarki 93, 96, 107, 121–2, 123, 149, 153
Tatev Monastery, Armenia 44
Taurus Mountains 51, 53
Tbilisi 10, 82
1907 Tbilisi bank robbery 173, 179
Baratashvili Bridge 304
Bridge of Peace 306
concert and exhibition venue 269
Georgia and 9, 15, 17, 40
Holy Trinity Cathedral or Tsminda Sameba 271
Iran and 135
mass demonstrations and riots 243
Mongols and 32, 40, 43
Mother of Georgia statue, Sololaki Hill 242, 264
Ottomans and 92, 107
papal visits to 260
peasant revolts 179–80
Public Service Hall 304
presidential palace 269
printing press in 103
Road and Highway Construction/ Bank of Georgia 245
Russian Empire and 136, 180
Safavids and 87, 96, 107
Timur e-Lang and 74–5, 76
see also Georgia
Tell Hamdun fortress (Toprak Kale) 66, 67
Terek Autonomous Region 224
Terek Cossack Host 218
Terek–Dagestan Government 217–18
Terek Soviet Republic 218, 220
Terek River 33, 75, 94, 121, 122
Battle of the Terek River 43–4
Terskaya Krepost fort 92, 121, 122
Tersky Gorodok fortified town 94, 121
Transcaucasian Republic 195–6
Transcaucasian Socialist Federative Soviet Republic (TSFSR) 224, 225
Transoxania 74
Trebizond Empire 27, 48, 81, 84

Tsorey-Loam Mountains 37
Turkey 170
1919–1920 Paris Peace Conference 207, 210, 211–12
2022–present Russian invasion of Ukraine 312
Armenia/Turkey relations 4, 212–14, 302
Armenian massacres 205, 206, 215, 216
attack against Armenian forces 212–13
Azerbaijan/Turkey relations 6, 254–5, 294–5, 312
Cilicia and 72, 216
Grand National Assembly 211
Kars and 212–13
Nagorno-Karabakh conflict: Turkey/ Azerbaijan cooperation 254, 260, 262, 294, 298, 299, 300, 301, 312
NATO 214, 240, 254, 260, 298
oil and gas industry 259–60
pan-Turkism 201
Soviet–Turkish Friendship Treaty 211
strong player in the Caucasus 6, 301
Syria and 301, 312
Turkish National Intelligence (MİT) 254
Turkish nationalism 4, 176, 184, 207, 210, 211, 212, 212, 215, 215, 330n172
Turkish–Russian alliance 210
US and 242
see also Ottoman Empire
Turkish–Azerbaijani Confederation 253
Turkmenistan 259, 297–8, 336n35
Tuvalu 272, 308, 337n81

U

Ukraine
2004–2005 Orange Revolution 334n105
2022–present Russian invasion of 227, 282, 293, 294, 298, 301, 303, 309, 310, 312, 336n22
Central Council of Revolutionary Ukraine 196
Commonwealth of Independent States (CIS) 337n73
EU and 312
famines 226–7, 331n19
the Kadyrovtsy in 293
NATO and 306–7, 333n32
Russia and 114
Russian 'Near Abroad' 333n32
Soviet Union and 226–7
Union of Soviet Socialist Republics (USSR) see Soviet Union
United Mountain Peoples (UMP) of the North Caucasus 196, 217–18, 217, 224, 330n191
Central Committee 217, 218
United States (US)
1919–1920 Paris Peace Conference 210
Afghanistan and 152
Armenia and 303, 333n44
Azerbaijan and 255, 259, 294–5, 333n44
civil war 165
Cold War 241
Georgia and 195, 272, 307, 309, 310
Iran and 241, 242

isolationist policy 207
League of Nations and 210
Nagorno-Karabakh conflict 262, 264
oil and gas industry 255, 259, 298, 336n36
Treaty of Versailles and 210
Turkey and 242
the Urals 255, 259, 331n50

V

Van 177, 178, *190*, 328n35
    Armenian Genocide and siege of Van 189–90, *189*
Vanuatu 272, 308, 337n81
Vardzia Monastery, Georgia *21*, 88
Vashpurakan 8, 10, 26–7, 50, 54
Vaziani, Russian military base at 270, 272
Venezuela 272, 308
Venice 48, 58, 109–10
    1714–1715 Seventh Venetian–Ottoman War 110
    French occupation of 110
    San Lazzaro Monastery *109*, 110
Vladikavkaz 130, 149, 153, 162, 269, 279, 294
    Chechen terrorist attacks 280, 294
    partition of 280
    United Mountain Peoples (UMP) of the North Caucasus 217
    Vladikavkaz fortification, 'Master of the Caucasus' 134
    Vladikavkaz Military District 165
Volga River 114, 130, 182, 297, 298

Y

Yelisavetpol 143, 165, 181
    see also Ganja
Yerevan 80, 143–4, 199, *203*
    Blue Mosque 145
    bronze figure at the bottom of Yerevan Cascade *311*
    Cathedral of St Grigor the Illuminator 263
    Government Building No. 1 *303*
    Mother Armenia statue 242, *243*
    National Museum and National Gallery of Armenia 249
    Turkish attack on 213
    Yerevan Khanate 145
    see also Armenia

Z

Zangezur 200
    Autonomous Syunik 214
    war in 205, 214
    Zangezur Regional Council 205
    see also Syunik
Zangezur Corridor 301, 303
Zeitun 175
Zorats 'soldiers' church', Armenia *46*

Map 12. The Caucasus in the 21st century

Status as per 1 October 2022

- ● Modern capital cities
- ○ Cities
- — International borders
- — Borders of Republics, krai or oblast within the Russian Federation
- ▨ Disputed regions

Scale (km): 0 50 100 150 200 250